Mickey Vernon

Bob Schmidt

Bill Mazeroski

Dick Schofield

Danny Murtaugh

Dick Groat

Vern Law

This book belongs to:

Marie Smiley

"This field, this game, is part of our past. It reminds us of all that once was good and could be again."
—Terence Mann in the movie "Field of Dreams"

MAZ
AND THE '60 BUCS

By Jim O'Brien

When Pittsburgh And Its Pirates
Went All The Way

Dedication

Foremost, for my wife Kathleen and our daughters, Sarah and Rebecca, who know my books by heart.

For all the Pirates, past and present, who have made so many summers that much more interesting and pleasant, and given us all more than our share of thrills.

In memory of Roberto Clemente, Danny Murtaugh, Smoky Burgess, Don Hoak, John Hallahan, Bill Burwell, Frank Oceak and Lenny Levy, who were part of the team in that wonderful World Series season of 1960.

In memory of Frank Gustine and Billy Conn, who were part of the scene at Forbes Field, and made Pittsburgh someplace special. Gustine taught me as much about life as any of my professors at the University of Pittsburgh. In memory of Bob Prince, who cared.

In memory of Art Rooney, who loved the Pirates as much as he loved his own Steelers, and boosted everybody.

In memory of my father, Dan O'Brien, who never took me to a game, but loved me just the same, and my brother Dan, who took me to games and showed the way.

To my mother, Mary O'Brien, and sister Carole and brother Richard, for keeping the faith.

—Jim O'Brien

Copyright © 1993 by Jim O'Brien

All rights reserved

Published by James P. O'Brien — Publishing
P.O. Box 12580
Pittsburgh PA 15241
Phone (412) 221-3580

First printing, July 1993
Second printing, July 1994

Manufactured in the United States of America

Printed by Geyer Printing Company, Inc.
Pittsburgh PA 15213
Typography by Cold-Comp
Pittsburgh PA 15222

ISBN Number ISBN 0-91614-12-0

Bud Harris

Author Jim O'Brien with his back to the wall

To order copies directly from the publisher, send $24.95 for hardcover edition and $14.95 for softcover edition. Please send $3.50 to cover shipping and handling costs. Pa. residents add 6% tax to price of book only. Copies will be signed by author per your request. Discounts available for large orders.

Acknowledgements

This is the fifth book in my "Pittsburgh Proud" series and, as always, I had plenty of support from many special people in writing and publishing this tribute to the 1960 Pirates. The Pirates public relations staff, Rick Cerrone, Jim Lachimia and Jim Trdinich, were so helpful and Sally O'Leary, in particular, was a godsend. Everyone who submitted to an interview for this book has my deepest gratitude.

Many of the photographs were provided by David Arrigo, the Pirates photographer, Michael Drazdzinski, Michael Fabus, Bill Amatucci, James G. Klingensmith and Ed Morgan.

I am grateful to my daughter Sarah, a second-year student at the University of Virginia, and Doug Miller, an assistant publicity director with the New York Jets, who both proofread the galleys and made many helpful suggestions.

Thanks to Stush "The Fan" Carrozza and Doug Hoerth of WTAE Radio for providing me with a tape of the 7th game of the 1960 World Series, and to George Von Benko for his taped interview with Whitey Ford, Mickey Mantle and John Blanchard of the Yankees.

I wish to thank the publishers of several baseball books for permission to reprint material.

Gayland Cook and John Williams of Integra Bank/Pittsburgh have been especially supportive of my book projects, and provided a base on which to build a library about accomplishment and sports successes in Western Pennsylvania.

I wish to thank these patrons: Arco Chemical, Baierl Chevrolet, Blue Cross of Western Pennsylvania, Bowne of Pittsburgh, Continental Design and Management Group, Daniell-Sapp-Boorn Associates, Inc., Ernst & Young, Bill Few Associates, Frank B. Fuhrer Wholesalers, The Gustine Company, F.E. Harmon Construction, Inc., Hawthorne Sports Marketing, H.J. Heinz, Jessop Steel, Local Chevrolet/Geo Dealers, Mascaro Inc., Meridian Exploration Corp., Miles Inc., North Side Bank, Nortim Corp., PNC Bank, Sargent Electric, Westinghouse Electric.

I wish to thank the following for their support: Dennis Astorino, Bill Baierl, Eugene J. Barone, Walt Becker, Michael Berlin, Tom Bigley, Dave Brown, Renny Clark, Ray Conaway, Carole Cook, Richard E. Farrell, Mike Fetchko, Gregory W. Fink, Patrick Fleming, Frank B. Fuhrer, Bill Gormley, Frank Gustine Jr., Bob Gustine, Michael J. Hagan, Bill Haines, Darrell J. Hess, Andy Komer, Michael C. Linn, Robert Lovett, Jack Mascaro, Del Miller, Carl R. Moulton, Thomas H. O'Brien, Alex Pociask, Bill Priatko, Jim Roddey, Ed Ryan, Stanley M. Stein, Dick Swanson, Earle Wittpen.

Special thanks to Tom Mariano and Pittsburgh Trane, Jay A. Miller and Richard J. Nesbit of Sutersville Lumber Co., Clark Nicklas of Vista Resources, Steve and Charlie Previs of Waddell & Reed Financial Services, W. Harrison Vail and Three Rivers Bank.

Pittsburghers who take tremendous pride in producing this series of books are Ed Lutz of Cold-Comp Typographers and Stan Goldmann, Bruce McGough and Tom Samuels of Geyer Printing.

—Jim O'Brien

Words of Praise

"Nobody has a passion for a community or its sports teams any more than Pittsburgh-area journalist Jim O'Brien. This is reflected in his latest book entitled Whatever It Takes, *a humanistic look at the glory days of the Pittsburgh Steelers. The real appeal of O'Brien's well-researched and document-ed effort is the personal touch. He relates upbeat stories about the Steeler families, upbringing and early influences, and even Chuck Noll's theories on child-rearing! This is a must book for all Steeler buffs and any fan of professional football and would make a great Christmas gift."*
—Doug Huff, Sports Editor
The Wheeling-Intelligencer

"I think the most interesting story in the manuscript is the author's own. His personal journeys through the Pittsburgh sports scene of the 1950's and 1960's, long before the successes of the Super Bowl '70s, are wonderfully detailed and quirky. He has a special awareness of and feel for the way in which the Steelers have fit into the fabric of this city's neighborhoods. I'd like to read a book by O'Brien about Sports in Pittsburgh Then and Now.*"*
—Review for University of Pittsburgh Press

"Jim O'Brien is a one-man cottage industry. He writes books. He publishes them. He markets them. He autographs them. He distributes them. He promotes them. He promotes him-self. His topic is the Pittsburgh Steelers. More to the point, his subjects are athletes who played for the Pittsburgh Steel-ers during their glory years. O'Brien has taken the public's infatuation with the Steelers and turned the infatuation into two books about the team and a job for himself."
—Richard Gazarik
The Pittsburgh Tribune-Review

6

Contents

BABE RUTH

*"On the last Sunday of his career, only a week before
his retirement — when he was fat and worn-out at forty-
one and had gone off to play for the Boston Braves
because no other team would have him — he came up to
bat four times against the Pirates at Forbes Field at
Pittsburgh, and hit a single and three homers. The last
home run — the last one of his career, No. 714 — flew
over the roof of the double-decked grandstands in right
field. It was the first ball anyone had ever hit out of
Forbes Field (over the right field stands).
Goodbye, baseball."*
—From "So Long At The Fair," 1981, by Roger Angell

Introduction
A roomful of smiles

"Baseball, more than any sport,
is a part of our lives."

Stories. So many good stories. Everyone was swapping stories. There were Pirates from the past, sports writers and sports broadcasters, sports photographers, newspapermen — administrators and executives — some spouses, publicity people, and insiders.

Some of the stories were as spicy as the Cajun chicken and salad that were served at the luncheon, some were sad, most brought smiles to everyone at each of the tables.

This was a roomful of nice people, some famous, some not-so-famous, but all with connections to the Pirates and sports, and all with stories. It was a roomful of smiles.

The ballplayers were telling baseball stories, the sportswriters and newspaper people were telling stories about their game. "You were talking about the good ol' days, and how great it used to be, right?" said my wife Kathie when I conveyed the day's activity to her that night at dinner. She was scolding me and smiling at me at the same time.

After more than 25 years of marriage, Kathie knows the scene well. She swears she knows all the stories, too.

The occasion was the induction of two sports writers from my youth, Al Abrams and Les Biederman, to the Pirates' "Media Wall of Fame."

Abrams and Biederman were both dead, but they were alive on this sunny afternoon as they were remembered by one and all at ceremonies in the media lounge behind the baseball press box at Three Rivers Stadium. Had they been there, they would have been in their 80s. It didn't seem possible they would be that old.

Plaques were unveiled with their images and brief bios on them. Abrams was the sports editor of the *Pittsburgh Post-Gazette* from 1947 to 1974. Biederman covered the Pirates for *The Pittsburgh Press* from 1938 to 1969, and was a correspondent for *The Sporting News* while he was on the Bucs' beat.

Rick Cerrone, then the Pirates' vice-president for public relations, offered praise for the two men, and their unique roles in helping to write the history of the Pirates. He spoke about how baseball was more than just the players. It was a game that belonged to the fans, to families, to the story tellers. It covered a large canvas.

"Baseball, more than any sport, is a part of our lives," said Cerrone.

He was right on the mark, I thought, as I reflected on how I had spent the prevous year, visiting and interviewing the Pirates of the 1960 team, the one that won the World Series against the New York Yankees.

9

So many who were in the room on this May day, May 5, 1993, for the record, had written and told stories about the Pirates, had captured their achievements and disappointments with words and photographs — some which grace the walls of so many areas throughout Three Rivers Stadium and in saloons all over town. But no one had ever written a book specifically about that summer of 1960, — not for adults anyhow — and what became of those boys of that summer, those young men who came to Pittsburgh and pulled off a feat that still ranks among the city's magic moments in sports.

That was the task I took on a year earlier.

Four members of that 1960 Pirates team were present in the room to help pay tribute to those who were honored, as well as all who were in attendance. They are still special, mostly because they never think of themselves as special.

Sitting at the table next to the one where I was sitting were Dick Groat, Bill Virdon and Bob Friend. At the other end of the room was ElRoy Face. They were among the many Pirates from that team I had talked to at length, and had them share stories about that experience, and what had happened to them since that special year in their lives, and in the lives of so many Pittsburghers, Western Pennsylvanians and Pirates' fans round the world.

There were others in the room I had spoken to as well, former Pirates such as Nellie King, Nellie Briles, Frank Thomas and Ronnie Kline. In his heyday, they called Kline "The Callery Pa. Hummer." They still rank among the fans' all-time favorites.

For this book, I had talked earlier to Roy McHugh, the former sports editor of *The Press*, as well as Jackie Powell, who had assisted so many sports writers from the *Post-Gazette* through the years, and they were also at the luncheon.

John Troan, who had been the editor of *The Press* and who made his mark by breaking the stories during the mid-50s of University of Pittsburgh researcher Jonas Salk's discovery of a polio vaccine, was sitting with me and Fred Landucci, a former executive sports editor of *The Press*. I had worked with these men when I was in high school, college and later as a sports writer. None of us could believe that *The Press* had gone out of business on the last day of 1992. It was still hard to comprehend. The *Post-Gazette*, which I had delivered as a youngster, was the only bona fide Pittsburgh daily remaining.

By the bar in the media lounge there was a handsomely framed photo of Willard "Diz" Bellows, who had been the press room attendant at Three Rivers and at Forbes Field, his association with the Pirates dating back to his schoolboy days of 1924. He had died during the winter, just two months after I interviewed him for this book.

Bellows could have written a book himself from all the time he spent with the sports media through the years. He knew all the stories, too.

No one knew those whose plaques were on the "Media Wall of Fame" any better than Bellows.

The charter six members of that celebrated group included Charles

"Chilly" Doyle, who covered the Pirates for the *Pittsburgh Sun-Telegraph* from 1914 to 1957; Charley Feeney, who covered for the *Post-Gazette* from 1966 to 1986; Art McKennan, who was the public address announcer at Forbes Field and Three Rivers Stadium from 1948 to 1986; Sally O'Leary, a member of the Pirates' public relations staff for 30 years; Bob Prince, the "Voice of the Pirates" from 1948 to 1975; and Rosey Rowswell, the Pirates' first radio broadcaster, who did the games from 1936 to 1954.

Feeney, O'Leary and McKennan were all present for the luncheon. When Mary Abrams accepted the plaque for her late husband, she said, among other things, "I don't know how the Pirates would run without Sally O'Leary."

I smiled. My sentiments exactly. She had been so helpful to me on this project, from start to finish, as had everyone on the Pirates' public relations staff.

It was she who supplied me with the names, addresses and phone numbers of the living 25 members of that 1960 championship team, and every name, number and statistic I needed as I wrote this book. The manager, Danny Murtaugh, had died, as had several of his coaches, Lenny Levy, Frank Oceak and Bill Burwell. Three of the players were also deceased, Roberto Clemente, Smoky Burgess and Don Hoak.

But I was able to communicate in some manner with the rest of the championship cast, and so many others who knew them well, and with fans who recall that team and their accomplishments as if they happened yesterday.

Many Pittsburghers and Pirates fans elsewhere have often boasted that at one time in their lives they knew all 25 players on the team's 1960 Pirates World Series roster.

Many more boast that they were at Forbes Field on October 13, 1960 when Bill Mazeroski hit the home run to lead off the bottom of the ninth inning to beat the Yankees, 10-9, to win the World Series.

They are not all telling the truth. There were 36,683 fans in attendance that day, and to believe everybody who says they were there would have swelled the turnstile count to about 366,800.

Everybody who cared about the Pirates, and some who did not, knows exactly where they were when Maz hit the home run. It is one of those red flag events in people's lives, like the assassinations of President John F. Kennedy, Dr. Martin Luther King and Robert Kennedy.

Some argue that Maz's home run is the single most dramatic event in Pittsburgh sports history, while others hold out for the "Immaculate Reception" by Franco Harris in the Steelers' 1972 AFC playoff victory over the Oakland Raiders.

The Yankees had won 18 World Series and the Pirates two prior to that 1960 classic.

Radio broadcaster Chuck Thompson said during the seventh game, "It's been a wacky sort of Series, unusual to say the least."

It was 78 degrees as Vernon Law took the mound for the Bucs for that seventh game. Stan Musial of the St. Louis Cardinals, particularly popular in Western Pennsylvania because he came from Donora, was

11

sitting in a box along the first base line that day. But he would not be the most heralded Polish baseball player in the place at day's end.

The Pirates had won their three games by scores of 6-4, 3-2, 5-2 and the Yankees had won by 16-3, 10-0 and 12-0. The Pirates were not hitting in the Series like they hit during the season when they were the best in the league with a team batting average of .276.

John Blanchard was catching for the Yankees because Elston Howard had broken his hand in the sixth game. Yogi Berra was in left field. This is the sort of trivia some fans still remember about that day. It is part of the lore real fans of the Pirates must be able to pull out of their minds to have any credibility.

I learned so much about that 1960 Pirates team and the 1960 World Series that I did not know before. The fun of writing such a book is the discoveries one makes along the way.

It was a super sojourn. I found the 1960 Pirates to be pleasant and enthusiastic subjects. They wanted to talk about those wonderful days of their youth. They have gotten old, of course, and in some cases it hurt to see them hurting. Most of them are doing just fine, though.

They take pride in their accomplishments, but are just as eager to talk about their wives and families. And some of their wives provided as many stories as they did. Most of them are still with the wives they had when they played for the Pirates. None of them lives in a mansion. Their homes are comfortable and clean, the pride is still evident everywhere one looks. Some of the homes, with all the baseball memorabilia and pictures from the past, are like mini-museums, extensions of the Baseball Hall of Fame in Cooperstown, N.Y. Most of them have returned to the communities where they grew up. They have no difficulty remembering where they came from. They remain close to their roots. They remain humble.

Spending time with the heroes of my boyhood days was quite a trip. I hope you will feel the same way when you read their reflections. I hope these stories make you think and laugh and cry. If they do, I will have been successful in my mission.

"The 1960 World Series and obviously Maz's home run are important to a lot of people in this area," said Groat, who grew up in Swissvale and has a special feeling for all things Pittsburgh and who was the National League's MVP and batting champion for the Pirates in the summer of '60.

"That's a very beloved baseball team for people who grew up in that era. It was a team that never knew enough to give up."

"Sports writers become cynics because they learn eventually that, while there are no villains, there are no heroes, either. Until you make the final discovery that there are only human beings, who are therefore all the more fascinating, you are liable to miss something."
—Paul Gallico

A special year

Sports scene changed dramatically in 1960

Pirates and Arnold Palmer led late charge

1960 was a special year for sports fans in many respects, and especially for those who followed the fortunes of the Pittsburgh Pirates.

Everyone over the age of 40 from Pittsburgh to Altoona, Greensburg to Johnstown, Erie to Youngstown, Morgantown to Uniontown, or Wheeling to Washington can tell you where they were when Bill Mazeroski hit the home run and the Pirates defeated the mighty New York Yankees to win the World Series in 1960.

That magic moment will forever be associated with 1960. Some younger fans recall it as well because their mom and dad or grandparents still talked about it when they were growing up.

It was a pivotal year for the Pirates, and for baseball, football, basketball and golf at large. It was a significant year for the likes of Arnold Palmer, Chuck Noll and Mike Ditka, who went from being local legends to being hailed as internationally known and respected sports heroes.

Television, still a relatively new medium, took hold of sports and changed the way games would be viewed and followed forever.

It was the year that Arnold Palmer put his stamp on pro golf. He won eight titles in 1960, including the Masters at Augusta and the U.S. Open in Denver and never looked back. He set a new one-year record for official tour earnings, $75,263, and began his reign as the game's best player. Imagine that — $75,263 for winning eight tour events. A golfer gets that these days for finishing in the middle of the pack in a single tournament.

It was the year that Palmer, "sweating, chain-smoking, driving balls through tree trunks, shirttail flying," in the words of golf writer Dan Jenkins, took golf to the masses. In 1960, Arnie got thousands of people hooked on cigarettes, golf, television — and Arnold Palmer. By 1990, *Forbes* magazine estimated that Palmer was making $10 million a year and was the top product endorser of all time.

On April 8, 1993, on the opening round of the Masters, a 63-year-old Palmer was the only golfer to birdie the first three holes, and he had the crowd roaring again as it did in his heyday. "Going up to the fourth hole," he said afterward, "I felt about 30 years old."

That was a very good age. At 30, in 1960, the golfer known as The King to the other touring pros, won his second Masters.

It started happening in 1960 at the Masters, when Arnie birdied the last two holes to win, and then he was truly ordained as America's golf darling at the U.S. Open at Cherry Hills in June. His finish in the U.S. Open that spring cinched his celebrity. Seven strokes behind the leader, Mike Souchak, starting the final round, Palmer strangled the field with a first nine 30 and a 65 for the 18. He seemed to be winning every tournament with a last-second charge, in much the manner that the Pirates were surprising people with one comeback after another to win the National League pennant that same summer. Palmer became a favorite of President Eisenhower, himself a golf freak, and the two frequently played together on the country's classiest courses. It did wonders to popularize the game.

It was a year when golfing great Ben Hogan was doing his best to hang on, and a 20-year-old chunky kid from Ohio State University named Jack Nicklaus was making his pro debut. Golf would never be the same again.

It was the year Arnie's Army was born, and Latrobe gained fame as his hometown. The Westmoreland County community would later become a dateline as the site of the Steelers' summer training camp when the team won four Super Bowls in six years, one of the great accomplishments in professional sports history.

The American Football League was also born in 1960, and things would never again be the same for the National Football League. A young man got his first coaching position that year with an opportunity provided by the birth of the new league. This was Chuck Noll, who was hired by Sid Gillman with the Los Angeles Chargers. This same Noll would come to Pittsburgh in 1969 and turn the Steelers into winners of the highest order. And the Steelers would end up competing, along with the Cleveland Browns and Baltimore Colts, in a conference made up otherwise of all former AFL franchises. The Steelers became the dominant team in the American Football Conference in the '70s, as well as the rest of the National Football League.

Mike Ditka, from Aliquippa, Pennsylvania, would become an All-America as a senior two-way end at the University of Pittsburgh in the fall of 1960.

I was a freshman at Pitt that September and I can still see Ditka, with a crewcut and wearing his blue and gold varsity letter jacket, standing on the porch on the Fifth Avenue side of the William Pitt Student Union. He was the Big Man on Campus in 1960. He went on to be a great player and coach in the National Football League.

Right from the start, I was a sports writer for the student newspaper at Pitt, which led to an opportunity to write home town feature stories for Beano Cook, the zany sports information director whose cluttered office was in the Pitt Field House. My first effort was on Fred Cox for the daily newspaper in Monongahela.

I remember being in Cook's office one Friday that fall when three famous football people passed by his desk within an hour's time to pick up their scouting credentials and press box seats for the next day's game at Pitt Stadium.

They were Bucko Kilroy of the Philadelphia Eagles, Emlen Tunnell of the New York Giants — great players I had known from listening to radio broadcasts of Steelers games — and Al Davis, a scout for

1960 was the best of years for Dick Groat and Arnold Palmer. They lit up the sports world as Groat was the National League's MVP for the championship Pirates and Palmer was the Golfer of the Year, winning the Masters and U.S. Open.

Palmer and Groat are grandfathers now, but still get together for a round of golf now and then on their own Westmoreland County courses.

the Los Angeles Chargers. Hard to believe that Noll and Davis — who would become arch-rivals when Davis directed the Oakland Raiders — got their start with the same AFL team.

Davis was a delight with his Brooklyn tough-talking, fast-talking, gum-chewing manner, and roguish laugh right from the start. Red Smith of the *New York Herald-Tribune*, one of the most famous sports writers in the country and later a winner of the Pulitzer Prize when he worked for *The New York Times*, was also a visitor that day to Cook's office. I volunteered to drive Smith to the airport following the next day's game just so I could have an hour in his hallowed company. Cook introduced me to a lot of celebrities in the sports world and sports writing game over the next four years.

Minnesota won the national championship in football in 1960, even though they would lose in the Rose Bowl to Washington, which claimed a future Steelers stalwart named Ray Mansfield in its lineup.

Ohio State won the NCAA basketball title with a team that included Bobby Knight, Jerry Lucas, John Havlicek, Mel Nowell and Larry Siegfried. Havlicek had played at Bridgeport, Ohio, High School, not far from Bill Mazeroski's home town. The following year, the Buckeyes would play Pitt in the first college basketball game held at the newly-opened Civic Arena. It was a game that was arranged by Les Biederman, the baseball writer for *The Pittsburgh Press*, and an alumnus of Ohio State. The game was played for the benefit of Children's Hospital. I remember attending a press conference at Frankie Gustine's Restaurant where Lucas, Havlicek and Nowell appeared to promote the game. I still have some pictures of them I took that day outside the restaurant.

To have the World Series conducted on our campus the second month I was at Pitt, in October of 1960, made for a glorious introduction to college life, as I look back upon it now. Back then, the Pittsburgh symphony and all top entertainment acts that came to town played at the Syria Mosque, across the street from the Cathedral of Learning and the student dorms, and the Pirates and Steelers both played at Forbes Field. The Steelers would later play at Pitt Stadium.

These were all perks for Pitt students.

The 1960 World Series was one of the strangest ever played. The Yankees set all sorts of records with ten home runs, 55 runs and a .338 batting average. Their three victories were by 16-3, 10-0 and 12-0. The Pirates scored only 27 runs, hit only four home runs, and batted .256, yet the two teams were tied after six games. The final game was a slugging match in which the Pirates took a 9-7 lead on catcher Hal Smith's three-run home run in the eighth inning, but the Yankees came back to tie it in the top of the ninth inning with a two-run shot by Yogi Berra. Then Bill Mazeroski, leading off the bottom of the ninth inning, got hold of Ralph Terry's second pitch and drove it over the left field wall to spark a civic celebration that may not have been rivaled in sports history.

Topped by that World Series finish, the 1960 baseball season was something of a turning point in major league baseball history.

1960 was Ted Williams' final season. He closed it out in grand style by stroking a home run, his 29th of the season, in his final at-bat at Boston's Fenway Park. He left the game with some gaudy numbers: a .344 career batting average, 521 home runs, 1,839 RBIs, 1,798 runs scored, and with fans wondering what kind of statistics he would have rung up if he had not missed four seasons because of military service. He was the last of the pre-World War II heroes.

And, after 1960, big league scouts were no longer able to recruit talent out of baseball-rich Cuba. At the end of 1958, Marxist-Leninist revolutionaries led by Fidel Castro overthrew the military dictatorship of Fulgencio Batista. In January 1961 the Eisenhower administration broke off diplomatic relations with Castro's government in an effort to isolate Cuba in the Western Hemisphere. That stopped the flow of baseball talent from Cuba coming to America.

Finally, the 1960 season ended a 56-year period in which the National League and the American League consisted of eight teams each and (except for 1919) scheduled 154-game seasons. Fans would no longer be able to refer to their teams as "first division" or "second division" teams. The scoreboard at Forbes Field would no longer be big enough to carry the inning-by-inning scores for all the games at the same time.

Branch Rickey, at age 78 in 1959, had tried to create a Continental League as a competitor to established baseball, but this only prompted the owners to expand the ranks for the 1961 and the 1962 seasons. The American League added two teams for the 1961 schedule and the National League added two teams for the 1962 schedule.

1960 was also the last year for Babe Ruth's record of hitting 60 home runs in a single season. Roger Maris would hit 61 in 1961, and Commissioner Ford Frick would put an asterisk after it because Maris had more games in which to do it. Maris hit his 59th home run in the 154th game of the American League's 162-game schedule.

There would be more teams and more games, and new heroes to replace Ruth and Williams, but there would never be another year quite like 1960.

Ohio State stars Mel Nowell, John Havlicek and Jerry Lucas at Gustine's Restaurant prior to first college basketball game at Civic Arena. The defending NCAA champion Buckeyes beat Pitt.

Jim O'Brien

Where Were You?

"I had no idea what had happened."
—John Rosato

Saul Finkelstein
Courthouse services for attorneys
Squirrel Hill
"I wasn't able to go to the seventh game of the 1960 World Series, but I stayed home from school to watch it. I was in seventh grade at the time. I gave up on the Pirates midway through the game, when they were behind by 6-4. My cat had died the night before, and I decided this was a good time to bury it. So I went out in my backyard and buried the cat under a tree. I got back to the game on TV about the eighth inning, and everything went crazy from thereon in. I go out to what remains of the outfield wall at Forbes Field each year on October 13. First, I go to the Original and get a hot dog. I bring a Pirates seat cushion and a tape of the seventh game by Bob Prince and Jim Woods, and one with Chuck Thompson, and I sit by the wall and listen to the tapes. I go at 1 o'clock and I sit under the flagpole. It's a lot of fun."

John Rosato
Landscape contractor
Assistant football coach, Duquesne University
"I grew up in Oakland, which was a great place to grow up, and I was a fourth grader at St. Regis Grade School, which was on Parkview Avenue, across the street from the house where Danny Marino grew up. I was watching the seventh game on TV at school. They let us out early and I took off and raced to Forbes Field, which was about a mile away, and close to my home. I was running by the Turtle Spit Fountain — it's really the Mary Schenley Fountain — but we called it the Turtle Spit Fountain. That's where I was when the ball came over the left field wall. I had no idea what had happened. People were just screaming. Frankly, it was scary. There were millions of people going after that ball. It scared the hell outta me. I'm only nine. I didn't want to go near that ball. Later on, I played Little League ball on that Schenley Plaza field, which is now called Bill Mazeroski Field. Balls used to come over the wall at Forbes Field and bounce through our field. We took it for granted. We used to sneak into the games with the Knot-Hole gangs, and we'd climb up the trees to look into the field. We did some bad things, too. We were always hustling outside the park, trying to make some money. We retrieved home run balls and sold them to people coming out of the park. I stayed in Oakland till I was 30, and I wouldn't trade that experience for anything in the world. We lived on Meyran Avenue. During the '60 World Series, my parents were parking cars in a corner lot at Bates and Atwood for about $5 a car, which was a lot in those

days. I still go down there where the ballpark used to be. I love to be there. I take my son down to the Mazeroski Field and hit balls to him. I tell him what it was like to be a boy when Forbes Field was there."

Jim Tripodi
Beaver Falls

"I was 11 and in the 6th grade at the 37th St. Elementary School in beautiful downtown Beaver Falls, and I was a patrol boy helping students cross at 38th St. and 3rd Ave. I had a Channel Master transitor radio, which was my confirmation gift that year. When Maz hit the home run, I ran home screaming. I have my own sports collectibles shop now, called Diamond Jim's, and I have an unused ticket from Game 7 of the 1960 World Series. It cost $7.70 then. I also have a tape of the 1960 World Series and when I'm on my way to a sports card show I pop it in to get me in the mood."

Angelo Vento
Monroeville

"I was a plumber working on a sewage plant out by the airport, and I was heading home to East Liberty. I was coming over the Fort Pitt Bridge into town when Mazeroski hit it out. I never was so happy in my life, especially being a fan of Mazeroski. It's a wonder I didn't wreck. My son, Phil, has always been a big fan of Maz, too."

Carnegie Library of Pittsburgh

Note the nun and barbed wire at the wall of Forbes Field.

Bill Virdon
They called him "Quail"

"I do what needs to be done."

There was a pall over Pittsburgh. The city was in mourning. Just when everybody thought the Bucs were going all the way — that 1992 was going to be their year — the Atlanta Braves broke their hearts. The Pirates had come within one out of going to the World Series, but the Braves scored three runs in the bottom of the ninth inning to deal the Pirates and their followers the most difficult of defeats.

The Pirates had lost three of the first four games, but bounced back to win the next two games, forcing a seventh game and giving hope to a miracle-like comeback. Alas, they came up short.

I asked Virdon where he was when former Pirate Sid Bream raced from second base to score the winning run for the Braves on a pinch-hit by Francisco Cabrera in the bottom of the ninth, beating a throw from left field by Barry Bonds and a lunging tag by Bream's good friend Mike LaValliere.

"I was standing in the dugout, where I stood most of the game," said Virdon. "It wasn't much fun watching it. You can't anticipate things going bad, even though you realize things can go bad. From the fifth inning on, you hope he (Doug Drabek) can finish the game. Things just didn't work out. It wasn't any fun. We were all sweating out the last inning, hoping that the two-run, then one-run, lead would hold up. You do that all season long. But you can't be satisfied till it's over."

It was a Saturday in October, three days after that stunning setback, and most Pirates and those who had been rooting for them were still in shock. Many were in seclusion. But Bill Virdon was still Bill Virdon, and he was gracious enough to agree to talk about it, as well as his long career in baseball. Virdon has always been an obliging fellow.

He has always returned telephone calls, and responded to written requests with well-thought-out letters of his own. While a quiet, reserved sort, Virdon has always had a quick smile, and behind those glasses there remains a twinkle in his blue eyes. He is of Irish and English descent, stands six feet and weighs 185, and looks like he could still slip into that No. 18 uniform and play ball. But he was 61 when we spoke, and had seven grandchildren, ranging in age from 19 to a year old.

During Virdon's playing days in Pittsburgh, colorful Pirates broadcaster Bob Prince tagged him with the nickname "Quail" because Bill not only liked to hunt game birds in Missouri and Arkansas in the off-season, but because of the way he often hit the ball. "He referred to my looping hits just over the infield as dying quails," explained Virdon, "and in turn gave me the name."

Bill and his wife Shirley were nearly finished packing their bags in the apartment they shared during the baseball season in Mt. Leba-

TV's Ed Sullivan hosts Pirates Bill Virdon and Yankees
Gil McDougald on popular Sunday night show.

Virdon with Pirates Hall of Famer Lloyd Waner

Virdon in 1960 at Forbes Field

① ② ③

Pittsburgh Pirates

Virdon's advice to young players: "Always give it your all. That is what the fans
ay to see."

non, a suburb to the south of Pittsburgh, about 15 minutes from Three Rivers Stadium. They were preparing to depart Pittsburgh in a few hours to fly back home to Springfield, Missouri, 850 miles away.

"It's home," said Virdon. "Springfield is in the southwest corner of the state, near the Ozarks. I grew up in a small town about a hundred miles from there. I bought my house after the 1960 World Series. I traded another house there to get this one; it's just outside the city limits.

"I've always gone back home. I never stayed. That's the only way you can get away from it for awhile. Somebody's always hounding you, wanting you to do something. That's understandable, but I always wanted to get away from it for awhile. Going home gives me that chance."

There would be writers hounding him, however, when he got back home. The telephone would be ringing off the hook for a few days as Virdon was regarded as a strong candidate for the managing posts at both of the new expansion franchises, in Florida and in Colorado. "There's nothing definite yet," said Virdon before leaving Pittsburgh, referring to reported rumors about who would be hired. "I'm still involved in both situations. I'm interested in managing one of the expansion teams; otherwise I would not have talked to them about the job."

As it turned out, Virdon was not picked as the manager in either place. Chalk up another disappointment for the fall of 1992. Shirley Virdon felt her husband would bounce back, as he always has. "I think that Bill has always felt that after anything disastrous happened to us, we were better off," she has said. "Bill has learned a lot from everything that's happened to him. He doesn't look back; only forward."

Virdon had rejoined Jim Leyland's staff in 1992 after spending the previous three seasons as a spring training instructor and a minor league hitting instructor in the Pirates organization. He served as the team's hitting instructor during Leyland's first season as manager back in 1986.

"What I've learned is you do what you have to do," Virdon said. "You want to teach people, you want to work with people, so you find a way to do it. I never got a bang out of authority. I do what needs to be done."

Always an unabashed admirer of Danny Murtaugh, Virdon is also impressed with Leyland. "He prepares himself well and he's a good communicator," avowed Virdon. "He likes to do it one-on-one. He likes to work with the individual. He touches base with individuals, somehow, in the clubhouse, or in the hallway. There's a saying in baseball about how you can smell something. You know when things get off track. Jim doesn't miss anything. He keeps things under control. This club has done very well under Jim Leyland. Just look at the record."

Virdon has worked for the Pirates in several capacities during his distinguished career, as an outstanding center fielder for 10 years, beginning in 1956, and as a manager for nearly two seasons, in 1972 and 1973, and as a coach on several other occasions. His face is a familiar one to baseball fans in Pittsburgh, and he has always been one of the most popular Pirates.

Whenever the TV cameras focused on Leyland in the dugout during the 1992 playoff series with the Braves, Virdon was often visible in the same picture, or in the background.

"I never saw you saying anything; I never saw your lips move," I said to Virdon. He wasn't even spitting, risking his membership card in the managerial and coaching ranks of baseball.

"It was not my position," he said. "You run things over in your mind, but I was not going to voice my opinion. You don't manage another man's club. When I was managing, the media would ask me about a decision the other manager made and what did I think of it. I didn't get involved with that. You shouldn't try to manage another man's club."

Virdon managed baseball teams in New York, Houston and Montreal. It was when he was managing the Yankees that I really spent the most time with Virdon, covering the club on occasion for *The New York Post*. Being a Pittsburgher, I thought, was a good door-opener for me with Virdon back then, and he was always cooperative, if careful with the words he chose to express himself in clubhouse interviews. New York writers didn't think he was a good interview, but they thought he was a good guy.

Virdon is the answer to a trivia question in that respect. Who was the manager of the Yankees who never lost a game at Yankee Stadium? It was Virdon. He managed the Yankees for a little more than one and a half years — 1974 and 1975 — and that is when the Yankees played their home games at Shea Stadium while Yankee Stadium was undergoing extensive renovation.

In his first year in New York, Virdon managed the Yankees to an 89-73 record and a second place finish. He was named Major League Manager of the Year by both *The Sporting News* and the *Associated Press* that year. It was the Yankees' highest finish in more than a decade. New York was 53-51 the next season when Virdon was fired by George Steinbrenner.

Virdon was a quiet sort, and he had a bad stomach. Some of the Yankees dubbed him "Mr. Milkshake."

Virdon was the second choice when he was named manager of the New York Yankees in 1974. George Steinbrenner had wanted Dick Williams, who was under contract to manage the Oakland A's. And A's owner Charley Finley refused to release Williams. So Steinbrenner had to settle for Virdon.

The New York media made much of Virdon being a runner-up selection at best, but Virdon said it didn't matter to him. "I was out of a major league job at the time," he told us at the end of the 1992 season. "I was eager to get a job. I had a chance to manage. That was more important to me."

Two of the coaches Steinbrenner provided Virdon with were Whitey Ford and Elston Howard, who had played for the Yankees against the Pirates in that 1960 World Series.

"That was as good an experience as you could have, managing in New York, if you were planning on staying in the field," said Virdon

23

when we spoke in October, 1992, and shared stories about our experiences in The Big Apple.

"The media attention and pressure was about 100 to 1 to managing in Pittsburgh. Here, you'd have the two beat writers and a few writers from the other team's city. In New York, there'd be 50 to 75 writers, depending on the significance of the game.

"The experience was good for me," said Virdon, continuing to get ready for his return trip to Springfield. "It was a good two years. We had some talent. We were in the race up to the last day my first year. We finished one game out. We had Piniella, Munson, Murcer, Lyle, Nettles. We got 'Catfish' Hunter the second year. He was the first big free agent signing. We had Pat Dobson, Tippy Martinez."

Virdon has known the best of days and the worst of days while wearing a major league baseball uniform, and this may have helped him deal with the stunning setback to the Braves in the 1992 NL championship series. He had been a pivotal figure both offensively and defensively when the Pirates beat the Yankees to win the 1960 World Series, a coach on Murtaugh's staff in the 1971 championship season and the manager in 1972 when the Pirates were just one out away from their second consecutive trip to the World Series.

Talk about difficult defeats . . .

The Pirates lost the National League pennant in 1972 when Bob Moose threw a wild pitch to allow George Foster of the Cincinnati Reds to score from third with the winning run. I was in Cincinnati covering that game at Riverfront Stadium for *The New York Post*, and I remember how disappointed the Pirates and Virdon were afterward on that infamous day in Pirates' history. It was a frustrating way to end a season.

In 1980, his Astros also lost in the final game of the National League championship series, so Virdon was familiar with the feeling of what might have been.

"I've done almost everything I've wanted to in baseball, although I missed a couple of times by an out or two of getting a team to the Series," said Virdon.

Virdon, it should be pointed out, has a fine record as a manager. He was hired to manage the Astros late in the 1975 season. In 1979 he was named the Manager of the Year by United Press International after the Astros finished second in the NL West. He guided them to the 1980 National League West championship and was again named Manager of the Year by *The Sporting News* after Houston won its division for the first time in club history. He was also in charge when the Astros won the second-half title during the strike-shortened 1981 season. His seven-year mark with Houston was 544-522 (.510), which makes him the winningest manager in the history of that franchise. His last managerial assignment was with the Montreal Expos in 1983 and 1984. His composite record in 13 years as a big league manager was 995-921 (.519). By coincidence, Leyland had the same winning percentage of .519 after eight seasons as Pirates manager.

"What I regret most about those teams were the players that were involved, the guys who never got another chance to go to a World Series," said Virdon. "That was the tough part about it. I've been in baseball a long time, but there's still no feeling like being in the playoffs or the World Series. It's like walking on a cloud."

Looking back on the loss to the Braves in that seventh game of the 1992 NL playoffs, Virdon said:

"What you have to remember is that until it is over there's always that chance of losing. That's why they have nine innings, and time limits and clocks. There was nothing wrong with the Pirates; it just didn't turn out in our favor."

"I knew it was trouble."

Virdon was the lead-off hitter in the 1960 World Series. In the seventh and deciding game, Virdon batted in two runs as the Pirates took a lead of 4-0. The Yankees went ahead, 7-4, but in the eighth inning Pittsburgh scored five runs, partly because of a ground ball off Virdon's bat that hit Tony Kubek in the throat.

Virdon cursed the moment he watched the ball leave his bat and bounce toward Kubek. Routine grounder, classic double-play ball, he thought.

Kubek would get Gino Cimoli at second, Virdon would be nipped at first and the Pirates' eighth inning rally would die right there. And New York, leading 7-4 in the seventh game at Pittsburgh, would go on to claim the 1960 world championship.

But the ball was never gloved, the throw never made. Instead, Virdon reached first base and looked toward second to see Kubek on the ground, near the bag, clutching his Adam's apple. Everybody was safe and Kubek, breathless and hurt, was on his way to a nearby hospital.

"I hit the ball well," Virdon once recalled, "but I hit the ball right at Tony. Fortunately, there was a clump of dirt out of place, a pebble or something, and just as he got ready to field the ball, it took a quick, short hop that wasn't expected, and it hit him in the throat, directly in the Adam's apple. Instead of the double play, I ended up getting a single, and we had two runners on and nobody out. There's no question it would have been a double play."

George Kiseda, an irreverent sports journalist at the *Pittsburgh Sun-Telegraph*, suggested that Eddie Dunn, the groundskeeper at Forbes Field, should have been named the MVP of the 1960 World Series.

From there unraveled a championship the Yankees had won, lost and won again — depending upon the day of the week — and finally would lose. The double play that wasn't led to five runs for the Pirates and after the Yankees had scored twice in their half of the ninth to tie the score, a miner's son named Bill Mazeroski hit the most dramatic home run in Series history to push the Pirates to a 10-9 triumph and its first world championship since 1925.

25

Where was Bill Virdon when Bill Mazeroski hit the home run that sunk the Yankees in the 1960 World Series?

"I was getting ready to go on deck," said Virdon, recalling the sequence of events. "I was next to the bat rack. Dick Stuart was on deck. He was going to pinch-hit for the pitcher."

Did Virdon know it was going out right away?

"No, but I knew it was trouble," said Virdon. "Immediately. You look to the outfield, and you look to see how the outfielder is moving."

That outfielder was Yogi Berra, who is better known for being a Hall of Fame catcher for the Yankees.

"You could see right away that he wasn't going to catch it," ventured Virdon. "You were hoping it would hit the wall, and get away from him. Then it was out."

I asked Virdon if the suddeness of the finish didn't compare somewhat with the way the Pirates had just lost the playoffs to the Braves. It was hard for anybody associated with the Pirates or Pittsburgh to appreciate the drama that had unfolded at Atlanta's Fulton County Stadium that Wednesday night, but it was baseball at its absolute dramatic best. It was good theatre. It was like something out of a movie about baseball — like Robert Redford hitting a home run to win the big game in *The Natural* — an unbelievable finish.

"This year's game was dramatic, but it wasn't the same," said Virdon. "In 1960 the bottom of the ninth inning was over before it started. This time things started to materialize. It took awhile. We had two outs. If we get one more out we win. This took longer to unfold than the way Maz finished the 1960 Series."

Maz's home run wasn't the only one that sticks out in Virdon's mind from that 1960 Series. He also remembers a shot by Mickey Mantle over the deepest part of center field.

Asked what player on the Pirates he admired the most, Virdon said, "Dick Groat. He always got more out of his ability than anyone in the game."

When asked to name his most cherished memory of his days with the Pirates, Virdon said, "winning the pennant and the Series in 1960, and Danny Murtaugh's guidance through the years. He prepared me to stay in the game."

There was a magic to Murtaugh's team in those days, and it was a close-knit club before such unity was hailed in song and banners as it was with "We Are Fam-a-lee" during the Pirates' championship season of 1979.

"There are lots of reasons why that 1960 team is so well remembered," said Virdon. "One reason for that is because we were such big underdogs. Another reason was because Pittsburgh hadn't had a winner in such a long time (the Pirates last won a World Series in 1925). It was the culmination of those things — and who we were playing."

What about Bill Mazeroski, the hero? Did his heroics sit well with the team?

"He was a favorite of anyone involved with that club," said Virdon.

26

Virdon with Manager Danny Murtaugh   With Bill Mazeroski at 30th year reunion.

During his days as manager of the New York Yankees, Virdon catches up with Willie Stargell and Richie Hebner.

Bill and Shirley Virdon flank their daughters, Deborah Ann, Linda Sue and Lisa Lee, during spring training stroll.

"Everyone would love to do something like that, but there wasn't one jealous person on that club."

Why not?

"Because it was Maz. He's good people. I think that answers it. Everybody liked Maz; he was good people. He was good-hearted, pleasant to be around, he was a clutch hitter and he could play second base with the best of them.

"He was *the* Pirate. Maybe he wasn't the most productive hitter, or a high average guy, and maybe he wasn't the most glamorous. But probably everybody liked him. Everybody was completely satisfied that he was the one who hit the home run.

"I roomed with him for three or four years. I knew him as well as anybody. We probably said less to each other than any two roommates in the history of sports. We weren't that talkative — both of us were on the quiet side — but we ate together, we had a few drinks together, we walked around town together, we went to the ballpark together. He later coached for me for a year or two with the Pirates.

"We had a really unique club. Everyone contributed. I think that club and this club and the one in '71 had a lot in common. Somehow, over the course of the year, when they had to come up with the runs they came up with the runs The only thing we didn't do this year was win that last one.

"This club (1992) had a lot of similarities. There was nobody involved with the (1960) club who didn't contribute. Everybody had a big part in it. They seemed to be able to get it done. That's what I remember best.

"We were especially tough in the late going. How often we'd come back . . . The writers used to say they didn't have to come to the ballpark until the sixth inning."

For the record, the 1960 Pirates on 29 occasions, when trailing after six innings, came on to win.

Virdon's advice for young players: "Always give it your all. That is what the fans pay to see."

Virdon was hailed for making game-saving catches in Game One and Game Four of that 1960 Series. Murtaugh had told the New York media in advance that they were going to see a great center fielder in action, and he didn't have Mickey Mantle in mind. Virdon made Murtaugh look like a true seer.

In the fourth inning of the first game, Berra came to bat with two on, nobody out, and the Yankees trailing, 3-1. Berra ripped into a Vernon Law pitch and sent it deep to center field. It looked like extra bases, for sure, a bases-clearing, game-tying hit. Virdon ran it down, leaped and caught it. The Bucs went on to win.

The Yankees killed the Pirates in the next two games, and then the Pirates evened the Series at two victories apiece with a 3-2 win. This time Bob Cerv crushed an ElRoy Face pitch and with the runners on the move from first and second, Virdon made a circus catch at the end of a long run.

Virdon was so impressive in the field that his efforts were compared to past World Series spectacular fielding by the likes of Willie Mays and Al Gionfriddo.

"People made a fuss about those catches because it was a World Series," said Dick Groat, shortstop on the Pirates' team for which Virdon was the defensive hero. "Actually, he was such a good outfielder, he made a lot of great catches look easy. I remember him pulling the ball out of the vines in Forbes Field that nobody believed.

"And the thing about his great catches is that he would come off the wall throwing. I played in front of Virdon for seven years and I can never recall him throwing to the wrong base. To describe Bill Virdon, you can say he didn't make mistakes.

"In my opinion," Groat continued, "Bill Virdon was the all-time greatest center fielder who ever played the game."

Even Virdon was embarrassed by that evaluation and cautioned a writer about buying that statement at face value.

"Dick is prejudiced," said Virdon. "He was not only a teammate but we roomed together, and were the best of friends. You better ask someone else."

Mazeroski may not have been a neutral observer, either. "There weren't many better than Virdon," said Mazeroski, who also roomed with Virdon. "Nobody worked harder at trying to be the best."

Groat would not give up. "Bill Virdon played the game intelligently," Groat goes on. "He had an unbelievable instinct and he worked extremely hard all of the time. He was a complete ball player, always thinking ahead — very, very team-oriented.

"Put a man on second and you could bet that Bill moved him over. He never missed a sign. Bring any hitter to the plate and Bill knew exactly how to play him. He had that instinct for every aspect of the game — running, hitting, playing defense. He always knew the precise stage of the game — the inning, the hitter, the pitcher, the score, the count — everything there was to know."

Groat flips the observation ball to Mazeroski:

"He never did let up," Maz said of Virdon. "He had a great jump, but he worked on that. During batting practice every day, he would spend time in the outfield, making believe that he was going after every ball, moving as the ball left the bat. You don't see players work like that often.

"He had it down so pat that we figured in a game he would take off before the batter made contact."

It was ironic that Virdon was at his very best in a nationally-televised Series with the Yankees because he could have been wearing the pinstripes himself. He originally signed with the Yankees.

Virdon has to smile when he reflects back on the spring of 1954. After a great season with the Yankees' Double A club in Birmingham, Alabama, Virdon was invited to try out for the parent team and he was placed on the major league roster.

Joe DiMaggio had been the Yankees' center fielder when Virdon was growing up and they had signed a young phenom named Mickey Mantle before Virdon came along.

"It was a spring to remember," Virdon recalled during an interview with Ian McDonald of the *The Gazette* in Montreal when he was managing the Expos. "Casey Stengel played me in several exhibition games and I was 0 for 19. I dropped a ball late in a game that caused us to lose.

"And to cap it off, I hit Casey in the ribs with a relay from the outfield during warmup. The throw had a lot on it and knocked the wind out of him. When he got his breath back he looked out towards where I was and hollered, 'If you could throw half that accurate in a ball game you might throw somebody out!' To make a long story short, two weeks later I was back in the minors."

And within a month he was out of the Yankees' organization. "It was actually a break," said Virdon at his apartment in Mt. Lebanon. "I was familiar with the people in front of me, and I didn't see an opportunity for me in New York."

Reflecting on his early days in the big leagues, Virdon offered another evaluation:

"This game has not been easy for me," Virdon said. "I've had to work for everything I've ever got. And it's been hard work.

"I worked in the outfield to make myself a good outfielder. I shagged flies until I felt I would drop. And I practiced throwing from the outfield so much I thought my arm would fall off.

"And the same goes for hitting. I was not a natural hitter. I had to work for every hit. Sure, I would have liked to hit .300. Who wouldn't? But when I hit only .250 it was not because I wanted to hit .250. It was not for lack of trying. I was always trying my best."

"There was a lot of room to cover."

There was no center field quite like the one that Virdon roamed at Forbes Field. He has gone out to the site in recent seasons, and it pleases him that a portion of the center field wall still remains intact, and is a tourist attraction. "I've been back out there, but not this year," said Virdon. "I'm familiar with what's left of Forbes Field.

"Forbes Field was ideal for a center fielder who had some speed and ability," added Virdon in our interview. "There was a lot of room to cover. You didn't have to worry about fences. No ballpark had a bigger area overall to cover. Some had deeper walls, but none had more ground to cover. I did it for ten years."

And he did it, according to New York baseball writer Maury Allen, a former co-worker of mine at *The New York Post*, "the way DiMaggio had played it in New York, effortlessly, stylishly and comfortably. They just don't make defensive center fielders like Virdon very often."

30

It is interesting to note that Virdon and Roberto Clemente both broke into baseball the same year — 1955 — and Virdon, with the St. Louis Cardinals, was named the National League's rookie of the year. Virdon hit .281 with 17 home runs and 68 RBIs and was also an excellent outfielder, whereas Clemente batted .255 with five home runs in 124 games. Virdon won the International League batting title the year before with a .333 average with Rochester in Triple A ball.

"What was it like to play ball next to Roberto Clemente?" I asked Virdon.

"I can't say anything bad about it," replied Virdon. "Nothing to my left side went undone. I knew if something went that way it would be taken care of."

"What sort of relationship did you have with Clemente?"

"We were friendly. There was a respect," answered Virdon. "He was one of the best in the business."

I mentioned to Virdon that Clemente was not as big a hero in Pittsburgh when he was playing as he was after he died in a tragic airplane crash. A local sports writer had suggested late in the 1992 season that Barry Bonds could become as big a hero in Pittsburgh as Clemente if he would change his attitude and be more sensitive to his image.

Certainly Clemente was not any more concerned about winning over the fans than Bonds. Clemente was never much of a public relations man during his heyday, but he was a Hall of Fame performer, no doubt about that. He played right field with the same flair and skills that separate the Penguins' Mario Lemieux from the pack in the National Hockey League.

"I think there were reasons for Clemente not being accepted as a hero when he was playing for the Pirates," offered Virdon.

"When he came up he was 19, right out of Puerto Rico, and he was not familiar with American ways. There was a language barrier at first. He wasn't sure what was expected of him. He was criticized for his ways. As he aged and matured, he gained and gained by the time he finished his career.

"I don't think there was anyone more respected. I credit that to his ability and his intelligence. I played with him, I coached with him, and I managed him, and I can't say enough about how much he matured. And he knew what was expected of him, and he did what was expected of him.

"At first, I don't think he had an idea of what it would be like for him in the major leagues, especially coming from a small Spanish-speaking island. He had the reputation of complaining about hurts all the time, but you can look at the record and he was there."

Clemente was just as complimentary of Virdon when he spoke of him in 1962: "I know more about Virdon than any other player because we're so close in the outfield. He doesn't get the headlines because he makes everything look so easy. Many times I look up on a tough chance and there is Virdon near me in case something goes wrong. If you don't want to take my word for it how valuable Virdon is, ask some of our pitchers. He has kept quite a few of them in the big leagues."

One of those pitchers, ElRoy Face, once said, "I could make mistakes and Virdon would solve them. He'd catch the ball."

The Pirates won a divisional title in 1972 in Virdon's first year as manager, and then Clemente was killed before the 1973 season (on Dec. 31, 1972), Mazeroski retired, Steve Blass, unexplainedly, went from being a 19-game winner to a 3-game winner, and the Pirates disappointed their fans and fell from first to third place in the NL East.

The Pirates' record was 67-69 when GM Joe Brown bumped Virdon in favor of Murtaugh. It was often said that Brown believed Murtaugh was the only man who could really manage the Pirates. The Bucs finished up 13-13 with Murtaugh in charge.

Virdon had come back to Pittsburgh as a coach in 1968 under Larry Shepard and then Murtaugh, and despite the unpleasantness of giving way as manager to Murtaugh in early September of 1973, he still credits Murtaugh for his development as a manager in baseball.

"The biggest thing I learned sitting next to Danny Murtaugh on the bench was patience," said Virdon in 1971. "He showed me that you have to have patience with the players. Also with patience, he showed confidence in the team and that confidence was reflected in the players' feeling toward the manager. Danny has had the patience to stick with his players when they make a few mistakes."

Before Virdon was released, he showed his firmness with two players — Rich Hebner and Dock Ellis — but it may have hurt him in the end. Joe Brown wasn't big on manager-player disputes, especially public ones.

Virdon accused Hebner of indifferent fielding following a game. Hebner roared back and cursed. Virdon got a public apology the next day. The only problem was that Virdon's venom was spit out in front of sports writers who were in the clubhouse. Brown was very upset with Virdon for this public outburst. Brown believed such criticism should have been offered in private.

Ellis liked to wear pink hair curlers in the locker room. Virdon told him, "I don't care what you wear at home, but you don't wear them at a ballpark." Ellis complained but left the curlers home.

"I'd rather have guys who want to play," said Virdon, "but if they're raising too much hell, you've got to collar them to keep it from snowballing."

Two people who came to his defense were Mazeroski and Al Oliver. "He's a fantastic guy," said Maz. Oliver offered, "He's the only manager who ever understood me."

Mazeroski had more to say on the same subject. "His honesty and fairness are the qualities that stand out. He treats everybody alike and only asks that you play ball and be a man about it. He won't get on you if you do your job, but he can be as hard as necessary."

"I always looked for a game."
— Bill Virdon

The story of William Charles Virdon began in Royal Oak, Michigan, where his father, Charles, worked for the Ford Motor Company. Bill was born in Hazel Park on June 9, 1931. To believe his mother, Virdon was destined to become a big-time ballplayer. "When he was still sitting in a high chair," Bertha Mae Virdon once said, "you could throw something to him and he'd catch it."

The Virdons liked their sports. "My folks took me to my first ball game when I was 10 days old," Virdon said. "We lived in the Detroit area and followed the Tigers." In his personal file in the Pirates' p.r. offices, when asked to list his childhood sports hero, Virdon chose Hank Greenberg of the Tigers. Greenberg, of course, finished up his career with the Pirates in 1947.

"I wanted to play the game ever since I was big enough to play," said Virdon. "I always looked for a game."

When Virdon was 13, his father decided he wanted a quiet life. He moved the family to South Fork, Missouri and a year later to nearby West Plains. He bought a farm. And then a grocery store. And then other businesses.

Like most of his teammates on the 1960 Pirates, Virdon was a multi-sports star in high school. His school didn't have a baseball team, but he excelled in football and basketball, and played baseball on a local amateur team. As a senior, Virdon was a quarterback and captain and once scored three touchdowns — on runs of 95, 65 and 60 yards — in a victory against a top rival. "A couple of those touchdowns were on punt returns," recalled Virdon.

"I liked to play any kind of ball, not just baseball. In fact, when I was younger, I played more football than I played baseball. I played only one game of baseball in high school."

He did play for hometown teams in West Plains, however, against teams from other communities like Pumpkin Center. He was a shortstop, at first, but later switched to the outfield.

The University of Missouri tendered an offer of a football scholarship, but Virdon accepted a basketball scholarship instead to Drury College in Springfield. He left after the first term when he was discovered by the Yankees, by the same scout, Tom Greenwade, who plucked Mickey Mantle out of obscurity in Oklahoma. Virdon was going to be a physical education major and thought he wanted to be a coach someday.

Bill met his wife when he was home from the minor leagues. She was a teacher in the West Plains high school and was introduced to Virdon by one of her students. "It sounds like a fairy tale, doesn't it," said Shirley Virdon, the mother of their three daughters.

With Mantle in the fold, however, there was no room in center field for Virdon with the Yankees. He was one of several players dispatched to the St. Louis Cardinals in exchange for Enos Slaughter in 1954.

He was named Rookie of the Year in the National League with the Cardinals in 1955 and a year later, on May 16, 1956, he was traded to the Pirates in exchange for Bobby Del Greco and Dick Littlefield. "It was the worst trade I ever made," confessed Frank Lane, the general manager of the Cardinals who had a long and colorful career in baseball.

In 1956, Virdon batted .319 for Pittsburgh, which was the second highest in the league. That was a bonus as far as Joe Brown was concerned because he said he made the trade for Virdon strictly to strengthen the Pirates' outfield.

Said Joe Brown at the time: "I always liked Virdon as a player and I thought a left-handed hitting outfielder (Virdon batted left-handed, and threw right-handed) would balance us somewhat. I'll be honest, though, I didn't think he was the outfielder he showed us. He has made some great plays in the field."

With his speed and fine arm, Virdon tied the major league record for most assists by an outfielder in one inning in 1958. Then in 1959 he led all National League outfielders in double plays. In 1962 Bill received the Gold Glove in recognition of his work in centerfield. Clemente and Mays were the other outfielders so honored that year.

Murtaugh often said he thought Virdon was right up there with Mays as far as his ability in the outfield was concerned. "And I think Mays is one of the best defensive ball players I've ever seen in baseball," said the Pirates manager.

Virdon lists the Gold Glove and his .319 batting average in 1956 as the personal highlights of his career with the Pirates.

"Virdon always gave $1.10 for every dollar you paid him as a player," said Brown. "It is impossible to manage or coach without character, and that's what Virdon has . . . character."

Pittsburgh Pirates

Bill Virdon and vacationing Pirates fans are flanked by Dick Groat, left, and Don Hoak at spring training.

Where were you?

"I'll never forget that day."
—Rich Nesbit

Vincent A. Sarni
Former Chairman of the Board, PPG Industries
Chairman of the Executive Board, Pittsburgh Pirates

"I remember Mazeroski's home run very well. I was living in Connecticut at the time. It ruined my day. You see, I was a Yankees fan at that time. But now, as a Pirates fan, I am thrilled when I see replays of that fantastic finish."

Eugene Barone
Chairman of the Board,
Blue Cross of Western Pennsylvania

"I was in San Francisco two weeks ago, and I went over to Tiburon for lunch. I walked into a store that had old sports pictures. What caught my eye was one of Honus Wagner. I always enjoyed Honus Wagner. I had friends in Carnegie when I was growing up, and we used to talk to Honus Wagner routinely. We never realized the significance of how big he was. I think his card is the most valuable of all the collector cards now. Look how many autographs we could have had. Behind the picture of Honus Wagner was one of Forbes Field during the 1960 World Series. I bought them both.

"I was at a dinner one year held by the Pittsburgh Pirates chapter of the Major League Baseball Alumni. I was seated between Bill Mazeroski and Dick Groat. How much better of a position could you be in if you grew up loving baseball in Pittsburgh?

"I was watching the seventh game of the 1960 World Series in an office at the Law & Finance Building. The thing I remember was — when the Pirates won — seeing all those IBM cards, everything was done on IBM cards in those days, flying out of office windows. It was quite a day in Pittsburgh. I remember seeing Maz on the Today Show the next morning. That was such a thrill for all of us."

John E. Wright, President
Wheeling-Nisshin Inc.
Follansbee, West Virginia

"I was at Forbes Field when it happened. I remember there were about five kids running around with baseballs after the game, trying to sell them, saying the one they had was the one Maz hit out. I was working at Wheeling-Pittsburgh Steel then, and our plant was 90 percent in Yorkville and 10 percent in Tiltonsville. The day after the game there was a parade down the main street of Yorkville — which was about six blocks long — and Maz was riding in an open-top convertible, waving to everyone. The fire trucks from both communities were in the parade, which means there were two fire trucks, and the bands from both high schools were in the parade. Neither school exists anymore. But he's an outright legend down there still. I've never met him, but I have played on Maz's golf course."

William Block Sr.
Chairman, Pittsburgh Post-Gazette

"I really have only a hazy memory. I remember that we were there at Forbes Field and I remember the excitement as Bill Mazeroski's home run went over the fence and how the crowd surged toward home plate and Maz got lost in the tumult. I recall that we stood in a daze, hardly comprehending that the game was over and the Series was won. The ending was so sudden that it took a while for the realization to sink in. It's something everyone here remembers. It still amazes me the way people in Pittsburgh still react to seeing a replay of Mazeroski's home run. It still excites them. They still cheer."

Rich Nesbit
Vice-President, Co-Owner,
Sutersville Lumber Co., Inc.

"I have a film that I made of Mazeroski's home run. I was too excited to film it from start to finish — I was jumping around so much — but I had a Kodak Brownie film camera, and I got him crossing the plate. I still look at it from time to time.

"My wife Peg and I were both at that seventh game, though we were not sitting together. Originally, we had a pair of tickets for the sixth and seventh games. My brother-in-law and I went to see the sixth game, just in case there wouldn't be any seventh game, and we agreed to give our tickets for the seventh game to our wives. The Yankees beat the Pirates badly in the sixth game, by 12-0.

"The morning of the seventh game, somebody associated with John Harris, the man who owned the Pittsburgh Hornets and started the Ice Capades, called our lumber company and asked if any of the salesmen wanted to go. We were doing some business with them at the time. None of the salesmen wanted to go. I said, 'I'll take them!'

"So my brother-in-law and I went to the seventh game. Our wives sat in the other seats. I was in a box hanging out from the third tier. It was a great view from above. Bishop Wright was in the same box. When Hal Smith hit that home run in the eighth inning to give the Pirates a 9-7 lead it looked like that would be the game. But that became anti-climatic after the Yankees tied it up at the top of the ninth inning.

When Maz hit the home run we all went crazy. I was too busy jumping around to film it. I'll never forget that day.

"Those players were great. I remember we went to spring training the next year. We really liked Vernon Law. I took a copy of the game program from the 1960 World Series and asked Law if he would sign it. But I had forgotten to take a pen. He went up to somebody else and borrowed a pen so he could sign my program. I don't think today's ballplayers would do something like that. I remember there was a Cadillac limousine sitting nearby, and Everett Taft Bensen was in it. He was the Secretary of Agriculture. He was an important figure in the Mormon church and he was there to see Law, who was a deacon in the Mormon church."

Christopher Passodelis
Owner, Christopher's Restaurant
Pittsburgh

"My wife Cathy and I were living in a little dinky apartment in Prospect Park in Whitehall at the time. We had been to two of the earlier games in the World Series, but I could not come up with any tickets for the seventh game.

"We were watching the game on TV. We had two of our four boys back then. Billy was two, and Michael was ten months old. We were holding them on our laps while we were watching the game. When Maz hit that home run we started jumping up and down, jumping as high as we could, and the kids started crying. The whole apartment was in an uproar. You could hear other families carrying on in the other apartments. It was where a lot of young couples were living, and they were so happy. I remember we paid $92.50 a month, and that included all the utilities. It was a great time in our lives."

Ed Ryan
Founder, Ryan Homes
Mt. Lebanon, Pa.

"I remember the thrill and the excitement just within myself, then what happened on the field. Geez, it was really great. If you asked me — like the 'Immaculate Reception' — the Mazeroski home run was the most exciting event I have ever witnessed in sports."

Jim Kosko
LTV Steel
Chagrin Falls, Ohio

"I was working at Westinghouse Electric Company in East Pittsburgh back then, after I'd gotten out of college. I was sitting on the second level on the first base side, above the Pirates dugout, for the seventh game of the 1960 World Series. I was there with my future father-in-law, John Rebol, who was the owner of the Pittsburgh Institute of Mortuary Science, which was on Forbes Avenue across the street from Magee-Womens Hospital. He had a secretary named Jean Coyne, and we went to Pete Coyne's Bar in Oakland after the game and celebrated. He knew everybody there. It was early in the day, and I decided to go home to Duquesne and take a nap. I was planning on going Downtown that night to really celebrate. I woke up the next morning on the couch and had missed everything."

Pat Williams
President, Orlando Magic
Former Minor League Baseball Executive

"I was at Wake Forest University at the start of my junior year when the Pirates played the Yankees in the seventh game of the 1960 World Series. We were watching the game on TV in the Monogram Club, a hangout for varsity athletes. I remember Norm Snead was a senior that year. He went on to a great career as a quarterback in the National Football League. We were walking out of the club together after Mazeroski hit the home run. Snead hated baseball. He thought it was the most boring thing imaginable. He turned to me and said, 'That was the most fantastic game I ever saw.' It's funny how things stick in your mind. You are doing a tremendous service for sports fans. It's important that these stories be saved for future generations. You have to talk to these people before it's too late. I am a hero-worshipper, so I envy you your assignment."

Pittsburgh Pirate

Bill Mazeroski follows through after hitting home run to win the World Series in bottom of ninth inning of seventh game.

38

Dick Groat
Hometown Hero

"Baseball owes me nothing.
I owe everything to baseball."

The corn stalks that remained standing appeared dry and brittle, and the spikes of corn that had been harvested were all shorn at the same height on the color-layered horizon. Pumpkins were scattered about the fields, and pumpkins were stacked neatly, by size, at the roadside fruit and vegetable stands. Those pumpkins were covered with dew, no doubt, in the chilly morning, but the moisture had been burned off by a bright sun as temperatures climbed toward the mid-'60s.

Apples were advertised by signs, some professionally painted, others of a homemade variety, along the road. There were several apple orchards in the area. I could smell apples through the open windows as I drove along the road.

It was an idyllic day, on October 26, 1992, and the fall foliage was spectacular. The woods were ablaze with the green leaves having given way to gold, red, orange, brown and burgundy. The trees were still rather full and draped over the winding road of Route 30 leading to Ligonier. It doesn't get any better in New England or North Carolina than it does in this Westmoreland County countryside.

It looked like a Nat Youngblood watercolor rural scene.

Now I was driving Route 711 north, looking for the Champion Lakes Golf Course, billed as "a country club open to the public," which is owned and operated by former Pirates Dick Groat and Jerry Lynch. It is located in the valley of the Laurel Highlands, seven miles north of downtown Ligonier and Fort Ligonier, a replica of a fortress that was originally built in 1758 by General John Forbes — Forbes Avenue and Forbes Field were named after him — and once occupied by General George Washington during the French and Indian Wars. In that same year, General Forbes drove the French from the Point and built Fort Pitt.

I had to smile when I recalled a visit there about ten years earlier when Kathie and I took our daughters, Sarah and Rebecca, to nearby Idlewild Park as well as Fort Ligonier. There are waxen figures at Fort Ligonier depicting scenes from the 18th Century, and my oldest daughter, Sarah, then about eight years old, was spooked and started crying when she saw bloodied waxen figures of soldiers who had been shot while defending the fort. She can laugh about it now.

The town square in Ligonier was decorated for Halloween, with colorful straw-stuffed figures, and witches and goblins attached to lamp posts and park benches and the gazebo in the center island. There is a Mellon Bank there, and there are Mellon-owned estates nearby, and old money all around this sleepy-looking storybook village.

Pittsburgh-born writer Annie Dillard described Ligonier in one of her books as "that pretty village in the distant mountains where the Mellons lived."

Champion Lakes Golf Course is located about 70 miles east of Pittsburgh. You take the Parkway East from the city, and hang a right on Route 30, just past the road signs for Edgewood, Kennywood Park and Swissvale. Groat was born and raised in Swissvale and has a home today in Edgewood, just east of the Squirrel Hill Tunnels. The trip, for the most part, was familiar to me, as Route 30 leads to Latrobe and St. Vincent College, the summer training camp site for the Pittsburgh Steelers. I had made that trip many times while reporting on the Steelers for *The Pittsburgh Press* in the late '70s and early '80s, and while researching books about the Steelers in the '90s.

Once you pass St. Vincent College, you see Latrobe Area Airport, Latrobe Steel and Latrobe Area High School on the right side of Route 30, and on the horizon just behind the high school is the so-green landscape of the Latrobe Country Club, owned and overseen by golfing great Arnold Palmer, a legendary figure throughout the world, but just another good guy in his hometown. His dad, "Deacon" Palmer, was the greenskeeper and the family lived in a small house on the course that Arnold now owns. Palmer's Cadillac dealership is also on the right side of the road, then signs for Youngstown, Pa., and Derry, then Idlewild Park and, at last, Ligonier and the Lord Ligonier Inn. You turn left on 711 to a paradise-like fall setting. If you turn right, and drive 711 South, which I did later on my way to speak at a workshop seminar hosted by Caremark, a home health care company, at Seven Springs in Donegal, you drive by the Laurel Valley Golf Club and the Ligonier Country Club, two very private and much-admired golf preserves about ten miles away from Groat's golf course. The layout at Laurel Valley, in particular, rates as one of the best and most exclusive in the nation.

Groat's 18-hole, par 71 course, which he believes is second only to Laurel Valley in Western Pennsylvania, is for the average guy who loves to play golf on a championship course. It is a demanding layout. The green fee was $15 during the week, and $20 on weekends when I visited. Golf carts were $18, or $9 per person.

"Our idea was to build a championship golf course for the public," said Groat. "It's a course for the man who loves the game and wants a challenge. And there's not a prettier layout anywhere."

As I was searching for Groat's place, I passed the Mill Creek Stables and saw beautiful dark brown riding horses grazing in a large, flat field, and a small roadside bar called The Wagon Wheel. I saw a headless man crawling in a front yard, another of those straw-stuffed Halloween figures. It turned out there was no sign in front of the Champion Lakes when I arrived — it was being refurbished and would be hanging out when I left two hours later — and I nearly missed the entrance. But I spotted parking spaces marked D. Groat and J. Lynch, and turned in to the lot. I thought Lynch had retired from operating the course several years earlier, and was surprised to see he still had a reserved parking place in front of the pro shop.

Lynch used to live in a house that adjoins the clubhouse, and now Groat lives there part of the year.

I found Groat sitting at a table in the center of the clubhouse dining room, talking to someone on the telephone. His only companions were Nancy Yeager, a waitress, who would make us both delicious cheeseburgers and french fries for lunch, and Dave Mahoney, the club bartender for many years. A few locals were out playing the 18-course, and later some teenage boys sneaked onto the course after school. Groat just smiled when he saw the boys swinging their clubs through a panoramic window.

There were so many leaves in the fairways that playing golf was like playing hide-and-seek, but these dyed-in-the-wool golfers were taking advantage of an unseasonably nice day to whack the ball around. Even when Groat goes back to Edgewood, his course remains open to play on such days. He drives up to look after business on those days.

"I live here from the first of May through the end of October," said Groat. "Then I go to my home in Edgewood for the winter. That way I can go watch basketball practice when I want to."

Groat was looking forward to his 13th season as the color analyst for University of Pittsburgh basketball, working with play-by-play broadcaster Bill Hillgrove of WTAE Radio.

Groat was a two-time All-America basketball player at Duke University and the 1952 College Player of the Year. I have seen his photo in the Basketball Hall of Fame in Springfield, Massachusetts, though he is not an inductee.

In a wonderful book about the Duke University basketball program of the late '70s called *Forever's Team*, writer John Feinstein referred to him as "the immortal Dick Groat." His jersey No. 10 was the first and one of the few ever to be retired at Duke. A replica of it hangs from the rafters at Duke's Cameron Indoor Stadium.

"He has the self-assured manner of a big man on campus although he's lost much of his crew cut," wrote Jim Brosnan, a pitcher-book author *(The Long Season)* from the Cincinnati Reds. In 1960, Groat was the captain of the Pirates, and no other baseball team in the majors had a captain. The Pirates were different, that's all.

Groat played two years in the National Basketball Association with the Fort Wayne Pistons before going on to star with his hometown Pittsburgh Pirates, where he was the National League batting champion and MVP in 1960 when the Pirates beat the New York Yankees to win the World Series. Interestingly enough, Groat has always regarded himself as a retired basketball player, rather than a retired baseball player.

Groat could be the greatest all-around athlete ever to come out of western Pennsylvania. He is competing in that respect with the likes of Arnold Palmer, Stan Musial, Johnny Unitas, Joe Montana, Jack Twyman, Tony Dorsett, Maurice Stokes, George Blanda, Danny Marino, Joe Namath and Honus Wagner, but Groat alone reached the pinnacle in two pro sports.

Groat has been a great fan of the University of Pittsburgh and its sports teams, going back to his youth, and the school does not have a more fervent or frustrated fan. "What's wrong at your alma mater, James?" began Groat when we sat down to talk.

He wanted to know how Pitt had been beaten so badly by East Carolina at its Homecoming Game at Pitt Stadium two days earlier. He was worried that the basketball team was not going to have the guards to complement an anticipated strong frontline to be a winner in the Big East. Groat is partial to backcourtmen because that was his position. I have had two Hall of Fame coaches, Red Auerbach of the Boston Celtics and Red Holzman of the New York Knicks, both rave to me about their high regard for Groat as a basketball player. Some say the great Bob Cousy hated to play against Groat.

Groat looked great, as usual. He was 10 days away from his 62nd birthday — on November 4. He still had that well-chiseled head, still balding, that firm chin, and the determined look of a guy who would be out to beat you no matter what the game. The brown hair that remains has gone gray for the most part. There is a sharp edge to all of Groat's Germanic features. He was wearing a black sweater over a yellow-gold golf shirt — Groat still looks good in a black and gold uniform — with a Champion Lakes logo over the left breast, and charcoal gray slacks, neatly-pressed, and well-shined black shoes. And there is still a gleam in his brown eyes. Groat has always taken pride in being a sharp dresser. At an even six feet, he weighed 175 pounds, "just three pounds over my playing weight at Duke, though I get heavier in the winter."

Groat is a gracious host, a good storyteller, and it is easy to feel comfortable in his company.

Sometimes I think Groat is taken for granted in his home area — like a prophet who is not honored in his home country — and that he is more appreciated outside of Pittsburgh. He is still an idol at Duke. Groat is a much more revered figure in North Carolina and ACC country than he is in Pittsburgh. A friend of mine on Long Island, attorney Bill Hodges, was so eager to meet him at a Pitt basketball game at St. John's University, and was so impressed with what a regular guy Groat was when they talked. New Yorkers have a high regard for Groat.

During our two hour interview at his golf club, Groat drank a Diet Coke and a can of Budweiser, and ate his cheeseburger.

My father-in-law, Harvey Churchman, has played a number of golf courses around the country, and he was most complimentary about Groat's golf course. He also recalled having a great steak in the clubhouse when he was there with a group for a golf outing.

Gerry Dulac, the golf writer of *The Pittsburgh Post-Gazette*, rated Champion Lakes the "best public golf course" in western Pennsylvania. "It isn't even a contest," he said of the 6,608-yard layout.

Groat smoked seven cigarettes from a pack of Marlboro Lights, and filled up an ashtray. When I admonished him about smoking so much — my wife, Kathie, a social worker in the oncology unit at Allegheny General Hospital, would have done the same — he shook his head, and said, "I know. I quit for about five or six days a few weeks ago, and I should stay off them."

Five former Pittsburgh basketball players who could hold their own on the hardcourt: Dick Groat, Brian Generalovich, Connie Hawkins, Ed Fleming and Dr. Don Hennon get together at Curbstone Coaches confab at Allegheny Club at Three Rivers Stadium.

Michael Drazdzinski

Duke University

Dick Groat during his glory days at Duke, and as color analyst on Pitt basketball broadcasts with WTAE's sports director Bill Hillgrove.

When Groat first signed with the Pirates after graduating at Duke, he did not smoke or drink. "Right down Rickey's alley," it was noted at the time.

He graduated from Duke in June, 1952 and then played in 95 games for the Pirates. He is one of the few major leaguers who never played an inning of minor league baseball.

When I asked about Jerry Lynch, his long-time partner best known for his power as a pinch-hitter for both the Pirates and Cincinnati Reds in his heyday, Groat replied, "Jerry retired from active participation in the club about five years ago. He's living in Lawrenceville, Georgia, just outside Atlanta, where his children and grandchildren are. He still owns 25 percent of the course. Would you believe it, we're into our 27th year?"

"I'm bigger than you and I'm bigger than Mr. Groat, so you better take my money."
— Bill Fralic, NFL Pro Bowl Guard

Groat volunteered that he had just hosted the annual Pirates Alumni golf outing, coordinated by Nellie Briles, a former Pirates and Cardinals pitcher who works as director of corporate sales for the Pirates. "We had about 20 guys who were associated with the Pirates out here a week ago Friday," said Groat. "We had a great time. Bill Virdon was here, and ElRoy Face, Bob Friend — Maz was in Florida with his son, Darren, who coaches college baseball down there. We also had Nellie King, Bobby Del Greco, Chuck Tanner, Ron Neccai, Kent Tekulve, Bob Robertson, Bruce Dal Canton, Doug Froebel, Bob Purkey, Grant Jackson and Tommy Qualters from the Phillies. Ray Mathews, the former Steeler, always comes to our outings, too."

For the record, Del Greco and his Hill District buddy Tony Bartirome were both on the Pirates when Groat came to the team in 1952. Some of his other first-year teammates were George Strickland, Gus Bell, Joe Garagiola, Clyde McCullough and Ralph Kiner.

"It was a most enjoyable day," said Groat of the Pirates' reunion. "We all took turns standing up and reflecting on our days with the Pirates. There was a lot of reminiscing, especially about Branch Rickey and Billy Meyer. There were some funny stories."

Reunions can be that way. I told Groat that I had a great time at Pitt's Homecoming that weekend, despite the Panthers' poor performance on the football field, because I had seen old friends, classmates and some of the people I worked with when I served as assistant athletic director and sports information director from 1983 to 1986, and as the director of Pitt's Outreach Program in 1987.

I told Groat how good I felt when I got hugs from Herb Douglas, an Olympic bronze medal winner in the long jump in 1948 and a boyhood hero of mine from our hometown of Hazelwood, who was honored at halftime ceremonies, along with Olympic gold-medal winner Johnny Woodruff of Connellsville.

44

I also got great big bear hugs from Craig "Ironhead" Heyward, then a running back from the New Orleans Saints, and later from Bill Fralic, then a Pro Bowl guard for the Atlanta Falcons. Both former Pitt stars were home on the weekend when their respective NFC West teams were enjoying byes. Both signed with new teams since then.

Heyward and Fralic were two of my favorites. They were the most talented players on their respective teams at Pitt, but they also got into the most mischief. They were much bigger than I had ever been in my youth, indeed they were like bulls in china shops whenever they flexed their muscles, but I could identify with them. And I liked them. I was constantly counseling them, inviting them to my office to discuss their behavior, their families, what was best for them. You never know how young people respond to that sort of advice, but their hugs, and kind words and smiles, assured me that we had made a positive connection. They could have ducked me.

"Buildings come and go," offered Fralic, looking about the campus from high on a hill near the Charles L. Cost Sports Center, where the Cathedral of Learning and Pitt's Medical Center were visible over the distant rim of Pitt Stadium. "It's the people who make Pitt."

Groat nodded in agreement as I told him my little Homecoming tale. "Bill Fralic is quite a special young man," said Groat. "This is his favorite golf course, he told me, in the United States.

"Bill comes out here and spends the day, and plays 40 holes or more. The Falcons couldn't find him once, and someone suggested they call Champion Lakes Golf Course. 'That's where you'll find him,' the man said. He plays from early in the morning, and all the way through the day. He might call at 10 p.m., and say, 'Can you get us off in the morning?' He's a class kid, a special kid. The last time he came out here, he insisted on paying, though I had always let him play for free. We have a young man in our pro shop named Bucky Mears, who's a student at Duke. He's a big Pitt fan, too. He told Fralic, 'Mr. Groat would kill me if I charged you.' And Fralic said to Bucky, 'Hey, I'm making more money today than Mr. Groat, and I'm bigger than you and I'm bigger than Mr. Groat, so you better take my money.' And he gave Bucky a $50 bill."

Groat and Lynch bought two different tracts of farmland during their playing days with the Pirates, and have developed one of them. "Jerry and I walked off the golf course for two and a half months, and we knew what we wanted before we put down hand money on the farm," said Groat. "We broke ground for the golf course on Christmas Eve, 1964. We cut the golf course out of the woods, and went back to baseball for spring training. We had no financing to build the golf course, and we laid it out ourselves. We knew exactly what we wanted. We worked with the construction company in opening the woods for the fairways, and greens.

"I think we came up with a great course. Arnold Palmer and Rocco Mediate share the course record of 68, which is three under par. Arnold was just here in July. He hadn't played our course in a few years, but he has always been most generous in his remarks about our operation.

45

"I'm very prejudiced, but next to Laurel Valley, I don't think there's any course close to it. We had a writer visiting here recently from *Golf Digest* who was evaluating it. He said, 'Your fairways are better than most country clubs.' We patterned it after one of the golf courses at The Homestead in Hot Springs, West Virginia.

"This area lent itself to the type of golf course we wanted to build — a wooded course, scenic and with water."

What's the best Groat ever did on his own course?

"I shot an 81 once. But I don't play much anymore, and my handicap is about 10 or 12 now. I played nine holes recently with my daughter Allison, and she beats my brains out. But I still enjoy it."

When Groat's baseball career was interrupted for two years (1953 and 1954) while he served in the military, he was stationed at Fort Belvoir, Virginia, where he worked with an engineering construction crew, building highways and airstrips. So he was familiar with bulldozers.

When he was playing for the Pirates, and for awhile after his playing days were over, Groat was employed in public relations and sales by Jessop Steel of Washington, Pennsylvania, so he knew how to handle business and, better yet, how to handle people. He was a natural, in that respect.

Groat pointed to some photos on display behind the bar in the clubhouse. A black and white one showed him standing next to Palmer, both with cigarettes in their mouths. "That one was taken in 1960," said Groat. "Arnie had just been named Golfer of the Year, and I had just won the MVP Award in the National League." Then Groat pointed out the photo below that one, a color print showing him and Palmer standing next to each other, and looking directly into a camera held by Groat's daughter, Allison.

"We've both aged a little in the last 32 years," Groat confessed.

A gentleman named Marty Statler stopped in to say hello to Groat after he had completed playing. Statler, who owns a driving range and a par 3 golf course on Rt. 30, likes to play Groat's golf course. "He grew up with Arnold in Latrobe and is a golf pro himself," said Groat.

While he was dropping some local names, Groat also mentioned that he had watched the final game of the National League playoffs on TV in the company of John Page. He is the son of Joe Page, who previously owned a bar on Rt. 30 for many years after retiring from baseball. Joe Page was once the ace relief pitcher for the New York Yankees, and one of the first and most prominent relief pitchers in baseball history.

"John had a chance to make it, too," said Groat. "He was a good-looking young hitter. He went with Eddie Stanky at South Alabama, and he had a chance to be a pretty good player."

Then, again, that is what they said about Paul Blanda, the brother of George Blanda, just down Route 30 in Youngwood, Pa. Paul played at Pitt at the same time as All-American Joe Schmidt, but his career was cut short with a knee injury. For every Joe Page there are ten John Pages, and for every George Blanda there are ten Paul Blandas. It is not easy to make it to the big party.

Groat said that John Page lived with his mother, Misty Page, in Ligonier. Groat looks for people like that to join in watching sports events on TV ever since his wife, Barbara, died of cancer in June of 1990. Barbara died a few days before the Pirates held a reunion of the 1960 championship team. Dick decided not to participate. He did not attend the banquet held for the team, but he was persuaded by his Pirates teammates to be with friends at such a time. So he donned his old uniform and played in the Old Timers Game.

Reflecting on the final game of the 1992 season for the Pirates, in which they lost a heart-breaker to the Atlanta Braves in the bottom of the ninth of the seventh and deciding game, Groat said, "Ironically, it was one of the few baseball games I've ever watched in my life where it never crossed my mind that the Pirates would lose.

"When Bream scored that winning run, I felt nothing. I was just absolutely stunned. No matter what happened that inning, even when Lind let the ball get away from him, even when the bases were loaded, I just thought there was no way the Pirates wouldn't come away with a win.

"When I was a ballplayer, I can remember that consistently, from the seventh inning on, I would count the number of outs we still needed to get the game over with when we had a lead. I'd say, 'Nine outs to go . . . eight outs to go. . .' So, obviously, I didn't think the same way as a ballplayer."

Groat preferred to praise Jim Leyland, the Pirates' manager, rather than second-guess him as many had done in the wake of the Pirates' third straight failure in the National League's championship series.

"I think Jimmy does a great job of handling people," said Groat, "very much like I felt Danny Murtaugh did. He's great at getting the best out of 25 players. Obviously, Bill Cowher does the same."

Groat was alluding to the Steelers' first-year head coach, who succeeded Chuck Noll after he had been at the helm of the team for 23 years.

"My boy, Jerry Olsavsky, even got to play some linebacker last night," said Groat, referring to a nationally-televised game at Kansas City the night before. Olsavsky is a former Pitt performer, which is how Groat got to know him so well.

"You are really a big Pitt fan, aren't you?" I asked Groat.

"I grew up here," said Groat. "I grew up with two brothers and a sister who all graduated from Pitt. I had another sister who graduated from Carnegie Tech. My brother Charley Groat was a great runner in track at Pitt. He and my brother Marty both went to Pitt on basketball scholarships for Doc Carlson. Both had problems with Doc, and dropped off the team. Doc could be difficult."

Carlson was a Hall of Fame basketball coach at Pitt, but he remains a controversial figure among those who played for him, or rooted for Pitt during his long stay there.

I mentioned to Groat that I had heard a similar complaint the week before from Bill Baierl, the owner of Baierl Chevrolet in Wexford, who received a basketball scholarship from Carlson, but found him difficult to get along with as a young athlete.

Sam David, who came out of Bridgeville as a big-time scorer but was stymied by Carlson's slow-down style, told me, "I started out hating Doc Carlson, but I ended up loving him." David also ended up becoming a priest in the Antiochian Orthodox Church, whose priests are permitted to be married. Groat had recently attended ceremonies at which The Very Rev. Sam David was elevated to the highest stature in his church. He is the pastor of St. George Orthodox Church on Dawson Street in South Oakland, a block away from Danny Marino's boyhood home. One of his children, Joey David, was a wonderful basketball player and an even better person, as a starting backcourtman for Pitt's basketball team in the mid-'80s.

Groat is a big fan of both Sam and Joey David. When he was playing ball at Swissvale High, he looked up to Sam and other local college stars. "Sam and Dodo Canterna both played for Pitt's basketball team, and they remain two of my favorite people. I was always a big fan of Pitt athletes," said Groat.

"I remember as a kid listening to the 'Dream Backfield' on the radio playing against Duke. The backfield consisted of Marshall Goldberg, Dick Cassiano, Curly Stebbins and John Chickerneo. I loved Dr. Sutherland, their coach. My brothers just worshipped him. He had a way about him, just the way he walked onto the field. I remember him coaching the Steelers. You had to respect this man, just the way he walked.

"Michelosen succeeded him as coach of the Steelers, before Michelosen coached at Pitt. It was Michelosen who helped me get to Duke. He and Sutherland had both gone to Duke regularly to observe their football camp, and they knew the people there. I had read an article about how they played big-time baseball at Duke. That's how I got interested in the first place."

Michelosen was a fraternity brother of Martin Groat, one of Dick's older brothers. They did not offer baseball scholarships at Duke, but there were three basketball scholarships available. Recruiting wasn't the big deal it is today. Somebody at Duke asked Martin Groat about his brother. "Can he play basketball?" Martin thought his brother was a pretty good all-around athlete, so he said he thought his brother could play both sports at Duke. Dick turned out to be an All-American in both. He went right from the campus to a starting position with the Pirates.

"I had some major league dreams growing up," said Groat, "and I guess I'm one of the fortunate people to fulfill every dream I've ever had in athletics."

"I'm so tired of reading negative writing."

I mentioned to Groat how I had spoken a few weeks earlier with Ernie Banks, the Hall of Fame shortstop from the Chicago Cubs, at a card collectors show at Three Rivers Stadium that was held concurrently with a Steelers Fanfest.

Bill Mazeroski and Dick Groat embrace after winning 1960 World Series.

Groat with partner Jerry Lynch at their Champion Lakes golf course in Ligonier.

Jim Leyland with Groat at 30th year reunion at Three Rivers Stadium in 1990.

Barbara, Carol Ann, Tracey and Dick Groat at training camp.

Banks asked me and those seeking his signature (at $15 a pop on pictures, bats and gloves) about several former Pirates, including Groat. "Groat beat me out for MVP honors in 1960," recalled Banks.

Banks had asked me about the well-being of about a dozen sportswriters who had worked in Pittsburgh when he was playing for the Cubs. Most of them are dead, a few retired. He also rattled off the names of New York writers to me. "I doubt that a ballplayer of Banks' stature who is playing today will be able to do that 20 years after he has finished his career," I suggested to Groat. He agreed.

"I had the nicest guys in the world writing about me," said Groat. "They wanted to write positive stories. Today, maybe it's the competition from TV, they feel compelled to write negatively. I'm so tired of reading negative writing."

Groat, by the way, also sent "thank you" notes to me whenever I wrote an article about him. He did the same with all writers, I later learned. "I was raised that way," he explained. "I think my sister had that influence on me. Even when there was a critical story about me it was deserved. I had booted a ball or made a mistake on the bases. And they pointed that out in their stories. I can't recall being upset with anything that was written about me. If it was negative, it was always justified. So I could accept that. I sent the 'thank you' letters because I think you owe it to someone who had been good to you all along. When I am speaking, I always thank the owners who provided me with opportunities — John Galbreath, Augie Busch, Bob Carpenter and Horace Stoneham — and with the news media, no matter where I played."

Thinking about what I had said earlier, Groat added, "Ernie Banks, by the way, called me when he was in town. Other guys call me and I call them. I called Tim McCarver when he was in for the playoffs. I see Timmy for lunch in Philadelphia when we (the Pitt basketball team) go to play Villanova. I called him after he did such a great job with the Olympics to congratulate him.

"We were teammates in St. Louis in 1963, 1964 and 1965. I call McCarver and tell him what a great job he does. When I see him call a game, I'm very proud of Timmy. I saw him grow up. He's a real student of the game, and he's a great competitor.

"When I'm speaking, I often refer to the four pennant-contending clubs I played with. I remember the '58 Pirates and the '60 Pirates, the '63 Cardinals and the '64 Cardinals. Two of those teams finished second, and two of them won the world championship.

"There's something about being involved in a pennant race. You became closer, and not only as teammates. Bill White and I are still very close friends. Curt Simmons and I are still close. Curt Flood . . . I think the world of him. He and Lou Brock are close friends of mine. There's a bond that never goes away.

"Looking back on it, those were the three happiest years I ever had in baseball, my three years in a Cardinals uniform."

"You never forgave Joe Brown for trading you away, or for not giving you a shot at managing the Pirates when they hired Larry Shepard (1968), did you?" I said to Groat. I also knew that Groat was

50

upset at the start of the 1960 season because Brown cut his salary considerably because he had gone from hitting .300 in 1958 to .275 in 1959. The negotiations had not gone well, though Groat managed to convince Brown not to cut his salary as much as he had originally planned.

When I brought all this up to Groat, he lifted his eyebrows and shrugged his shoulders. "One of my greatest thrills in the world was being in the 1963 All-Star Game — when it really meant something — in my first year with the St. Louis Cardinals. That's when the players picked the teams. I got more votes than anybody in either league. And then the next year we won the pennant. This all came after Joe Brown said they (the Pirates) couldn't win a pennant with me at shortstop.

"By the way, that was also the only time in the history of baseball that one team had the entire starting lineup for the infield in the All-Star Game."

Ken Boyer was at third base, Groat at shortstop, Julian Javier (another former Pirate) at second base and Bill White at first base for the National League in the 1963 All-Star Game.

"In 1964, Boyer, White and I started, with Mazeroski at second base, and that's when the National League started to dominate the All-Star Game."

I asked Groat what it was like to be a teammate of Stan Musial in St. Louis.

"I played with Musial my first year in St. Louis. It was his last year. I remember when Musial announced his retirement. It was late August, and the Cardinals were in fifth or sixth place. The Busch family did a lot for its players, and they had a party at Grant's Farm, which was owned by the Busch family. It was a miserable hot day, and the TV trucks showed up.

"That's where Stan announced his retirement. From that day forward, Stan hit between .370 and .400. We came from sixth place, and won 19 out of 20 games, and came within a game-and-a-half of the Dodgers. We lost a series with the Dodgers at the end of the season to end our chances. Johnny Podres beat us 3-1, then Sandy Koufax shut us out, 4-0, and then the Dodgers beat us in 12 or 13 innings when a guy named Noone came off the bench to beat us with a home run. They beat us in our own ballpark, and we were out of the pennant race with a week to go.

"That was some year, though. I was hitting second and Musial was hitting behind me. I never saw an individual hit the ball so hard. He had tremendous extra base power. It was the damnedest stretch drive I ever saw a human being have. At age 42, he was unbelievable."

Musial also came from Western Pennsylvania, calling Donora home, and was always a big favorite at Forbes Field.

"I've always been impressed with Stan Musial," said Groat. "He not only was the greatest hitter in the National League, but he was the best person in the league. He was always nice to me. He couldn't believe the Pirates had given up on me.

"In 1963, I had the greatest year of my career. I was hitting in front of Musial, and I did better than when I won the batting title (in

1960)." In 1960, Groat raised his batting average 50 points from the previous year to .325 and won the batting title on the final day of the season. In 1963 with the Cardinals, Groat batted .319, but he had 73 RBIs (compared to 60 in 1960) and he had a career high 201 hits and led the league with 43 doubles.

Some years were better than others, but none was really bad, as Groat looks back on it.

"Baseball owes me absolutely nothing. I owe baseball everything," he said. "I never made the kind of money that the poorest players make today, but they treated me well. I met my wife through baseball, and I started my family when I was in baseball.

"There are still people who play Champion Lakes Golf Course because Jerry and I played major league baseball. We are still benefiting from the association."

Groat was nearly traded before the 1960 season. After the 1959 season, the Kansas City Athletics offered Roger Maris for Groat, but the Pirates backed off the offer and acquired Gino Cimoli to play left field. Imagine Maris hitting at Forbes Field. That would have been Brown's best-ever trade.

The Athletics traded Maris to the Yankees for Hank Bauer and Don Larsen. Coincidentally, Groat and Maris were MVPs in 1960 and met in the World Series. And, of course, Maris hit 61 home runs in 1961.

Groat was sidelined late in the '60 season, but returned to win the batting title.

On September 6, Groat was hit on the wrist by a pitch from Lew Burdette of the Braves. He suffered a broken bone, and was sidelined for a month. It made him look doubtful for the World Series. He was leading the league in hitting when he was hurt.

On the last weekend of the season, Groat was hitting .325 and Norm Larker of the Los Angeles Dodgers was batting .322. The Pirates had already clinched the pennant and Groat could have won the title by sitting out the series with the Braves. He batted ten times, collected three hits and finished at .325. Larker finished at .323. But Groat wasn't jeopardizing his batting title, he was just getting ready for the World Series.

In his first at-bat of the World Series, Groat hit a run-scoring double, and he scored on Bill Virdon's single and the Pirates won, 6-2.

"New York and the Polo Grounds were always special to me."
— Dick Groat

Groat's family includes three daughters and six grandchildren. His daughters are Tracey Lynn Goetz, 36, who lives in Durham and is married to former University of Richmond head basketball coach, Lou Goetz; Carol Ann Scorpion, 34, who lives with Dick at his home in Edgewood; Allison Morrow DeStefano, 29, who lives in Latrobe and manages her dad's golf course.

His wife, Barbara, died after a lengthy illness. "We would have been married 35 years this November," said Groat. He and Barbara Womble were married on November 11, 1955. She had dark blond hair and blue eyes and was a real beauty.

Since Barbara was from Wilmington, North Carolina, I figured they met when Dick was a student at Duke.

"No, we met in 1955 in New York," he said. "I was warming up at the Polo Grounds, and I heard somebody calling me by name from the third base seats. It was a mature voice. This nice, gray-haired man said he wanted to meet me. He said, 'This is my daughter; she's modeling here in New York. Her name is Barbara.' I chatted with them awhile, and then watched as they went back to their seats. There wasn't a big crowd at the ballpark that day; the Giants weren't drawing that well. So I could track them.

"I got hold of Bob Prince. I said, 'Bob, I need a favor. Would you mind going up there and getting her phone number for me? I want to call her.' He said, 'You think I'm crazy?' I said, 'She's with her father.' He said, 'That's worse.' But he did it. I can still see him walking up the steps toward them, wearing one of those wild plaid sportscoats he wore, and he got me the telephone number.

"That's why Bob and Betty Prince always took credit for Barbara and my three children and my six grandchildren.

"I guess that's why New York and the Polo Grounds were always special to me. I got my first major league hit there. I got my first home run there and, more importantly, I met my wife at the Polo Grounds.

"The ballplayers thought I was crazy because I was buying all these fashion magazines at the airport, because Barbara was on the cover and in the pages of some of them."

Groat let that sink in awhile. He was looking out the expansive window at his golf course, and he had a faraway look. "I guess you miss Barbara a lot," I said.

"I guess I miss her more than ever at this time of the year, more than any other time. During the summer, there are people here all the time. Now everyone's gone by six o'clock. I become tremendously lonely.

"Last night, I stayed at the clubhouse and watched the Steelers' game. Usually, I go to the local bars just so I don't have to watch the games alone. I feel fortunate to have a daughter here in the summer, and I go home to Pittsburgh and have my other daughter watch over me all winter time."

"He is definitely a man's man.
Mazzie has fun in life.
— Groat on Mazeroski

Why were the '60 Bucs so special? Why do they have such a hold on Pittsburgh sports fans? How did they manage to remain so close through the years?

"I always said my biggest thrill in sports was seeing Bill Mazeroski hit the home run that won the World Series," began Groat. "To play on a championship team in my hometown, after growing up a Pirates' fan, was the answer to my dreams. I was a great Pirates' fan; my older brother Martin took me to a lot of games when I was young, and I thought those days at the ballpark were the greatest days.

"In that World Series, we lost three ballgames that we were never in, so there was no second-guessing. You couldn't look back at a boot, or say, 'If I'd done this or that.' Every game that was close we won.

"That was something we were taught. In previous years, we lost a lot of games by one run. That year we won the close games. Mr. Rickey emphasized over and over that bad teams lose one run games. I told Moose Skowron of the Yankees, when he got on me recently about how the Yankees were so much better than us that year, that the great teams win close games. I told him what Mr. Rickey said.

"We came from behind a phenomenal number of times that year to win games. We came back a couple of times in that final game. Then Maz hits the home run to win it. That's the only time it ever happened like that in the history of baseball. Plus, it's because we beat the mighty Yankees.

"I think that home run has hurt Mazeroski more than it helped him when it came to the Hall of Fame. I hate to say this, but I'm firmly convinced that it became a detriment. It overshadows that he was the greatest fielding second baseman in the history of baseball. He had to be."

Groat has gone on record many times saying that Mazeroski should be in the Baseball Hall of Fame.

"That's absolutely correct," said Groat. "I've spent a great deal of time discussing with writers that this man should be in Cooperstown. All the younger writers remember about him is him hitting the home run."

"Why has Maz always been so special in your mind?"

"I've grown up with Maz. He came up with the Pirates. I was supposed to be a veteran when he joined the Pirates, but I was probably only two seasons ahead of Billy in the big leagues.

"There's no way to describe to you the kind of relationship we had. I really studied hitters. I had to play hitters impeccably because I didn't have the great speed to cover a lot of ground. I'd tell Maz where to move to, as far as playing the different hitters. I never had to move him a second time. He remembered, and he'd be in the right spot the next time around. He had quick hands and especially quick feet. To this day, we're still exceptionally good friends.

"At the end of September, Maz, Bob Friend and I were all flown by Delta Airlines down to Pinehurst, North Carolina to participate in a National Legends Golf Tournament that was co-sponsored by National Car Rental. People like Ernie Banks, Brooks Robinson, Willie McCovey and Al Kaline were there. Vinegar Bend Mizell was there; he lives in Winston-Salem.

54

"Maz was among the most popular guys there. He is definitely a man's man. Mazzie has fun in life. He wakes up in the morning and he has a major decision to make. Is he going to play golf, go fishing, or hunting? He's very close to his wife, Milene, and their two boys, Darren and David."

I had recently talked over the telephone to Milene, and she was so pleasant. She told me, "Billy has always been very content. He doesn't need much to be happy. How much do you need to be happy?" I repeated this exchange to Groat.

"We're from a different era," said Groat. "I feel fortunate. My mother and father didn't raise me to worship the almighty dollar.

"I remember something Bill White told me at one of the Cracker Jack Old-Timers All-Star Games. He said, 'I could go back to the hospitality suite and have a great time with you guys. Today's ballplayers won't be able to do that in 30 years. They don't really have any relationships.'

"Bill was working with the Yankees at the time, and he said they all have their own rooms on the road, and they all go their own way. They don't pal around or have anything to do with one another.

"We all had roommates and we went everywhere together. There was always a group of us going somewhere together. Those relationships are still special.

"As far as the money today, I can't even relate to it. I don't know how you spend it. Yet guys go bankrupt. What kind of investments do they make?

"We all had roommates. My first roommate was Ralph Kiner. Can you believe that? In high school, I was a Kiner fan. And I ended up rooming with him. It was a great experience for a young player. He looked after me and showed me the ropes. It was an education.

"I remember one time we arrived at the Knickerbocker Hotel in Chicago, and I couldn't find my name on the room list. Until I turned to the second page, and there was just one line, for Kiner and me. It had a note after our names: 'air-conditioned, if possible.' He got special treatment from management, but he didn't expect it from any of us. He was the nicest man in the world to room with.

"I had the bellboy take our bags up to the room, and I tipped him. I remember when I got to our room, I was afraid to pick a bed out until Kiner came and told me which one he wanted. He's funny. When he sees me, he still calls me Roomie."

What others said about Dick Groat in 1960 . . .

Danny Murtaugh, Manager, Pittsburgh Pirates:
"His batting average doesn't begin to tell the story. He can handle a bat as well as anybody I've ever seen. If you want a runner moved along, he does it. Pitchers fear him. He's the best No. 2 hitter in the league."

Joe Brown, General Manager, Pittsburgh Pirates:
"Dick was never blessed with great talent, but he played at a level above many players of greater talent. He was successful because of his consistency of performance and intelligence and because he was highly motivated. Defensively, he was always in position. He knew the hitters. He knew the patterns. Offensively, he knew the pitchers, he knew what the situation demanded of him, and he always came through."

Alvin Dark, Manager, Milwaukee Braves:
"He has a radar bat."

Gene Mauch, Manager, Philadelphia Phillies:
"He holds the Pirates together."

Fred Hutchinson, Manager, Cincinnati Reds:
"He kills us. I wish to hell he'd go away."

Pittsburgh Pirates

Danny Murtaugh and Dick Groat look to bullpen for help.

"Baseball is played by men of normal build doing something magic. Unlike other sports, baseball's past is always relevant; its distant mirrors renew the present, and the present revives the past."
—Luke Salisbury, Author
"The Answer Is Baseball"

Hall of Fame
From Pittsburgh To Cooperstown
And Its Fields of Dreams

*"Of all the places we've been,
we liked Pittsburgh the best."*

Bill Guilfoile calls Cooperstown "a nice place to raise a family." Guilfoile and his family have lived there for 15 years, or since he became the public relations director and (in 1991) the associate director of the National Baseball Hall of Fame and Museum.

He lives on Lake Street in a storybook white cottage house, and has a boat in a slip across the street behind the Otesaga Hotel. There is a tennis court two doors away, and the Leatherstocking Golf Course within walking distance. It is a quiet community of 2,400 citizens named after author James Fenimore Cooper. He can walk to work. Not bad.

Before that, Guilfoile and his family lived in Bethel Park for nine years — from 1970 to 1978 — when he was the public relations director of the Pittsburgh Pirates.

"We miss Pittsburgh," he said, when we visited the Baseball Hall of Fame in September of 1990. "We made some special friends there, and we think it's a pretty special place. Of all the places we've been, we liked Pittsburgh the best."

Guilfoile first came to Pittsburgh in October of 1960, when he was the assistant publicity director of the New York Yankees, when the Pirates won the World Series by defeating the Yankees on Bill Mazeroski's ninth inning home run in the seventh game.

He wears a Pirates' World Series ring from 1971. He left before the 1979 season when the Pirates won another World Series championship. He still roots for the Pirates.

The Pirates were in first place in the National League East in the stretch run — they would go on to win the National League East title — and Guilfoile was among their many fans pulling for them to hold off the Mets, even though he is a native New Yorker. He spent his boyhood in Brooklyn. He also roots for Notre Dame, his alma mater.

Guilfoile asked about friends back in Pittsburgh, especially Betty Prince, the wife of the late Bob Prince, who broadcast the Pirates' games when Guilfoile worked for them, and about Nellie King, Prince's sidekick.

Among the many displays at the Baseball Hall of Fame, there is an enlargement of the front page of the sports section of *The Press* of July 23, 1974 that features a headline article by Bob Smizik when the National League defeated the American League in the All-Star Game at Three Rivers Stadium. There is also a column by Pat Livingston, the former sports editor, who continues to reside in Bethel Park.

The day before I traveled to Cooperstown, I participated in a book signing promotion for Smizik's history book on the Pirates at Border's Book Shop in Norman Centre II in Bethel Park.

Four former Pirates were present to autograph the book — Frankie Gustine of Green Tree, Dave Giusti and Kent Tekulve of Upper St. Clair, and Bob Friend of Fox Chapel — and they all asked to be remembered to Guilfoile, a nice guy and a good friend.

Those four also swapped stories about their days in baseball. They had one ear on the KDKA broadcast of the Pirates-Cardinals game, trying to catch the details offered by their buddies, Lanny Frattare, Steve Blass, Jim Rooker and Kent Derdivanis, and another on the customers who wanted their autographs in the books. They were all caught up in the excitement. Pennant fever had infected everybody in Pittsburgh.

In February of 1991, I attended the Piratefest at the Expo Mart in Monroeville, along with Smizik, and had coffee and donuts with King, Friend, Gustine, ElRoy Face and Vernon Law. This was when Barry Bonds was balking about his contract, and other Pirates were pushing for bigger salaries and taking the club to arbitration, and it prompted a Pirates' official to remark, "Geez, these guys here are so easy to work with. I wish the players today were as cooperative and kind."

I went to Cooperstown for the annual sales meeting of *Street & Smith's Sports Group*. Cooperstown is about 460 miles from Pittsburgh, or a nine to ten hour drive. It's beautiful in the fall.

A Pittsburgher has to feel proud when he visits the Baseball Hall of Fame. One of the first exhibits as you enter one of the wings is of Honus Wagner of Carnegie, who was voted into the first class of the Hall of Fame in 1935.

Wagner enjoyed 17 consecutive .300 seasons, including eight as the National League batting champion. He led the Pirates to three consecutive pennants in the early 1900s. His baseball card, which is on display, is the most valuable of its kind. Stan Musial of Donora is the other local product in the Hall of Fame. Josh Gibson and the Homestead Grays and Pittsburgh Crawfords of the black baseball leagues are also honored.

I had been to the Baseball Hall of Fame twice before, in 1975, to see boyhood hero Ralph Kiner be inducted, and in 1977. Now there are bronze plaques for Roberto Clemente and Willie Stargell, as well as Arky Vaughan, Pie Traynor, Kiki Cuyler, Lloyd and Paul Waner, Max Carey and Fred Clarke. Manager Bill McKecknie and GM Branch Rickey are also Pirates' representatives enshrined.

While there, the *Street & Smith's* staff had an opportunity to play a pick-up baseball game for two hours at Abner Doubleday Field. I was never very good at baseball, but anything seemed possible on this particular sunny afternoon.

We had girls and guys in our game. Nobody was keeping score. We took turns running and batting and pitching and fielding, and pretending we were big-time players. It was pure fun. The field has real grass, the greenest grass, and the infield diamond is rich orange-red clay.

It sticks to your white stockings, hopefully forever. The grass had just been manicured and the clay freshly raked, according to the caretaker.

I had a buddy of mine with me. John Fadool of Mt. Lebanon said he hated to clean his sneakers after running around Doubleday Field. "I had red clay in the tread of my sneakers, and I hated to knock it out," he said. "Somehow it seemed sacrilegious."

I remembered that on an earlier visit I had been accompanied by a pal from Long Island, an attorney named Bill Hodges, who loved mixing with the Hall of Famers in a cocktail lounge at the Otesaga Hotel. He didn't want to change his clothes after brushing against ballplayers from the past who have been enshrined in the Hall of Fame. You have to be a dyed-in-the-wool sports fan to understand those sentiments.

It also seemed a sin to mess up the infield at Doubleday Field. What a ball. It was, indeed, a blessing to play a baseball game on Bill Guilfoile's "Field of Dreams" just for one day in your life. For one sunny afternoon, you felt like a Hall of Famer.

Baseball Hall of Fame/Pioneer Photo Inc.

Roberto Clemente (#21) is featured, along with Willie Stargell, in Pirates exhibit at Hall of Fame. Bill Guilfoile (upper right) is associate director at Cooperstown shrine.

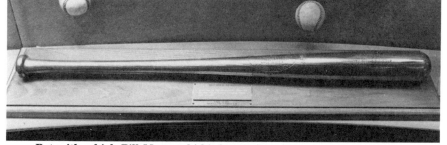

Bat with which Bill Mazeroski hit heroic home run is at Hall of Fame.

Where Were You?

"Not everybody was happy that day."
—Sal Farina

Orville "Dutch" Hemminger
Pleasant Hills
"My dad was the assistant postmaster, and he was the only one who got tickets for the seventh game. It was strictly a lottery deal, and you didn't know what game you were going to get, if any. Everyone laughed at him. 'You're not going to see any game, Dutch,' they'd say. But he got to see it. My dad and I always went to the home opener."

Mary Coles
Irwin
"I had just come home from the Westmoreland Hospital after having a baby daughter. When I saw Maz hit the home run on TV, I was jumping up and down. I'm sure my doctor wouldn't have approved."

Dr. Ed Sweeney
Internist, St. Francis Hospital
Shaler
"I was a seventh grader at Charleroi High School, and I was kept after school that day and missed it. I did get a baseball signed by everyone on the '60 team, and I've been to the Dream Camp because I really love baseball."

Rick Sarazen
Franklin Park
"My uncle, Ron Sarazen, who was from the North Side, and went to North Catholic High School, sang the National Anthem before that seventh game. Nobody remembers that. He lives and performs in Las Vegas now. All the nuns at St. Andrew's Grade School in Manchester let us watch on TV when Uncle Ron was singing. There were seven little Sarazen kids in the school at that time. We had to go back to our classes after he finished singing. We didn't know till we got home how the game turned out."

Jean Styen
Squirrel Hill
"I was making up an algebra test after school. The ballgame was broadcast over the p.a. system into the classrooms at Mt. Lebanon High. When Maz hit the home run, we all went crazy, and we were all jumping up and down. The schoolbus came at 3:20 p.m., so most of the kids were on the bus when he hit the home run."

60

Sal Farina
Insurance Salesman
Wexford

"I was born in Brooklyn, and I was seven years old, and I was a Yankees fan. I still have some seats from Yankee Stadium. I paid $25 for a pair of them I have a jersey from Whitey Ford, a Mickey Mantle bat. I loved Mickey Mantle and we thought for sure the Yankees would win. I was in second grade at St. Cyril & Methodius Grade School. We got home from school that day about the fifth inning. And, boy, when Maz hit the home run my dad and I both cried. The Yankees should have won. Believe me, not everybody was happy that day."

Rose Ellen Salopek
Masontown, Pa.

"I was a student at Canon-McMillan and they piped the game into our classes. When Maz hit the home run it was unbelievable. I have a photo of myself with Clemente when I went to a game. He was the only one who stopped and posed for a picture for me."

Debby Thomas
Ross Township

"I grew up in Tiltonsville, which is Maz's hometown. I was in first grade when they had a parade in his honor after the World Series. They let us out of school and we were all waving little American flags when he rode by in a convertible. My dad has a home movie of it all. My dad was a Maz fan. He'd go to Pittsburgh and to Cleveland to see baseball games. That was the biggest thing that ever happened in Tiltonsville. His picture in a Pirates uniform is in our school. When I graduated in 1972, it was still there. Maz used to come to a basketball game at our school now and then, and people would always make a fuss over him."

Pittsburgh Pirates

Bill and Milene Mazeroski wave to fans in his hometown of Tiltonsville, Ohio following his World Series-winning home run in 1960.

Reflections on Forbes Field

"Is the ivy still on the wall?"
—Ralph Kiner

I entered the University of Pittsburgh as a freshman in the fall of 1960. Talk about timing. I signed up for the student newspaper, *The Pitt News,* in August, before I even made my course selections. I started classes in September. In October, the Pirates played the New York Yankees in the World Series on our campus.

Forbes Field was just across the street, a short block from Forbes Avenue and the William Pitt Student Union, which had been the Schenley Hotel. The student publications were housed on the fourth floor of the building. It was my home away from home during my four years as a student at Pitt.

Visiting baseball players and pro football players had stayed there for years when they were playing the Pirates or the Steelers at Forbes Field. So did the biggest entertainment stars, who played at the nearby Syria Mosque, on the other side of the hotel, just across Fifth Avenue, behind the Pittsburgh Athletic Association (P.A.A.).

Oakland was then the sports and cultural center of the city of Pittsburgh. It had no rival. Pitt students were spoiled by their surroundings, and some took the scene for granted. The Pitt baseball team even played some of its home games at Forbes Field, especially after the Pirates departed for Three Rivers Stadium in the summer of 1970.

What a setting Oakland was for a seventeen-year-old who wanted to be a sports writer. I worked in an office on the fourth floor of the Student Union, the one designated for the sports department. It was surrounded by three bathrooms. It was the size of a hotel room, which is what it was originally. Who knows what opposing ballplayers stayed in that same room through the years? Who knows who slept there? How about Babe Ruth? Or Red Grange?

I was not much of a baseball fan back then — I thought the game was too slow, and I had never been any good at it — but I did get into see a few Pirates' games that year. I wrote hometown stories on Pitt athletes for Beano Cook, the sports publicity director, and he looked after me as best he could, as long as he did not have to pay me.

Cook knew most of the ushers at Forbes Field, so we successfully slipped into the ballpark a few times together. One of the ushers, "Big Bob" DePasquale, would dust off some unoccupied reserved seats in the boxes on the third base side, and sit and chat with us. We received V.I.P. treatment, and the price was right. Bob's brother, Jeep DePasquale, was the head of the ushers' union, and would later become a controversial figure on City Council in Pittsburgh.

Cook also introduced me to a lot of intriguing characters who were big sports fans, and liked to wager on every sports event they could get wind of, in watering holes and restaurants that surrounded Forbes Field such as The Home Plate Cafe, The Clock, Jack Canter's Restaurant, Pete Coyne's Cafe, Cicero's Restaurant, The Interlude, Pitt Tavern, The Oakland Cafe, Weinstein's Restaurant, Scotty's Diner, a few after-hours spots like the Greek Club and Sandscratchers, and especially at Frankie Gustine's Restaurant. They are all gone from the local landscape, or have been changed to something else. Most of them are now fast-food outlets. The Home Plate Cafe is now a community theatre. Gustine's is now Hemingway's, and still has a special hold on me. We could never afford to go into Jimmy Blandi's Park Schenley Restaurant, which also gave way to what is now the Hillman Library.

I did not personally attend any of the games in the 1960 World Series. I watched them on TV at the Student Union, either in the lobby, or on a TV set someone had brought to the offices of *The Pitt News*. To be honest, I'm not sure where I was at 3:36 p.m., October 13, 1960, when Maz hit the home run, but I think I was in the Student Union. I do remember where I was when President John F. Kennedy was killed on November 23, 1963 — walking by the University Shop, a men's clothing store, on Forbes Avenue, between Gustine's and the Student Union. A student employee there told me the bad news.

It was Tuesday, October 27, 1992, about 2:45 p.m., and I was killing some time before a 3 p.m. appointment for an interview with an official of the Joseph M. Katz Graduate School of Business. I was standing at the top of a stairway on the third floor of Lou Mervis Hall, gazing out through a two-story window at a special panorama, and looking back in time.

Katz came to Pitt from Peabody High in the east end of Pittsburgh back in the mid-'30s and was a journalism student. He worked at the local daily newspapers after school and on weekends, and soon came to the conclusion that you could not make a lot of money as a newspaper reporter. He never gained a degree at Pitt, either, as he went into business for himself. Many successful entrepreneurs followed the same route.

He was ambitious, so he started a stationery business with a small printing press in his family's garage in East Liberty, taking advantage of some contacts he had made at Pitt to land his first clients, and that grew into Papercraft, once the world's largest gift wrapping company. If you ever wrapped a Christmas present, there is a good chance you contributed to the Katz coffers. He was grateful to Pitt and gave his alma mater $10 million in the mid-'80s, so they named a graduate school after him.

Lou Mervis was a football player at Pitt, who lettered in the 1918 and 1919 seasons, and was a standout lineman. As the story goes, one day he swapped uniforms with a teammate before a game and had a great performance. A New York sportswriter who picked All-American teams in those days thought he was great, and put Leonard Hilty —

whose jersey number Mervis was wearing that day — on his post-season team. Hilty is still listed among Pitt's All-Americans.

It was a less sophisticated time, that's all. Mervis made a lot of money after he left Pitt and, despite the All-America mess-up, still had fond memories of his old school, and felt he owed much of his success in business to Pitt. So he donated a significant sum of money and had a building named after him.

The building is one of my favorites at Pitt. It has mirror-like glass on its facade. It glistens on sunny days, and is a jewel in the southernmost end of the Pitt campus. It reflects part of Forbes Quadrangle.

It is located where the right field stands used to be at Forbes Field.

A portion of the center field wall remains there, and runs above a grassy, well-kept knoll, just to the left as one enters the Katz Graduate School of Business. It is a wonderful setting, especially when the flowers are out, a nostalgic setting. The flag pole that was there when the Pirates played there is still there, as are the distance markers, painted in white and outlined in black on its red bricks. On the other side of the wall is the Bill Mazeroski Field, used by Oakland Little Leaguers.

After Forbes Field was leveled, someone had the vision to preserve something of its specialness. Some of the bricks from the outfield wall were re-set in a sidewalk, and the in-laid brick shows where the left field wall once stood. It's fun to tip-toe along the red-brick line and think back to the days of our youth, and the glory of our times. There is a plaque in the ground marking the spot where Mazeroski's 9th inning home run went over the wall to win the 1960 World Series. The plaque is on the corner of a sidewalk on the other side of Clemente Drive from the Katz Graduate School of Business.

Home plate is preserved under plexi-glass in a hallway of Forbes Quadrangle. It supposedly is in the same spot where home plate was at Forbes Field. I recall, when I was working as the assistant athletic director for sports information at Pitt, that I took some newspaper guys there who were following the Florida State University football team. They were so excited about seeing the remnants of Forbes Field.

There were no major league baseball teams in Florida back then. It was where teams like the Pirates prepared themselves for the real stuff, where spring training camps were conducted. Major league baseball sites were real shrines for sports followers who grew up in Florida. Some of the fellows, even though they were wearing suits and sports coats and dress slacks, went running down the hall and slid across home plate, just for the hell of it.

The Schenley Fountain is also nearby. One of my favorite photographs of my childhood shows me standing, at about age four, wearing a military uniform, posing in front of the fountain, with Pitt's Cathedral of Learning looming high in the background.

Back in 1972, when they were tearing down Forbes Field to make room for new buildings on the Pitt campus, I returned from New York, where I was working at the time, to survey the scene. When I got back

Forbes Field was built in 1909 for baseball right in the heart of Oakland. It was leveled during the spring of 1972.

Author Jim O'Brien at the wall that remains from Forbes Field during the summer of 1993

to New York, I talked about my visit home to New York Mets' broadcaster Ralph Kiner, who had been a home run hitting hero for the Pirates and the team's biggest draw at Forbes Field.

I mentioned that they left part of the wall as a memorial of sorts. "Is the ivy still on the wall?" asked Kiner. The answer then was yes. The answer on the day of my visit in the fall of 1992 was still yes. Those ivy-covered walls were one of the distinctive touches that set Forbes Field apart from other ballparks. Chicago's Wrigley Field and Boston's Fenway Park are similar in size and style to Forbes Field.

As I stood at the top of that stairway in October of 1992, I looked out on Schenley Park — its fall foliage was both warm and spectacular — and at the homes below in what was once known as "Little Italy" and remembered watching old men play bocce on a court cut out of the side of the hill. I looked to the skyline above where I swear I could see the backend of the two-story home where my wife, Kathie, lived above a family when she was a graduate school student at Pitt in 1966 and 1967.

I was standing where the back of the right field stands had once stood. I remembered hearing how a friend of mine, Tom "Maniac" McDonough, a highly-successful insurance salesman who was an incurable gate-crasher, used to climb up the back of the right field stands to sneak into Forbes Field for free. It was like climbing a giant set of window blinds about ten stories high, and had to be a risky climb. McDonough now lives in an apartment that is a cliff-side affair on Mt. Washington, overlooking the Golden Triangle and Three Rivers Stadium. McDonough is still not afraid of heights.

When there was a night ballgame at Forbes Field, the light standards lit up the living room of the second floor apartment Kathie shared with two other graduate school students. We introduced one of them, Nancy Homer, to Bob Smizik, who succeeded me as the sports editor of *The Pitt News*, and looked after *Pittsburgh Weekly Sports*, an irreverent tabloid newspaper I had founded along with Beano Cook, the sports publicist at Pitt, while I was away in the U.S. Army for nearly two years. Smizik later became a sports writer and then a columnist for *The Pittsburgh Press*. Smizik and I worked together on the Pitt student newspaper for four years, and later for a similar span at *The Press*. He and Nancy were scheduled to be paired in our wedding party, but were both late dropouts because he broke his leg and she had her gown stolen while visiting New York. It was not until years later that we succeeded in introducing Bob and Nancy to each other, and the rest is history. They enjoyed each other's company from the start.

Smizik was with me on a November night in 1966 when we attended a party held by Josie Grossman, who had been the editor of *The Pitt News* in our senior year, and was now in the Graduate School of Social Work at Pitt. The Oakland branch of Independence Court, an assisted care residence for senior citizens, is located on the same site as the apartment where Josie held her party, next to Central Catholic High School.

Forbes Field was adjacent to the Pitt campus.

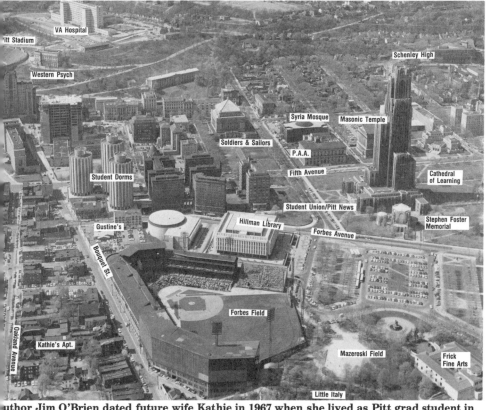

VA Hospital

Pitt Stadium

Schenley High

Western Psych

Syria Mosque   Masonic Temple

Soldiers & Sailors

P.A.A.

Student Dorms

Fifth Avenue

Cathedral
of Learning

Student Union/Pitt News

Gustine's

Hillman Library

Stephen Foster
Memorial

Bouquet St.

Forbes Avenue

Forbes Field

Oakland Avenue

Kathie's Apt.

Mazeroski Field

Frick
Fine Arts

Little Italy

Author Jim O'Brien dated future wife Kathie in 1967 when she lived as Pitt grad student in apartment on Oakland Avenue. They often met at Gustine's, midway between the apartment and the Student Union and The Pitt News offices.

That is the night I met Kathie. It was love at first sight, for me anyhow. Kathie was not so sure. I punched a fellow in the nose that night, and bloodied it, for getting out of line with a female cousin of mine named Pat Burns. Smizik whispered in my ear that night that it was one of the best punches he had ever personally witnessed.

Kathie and I had our first date a week later aboard the Gateway Clipper. It was after a Steelers game, and was tied in with the game, and was promoted by Baldy Regan, a sports promoter and hustler from the North Side who would later serve on City Council. Harold Betters and his group provided the music that night on the Gateway Clipper.

One of my early dates with Kathie took place at Forbes Field. I invited her father to join us for a professional soccer game at Forbes Field. A team called the Pittsburgh Phantoms, with a star player named Co Prins, was a single-season entry in a professional soccer league. They were owned by the same people who had purchased the new franchise in the National Hockey League, the Pittsburgh Penguins. Kathie's dad sat with her in the stands, high above home plate, and I spent most of my time in the press box, taking notes for a story for *Pittsburgh Weekly Sports*. Kathie stayed nearly the entire game, before retreating to her apartment. That is when I knew she had the right stuff to live with a sports writer. She would make a good wife.

Much of our courtship was conducted in late-evening meetings at Frankie Gustine's Restaurant. I would go there after putting the sports section of *The Pitt News* to bed. When the other guys would call it quits and go back to their dorm rooms, I would call Kathie.

"Come on over for awhile, I'd like to see you," I'd say. And she would usually come over. We would have a beer and a sandwich and sit and talk for awhile and then I would walk her to her apartment. We met in November and we were married on August 12 of 1967.

Pitt students still live in that neighborhood. Once upon a time, many of the Pirates lived in that neighborhood, too. It was the best they could afford, and they were comfortable there.

Danny Marino grew up farther south in Oakland, on Parkview Avenue, and I remember when I visited his family's home there when he was a senior at Pitt that he spoke of playing catch in a street nearby with Willie Stargell of the Pirates. Stargell lived near Marino's grandmother. Bruno Sammartino, the world wrestling champion at the time, also grew up in that neighborhood, as did Joe Gordon, the public relations guru of the Pittsburgh Steelers. It is probably one of the reasons Gordon grew up to love the Pirates, the Steelers, the Pitt Panthers and the pro hockey team, then called the Pittsburgh Hornets, who all played their home games in Oakland back then.

Walking through those neighborhoods on the way to a Pirates' baseball game in my youth was always a special time. There was a different feel to that neighborhood. Whoever was driving you to the game had to park about a half mile or more from Forbes Field. It was a catch-as-catch-can deal, parking in the street, or in somebody's driveway, for a small fee. In the neighborhood around Forbes Field, everybody it seemed was picking up a few bucks parking cars in their backyard or driveway. The locals sat on the stoops of their homes, or on swings on their porches, and watched the fans walking by on their way to the ballpark.

You could also go to the ballpark by taking a streetcar. There was a streetcar barn just a block from my home in Hazelwood, and my Grandpap O'Brien had been a streetcar motorman for the Pittsburgh Railways Co., and we never had a car when I was a kid, so we took the streetcars everywhere in the city, especially to the Pittsburgh Zoo in Highland Park and to Kennywood Park. That was about as far from home as we ever got in my youth.

My dad was not a sports fan. I do not remember him ever taking me to a baseball game at Forbes Field or a football game there or at Pitt Stadium.

A fellow named Frank Casne took me, and several other youngsters in our neighborhood, to a few baseball games at Forbes Field. Casne was a recreation director at Burgwin Park, several blocks from my home. I remember Casne wore sneakers, khaki slacks and a white T-shirt and always had a whistle dangling from his neck with which he commanded our attention and respect.

He enrolled us in something called the Knot-Hole Gang and, for 50 cents, we could go to Pirates games on specially-designated days during the summers of our youth. We entered Forbes Field through a gate on the outside of the wall in right-center field, and sat in the right field stands.

I remember being out there one day with the Knot-Hole Gang when a Pirates outfielder named Carlos Bernier hit three triples in the same game. I looked it up, as Bernier remains one of five Pirates to pull off that feat, and it happened on May 2, 1953 against the Cincinnati Reds. I can remember that Bernier hit two of the three triples off the top of the batting cage in center field. They rolled that batting cage out to the wall following pre-game hitting practice for each game. There were also tombstone-like momuments out there to challenge the center fielders.

I remember how close we got to see some great right fielders like Carl Furillo of the Brooklyn Dodgers and Stan Musial, my personal favorite, from the St. Louis Cardinals. They could all play balls off that right field wall like it was their own backyard. They knew just how the ball would bounce and were unerring in positioning themselves. They all had strong arms. Later, when I was a student at Pitt, I liked to sit out there and watch Roberto Clemente play in right field.

Clemente would come into my life at a later time, and in a disturbing way.

Just before Kathie and I were to get married in 1967, we had put down the first month's rent on a two-bedroom apartment in the Pennley Park Apartments in East Liberty, at the corner of Penn and Negley, not that far from Forbes Field.

Many of the Pirates lived there, like Alvin McBean, Maury Wills and Matty Alou, I remember, and, of course, Clemente. I think the apartment cost me about $175 a month.

Kathie was going to live there for a month before we got married. I was editing and publishing *Pittsburgh Weekly Sports* at the time, living with my parents and making about $3,000 a year, if I was lucky, and Kathie was a social worker at Presbyterian University Hospital, making $8,500 a year. I was trying to scratch up $25 for a tuxedo for our wedding. Beano Cook came to me one day and said he had a great story for our paper. "This is going to make us," he said. He gave me his notes that he had scribbled out on a sheet on a clipboard he has always carried with him.

He had gotten wind of a fight in the Pirates clubhouse — "Big Bob," the usher, gave him this great scoop — between Clemente and Willie Stargell. So I wrote the story, using all of Cook's information, and we ran it in the usual "World War II Declared" headlines we reserved for such scoops.

There had been a fight in the Pirates' clubhouse, all right, but it was between two other players.

Clemente sued us for $1 million and Stargell for $750,000 for damaging their reputations. One of our *PWS* subscribers, an attorney, had urged the players to take such action. Talk about an ambulance-chaser.

I remember coming home one day to our house in Hazelwood, 5410 Sunnyside Street, as it said in the masthead of *Pittsburgh Weekly Sports*, and finding my father sitting at our kitchen table with a representative of the sheriff's office at the other end of the table.

The sheriff was there to serve me with the papers for the law suits.

My father was on sick leave from Mesta Machine Company at the time. He was suffering from arthritis, particularly in his hands. His finger joints were all swollen and sore. He was unable to work. He had been a drill press operator for over 35 years at Mesta, in West Homestead, and he had to do close work with his hands.

He had the oven turned on and the oven door opened to make the kitchen warmer. It was like a waiting room to hell. The sheriff's deputy was sweating. I am sure he didn't know what to make of the situation. Our home cost my parents $2,800 to buy in 1947, and it took them about 18 years to pay off the debt. My mother would be selling the house in about two years, after my dad died, for $4,500, and she had to hold the mortgage.

I nearly checked out of this world just before my third birthday, so every day of the next 47 years was a bonus. Every sports event I have witnessed has been one more than I might have expected to witness.

The Glenwood Bridge has always been a monument to my life, though there is no plaque designating it as such. It spans the Monongahela River and connects Glenwood with Hays and West Homestead. I have never crossed it that I didn't think about what had happened to me there in my earliest years.

I fell from a moving taxicab on that bridge as a child and was almost killed in the accident. Several doctors at Mercy Hospital told my parents that my head injuries were so severe they did not expect me to survive.

My parents were told to keep talking to me and not to allow me to fall asleep or I might not awake, so they kept several all-night vigils. Fortunately, talking has always come naturally to every one in my family.

We had planned a celebration that day. My father worked at Mesta Machine Company in West Homestead. He was a machinist for a company that boasted it was the largest builder of steel mills in the world. He had gotten a raise.

So we were going to take a cab and go to Poli's Restaurant in Squirrel Hill to mark the occasion. But the weather came up bad, and it was raining hard, and the dinner plans were scuttled. After picking up my dad at work, we were returning home in a green Iron City taxicab.

The cab driver was drunk, according to the tale that was told to me often in my youth, and he was driving too fast on the Glenwood Bridge. The bridge, with its floorboard surface, was always slick when it was wet, and the steel street car tracks were particularly slippery under spinning tires.

The cab got caught on the street car tracks, and whipped sharply as the cabbie tried to recover control of the cab. It whipped so sharply that the door on the left rear side flung open, and I, sitting between my mother and sister and brother in the backseat, was catapulted from the cab and soared headlong into the top railing along the side of the bridge. I struck my head on the steel railing, and bounced back into the street car tracks on the other side of the bridge. I was fortunate that no street car, or any car, for that matter, was coming in the opposite direction, or it would have run over me.

I was also fortunate that I did not fly a little higher or I would have soared over the railing and right into the Monongahela River below. Years later, a huge military airplane went into those same waters, on the other side of the bridge, and was never seen again. That remains one of the Mysteries of Pittsburgh.

My father was riding shot-gun alongside the cab driver. He screamed at the driver to stop the cab, and my dad, or so I am told, jumped out of the cab before it came to a stop, and rolled over a few times before he gained his footing. He raced over to my bent form and picked me up, and brought me back to the cab. Then he ordered the cabbie to take me to Mercy Hospital, where I had been born almost three years earlier on August. 20, 1942.

I am told that I bled all over my brother Dan's brand new powder blue suit while being transported to Mercy Hospital. My Aunt Mary O'Brien was a nurse at Mercy Hospital in those days, and she told me when I was an adult that I was really in bad shape when I came to the hospital. Her story sort of certified what my parents had been telling me for years.

I had a fractured skull and I required 48 stitches to close the wounds on the top of my head. It helped me remember that there were 48 states in the U.S.A. There was a hole about the size of a nickel on the left side of my upper lip and the surgeons had to graft skin from my left knee to fill the void. There is still a bump on the inside of my mouth that I trace with my tongue from time to time.

When I returned home from the hospital in time for my birthday my picture appeared in the local daily newspapers. One showed me holding a ball in my lap. The other showed me sitting at a piano with my fingers on the keys. I have always wished I could play a piano, but I never could. So I have no idea why they propped me up in front of a piano for that picture. They should have had me in front of a typewriter. It would have made more sense.

Our home at the time was 5413 Sunnyside Street in Glenwood. My father was born on the couch in that home. His father had been a street car motorman for the Pittsburgh Railways Company, which had a car barn at the bottom of the hill from our home.

My mother's father had been the yardmaster at the B&O Rail Road, which was also located at the bottom of the hill. That hill was Almeda Street. As teenagers, my parents lived in the adjoining sides of a duplex house at the top of Almeda Street. They used to talk to each other once in a while by opening the medicine cabinets in their respective bathrooms, which were on opposite sides of a common wall. During the spring of 1993, police confiscated crack cocaine in a Cadillac that was parked on Almeda Street. The neighborhood has changed.

My family was very familiar with that neighborhood. My grandparents had homes within a block of ours, but only my Grandmother O'Brien remained when I was growing up. The others had died before I could know them.

When I was five, we made a big move. We left our house at 5413 Sunnyside Street and moved across the street to 5410 Sunnyside Street. It was a larger house and we needed the space. Two families were living at 5410 when we moved in.

It was a row house, at the end of four attached houses. It was a three story building, at least on the back side, facing an alley called Gatelodge Way. There were two bedrooms on the top floor. My parents shared one. My brother Dan and I shared the other. My sister Carole slept in a room below us. Our living room, or front room, as we called it, was beneath my parents' bedroom.

Our kitchen was on the first floor. You had to walk up four steps from the kitchen to enter our basement, where we later built a legitimate bathroom. When we first moved in there was a commode in a corner of the basement, and a hose was hung in the rafters with a shower curtain suspended somehow around it to give us some sort of a shower. We took baths in a galvanized tub, which you had to fill by carrying and emptying buckets from the kitchen sink.

I did not leave Sunnyside Street until I got married on August 12, 1967.

As a child, I took a deep interest in sports, and was kind of the coordinator of athletic events in our neighborhood. I set up teams and leagues for several sports, such as basketball, softball, track and field, football, and kept statistics, and did publicity. I formed an organization called the Sunnyside A.C. and got us black and white T-shirts. I would organize sessions where we prepared sandlot fields for play, cutting down weeds, and lining the bases, shoveling snow off the street so we could play basketball in the winter, putting up lights so we could play at night. I sold space on ad cards to help raise money to pay for our uniforms and expenses. I bought a small printing press when I was nine, and started printing tickets and programs for our sports activity. I also began to publish an occasional one-page newsletter about the sports activities on Sunnyside Street. I would post it on the door of our home from time to time for the other kids to read.

I would cut photos from sports magazines and change the cutlines so that the kids on our street would be mentioned.

I started helping my brother Dan deliver the *Pittsburgh Post-Gazette* when I was 10 or 11. I succeeded him as the newscarrier for our neighborhood route. We loved to read the sports pages. We bought the baseball and football bubble gum cards, collected and traded them and — something today's kids never do — we played with them. We flipped them and sailed them, won some and lost some, and didn't cringe when our cards got scuffed up a little. Plus, we knew something about the ballplayers on the cards. We cared about the ballplayers more than we cared about our cards. We didn't keep them under glass.

When I was 14 I was hired to be the sports editor of our local bi-weekly newspaper, *The Hazelwood Envoy.* I was responsible for nearly two full pages of the newspaper. I did that until I was a sophomore at Pitt and became the sports editor of *The Pitt News.*

That led to *Pittsburgh Weekly Sports*, and a lifetime of writing for newspapers like *The Miami News, The New York Post* and *The Pittsburgh Press.*

Everything I have done since I have been an adult started on Sunnyside Street with the activities of my youth. I have always enjoyed playing games and writing about them.

Jim O'Brien wore his Pirates uniforms proudly as youngster on Sunnyside Street.

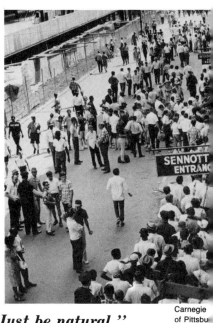

"Don't be sharp or flat. Just be natural."
—Willie Stargell
Pirates Hall of Famer

Where Were You?

"I'll never forget that moment."
—Dr. Thomas Starzl

D. Michael Fisher
Pennsylvania State Senator
Upper St. Clair, Pa.

"The two greatest moments in Pittsburgh sports were Bill Mazeroski's home run that won the World Series, and Franco Harris' 'Immaculate Reception' against the Oakland Raiders. I was in the stands for both. A few years ago, I was invited to play in a Mellon Bank golf outing at Laurel Valley. I was paired with Mazeroski in a foursome, and rode around with him in a golf cart. I had never personally met him before. He was just a nice, decent, ordinary guy. It wasn't until after it was over that the significance struck me. I had spent four hours golfing with one of my boyhood heroes. So I asked Maz to sign my scorecard."

Larry Dunn
Commissioner, Allegheny County

"It was 1960. I was in my first year of college at Johns Hopkins University in Baltimore and I was the lone Pirates fan among a school full of Yankees rooters.

"As the Pirates and Yankees alternated victories, my emotions kept changing from high to low, so by the seventh game, I felt my standing with my classmates as well as the Pirates' glory was at stake.

"I was the only student in my calculus class listening to the game on a portable radio, and when Bill Mazeroski hit his game-winning home run, I couldn't help standing up and boasting to the class . . . and a bemused professor . . . that the Pirates had defeated the mighty Yankees.

"The Buc victory brought a large touch of Pittsburgh to me and helped to lessen the home-sickness I was feeling at the time. It also allowed me bragging rights for the rest of the year with my classmates.

"Incidentally, I was out of town both times when the Pirates won the 1971 and 1979 World Series, so I have yet to see a Series game in person. The Pirates beat the Baltimore Orioles in both of those Series. Imagine what it would have been like to be a Pittsburgher at Johns Hopkins when that happened."

Dr. Thomas E. Starzl, Director
The Transplantation Institute
University of Pittsburgh

"I was in San Francisco the day Maz hit the home run. Everyone was going crazy. What the hell happened? It was three hours behind Pittsburgh time. That game had just ended as we entered a barroom at the hotel. I was at the convention of the American College of Surgery. The Yankees were supposed to win. I didn't know then I'd end up being a Pittsburgher, but I'll never forget that moment."

"It's like Kennedy's assassination."
—Doug Hoerth, WTAE

Joe Luxbacher
Head Soccer Coach
University of Pittsburgh
Beadling, Pa.
"The book on the 1960 Bucs should be a big seller. I was only a kid at the time, but I remember all those players. In fact, if I ever had one idol in the sports world it was Roberto Clemente."

Dave King
State Representative
Greenville, Pa.
"I was in dental school at Pitt, and working in the clinic at the corner of Thackeray and O'Hara, just three blocks from Forbes Field. We had color TV sets in the clinic, and we were watching the game. We knew that the gate would be opened out in left field after the sixth inning. We ran down in time to watch the seventh, eighth and ninth innings. We saw the ball hit Kubek in the throat, saw Hal Smith hit the home run, and saw Maz hit the home run. We saw some great action. There were four of us, and we squeezed in some space below the bleachers. And we know the answer to the trivia question: Who was in left field for the Yankees when Maz's ball went over the wall out there? It was Yogi Berra."

Doug Hoerth
Talk Show Host
WTAE Radio
Pittsburgh
"If you want to have a great sports nostalgia show on the radio just mention Mazeroski, and you'll jump-start the show. Everybody in this area remembers where they were when Maz hit the home run. It's like Kennedy's assassination. In my neck of the woods in New York-New Jersey, everybody remembers Bobby Thomson's home run. They remember everything they did that day. There are certain days that you remember everything that there is to remember. My wedding day and all the assassinations — John Kennedy, Robert Kennedy, Dr. Martin Luther King — and the 'shot heard round the world' are like that for me. Thomson's home run was a lesson in life: that the good guys don't always win. The New York Giants beat the Brooklyn Dodgers. The hated Leo Durocher came out a winner. The guy with the black hat won. I was brought up on western movies, and that never happened in those movies. Yet Thomson and the Giants beat Ralph Branca. I cried. I cried like a baby. I was seven years old at the time, and I had taken off the day at school to see it. I told my mother, 'I thought the good guys always won.' "

Kathie O'Brien, Social Worker
Allegheny General Hospital
"It was a Thursday, I think, and we were in school. It was a beautiful day. We were allowed to listen to the game on the radio. Some kids had brought transistor radios to class. They were fairly new. I know we didn't have one at home."

Linda Seeley
Greenville, Pa.
"I'm not a sports fan, but is he (Bill Mazeroski) the one responsible for that funny little brick walk where Forbes Field used to be?"

Pittsburgh Pirates

Streamers and computer cards fill Forbes Avenue in Downtown Pittsburgh in wake of World Series victory by the Pirates in 1960.

Bill Mazeroski
"I was never one to be a big shot."

"How much do you need to be happy?"
— Milene Mazeroski

"The last half of the ninth inning . . . And Ralph Terry, of course, on the mound, will be facing Mazeroski . . . Here's a ball one, too high, now to Mazeroski . . . Now the Yankees have tied the game in the top of the ninth inning . . . Well, a little while ago when we mentioned that this one, in typical fashion, was going right down to the wire, little did we know . . . Art Ditmar throws. Here's a swing and a high fly ball going deep to left . . . it may do it! Back to the wall goes Berra. It is over the fence! Home run! The Pirates win! (Continuous cheering without comment for 35 seconds.) Ladies and gentlemen . . . Mazeroski has hit a one-nothing pitch over the left field fence at Forbes Field to win the 1960 World Series for the Pittsburgh Pirates by a score of 10-nothing. Once again, that final score: the Pittsburgh Pirates, the 1960 World Champions, defeat the New York Yankees, the Pirates 10 and the Yankees 9. It is all over in one of the most dramatic finishes on (sic) history. Bill Mazeroski has hit his second World Series home run over the left field barrier, 406 feet away, and the Pirates are the 1960 World Champions of baseball."
— Broadcast by Chuck Thompson
at 3:36 p.m. on Oct. 13, 1960

Bill Mazeroski was sitting in a rocking chair in the family room of his home in Greensburg, Pennsylvania, just off Route 30, about 30 miles east of Pittsburgh. Mazeroski was rocking back and forth and smiling like a Cheshire cat as he listened to a tape recording of Chuck Thompson's call of his famous home run. Mazeroski's wife, Milene, sat silently in a chair nearby. Bill chortled every now and then, positively purring, whenever Thompson made a mistake in his commentary, like having Art Ditmar instead of Ralph Terry throwing that fateful pitch, or the final score (10-nothing) the first time around. Mazeroski memorized the script long ago. His eyebrows shot up knowingly each time Thompson said something wrong, and Maz seemed to be talking under his breath.

Thompson was one of the best in the broadcasting business, the voice of the Baltimore Orioles and the Baltimore Colts, and the man who described the action in 1958 when the Colts, led by Pittsburgh-bred Johnny Unitas, defeated the New York Giants in sudden death overtime for the National Football League championship in what was called "the greatest football game ever played." Thompson was orginally from Reading, Pennsylvania, and had gotten his professional start in the late '30s doing a college football game at Carnegie Tech, when the Tartans were a national power, and he later appeared on Pittsburgh television doing national telecasts of NFL games on Saturday night over the Dumont network. But he stumbled down the stretch in the Pirates

Bill Mazeroski celebrates
game-winning home run.

World Series victory over the Yankees in what may have been the most dramatic moment in Pittsburgh sports history.

"He sounded more excited than I was," said Mazeroski, smiling at his own line, remembering how he had run around the bases waving his ballcap and carrying on like a kid in a playground.

When Thompson said the crowd was 36,683, Mazeroski smiled once more and said mockingly, "And I've talked to every one of them."

Mazeroski continued to smile as he listened to what he quickly recognized as a re-created post-game interview with broadcaster Bob Prince. "Bill, how's it feel to be the hero of the World Series?" Prince asks Maz in the tape that was done after the fact. In truth, at the time Prince had no idea how the 1960 World Series had ended, and brushed off Mazeroski, the first player to come by him in a crazy clubhouse at Forbes Field following that game.

"I didn't think I remembered him talking to me like that after the game," said Mazeroski. "I was pushed toward Prince, and he asked me a few questions. He said, 'How's it feel to be on the world championship team?' I always wondered why he didn't ask me about the home run. I asked him a year later, 'Did you want Dick Stuart to hit the home run or me?' The truth is that, at the time, he didn't know who hit it."

I had borrowed my daughter Rebecca's portable tape player and brought it with me when I visited the Mazeroskis at their home on Saturday morning, November 21, 1992. Doug Hoerth of WTAE Radio, a real nostalgia buff, especially when it comes to the broadcasting business, had been thoughtful enough to send me a tape recording of the seventh game of the 1960 World Series after learning of my book project.

I thought it would be a good way to set the mood for my Mazeroski interview. It worked. It lit up Maz and set the tone for two-and-a-half hours of pleasant and insightful conversation. He remains the only man to ever end a World Series with a home run.

"I wish somebody else would do it," said Mazeroski. "Maybe they'd be more outgoing and they could explain it better."

But Mazeroski did just fine, in my opinion, and it is his humble, unassuming manner that made him such a popular and enduring hero. He was the starting second baseman for the Pirates from 1957 through 1970, and there was none like him. "He became the most proficient second baseman the Pirates or possibly anyone else ever had," wrote Roy McHugh.

"He's a real down home guy, that's why everyone liked him," said Joe Scalise, a man who ushered at Forbes Forbes, and now heads the ushers at Three Rivers Stadium, and was an eyewitness when Maz hit the home run in 1960.

"As a kid, you always dream of hitting the home run to win the World Series," said Mazeroski. "It just happened to come true for me. A day doesn't go by during baseball season that someone doesn't come up and mention the home run to me. At least, it seems that way."

Maz leads a simple, untarnished, almost philosophical life. "I look for the easy way to do things," he once said during his playing days.

He hasn't changed. He lives in solitude for the most part, picking his spots when he wants to tune in to the real world. "I am just myself . . . the same person I have always been," he assures you.

Maz, at 56, appears much stouter than in his playing days, but he had a weight problem even when he was playing. He has a full head of hair, but it is gray on the sides, and salt and pepper on top. He and Milene had been married for 34 years, and they played well off one another — like Mazeroski and Dick Groat on a double-play maneuver — and Milene, who is more comfortable in conversation, provided cues to bring out the best in Bill. They bounced lines off each other beautifully like they were playing pepper ball.

Maz was always regarded as a tough interview. He was pleasant enough, mind you, but he said little. Myron Cope wrote a series of articles about the Bucs before the 1960 World Series, and profiled all the starters individually except Mazeroski. Cope lumped him in with several others because "he's so difficult to get anything out of."

That's why I wanted Milene to remain in the room to prompt her husband in our interview.

"Is this the same home that I was in when I interviewed you for that story in *Sport* magazine back in the winter of 1968?" I asked as I entered their family room.

"Same home, probably the same furniture," said Milene, just as modest and easy to be around as her husband. They live in a spacious three bedroom brick ranch home set on 20 wooded, mostly hilly acres. There is a working farm next door where cows and chickens can be seen from the road. "Every once in a while we get them in our yard," said Maz.

"Every once in a while they come in and fertilize our garden," said Milene.

"We liked it here because it was country and away from the hustle and bustle," said Maz. "It was quieter back then, now it's getting civilized."

"Now there's a lot going on nearby," said Milene. "We're close to shopping; there are malls in both directions, and we're not far from downtown Greensburg."

"We're close to the mountains," said Maz, "and we're close to the city. It's ideal."

The family room in their home is spacious, but full of baseball memorabilia. Two of the eight Rawlings' Gold Gloves Mazeroski had won as a slick-fielding second baseman for the Bucs over a 17-year span are on display atop the mantel. He played on what was regarded as the worst infield in baseball at Forbes Field, yet was flawless in his glove work. There was a large Kuzma oil painting of Maz on one wall. On top of the TV was a framed photograph of him and his family from August 7, 1987, the night they retired his No. 9 at special ceremonies at Three Rivers Stadium. There were family photos and lots of knick knacks. This had not been done by a decorator; it had a lived-in look. It was a great place to be on an otherwise gray, dank day.

The furniture was well-stuffed and comfortable, Early American in design, and many of the cushions were covered, as well as many of the tables, with white doilies. Several colorful afghans draped some of the couches and chairs as well.

"Did you do these?" I asked Milene.

"No, they're just things we've picked up through the years," she replied, almost apologetically.

"My mother is 85 and she still embroiders and crochets," I told Milene. "We used to have doilies like this in our home in Hazelwood."

"Everybody used to," said Milene. "I still do."

The furniture was mostly browns and beiges, and the room was a warm one. Bill seemed quite comfortable, rocking back and forth in that rocking chair, wearing soft black loafers over burgundy socks, dark slacks, and a V-neck sweater over a golf knit jersey. He was sitting next to large sliding glass doors that led to a backyard patio. The cloth awning had been removed from the support frame for the winter. It had been raining all morning, and there was a large puddle on the patio. Gray squirrels scurried across the patio, skidded through the puddle, and all about a hillside behind the Mazeroski home. It was a perfect backdrop for Bill Mazeroski, but the weather put a damper on his day's schedule.

"No golf today," said Maz, mournfully.

"I don't think so," said Milene, softly.

"Have to go fishing," kidded Maz.

"You can watch the college football games on TV," suggested Milene.

"It's Temple and Rutgers," said Maz in a semi-grumble.

"They're not showing Ohio State and Michigan here," I interjected. "Can you believe that?"

"Yeah, and Ohio State is so close," said Maz, an Ohioan by birth. "There won't be too many people watching Channel 4 today."

These are the kinds of decisions and options Maz must make just about every day of the week, not just on Saturday.

Dick Groat had told me in an earlier interview, "Maz has to make a major decision every day when he gets up: Is he going to play golf, go fishing or go hunting?"

Maz laughed when I related Groat's comment to him. He can live with the teasing. He is doing just what he wants to do.

Sally O'Leary, who looks after the alumni in the Pirates public relations office, and produces a slick newsletter called *The Black and Gold*, to keep former Pirates informed about each other, gets a kick out of Mazeroski, whom she dearly loves.

"I get lots of requests for Bob Friend and ElRoy Face to make appearances and talks and card signings, but I get the most for Maz," she says with a chuckle, "but Maz just doesn't want to do anything. I have to pick my spots with him."

Maz is more content and comfortable in the company of family and friends, and prefers his sports on TV these days.

"Hey, I'm a sports fan," said Mazeroski. "I watch it all. I follow Pitt. I've been very disappointed in their football team and their basketball team."

I left my home at 8:30 that morning, about a half hour later than I had originally planned. I passed the basketball courts in Upper St. Clair where I usually play basketball with an over-the-hill gang on weekend mornings during the summer months. They were still at it. Sure enough, there were 11 of them out there playing in a steady rain. One of my neighbors, Jack Curley, who is in his early 60s, was running in the midst of the pack in his familiar burgundy sweatsuit. I call him The Scarlet Pimpernel. I had to smile. They looked crazy out there, playing in the rain. Now I know how I looked to my disbelieving neighbors when I was out there on similar wet days.

But Maz still enjoys playing games as well.

You have to like the Mazeroskis. I missed their home on the first pass, and thought I had gone too far, after passing a farm, so I stopped at a service station, and asked where I might find Bill Mazeroski. Two fellows quickly told me how to get to the Mazeroski manse.

"Our home is back off the road a good bit," Bill had told me in advance. "But, at this time of the year, you should be able to see it. I have a big ol' blue van in the driveway."

When I drove down their long driveway, I was greeted by the sound of a barking dog. I learned that the barking dog was named Muttley, a mutt or mongrel, which is just the sort of dog you would expect the Mazeroskis to have. Milene and Bill were both tugging at Muttley's collar to keep him from darting at me when I stepped on their porch.

The Mazeroskis had been sitting on a bench on their front porch waiting for me. They were concerned that I would miss their place, and were watching for me. It was damp and there was a chill in the air, but they were wearing sweaters, and sitting together on lookout. It was considerate of them. They are old-fashioned in their concern for others.

I had not been to their home in 24 years, yet it seemed like yesterday the way they greeted me and made me feel at home. You would have thought I was a long lost cousin.

Can you imagine what a ballplayer like Billy Mazeroski might command today?"
— Ralph Conde on WHJB

I was listening to Ralph Conde's Saturday morning sports talk show on WHJB Radio in Greensburg as I drove to the Mazeroski home that morning. I had been a guest on that same show two weeks earlier, prior to selling and signing my books *Whatever It Takes* and *Doing It Right*, about the Pittsburgh Steelers, at a "Celebration of Authors" at the Greensburg Garden and Civic Center. There had been 54 Western Pennsylvania authors present at that prestigious event.

Conde was decrying the current state of sports in this country, dwelling on negative news about Pitt's sorry football team, some off-the-ice hanky panky on the part of Penguins' star Mario Lemieux while on the road in Minnesota, and the Pirates' ongoing fire sale of high-salaried ballplayers. The Pirates were cutting their payroll dramatically in reshaping their squad.

Conde was critical of the kind of money Jose Lind was making as the Pirates' second baseman. Lind had recently won his first Gold Glove, and had made only six errors during the season. But he made an error in the bottom of the ninth against the Braves in the final game of the playoffs, and will be best remembered for a mistake he made that opened the gates for the Braves in what turned out to be the final game he would ever play for the Pirates. The Pirates had just traded Lind to the Kansas City Royals rather than have him take them to arbitration to the tune of a $3 million annual salary.

"Three million for a light-hitter like Lind!" cried Conde. "Can you imagine what a ballplayer like Billy Mazeroski might command today?"

I thought it was ironic that Conde mentioned Mazeroski on his show as I was driving to interview him. Maz is still in the news, I thought, never to be forgotten.

"That Conde is a real character," said Mazeroski, when I mentioned it to him. "He has a real following around here."

What goes through Mazeroski's mind when he hears about how much money he would be making today?

"I block that out," he said. "I don't worry about it. It would be nice, but. . ."

I suggested to Mazeroski that he was much richer than most of today's ballplayers, like Jose Canseco, Ricky Henderson, Bobby Bonilla, Doug Drabek and Barry Bonds, none of whom seem as contented as Mazeroski.

"I think you're a rich man," I said to Mazeroski.

"Me rich?" he said. "How's that?"

"You still have Milene, some business interests, a pension, a paid-off home, and your children are doing fine, and you do what you want to do every day," I said. "And you're happy."

Milene and Bill both nodded in agreement. I had spoken to Milene the month before on the telephone and she had said to me, "Bill doesn't require a lot. He's content. How much do you need to be happy?"

Mazeroski is doing just fine financially. He owns Bill Mazeroski's Golf Course, a nine-hole golf course, in Rayland, Ohio, which used to be the Vine Cliff Golf Course, and Bill's Bar, a restaurant and bar in Yorkville, Ohio. He lends his name to a national baseball magazine done by Peterson Publishing. He gets some paydays for public relations appearances, but more often than not he participates free of charge in countless charity-related golf outings in the tri-state area, as well as an occasional event around the country. "Bill doesn't know how to say 'no' to too many people," said Milene. "But he likes to play golf and to see his old teammates so it works out OK for him."

As Maz sees it, he is still leading the good life.

"I always knew baseball was going to end sometime," he said. "I never looked for anyone to help me when it was over. We've been very comfortable ever since we've been married."

Milene Mazeroski is surrounded by reporters after husband's 9th inning home run.

Bill and Milene Mazeroski pose with their sons David, on lap, and Darren, at Fort Myers.

Maz with mother at victory dinner after hitting HR in first game of the 1960 World Series

Bill and Milene Mazeroski are flanked by sons Darren (left) with wife Jill, and David at Three Rivers Stadium when Maz's No. 9 uniform was retired.

He looked Milene's way for approval of his comment.

"We have everything we need," he said.

Maz gave that some more thought, and then added, "If I were playing today, I'd never want to be the highest paid player. I'd like to be somewhere in the middle, and not have as great of expectations."

He didn't think Bonilla, Bonds and Drabek had made the best decisions by leaving Pittsburgh and going where they could make the most money.

"Playing for the Pirates in Pittsburgh is still a good situation," he said. "It's important to win in baseball. If you're on a bad team, you don't have nothing to play for except yourself. You end up with a poor attitude."

He owns Bill's Bar in Yorkville. Why not Maz's Bar? Why not capitalize on his unique name? Bill smiled. "My partner is an accountant named Bill," he said. "His name is Bill DelVecchio. It's named for him, too. After all, he runs it, as well as our golf club. Right as you go in the door, there's a big picture of him on one side of the wall, and another one of me."

That makes perfectly good sense to Mazeroski, if not the best business sense to anyone who has worked on Madison Avenue as I have. His way, though, is probably the best way.

"We have great barbeque ribs there," he said of his bar. "In fact, we had some last night. I brought some home for us. Great baby backs."

Bill would enjoy that take-home meal more than another banquet in his honor.

"You don't need much," said Bill. "I was never one to be a bigshot. Not from where I come from. You have to have your privacy, too, so I never looked for a lot of public attention.

"I have often said I'd hate to be like Joe DiMaggio, Mickey Mantle or Willie Mays who can't go anywhere without being recognized. I would never want to be that big."

Maz used to have some of his Gold Gloves on display at his bar. "But I had to take them out; they were too valuable, and I heard about other guys having their stuff stolen from places like that. It happened to Groat."

He mentioned that Milene worries about all his baseball memorabilia. "It's a wonder she doesn't have gray hair; she worries so much," he said.

"He likes us and we like him."
— Ron DeNunzio

Maz is happy that he can go to dinner at DeNunzio's Restaurant in nearby Jeannette, take his family, and have a good meal without being unduly disturbed by the other patrons. Everyone there knows Maz is there, and they are happy to have him, but they do not pester him. Owner Ron DeNunzio shares Maz's passion for playing golf so they get along beautifully. Ron's father, Tony DeNunzio, a local bank executive with Community Savings, always wants to take just one more picture with his omnipresent camera, but Maz understands. He just smiles.

"He likes us, and we like him," said Ronnie, "and people are pleased that he's here when they're eating dinner, but they don't go over and bother him and his family."

There are several photos of Maz on the walls in the bar room at DeNunzio's, as there are of two other local sports heroes, golfing great Arnold Palmer of neighboring Latrobe, and long-time Steelers football player and coach Dick Hoak, who grew up in Jeannette and now lives in nearby Greensburg. They are up there on the Wall of Fame along with all the local patrons.

Maz is happy to drive down Route 30 a few miles west to Fontana's Cafe on the border of North Huntingdon and Irwin. Maz and owner Jimmy Fontana go fishing and hunting together. It's a no-frills family restaurant and bar. There is a big portrait of Maz behind the bar, and photos of some other local favorites, like former Pirates' relief pitcher Dave Giusti, former Chicago Bears defensive stalwart Doug Plank of Irwin, and Steelers' Hall of Fame linebacker Jack Ham, who have all enjoyed a beer or two at the bar on Pennsylvania Avenue in their heyday. Maz has even tended bar for his buddy Jimmy just for kicks.

A good friend, former Pitt and NFL football player Bill Priatko, who lives in North Huntingdon, took me to Fontana's Cafe just before Christmas in 1992.

"Maz and I have played lots of golf and gone fishing together many times," said Fontana. "He used to stop in my place with Tony Bartirome, and we just became friends. I never paid no mind to them, at first, but I got to know them in 1961. Maz and I sat down and we played cards, and he had a beer and I had a beer, and he chewed and I chewed, and he just said, 'What are you doin' tomorrow?' We made a date to play golf at Lincoln Hills the next morning, and we ended up playing cards till 6:30 in the morning. I wasn't sure he still wanted to play golf at 10 a.m. He said, 'Let's get something straight. When I tell you I'll be there, I'll be there.' He just came on to me and we've been friends ever since. He said, 'I don't make too many friends.' His wife Milene told me I'm one of his closest friends. I relish that. We almost went together to buy the Irwin Country Club, but changed our minds. It would be too much work.

"Milene is a special person; so is he. He's soft. He called me a soft touch, but so is he. He can drop a tear or two. He may not make friends right away, but if he's your friend he's your friend. At the beginning, he was very different. You had to open him up to get him to say anything.

"He ate anything we cooked here. He especially loved salads. He said 'You Dagos put sauce on everything to cover it up.' But he always has an appetite. People would come in and ask me, 'Is Maz comin' in?' Yet they were smart enough to let him alone when he was here. They'll ask me, 'Hey, Jimmy, can I talk to Bill?' The people at my place love him. It was the same way with Jack Ham of the Steelers. The people here are warm people, and those guys are easy to become friends with.

Guys like Steve Blass and Dave Giusti were real close with me. Steve Blass' dad, Bob, has been here. Manny Sanguillen, Willie Stargell and Kent Tekulve have all come here. We'll play cards, and sometimes they've stayed over at my place. We've just had a ball with those guys.

"People are always after him to do things. I run it by him, but I never push him. If it's for kids, he'll usually do it. I'll go with him. He's good when it comes to anything that raises money for young kids.

"He never talked about the home run. I've never brought it up to him. A lot of people say to him, 'Hey, do you know where I was when you hit that home run?' Or they'd say, 'Do you know how much money you cost me?' I had tickets to that seventh game of the Series, but I gave them away because I had to be here to work the restaurant. I didn't know Maz then.

"But this has always been a good sports bar. We watched it on TV. We still watch it on TV. If they show him hitting that home run, the guys here will razz Maz about it. They'll holler, 'Way to go, Mazzie.' He takes it in stride. Not too much excites him.

"He's a good man. He looks after his family. His dad had some problems after a mining accident wiped out his chances to be a big league ballplayer, and sometimes it was difficult for Bill when he was growing up. So he appreciates his friends. He told me if you have two good friends you've got a lot. He never thinks of himself as a hero. Bill is a super, super guy."

"He's soft. He called me a soft touch,
but so is he. He can drop a tear or two."
— Jimmy Fontana

Maz belongs to the Lincoln Hills Country Club, located about five miles west on Route 30 from his home, where he likes to play golf. He has no trouble getting a game or tee time.

"It wouldn't be much of a life," said Maz, "if you had to hide from people all the time. That's not what life is about. That's why we moved out here in the first place back in 1961. We had 20 acres, mostly hillside, and it was away from everything. The place has built up around us quite a bit, but it's still private and we like it that way. We got a 30-year mortgage on the place. Now it's paid off."

"It (30 years) seemed like an eternity at the time," said Milene. "Life has been simple, but it's our life."

Milene grew up in the steel town of Braddock, located between Greensburg and Pittsburgh, along the Monongahela River, between Homestead and Kennywood Park. It was once a bustling steel town; now it's more of a boarded-up ghost town.

Life was difficult for Milene as a child and that's when business was good in Braddock.

"My dad's name was Walter Nicholson, and he was a craneman in the U.S. Steel Edgar Thomson Works in Braddock," she said. "My

Bill Mazeroski tags out Willie Mays of San Francisco Giants.

Mazeroski is honored by former mates Bill Virdon, at left, Bob Skinner and Danny Murtaugh, at ceremonies at Three Rivers Stadium.

Mazeroski hugs Dick Groat.

Maz with Arnold Palmer in 1965

mom's name was Gladys. She died when I was a baby, an infant. There were five in my family. We lived with my dad's family. His mother and my dad's sister raised us. I remember how families stuck together in those days.

"I think we have a sense of values we both share. We have a strong sense of family."

Bill was born in Wheeling, West Virginia. "My mother went across the bridge to the hospital in Wheeling, and then she went back home to Ohio," said Maz. "It was a little place called Witch Hazel. It was near Adena, Ohio. It's back in the hills between Steubenville and Wheeling.

"We didn't have electricity. We had outhouses. We didn't have a refrigerator. We just didn't have much where I came from. I dug my uncle's outhouse for my first glove. And you go down pretty deep when you dig an outhouse. He got the glove for me as a reward for my work. It might have been one of those three-finger gloves."

It might also help explain why Mazeroski was always so reluctant to discard any of his gloves when he played for the Pirates. No one else on the team stuck with a glove the way Mazeroski did. He wore them thin.

"I always used an old glove," he said. "I probably used the same glove for five or six years. I'd break it in for a year before I'd use it in a regular game. I was always breaking in a new glove. I'd have three gloves. I always wanted to have one ready to take the place of the one I used. You had your 'gamer.' And you didn't use it just to catch or warm-up. Someone like Virdon, on the other hand, broke in a new glove every year."

I had heard that his dad was a promising ballplayer, but lost his chance when he suffered a disabling injury in a coal mine accident.

"Yes, my dad was a coal miner," said Mazeroski. "Something fell off the ceiling of a coal mine one day, and cut his toes off on one of his feet. He could still get around, and run a little, but nothing like he used to. It happened in the winter time. He was supposed to go to spring training for the Cleveland Indians that year. He was about 19 or 20 at the time.

"My dad's name was Louis. I wasn't born when he had the accident, and he never talked about it, or about losing his chance to play big league baseball. My dad was a lot quieter than I was, if you can believe that. He didn't talk a whole lot."

"Did he play ball with you, and teach you the game?"

"We tossed the ball around a lot in the backyard, but he wasn't pushing me to play ball or anything like that. He got to see me play with the Pirates. He liked that. But he died in 1959, the year before we won the World Series."

"Did you have a close relationship?"

"I don't know," said Mazeroski. "Like anybody else, I guess."

"After you were the hero in the World Series, did you think about how proud he would have been to have witnessed that, to see his son win a World Series?"

"You always think about things like that, sure."

92

"When did your mom die?"

"Seems like it was about ten years ago. She was a big baseball fan, too. She really enjoyed it."

"You were a big fan of baseball early in life, I'm told. What do you remember about that?"

"I grew up as a fan of the Cleveland Indians. I was a big fan of Lou Boudreau and Joe Gordon, their shortstop and second baseman. They were a great combination. I liked that whole 1948 team. Al Rosen and Larry Doby were heroes of mine, and I always got a kick out of mixing with them at oldtimers games later in life. I loved listening to Jimmy Dudley and Jack Graney doing the Indians games on the radio."

When I was a high school and college student, Mazeroski was always a big hero in my home because of where he came from. My mother was born and bred in Bridgeport, Ohio, just across the river from Wheeling. As a teenager, she worked at the Howard Wilson Funeral Home in Wheeling. So John Havlicek and Allan Hornyak, who came out of Bridgeport and went on to Ohio State and the National Basketball Association, were also big favorites. My oldest brother, Richard, has lived most of his life in Bridgeport. He also tipped me off early about Bill Hosket, who came out of Bridgeport and played at the University of Dayton before joining the New York Knicks when I was covering the team for *The New York Post*.

So the story was familiar to me when Mazeroski said, "I remember how the river used to flood the island at Wheeling, near the race track. That was about eight to ten miles from my home. That was a long trip, so I seldom got there. I got to go to Martins Ferry, which was about four or five miles away. I'd go there on a bus."

Lou and Alex Groza grew up in Martins Ferry, and the Niekro Brothers, Phil and Joe, grew up nearby in the same valley. "We all grew up the hard way," said Maz, "but the Valley Boys are better the tougher it gets."

Guys from Braddock used to talk the same way, so Milene smiled knowingly when her husband made that observation.

Milene explained how she met Maz in the first place.

"I went to work for the Pirates right out of high school," said Milene. "Someone called and told me about a vacancy in their front office. I was interviewed and I got a job as a secretary in the scouting department. I was a secretary to Rex Bowen, the head of the scouting department. During the baseball season, the ballplayers came through the front doors and passed by my office on the way to the locker room."

"Murtaugh stopped me, and introduced me to her one day," remembered Bill. "He said, 'You take this girl out.' I wouldn't have known what to ask her if he hadn't intervened."

"Murtaugh, the old match-maker," interjected Milene.

"We met under the clock at Kaufmann's for our first date," she continued. "We had Chinese food at a restaurant on Second Avenue Downtown in old Chinatown."

"Did Bill talk to you that night?" I asked.

"Sure he did," said Milene.

"Not much," said Maz. "Not in those days."

"Says you," shot back Milene.

"Did you hit it off right off the bat?" I asked.

"Did I?" asked Milene. "I think we got along well."

She said they dated for a couple of years. "We became engaged in 1957 and we were married in 1958," said Milene.

"I was in the Army for six months after the baseball season," said Maz. "And we got married when I came back home."

I asked Milene what it was like to be married to a major league baseball player all those years. "I'd listen to all the games, but I couldn't just sit," she said. "I'd do the ironing. I couldn't just sit still."

That brought back a memory. My mother used to have the radio on to the Pirates' baseball game when she was doing her ironing in our kitchen when I was a kid. She still always has whatever ballgame is on — football, baseball, basketball or golf — when I visit her in her apartment.

She's the one who got me hooked on sports in the first place.

"That was all before my time."
— David Mazeroski

The month before, Mazeroski had gone to Florida to spend time with his son Darren, who is a baseball coach at Gulf Coast Community College in Panama City. "He just got the head coaching job this year," said Maz, proudly. "He was an assistant there for four or five years.

"He had played there for two years, and then two years at Northeast Louisiana University. He played one year in the minors for the Montreal Expos at Jamestown, New York. He batted .245, but he was released.

"He was short in some areas. He didn't have enough power, he didn't have enough speed. He could catch it and hit it a little bit."

"He could make the double play beautifully," interjected Milene.

Maz smiled. "He could always do that," he added. "He could turn the double play; we worked on that a lot right from the beginning. But he didn't have enough power, and he couldn't drive the ball to the opposite field. I don't think he had enough."

Milene just wagged her head as her husband handicapped their son's baseball ability, too honestly to suit her perhaps. "I knew he wanted to be a big league ballplayer so badly," she said. "In his high school yearbook, Darren said he wanted to be a pro baseball player and make beer commercials.

"When he came home after he was dropped from the minors, he was crushed. But he got his act together in a hurry. He went to Western Kentucky University and got his master's so he could coach on a college level. His world was shattered, but he picked up the pieces.

94

Nobody turned the double play at second any better than Bill Mazeroski.

Mazeroski with Willie Stargell and Bob Friend

"When that happens to your kid you hurt right with them," Milene continued. "David didn't want to be a ballplayer. He came along later, and he just didn't share the same interest in the game. David is 22 and Darren is 30. David graduated last year from Grove City College, and now he is seeking a master's in Management Information Systems at Pitt. He's really into computers. He lost me somewhere in the sixth grade. He is commuting to Pitt from home, and he is real excited."

I asked David if he ever walked across the campus to check out what remains of the wall from Forbes Field, or the Bill Mazeroski Field for Little Leaguers that is located on the Schenley Park side of the wall. David said he had been there, but it didn't seem to mean much to him. He offered little in the way of a comment when I asked him if he took any special pride in the place. "That was all before my time," he said.

"Suppose I really am somebody.
And it was the first time I ever remember
being on the earth as opposed to a part
of the earth. I was aware . . . at that moment,
of being on a ball."
— Maya Angelou, writer, poet

Bill and Milene Mazeroski can remember retreating to Schenley Park after Bill had hit the home run to win the World Series in 1960. They can remember how excited everyone was in Pittsburgh that day.

"There was no destruction of anything that day," said Bill. "It was just joy and true celebration."

"Right, just happiness," said Milene.

"I had been interviewed for an hour and a half after the game," said Bill, "and that gets old. The reporters were ten deep around me. They were asking me questions I had never been asked before. They wanted to know about my family, my dad, my mother, and they wanted to go way back. I wasn't used to that. It had just been about baseball before that, and I wasn't used to that. I had enough of that, and I wanted to escape from it all.

"I met Milene outside the clubhouse and we lowered our heads, and moved through the mob. It was pretty rough. We were by ourselves, and the fans just wanted to maul you."

"It was a happy crowd, though," said Milene.

"Nobody wanted any autographs," said Bill.

"No, they were just happy," said Milene.

"We went to a parking lot at a service station called Stuckert's, just across the street from Frankie Gustine's Restaurant after we left Forbes Field," recalled Bill. "Everybody knew us. Somebody gave me a beer. I toasted it, but somebody hit it and it nearly broke my tooth. I got into the car we had — it was an old, used black Lincoln — and drove away.

"We drove up to Schenley Park to get away from it all. There was nobody there. Not any cars. Not a soul. It was so quiet. Even the squirrels had disappeared. Maybe they were out celebrating."

"We had to go somewhere," said Milene. "We were planning on going to my family's house in Braddock first, and then we were going to Webster Hall that night for a celebration. When we got to Schenley Park, I just said, 'Let's stop here.' So we did."

"We really didn't talk about the home run," said Bill. "It was just another home run."

"We won, that's what we were thinking," said Milene. "It wasn't anything individual. We won. Our team won the World Series."

I mentioned to Bill that several of his former teammates, like Groat and Virdon, had said they were glad he was the hero of the World Series, and that no one on the team resented his starring role.

"I remember Skinner and Virdon . . . they got me in the hallway," said Bill. "They said they were glad I hit the home run, and not anybody else. I didn't think it was such a big deal. I didn't realize then the proportions it would reach. But, hell, it's lived with me for 32 years."

I mentioned to Mazeroski about his joyous trip around the bases.

"It was the first time I ever showed emotion on the field," he said. "I couldn't hold it down this time. We beat the Yankees, and I always hated the Yankees. They were always beating my Cleveland Indians.

"I wouldn't have wanted to play them every day. They had an awesome team. They had been winning a lot of championships before then, and they won big for four or five years after that. They had a dynasty. People say to me, 'You beat the Yankees.' But we beat the Yankees. It was the whole Pirates team."

As a player and later as a coach, Mazeroski swallowed hard when he would hear other players speaking in a selfish manner. Mazeroski could not understand anyone who was cheerful because they had three hits when the team had lost, and he had little patience with a player who was dejected if he went hitless in a Pirates' victory.

Mazeroski was a team man all the way, and he still is. He takes pride in the fact that he didn't sit down when he was in a batting slump because he felt the team could benefit from his fielding.

"Our pitchers wouldn't let me sit down," said Mazeroski, when I brought up the topic from a conversation we had years before. "They wanted that double play. They'd say, 'Maz, you can't sit out today. You've got to play. I don't care if you don't get any hits. We need that defense.' "

The argument persists that Mazeroski was robbed by not being voted into the Baseball Hall of Fame. I was among those who voted religiously for him, as well as ElRoy Face, for the 15-year period that his name appeared on the ballot. But he never came close to getting the number of votes necessary for induction from the members of the Baseball Writers Association.

At the same time, Mazeroski is more famous than many members of the Hall of Fame. His home run is shown on the highlights before and during the World Series each fall. And I have been to the Hall of

Fame on several occasions and know first hand that Mazeroski's image is well documented at the Cooperstown shrine, even if he is not officially honored there.

I mentioned this to Mazeroski. Oddly enough, he has never toured the museum and seen any of his stuff on display. "Somebody else told me they were there and that they saw as much of me as anyone else," said Mazeroski. "They said my old glove and my bat are there, and there's a picture of me hitting the home run. They thought I was in the Hall of Fame. There's enough stuff there.

"I've been there, but I've never been through it. We played two exhibition games there during induction ceremonies, and I played in an Old Timers Game there. I was just in and out; I never toured it."

Why not? Surely, somebody who was as big a baseball fan as Mazeroski all his life would want to look around and check out all the baseball memorabilia and history.

"At that time I had no desire to do it," said Mazeroski. "Maybe I could go there now and enjoy it. To have no one know you, that would be fine. I wouldn't want to go there with a crowd. I never did wait in line. If there's a line in a restaurant, I'll go down the street to Eat'n Park or McDonald's."

There is no bitterness in Mazeroski regarding what some see as an inexcusable oversight by the baseball writers. Groat is one of those most vocal about it. At the same time, Groat is grateful for his own baseball experience and all the doors it has opened for him in his life. Maz agrees.

It is enough for him to be honored in the Westmoreland County Chapter of the Pennsylvania Sports Hall of Fame as far as he is concerned. Plus, the Pirates have retired his jersey No. 9. He has no complaints.

"What the hell does baseball owe us?" he said. "We were just fortunate enough to get the chance to play. If I hadn't been a big league ballplayer I'd have been playing for some bar team and getting beer and spaghetti for doing it. I just enjoyed the game.

"A lot of people have dreams, but they don't get to live them. I'm one of the few who lived it to the hilt.

"I can remember walking down dirt roads and picking up a broom stick and hitting stones and pretending to be Babe Ruth and winning a World Series. Just about every kid who ever lived did that, or who lived on a dirt road and picked up stones.

"You just dream about being somebody. You have to have something to make you concentrate. You'd make up boundaries in your mind: where you'd have to hit it for a single, a double, a triple, a home run."

I told Maz that kids who were born after he hit the home run still idolized him as they grew up, and pretended to be Bill Mazeroski. Milene smiled and shook her head affirmatively. "They say their dads were always telling them about him all the time," she said.

"And they probably had a big wad of bubble gum puffing out their jaw," said Maz. "Pretending to have a wad of tobacco in their cheek. You had to have that to be a real ballplayer."

"I can remember walking down dirt roads and picking up a broom stick and hitting stones and pretending to be Babe Ruth and winning a World Series."

Pittsburgh Pirates

Bill Mazeroski made his mark as an Ohio schoolboy for Warren Consolidated High School in Tiltonsville during tournament game at nearby Bridgeport.

Ralph Terry
The answer to a trivia question

"It was like a slow-pitch softball game."

Bill Mazeroski says he sometimes wishes that someone else had hit that home run, "somebody who could have explained it better than me," and he never dreamed that it was a feat that would follow him for the rest of his life.

"I thought it was a home run, that's all," said Mazeroski. "All I could think about was that we beat the Yankees."

Ralph Terry would rather be in Bill Mazeroski's shoes than in his own over that fateful moment in baseball history. Terry was the one who threw the ball that Mazeroski hit over the left field wall at Forbes Field at 3:36 p.m. on October 13, 1960. Better to be the hero than the goat in that game.

Just as Pirates fans will forever remember that it was the Mets' Jon Matlack who unleashed the pitch that Roberto Clemente hit for a double and the 3,000th hit of his career they will always remember Ralph Terry.

His name will forever live in infamy.

As soon as Terry picked up a telephone in his Larned, Kansas home and realized the call was coming from Pittsburgh, he offered an answer before he ever heard any question.

"I should have curved him. I know now I should have curved him."

Instead, he threw a slider. In many reports it has been recalled as a fastball. But it was not a fastball. That is what the Yankees wanted Terry to throw — a fastball — but he shook off several signs by John Blanchard for a fastball, according to the story Blanchard tells about it — and went with his slider.

Whatever he threw, it was the wrong pitch.

"I don't have any regrets," he said. "Maz isn't a hot dog. That home run couldn't have happened to a nicer guy. I just wish it would have happened to someone besides me."

No one was more upset by the home run and the 10-9 defeat for the Yankees than Terry.

"I must have warmed up five times in that game," recalled Terry, "and I was pooped by the time I got in. Both pitching staffs were shot by then. The only time we got anyone out was when they hit 400-foot fly balls or line drives at people. It was like a slow-pitch softball game.

"I can still hear Whitey Ford telling me afterward how he was going to get a Cadillac with his World Series check, but that he would have to get a Ford because of me. And I can hear Jim Coates (who gave up Hal Smith's three-run, eighth-inning home run, which gave the Pirates a 9-7 lead) telling me he hated to see it happen to me, but that it was better I was the goat than him.

"I didn't really feel too bad because it was my first World Series, and I loved just being there. I always knew I might get another shot at it. The guy I really felt bad for was Casey Stengel. We all knew that was his last year."

How Terry knew it was Stengel's last season as the manager of the Yankees is another question. Stengel's firing after that game was a surprise to most baseball people.

The Yankees would get to the World Series the following season with Ralph Houk as the manager. The Yankees won in five games against Cincinnati. Terry was the losing pitcher in the only setback. He was oh-for-October.

Terry had a chance to redeem himself in a World Series the following year, 1962, going up against the San Francisco Giants of Willie Mays and Willie McCovey. Terry won two games that time around, including the seventh game, and was named the World Series Most Valuable Player, taking home a new Corvette from *Sport* magazine as his prize. Terry was carried off the field by his teammates after his 4-hit, 1-0 victory.

That game came down to the ninth inning, too. There were two outs and Felipe Alou was on third base, and Mays was on second, with McCovey coming to bat. Mays had doubled to deepest right, but admitted he had been trying to hit a home run. "I was going for the bomb," said Mays. "We needed a home run. I was going for it."

Houk went to the mound and asked Terry if he wanted to pitch to McCovey or walk him. If he walked McCovey, he would be pitching to Orlando Cepeda, not exactly a drop-off in hitting talent.

Terry wanted to pitch to McCovey. His first pitch was a curve and McCovey hit a foul ball down the right field line. The second pitch was an inside fastball and McCovey ripped it chest high right at Bobby Richardson. Like a rocket. McCovey would tell Richardson a decade later that it was the hardest ball he ever hit. Richardson gloved it without moving, then dropped to one knee just to make sure.

"There is very little difference between winning and losing," Terry said. "You just have to go out and do your best every time."

Terry threw his glove, and then his cap in the air. He knew the joy that Bill Mazeroski felt in 1960. McCovey could have ripped one into the right field stands just as well. Even a single up the middle would have scored Alou and Mays, and the Giants would have gone home the winner.

As Terry was guzzling champagne at his locker, Joe DiMaggio spotted him, and came over to him. "You can forget that Pittsburgh thing now, Ralph," he shouted. Terry nodded.

"I want to thank God for a second opportunity," he would say. "You don't often get a second chance to prove yourself, in baseball or in life."

For Terry and his teammates the championship was a reaffirmation that Terry, who'd won 39 games in two years, was one of the finest right handers in the game. And that the Yankees dynasty, interrupted by Chicago in 1959 and Pittsburgh in 1960, had been fully restored.

Vernon Law with Ralph Terry before 1960
World Series. Terry was goat of Series

Terry with Tom Tresh after victory o⟨
Giants in 1962 World Series. Terry was M⟨

"One out of two isn't bad," Terry said. "You're only as good as your last performance."

Yet more people remember what Terry did in the 1960 World Series than they do from the 1962 World Series.

Terry told a wonderful story to Pittsburgh sports columnist Ron Cook back in the summer of 1985:

"I can remember playing golf in a pro-am tournament in Portugal," said Terry, who has been a golf pro and has played on the senior circuit, ala John Brodie of the San Francisco 49ers.

"My partner was an Englishman who was in the steel business. As the day progressed and we drank a few bottles of port, this fellow says to me, 'I understand you played a little rounders in your day.' I tell him I did and he proceeds to tell me he saw one game in his life, in Pittsburgh in 1960. Well, my ears perked up at that.

"He goes on to say that he was part of a group brought to Pittsburgh by U.S. Steel and that they played golf at Oakmont in the morning. He said their host then told them they had to make haste to get Downtown, that they were going to see an American classic, the seventh game of the World Series. All this time I'm thinking that this guy knows who I am and he's pulling my leg, then I realize he's not because he's getting more and more excited.

"He says, 'You wouldn't believe what happened. In the final chukker, this bloke hits the ball clear out of the lot and pandemonium breaks loose. We were lucky to escape with our lives.'

"I just looked at him for a second, then told him, 'You know someone had to bowl that ball up there for the bloke to hit? Well, that was me.'

"What a party we had that night, celebrating the coincidence."

"Maz isn't a hot dog. That home run
couldn't have happened to a nicer guy.
I just wish it would have
happened to someone besides me."
—Ralph Terry

Celebrating Maz's home run
They, too, ran the bases

*"To be from Pittsburgh in those days
was to be from a town of losers . . ."*

Tad Potter
Consultant
Fox Chapel

"As a young boy, who was born and raised in Pittsburgh, I was fortunate to have parents who could afford to send me to a summer camp located in the Pocono Mountains of northeastern Pennsylvania. As one of five boys in our family, I often wondered whether our parents were sending us to a summer camp for our benefit or theirs. The years we spent away from home in July and August began in 1940 and ended in 1950. Obviously, at this time of the year the baseball season was in full swing, and the daily results of the baseball games were discussed endlessly. Almost every boy attending that camp was an avid fan of his hometown baseball team. Since the camp was located in the Poconos most of the other boys were from areas other than Pittsburgh, notably Philadelphia, New York and New Jersey. Those few of us from the Pittsburgh area were teased unmercifully all summer long as the Pirates continued to lose to the Phillies, Giants and Dodgers. We never ever mentioned our beloved Steelers during those summer months because they too were experiencing their losing ways every season. To be from Pittsburgh in those days was to be from a town of losers and as young boys do, they never let us forget that fact. The only thing we could counter their bragging and teasing with in those long days of summer was Ralph Kiner — the home run king of the National League. What a hero he was to us! Later in life, while attending Valley Forge Military Academy located near Philadelphia and then Penn State University in State College, Pa., plus my two years of military service in the U. S. Navy, I was constantly ribbed, teased and hounded about the losing ways of the Pirates and the Steelers. Being a sports fan from Pittsburgh in those earlier years of my life was a tough cross to bear. Being humble became a way of life when the topic of sports teams was discussed.

"With those kinds of experiences firmly established in the memories of my early years, the accomplishments of the 1960 Pittsburgh Pirates and especially the events that occurred on that wonderful day of October 13, 1960 now live forever in my mind as a Day of Ecstasy.

"I was 27 and I was a marketing analyst, working for Peoples Natural Gas Co. Jim Coleman was a neighbor of mine and we were also in the Navy Reserve together. Anybody who was a Pirates fan then had to be nuts because they hadn't won for so long. When they pulled that off in '60, I didn't miss a game of the World Series. Coleman had a connection at the Hilton, and that's where the Yankees were staying.

Dan Topping, one of the Yankees' owners, was a business partner of Nicky Hilton. That's where Coleman got my tickets. I already had tickets way out in right field. My wife, Jean, who's also a baseball freak, went with me. We had seats AA, 1 and 2. It was along the third base line. This was unreal. We ended up in the third base box with the Yankees' brass. Topping and Del Webb, the owners, and Roy Hamey, the general manager, and Mayo Smith, who had scouted the Pirates, were in there with us. It was so interesting listening to them talk. When the Pirates did something, Jean and I would be screaming and jumping up and down. Some of the Yankees were looking at us like 'who the hell are those people sitting with the boss?' When Maz hit the home run, I said, 'Jean, you stay here, I'll be right back.' I was right there at home plate. The umpire at home plate was holding back all the Pirates so that Maz could touch the plate. I was the first one to greet Maz at the plate. I was jumping up and down with him. I showed up in the *Sun-Telegraph* and in *Sports Illustrated*. I tell my kids, 'Your dad is in the Baseball Hall of Fame.' Every World Series, they see me in the highlights. That was one of the best days in my life. The darkest day came when I was a general partner for the Pittsburgh Penguins (1971 to 1975) and the IRS pad-locked our doors and put us out of business."

Tom Ward
Truck Driver, Duquesne Light Company
Monroeville, Pa.
"I was 15, living in Shadyside, and I was a 9th grader at Peabody High School. I didn't go to school that day and I bought a standing room ticket for $4.40. You were supposed to stand behind the seats out in right field. Late in the game I walked around to the other side of the field, up behind third base, and little by little I made my way down closer to the field. In the seventh inning when Hal Smith hit the home run, I moved behind the Yankees' dugout. I squatted down right behind the dugout. When the ball hit by Maz cleared left field I leaped out over the Yankees dugout and raced onto the field. I grabbed (third base coach) Frank Oceak's hat. Maz was holding his helmet in his left hand and I tried to grab it and he nearly tore my hand off. I just followed Maz to home plate, running behind him. All the Pirates had come out of the dugout to greet Maz. I have played golf at Dick Groat's course at Champion Lakes, but I have never met Maz."

Bill Mazeroski is mobbed at home plate after game-winning home run.

Among those who welcomed Mazeroski at home plate were (from nine o'clock to midnight clock-wise) Tad Potter (in white shirt with tie), Domenic Varratti and Tom Ward.

Domenic "Woo" Varratti
Retired, City Truck Driver
Former Usher, Forbes Field
Swisshelm Park, Pa.

"We were born and raised on Bouquet Street. We followed baseball from the time we could walk. We sold newspapers and ran errands for Dizzy Dean. The Pirates came close a couple of times, but they never won nothing significant until they won that World Series.

"When Maz hit that home run, I just couldn't take it anymore. We used to play an Italian game, where you matched fingers, by tossing them out on a signal, and you'd bet on it — odd and even — maybe for a quarter. Maz loved to play that game, it was called 'more'. I told Maz he loved to play that game more than he loved to play second base. So he was our buddy.

"I was working the first base side that day. I was sorta responsible for the ushers on the field at the end of the game. We were supposed to keep the fans off the field because the Bears were coming in to play the Steelers in three days, and we didn't want the grass chewed up.

"But when he hit the home run, there were more people on the field than you could shake a stick at. Some people were pulling up the bases, somebody dug up home plate, some grabbed at the mound. Everything was up for grabs. I just lost it.

"And I went for Maz. I was the guy at his heels as he hit home plate (see cover of this book), the bald-headed guy. I was about 35 at the time. It cost me $3.50 to get a copy of that photo from the AP. I have a copy framed in my front room, and in my TV room at our home in Swisshelm Park, which is just on the border of the city by Swissvale, Dick Groat's hometown. I was a city truck driver, 4th Division, Highways and Sewers, before I retired in 1985.

"It was a great day for us. We loved baseball. We used to chase Dizzy Dean back to the Schenley Hotel, which is now the Pitt Student Union, and he'd talk to us. One day he told us he never learned how to read, and I believed him. But he bought papers from us anyhow, and he'd give us a buck, which was a big deal back then.

"Maz would never do that. I hate to say this, but Maz was tight with a buck. He loved to play our games, but he never wanted to pay. If he owed you a buck he'd owe it for a long time. Dick Stuart would get on him about it; Stuart was crazy. But Maz would pay, eventually, and I'd go out of the park to Quinque's, a food stand right across from the press entrance, and get something to eat, and come back and eat it in front of Maz. I'd tell him he'd paid for it, and he'd make faces at me. We loved the guy."

This scene is unlikely to ever be repeated in a World Series game. As Mazeroski rounded the bases, Fritz McCauley of Hazelwood (in dark blazer), was first to reach him. Tom Ward waited for him on third base line and grabbed third base coach Frank Oceak's ballcap before crush at home plate.

Dick Farrell, Sewickley
Farrell Benefit Consultants, Inc.
Foster Plaza, Green Tree

"Billy Hammer and I went in together when they opened the gates in the seventh inning. We had graduated from Central Catholic High School that year and we were getting ready to enter the military service. We squeezed our way into the left field bleachers, but being from Greenfield we weren't satisfied to stay there so we worked our way down behind the Yankees dugout. As soon as Maz hit the home run I ran out on the field. I grabbed him around the neck and rode him right to the dugout. I showed up in a lot of the pictures of the celebration. You can see the back of my head in one of those sequence shots of Maz running the bases that's in the Allegheny Club at Three Rivers Stadium. He had a gold chain around his neck and I started to pull at it. He said something like 'Don't do that,' and that was that. I played in a golf tournament for the Easter Seals last year at the Field Club and Mazeroski was in the foursome right behind us. I didn't bring up what happened in the '60 Series."

Fred "Fritz" McCauley
Restaurant and Apartment Owner
Pittsburgh, Pa.

"I was 22 at the time, and I was a bellman at the Hilton Hotel in Downtown Pittsburgh. I was living in Hazelwood. I got into Forbes Field at 8:30 in the morning on the day of the seventh game of the 1960 World Series.

"A Pinkerton guard named Riley, a short, fat guy, left me in, and told me to stay in the bathroom until the game started. I was wearing a T-shirt and jeans. I called my brother on the telephone and he brought me a dark blazer, a white shirt and a pair of slacks, and he slipped them through the gate to me.

"I changed and went to a runway at the end of the box seats by third base. I sat on a milk carton that had a pillow on it. (He was in a section looked after by "Big Bob" DePasquale, a long-time usher from Oakland). I had been to 33 Pirates games that year, and I always sat in the bleachers out in left field. That's how I knew, as soon as Maz hit the ball, that it was going out of the ballpark. I knew what a home run out there looked like. Soon as he hit it, I started running for the field. I might have been the first person out on the field. How can you say it? I was just blinded with delight.

"I caught Maz at shortstop, and had him briefly around the waist, but he threw me off. I think he took his cap off because he thought I was going to grab it. I ran after him from third to home. I'm the guy with the dark jacket flapping and my hair flying in the breeze, to Maz's right. I see myself on TV and on the scoreboard from time to time, and in commercials. I saw Maz recently and he's put on a lot of weight. I know I can beat him to home plate now. But I've never met him personally since then.

108

"I'm in the picture of him heading for home that's in the Allegheny Club at Three Rivers, and at bars all over Pittsburgh. There was once a big copy of it in the J&L Steel Mill in Hazelwood. I'm opening a restaurant in Conneaut Lake called Leah Marie's Pizza Parlor, and I'm going to have the picture in my place. It's nice to be a little part of history. Hey, I'm the only guy from Hazelwood in the Baseball Hall of Fame."

Mazeroski is mugged by Fritz McCauley as he races toward third base after hitting winning home run.

James G. Klingensmith/Pittsburgh Post-Gazette

Setting the scene
Pittsburgh and the world were on alert

*"Pittsburgh seethed in celebration for the team
that should have lost but wouldn't."*
—LIFE, October 24, 1960

We were worried about Communism and THE BOMB in 1960. Russian leader Nikita Kruschev kept barking at us about one thing or another, and he came to New York and stormed the U.N. with his complaints. He made us nervous. He wasn't happy about an American U-2 spy plane being captured over Russia. We were up to our eyeballs in the coldest of cold wars. Dwight D. Eisenhower was our President, and John F. Kennedy and Richard Nixon were squaring off that fall season in a series of four TV debates as they campaigned to succeed Ike. Broadway bookies were favoring Nixon in the opener.

The U.S. and Russia, despite our differences, both sent teams to Rome for the Summer Olympic Games.

Some copies of 1960 issues of *LIFE* magazine, an outsized (10½" x 13") photo magazine, bring that period into sharp focus. The issue cost 19 cents.

Nancy Kwan, a new star of *The World of Suzie Wong*, was on the cover of the October 24, 1960 issue wearing a gold Oriental gown with a large slit up the side of her leg. She was a naughty girl of the night-clubs who falls in love with an American, played by William Holden, and accepts the odd idea that not being naughty can be nice, too.

Another blockbuster of a movie, *Spartacus*, starring Kirk Douglas, Sir Laurence Olivier, Jean Simmons, Charles Laughton, Peter Ustinov, Tony Curtis and John Gavin, was previewed in *LIFE* as well.

Several features were listed as coverlines, including this one:
Spectacle of Violence —
MOST PHOTOGRAPHED ASSASSINATION IN HISTORY
There were eight large photos inside showing the assassination of Inejro Asanuma, chairman of Japan's Socialist party, by a 17-year-old student who repeatedly thrust a foot-long sword into his body.

How were we to know in 1960 that it would not remain the most photographed assassination in history? Or even during my four years in college?

In that same issue, the next photo story after the assassination story, was one entitled:
THE BUCS HEIST SERIES AND THE LID BLOWS OFF
There was a photo of the "goggle-eyed hero" Bill Mazeroski. There was a photo showing University of Pittsburgh students and staffers atop the Cathedral of Learning — it had to have been set up by the *LIFE* photographer — supposedly cheering on the Pirates at Forbes Field far below. That picture is now a popular poster at art galleries around Pittsburgh. The other photo shows the celebration at home plate as Mazeroski

110

scores after hitting the home run in the bottom of the ninth inning to defeat the New York Yankees.

Here's an excerpt from the text:

"Then Bill Mazeroski hit a home run — the fifth in that incredible final game. While he was circling the bases, frenzied Pittsburgh citizens surged onto the field and practically carried him the last few steps to home plate.

"This was only the beginning. For the next 12 hours Pittsburgh seethed in celebration for the team that should have lost but wouldn't. The people felt an uncontrollable urge to let go — and loudly. Automobile horns began non-stop honking and attics were ransacked for whistles, tubas and Halloween noisemakers.

"The hordes converged on Downtown Pittsburgh where paper hurled from office windows had bogged down trolley cars. Snake dancers bearing signs torn from Forbes Field and beer bottles added to the traffic snarl.

"At 9 p.m. a police lieutenant viewed the chaos in Downtown Pittsburgh and radioed headquarters: 'This is preposterous!' Bridges and tunnels leading to the city were closed to incoming traffic. In self-defense, hotels barred their lobbies from anyone without a room key.

"When the sun rose on the home of baseball's new world champions, the city was a shambles. The clean-up job would cost $50,000."

Changing Times

1960 was a turning point year in politics. The population grew more in the '50s — 18 percent, from 151.3 million to 179.3 million — than in any other ten-year period in American history.

Most of the population growth was in the suburbs and there were less people living in rural areas. For the first time in history, white-collar workers outnumbered blue-collar workers, and there were more people with more free time and more money to pursue recreational and entertainment interests.

What was the going price?

Hahn's had a World Series special on TV sets. A week before the Series would start in Pittsburgh, Hahn's was advertising 19-inch sets for $169, and 23-inch sets for $239. The local department store was also selling a five-piece triple dresser suite for $199.

A brand new Dodge was on sale for $2,007 at Coleman Motors in Wilkinsburg. A Biscayne sedan was selling at Baierl Chevrolet in Ambridge for $3,000. A 6-cylinder, two-door Biscayne sedan or an Impala convertible cost $2,600. A Chevy station wagon was going for $2,735.

The average house in the U.S. was selling for $18,000. In 1950 the average price was $10,000.

There was a sale at Horne's for "elegant fashion coats," fur-trimmed with mink, fox, beaver, squirrel, muskrat or fitch at $59. The ad pitch went like this: "Look truly elegant, dress up in the glamour of a beautiful fur-trimmed coat." The price was $4.40 for matching millinery "stunning hats."

111

A men's suit at Kaufmann's, billed as "the dynamic look," was on sale for $59.50. Men's T-shirts and shorts were $1.25 apiece.

Hughes & Hatcher at Wood near Oliver had a great deal: a suit with two pair of slacks for $65. (It's a shame they don't still sell a suit with two pair of slacks.) Bond's on Fifth Avenue was advertising "a two-trouser suit" for $59.95, while Richman's had a $39.95 suit special.

A pint of Sam Thompson rye was selling for $2.59 and a half-pint for $1.34.

Giant Eagle was offering P.S. Blue Stamps with every purchase, and Thorofare was offering extra P.S. Blue Stamps. Remember licking and sticking those stamps religiously in those books the stores also provided? Save so many books and you could turn them in for all kinds of prizes. As a kid I had done something similar in purchasing Liberty stamps to get enough to convert the same kind of book into a $25 U.S. Savings Bond.

Anyone wanting to hear the Series on a transistor radio could get a new model, complete with case, earphone and rod antenna, for only $9.95, and they could pay for it with 50 cents down and 50 cents a week.

Round steak was selling for 75 cents a pound at the A&P. You could get a knit dress at Penney's for $8.88, or sheer nylons for $4.32 a dozen. A velvet hat could be had for $3 at Kaufmann's. Bridge mix was selling for 43 cents a pound at Kresge's.

What was on TV?

There were lots of game shows on TV in 1960, such as "What's My Line?" and "The Price Is Right" and "I've Got A Secret." There were giants delivering the news with Walter Cronkite on CBS and Chet Huntley and David Brinkley on NBC. There were westerns — "Maverick," "Gunsmoke," "Bonanza," "Bronco" — and cop shows — "Dragnet" and "Highway Patrol" — and situation comedies — "Love That Bob!" "Make Room For Daddy," "My Little Margie," "I Love Lucy," and old movies. Most of it was cotton candy fluff.

There was a nervous gentleman named Jack Paar who hosted his own late-night variety program called "The Tonight Show," and it was the first modern TV talk show. He had a sidekick he chatted with named Charlie Weaver.

The Pittsburgh Press radio-TV writer Fred Remington was in Hollywood interviewing Debbie Reynolds who was doing a TV special. Bing Crosby, who owned a small piece of the Pirates, was also doing a TV special.

The TV fare that fall featured shows such as "Twilight Zone," "The Flintstones," "Rawhide," "The Donna Reed Show." "The Real McCoys," with Walter Brennan as Grandpa McCoy, was a hoot in those days. Fred MacMurray and Bill Frawley were the featured stars in "My Three Sons," a popular sitcom.

Pa. Governor David L. Lawrence throws out first ball in opener of '60 World Series.

Oakland institution Gus Miller, former head of ushers at Forbes Field, throws ceremonial pitch.

Mayor Joe Barr got doused with beer by Dick Stuart in Pirates' clubhouse celebration.

Benny Benack and his Iron City Six played their music all the way.

Roberto Clemente signed some game programs for young fans.

Patriotic bunting in place at Forbes Field for '60 World Series. Main gates were on Sennott Street.

Tabloid fare:

Bridget Bardot, depressed on her 26th birthday, tried to commit suicide by swallowing barbituates near Nice, France.

On September 30, Clark Gable announced that he would become a father for the first time. He was in Reno to film "The Misfits" with Marilyn Monroe. Gable, known then as "the king of the movies," was 59 years old. His fifth wife, Kay Spreckles, 42, was expecting.

Bing Crosby was touring Europe with his wife Kathy, and would not be able to attend the World Series in Pittsburgh to root for his Pirates. But two of Bing's brothers, one of his four sons, and a Hollywood delegation led by Phil Harris and his wife, Alice Fay, were expected to come to Pittsburgh to pull for the Pirates. Joe Duddy, the manager of the Pittsburgher Hotel, said 11 rooms had been booked by the Crosby family for the World Series.

Tony Grosso was being investigated for bribing a policeman.

Fred Astaire turned 60 in 1960.

Headshot photographs of the new stewardesses for TWA appeared in the local dailies.

Local Tidbits:

Eligibility rules were announced by the United Way campaign for a "Miss Torch" competition. "She will be between 18 and 25, single, a working girl and a resident of Allegheny County."

Charles Carey, the manager of the Penn-Sheraton, denied rumors he was sealing off an entire floor for Frank Sinatra.

All the big steel companies and manufacturing plants planned big TV parties at Pittsburgh hotels. They were having a drawing for the few tickets they had, and as one report put it, "the losers would have to go to Forbes Field." One of the steel companies booked LeMont for a TV party one afternoon.

None of the companies could get enough tickets to satisfy their customers.

Nobody wanted to work.

Justice took a holiday when Judge Wallace S. Gormley said the Federal Court would be on a half-day schedule, from 9:30 a.m. till 11:30 a.m. on the days World Series games were played. Most judges had tickets for the Series somehow.

"It's the first time in 33 years we've have a thing like this and it might be another 33 years until we have it again," declared Judge Gormley, defending his action.

President Judge William H. McNaughton followed suit with a half-day schedule for the Common Pleas Court.

Postal service workers were permitted to listen to the World Series on radios during working hours.

The Golden Triangle was festooned for the World Series. A North Side flag firm, headed by Raymond G. Flynn of Liverpool Street, was the successful bidder at $2,130 to put appropriate bunting on light poles throughout Downtown Pittsburgh.

114

Safety Director Louis Rosenberg warned Pittsburghers about scalping World Series tickets. They were threatened with three months in jail and a $50 fine or both if they were caught selling tickets.

It was a different era, with a different newspaper slant, and there was a front page story about all the parties around town.

"One of the more convivial affairs," one report read, "will be a round-robin at the Hilton Hotel presented by the Pittsburgh Baseball Club through the good graces of its president, John Galbreath. He will fete baseball writers and sundry sports figures at the Pirates' Hospitality Room where both drinks and typewriters will be available in volume."

One wonders why the newspaper wrote about a private intramural event for everyone in town to read about, which only let everyone know that the reporters and press people would be getting free booze and food as usual.

A manufacturer of burial vaults invited 300 funeral directors to an "old-fashioned" baseball rally with liquor and buffet at his plant in Dormont.

U.S. Representative Adam Clayton Powell was speaking in Pittsburgh on October 10 at a national conference on urban problems. Powell praised John F. Kennedy and blasted vice-president Richard M. Nixon as a "great pretender" on civil rights and housing legislation.

Teamsters President James R. Hoffa was coming to Pittsburgh in late October to address district Teamsters members and their families at Soldiers & Sailors Memorial Hall in Oakland, a block away from Forbes Field

Margaret Lee Walgren, a South Hills resident running for Congress in the 27th district, spoke out on WTAE about unemployment.

City Council decided to raze the crumbling Market House where farmers sold their produce in Downtown Pittsburgh.

The 1954 graduating class of Mt. Lebanon High School was planning an October 29 reunion at South Hills Country Club.

The Chamber of Commerce and fraternal organizations were after city officials to ban bingo games in McKeesport. Mayor Andrew J. Jakomas responded sarcastically, "It's nice we have so many people interested in the welfare of our community. We will watch this situation carefully and if we find something to worry about we will take appropriate action."

The City of Pittsburgh bought the old *Post-Gazette* building at the corner of Grant Street and the Boulevard of the Allies for $900,000, and turned it into a Public Safety Building.

National Headlines:

Five world leaders called for a summit meeting between Eisenhower and Khruschev. They were: Premier Nehru of India, President Nassar of United Arab Republic, President Sukarno of Indonesia, President Tito of Yugoslavia and President Nkrumah of Ghana.

World Series Fare:

Joe Garagiola, who had played for the Pirates during their worst span, had a book out called *Baseball Is A Funny Game*. And *The Press* was sponsoring a write-in contest where the prize was two tickets to the World Series. The judges, if you can believe this, would be Garagiola, Stan Musial and Willie Mays. It is difficult to imagine "The Say Hey Kid" checking out the entries, or "Stan the Man" musing over which was the best of the 25 words-or-less offerings.

The *Post-Gazette* lined up Don Hoak as a guest columnist for the Series, while *The Press* secured the services (reflections) of Vernon Law and Dick Groat. Groat was also doing a show on KDKA Radio.

The Press also lined up guest columnists to preview the World Series. Al Lopez, the manager of the Chicago White Sox of the American League, was picking the Yankees to win.

"In my opinion, the Yankees have too much power and are too deep and have too good a bench for Pittsburgh," allowed Lopez when interviewed by a ghost writer.

"I consider this the best job that Stengel has done in his long career. The Yankees pitching doesn't look as strong as that of Pittsburgh, but you must remember that the New York pitching is good enough for a short series. The fact that Pittsburgh had a better staff for the long haul is not so important in a series which might end in four games and can't go more than seven games."

Lopez singled out Yogi Berra in left field as a defensive liability for the Yankees. "Casey Stengel holds his breath every time a ball is hit in that area."

Certainly Stengel held his breath when Mazeroski hit that last ball of the Series out in that area.

Solly Hemus, the manager of the St. Louis Cardinals of the National League, the other guest columnist, picked the Pirates to win the World Series.

"All games are won on defense and the Pirates' (defense) is vastly superior to that of the Yankees. Any baseball man will tell you that Dick Groat and Bill Mazeroski form the slickest double play combination I ever saw.

"No one goes farther for a ball than Bill Virdon in center field and he is flanked by superlative flychasers (I can't believe Hemus actually said that) in Roberto Clemente and Bob Skinner."

Hemus also praised the Pirates' pitching staff led by starters Vernon Law, Bob Friend, Vinegar Bend Mizell and Harvey Haddix, and ElRoy Face and Clem Labine in relief. Hemus labeled Friend an outstanding fastball pitcher, and mentioned that Mizell, who had previously pitched for the Cardinals, had just learned how to pitch in recent years. Before that, he was just throwing as hard as he could. "As a fireman, Face is second only to our own Lindy McDaniel," observed Hemus.

Waite Hoyt, who broadcast the Cincinnati Reds game and had pitched for the Yankees when they swept the Pirates in four straight in the 1927 World Series, told *Press* columnist Pat Livingston that he liked the Pirates in six games.

116

Mickey Vernon was put on waivers and released to full-time duty as coach of the Pirates.

Bill Burns and Tom Bender were TV newscasters.

Benny Benack and his Iron City Six were riding around Pittsburgh streets on the back of a flatbed truck playing "Beat 'Em, Bucs" to rally Pittsburgh around its Pirates.

There was a sidebar in the paper lamenting the fact that Johnny Craig, a Pittsburgh grocer who had watched the Pirates play in every game since 1946, had failed to get a ticket in the lottery for the World Series.

Because of the ticket shortage for fans at Forbes Field, a hue and cry was resumed that called for a new stadium on the city's North Side with a larger seating capacity.

Rev. Walter M. Trogler, the president of the Businessmen's Association of the North Side, said, "With the Pirates now pennant winners it becomes increasingly apparent that Pittsburghers need to have at least a 50,000 seat stadium with more parking space.

"It is heart-breaking to disappoint so many local Pirate fans seeking a World Series ticket and having those who do receive them pay $5 for parking space.

"The North Side is the only logical place for such a stadium. It is convenient and geographically perfect."

Mel Allen, the veteran New York Yankees announcer, and Bob Prince of the Pirates were hired by NBC to handle the TV play-by-play of the World Series. Chuck Thompson of the Washington Senators and Jack Quinlan of the Chicago Cubs were picked to be the radio commentators.

Extra air flights were scheduled between New York and Pittsburgh for fans wanting to follow the Series. Hotels were booked up in the Pittsburgh area as far away as Steubenville, 35 miles from the city.

A Pirates' TV Pep Rally was scheduled for the World Series Eve, at the Schenley Plaza near the statue of Honus Wagner. ElRoy Face, Harvey Haddix and Hal Smith appeared in the WTAE-TV promotion. Face and Dick Stuart made a promotional appearance at Kaufmann's. The Pitt and Carnegie Tech bands played at the pep rally.

Forbes Field employees threatened to strike over World Series pay, but eventually agreed to terms.

Chuck Connors, TV's "Rifleman" and a former major league baseball player, came to town for the World Series.

Pittsburgh-born Billy Eckstine sang the National Anthem at the World Series opener.

Sports Shorts:

On September 31, Purdue was playing a big football game at Notre Dame, and two former classmates and teammates from Charleroi High School would be pitted against one another. The Irish captain was Myron Pottios, who would later play for the Steelers, Rams and Redskins in the National Football League, and the Purdue co-captain was Maury Guttman.

117

Paul Kurtz was the scholastic sports editor at *The Press* who chronicled the performances of all the local prep stars. Doc Giffin was covering small college sports.

Hall of Famer Harold "Pie" Traynor was pictured in "Who Can? American!" ads, with his glove on his right hand, promoting American Heating Company.

The Steelers were playing the Browns at Cleveland Municipal Stadium. A special train for Steelers fans was leaving the Pennsylvania & Lake Erie Rail Road Station at 9:30 a.m. and was scheduled to arrive in Cleveland at noon. The ad for same boasted "best tickets, best food, best time, free refreshments, free entertainment" — all for $15. Fans were urged to call the Steelers ticket office at the Roosevelt Hotel, at 139 Sixth Street. The telephone number for the Steelers then (and now) was 323-1200.

Penn State football was on KDKA Radio, sponsored by Gulf Oil Corporation.

Sword Dancer was the swiftest race horse in the land that year.

Ted Williams batted .344 in his final season.

St. Bernard's beat St. Stephen's, 39-0, in City Catholic Grade School Football League action.

In boxing, Tommy Schafer, a grave digger from the North Side and, of course, a sports writers' favorite in those days, scored a TKO in the third round over Rudy Richardson at the McKeesport Palisades. Freddie Martinovich of Soho defeated Carmie Price of Ambridge on the same card in Bill Speney's promotion.

The Pirates were finishing the regular season with three games at Forbes Field with the Milwaukee Braves. The Braves would be going with Bob Buhl, Warren Spahn and Lew Burdette, the same three that dealt the Pirates three straight setbacks the weekend before in Milwaukee.

Pitt was playing its third game of the 1960 schedule at Oklahoma, where they would lose by 15-14 to the Sooners, coached by Bud Wilkinson.

Prior to that game, an Oklahoma scout named Rudy Feldman had been raving about Pitt's senior end Mike Ditka. "Iron Mike," as the two-way standout from Aliquippa was known in those days, had caught a touchdown pass the previous week against Michigan State. He had scooped up a low throw by quarterback Dave Krause to score against the Spartans.

But Feldman was more impressed with Ditka's defensive play. He told Roy McHugh of *The Press*, "If the action comes toward him, he makes a beeline for the ballcarrier and tries to hurt anybody in his path. Michigan State has a rugged team, but on one play Ditka knocked down a Pitt man and two Michigan State men and then caused the ballcarrier to fumble."

It brought to mind a better story about that particular game. Pitt trailed at halftime because Herb Adderly, an All-American and future Hall of Famer with the Green Bay Packers and Dallas Cowboys, had

Pirates placard lineup at Forbes Field includes (left to right) Frank Oceak, Bill Virdon, Dick Groat, Bob Skinner, Dick Stuart, Roberto Clemente, Gene Baker, Hal Smith, Bill Mazeroski, Vinegar Bend Mizell and Sam Narron.

Championship squad poses behind batboy Bobby Recker at Forbes Field: (front row left to right) Burgess, Baker, Clemente, Vernon, Narron, Murtaugh, Oceak, Burwell, Schofield, Hoak, Smith. (Second row): traveling secretary Bob Rice, Friend, Haddix, Nelson, Law, Green, Stuart, Mizell, Gibbon, Christopher, hitting instructor George Sisler, trainer Danny Whelan. (Rear row): Cheney, Groat, Cimoli, Mazeroski, Witt, Labine, Skinner, Virdon, Face, Oldis.

caught a pass at midfield and broken a tackle by Chuck Reinhold, a defensive back from Pittsburgh's Mt. Lebanon, who wanted to become a minister some day.

In the locker room at halftime, Reinhold exhorted his teammates to do better in the second half. The next sound heard in the locker room was the sound of Reinhold's body being tossed into a metal locker door. "If you hadn't let Adderly get away, we wouldn't be behind," shouted an incensed Ditka, who had seized Reinhold and heaved him into the heavy metal section of the room. Ditka's second half TD catch enabled Pitt to tie Michigan State, 7-7, that afternoon.

In another game that season, Ditka punched out two guards on the team, Ralph Conrad and John Draksler, in the same huddle because he didn't think they were giving their best. And you thought he was tough as the Chicago Bears' coach.

The Pitt freshman football team, enroute to a perfect 6-0 season, beat Indiana University of Pennsylvania, 27-0. Rick Leeson, a fullback from Scott Township, scored on a 28-yard run and on a pass thrown by Paul Martha of Shady Side Academy. The other TDs were scored by John Gregg of Mt. Lebanon and Peter Billey of Hurst.

There was a highly-publicized court case in which Dr. Edward H. Sebastian, a dentist from McKees Rocks and a former faculty member at the Pitt Dental School, was found guilty of offering money and special favors to two Pitt basketball players, John Fridley and Dick Falenski, to fix the outcome of, or to shave points, in basketball games.

Gene Fullmer won a 15-round decision over Sugar Ray Robinson for the NBA middleweight title in Los Angeles.

Jim Brown of the Browns was arrested for speeding in Cleveland.

Checking Out Books and Micro-Film:

The Oakland branch of the Carnegie Library is the biggest one in Pittsburgh. It is located about 200 yards from where Forbes Field once stood, just across the Schenley Plaza from Forbes Quadrangle and the Hillman Library, just across Forbes Avenue from the University of Pittsburgh's Cathedral of Learning.

During the year and a half that I attended Central Catholic High School in 1957 and 1958, I often stopped at the library on the way home to Hazelwood. I would hitch-hike through Schenley Park after I had finished my research there. I always enjoyed going to the library. I often went there when I was a student at Taylor Allderdice High School in nearby Squirrel Hill.

During my four years as a student at Pitt, I spent a lot of time at the same library. It has always been a favorite haunt of mine.

It hasn't changed much. I enjoyed returning there to do research on the 1960 World Series and surrounding news events and advertisements to do this book. It is still a wonderfully warm place to spend several hours on a winter's day. You never leave without learning something you didn't know when you first entered its halls.

I love to look at the microfilm of old newspapers, to look at the photos in the library's collection, and to soak up the scholarly atmosphere. It is like entering a time machine.

Local Entertainment:
Jackie Heller was singing at the Town House for two weeks. Once a local favorite at the Show Boat and at the Carousel, he had come in from Miami for this local gig. The Skyliners would be following Heller to the Town House, which was offering a special bus to Forbes Field.

William Steinberg was the director of the Pittsburgh Symphony Orchestra.

Pearl Bailey was appearing at the Twin Coaches, and she was also in a movie *All The Fine Young Cannibals* at the Penn Theatre. Roy Liberto and the Bourbon Street Six were at the Riverboat Room of the Penn-Sheraton Hotel. Baron Elliott and his Orchestra were appearing at the Grotto Ballroom on the North Side. Artie Arnell and his Orchestra were at the Grand Ballroom of the Penn-Sheraton. Les Kelton's Orchestra was at the English Room of the Fort Pitt Hotel.

Art Pallen was the deejay for "The Big Dance" on Friday night at the Sherwyn Hotel.

Singer Jeanne Baxter was in the Press Club in the Sherwyn on Friday nights. Pianist Ray Crummie and his group were accompanying her.

There were more than 30 drive-in movie theatres in a listing of their latest attractions. They included the Ardmore, Blue Dell, Colonial, Echo, Fair Grounds, Greater Pittsburgh, Green Tree, Miracle Mile, Monroeville, Mt. Lebanon, Penn-Lincoln, Route 19, Silver Lake, South Hills, South Park, Super 71, Wexford, Starlite, Woodland.

What was at the movies?
Ben-Hur, starring Charlton Heston, Jack Hawkins and Stephen Boyd, was playing at the Warner.

All the Fine Young Cannibals, starring Natalie Wood and Robert Wagner, was at the Penn.

The World of Suzie Wong, with Nancy Kwan and William Holden, was at the Nixon.

September Storm, starring Joanne Dru in Stereovision, was at the Fulton.

All The Young Men, with Alan Ladd and Sidney Poitier, was at the J.P. Harris.

The House of Usher, with Vincent Price, was at the Stanley.

Popular Movies in 1960
"The Apartment," Jack Lemmon and Shirley MacLaine

"Psycho," Alfred Hitchcock thriller with Anthony Perkins, Janet Leigh The advertisement included this warning: "No one will be admitted after the picture has started."

"Elmer Gantry," Burt Lancaster and Jean Simmons. Adults Only.

"Peyton Place," from Grace Metalious novel, with Sandra Dee, Dorothy McGuire

"The Sound of Music," with Julie Andrews, Christopher Plummer, Eleanor Parker, Peggy Wood

"Never On Sunday," Melina Mercouri
"Butterfield 8," Elizabeth Taylor
"Spartacus," Kirk Douglas
"Exodus," Paul Newman
"The Sundowners," Robert Mitchum and Deborah Kerr

Leading Recording Artists:
Anita Bryant ("Paper Roses")
Hank Ballard and the Midnighters ("The Twist")
Ray Charles ("Georgia on My Mind")
Bobby Darin ("Beyond The Sea")
Mark Dining ("Teen Angel")
Everly Brothers ("Cathy's Clown")
Hollywood Argyles ("Alley-Oop")
Bryan Hyland ("Itsy Bitsy Teenie Weenie Yellow Polka Dot Bikini")
Brenda Lee ("Sweet Nothin's," "I'm Sorry")
Elvis Presley ("It's Now Or Never")
The Shirelles ("Dedicated to the One I Love," "Tonight's the Night")
Bobby Vee and the Shadows ("Devil or Angel")
Jack Scott ("What In The World's Come Over You?")
Maurice Williams and the Zodiacs ("Stay")
The Ventures ("Walk, Don't Run")
Bobby Rydell ("Ding-A-Ling" and "Volare")

Humphrey Bogart and Lauren Bacall (in Key Largo, 1948) became cult figures for college students in '60s.

Marilyn Monroe

Jimmy Dean

Elvis Presley

Lucille Ball

Whitey Ford
He's still smarting over Game 1

*"We still think about it
and it happened 32 years ago."*

Whitey Ford was in a ballpark in Pittsburgh. Instead of competing with the Pittsburgh Pirates, however, he was competing with the Pittsburgh Steelers.

This was Saturday, October 3, 1992, and Ford was affixing his signature to whatever fans put before him — for $11 apiece — at a table in the Pirates Dugout Club restaurant out in left field at Three Rivers Stadium. Ford was one of the famous baseball players who had been imported to participate in one of an ongoing series of U.S.A. Sports Celebrity Card Show events promoted by DiCesare Engler. Ernie Banks and Frank Robinson, two of the great power hitters in baseball history, took their turns at signing bats and balls and game programs and photos as well. They drew about a thousand customers apiece.

At the same time, the Steelers were taking advantage of a bye in their schedule to sponsor a two-day promotion of their own at Three Rivers, hosting their fans on the stadium turf with an assortment of displays, games and a lineup of former stars to sign posters and other items the Steelers distributed. It was a fan appreciation gesture on the part of the Steelers, and it was a popular success. So it was a double-header for sports fans in Pittsburgh. They could get their fill of football and baseball on a weekend when there would otherwise have been little sports activity. The sun was shining and as Banks often put it during his playing days in Chicago, "It's a great day to play two."

Ford is a confident New York-born and bred ballplayer who can be as charming as Banks, but not if a visitor insists on reminding Ford of the 1960 World Series.

It was 32 years later, and Ford was trying to forget it, not reflect on it one more time.

Back in 1960, Ford watched from the bullpen as Ralph Terry threw the fateful slider, up across the letters, and Mazeroski blasted the ball out of the ballpark in the most dramatic finish in World Series history. Mazeroski's game-winning home run in the bottom of the ninth inning gave the Pirates a comeback 10-9 victory.

It left the mighty Yankees in a state of shock.

Ford didn't pitch in Game 7.

He is more bugged when he thinks about Game 1 of that 1960 World Series.

"I was mad that I didn't start the first game," Ford said for starters during his visit to Three Rivers Stadium.

Ford started Games 3 and 6, earning complete-game victories in 10-0 and 12-0 victories. Had Ford started Game 1, some feel there would not have been a Game 7. Then, too, Ford had been warming up in the bullpen alongside Terry in the late innings of that final game of the year. So Stengel was faulted by some for not giving the ball to Ford as a relief pitcher in that last game.

After all, there was no tomorrow. Why not go with your best?

"Casey always had his best pitchers start," Ford said in another interview. "There was no such thing as middle relief. Just four or five starters and Joe Page. He let his pitching coach run the staff. If Casey came out to the mound, it was to take you out. The only time I got mad at him was when he didn't start me in the first game of the 1960 World Series. He started Art Ditmar. Casey never said a word, and I never knew the reason."

From all reports at the time, Casey thought Ford's arm was tired and needed an extra day's rest. Ford pitched shutouts in the third and sixth games. He wasn't rested enough to start the series-deciding seventh game, and the Pirates won, 10-9. Casey later told his business manager that his greatest regret was not using Ford to relieve in Game Seven.

Jim Murray of the *Los Angeles Times* once wrote "Edward Charles Ford is the greatest Yankee pitcher in history —not Lefty Gomez, Red Ruffing, George Pipgras, Herb Pennock, Allie Reynolds. He's won more games in history, struck out more people, pitched more shutouts, won more World Series games. Whitey wasn't lucky he was a Yankee, the Yankees were. He's the spirit of the Yankees."

Stengel should have known better. After all, it was Stengel who once observed of the fearless Ford, "With him on your side, you'd think you just bought the business."

Art Ditmar, who was one of the most undistinguished pitchers ever to start a World Series, had the most wins on the Yankees staff that season with a 15-9 mark, and Stengel selected him to start the opener. Ditmar did not last the first inning, giving up three runs in a hurry, and the Pirates went on to win, 6-4.

Ford was 12-9 during the 1960 season, but missed a big chunk of the season and many starts because of an injury.

Ford has kept his ties with the Yankees in one capacity or another through the years since he retired as an active player in 1967. Each year he and former teammate Mickey Mantle host a fantasy camp in Fort Lauderdale, Florida, and Ford also works with Yankees' pitchers there in spring training.

He also owns a couple of Blockbuster Video stores and an indoor batting range on Long Island. Today, Ford prefers nine holes of golf to nine innings of baseball. And he can handle 18 or 36 holes if he is having fun. During his visit to Three Rivers Stadium, he spoke to reporters about having recently joined Yogi Berra for a golf outing at former President Ford's tournament in Vail, Colorado. He also mentioned that he had played golf in Bethlehem, Pa., with entertainer Perry Como, the pride of Canonsburg. Asked what he missed most about baseball, Ford said, "I don't really miss it. I go to spring training for seven weeks. That's plenty."

Vinegar Bend Mizell vs. Whitey Ford in Game 3 at Yankee Stadium.

Ford appeared on George Von Benko's sports talk show over WASP Radio in Brownsville before he came to town to appear at that sports card show at Three Rivers Stadium.

Ford's unhappiness about being bypassed as the starting pitcher in that first game is well known. Ford has made no secret about it through the years. Ford's name is still in the record books for his work in the World Series. He has the most starts (11) and most victories (10) of any pitcher in baseball history. He also has the most strikeouts (94) in World Series competition.

So Ford figures Stengel would have been smart to start him in Game 1. Many of his teammates expressed similar shock when Stengel decided on Ditmar.

"Quite a few of them have told me that," offered Ford. "But I was a little annoyed myself." He laughed at that remark, and continued. "It's probably the only time in the 11 or 12 years I was with Casey Stengel . . . maybe the only time I was annoyed at him. We lost the first game and I thought I should have started that one."

Stengel was famous for playing hunches. He had considered starting Bill Stafford, but his coaches, Ralph Houk and Frank Crosetti, talked him out of it, feeling a rookie should not start a World Series opener.

"Casey never explained anything," said Ford. "He just went ahead and did it. He was so successful most of the time we didn't say much about it.

"I missed part of the season. I was out a couple of months. I was pitching the last month and I was pitching well."

Many fans of the Yankees felt that the Pirates were lucky to win the World Series, that the Yankees were definitely the best team. How did that talk affect Ford?

"They won," he said. "That's what counts. It's something we still think about once in a while. And it happened 32 years ago. There's no getting around it. They played good baseball when they had to, and when the chips were down. Hal Smith hit the home run and, of course, Mazeroski hit the home run. When they had to perform they did. So you can't take anything away from them. They had a fine ball club.

"Gino Cimoli said it best. He summed up the whole Series when he said, 'The Yankees set all the records and we won the Series.' That says it right in a nutshell. We did everything right except win the World Series.

"And that's what I mean. When the chips were down, they came through. They didn't let that 16-to-1 setback bother them. Most clubs would have folded up and said, 'Let's just get this thing over with and go fishing.' But, no, they didn't. They hung real tough every day. You can't beat that, and we didn't."

"Was it the most disappointing part of your Yankees career?"

"Yes, that was the most disappointing thing that ever happened to me," offered Ford, "and, you know, I played in five World Series with Mickey Mantle, and we lost three of them and won two of them. After that Pittsburgh World Series was the time Mickey cried.

126

"He sat in his locker and the big tears were coming down his cheeks. I know what he was going through. There were several of us who weren't feeling too good at the time.

"For me to see that, coming from him, a man like that, that meant a lot to me. He was hurt by that World Series there. He just shook his head. He didn't say anything derogatory at all toward the Pirates. It was just that we should have won that World Series. That's what he felt badly about. We all did. It was a downer."

Yankees shortstop Tony Kubek clutches throat where he was struck by ball that took a weird bounce after coming off the bat of Billy Virdon while second baseman Bobby Richardson calls for help.

Yankees star Mickey Mantle

Yankees starter Art Ditmar

127

Bob Prince
"We had 'em all the way."
"I had more fun than any of them."

Bob Prince, the lean and lively sports broadcaster for the Pittsburgh Pirates, must have been caught up in a midtown mob of fans asking erudite questions like "Who's going to win tonight, Bob?" or "Are we going to have a game tonight, Bob?"

Prince was nearly an hour late for our mid-afternoon meeting in the summer of 1963 at the Pittsburgh Athletic Association (P.A.A.) in Oakland, just two blocks from Forbes Field, where he said we could have a few drinks and chat. Somehow Prince could not quite catch up to his appointments.

He was 45 minutes late, but he walked in with a let's-get-going stride, and a smile and a wink. I was soon to start my senior year at the University of Pittsburgh, and I was interviewing Prince for the first edition of *Pittsburgh Weekly Sports*, a tabloid that Prince was eager to see come off the presses. I was grateful that Prince was giving me his time, even if he was late.

Prince was a popular figure in the P.A.A. and always created a commotion when he moved through the lobby. Prince loosened up the otherwise often staid atmosphere of the private club, just across Fifth Avenue from Pitt's Cathedral of Learning. I was a little nervous because I had always regarded the P.A.A. as a rich men's citadel, but he made me feel instantly at home and at ease. Prince had the run of the P.A.A. After all, he had been the Pirates broadcaster since 1947, starting out as a sidekick to Rosey Rowswell, so everybody in Pittsburgh knew him, or thought they did, anyhow. Rosey died four years later, and Prince took control of the buttons on the baseball broadcasts. Prince was friendly to everybody, and his name suited him well.

While baseball was his best sport, by far, he also did football, basketball, swimming, golf and, near the end, hockey. He never took any of those sports or himself seriously. He always sounded like he was having a good time, and his listeners loved going along for the ride. "How sweet it is!" Prince would say, and his listeners would nod in agreement.

He was involved in many charity activities, notably the Ham-Am golf tournament for the benefit of the West Penn Caddie Scholarship Fund, the annual HYPO game which benefited amateur baseball, and he was a major magnet in raising money for the Allegheny Valley School, which became his pet project. It is a private, non-profit multi-campus residential care and educational agency serving mentally retarded children and adults, many of whom are also physically handicapped. The school's main campus in Robinson Township contains many mementos and plaques memorializing Prince's special contributions to its successful operation. His good friend Myron Cope replaced Prince as the prime fund-raising figure for Allegheny Valley School.

Bob Prince — "The Gunner"

On his dizzy whirl on the hand-shaking merry-go-round at the P.A.A. that day we got together, Prince peeked into every nook and cranny of the club, making sure he did not miss anyone.

He apologized for being late, autographed a baseball at the desk, and asked the manager there if anyone had called for his tickets. "Now let's go downstairs and get away from all these crazy people," he said, and moved out three paces ahead in his dark dressed-for-action slacks.

He cracked two quick jokes and then descended a semi-circular stairway as if he were trying to get a running start for a parachute jump.

Prince seated himself at a table near the bar in a new wing of the P.A.A. There was a meticulous setting for four for dinner. "You don't want this stuff in front of you," he said, piling the plates and silverware on a corner of the table.

Seated there, he stirred up an image of King Arthur greeting his knights at the Round Table, as a few score of his friends digressed from their original path to walk by his table.

"Can you bring Murtaugh and Casey Stengel over Friday?" one asked.

"I don't know," Prince sighed. "I'll have to ask them."

"How about stopping back later on in the Walnut Room, Bob?" another inquired. "We need a quorom for our meeting, and we're a few short. Just make an appearance, huh? You know a man like you counts five."

"Flattery will get you nowhere, brother," Prince said in that familiar velvet-like tone, grinning. Prince made the meeting, although he was a bit late.

An old schoolmate of Prince approached him and asked him to take a $25 chance on $2,000. "The Bishop will probably win it, but I'll take one," said Prince. This was typical Prince. He had a hard time saying no to anyone, and he was always tossing money and gag lines around.

Prince drew a cigarette from his pack, and the waiter was there to strike a match. Now Prince was ready to talk. In between standing up and down like a schoolkid practicing for a fire drill, while I shook the hands of another dozen friends, I learned that Prince was the best-known man in town.

Prince affected worldliness in his manner and speech. Some said he was a show-off and too gabby. His craggy face grew warm and his lips moved like a flying carpet as he talked about his life.

"I had a helluva youth!" Prince exclaimed, twisting in his seat, and fetching another pretzel.

Prince was the son of a regular Army officer, and he moved from one Army post to another as a youth and then from school to school (Pitt, Stanford, Oklahoma, and Harvard Law).

"One day I counted them up," he said, "and I found that I've been to 18 schools in my life. We moved every two years, and we lived in ten different states. Man, I lived like a king — even during the Depression. People in the Army had no trouble. I even took care of my father's polo ponies (he had 12 to 14). I had to get up every morning and exercise those damn things at four o'clock before I'd go to school.

"I even went out and broke wild stallions at Fort Lewis, Washington. There aren't too many places you can do that today. I had all the fine horses I ever wanted. I rode in steeple chases and fox hunts.

"I lived like a millionaire. I could play all the golf I wanted to. Swim all I wanted. I fired thousands of rounds of ammo on the machine guns. And even learned to fence with a champion. I'm pretty good at the epee and foil.

"If my father had been a civilian I couldn't have done it," Prince added, and paused for his second wind. "I got to play golf on the finest courses. Heck, I shoot in the '70s now. And, man, I can really whip 'em in table tennis."

After running the gamut of American high schools, Prince finished up at Schenley High School in Pittsburgh, but never actually graduated. "I was a half-credit short," he explained. "But my father was a man of influence here in Pittsburgh in those days. And he exerted his influence, and promised I would make up the missing credit in night school. But I never did.

"You know," Prince pointed out with an extended finger, "my father had this town under martial law during the flood of 1936. He gave all the orders in that crisis. He was running the show. I remember going in a row boat with my father down Liberty Avenue."

Well, Prince entered Pitt where he was "sensational in writing," by his own admission, and distinguished himself as the "craps shooting" champ in the hallways during his free periods.

He belonged to the Phi Delt fraternity chapter and was on the men's council as a sophomore.

He was on the swimming team at Pitt where he tested the patience of Coach Pat Corr on a regular basis. Prince was a sprinter on the swim team and was known as "Rapid Robert."

On a bitter winter day, Prince arrived late — as usual — for practice, wearing a full-length fur coat that was a mark of distinction on campus in those days of jazz, flappers, gold fish swallowers and stuffing guys in phone booths.

Coach Corr sternly chewed out Prince. "You're always late! Where the hell have you been?"

Prince flipped off his fur coat, revealing only swim trunks and the skinniest of long bodies underneath, and informed the startled coach, "Hey, Pat, I'm ready!"

At a meet with CCNY, "Rapid Robert" arrived with a cigarette dangling from his lips. Before Corr could admonish him for smoking, Prince disarmed him by saying, "Here, Coach, hold this fag for me. I'll be back in 51 seconds." Which was close to Johnny Weismuller's world record at the time in the 100 yard freestyle event.

Prince may have been Pitt's most famous swimmer because he publicized his involvement through the years at so many sports banquets, mostly poking fun at himself and his stick-like body.

"I never set any records until I reached Oklahoma," he said.

He would save his most celebrated performance at a swimming pool for a high dive act from the balcony overlooking the Chase Hotel pool in St. Louis when he was broadcasting Pirates games. He cleared a good 50 feet of concrete with his "Swannie" on a dare wager, noting "I'll do anything for twenty bucks."

He balked when his father was uprooted again, and he was to enroll in Stanford. He went there, however, and deliberately flunked out. Then his father was transferred to Fort Sill, Oklahoma, and young Bob enrolled at the University of Oklahoma. "Greatest school I ever went to," Prince volunteered. "They were a real friendly bunch of people. Stanford was snobbish."

Prince ended his educational swing at Harvard Law School. He was there the same time that John F. Kennedy was an undergraduate student. Prince won an audition for a radio broadcaster's job by "accident" and quit Harvard just shy of a degree.

"About eight of my relatives went through Harvard with flying colors," Prince remarked. "I failed in the family tradition. But I've had more fun than any of them."

Prince was fun to be around.

He was a booster. He was always trying to help other people. His wife, Betty, a Grove City College grad who was always active in alumni affairs, is a lovely woman. They had two children, Bobbie and Nancy. Betty still chuckles when I relate stories to her about her husband. His name and his stories still pop up at sports banquets, and still draw laughs. Betty has always been a good sport about Bob.

Her husband's ashes are in a columbarium in the courtyard at Westminster Presbyterian Church in Upper St. Clair, where the Prince family lived for many years. "It's nice that he's here," Betty once disclosed. "The grandkids drive by on Route 19, and honk the horn to Bob."

Prince and I teamed up as the co-emcees when the Curbstone Coaches were reactivated at the Allegheny Club in the early '70s under the sponsorship of The Pittsburgh Brewing Company and *The Pittsburgh Press.*

Every time I was with him, whether it was in the P.A.A., the St. Clair Country Club, the Allegheny Club or Toots Shor's in New York, Prince always picked up the check and usually bought the bar a round or two. He spent money like it was burning a hole in the pocket of his latest wild slacks.

In the off-season between 1975 and 1976, the Pirates announced that Bob Prince and Nellie King would no longer serve as their broadcast team. Prince had ruffled the feathers of some of his bosses. The fans were shocked and upset. Prince was more than a radio broadcaster in Pittsburgh. He was an institution. He was unique, an original, and he was as closely linked to the Pirates as the team's nickname.

Prince had rooted for the Pirates on the air, and never apologized for it. He was remembered for several phrases he repeatedly used on broadcasts such as: "You can kiss it goodbye." "Closer than fuzz on a tick's ear." "By a gnat's eyelash." "We had 'em all the way." "Sufferin' catfish." "Can of corn." "He picked that up like a Hoover sweeper." "Alabaster blasters." "A bloop and a blast." "Bug on a rug."

132

Bob Prince announcing game in August 1960

With Art Rooney at banquet in 1975

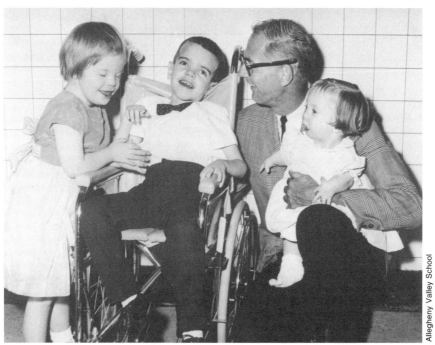

Prince was primary fund-raiser for children at Allegheny Valley School.

He also created the "green weenie" and popularized "babushka power."

He delighted banquet audiences with his quick wit, such as when he introduced Stan Musial by saying, "I think it is ridiculous that we are gathered here tonight to honor a man who made more than 7,000 outs."

There has never been a better banquet emcee than Prince in Pittsburgh. He had a remarkable voice, a wonderful way of saying things, sometimes outrageous things, sometimes irreverent things. He knew how to tell a story, how to set the scene during a baseball game. He was a delightful entertainer. His voice was unmistakable, and there was a reassurance about it, especially late at night listening to him in the dark as he was doing a game out on the west coast.

The Pirates were never the same without Prince, and Prince was never quite the same without the Pirates.

He continued to make appearances on local radio and TV, and got involved with other sports and commentaries, but it was never what it used to be. Pittsburgh and the Pirates were the poorer for Prince not being at the mike. And Prince was poorer for not making as much money, and lacking the vehicle to carry on his public career. He was finally brought back to the Pirates broadcast booth on May 3, 1985. Incredibly, the Pirates scored nine runs against the Los Angeles Dodgers in the first inning he worked, and went on to win the game, 16-2.

Prince was dying of cancer at the time, though it had not yet been made public. He died before the season was over. He was inducted into the broadcasters wing of the Baseball Hall of Fame in Cooperstown, New York, on August 3, 1986.

In his autobiography written with Tom Bird, Willie Stargell said the following about Prince:

"But something I found hard to accept was the firing of the Gunner and his partner Nellie King . . . the city was shocked. His life was thrown into total disarray. He never even felt it coming. The reason given for his release, which I found to be incredible, was that his rating had slipped. He was the city of Pittsburgh's number one son. He was loved by everybody in the organization and in the stands.

"We as players enjoyed the Gunner's stories and antics. He was a constant flow of motion. He dressed to be absurd. He usually wore bright summery colors, with a $500 pair of Gucci shoes and no socks. And he was a brave man not to wear socks with his ugly ankles. 'It's gauche to wear socks with Gucci,' he used to tell me.

"No announcer could ever be a bigger hype for Pirate baseball than the Gunner. He invented the Green Weenie, a green plastic hot-dog shaped object he'd lead the fans in shaking at the opposition. Such behavior was supposed to spur bad luck for Pirate opponents. He'd draw thousands of women to the games with his Ladies Nights. And he thrilled the fans with his 'babushka power.'

"Pirate fans loved Bob and he loved being their announcer."

Lanny Frattare
Memories of Maz and Prince

*"I was a great Yankees fan . . . and Yogi Berra
was my favorite ballplayer because
he looked like my dad."*

Pirates broadcaster Lanny Frattare is a fervent fan of America's pastime and American history, especially Presidential history. Frattare believes that what goes around comes around. That both baseball and history go in cycles.

Frattare felt as badly as any baseball fan in Pittsburgh, probably worse than most, when the Atlanta Braves beat the Pittsburgh Pirates in Game 7 of the 1992 National League championship playoff series.

It was a familar feeling to Frattare, however, one he had first experienced as a seventh grader at Charlotte High School (grades seven through twelve) in his native Rochester, New York.

Frattare felt the same way when Bill Mazeroski hit the home run to lead off the bottom of the ninth inning in Game 7 of the 1960 World Series.

"I was a great Yankees fan back then," said Frattare. "Yogi Berra was my favorite ballplayer because he looked a lot like my dad, who had also played catcher when he was younger.

"I used to help set up audio-visual equipment in school, and I was in the big room where they kept all the equipment. It was the only place in the school where there was a TV set, and I was able to watch some of that game. I saw Maz hit the home run.

"I was on the other side of the fence from the Pittsburgh fans back then. I was devastated. So when I talk to Pirates fans now, and they talk about how low they felt after the Braves beat the Pirates and kept them from advancing to the World Series, I tell them how I felt back then. Now they have some idea of how the Yankees fans felt in 1960.

"We now have a sense of what the Yankees experienced back in the '60 World Series to be out in the field like that and see a game and the Series get away from them on one pitch."

Frattare has not changed much from those school days. He still enjoys helping set up things at school. Only now, as the father of a senior, David Frattare, Lanny was working backstage at Upper St. High School in a suburb ten miles south of Three Rivers Stadium, helping the students get the sets ready for their spring musical "Oliver." Frattare has been helping out with the painting of scenery for such productions for several years. His wife, Liz, has been an active parent in the school system for a long time, too. They also have a daughter Megan in one of the local middle schools, and I have seen Liz and Lanny at a lot of school activities through the years.

Lanny Frattare is a friend and good neighbor to all who meet and know him in Pittsburgh.

And many of those who listen to Lanny Frattare when he is broadcasting Pirates baseball games feel the same way. He is an easy-going, down-to-earth fellow, and he makes you feel comfortable in a hurry.

1993 would be his 18th season with the Pirates, and only Bob Prince and Rosey Rowswell described Pirates action over a longer span. He wears well. He is a straight arrow in a business where there are lots of curve balls.

Frattare feels particularly indebted to Prince whom he credits for teaching him so much about the business.

To his credit, Frattare has never tried to mimic Prince. It would be an impossible task, in and out of the broadcast booth. "Bob tried to pass along some of his old wild plaid sports coats to me," offers Frattare with a winning smile, "but I resisted the idea."

Frattare said he wanted to be a baseball broadcaster since he was ten years old, and growing up in Rochester.

"There will never be another 'Voice of the Pirates' as that title will always belong to Bob Prince," Frattare told an early morning gathering at a media seminar at Westminster Presbyterian Church in Upper St. Clair, where Prince lived when he was doing the Pirates broadcasts.

"I wouldn't be here today if it weren't for 'The Gunner' helping me," he said. "He taught me about the importance of getting out and getting to know the people in the community, and of giving back.

"I think of him a lot. I hope he looks down and approves of the way I conduct myself, and the way I broadcast Pirates baseball.

"Bob Prince taught me some rules. For instance, he said when you go from radio to television think about shutting up right away.

"I don't think you can give the score too much. Bob Prince said to give the score every time a new batter comes up, and every time the count is three-and-two. And if you think you haven't given the score enough then give the score again."

Prince was the most popular toastmaster for sports dinners and public gatherings in the history of Pittsburgh. He had a loosey-goosy style, a flair about him that came naturally, and there will never be another one like him. He was often outrageous, and always unforgettable.

Prince also told a lot of saucy stories and off-color jokes, and Frattare wouldn't touch such blue material at any price. It's simply not his style.

But Frattare has followed Prince's lead in getting to know people in the community and for giving back. Frattare does charitable work for the Cystic Fibrosis Foundation, Goodwill Industries and Bob Prince Charities.

He also hosts a celebrity golf tournament at St. Clair Country Club each July for the benefit of the Parent and Child Guidance Center in Banksville, and he is a member of the board of directors for Pirate Charities.

Frattare has often recruited Pirates to play in fundraising basketball games. I have been most impressed with his annual participation in preparing scenery for the high school musical. He does whatever work with a paint brush he is asked to do, and helps out backstage.

His good friend Kent Tekulve, the former Pirates relief pitcher, and Kent's wife, Linda, contribute in similar style to school activities on every level in the Upper St. Clair School District. Frattare and Tekulve don't feel like celebrities, which is the key to their popularity.

Frattare is a fan above all else, and he couldn't shake that playoff memory of Sid Bream scoring from second base with the run that sent the Atlanta Braves rather than the Pirates to the 1992 World Series.

"We won't soon forget the name of Francisco Cabrera, either, will we?" asked Frattare. "I ached so much for Jim Leyland and the players. It was a depressing couple of days. I talked to Pirates fans and they were walking around in a trance."

It was a mixed blessing, however, for Frattare and his family.

"A week later my son, David, participated in a cross-country meet and I video-taped the race," Lanny related. "David won the race. As I was driving away, I said to Liz, 'Do you realize if we had won that seventh game, we'd have been in Toronto today?'

"As much as I would have liked that, I wouldn't trade it for seeing my son win that race. It lifted me."

Frattare credits his father for being the man who most shaped his life. "He was the one who taught me what was the right thing to do, and not to worry about things you can't control.

"I have been fortunate in my lifetime to have been surrounded by individuals like Jim Leyland, Willie Stargell, Bob Prince and Kent Tekulve. I have learned from all of them."

Frattare feels that Prince promoted him as a possible Pirates broadcaster when Lanny was learning the trade, serving as the broadcaster for the Pirates' Triple A team in Charleston, West Virginia, during the 1974 and 1975 seasons.

"The Pirates played an exhibition game in Charleston in 1974," recalled Frattare. "Bob Prince and Nellie King didn't come down for that, but I had a chance to talk to Bill Guilfoile, the team's public relations man who, as you know, is just the nicest guy in the world.

"Bill suggested I stop in Pittsburgh on my way back to Rochester at the end of the season. The minor league season is over on September 1st. So I did just that, and Bill introduced me to Bob and Nellie. Bill gave me a press box pass, and I sat in Bob's booth during the game.

"Steve Blass was pitching for Charleston that season, trying to get his control back so he could return to the Pirates, and he and Karen lived above Liz and me in the same apartment complex.

"When Steve heard I was coming to Pittsburgh, he invited me to stay overnight at his home. So I did. When I woke up in the morning, Steve was blackcoating his driveway and I felt so indebted to him for giving me a place to stay that I helped him do the driveway. I really didn't have any work clothes, so Steve gave me some. I always tell him that he owes me on that one, and that one of these days he should come over to my place and help me blackcoat my driveway.

137

"I was keeping score in the press box that first night, and Bob Prince came up to me, and asked me if I would like to do a half-inning on the air. I was shocked. The next day I went to the ballpark early and I was talking to the ushers and so forth, and I was amazed at how many knew I'd been on the radio the night before. 'So you're the kid who was on with Prince last night?' they'd say. Bob asked me if I wanted to do a half-inning again the second night. But Mudcat Grant showed up in the press box that night, and went on with Bob, and I didn't get on the air that night."

That was a telling anecdote about Prince because it pointed up how he was always trying to help young people get started, and how he was always boosting promising young people in the media business. Prince was popular and felt secure about his own position. Many people in his business would have been reluctant to give a young talent an opening for fear that the youngster might steal their job.

"Bob and Nellie both told me they were interested in having me come in as a third announcer the next year," recalled Frattare. "That's when Bob got fired. I thought my chances of coming to Pittsburgh were over. I figured my career was over with his firing. And I didn't know if I was coming back to Charleston for the 1976 season.

"After Bob was fired, he called me in Rochester about every ten days to tell me what was going on regarding his replacement. He cared enough to do that. He might have been calling some other young announcers as well, but I was impressed with his personal concern for me. He was the most caring and giving individual I ever met, with the exception of my father.

"The Pirates brought in Milo Hamilton as the No. 1 announcer to replace Bob. And I came in as the No. 2 announcer; I think I was sort of a compromise choice for that slot, from all that I later heard about the situation. John Steigerwald went to Charleston and replaced me.

"I was amazed when I went around the league and learned of how many people had been touched by Bob's generosity, whether it was the host of the press room — Bob was notorious for giving big tips wherever he went — or a bellman at a hotel. I was amazed at how many charities he helped in one way or another. Milo Hamilton and I were the broadcasting team through the 1979 season. But Milo had an impossible situation trying to replace Bob. Nobody could have done it."

Frattare has also come to appreciate the special magic of Mazeroski and the '60 Bucs in Pittsburgh. Talking about the ninth inning home run by Mazeroski, Frattare said, "I believe it was the single-most outstanding event in Pirates history. I think the '60 World Series is the achievement by which everything about the Pirates is measured, till this day.

"It was an event that happened at a time when baseball probably enjoyed its greatest popularity in this country, and the fact that the victory came against the great Yankees team was also really significant.

"And Maz is truly amazing with his attitude about the whole thing. Bill has not been overexposed because he has never sought the spotlight.

He's been somewhat bashful about it. I've seen him at some banquets and celebrity golf outings, and he always seems to stay out of the center of the room. Sometimes I think he's embarrassed by any attention that's paid him.

"I'm a lot like Maz. When I'm at a public gathering, I tend to back off into a corner somewhere. Bob Prince could come into any place and get the room's attention immediately. He would dominate a room. But I'm not like that."

I recalled hearing Frattare speak at a church seminar a few months earlier, and how he confessed to having a nervous feeling about talking to people outside of the broadcast booth. It took him awhile to warm up to the task and to get comfortable with the crowd.

"Most Pirates fans know that Maz would rather be remembered for his defensive abilities," said Frattare. "They have trumpeted his call to be inducted into the Baseball Hall of Fame because they believe he is the greatest second baseman.

"When Lee Mazzilli came to the Pirates in 1983, I referred to him once on the air as 'Maz.' He was called that by his teammates from time to time. But I got several letters taking me to task for that. I was told, in no uncertain terms, never to refer to him as 'Maz' again. I was told that there could only be one Maz in Pittsburgh. And I bowed to that, and never did it again."

Lanny Frattare is flanked by two of Pittsburgh's favorite broadcasters, Jack Bogut and Jim Rooker. They all provide community service.

Bob Friend
The pitcher from Purdue

"I was lucky. My dream came true."
—Bob Friend

"My God, were we ever really that young?
Oh, Bob, look how young you look.
Look how young we all look."
—Pat Friend

Bob Friend is a fascinating fellow. Bob boasts of having a photographic mind, and he has plenty of photographs on hand at his home in Fox Chapel to challenge himself to the delight of a visitor.

Bob glances at a photograph and can provide uncanny detail as to what happened on that particular occasion. Talk about capturing the moment. Forever. He not only can provide details on the score of the game, but the count on the pitch, its outcome, the site and how the weather was. It's mind-blowing stuff. Click, click, click. It all comes back so vividly for Friend. His eyes light up when he sees a familiar photograph. He has a high-energy voice and he enjoys reminiscing.

The images come sharply into focus. And fast. He can slow it down, like in the movies. He's a big movie fan, by the way. He had just seen a made-for-TV movie on the TNT cable channel called "Cooperstown," which begins with a panoramic shot of Forbes Field in Oakland. The camera scans a black and white photograph of the former home of the Pirates. For Friend, it brought back balls and strikes of the past, ballgames won and lost. Teammates who have moved on. Teammates who are no more.

"I try to recall the moment, the games," said Bob. "I'll think about things like Vernon Law and I going over the hitters together before the Series, or I'll think about Hollywood stars like Joe E. Brown and Bing Crosby, and what it was like to meet them from time to time when I was playing for the Pirates. I was always around good people. To me, as great as the Yankees were those years, I think the '60 Pirates were destined to win. We just wouldn't let ourselves lose. The whole team was that way. That's why no one was scared off by the Yankees.

"When I see a movie like 'Field of Dreams' . . . When I saw those great players coming out of a cornfield to play ball, I can relate to that. Because we cleared fields like that to play ball when I was a kid back in Indiana."

The reflective Friend was always considered one of the more cerebral of the Pirates' cast of the '50s and '60s. He and Dick Groat were both college graduates, Friend from his hometown Purdue University and Groat from Duke University, and they were different in that regard.

140

Everyone was always saying how smart they were; they still do. College men were rare in baseball back then.

Friend was one of the best pitchers the Pirates ever claimed as their own. There was a point midway through his career, where Friend, ol' No. 19, was the best right-handed pitcher in the National League. He won 197 games, 191 as a Pirate. That is more than any Pirates pitcher in the past 65 years. He had more complete games (161), shutouts (35) and strikeouts (1,682) than any Pirate since 1929. His 22 victories in a season (1958) have not been equaled since then.

"That was not my best year," Friend is fast to tell you. "I was lucky as hell that year. My best year, by far, was 1960. I had four strikeouts to every walk that season. I should have won 25 games that year, but I had a lot of no-decision affairs. There were a lot of struggles. I only had two bad games all year. But the important thing is that we won the pennant.

"I played for the Pirates during the early and mid-'50s. In those years, we used to lose 90 to 100 games a year. To go through that, and then win the world championship in 1960 made it even more meaningful."

Back in 1960, Friend captured the special feeling in the stands that season when he observed, "The fans cheer when you strike a guy out. They explode when an easy fly ball is hit to the outfield. You'd never know they've had baseball here for sixty years."

In compiling his 22-14 record in 1958, Friend became the first Pirates pitcher to win 20 since Murry Dickson turned the trick in 1951. It was the most games any Pittsburgh pitcher had won since Burleigh Grimes wound up with 25 wins in 1928.

Whereas ElRoy Face had a fantastic season (18-1) and Haddix had that 12-inning perfect game in Milwaukee (he lost 1-0 in the 13th), both in 1959, Friend has no single season or single pitching performance that is still talked about.

Friend said he never missed a start in 16 years as a Pirate, 477 altogether. That's an average of 31.8 starts per season. Writer Bill Utterbeck suggested in an article about Friend that this is "Hall of Fame dependability." Of the 32 pitchers from the past 65 years inducted into the Hall, only Don Drysdale (33.2), Tom Seaver (32.4) and Robin Roberts (32) had higher averages for starts. Two other recent inductees, Gaylord Perry (31.4) and Ferguson Jenkins (31.3) came close.

Utterbeck wrote in *The Pittsburgh Press*: "Curious how Haddix, who won 45 games with the Pirates, is more often recalled for a single loss than Friend is for 191 victories."

Dick Groat was asked about that.

"What Harvey did was unique. What he did that night may never be duplicated," said Groat. "But what Bob did was unbelievable. He went out day after day, year after year, and did the job. The whole time I was in Pittsburgh, he never missed a start. Not once."

Talking about Friend's consistency, Haddix had this to say: "That's not something that people notice. You don't get a lot of publicity for it. But to the players and the manager, durability may be the most important thing."

"Maybe Bob didn't have a lot of great nights," said former Pirates general manager Joe L. Brown, "but almost every night was a good night. He didn't have many bad outings. He pitched well every time out. Bob was a very highly regarded pitcher. The amazing thing about him is that he won so many games while playing for a last-place club. There is no telling how many games he would have won if he had played for another team."

Utterbeck went to the record books to come up with these interesting stats: In his first seven seasons, when Friend was 20 to 26 years old, the Pirates finished seventh or eighth in an eight-team league. Friend averaged 10 victories per season. He allowed nine hits per game while striking out four and walking two.

In Friend's final eight seasons with the Pirates, when they were competitive, "but not a dominating team," he averaged 15 victories. He still allowed nine hits, four strikeouts and just under two walks a game.

Based on those figures, if he had pitched for a competitive team every year in Pittsburgh, Utterbeck believes Friend would have won 231 games. That's more than Hall of Famers like Drysdale, Jim Hunter, Bob Lemon, Rube Marquard, Stan Coveleski and Chief Bender.

In truth, though, Friend lost 230 games.

"Looking back, I think the thing I'm most proud of is that I was able to work on a consistent basis," Friend said. "It was important to me to go out to the mound when it was my turn and keep the team in the game."

"This is it tonight.
I'm going to do it for you."
—Dick Stuart

Robert Bartmess Friend — Bartmess was his mother's maiden name — was born on November 24, 1930 at Lafayette, Indiana, and marked his 62nd birthday two months before I talked to him. His brown hair was thinner, but his blue eyes were as bright as ever. It is unlikely he was still six feet, 190 pounds — his playing weight in 1960 — but he looked just fine.

He still had those chipmunk cheeks and that Friend-ly smile. His heritage is Scotch-English, and he looks and plays the part.

He wore a brightly colored shirt, black slacks, black socks, black shoes. And a bemused look. He was eager to talk. "I've never felt that our '60 team got its full due, and I'm pleased that you're doing this," he said in the way of openers.

Seeing a photo from the 1958 season, in the hallway just off the kitchen, that showed him smiling, and writing in 20 victories on a clubhouse chalkboard, brought back a memory of one of his favorite outings.

Such photos were once routine in the newspapers, but are now considered corny.

"Dick Stuart hit a three-run home run off Marv Grissom of the Giants to get me my 20th," said Friend. "Dick hit it out in the tenth inning. Grissom was doing well up until then. That's one game I won't soon forget.

"I tried eight or nine times to get that 20th victory, and it was getting frustrating. I got my 19th in mid-August and didn't get my 20th until mid-September. Stuart came up to me before the game and said, 'This is it tonight. I'm going to do it for you.' He wrote '20' on my locker before we left the clubhouse."

Friend finished with 22 victories during that 1958 season, tying for the league leadership in that category with Warren Spahn of the Milwaukee Braves, who was the ace of a championship team and beat out Friend for the Cy Young Award.

Bob and his wife Pat were in the process of picking out favorite photographs, illustrations and cartoons that he has collected during a 43-year career in Pittsburgh, first as a pitcher for the Pirates, then as a local politician, and as a civic-minded insurance broker when I visited their comfortable three bedroom red-brick ranch home on a cul-de-sac near Fox Chapel High School. Bob has been with Babb, Inc., insurance brokers, for 18 years, with offices on Ridge Avenue on the North Side, near Art Rooney's old house. His title is vice-president. Ron Livingston is the president of the firm.

"We were never allowed to put these pictures up on the walls before," explained Pat in a near-whisper when Bob left the room for a moment. "Bob was always too bashful to do that. But our son Bobby got after us recently about it, and urged us to display these pictures. He said we should be proud of them. He said it was time to get them out of the closets."

Bobby Friend, 29, called home to his parents, coincidentally enough, during my visit. He was calling from the home of his sister, Missy, 32, out in Costa Mesa, California. Bobby was in his second year on the Professional Golfers Association (PGA) tour. He was playing in a pro-am at Newport Beach, and would be moving on to the renowned Pebble Beach links to compete the following weekend in the AT&T Pro-Am Tournament, which used to be the Bing Crosby Invitational. He was paired with Johnny Bench, the Hall of Fame catcher from the Cincinnati Reds. Bobby made the cut in the pro part of the competition, but was not pleased with his play in the stretch run.

Bobby's sister, Missy Alexander, has two children, Michael, 8, and Brynne, 6. So Bob and Pat Friend are proud grandparents, and are just as eager to show off pictures of their grandchildren as they are Pirates paraphenalia.

Bobby had gotten married on January 9, 1993. He had proposed the previous year to Leslie Minard, a United Airlines attendant he had first known in high school, during an interview about "the new breed" in golf with sports broadcaster Jim Nantz on national TV during a tournament in Memphis. The wedding preparations prompted his parents to paint their basement game room in advance of the event, and to start putting up prized photos, paintings, prints, cartoons and framed newspaper pages from Bob's baseball and political career, and Bobby's budding pro golf career.

Both the gameroom and a family room and hallways upstairs were dominated by color prints of the same large photograph of Forbes Field during a night game, with a dramatic dark blue sky above the double-deck facility that was leveled in the early '70s after the Pirates and Steelers shifted to Three Rivers Stadium. In the photo, the green grass gleams under the bright lights of the light banks overhead. "Isn't it beautiful?" asked Pat. "I just love that picture."

Bob pointed to a black and white photo of Forbes Field, where the sky is dominated by smoke from the nearby Jones & Laughlin (J&L) steel mills along the Monongahela River. They stretched from the South Side to my hometown of Hazelwood in the photograph. That smoke and those mills, and so many jobs, are missing from the Pittsburgh landscape these days.

"That's the way it was in the '50s when I first came here," offered Bob, who made his debut with the Pirates in 1951. "There's nothing doctored up about this photo. That's just the way it was. That's the way I liked it. It was colder than hell when I first came here. But I got used to it."

Friend pointed to spots around the Pirates dugout in the photo. "When I got here, Honus Wagner would be sitting in the dugout here — he was an emiritus coach — and Pie Traynor would be there. You talk about a Field of Dreams. . ."

The largest rendering on the gameroom walls is an enlarged reproduction of a story on the outcome of the 1960 World Series that appeared in the *New York Times*. The story, or ode to Bill Mazeroski — he was referred to as "Big Bad Bill" Mazeroski in the story — was by Scotty Reston, then a sports writer and later one of the most respected political columnists in the country. A picture above the story was the familiar one showing Mazeroski following through on the swing that sent Ralph Terry's final throw of the seventh game of the Series out over the left field wall at Forbes Field. You can also see the scoreboard and the Carnegie Museum and Library, and what are now Carnegie Mellon University buildings in the background.

The Mazeroskis, Bill and his wife, Milene, had attended the wedding of Bobby Friend, which pleased his parents to no end. "It meant a lot to me to have the Mazeroskis here," said Bob. "They have always been special to us."

The Mazeroskis and Friends have more in common than playing for the Pirates. Branch Rickey was partly responsible for pairing up both couples. Milene was working as a secretary for scouting director Rex Bowen at Forbes Field when Rickey, and Danny Murtaugh, directed Mazeroski to ask her out for a date. Pat was a nurse to Dr. Joseph Finegold, the Pirates team physician.

She was Pat Koval then, from Washington, Pennsylvania, when Rickey, the team's front office boss who was not adverse to shaping his

144

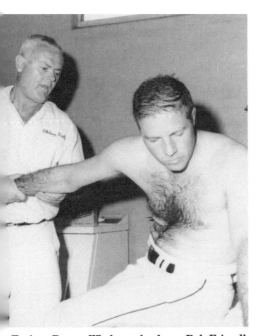

Trainer Danny Whelan rubs down Bob Friend's throwing arm.

Pat and Bob Friend with daughter Missy and son Robert Charles.

'riends on St. Patrick's Day

Friends campaign for City Controller's office. Bob won the election.

players' personal lives, decided she and Bob would make a perfect couple. They were married in New Jersey on September 30, 1957 — the day after the season ended.

"Rickey heard we were dating and he kept pushing me to get married," said Bob. "He thought we were a good pair. He liked his players married young and I was 27 by then. He called me a matrimonial coward."

"We have always gotten along well with Bill and Milene," said Pat with more than a hint of pride. "They're just nice people. They've always been easy to be with."

"I think the Mazeroskis like to be around us," said Bob.

"They know we're never going to exploit or use them," added Pat. "I hate people who do that. To us, they're just good friends."

Pat remembers where she was when Maz hit the famous home run. "I was at Forbes Field having false labor pains," she said. "That was just before Missy was born. We went to a party at Webster Hall that night, and we were all so happy."

Bob produced a photograph from a pile on a table in the middle of the gameroom. "Here's another great old ballpark," said Bob. "That's Griffith Stadium in Washington, D.C."

That was the site of the 1956 Major League All-Star Game. Friend, who finished that season with a 17-17 record and a league-leading 314 innings pitched, worked three innings in that All-Star Game.

He gave up three hits, struck out three batters, and gave up no runs in that All-Star Game stint. He struck out Mickey Mantle and Yogi Berra of the New York Yankees, and Ted Williams of the Boston Red Sox at Griffith Stadium.

"I struck out Williams with the bases loaded for my last out," said Bob. "I have a photographic memory of everything I did in baseball; I had a photographic eye. The count was three-and-two and I threw him a curve ball inside. It was a hard curve. He swung and missed. I can see it like it was yesterday."

"Tell him the story," urged Pat, "about when you and Bobby bumped into Ted Williams at the airport in Atlanta." The story Pat had in mind demonstrates that Friend was not the only ballplayer with a photographic mind.

"Bobby and I were walking throught the airport about 15 years after that All-Star Game, and I spotted Williams and went up to him. I said, 'Hi, Ted, I'm Bob Friend; it's nice to see you. This is my son, Bobby.'

"And Williams looked at me, and said, 'I remember you. You know, I never thought you'd curve me.' Bobby just stood there with his mouth open. He couldn't believe what he had just heard Williams say."

"You remember pitches like that?" I asked.

"I'd remember it because it was Ted Williams," said Bob. "That was my last out in the All-Star Game that year."

Bob was the starting and winning pitcher in that All-Star Game, and a year later he worked the middle three innings of the mid-summer classic and was charged with the loss.

146

"I'd remember it because
it was Ted Williams."

Friend kept finding one photograph after another that sparked a special memory. He showed one to Pat, one of them and their children. "My God, were we ever really that young?" asked Pat. "Oh, Bob, look how young you look. Look how young we all look."

Another photo showed Friend with Ralph Kiner, who was the National League's leading home run hitter with the Pirates when Friend first joined the team.

"Kiner hit his 250th home run at Braves Field in Boston," recalled Friend. "He was married to the tennis star Nancy Chaffee at the time, and he took me with them to celebrate. I was 19. He took us to the Copley Plaza — that was big-time — and he bought champagne. I pretended like I had my share of champagne in the past. I puked later that night. I was a rookie, and he picked up the tab. Kiner took good care of all of us."

There was a photo which showed Friend flanked by Arnold Palmer and Ted Kluszewski at a pro-am golf outing at the Field Club in Fox Chapel. Another photo showed Palmer and Jack Nicklaus in a playoff for the U.S. Open title at Oakmont in 1962. That brought back memories for both of us. Bob had been there. So had I, after my sophomore year as a student at the University of Pittsburgh, when I was working as a summer intern at *The Pittsburgh Press*. I had gotten to go to the Open by volunteering to write photo cutlines as the photos were taken by *Press* photographers.

A photo showed a meeting on the mound involving Friend, Groat, Hal Smith, Murtaugh and Stuart. "That was at Wrigley Field," said Bob, without missing a beat. "They had the smallest clubhouse in the league. Clemente hit like hell there. I'd like to see what his batting average was in Chicago."

Another photo showed Bob with broadcaster Ray Scott and Don Hoak.

There was a picture of Friend firing his fastball off the mound at Forbes Field, with Stan Musial of the St. Louis Cardinals at the plate. "He was so great," recalled Friend, "and he loved to play at Forbes Field and Ebbetts Field. He was popular in Pittsburgh because he came from Donora."

Friend was pictured with the likes of Lew Worsham, the 1947 U.S. Open golf champion from Oakmont who also won the Tam O'Shanter World Championship in Chicago in 1960; Del Miller, one of the all-time harness racing greats; and Kiner. "That was in the King's Room at the Hilton Hotel before the Dapper Dan Dinner in 1985," said Friend.

A photo showed a young Willie Stargell standing between Mazeroski and Friend. "Stargell hit a home run in his first game with the Pirates," offered Friend. "It happened in Milwaukee. Look how slim he was then."

A 1956 photo showed Friend and Dale Long pointing to the No. 8 on the back of the uniform of infielder Gene Freese from Wheeling

147

after Long had hit a home run in a record eighth straight game. They don't take photos like that anymore, either.

"I pitched the day Long set the record," said Friend. "We won 3-2. I gave up only two hits. The two runs were produced by Duke Snider's home run. He hit one over the iron gate in right center field at Forbes Field. You remember that? That's big time.

"I gave him my best shot and he gave me his best shot. I threw a good fast sinkerball, and he had a good fast swing and it was gone. It was as hard as I've ever been hit."

I had to smile once more at Friend's fantastic recall ability. When I called attention to it again, Pat smiled and shook her head. "I have to laugh," she said. "I can't believe this. I don't know how he does it. He comes up with every pitch he threw, and Bobby remembers every golf ball he hit."

Bob observed, "Most ballplayers are like that."

"But, good God, it was 50 years ago!" replied Pat.

Friend's remarks about Snider's home run prompted me to bring up a pet peeve of mine.

"How come," I asked, "these baseball analysts tell you it was a great pitch when a pitcher fires one down the middle and a batter swings and misses, and then when a pitcher throws the same pitch and a batter hits it out of the park that we're told the pitcher made a mistake?"

Friend recognized what I was talking about. "I think you make a mistake when you're throwing an 0-2 pitch and someone hits you. There's no reason to let anyone hit a no-ball, two-strike pitch."

"Steve Blass told me that Murtaugh would fine you if you gave up a hit on an 0-2 pitch." I said.

"If you have control," offered Friend, "you should be able to place the ball where they'd have a hard time hitting you. Of course, the great ones could deal with anything you served up. Guys like Aaron, Musial and Clemente could get good wood on a ball right on their fists."

We ended up talking about some momumental home runs, one that Mantle hit at Yankee Stadium in the World Series, and one that Dick Stuart hit over the deepest part of center field at Forbes Field.

"Mantle hit his off Mizell; it went into the second deck," said Bob. "Stuart hit his off Glen Hobbie of the Cubs. It went out like a golf ball. It was on a line and it just kept rising. It flew out over the 457 foot mark. And it still had plenty of steam on it. Kiner hit one high over the scoreboard and it hasn't come down yet. Frank Howard hit one off George Witt — he'll get mad at me about this, but heck I gave up plenty of dingers in my day — and it went over the 406 mark and kept going."

Friend said fans don't forget certain games, either, even if you wish they would.

"A guy stopped me in the street and asked me if I remember a no-hitter I had going in Brooklyn," offered Friend. "In the seventh inning I knocked down Junior Gilliam and he got back up and singled. Then Duke Snider hit a home run and we lost, 2-0. Yes, I remember it. He (the fan) was in the stands that night and, for some reason, he remembered it, too."

"I'll make sure I'm out there."
— Yogi Berra

Friend seems to find the greatest satisfaction from talking about Bobby, his son, the pro golfer.

"It took him five years to get his PGA card," said Bob. "He played on the Canadian tour, and he spent two years on the Ben Hogan Tour. He played all sports when he was younger. He was a good wrestler, and he played football at Fox Chapel High. I got him into golf. He won a golf scholarship to LSU. That's where he really developed his game."

I asked Friend if he had compared notes with another Fox Chapel citizen of note, Frank Fuhrer, whose son Frank III, had spent several years on the PGA Tour before turning to business a few years back. "Oh, yeah, Frank and I are good friends," said Bob. "He's real familiar with our Bobby's golf pursuits. I've often talked to him about it. He's given us good advice."

He also saw up close the heart-rending difficulties suffered by Bill and Milene Mazeroski when their oldest son, Darren, tried in vain to become a big league baseball player.

Friend mentioned how he and Mazeroski, Dick Groat and Jerry Lynch had all flown together to Monroe, Louisiana to help dedicate a new baseball field at Northeast Louisiana University when Darren Mazeroski was playing on the team there. Former Steelers quarterback Bubby Brister had once played baseball and football there as well. "Even then, Maz was pretty objective in his observations about Darren," said Friend. "He just didn't think he had everything you need to make it in the majors. He made some comments that day when we sitting in the stands. But he was so proud of both of his boys."

"The other one, David, is really smart," said Pat. "He's into computers and is going for a master's degree at Pitt. He was a good student at Grove City College. Your kids give you different kinds of satisfaction. Our Missy is a good kid, too. We've been so lucky to have two good kids."

Bob mentioned how Yogi Berra had come out to watch Bobby play in the U.S. Amateur when it was held at Berra's club, the Montclair, New Jersey, County Club, back in 1985. "I'd run into Yogi somewhere, and I told him that Bobby would be playing at his place.' Yogi told me, 'I'll make sure I'm out there. Hey, they have four of the toughest nines there.' Yogi always has a way of saying things differently. But he came out, like he said he would, and followed Bobby for a few holes."

That prompted Bob to mention that Ralph Terry, who threw that fateful home run ball to Mazeroski in the 1960 World Series, was playing on the senior golf tour.

Friend feels that the Pirates put that World Series triumph in motion early in the season, by constantly coming back from defeat to pull out late-inning victories.

"I can remember early in that '60 season that things just always seemed to turn our way," said Friend. "We came back so many times

149

that year to win games. Cincinnati was leading 5-0 in the eighth inning of one game. We had two outs. Fred Hutchinson, the Cincy manager, decided to give one of his top relief pitchers some work. It was early in the schedule, in the spring, so he brought in Bill Henry. He was an outstanding relief pitcher, a real flame-thrower. He came in and Hal Smith hit a three-run pinch-hit homer. Then Bob Skinner bombed a two-run homer. It was the second game of a doubleheader and it was getting dark, and they couldn't turn on the lights because it was Sunday and there were blue laws prohibiting that back then. Henry was a lefty and it looked like a mismatch in favor of the Reds. It was hard to see the ball. We went on to win, 6-5. I saw Hutchinson going through the runway after the game, and he punched out every light bulb — about five of them overhead, with his bare fist — as he walked to the clubhouse. Boy, he could get hot! He could tear up a clubhouse. That was the way the season went."

"What do you think was the secret to the team's success?" I asked Friend. "What set the Pirates apart from the pack?"

"We had great chemistry," he replied. "We were all different, but we all played as hard as we could. We had some veterans from other clubs who appeared to be on the downside of their careers, like Gino Cimoli. But he teamed up with Bob Skinner to give us a solid twosome in left field. Rickey had first base covered with Dick Stuart and Rocky Nelson. Rocky was a character in his own right, not like Stuart, but a character just the same. He was a solid family man, a true professional who never quite made it in the majors, but was a great home run hitter in Canada. Each was used just enough to take advantage of their strengths.

"We had a team that didn't make mistakes; we always threw the ball to the right base, and we ran the bases well. Our pitchers got the ball on the plate. Even in spring training, we felt like we were going to win.

"We saw it coming in 1959. That's the year we started to put it together, and became a legitimate contender. Groat and Maz were such a great double play combination. If I had a good year in '59, we might have had a run at the championship.

"There was a lot of pressure on me. I had a bad season in 1959, a real disappointment, and I was fighting to make a comeback. But there was no question about my status as far as Danny Murtaugh was concerned. To Murtaugh, I was his man, and was the starting pitcher in the season opener.

"I had a great year in 1960. Vernon Law had a helluva year, and Haddix was as good a spot-starter as there was in the league. Mizell was 1-3 when we got him, and he went on to win 13 games for us with that fastball and big overhand curveball. It all came together."

"We had great chemistry."
— Bob Friend

150

"I struck out Willie Stargell."

Friend pitched for the "old rinky-dink Pirates," as he calls them. He pitched for 16 years with the Pirates and spent a year in New York, finishing up his career with the Yankees and the Mets.

When he went to the Mets, he was struck by the strong support given the team by New Yorkers. "The thing that amazed me was that we were so bad, yet there were 45,000 at every game. I beat the Pirates when I was pitching for the Mets. I struck out Willie Stargell. I saved the game for Tug McGraw's first win. Wes Westrum was my manager there. I threw the last pitch in the last game the New York Giants played at the Polo Grounds. I remember Mrs. John McGraw was there. I have a picture of it. I pitched to Dusty Rhodes. Frank Thomas was at third base, Groat was at shortstop and Maz was at second. I got married the next day in New Jersey, so I won't forget it. So I've been in on a few firsts, and a few lasts."

I mentioned that Dick Groat had a special affection for the Polo Grounds.

"That's because he met Barbara, his wife, at the Polo Grounds," said Pat Friend. "She was a classy woman."

"I remember that Groat got his first hit at the Polo Grounds," said Bob. "Dick came up against 'Big Jim' Hearn and got his first hit."

Friend was an 18-game winner with the World Series Pirates, but didn't win a World Series game. "That was a personal disappointment, but winning like we did against the great Yankee team mellowed it quite a bit," he said.

In 1955, he became the first pitcher in history to lead the National League in ERA (2.84) while performing for a last-place team. He also came within a whisker of pitching baseball's first perfect game in 33 years.

"We had some bad ball clubs," said Friend. "Then we got better and nobody can take that memory of 1960 away from me."

He was a player rep for the Pirates for ten years, served as the National League player rep for five years and also on baseball's pension committee for five years.

Just to prove he wasn't perfect, when he was with the Mets, he charged at Pirates manager Harry Walker late on a Sunday afternoon at Forbes Field because he felt that Walker was pouring it on when he ordered a Buc to squeeze bunt in a lop-sided game. "I shouldn't have done that," Friend offers now. "But we patched up our differences over that one."

Friend is hopeful that baseball will survive despite an economic structure that turns off a lot of fans these days, as well as some former players.

"I think today's players have held up very well under the tremendous pressure of public opinion about those big salaries," he said. "And, what's more, they've kept themselves motivated to keep playing ball.

"We had plenty of motivation to play well. When I was playing, if you had a slump, you could get a 25 percent cut in salary in a bad year."

But Friend does not fret about the easy-come, easy-go economics of today's game.

"Baseball was good to me," said Bob. "I had the dream as a kid to play baseball in the majors. I was lucky. My dream came true."

His boyhood hero was Bob Feller, and Friend ended up seeing his name in some of the same listings as Feller. Both were strong-armed throwers who often finished what they started, and started every fourth day.

Friend was an outstanding athlete in high school, lettering in baseball, football, basketball and golf. He suffered a right shoulder separation in high school, which prompted him to give up football in favor of baseball. He had been captain of the football team and an all-state halfback in 1948 and an all-star baseball player in 1949. He played American Legion baseball for four years. He worked harder than most pitchers.

"He was always concerned about his legs," recalled Steve Blass, who roomed with him on the road for a spell. "He always wanted to walk to the ballpark, no matter how far it was from the hotel, or how hot or cold it might be."

Friend used to go to spring training two weeks before his teammates. He walked six miles to practice each day in spring training. In Pittsburgh, he walked five miles to Forbes Field every day the team was in town.

During his playing days, Friend's formula for pitching success went like this:

"I rely mainly on my sinker and fastball," he once wrote. "I throw five pitches: fast, faster, slider, slow curve for a change and a slip pitch. My best pitch is my sinking fastball, which is my double play pitch. I use it fifty percent of the time . . . try to keep the ball down all the time — use it when in jams."

"I throw every day definitely. I lob some for 15 minutes in the outfield every day, and I pitch 10 or 15 minutes (not hard) every day.

"I like to pitch with three days rest as control is sharper, but I feel I can come back occasionally with two days rest."

Pitching for the Pirates was a dream come true for Friend.

"When I was seven or eight, I began dreaming about playing in the major leagues," he said. "In Lafayette, Indiana, where I grew up, I used to listen to every Cubs and White Sox game."

Friend left Purdue early to become one of Branch Rickey's kiddies in Pittsburgh, but went back to school each winter and, finally, after eight years, his persistence paid off in the form of an undergraduate degree from Purdue.

By attending classes one semester a year it took him eight years, but he got his degree, a b.s. in economics. He was the eighth member of his family to get a degree.

He joined his late father, three sisters and three brothers as Purdue graduates.

"I always had my heart set on a college degree because it's been sort of a tradition in our family. My father was graduated in 1909 with a degree in animal husbandry."

Throughout his career, Friend was a model for any athlete in that era. He knew he could not count on throwing a baseball for a living for too many years. From the day he signed with the Pirates, he prepared himself in the off-season for his future beyond baseball.

Whereas many athletes spend their off-season hunting, fishing, drinking beer and drifting about, Friend had a game plan. After he earned his degree at Purdue, he also took courses in economics and finance at the University of Pittsburgh. He has always been a gentleman and a tremendous ambassador for the Pirates and Pittsburgh. He has always had a knack for public relations, and the good sense that reflects his solid midwestern breeding.

In his business life, Bob worked in the securities business, and with Commercial Bank of Pittsburgh (later First Seneca), ran successfully for Allegheny County controller in 1967 and was re-elected in 1971.

Wherever he went, Friend either ran or he walked.

Tom Johnson, vice president of the Pirates, got him into politics, along with Republican County chairperson Elsie Hillman. They wanted Friend to run for public office, and he went along with the idea.

Friend found out he had a knack for politics, and as a sales person. He got along well with people, and he did his homework to make sure he knew what he was talking about.

"The discipline of being a professional athlete has a carry-over into business, especially sales," said Friend.

Friend tries to stay active.

For recreation, Bob has played squash, he can play the piano, and he has always been a big barbershop quartet fan. It doesn't take much to get Friend to break into a song. He used to sing at Variety Club fundraisers.

He always had a good mind for business, and he believed in investing and saving for the future.

As a small boy in Lafayette, Indiana, he negotiated the mowing rights to sixteen lawns and started to stash away his money for college. By the time he was in high school he had acquired an annual summer job — at the Ralston Purina Mills in Lafayette. He worked 12 hours a day, from 5:30 a.m. to 5:30 p.m., throwing sacks of feed and other tasks calculated to build his muscles and his bank account.

Bob took piano lessons from age 5. His dad conducted a local orchestra. Bob's father was a farmer and milk broker. Bob was the youngest in his family.

The Pirates landed him for a $15,000 bonus. The Dodgers offered $20,000 to him when he was 19, but he signed with the Bucs because he thought it was a "better opportunity" for him.

153

"I have no regrets about signing with Pittsburgh. I was a little discouraged at times when we were losing so often, but I never wanted out of Pittsburgh. This town has always been good to me. Eventually, I could see that we were building something here. I got to be part of a world championship team with the Pirates and I'm very proud of that."

Victorious Pirates in clubhouse after 2-1 victory over Milwaukee Braves were (left to right) Roberto Clemente, Bill Mazeroski, Bob Friend and Jack Shepard.

Friend joins Warren Spahn and Johnny Antonelli at 1956 All-Star Game.

Oakland Characters
They had a birthright to the ballpark

"Everybody who worked at Forbes Field
came from Oakland. We thought it was
our playground."
—Joe Scalise

There were more characters per square inch in Oakland, and they all grew up thinking Forbes Field was their second home.

Willard "Diz" Bellows,
Bartender, Media Lounge
Three Rivers Stadium

"I was in the clubhouse when Maz hit the home run. I went down to set up things for the TV people who would be coming in after the game. I never saw the home run. Because Gino Cimoli was in the clubhouse watching it on a small TV. When the Yankees tied the score in the top of the ninth inning, Cimoli picked up the TV and threw it against the wall. It broke into pieces. So we never saw it. To this day, the only time I've seen Maz's home run is on baseball highlight shows, or shows about the World Series.

"I grew up on Ward Street in Oakland, just three blocks from Forbes Field. I started working there at the age of 14, and I have been here since 1924. I turned the turnstiles; that was my first job. At that time, the ballgames didn't begin until 3:30 in the afternoon. I was going to Schenley High School, and I didn't have any classes during the last two periods. A fellow in my neighborhood named Larry Collier was an assistant to Sam Waters, who was a vice-president of the Pirates, and I asked him, 'Is there any chance of me working there?' And he got me a job.

"Three-fourths of the kids or fellows in Oakland worked there. We thought it was our own private playground. By the time the World Series came around in 1960, Jack Berger, the p.r. man then, had me working in the press room. I worked in the Steelers' press room a few years before that. Les Biederman of *The Press* looked after things, too, as the head of the local chapter of the Baseball Writers Association. He thought he was the top writer. I have no idea how I got the nickname 'Diz,' but maybe it was because I thought Dizzy Dean was such a great pitcher. They started calling me that before I went to high school.

"Of all the players on the Pirates, Dick Groat was my favorite. We talked a lot; he was easy to talk to. I used to like to talk to the players in the clubhouse; you didn't need a special pass back then to get in. It's

155

been great working here, especially when the Galbreaths owned the team. I got along great with John and the son, Dan. They always took me and my wife Henrietta to the World Series. My wife is dead now.

"Jack Hernon and Charley Feeney, from the *Post-Gazette*, were two of my favorite writers. I liked Al Abrams and Jack Sell. What's the difference in the sports writers then and now? They aren't like they used to be. In the old days, they were more friendly, and they stayed around longer after the game. They socialized more. They didn't take themselves so seriously. My best friend in the broadcasting business among the out of town guys was Jack Buck. Bob Prince was good to me. He liked Canadian Club and Coke. After he had his health problems, though, he switched to vodka. He liked Screwdrivers. Prince was always great with me. Every Christmas, Prince would give me a $350 Christmas present. Course, I took care of him all year. That's the way he was. Any time any fans came up and wanted to see him, he wanted to see them.

"Maz has been back a few times since. He's getting big and fat; he better watch it. I always got along good with Maz. ElRoy Face and I were good friends. ElRoy still comes around. They were great players and they're still great people."

Bellows died two months after our interview.

Jackie Powell, 80
Hockey Goal-Judge from 1937 till 1991 in Pittsburgh
Longtime sidekick to Jack Sell, Post-Gazette Sports Writer

"I was 48 at the time, living in Lawrenceville, and I was an egg buyer for A&P. That's what I did for a living, and I helped Jack Sell, the sports writer, keeping stats and running copy for him whenever he covered a sports event. And I was the goal judge for the Hornets at the old Duquesne Gardens in Oakland. I started helping Jack Sell when I was a student at Schenley High School. I was with Sell in the third tier auxiliary press box that day. He was there to write a secondary story for the *Post-Gazette*.

"I was at all the games, but, of course, I remember that last one the best. I just remember the bedlam when Maz hit that ball out of the park. Everything happened to me afterwards. I was with Joe Brown in his office when he called his dad out in California. There were tears in his eyes when he was talking to his daddy.

"He invited me to a celebration party, which was supposed to be a well-kept secret, at Webster Hall. He asked me to take his secretary, Jeanie Donatelli, out to the airport to pick up some relatives who were coming to town. The traffic was so bad after the ballgame. They were celebrating in the streets all over Pittsburgh.

"I'm driving and my wife kept reaching over and blasting the horn. She kept doing that over and over again. Until the battery went dead on me. The car stopped right in the middle of the street on the Boulevard of the Allies."

Buddy Diulus and Joe Scalise share stories in press box at Three Rivers.

"Most people are on the world, not in it."
—John Deer

Jackie Powell

Willard "Diz" Bellows

Joe Scalise, Adelphia Cable
Head of Ushers Union
Three Rivers Stadium

"I was working the third floor at Forbes Field during the seventh game of the World Series. I was by the press box up there. That press box was built in anticipation of a World Series in 1938 that never came off here. Rosey Rowswell used to broadcast from up there. I got down to the first floor by the ninth inning, however, so I had a good view of Maz's home run. One of our ushers, Domenic 'Woo' Varratti, who lived on Bouquet Street in Oakland, is the guy at Maz's heels as he headed toward home plate. Buddy Diulus here (at his side) worked the third base section that day for the seventh game. Everybody who worked at Forbes Field came from Oakland; we thought it was our playground. There was a guy named 'Ditty' Rittmeyer who used to climb over the roof all the time to get in. One time they were holding a Holy Eucharist Rally, and it was free admission. But he went over the roof anyhow, just to stay in shape. The cops would slap at those guys' heels with night sticks as they were scurrying up the wall, but that didn't deter them. My home was on Ward Street, about ten blocks away. Buddy lived on Bouquet, about five minutes away. I sold newspapers there, inside the first base runway, when Ralph Kiner was playing for the Pirates. I was a star hustler. Some of the players would get upset because they thought we knew more about baseball than they did. Some question would come up, and one of the sports writers would say, 'Ask the ushers, they'll know.' I'll never forget another homer besides Maz's in that World Series. Mickey Mantle hit one over the iron gate — right-handed! — and it was like a rocket. I couldn't believe it. The win in '60 was on a par with the Mets winning it all in '69. Oakland was a great place to grow up in. We had the Duquesne Gardens, Pitt Stadium, the Syria Mosque. Everything went on in Oakland — the ice shows, the symphony, the top entertainers, and we had great places to go like the Sandscratchers, the Young Men's Thinking Club, the Greek Club, the San Lorenzo Italian Club, the Irish Club, the Oakland Cafe, Pete Coyne's, the Hideaway Bar — that was a cheaters' hangout — the Black Angus, Gustine's, Weinstein's, Canter's, The Clock, so many places, a lot of great restaurants. Now it's all fast food joints. Everything was there. Why did we always find parking spaces? Why did 30,000 people manage to find parking spaces? The trolley line went by the ballpark; that was important."

Steve "Dirt" DiNardo
Retired 1993, Head Groundskeeper
Three Rivers Stadium
Brookline

"I grew up living on Gonciar, just off Bouquet Street next to Forbes Field. I was born in Panther Hollow. My father moved there from Italy, and that section down behind Forbes Field became known as Little Italy.

Babe Ruth hit a home run that landed near our place, and a neighbor Henry DiOrio, who worked for DiNardo Construction, got the ball and turned it over to the Baseball Hall of Fame. I was in the third tier when Maz hit the home run. No, I didn't pay to get in. I lived right next door to the place. We never paid to get in. We went through Myron O'Brisky's concessions place to get in the ballpark. I started out working on the ground crew there, and continued here when Three Rivers Stadium opened in 1970."

Paul Tomasovich
Greatest Home Run Hitter
In Softball History
Greenfield

"I was 25 or 26 at the time. I was driving a truck for Continental Transportation, and I was driving down Forbes Avenue. I was coming around that S-curve in front of St. Agnes Church in Soho and heading downtown. I didn't have a radio in my truck, but I could hear the game because everybody had the radio on and everyone was sitting on their porches or front steps. When Maz hit that home run, people came off their porches and converged in the middle of the street. People ran out of their houses and out of the bars. You could just see the street filling up with people, like a swarm of locusts. People were jumping up and down. People didn't know what to do. Everybody started marching downtown. People were walking over cars. Nobody was in pain before long. All of a sudden, everyone in Pittsburgh was Polish. I called my boss on a telephone and told him, 'I can't move. What do you want me to do?' I got three hours overtime that day, just trying to get back to the office. It was unreal. A friend of mine got the ball that Mickey Mantle hit out of the deepest part of Forbes Field in that Series. And Mantle hit that one right-handed. My friend got it in Panther Hollow and he gave it to the Hall of Fame."

Bob "Big Rip" Rittmeyer
Mars, Pa.

"My brother, Carl, or 'Ditty,' as we called him, and I used to sneak into the ballpark a lot. Sometimes we'd climb up the side of the ballpark and over the roof to get in. We lived on the Boulevard of the Allies, near the Isaly's headquarters, so Forbes Field wasn't far from our home. My brother and I were both there for the seventh game of the World Series, on the second tier, watching from the back. We sorta had a way of getting in there. We used ushers passes. They'd let us in. I'm 72 years old and my brother, who lives in Plum, is 70. Oakland was a real good place, and we were proud of it. We enjoyed having things around us in Oakland. We went to all the sporting events. When they had fights there, we'd scale the wall on the Bouquet Street side of Forbes Field. Sometimes my brother and I would scale the right field, going up what we called the rafters, which were like climbing giant window blinds.

159

Sometimes we'd do things just to show the guys we could do it. We both ended up doing construction work. We just attended a funeral in January of one of the guys who used to scale the walls with us, Danny Walsh. Joey Diven and Jim Lally and some of the other guys from Oakland were there. We all swapped stories, and we laughed like the devil. We used to play out in Schenley Park. We'd hear Kiner was up over the P.A. system, and we'd go over by the wall and hope he'd hit one out. We enjoyed doing those things. Some people thought we were crazy."

Carl "Ditty" Rittmeyer
Plum Boro, Pa.

"I scaled the walls at Forbes Field frequently. We'd get into Duquesne Gardens by the fire escape to see the Pittsburgh Hornets and the Pittsburgh Yellow Jackets play hockey there, and we'd get into Pitt Stadium. Danny Walsh and Jimmy Driscoll would usually go over the wall with me. We probably went from bottom to top at least 50 times. If the cops caught us they'd start banging their sticks against our feet or legs. Oakland was a great place; we never paid to get in to see anything. We scaled the wall one night to see Billy Conn fight there."

Local Legends: Paul Tomasovich and Baldy Regan

160

Joe L. Brown
Always trying to make the Bucs better

"The main reason we won was we had a professional club. They were dedicated to the game. They played it right."

B aseball seems to be about family, and many recall days and nights spent at the ballpark with fathers and mothers, or with sons and daughters. Joe L. Brown, who built three championship teams as general manager and had an impact on the Pirates organization over a 30-year plus period, has a vivid memory along those lines.

"My son was 13 when we played the Yankees in the 1960 World Series, and he was sitting down in my box by the Pirates dugout at Forbes Field for the seventh game," began Brown. "He was sitting with Branch Rickey Jr.'s son, whose grandfather had been my mentor in baseball. I was upstairs where I preferred to be, watching the game without anyone distracting my attention. About the seventh inning, after Yogi Berra hit a three-run homer in the previous inning to put the Yankees ahead, 5-4, my son came upstairs to see me. Tears were running down his face. 'Oh, Dad, I feel so sorry for you,' he said to me. 'We're going to lose.'"

Brown mimicked the trembling tone of his son's sobbing voice as he retold the story, perhaps showing a trace of his own father's acting ability. His dad, you may recall, was Joe E. Brown, the Hollywood actor and comedian, who was a big sports fan.

"I tried to calm my son down, and I told him, 'We haven't lost yet. Don't you feel sorry for me. You'll find out today that the game isn't over until the ninth inning is over.'"

And sometimes not even then, as Harvey Haddix of the "12 perfect innings" game fame could certainly attest.

When I asked Brown to repeat his phrasing, to make sure I had it right, he said, "I'm not sure that's exactly what I said, but something like that. It was like Berra's 'it's not over till it's over,' but not as catchy perhaps. It's the truth, though. My son couldn't conceive then that we could come back. After Bill Mazeroski hit the home run to win it for us in the bottom of the ninth, my son learned the lesson I wanted to teach him. He knows better now."

There was an energy to Brown's voice as he spoke, and he punctuated his points with great emphasis and that came across loud and clear, even long distance. Brown was the Bucs' general manager for 21 seasons, from 1956 to 1976, and served as a special assignment scout up until 1992. He enjoyed staying involved. He remains a member of the team's board of directors. Brown may be retired, but it was obvious by his vibrant voice that he still has a gusto for the game. For Brown, it is still the bottom of the ninth.

Ty Brown has made baseball his life, just like his dad. He had a new job, as a scout for the 1993 season for the Miami Marlins, one of the new entries in Major League Baseball. He and his family had been to see Joe during the Christmas holidays in Mexico. Ty's given name is Don, after his dad's brother. Joe also has a daughter, Cynthia, who is married to Ron Steiner, who once worked in sales at Channel 11 in Pittsburgh. The Steiners are at home in Albuquerque. They have two children, Michael, a teacher and coach at Durham (N.C.) Academy, and Amy, a junior at Pomona College.

"I gave Ty my 1960 World Series ring when he became an adult," said Joe. "He wears it all the time; it's his most prized possession."

Brown wanted to say something else about that 1960 World Series. "People say to me, 'I know your biggest thrill must have been Mazeroski's home run' . . . and Maz's home run was a big thing. To me, though, Hal Smith's home run in the eighth inning was a more shocking thing. We were down the drain at that point. We were out of it; we were losing. He gets a three-run homer and we score five runs in the eighth. So Smith's home run, and the many late-inning rallies we put together in 1960, were my biggest thrills."

Joe L. and Ty Brown should have known by then that it was impossible to count out the Pirates no matter how far behind they were during that magical 1960 season. The Pirates made a habit of getting behind in the early innings only to rally and pull out games in the late innings with players taking turns providing the game-winning histrionics. A check of the records reveals that 21 of the Pirates' victories that year came in the ninth inning, twelve of those after two were out.

Frankie Gustine, a former Pirate who owned a popular restaurant-bar near the ballpark, complained that year in jest, "The fans used to start coming into my place in the eighth inning. Now they wait till the last man is out." Brown had no pity for Frank Gustine's plight.

"I'll tell you why we won that year," said Brown. "The main reason was that we had a professional club. They knew how to play baseball and they were dedicated to the game. They played it right. They never gave up. The two things I remember about that team are the spirit it had and the professionalism it displayed. There were teams with more talent, but none that played the game more properly.

"They gave themselves up for the good of the team. They could handle the bat, hit behind runners, put down the bunt. When we got runners on base, we believed we were going to score the run. We did what we had to do to advance the runners, to get that run. We didn't have a lot of team speed, but we ran the bases well. We made good decisions. We didn't play cautiously. We didn't have a lot of power, but Forbes Field was a spacious place, and we weren't looking for them to hit home runs.

"This was a team. Most of them were mature. Maz and Stuart were the only regulars who were young. Some of them had been around the block. Some of them had their best years, their only big years, for some it was their last hurrah. But, for that year, everything came together."

162

I mentioned to Brown that earlier in the day I had read a book called *Mick*, by Mickey Mantle with Herb Gluck (Doubleday, 1985), in which Mantle had said the 1960 World Series was the biggest disappointment in his career with the Yankees because he knew the better team had lost.

Brown allowed that comment to sit for awhile before responding, as if he were marinating beef before putting it on the grill.

"I think our team was underrated," said Brown. "We didn't have the big stars like the Yankees did. On paper, we didn't have the best team in the National League. But we were the best team. And baseball, like football and basketball, is still a team game.

"They had four Hall of Famers in Mantle, Berra, Maris and Ford, and we had one, in Clemente. We had players who played the game as skillfully, competitively and as professionally as any team I've ever seen. Guys came through for us that year, like Hal Smith and Rocky Nelson and Vinegar Bend Mizell. I got Mizell from the Cardinals and he came in and won 13 games for us. We don't win without Mizell. Two years later, I traded him to the New York Mets. He couldn't get anyone out."

"The Mets didn't hold on to him too long, either," I interjected.

"No, he just didn't have it any more," said Brown. "But he had it when we needed it. He's such a nice man, too."

"Man was meant to be challenged."
— Joe L. Brown

Brown was talking about the Pirates from his home in Monarch Beach, California. He had just officially retired two months earlier from an active consultant position he has held with the Pirates ever since he departed Pittsburgh as the team's general manager in 1976. He would be leaving in the morning to spend a week in Scottsdale, Arizona, with baseball people from the past he had befriended, such as Chub Feeney and Herman Franks, formerly with the San Francisco Giants. He had been going to Scottsdale the previous 18 years at the same time checking out players for the Pirates.

"I used to hate to go into the Giants dressing room because of Herman Franks," I said. "He set a bad tone for the team in the way they dealt with sports writers. He was always ripping into one writer or another in front of the team," I said. "Guys like Willie Mays took their cue from Franks."

"I know," said Brown. "When we were both in baseball, I thought Franks was an old curmudgeon, but we have become close friends. He's mellowed. We all have."

Brown was going to Scottsdale with his wife of two years, Paulita Jenkins. "My first wife, Din, died three and a half years ago," explained Brown. "She died of cancer 11 months before our 50th wedding anniversary."

163

"When you're sitting out in the sun in the stands at the ballpark in Scottsdale, watching a baseball game, kibitzing with your buddies from the old days, does it get any better than that?" I asked Brown.

"Yes, it does," said Brown, begging to differ, and considering his words before he continued. "The best is when you have something to do with what's going on on the field. The thing I miss is the camaraderie with players, though much of that is gone from the game today. The administrative side and the players don't have much to say to one another anymore.

"The big thing, though, is the competitive aspect of it all. That's what I miss. The trying to improve the ballclub, some way or another. How to make us better. What could I do to improve the minor league operation, or what player could I get from here or there, and what would I have to give up to do that? Those were the things that concerned me. All of those things were fun."

Brown thought about that awhile and added, "Man was meant to be challenged."

Just to show he did not live in the past, Brown said, "By the way, I absolutely think we have a dandy fellow in Pittsburgh in Ted Simmons. I think he's doing a great job under difficult circumstances."

Brown made that observation before Simmons suffered a heart attack at age 43, and ultimately resigned his position because of health concerns.

I brought up the subject of the 1992 National League playoffs, and how disappointing it was when ex-Buc Sid Bream scored from second base with the game-winning run that robbed the Pirates of a trip to the World Series.

"Paulita and I were sitting behind Ted and his wife in Atlanta," recalled Brown. "It was like we had all been hit by lightning."

"Joe L. Brown was the best general manager in baseball."
— Dave Giusti

A few hours prior to talking to Joe L. Brown on the telephone, I bumped into Dave Giusti, one of the heroes of the Pirates' 1971 World Series, indeed, the Fireman of the Year, and someone who put in 17 seasons in the big leagues. Giusti and I were participating in the playoffs for a platform tennis league in Greater Pittsburgh. Giusti, still a great competitor, lives next door to Steve Blass in Upper St. Clair, a suburb 10 miles south of Three Rivers Stadium. He was living in the same half-mile stretch as Steelers Hall of Fame coach Chuck Noll and sportscaster Myron Cope.

Giusti was a player representative with the Pirates, not always the best way to remain popular with the front office. A grizzled, outspoken type, Giusti always spoke his piece and he still does. There is nothing political about Giusti. When I asked him about Brown, however, he quickly offered, "Joe L. Brown was the best general manager in baseball. He knew what he was doing, and he was fair. He cared about you. He took the time to get to know you. He wanted to know what you were all about, what you were thinking, how you felt.

"I remember once I was really pitching lousy over a two-week spell, and he sat me down in his hotel room in San Diego and said, 'How can I help you? What can we do to help you get through this?' I had no idea what the hell was going wrong with me at the time. But it was important to have the boss talk to you one on one, and show genuine concern.

"He asked Clemente about me before he got me from St. Louis. And he asked me about Nellie Briles before he got Nellie from St. Louis. He valued our opinions. He'd do things like that. He wasn't afraid to ask his players for input. He didn't pretend like he knew it all, as some guys do at that level."

Giusti, a starting pitcher while with Houston and St. Louis, switched to the bullpen for Pittsburgh when he arrived in 1970. His 30 saves in 1971 led the league and he saved two games for the Pirates in the NLCS against the Giants and one in the World Series victory over Baltimore.

"When you talk to Joe," said Giusti, "please give him my best wishes."

Brown sounded pleased when I passed along Giusti's good wishes and his compliments. "Yes, I would seek information from the fellows I felt had good judgment, not everyone," said Brown, making sure he set the record straight on that one.

Brown was 37 when he took command of the Pirates, succeeding the 74-year-old Branch Rickey when Rickey retired after the 1955 season. Brown was a tall, erect man, usually well tanned, who favored close-cropped haircuts, gaucho shirts and sports jackets. He was never inhibited by the unwritten rule that general managers should not fraternize with the help.

"If I don't go down to the dugout," he once told Myron Cope for a story in *The Saturday Evening Post* (September 17, 1960), "how the devil am I supposed to know what's going on? Besides, this is how I learn how you make the double play, how you hold the ball. I like to nose around."

When I mentioned this to Brown, about his approach, his penchant for mixing with his players, playing cards with his managers and coaches, he said, "It wasn't a philosophy I adopted or anything like that," he said. "It was just natural for me. I got into baseball in the first place because I fell in love with baseball players.

"The most important part of the game was the player. If you sit in the office you can't tell what your players are all about. I watched the practices, and I made a lot of road trips. I took a few players, or one player at a time, out to dinner. At spring training, I was always out on the field, observing and doing stuff like putting the balls in the pitching machines, anything to be around the players.

"I wanted to know what their approach was to the game. You win with attitude, not just talent. It takes a dummy not to know what a ballplayer looks like, but I wanted to know what they thought like. To me, that was critical."

Getting Giusti and Briles were just two of the many successful player transactions pulled off by Brown during his long tenure in the Pirates front office.

Always a free-wheeler on the baseball talent market, Brown will tell you a series of trades he engineered that made pennant winners and world champions out of his Pirates in 1960.

In May, 1956, in Brown's first major deal, he sent the St. Louis Cardinals Bobby Del Greco, a fine defensive outfielder with limited offensive ability who grew up on the Hill district with his buddy Tony Bartirome, and pitcher Dick Littlefield in exchange for outfielder Billy Virdon. Frank Lane, who was then general manager of the Cardinals, later called it "the worst deal I ever made." Brown acquired a young fellow who was to be one of the game's most stylish outfielders and a clutch .270 hitter, and a class individual.

Brown made a second killing in January, 1959. He gave up another home-grown favorite in Frank Thomas and Jim Pendleton, who both could play the outfield as well as the infield, and pitcher Charles Douglas to the Cincinnati Reds in return for third baseman Don Hoak, catcher Smoky Burgess and pitcher Harvey Haddix. There would have been no pennant or World Series without this trio, no doubt about it. They all played major roles in the triumphant march by the Buccos.

The immediate reaction to that trade, however, was not a positive one among Pirates fans. News of the trade flashed over radio and television near midnight. At Brown's home in Mt. Lebanon, the telephone began ringing and did not stop until 3 a.m. "Has your husband gone crazy?" Pirate fans kept demanding of Joe's wife, Din.

Upon his return home, his wife told him, "Next time you swing a big deal, Trader Brown, kindly be at home to answer the telephone."

Nobody heckled Brown for too long about that deal.

With the 1960 season a month old, Brown and manager Danny Murtaugh concluded that they were badly in need of another starting pitcher. They gave up a fine prospect in second baseman Julian Javier, who would go on to play in the All-Star Game but could not move Mazeroski out of the starting lineup in Pittsburgh, sending him to the St. Louis Cardinals in exchange for Mizell. It was a good trade for both teams. Mizell helped the Pirates win the World Series, and Javier helped the Cardinals win two pennants, and a World Series.

Brown made another move in the midst of all that in which he takes immense pride as well.

Brown got lucky a few times, too. During the interleague trading period prior to the 1960 season, he gave the Athletics catcher Hank Foiles and two farm hands — shortstop Ken Hamlin and pitcher Dick Hall — in exchange for cash and Hal Smith. With the Pirates, Smith proved to be a capable catcher, platooning with Burgess, and he hit close to .300 for most of the season. And, of course, he hit that critical home run in the seventh game of the World Series. That one home run made it a great trade.

166

GM Joe L. Brown

With Dick Groat at contract signing in 1957

With dad Joe E. Brown

With Manager Danny Murtaugh

Front and center with Roberto Clemente, Billy Mazeroski, Billy Virdon and Frank Oceak at spring training camp.

Twelve days later, Brown struck what many thought was a strange deal with Bing Devine of the Cardinals, swapping starting pitcher Ronnie Kline for a minor league pitcher, Tom Cheney, and an outfielder, Gino Cimoli, who was hardly the long-ball hitter the Pirates seemed to need. Cimoli backed up Virdon and Skinner in the outfield, and did a fine job. Cheney was a capable spot pitcher.

"Power does not win pennants," Brown defended himself at the time. "Balance does."

A month prior to the big trade with Cincinnati, Brown stood up at the winter draft meetings, sucked in his breath, and called out, "Rocky Nelson!" There were snickers and guffaws throughout the room when he announced the Pirates pick.

Nelson, a bald, craggy-faced, garrulous veteran, had been in professional baseball since 1942 and had nine major league trials. But he never stayed up too long. He was a big star in the minor leagues, hitting home runs and driving in runs in large numbers, yet he could never stick for long in the bigs.

Brown had put in a long apprenticeship in the bushes, too, and maybe he had a soft spot for a player who needed another break. At the age of 20, when he was an end on the football team at UCLA, Brown quit college to become assistant business manager of a Class D baseball club in Lubbock, Texas. During his 17-year climb to being the Pirates' GM, Brown had dragged infields, taken tickets, driven team buses. Along the way, he learned something about evaluating ballplayers.

"Nothing at Pittsburgh gave me as much personal satisfaction as drafting Rocky Nelson," said Brown. "I was the only man in our organization who thought of him. Our scouts spent more than a month going over reports on possible draftees, but Rocky's name was not on their lists. I simply could not believe that a guy would have his minor league record and not have ability."

Reflecting on it now, Brown said, "I felt certain we needed a left-handed hitter. So I asked George Sisler to go out and check out the possibilities. I respected his opinion a lot. I asked him who was out there. 'There's nobody out there,' he said. 'Who's the best left-handed hitter out there?' I said, rephrasing the question. He mentioned Rocky Nelson. 'Is he the best left-handed hitter?' I asked again. Sisler said, 'Yes.' And I said, 'Then we have to draft him.' I was sitting in front of Chub Feeney from the Giants when I made Nelson our draft pick. *Ozzie and Harriet* was a popular TV show at the time, and after I announced that the Pirates were picking Rocky Nelson, Feeney smiled at me as I turned to sit down and said, 'Don't you mean Ricky Nelson?' Oh, they all laughed at my expense that day. But he was a good ballplayer."

Brown didn't add that he had the last laugh on that one. Like his dad, though, he knew if you had to spell it out then it wasn't a good story, or a good line, to begin with.

"I play the game."
— Danny Murtaugh

When I asked Brown what was the key to his club's success in 1960, he did not hesitate. "Danny Murtaugh more than anyone else, no doubt about it," said Brown, and then began a tribute to Murtaugh that only reinforced all that I had heard about one of Brown's shortcomings: that he thought Murtaugh was the only man who could manage the Pirates.

"He wasn't the only manager, I never felt that, but he was one of the best managers, and certainly the best manager for our ballclub," said Brown, bristling maybe at the tone of the observation I threw his way. Brown turned the ballclub over to Murtaugh on three different occasions. He kept coming back to him the way George Steinbrenner kept re-hiring Billy Martin, a second baseman of Murtaugh's time.

In the conversation that ensued, Brown alternately referred to his favorite manager as "Murtaugh" and as "Danny." It was obvious he was talking about a long-time friend as well as a baseball man whose savvy and strength he still admired.

"Murtaugh was maybe the most underrated manager in baseball," he said. "They wrote about him spittin' tobacco, and rockin' in his rockin' chair and drinkin' milk, and being a leprechaun and the like. But he was a thinker.

"For a night game, Murtaugh would get to the ballpark between 11 and 1. He liked to play pinochle for an hour or so with some of his coaches, and just relax and have some fun. I'd join them sometimes.

"At 2, he'd go into his office, and he'd close the door. He'd chew his tobacco and spit. He'd sit in that rocking chair. That I knew. One day I said to him, 'Dan, what do you do in there all by yourself?' He looked at me with a wink and said, 'I play the game.'

" 'What do you mean you play the game?' I asked him. 'When we play the Cardinals, for instance,' he said, 'I know who's going to play for them. I know who's pitching, and who's already pitched, and who they might have available for relief in different situations. I know who's hurt and who can't play. I'm thinking about who'll they'll bring in. Who do I call on if we get in trouble? What are some situations we might find ourselves in? Then when everything happens in the game, I know what I'm going to do. I've already played the game.'

"Murtaugh was not just into strategy. Murtaugh was the best handler of pitchers for a non-pitcher that I ever knew. Whenever Danny made a decision regarding pitchers they were all his. We had a relationship that was rare in baseball. I don't think any general manager and manager were ever closer. We were together in New Orleans for three years, in 1952, 1953 and 1954. We were poor together. We knew each other well. We were friends. I could say anything I wanted to Dan and he listened. He didn't always agree with me and he'd tell me so. It was an open-ended dialogue. I could make suggestions to him. Sometimes he'd go along with it, and sometimes he didn't. I'd tell him, 'I'm going to do so-and-so or such-and-such,' and he'd say, 'You can't do that!' We were sounding boards for each other.

169

"We had a rule in our organization. I wanted him, or any of my managers, to stop in my office for awhile sometime before each game. I wanted to know how they felt about the players on the team. That went for Bobby Bragan, for Murtaugh, for Larry Shepard, for Harry Walker, for Bill Virdon. At a home game, they were expected to stop by. On the road, I'd go to dinner with the manager, or play pinochle with the coaches. I wanted to know what our problems were as early as possible, not two thirds of the way into the season. I didn't want to hear about anything third hand. I wanted to now what was going on, what my guys thought of our personnel, and what we needed to win.

"Danny had a knack for handling players without them knowing they were being handled. He had rules, not a lot of rules, and he knew he had to handle different players differently. In 1960, most of the players really enjoyed playing for him. He had some rough times with Clemente for awhile, but when I brought back Murtaugh as the manager a second time (in 1970), they got along fine.

"One of the things Dan did was that if they had a bad day Dan didn't quit on them, or give up on them. Murtaugh never asked a player to do something he couldn't do. He didn't ask Dick Groat to hit home runs, for instance, or ask Stuart to bunt. Danny had the patience to go along with a player not until he fails, but until he succeeds.

"With Murtaugh as manager, we were never out of ballgames. We always had a chance to win. People didn't leave our games in the late innings, no matter what the score was. Forbes Field could hold about 34,000 in those days, and we had 30 to 34,000 fans there every day after a while that summer. We really caught on with the Pirate fans."

The Pirates averaged just over 22,150 fans that summer in posting a record 1.7 million attendance. The Pirates did not surpass that until they pulled in over 2 million in 1990 and 1991 at Three Rivers Stadium, when they averaged nearly 25,500 a game.

"Early in the season (April 17), we were playing the Cincinnati Reds," said Brown, recalling a game that several of the 1960 Pirates had pointed to in earlier interviews as a game that began a summer-long series of sensational comebacks. "At the end of eight innings, we were down five-nothing. Fred Hutchinson was the manager of the Reds. He wanted to take it easy on his starter, and get some work for one of his relief pitchers, Bill Henry. He was a big, hard-throwing left hander. He looked like a real mismatch for our guys. Hal Smith hit a three-run pinch-hit homer. And Skinner hit a two-run homer, hitting a line drive against the piping at the top of the screen in right field and it skipped off into the stands. We scored six runs in the ninth to win that one. Both teams dressed in clubhouses that were on the first base side of the ballpark back then. There were five or six exposed light bulbs on the runway that led to the clubhouse, and Hutchinson punched out all of them with his fist as he passed under them after that game."

There was a lot of leprechaun in Murtaugh, though, and he had a much-needed sense of humor that helped him get through many a summer.

170

I mentioned a story about Murtaugh that ElRoy Face had related to me, and Brown picked up on it quickly, and even added details that improved on Face's reflections. "That's one of my favorite stories," said Brown. "Murtaugh had pitched Face in five straight games. Murtaugh told him, 'I've been pitching you too much; don't come to the ballpark tonight.' And Face said, 'I can't do that. You might need me.' And Murtaugh told him, 'Then don't warm up or do anything out in the field before the game. Sit this one out.' We're in St. Louis and late in the game, he's got two relief pitchers up in the bullpen. Sure enough, one of them is Face. Murtaugh ends up bringing in the relief pitcher he knew was his best. After all, Face had pitched something like 18 consecutive innings without giving up a run. He brings him in and Face pitches the ninth inning, the tenth, eleventh and twelfth inning. In the 13th, Musial hits one on the roof to win the game for the Cardinals. And Musial wasn't a bad hitter. So Murtaugh walks by Face in the clubhouse, and as he does, he sneers and says, 'Relief pitcher my ass!' That was Danny."

"You might need me."
— ElRoy Face

Brown did not give Murtaugh all the credit for the 1960 success. "We had several players who had great years and several who might have won the most valuable player award that year," said Brown.

"Dick Groat was the most valuable player in the league that year, and he certainly was deserving. But Don Hoak, Roberto Clemente, Bill Mazeroski, Vernon Law and Bob Friend had fine years, too. Law won the Cy Young Award as the outstanding pitcher."

I mentioned to Brown that I heard Clemente felt he should have won the MVP award and that he did not attend the Pirates' post-game championship celebration because of what he regarded as a slight. "I knew Roberto didn't come to the party," said Brown, "but I didn't know that was the reason.

"The thing that hurt Clemente more than anything else was that Les Biederman, the baseball writer for *The Press* was plugging for Groat with the writers around the league, and knocking Clemente. Clemente was never close to Biederman again because it got back to him what Biederman had been doing."

Biederman covered baseball in Pittsburgh from 1938 to 1969, and was the major domo in the baseball press box, believing it to be his own private domain, and attempting to bar anybody in the media who displeased him.

"I guess you heard about how Hoak got hurt at a swimming party that year," volunteered Brown. "That was at Dr. Henry Sherman's home near the 18th green at Oakmont Country Club. He was an eye, ear and nose man, and he moved his practice to Latrobe in recent years. Several of the Pirates went there this one night, and Hoak slipped coming up the ladder and tore the sole of his foot on the metal. He swore everyone to secrecy. He got Dr. Sherman to stitch it up for him. The Cardinals came to town for a doubleheader the next day. Hoak played and he had some big hits. When he came in after the first game, I later learned, his socks were soaked with blood. He swore our trainer, Danny Whelan, to secrecy, too. Hoak didn't want to come out of the lineup. That's the kind of fighter he was. Dr. Sherman and I are still good friends."

Bob Friend eventually gave that story, with Hoak's permission, as a scoop to Milton Gross of *The New York Post* during the 1960 World Series. Biederman was furious with Friend for giving the story to an out-of-town writer. *The Press* carried the nationally-syndicated story by Gross. It made Biederman look bad, or at least Biederman thought it did.

Brown bounced around with some personal memories after that. Reflecting on Forbes Field, Brown observed, "It was a great old park. It was a beautiful setting, with Schenley Park in the background, especially when the flowers came out and all the trees were green. You had the Schenley Hotel. The players loved it. They'd sit out on the porch and watch the students walk by. They could walk across the street and they'd be in the ballpark.

"A story I remember is that Bill Turner, one of the front office assistants, said after Maz hit the home run, 'We had to win this one. We had three outs we still hadn't used yet.'"

I asked him what it would have been like if it had been Dick Stuart instead of Mazeroski who hit the game-winning home run.

"Stuart was on deck, of course, and he grabbed Maz in the clubhouse and hollered at him, in jest. He said, 'You cost me about $10,000. I was going to hit the home run and I'd have been the hero.'"

Did he think Maz made for the better hero?

"Maz was such a modest young man," said Brown. "He was like Musial. He never changed. He was still a good guy."

"People didn't know how to take him, and he didn't know how to take people." — Brown on Clemente

I asked Brown to talk about his stormy relationship with Groat. It seemed that Groat still held a grudge against Brown for several reasons: for cutting his salary prior to the 1960 season, for trading him to the St. Louis Cardinals, and for not considering him as a candidate to manage the team after Murtaugh had to give up the post for health reasons in 1968.

"I had a great regard for Dick Groat," said Brown. "I thought we had a great relationship until I traded him. I think he felt he'd always stay in Pittsburgh. But those things don't happen that much."

For the record, Brown traded away three hometown products in Frank Thomas and Bob Purkey, to Cincinnati, and Bobby Del Greco, to St. Louis. They, too, preferred playing in Pittsburgh. The trade of

Thomas worked out in the Pirates' favor, but the trades of Purkey and Groat did not. They were both trades that backfired on Brown.

"Dick's feeling for me changed considerably after I dealt him to St. Louis," said Brown, sounding like he wished it had not happened that way. "He had a complete change of attitude. And he said some harsh things about me to the St. Louis writers. He's never been real happy since.

"He thought I traded him because I thought he was through. That was not the case. In Dick Schofield and Gene Alley, I thought we could replace him. Alley was a year or two away from being a full-time shortstop, and he was a good one. He and Maz were a great double play combination.

"Dick thought that my trading him cast aspersions on his ability. I traded him and Diomedes Olivo (in 1962) for Don Caldwell and Julio Gotay. It wasn't a good trade, as it turned out, but I thought it was at the time. I had hoped to get Larry Jackson, who was a terrific pitcher, but they pulled him off the table on me.

"I was pretty much committed to making a change. I thought Schofield and Alley could play close to what Groat had given us, and I was trying to strengthen our pitching and provide an opportunity for two infielders who merited more playing time.

"Dick was pretty typical of the '60 team. He used his ability to the maximum, and he was intelligent. He came to us right from the campus of Duke and became an excellent player and an excellent contributor."

Brown later sent Schofield to the Giants. While Alley was a fine shortstop, he never hit as well as Groat, nor did he provide the same spark.

Brown never said he owned a crystal ball.

I asked Brown if he had any idea in 1960 that Clemente would continue to get better, and become the Hall of Fame performer he became.

"No, not really," he said. "Everybody recognized his talent. It was really a matter of Roberto settling down, and becoming more stable in his approach to everything. Roberto's early years were not starring years. While Roberto spoke English, he didn't communicate well. People didn't know how to take him, and he didn't know how to take people. He was called a malingerer, and people though he had imagined illnesses and injuries. But he didn't. He really had them.

"Harry Walker had a big influence on him. In the two full seasons that Walker managed the Pirates, Clemente had his only two years that he drove in over 100 runs (119 in 1966 and 110 in 1967). Harry had him hitting with more power to right. Harry used to tell Clemente, 'You're a great player, but you have the talent to be the greatest player in baseball.' Roberto, like most people, lapped it up. He listened to what Walker wanted him to do, and nobody but Ted Williams talked more about hitting than Walker did.

"Keep in mind that Clemente had almost no major league experience when he came to Pittsburgh. He had played one year in Montreal, with about 200 at bats. Most of his experience was in the Puerto Rican leagues. They were good, but they weren't major league by any stretch of the imagination. It just took Clemente awhile to blossom. He became such a great player in all phases of the game."

As he was talking, I could picture Brown beaming. Those '60 Pirates were still so special to him, and he could talk about them all night.

Joe L. Brown looks after his mentor Branch Rickey at training camp.

Where Were You?

"We could hear the roar of the crowd
for Mazeroski's home run."
—Bernie Fix

Ed Harmon, Home Builder
F. E. Harmon Construction Co.
Upper St. Clair, Pa.
"My grandfather, W. T. Foraker, lived in the 'Little Switzerland' area of Ohio, between Woodsfield and Marietta. He had a 150-acre farm there, and Bill Mazeroski used to go down there and stay in an outbuilding for a week and go squirrel hunting in 1959 and 1960. My grandfather loved baseball and he loved to talk about it. I loved to play baseball, so we got along great.

"I played on the baseball team at Mt. Lebanon High School before there was a high school in Upper St. Clair. We played against Paul Smith from Wilkinsburg, Dick Groat from Swissvale in high school, and Tony Bartirome and Bobby Del Greco in sandlot ball. We beat Swissvale once, 6-1, but Groat was great. He had a home run and a triple, and he was truly the best young ballplayer in the Pittsburgh area.

"My father, Ferl Harmon, was a home builder, and he took me and a few other fellows to the sixth game of the 1960 World Series. We left the house at 9:30 in the morning and took a lunch. We wanted to get out there as early as possible and watch batting practice. I never saw guys hit the ball like the Yankees did. They had Mantle, Maris, Skowron, Berra, Howard and they were all hitting balls into the stands and over the wall. I never saw such power! I loved watching that batting practice more than the game. Whitey Ford pitched for the Yankees that day and they killed the Pirates, 12-0. We went away that day writing off the Pirates.

"We were working on a home the next day in Upper St. Clair, for a Mrs. Hunter on Lambeth Drive, I'll never forget it. She was a big baseball fan. She turned the volume up on the radio and we could hear it over the power saws. She was so excited and she kept screaming and hollering. It was like being at the ballpark. When Maz hit the home run she went crazy, and I thought one of our guys was going to fall through a pane glass window. We were all so excited. It was great."

Gladys Wagner
Retired teacher
Friendship Village
Upper St. Clair, Pa.
"I was a fifth grade teacher that year at Burgwin Elementary School in Hazelwood. There was a boy in my class who had brought a transistor radio to school. Every so often, he would ask me if he could listen awhile to get a score. We were walking down the school hall at the end

of the day, and he asked me again if he could turn on the game. I wasn't supposed to, but I let him do it. He had it on loud when Mazeroski hit the home run at 3:36 p.m. A big cheer went up as they were running out of the school building. They were so happy! I was always glad I allowed them to do it."

Bernie Fix
Bethel Park

"I was a student in the nursing school at Presbyterian-University Hospital. I was Bernie Patla back then, and I was from Level Green, out near Monroeville. We wanted to get to the seventh game by the sixth inning because they let students in for free at that time, even for the World Series. Our instructor wouldn't let us out of class to go to the game. When class let out, several us were running down the hill to get there before it was over. As we neared Forbes Avenue we could hear the roar of the crowd for Mazeroski's home run. I was dating a young man who lived in Mt. Oliver at the time, and we were to meet that evening Downtown. But he couldn't drive over the bridge into town because they closed off the bridge because of the crowd Downtown, and he had to walk into town from the South Side. I remember we followed a man up the avenue who'd been drinking, and he was just banging away on a pot. There was lots of excitement in the city that night.

"We went to lots of games that year, getting in during the sixth inning. ElRoy Face pitched a lot in the late innings, and he was our favorite. I remember all the 'no parking' signs on the meters when you got near the ballpark. I just loved the feeling of the crowd moving toward Forbes Field. All the bar doors were open, and there was just a certain feeling of going to Forbes Field."

Fans get caught up in excitement of '60 World Series at Forbes Field.

176

Danny Murtaugh
A tough Irishman from Chester

*"He'd go to each of us and
get the most from all of us."*
— Smoky Burgess

Danny Murtaugh was the perfect manager for the Pittsburgh Pirates. For one thing, he looked like a Pittsburgh guy. Murtaugh's mug was that of a millworker, which he had been in his teens in a shipyard back home in Chester, Pennsylvania, or a coalminer. It was not difficult to picture him with a hardhat, soot on his face, and sweat on his brow and cheeks, and a lunchpail in hand. He was 5-9, 170 pounds, and fit in with the crowd. He was hardly handsome, but his face was inviting, and easy on the eye. Anyone could get comfortable in a hurry in his company. Murtaugh knew how to smile. He was generous about it.

He was Irish and proud of it. His eyebrows were huge and bushy and as black as the smoke that poured out of the nearby mills when he first came to Pittsburgh to play the infield for the Pirates in 1948. His five o'clock shadow always showed up on his heavy jowls around two o'clock. The mask suited him when he was in one of his dark moods.

Myron Cope, writing in the *Saturday Evening Post*, described him as looking like a dogface in one of Bill Mauldin's World War II cartoons.

Late in his career, the skin was puffy about Murtaugh's hazel eyes, and sometimes he would allow the heavy hoods to cover his eyes when he wanted to tune somebody out, or to show boredom with a particular line of questioning. Murtaugh, at times, drove reporters nuts because there were days he didn't give them much in the way of material.

He loved to shove a big wad of Beech-Nut Chewing Tobacco deep into his cheek, and he had lasar-like accuracy when it came to spitting a stream on an unsuspecting sports writer's shoes. He would do the same to his players and even umpires when he got into their faces — and he was good at that — when he was upset with something they did. Fans got a kick out of Murtaugh jawing with an umpire. But the umpires liked Murtaugh, too, and they might be more patient with him than they would be with Leo Durocher, Herman Franks or Billy Martin. Murtaugh was an incorrigible practical joker. He loved to play pranks on people, anything for a laugh. He would carry cherry bombs around with him when he was playing golf, for instance, according to Bob Friend and Jack Berger, and set them off when somebody was about to strike the ball off the tee.

He was a family man, faithful to his wife and children, a practicing Catholic, and he did not drink any liquor. He smoked as many as six or seven big cigars a day. It is no wonder he was such a big favorite of Steelers owner Art Rooney, whose first love was baseball and who was a frequent visitor to the Pirates' games and to Murtaugh's office. Rooney would send Murtaugh cigars from his own supply.

Ralph Kiner, a former teammate, told us Murtaugh was the last man he ever thought would be a big league manager. And he ended up being one of the best in the business. The majority of his former players speak of him kindly, and credit him with a great deal of the team's success.

Baseball managers do a lot of loafing; it's the nature of the game. None did it better than Murtaugh. There is a lot of idle time in this sport, that is why it is called the national pastime. Webster's defines pastime as "something that amuses and serves to make time pass agreeably, a diversion."

That's baseball, all right. Murtaugh could get comfortable in a hurry in the dugout, or in the clubhouse. He sat well, knew how to cross his legs, and flip flop them from time to time so he didn't turn to salt. He was known for his patience. Baseball people like to hunt and fish, they're not always the most ambitious people in the world, and Murtaugh fit the mold.

Baseball managers and coaches are not as active as, say, basketball coaches, football or even wrestling coaches. Baseball managers are not screaming from start to finish, and they can't stalk the sidelines. They can't even walk behind their bench the way hockey coaches do. Baseball managers sit and study and spit and who knows what else and, late in his career, Murtaugh even dozed off a few times on the bench. It is a sedentary life, and Murtaugh enjoyed it to the hilt. He even took it to extremes. He had a rocking chair in his office off the clubhouse, and spent some of his best moments in it. He did some of his best thinking, and some of his best sleeping, in his rocking chair.

He did not have a rocking chair on the road, but he still liked to get to the ballpark six to seven hours before a game and play some cards with his coaches, or Joe Brown, the team's general manager, settle on his lineup and pitching rotation for that day, and take a nap.

"I didn't particularly like sitting in my hotel room," he explained. "I'm not much for sitting in a hotel lobby, either. I'd rather go to the park and play cards or just relax. This is my office, this is where I work. I can relax here and think."

On a Pirates' personnel questionnaire, he listed his hobbies, interestingly enough, as basketball and watching movies.

"He's been able to keep a fairly happy ship."
— Joe L. Brown

The images persist. Going to interview Danny Murtaugh was like going to visit your grandfather. There he would be, after a ballgame, sitting in a rocking chair in his office at Three Rivers Stadium, sipping on a glass of milk. Or spitting chew tobacco. Or both. What a mixture, maybe Murtaugh's answer to a Molotov cocktail.

Murtaugh had a marvelous sense of humor, a twinkle in his dark Irish eyes, and he enjoyed jousting with sports writers. Most of the time, anyhow. During the summer of '76, quite often he looked pale and tired when you came upon him in his rocking chair. I only saw him twice that summer, as a visiting newsman from New York, but he did not look well, and the local writers expressed concern about his health.

He was not well, not really. We knew that. But none of us realized that his days were numbered. He had been ill before, on several occasions, but he had always bounced back, usually to manage his beloved Bucs once again.

He retired after that 1976 season. He suffered a stroke and died on December 2, 1976, at age 59. He may have hastened his departure by coming back to manage once too many times.

Murtaugh managed the Pirates on four different occasions — something no one had ever done elsewhere in baseball at that time — and led the team to four Eastern Division titles and two World Series triumphs — in 1960 and again in 1971. He always said the '60 team was his best.

"Managing a ballclub," he once explained, "is like getting malaria. Once you're bitten by the bug, it's difficult to get it out of your bloodstream."

Ol' No. 40 managed 15 seasons altogether between 1957 and 1976. During that time he became one of only 36 managers to win 1,000 games, compiling a record of 1,115-950 and a .540 winning percenage. His win total ranks second on the Pirates' all-time list to Fred Clarke's 1,422. Murtaugh was named *The Sporting News* Manager of the Year in 1960 and 1970. His number was retired by the Bucs in 1977.

He was asked in a pre-game broadcast in 1971 if he had realized he had nine blacks in the starting lineup. "Once a man puts on a Pirates uniform, I don't notice the color of his skin," dead-panned Murtaugh.

His boss and best friend, Joe L. Brown, once said of the dark-jowled Murtaugh: "He's not a flashy manager, but he always has a reason — a sound reason — for everything he does. And I think he's been able to keep a fairly happy ship."

In the third year of his first tour of duty, Murtaugh managed the Pirates to an unbelievable 1960 World Series victory over the New York Yankees. The team slipped to sixth place the next season, though, and then finished fourth, eighth and sixth again before Murtaugh was removed.

His successor, Harry Walker, was into his third season when Murtaugh was brought back to the bench. Murtaugh managed at a .500 pace in the Pirates' final 78 games, but they still finished sixth. He had been managing on an interim basis, and he gave way to Larry Shepard who had a two-year stint before Murtaugh came back a third time.

He came back in grand style. He directed the Bucs to an Eastern Division title in 1970. Murtaugh was named the Man of the Year for 1970 by the Pittsburgh Jaycees and won the Dapper Dan Award as the sports figure who did the most to promote Pittsburgh that year. He capped that off by managing the Pirates to another World Series championship over the Baltimore Orioles in 1971.

Asked by Arthur Daley, the Pulitzer Prize-winning sports columnist for *The New York Times*, about the secret behind his success that season, Murtaugh replied, "Brilliant managerial thinking and dumb Irish luck."

He was not in good health, however, and he stepped down in favor of his right-hand man, Bill Virdon, who led the team to another Eastern Division title in 1972. Virdon's team was struggling the next season, and Murtaugh was brought back for the final 26 games.

He had several health scares along the way, chest pains, arm pains, signals of possible cardiac distress. "These games are tough on my boiler," he said.

Murtaugh's finest managing job may have come in the 1974 season. The Pirates lost 10 of their first 12 games, and were 18-32 at one point. They put on an incredible drive and won 51 of their last 76 games and won the pennant on the final day of the season. It was their fourth division championship in five years.

Murtaugh made it five for six the next summer as the Pirates won another pennant. His team finished second in his final season of 1976.

> ## *"Danny was a much underrated manager.*
> ## *He knew what he was doing."*
> ## — Joe L. Brown

It was early April, 1993, and Joe Brown had just returned to his home in Monarch Beach, California following a 10-day visit to Arizona to check out some spring training activity in the company of old friends. He still misses Murtaugh. It would have been nice if Murtaugh had been sitting next to him in the stands at Scottsdale, sharing the sunshine and reminiscences, offering opinions about the players on the field before them. Brown had relinquished all responsibility for providing the Pirates with talent scouting reports only three months earlier, and did his best to say he preferred having more time for his wife and family.

During a lengthy telephone conversation, Brown laid two stories to rest that are part of the Murtaugh mythology. In every report I read about Murtaugh's career, he was considered a second choice to Clyde Sukeforth when he was first hired to manage the Pirates during the 1957 season.

Then, too, following Murtaugh's death in 1976, several sports writers suggested that maybe Murtaugh put his health, indeed, his life, at risk when he returned too many times to manage the team. I asked Brown if he felt any remorse, or blame, for bringing Murtaugh back three times after his original hiring.

"He came back the last two times because he wanted to," said Brown. "I only asked him back the second time. When I fired Larry

Murtaugh tweaks Mazeroski's cheek.

A real second baseman

Murtaugh towels off after victory.

Pittsburgh Pirates

Dan and Kate Murtaugh with sons Timmy, 8, and Danny, 4, and daughter Kathy, 2, in 1951 at their home in Chester, Pa.

Shepard (near the end of the 1969 season), I went to the winter instruction league and talked about our managerial situation to Danny because I valued his opinion so much.

"After we talked, he went to his room. He came back to my room the next morning and knocked on the door. He said, 'We talked about four guys last night. What about me? I'd like to manage again.' I said, 'I couldn't even consider it unless you got a complete clearance from your doctor.' Murtaugh said, 'I already got it.' 'OK,' I said, 'but I won't consider it unless you get one more clearance.' He said, 'From who?' I said, 'From Kate.' So Danny left my room and returned to where his wife Kate was, and came back and said, 'She said it's OK, that she'll be glad to get me out of the house.' And I said, 'Danny, if everything is OK, I don't want anyone but you.' And he came back and managed us to a division title in 1970.

"As far as the Sukeforth story . . . I asked Clyde if he wanted to manage the team more as a courtesy than anything else when we replaced Bobby Bragan two-thirds of the way through the 1957 season. Sukeforth was the senior coach in terms of service, and I thought he would be insulted if I didn't at least ask him. I knew in my mind he wouldn't take the job. He had turned down the Brooklyn Dodgers and that would have been a much cushier job at the time. The Dodgers had much more talent than we did. We had been losing, and our talent was very young; we didn't have too many veterans. He had said privately that he didn't want to manage.

"But, in my own mind, I wasn't sure Dan was the man to manage the team, either. I thought he was too concerned about his players, and too worried about their feelings, from what I had observed when we worked together at New Orleans (1952-54). He later managed in an independent situation at Charleston, West Virginia (in 1955), and I thought he got better about that. He found out you have to do what's good for the club. That you had to do what the situation dictated, and not worry about what the players would say. I'm not saying you shouldn't be concerned about the players' feelings, or be a despot, but you had to do what you thought best. I knew he was a good baseball man.

"Danny was a much underrated manager. He was made out to be the good humor guy, the spit-tobacco-juice, little- Leprechaun-on-the-shoulder, kiss-the-Blarney-Stone sort of guy. But nothing happened that he didn't plan. He knew what he was doing."

"He was a man's manager."
— Bob Friend

Bob Friend, a former Pirates pitcher who is now a vice-president at Babb, Inc., insurance brokers with offices on Ridge Avenue, not far from Three Rivers Stadium, smiled at the mere mention of Murtaugh.

"He was one of my friends," offered Friend. "He was a friendly guy. He could hit you with his tobacco juice from a hundred yards away, right?"

Well, at least from ten yards away, but why nit-pick when you are talking about a Pirates legend?

"A lot of guys on the team didn't like him," continued Friend. "He didn't get along well with Clemente for the longest time, but they both came around. And they got along, too. I remember Murtaugh shouting at Clemente when he came into the clubhouse late one day. 'If you're late, don't dress!' Murtaugh screamed and they got into it pretty good. Murtaugh was a tough Irish fighter. But that incident passed.

"He was an unlikely manager. He acted like he didn't know what was going on, but he was pretty sharp. He had great patience, especially with pitchers, and you need that. He was a man's manager."

Bill Mazeroski remembers Murtaugh fondly, even if he is not expansive on the subject.

"I always stayed away from the bosses; I just did what I thought I was supposed to do," said Mazeroski.

"Since Murtaugh was a second baseman himself, did he talk to you much about how to play the position?" I asked.

"No, he never talked to me about playing second base," said Mazeroski. "He left me on my own about that."

"What did you think of him?"

"I thought he did a good job. He got along well with his players. Everybody liked him. A few times, when he was going to have a team meeting, he'd say to me, 'I'm gonna pick on you today; I know you can take it. You're gonna be my whipping boy.'"

"Joe Brown must have thought the world of him as a manager, to bring him back so many times?" I said.

"Yeah, like Steinbrenner," Mazeroski said, "and the way he kept bringing Billy Martin back."

"I guess Murtaugh didn't talk as much as Harry Walker?"

"No one did. Walker talked a lot more."

Reuben Gomez of the Giants hit Mazeroski on the arm with a pitch on May 24, 1958. Earlier in the season, Gomez hit Hank Foiles with a pitch. So Murtaugh went to Vernon Law and ordered him to hit Gomez the next time he came to bat.

"Hit him on his right knee," said Murtaugh.

Law was reluctant to do so. "The Good Book says to turn the other cheek, Skip," said Deacon, an ordained minister in the Mormon church.

Murtaugh spit a stream of tobacco into the dugout in disgust. He looked Law in the eye and said, "It'll cost you a hundred if you don't!"

Law decked Gomez with his first pitch. "He who lives by the sword shall perish by the sword," Law allowed later, perhaps to relieve himself of any guilty feelings.

At the plate, the umpire warned Law about beanballs, and Gomez waved his bat angrily in Law's direction. Murtaugh leaped from his seat in the dugout and rushed the bat-wielding Gomez. Orlando Cepeda ran to intercept Murtaugh, but was felled by a flying tackle by teammate Willie Mays. It was a real riot.

"The fans never knew
the real Roberto Clemente."

Murtaugh managed Clemente for ten years. Less than two months after Clemente was killed in a tragic airplane crash, Murtaugh was asked to accept an award on Clemente's behalf at a big sports dinner in New York.

"You know what we used to call him?" Murtaugh told the audience. "We called him 'The Great One.' He was the best ballplayer I've ever seen and I say that with all due respect to Aaron, Musial and Mays. Clemente also was my intermediary. He had an important influence on the other young Latin-American players on our club. If I saw one was going astray, I'd call Roberto into my office. He'd say, 'Give me two or three days,' and that would be the end of the problem.

"Roberto Clemente, to me, was a compassionate man. He was a man of two faces. In the clubhouse, he was the center of all the funny stories. He'd hold court in front of his locker and there was always gaiety and laughter. When the time came for the game, Roberto would put on his other face, the disturbed face he always wore when he was concentrating completely on winning a baseball game. That's why I say the fans never knew the real Roberto Clemente."

Here is a twice-told tale, and perhaps it's apocryphal, that was related by Bob Broeg of the *St. Louis Post-Dispatch* upon the death of Murtaugh.

It concerns an incident in St. Louis when Jocko Conlan, umpiring at home plate, got upset with something Murtaugh said to him in protesting a call, and gave the Pirates' infielder a quick heave-ho. Murtaugh thought a third strike on a full-count was too high.

Joe Garagiola was catching for the Cardinals, and he was the teller of the tale, so it was probably embellished quite a bit to serve up at sports banquets for dessert.

"Look around, Jocko," Murtaugh is supposed to have said. "There's that punishing Polack, Musial, at first base, and Schoendienst, a Dutchman, at second. Marion, at shortstop, hell, I don't even know what he is, and Kurowski, another Pole, is at third.

"Pollet, a Frenchman, is pitching, and look behind the plate — Garagiola, a spaghetti-bender.

"There are only two Irishmen on the field, and you want to throw out half of us!"

Conlan changed his mind, and did his best to keep from chuckling, and allowed Murtaugh to stay in the game.

"I'm going to go home and listen to
some music and rock in my rocking chair."
— Danny Murtaugh

A World War II veteran, Murtaugh played nine seasons with the Philadelphia Phillies, Boston Braves and Pittsburgh Pirates, and was a career .254 hitter. He was considered a journeyman infielder in his day. Today, he would make millions with those numbers. He didn't do anything spectacular during his major league playing career, but he had spirit and a strong desire to win and he managed to hang on longer than his natural talent might have warranted. Unlikely as it seems, Murtaugh led the National League in steals with 18 as a rookie with the Phillies, even though he played in only 85 games.

He was a second baseman for the Phillies during the 1941, 1942 and 1943 seasons before he was inducted into the U.S. Army in 1944. Serving with the infantry, he was ambushed by German snipers near a farmhouse in Czechoslovakia. He saw service in both the European and Pacific theaters of war. He returned home in 1946. His sister's husband was a pilot in the war and was killed in action. So Danny moved his sister and her three children into his home until she remarried.

Murtaugh played for the Braves before he was traded to Pittsburgh.

On November 18, 1947, Murtaugh and outfielder Johnny Hopp were traded to the Pirates by the Braves for pitcher Al Lyons, catcher Bill Salkeld and outfielder Jimmy Russell.

He had his best season in 1948, hitting .290 for the Pirates. He teamed with Stan Rojek, a one-year wonder at shortstop, to give Bill Meyer a pretty good double-play combination in a four-way National League race won by the Braves.

Murtaugh remained with the Pirates through the 1951 season and the following year he became a player-manager at New Orleans in the old Southern Association. It was in New Orleans that Murtaugh first came in contact with Joe L. Brown, who was general manager of the New Orleans club.

Ballfans remember Murtaugh best as the manager of the 1960 World Series winners in Pittsburgh. Outhit by the Yankees, .338 to .256, and outscored by more than a 2-to-1 ratio (55 runs to 27), the underdog Pirates pulled a major upset in seven games. Mazeroski climaxed an incredible game with a tie-breaking home run that gave the Pirates a 10-9 triumph.

After the game, Murtaugh was sitting in his rocking chair, chewing tobacco, smoking a cigar and sipping on milk to calm an angry ulcer, and ruminating about his beloved Bucs.

Behind his desk, framed just above his head, was a bit of verse written by Edgar Guest, long-time newspaper rhymester who offered these lines:

"There are nine men out on the field of play,
"Nine men trying to win.
"But if you are a star, as the paper says,
"Who gets the run that brings you in? . . ."

Joe L. Brown burst into Murtaugh's office after that seventh game, hugged him and said, "You're the greatest manager in the world."

"Not the greatest," said Murtaugh, "but the most grateful."

As the 1960 season got underway, the Pirates were picked to finish in fourth or fifth place. But the Bucs beat back the challenge of, first, the San Francisco Giants, then of the Milwaukee Braves and, finally, of the St. Louis Cardinals.

As the Pirates appeal grew that year, Murtaugh became more and more in demand. He turned down money for interviews, and declined to do a paid TV show of his own for a Pittsburgh station. If there was any money to be had for public appearances, he had them send it to Children's Hospital in his behalf. He was always suggesting that they get the players to do interviews, commercials, shows and paid appearances. Shades of Chuck Noll, huh? Like Murtaugh, Noll also took in his sister and her children after his brother-in-law died.

Leo Durocher didn't know what he was talking about when he said, "Nice guys finish last."

After the seventh game, Murtaugh said, "Of course, it's my biggest thrill. What bigger thrill could a baseball manager have than to win the World Series? No, I can't put into words how I feel. Right now it would take a man with a better education than I have. Just let's say I'm mighty proud and mighty happy."

As the celebration whirled around him, Murtaugh announced, "I'm going to go home and listen to some music and rock in my rocking chair."

Murtaugh went home again . . . and again.

Daniel Edward Murtaugh returned to his home town of Chester each off-season, during his days as a player and as a manager. He was comfortable in Chester, like an old shoe.

He was born there, and he died there. There was a permanence about returning there each year that appealed to Murtaugh, a man not comfortable in the big city social scene.

When he was managing the Pirates, during the off-season, he still would help out on occasion behind the counter of his friend Jack McGovern's clothing store in Chester. McGovern had given him a job when he was a minor league second baseman, and Murtaugh didn't forget such kindnesses too quickly. So when McGovern needed an extra hand, Murtaugh just pitched in. He knew the routine. He knew how to mark up a suit for the tailor to make proper alterations. He knew how to ring up the cash register. To him, it was no big deal.

He met and married Kathleen Patricia Clark in Chester (on November 29, 1941), and they had their kids there, and their kids had their kids there.

He was born on October 8, 1917 in the ship-building and industrial city on the shores of the Delaware River near Philadelphia. His father was a shipyard worker, and Danny was the only boy in a family of five children. He grew up in a modest house in the Seventh Ward, a brawling Irish neighborhood populated by workingmen and politicians. It sounds just like The First Ward in Old Allegheny where Art Rooney resided in his youth.

Danny Murtaugh
at ease in clubhouse
office at Three Rivers

Murtaugh came up the hard way, and often said he came from the other side of the tracks. As a boy, he walked along rail road tracks picking up coal that had spilled out of passing cars so the family would have heat at home.

According to *Current Biography*, "Danny followed his father into the shipyards, where he worked for 34 cents an hour as a passer boy in a rivet gang and came to know what it felt like to have hot rivets flung inside his shirt. One day he was pinned down by a metal plate that had been dropped off a crane. On another occasion, two of his fellow workers were blown apart by a gas explosion fifty yards from where he was standing. At one time, he worked in a cereal factory as a wheat puffer, watching wheat kernels shoot from a cannonlike machine. At 21, he became a volunteer for the Franklin Fire Company in the Seventh Ward of Chester and narrowly escaped being trapped in a burning building."

Murtaugh played basketball for a team representing the shipyard in a local industrial basketball league. His ability as a basketball player, some say, was the main reason he got the job in the first place.

He broke into professional baseball in 1937, signing a contract with the St. Louis Cardinals after participating in a tryout camp, and was assigned to Cambridge, Maryland in the Eastern Shore League.

"You learn the lesson. As long as you manage, you're always going to be a rotten bastard. Or, in my case, a rotten little bastard."
— Earl Weaver of the Baltimore Orioles

The older he grew, the better Murtaugh managed. Of course, better talent may have had something to do with it. He was first in his division four of his last six seasons. The more he won the more he liked what he was doing.

"It's the players, not the manager, you know," Murtaugh might say when anyone asked too many questions about his role.

He had a run-in with Dock Ellis and had to put him in his place. Dick Stuart was a constant challenge. Murtaugh had a few rough times with Roberto Clemente. Early in his career, Clemente felt that Murtaugh considered him a malingerer. Later on, Murtaugh went out of his way to compliment Clemente and sound his praises to the press.

"But Roberto and I got along all right," Danny once declared. "I'm old enough, intelligent enough and, I think, smart enough to get along with anybody on our ballclub, especially if he's a .340 hitter.

"Roberto always gave me a hundred percent as a ball player. Our differences never have interfered with his performance on the field."

Murtaugh seldom cursed, and levied small fines for certain dugout cussing. "That will cost you," he simply told the offending player.

188

He platooned his players and that didn't always make him popular with whomever was sitting out that particular game. "I believe if you have 25 players on a ballclub, you should utilize them," he said, defending his handling of the lineup. "You shouldn't have a player on the bench you are afraid to use in a game."

He was loyal. He set a record by managing the same club four different times. Brown kept calling and he kept answering.

Bill Virdon, one of his loyal lieutenants, suggested his boss was improving. Virdon, who once played for Murtaugh, said of Murtaugh in the '70s, "Danny has a much better grasp of the game now than he did then. He has the game in his hands, and there isn't much that he misses."

Some sports writers wrote that he came back once too often, and remained too long. He said he wanted to go home and spend more time with the grandchildren. They were the biggest losers.

When Danny died, he drew praise from sports writers, Pirates administrators, and his former players.

"There was something so downright American about Danny Murtaugh, it makes you want to cry to think that he's gone," wrote Furman Bisher, the sports editor of the *Atlanta Journal-Constitution*. He called Murtaugh "a genuine soul."

Les Biederman, who covered the baseball beat for *The Pittsburgh Press* when Murtaugh was a player as well as a manager, wrote of him: "Murtaugh is a dutiful husband, a proud father and a man with a heart that beats as a human."

Bob Smizik, who later covered the Pirates for *The Pittsburgh Press*, wrote, "Danny Murtaugh will be remembered for many things. His success as a manager will be one of them, but not the foremost. Mainly, he will be remembered for his wonderful human qualities. He loved a good story, a good joke and a good time. And he loved people. Everywhere he went, Danny Murtaugh had friends."

During the 1960 World Series, what would appear to be a serious situation, Murtaugh found occasion to play a joke on John Drebinger of *The New York Times*, a veteran sports writer who wore a hearing aid. Drebinger could be a bit stuffy. He was a literate man who could have written his sports reports in Latin if he cared to. But he was a nice man, a good sport, and Murtaugh couldn't resist sticking pins into sports writers.

Murtaugh talked a few other sports writers into going along with his gag. Murtaugh appeared in front of a group of newsmen and started moving his lips, like he was talking, and the clued-in writers started scribbling notes feverishly in the front of the group. Drebinger removed his hearing aid and banged it a few times before he realized he had been had.

Murtaugh might stop an opposing team's sports writer in the morning at the coffee shop and ask him what he thought about his team's latest trade, a trade that had never been made, but had the sports writer wondering if he'd gotten up too late and missed a team transaction that his editor would be soon calling about to reprimand him.

When he traveled with the Pirates, Murtaugh enjoyed joking with waitresses and airline stewardesses. He found it difficult to hold late-night bed checks on his players because, as he used to say, "I can't stay up that late. They're all big boys and they should know what they're doing."

Some failed to find much humor in Murtaugh. Some saw him as a stoneface, who too often failed to respond appropriately with any answers of substance to their questions. They would hear about his rich humor from their peers in the press box, then catch Murtaugh after the game and get little to work with but a bunch of cliches, and over-boiled bromides.

"Do you have to have reasons for everything?" Murtaugh once scolded a reporter who was pressing him for information. "There's a lot of things I do and a lot of things I don't do without having reasons. That's the type I am."

Stan Isaacs of *Newsday*, liked Murtaugh, even though he wished the man were a little more colorful. "There's little that is lordlike and chest-thumping about Murtaugh," he wrote. "That's no exalted leader you see standing in the clubhouse amongst his players, quietly kibitzing a game of cards, looking like a man content just to be allowed in the joint."

Larry Merchant, an outstanding sports columnist for *The Philadelphia Daily News* and *The New York Post* before becoming the boxing analyst for HBO Sports, didn't share his colleague's enthusiasm for Murtaugh. "As a conversationalist and lecturer," wrote Merchant, "Murtaugh is in the same league with the statue of Honus Wagner behind Forbes Field."

Murtaugh even had critics at home. "My wife bawled me out the other night," Murtaugh once said. "She said, 'The least you can do when you go on TV is take the tobacco outta your mouth.'"

For that matter, Pirates managers have never been too concerned about how they looked on television. It's a team tradition to come off a bit seedy, or just plain bored.

No one was closer to Murtaugh than Joe Brown. When reporters complained to Brown about Murtaugh's reticence to discuss ballplayers individually, Brown responded by saying, "I can't put myself in Danny's mind. If it's true that he seldom discusses his players publicly, I haven't talked with him about it and, frankly, I don't care.

"There are some managers who feel their job is to be colorful for the press. Well, that's secondary or even tertiary."

Brown gave up his post as general manager of the Pirates just a few days before Murtaugh's retirement. Three months later, soon after he learned of Murtaugh's death, Brown was sobbing when he spoke to Pohla Smith of Pittsburgh's UPI bureau.

"I don't know the words," he said. "I haven't been close to many men as I was to Danny. He was my very dear friend and I said when he was alive that he was like my brother. I feel like I lost a second brother."

Brown's brother was killed in World War II.

"Danny was also my brother," Brown continued. "I loved him and I can't say anymore than that. He was an unusual human being, a fine, fine fellow. I ache for his family."

His players offered praise when they learned of Murtaugh's passing.

"I know there are a lot of great managers around," said Smoky Burgess, "but I've never seen a manager in the same category as Danny Murtaugh. He studied everything and got the most talent out of his players.

"You had to treat a Dick Stuart or a Dick Groat or myself differently. Danny did. He'd go to each of us and get the most from all of us."

Murtaugh chats with two Pittsburgh favorites, Bobby Del Greco (left) and Billy Mazeroski at Fort Myers.

Where Were You?

"I got confetti in my eyes."
—Gary Runco

Miles Span
Monroeville

"I gave away my tickets for that seventh game. I came into the park that day through Myron O'Brisky's office with Stuart and ElRoy. I was close to the players, and a good friend of Al Abrams, the sports editor of the *Post-Gazette*, and I could go into the locker room any time I wanted to."

Bill Spinella
Shaler Township

"I was self-employed at the time, and I had been listening to the seventh game on the radio when I went to the Keystone Lumber Company on Babcock Boulevard to get some building materials. It was in the ninth inning and the score was tied, 9-9. The guy at the desk was watching the game on TV. As I was standing there, Maz hit a home run. The man said, 'It took a Hunky to do it!' And he almost crawled into the TV set. He wouldn't even wait on me. I never got the materials."

Gary Runco
Glenshaw

"I was five in 1960, and we were riding in our family car with the windows open, trying to get from Bloomfield to Bellevue, and people were tossing all kind of stuff into the streets after the Pirates beat the Yankees. I got confetti in my eyes, and I cried all the way to my Grandma's house in Bellevue. But I became a big fan of Maz."

Stephen Bornyas
McKeesport

"I was in third grade at St. Nicholas Grade School in McKeesport. We were listening to the game on the radio in the schoolbus, but we got off the bus before the game was over. When I opened the door of our home, my mom was bouncing all over the floor on her backside. That's how I knew Maz hit the home run."

Mark Adler
Manufacturers Representative
Sewickley

"I grew up in the Bronx, at 163rd and Sheridan Avenue, and I was a big Yankees fan. I was ten at the time, and in the fifth grade at P.S. 35. That was my first World Series. We could sit in the bleachers at Yankee Stadium for $3. My mother sat by the TV each day and watched the games. I was in school when Maz hit the home run. We watched it on TV. I can remember Yogi turning his back and watching it go.

192

I had just become aware of baseball the year before. I had never heard of the Pirates. I didn't know who Roberto Clemente was. We were American League fans. I would go to Yankee Stadium by myself. It was difficult. We were used to the Yankees winning. I just bought four photos of Mickey Mantle; I'm still a Yankees fan. But I've had season tickets for the Pirates the past five years."

Diane Laughner Esswein
Bellevue, Pa.

"I was born on October 13, 1960 at Butler Hospital. My dad wanted to call me Mazzie. I went to a party for Pirates season ticket holders in 1990 at the Allegheny Club at Three Rivers Stadium and Maz was there. I won a lithograph showing all the great players in Pirates history, including Maz. Maz presented the lithograph to me, and I told him that I was born on the same day he hit the home run. He said, 'Now it's finally worth something to you.' I have a blow-up of a photo that was taken of the presentation with Maz, and it's on display in my living room. Someone asked me if Maz was my dad. Today, that lithograph is worth as much as $1,200."

Brad Simon
Chester Environmental
Bethel Park, Pa.

"Roberto Clemente really got me interested in baseball. I still have a batting helmet that belonged to him. I watched a lot of games at the ballpark and on TV with my grandfather, and he knew I loved Clemente. I played baseball at Gannon College, and in the Appalachian League. I was also on the Al's Cafe team that won the national slow-pitch softball championship in the '70s. Clemente gave me a tip on how to grip the ball and get it out of your glove quickly, and I never did it any other way after that. My father and his father all loved Bill Mazeroski. It was awesome when he hit that home run and they never stopped talking about it."

Ed Lutz
President, Cold-Comp Typesetting
Pittsburgh, Pa.

"I was working as a pressman at Reliable Printing Co. and going to night school at Carnegie Tech. When Maz hit the home run everybody went crazy at the printing plant and the owner shut down the business and sent us home. Everyone went out to party. I went home to Baldwin and changed to go to class. It was impossible to get back into town, so I drove through Hays and up through Homestead and across the High Level Bridge and through Squirrel Hill to Carnegie Tech. I had a class in layout and design. I was hoping the class would be cancelled, but it wasn't. I didn't celebrate till later that night."

Stan Goldmann
Chairman, Geyer Printing
Oakland

"My daughter Randi was four months old, and my wife and I dropped her off at my mother-in-law's before we went to Forbes Field. We had reserved seats on the third base side, in the last row. I just about jumped out of the stadium when Maz hit that home run. I dropped my wife off at my mother-in-law's and I picked up a good friend of mine and we went Downtown to celebrate, and we didn't get home till the next morning. One of the places we went to was Robert's Restaurant, a deli on Liberty Avenue between Sixth and Seventh, which was owned by my brother-in-law, Bobby Weinstein. Bobby Layne of the Steelers was there, along with Ernie Stautner and Tom 'The Bomb' Tracy and they were, literally, drinking the place dry. I got Layne to sign my World Series ticket stubs. I still have them. They were first floor reserved for $7.70 apiece. My seat was Section 18, Row Y, Seat 28. Who else has tickets from the seventh game of the 1960 World Series signed by Bobby Layne?"

Rich Corson
McMurray, Pa.

"I lived in Beaver back then. I was 18 and I was just starting out at Robert Morris College. My dad got tickets and we were sitting in the upper deck in right field, near the foul pole. When Yogi Berra hit a home run in the sixth inning the ball went just past us and just inside the foul pole. It put the Yankees ahead, 5-4. Everyone was so down. It was such a mood swing when Hal Smith hit the home run in the eighth inning. When Maz hit it, I had a perfect view. It looked like a rainbow. Everybody was ecstatic. We asked the streetcar motorman if he was going Downtown. He said, 'Hop on, we'll get there eventually.' Everybody was just so happy. There was nothing but joy in the city that day — no riots — everybody was everybody's friend. I still have my ticket from that seventh game of the World Series."

MERRY CHRISTMAS — HAPPY NEW YEAR

Rich Corson shows off painting of Maz's Series-winning home run in his family room McMurray. Corson's 1960 Christmas card is shown at right. He remains a big fan of the Bu

194

Casey Stengel
An Amazin' Manager

"He made more fans for baseball
than any man who ever lived."
— Bowie Kuhn, Former Baseball Commissioner
Eulogy to Stengel, October 6, 1975

Casey Stengel's last game as manager of the New York Yankees was the seventh game of the 1960 World Series in Pittsburgh. A week later, at age 70, he was pushed into retirement by Yankees' management. They said he had resigned, but that was merely a euphemism for being fired.

Two days after the cheering stopped in Pittsburgh, the news of Stengel's dismissal was announced in New York.

"You're goddamn right I was fired," Stengel growled at his press conference. It ended the most successful run in the club's history.

That is how upset the Yankees were about losing to the Pirates. They felt they had the best team in baseball, and that Stengel had somehow come up short with it. He had helped build a dynasty that would win four more American League flags before the talent ran out in 1965, but he became the scapegoat.

His teams had won ten pennants in 12 years, and seven World Series championships, but suddenly he was too old. "I'll never make the mistake of being 70 again," he said.

"They examined all my organs," Stengel said proudly, trying to make the best of a bad deal. "Some of them are quite remarkable and others are not so good. A lot of museums are bidding for them."

Two years later, Stengel surfaced as the manager of the newborn New York Mets. Suddenly he was young again.

When Forbes Field was leveled in the early '70s, I was able to salvage some souvenirs from the wrecking company. A night watchman gave me a clump of bricks, about three bricks worth, from the outfield wall, a signboard listing ticket exchange prices, and a nameplate that was slipped over Stengel's dressing stall whenever the Mets came to Forbes Field.

It is a black metal plate that says simply CASEY on it. It is a prized possession.

A lot of people don't know this, but Stengel played right field for the Pirates during the 1918 and 1919 seasons.

I had two brief encounters with Stengel in my life and both were enlightening and memorable. At least to me.

The first came in 1962 when he was the manager of the Mets. His team had lost its initial nine games of the season before winning for the first time against the Pirates in Pittsburgh.

I was a junior at the University of Pittsburgh at the time, and had an office in *The Pitt News* office in the Student Union, just a block away from Forbes Field. I had an assignment from a local scholastic sports magazine to interview Stengel about a batboy he once had when he was with the Yankees. This batboy had been special, so special the Yankees paid his way to attend college. His name was Carmello Villante, and he went to Lafayette College courtesy of the Yankees.

It boggles my mind now to consider what I did that day. Here's the Mets winning for the first time in their first ten outings, and I am in the clubhouse after the game to speak to Stengel about a batboy from the Yankees.

Later in life, I would cover baseball and the Mets and the Yankees for *The New York Post*, and I got to know all the New York sports writers. They were an intense group, and they took themselves quite seriously.

No one could handle sports writers more skillfully than Stengel. He had those big floppy ears, like those of a basset hound, and he was something of a caricature of himself. But he was a lovable figure. He suffered sports writers well. He was a decent man.

Looking back, as best I can, I think I had the good sense to wait until all the sports writers were finished talking to Stengel about the ballgame before I brought up the batboy business. I hope so. If I had interrupted the regular questioning to ask about a Yankees' batboy, I believe I would have been tarred and feathered right on the spot by the New York newsmen.

Now I know the kind of looks, or comments they would make, whenever a newcomer to the clubhouse exchanges would change the subject to something that had nothing to do with that particular contest. Or when someone went off on a sidebar subject, or something for a doctoral thesis.

I remember standing in the back of a pack of reporters, waiting for my turn, when the Mets' Frank Thomas, who had formerly played for the Pirates and had been the team's best home run hitter since Ralph Kiner, started hollering at the reporters from across the locker room.

"Lookit all those friggin' frontrunners!" shouted Thomas. "Where were they before? Now that we're winning, they want to kiss up to us!"

Stengel flinched and closed his eyes in a theatrical manner when he heard Thomas ranting and raving. He held up his hand to quiet Thomas. Then he went about the business of fielding all the questions that came his way.

I remember that Stengel spoke to me at length about the batboy. He gave me some delightful stories. He dressed as we talked, sitting on a stool to pull off his long blue stockings, but I felt like he was giving me quality time. After losing the first nine games as manager of the Mets, maybe Stengel was glad to talk about his days with the Yankees. He was animated, funny, and helped me out a great deal with my assignment.

It was not the last time he would come to the rescue of a young journalist.

About ten years later, I attended an Old Timers Game at Yankee Stadium as a reporter for *The New York Post*. The Yankees were the first team to hold Old Timers Games. No one did it better. I have always enjoyed such gatherings.

I was in the stadium's dining area after the game at a special party held for those participating in the Old Timers Game. It might have been in 1972, but I'm not sure. Among the special guests were the wives of Babe Ruth and Lou Gehrig. I should say the widows of Ruth and Gehrig. I sat with both of them at a table in the middle of the room, and just eavesdropped on their conversation.

I was just enjoying it. I was there as a reporter, but also as a fan. This was as close to Ruth and Gehrig I was ever going to get. Mrs. Ruth and Mrs. Gehrig were not good friends. They were too different for that. Mrs. Ruth liked to drink as much as her husband did, and Mrs. Gehrig was as straight an arrow as her late husband.

I made the mistake of trying to keep up with Mrs. Ruth instead of showing the temperance of Mrs. Gehrig. Had I stayed longer, I feel that Mrs. Ruth would have drunk me right under the table.

I had an awful looking Fu Manchu mustache adorning my upper lip in those days, and my hair was long, neck-length if not shoulder-length. I looked like Pancho Villa, or one of his sidekicks. I shudder when I see photos from those days. But it doesn't, strangely enough perhaps, make me any more tolerant of some of the haircuts of today's young people.

That mustache and hair got me into a jam with some of the Yankees of the past. Two in particular come to mind. Don Larsen, who had pitched the perfect game in the 1956 World Series against the Dodgers, and Hank Bauer, whose face had once been described as looking like "a clenched fist," both had crewcuts, just like they wore when they were starring for the Yankees.

Larsen, like Bill Mazeroski, did something in a World Series no one else had ever done, before or since. Just as everybody who saw the 1960 World Series game will remember seeing Yogi Berra motionless at the base of the wall as Maz's home run disappeared into Schenley Park, they also remember Berra running out and leaping into the arms of Larsen after Larsen's perfect 2-0 no-hit, no-run game on October 8, 1956.

Larsen and Bauer both started giving me a hard time, and ridiculing my hairlength and my mustache. They got brutal. I was debating the issue with them, and losing, and looking for a way out when Stengel stepped into the midst of the argument.

"Hey, lay off this young man," said Stengel, scolding them. "He's OK. Quit giving him a hard time over his hair. I tried to grow a mustache once . . . But it came in green. So I gave up on it."

With that, both Bauer and Larsen started smiling, then laughing out loud. Stengel had suceeded in breaking the tension, as he must have done on so many occasions in his clubhouse. He knew I was in trouble and he knew the best way to get me out of trouble.

I have never forgotten Stengel's kind gesture.

I scolded myself the next day because I thought I had stayed too long and drank too much in the company of those Yankees. I remember leaving Yankee Stadium that night, and stopping at a bar on the East Side of New York. I spent some time with another sports writer, Pete Alfano, before driving home to Long Island. It was risky business. The Yankees were not good models in that respect.

Larsen and Bauer both liked their booze. Larsen once fell asleep and hit a bakery truck and wrapped his car around a telephone pole at 4 a.m. in St. Petersburg, Florida. That telephone pole "which jumped out at him," as Stengel said late in the 1956 season.

Larsen recalled that incident during the 1978 season. He was grateful to Stengel for getting him out of a jam. "I knew he stuck up for me," said Larsen. "I always tried to pitch my hardest for him after that."

Stengel liked to drink. Bourbon and soda was his personal poison. He always had a drink or a cigarette in hand. Most times, he nursed his drink because he was too busy talking. Stengel knew something about drinking.

"I had this player in Brooklyn," Stengel once said, "and you could ask him for a match and find out what bar he was at the night before by the matchbook he was holding. After we traded him to another club I always went up to him before the game with a cigarette and asked him for a match. If he pulled out a match from some bar, I knew he had been out late and I could pitch him fastballs."

"I can't believe it."
— Yogi Berra

The Pirates were a surprise opponent for the Yankees in the 1960 World Series. The Pirates had not won the National League pennant since Babe Ruth and his "Murderers Row" colleagues had swept them in the 1927 World Series. The Pirates had not won a World Series since 1925.

The Yankees still had an awesome lineup. The Yankees set World Series records in 1960 for runs (55), hits (91), extra-base hits (27) and batting average (.338). They had drubbed the Pirates 16-3, 10-0 and 12-0. They did everything possible in a Series — except win it.

Stengel is still second-guessed for using Art Ditmar, a seven-year veteran who had pitched in three previous Series games in relief, as the starter for the opening game. The Pirates piled up three runs in the first inning and knocked him out en route to a 6-4 victory. Whitey Ford has never forgiven Stengel for not giving him the ball for that game. Ford won his two starts in the Series, but would have had a third start if he had been picked to pitch the opener.

It came down to the last innings of the last game.

In the home half of the eighth inning, Bill Virdon hit a hard ground ball that bounced off the concrete-like Pittsburgh infield and struck Tony

taugh and Stengel at '60 World Series

Stengel as a Pirate (1918-19)

Stengel with Clemente

Author Jim O'Brien with some of his personal
souvenirs from Forbes Field

Kubek in the throat. It was a double play ball that would have ended the inning. But the Bucs capitalized on that lucky bounce, and managed to stay alive. Hal Smith hit a two-out three-run homer to put the Pirates ahead again, 9-7.

The Yankees scored two runs at the top of the ninth to tie the game. And, of course, Bill Mazeroski hit the home run to win the game in the bottom of the ninth inning.

"I can't believe it," moaned leftfielder Yogi Berra.

"I'll never believe it," said Yankees' pinch-hitter Dale Long, a former Pirate.

After the game, Stengel was seen heaving a soaking-wet uniform shirt into his locker. Mickey Mantle was weeping. He would later say it was the most disappointing defeat of his baseball career. He knew the Yankees were the better team. Ralph Terry, the victim of the most memorable home run ever, sat immobile against a wall, his face buried in his hand, his shoulders bent in pain. Blood was seeping off a cloth on Kubek's neck. He had come back from a nearby hospital.

It was Stengel's neck, though, with its loose-hanging flesh, that was really at risk.

Stengel walked around the clubhouse. He threw his shoe to the floor, and walked around with one shoe on, and one shoe off, according to a report by Maury Allen of *The New York Post*. Stengel checked on Kubek.

Terry told his manager, "I hate to have it end this way."

"How were you operatin'?" Stengel asked him. "What were you tryin' to throw him?"

"I was trying to keep it low," Terry replied.

"As long as you were trying to pitch him the right way, I'm gonna sleep easy at night," said Stengel.

His appearance belied his upbeat remarks, however. Sweat was pouring from his head. The visitors' clubhouse at Forbes Field was as warm as the room where they had the cactus plants at the nearby Phipps Conservatory in Schenley Park. It was small, cramped and steamy. Stengel walked around muttering to himself.

"What about next year?" screamed a reporter.

"How do I know about next year?" said Stengel. "Some people my age are dead at this point in time."

"Will you be back?" a reporter persisted.

"God damnit, I just told ya, I ain't gonna tell you anything about it because I don't make my living here. Now go back and tell that to your editors."

He wouldn't discuss his future or the game. "Go ask the players," he said, "they lost it."

The man had just passed his 70th birthday. He had won ten pennants in 12 years, and had won the World Series seven times, but his days with the Yankees were nearly over. On October 18, 1960, he stepped down as the Yankees' manager.

That ball that bounced into Kubek's throat was still sticking in his own throat. "What if the ball don't hit him in the throat, dontcha think we win it and I'm out with a championship even though I'm discharged," said Stengel.

Branch Rickey was busy at the same time trying to put together a new baseball league, the Continental League, but Major League Baseball nipped that in the bud. The American League was expanded by two teams in Minnesota and Los Angeles for the 1961 season. With the aid of a New York lawyer named Bill Shea, a new franchise was formed in New York, and another National League franchise was added in Houston. They were to start play in 1962.

Charles D. Stengel was then working for his brother-in-law as the vice-president of a bank in Glendale, California. During that same 1961 season, Mantle and Roger Maris had a great home run race, and Maris ended up hitting 61 home runs to break Babe Ruth's one season record. Mantle finished with 54.

Construction soon started for Shea Stadium, named in honor of that New York lawyer, and next door buildings were going up for the World's Fair, to be held in 1964. I went to that World's Fair twice.

On October 12, 1961, just one day shy of a year since he last managed the Yankees in Pittsburgh, Stengel was named the manager of the New York Mets by George Weiss, who himself had formerly been a Yankees' front office executive. Stengel signed a one-year contract calling for $100,000.

Some of his original players were former Pirates like Frank Thomas, Gus Bell, Lee Walls, Joe Christopher and Clem Labine. The Mets soon became known as the "Amazin' Mets," and Stengel was the perfect manager for this strange assortment of ballplayers. Of Stengel, the team's traveling secretary Lou Niss said, "He was the world's greatest salesman."

The outfielders in the team's starting lineup were Thomas, who had six children, Bell, who had eight children, and Richie Ashburn, who had three children. Before the season started, Stengel said, "If they produce as well on the field as off, we'll win the pennant."

The Mets played their first game against the Pirates at the Polo Grounds, which had formerly been the home of the New York Giants. Bob Friend was the starting pitcher for the Pirates. Alvin Jackson, a small pitcher originally from the Pirates' organization, started for the Mets. History has it that someone showed up with a banner in the stands that day that read: "Let's Go, Mets." It was the beginning of a banner existence for the Mets in New York. The Pirates won that game, 4-3.

The Mets lost nine in a row before Jay Hook beat the Pirates, 9-1, in Pittsburgh. Backup catcher Joe Ginsberg raced through the clubhouse shouting, "Break up the Mets!" That was the day I first entered a major league baseball clubhouse with a notebook in hand.

Who would have known that ten years later I would be going to St. Petersburg, Florida with my wife, Kathie, to cover the Mets for *The New York Post*. The custom in those days was to switch beats at midseason after the All-Star Game break, so I swapped the Mets for the

201

Yankees with Maury Allen. No sports writer ever wrote about baseball with more enthusiasm and joy than Maury Allen. Some cynics in the business looked upon his love for the game and its combatants as a weakness in his makeup. I never bought that.

Stengel floated around the locker room after his Mets won their first game in ten outings. according to Allen's book, *You Could Look It Up* (Times Books, 1979). "I'm gonna let Hook pitch every day," said Stengel. "He'll go in the next hundred games so I can win the pennant. We shouldna lost the first nine and I don't see how we lost a game. That darn streak cost us the pennant. We might win the next twenty straight."

He admitted his Mets had messed up quite a bit when they were losing all those games at the outset of the 1962 season. "When you're losin', everybody commences playin' stupid," said Stengel.

That Mets team got off to a 5-16 start. As bad as they were, one of their broadcasters, Ralph Kiner, insisted that the 1952 Pirates (42-112) that he played for were even worse.

Stengel was good at getting laughs and taking the media's focus away from his team's ineptness.

"Can't anybody play this here game?" he asked at one point. It became the title of a book by Jimmy Breslin, with a few words switched around, as in *Can't Anybody Here Play This Game?*

Stengel smoked a lot. "No, I don't smoke all the time," he said, when questioned about his bad habit. "I stop when I go to sleep."

In Pittsburgh, he pointed up one of the city's own shortcomings. He liked to talk about the Bridge to Nowhere, the Fort Duquesne Bridge that stopped at the edge of the Allegheny River, and went a long time before being completed.

The Pirates beat the Mets, 4-3, in their first game at Shea Stadium before a crowd of 50,312. It was the same score by which the Pirates had beaten the Mets in their debut at the Polo Grounds. The Pirates won the second game as well. But the Mets, with Al Jackson pitching a shutout, beat the Pirates, 6-0, in the third game. This time it was Rod Kanehl who cried out in the clubhouse, "Break up the Mets!"

They came to Pittsburgh for a followup series, and the Mets' bus pulled up in front of the Hilton Hotel at the Point. There were helmeted policemen all over the place. Stengel said, "Whatta we done now?"

One of the policemen told a club official, "We just had President Johnson here. He gave a speech on poverty."

When Stengel heard that, he said, "He picked the right team."

One day a fan came up to Stengel in the lobby of the Hilton Hotel in Pittsburgh, and asked him for his autograph. Stengel obliged him. "I'm a Yankee fan," said the man, proudly. "I loved it when you managed the Yankees."

Stengel's jaw stiffened and he scowled, "I work for the Mets." And he turned and exited the lobby in a rush.

Yogi Berra became the manager of the Yankees in 1964, but it didn't work out. The next year, Berra and Warren Spahn both became coaches on Stengel's staff. "I got 'em because they add brains to the team," said Stengel.

The Mets held a party in Stengel's honor to help him celebrate his 75th birthday. It was part of an Old Timers Game promotion at Shea.

Stengel slipped on a wet floor in the bathroom that night and broke his hip and underwent surgery the next day.

In 1968, Gil Hodges took over as manager of the Mets.

In August of 1970, the Yankees held an Old Timers Game and Michael Burke, the team's president, prevailed upon Stengel, who had refused earlier invitations to come back to Yankee Stadium, to attend ceremonies at which his No. 37 would be retired. Among those present were Mickey Mantle, Whitey Ford, Yogi Berra, Tony Kubek, Bobby Richardson, Hank Bauer and Don Larsen.

"Don't worry none about Yogi," Stengel said that night at a post-game party. "They ain't throwin' no benefits for him."

I covered the Mets at spring training in 1972. On April 2, just before the ballclub was to break camp and head north to start the season in Pittsburgh, Hodges suffered a second and fatal heart attack. Berra became the manager of the Mets.

In early October of 1975, Stengel died. In delivering a eulogy, baseball commissioner Bowie Kuhn said, "He made more fans for baseball than any man who ever lived."

Casey Stengel at '60 World Series

Ralph Kiner
Kiner's Korner Started With '60 Series

*"He had a home run swing. When he made
contact with the ball, it went somewhere."*
— Hank Greenberg

R alph Kiner's career as a baseball broadcaster began with the
1960 World Series in Pittsburgh. And he has been at it ever
since.

In early October of 1960, Kiner came back to Pittsburgh, where
he had been the biggest of sports heroes and the National League's leading home run hitter all seven seasons (1946-1952) he played for the
Pirates. His assignment was to work the World Series pitting the Pirates
against the New York Yankees. He did a post-game interview show with
the star of the day for Channel 11.

It was strictly a free-lance assignment, a four-game stint as it
turned out, because he did the show only after the games in Pittsburgh,
but it was a World Series he won't soon forget. "It was a weird World
Series," recalled Kiner.

He was then in his fifth year as the general manager of the San
Diego Padres, then a Triple A team in the Pacific Coast League, and
he had planned on attending the World Series games anyhow. So broadcasting them was a real bonus.

"Part of my job in San Diego was to get ballplayers for the team,
so I'd go to the World Series and all the major league meetings to talk
to baseball people, and to make contacts," said Kiner. "It was a good
job, and I was planning on staying in baseball in the front office. I forget which TV station asked me if I was interested in working the World
Series, but I know that Bob Prince suggested they call me.

"I was going to be here anyhow, so I thought it was a great chance
to make some extra money. I had never done any TV, other than being
a guest, but I thought I could handle it. It was the kind of thing I'm
doing now with Kiner's Korner."

It was the first time he had ever done anything like that, and his
four-game effort led to offers to join the broadcasting teams with the
Chicago White Sox and the Cincinnati Reds. Executives of those teams
had caught his act in Pittsburgh and liked what they saw.

"I got lucky," said Kiner. "They had been looking for somebody
to do that show in Pittsburgh, and I think they tried everybody. Nobody was available. Bob Prince was involved somehow and he said, 'Why
don't you ask Ralph Kiner?'"

The 1960 World Series was an audition in baseball announcing
for Kiner, so to speak, and he benefitted from it, amazingly enough, even
more than Bill Mazeroski, the hero of the Pirates' championship series.

Kiner chose to work with the White Sox, and a year later he left Chicago in favor of New York and an opportunity to broadcast the ballgames for a new franchise in the National League, the Mets. It was the beginning of an amazin' run for Kiner and the Mets.

Kiner was completing his 31st year with the Mets when we met on a beautiful fall day, Saturday, September 26, 1992 — it was sunny after an early-morning drizzle, with the temperature at 78 degrees — for an enjoyable three hour chat about his baseball career.

The Mets were playing the Pirates at Three Rivers Stadium during our interview, but Kiner had the day off. The game was on the CBS-TV network, so the Mets' regular station, WWOR-TV in New York, was not carrying it. One of Kiner's cohorts, Tim McCarver, moved over to CBS-TV for the assignment, working with play-by-play announcer Sean McDonough.

Kiner had begun his career with the Mets in 1962 along with Lindsey Nelson and Bob Murphy. That trio stayed intact for 17 years. Nelson left the Mets' broadcast booth in 1978 and has since died. But Murphy and Kiner continued to call the shots at Mets' games. "I still enjoy it, and I'm looking forward to working again next season," commented Kiner.

Kiner was an icon from my youth, one of my first sports heroes. So it was still a thrill to talk to him at such length, if I remembered how I felt about him when I was first learning how to play ball. When I mentioned to him that I recently spent some time with "Bullet Bill" Dudley, a Pro Football Hall of Famer who had seen early service with the Steelers, I was surprised when Kiner said, "Hey, there's one of my contemporaries." I didn't think Kiner was quite as old as Dudley.

But, as Casey Stengel would say, you could look it up. Dudley and Kiner were both playing in Pittsburgh in 1946 — it was Kiner's rookie season in the big leagues and Dudley's last with the Steelers before he was traded to the Lions — and both were 69 when I spoke with them. "I'll be 70 on October 27," said Kiner. "It's been quite a run, a great run.

"I've never missed a Mets' game in 31 years because of health problems; I've missed a few because I took days off, but that's it."

Kiner's countenance showed considerable mileage. His face was fuller, and more lined, than when he put fear into opposing pitchers during his days with the Pirates, Cubs and Indians. It was freshly sunburned as he had been out playing golf that day with Gil Lucas, a Pittsburgh-based executive with the KBL sports channel, at the Alcoma Golf Club in Penn Hills.

We met at Motions, a classy bar-grill off the lobby of the Vista International Hotel at the north end of Downtown Pittsburgh. The Mets were staying there. Kiner was counting his blessings over his good fortune in not having to broadcast this particular ballgame. The Pirates blasted the Mets, 19-2, behind Bob Walk — one of the slowest-working pitchers in the major leagues — to close within one game of clinching the National League East pennant for the third straight season.

Kiner was round-shouldered, but still a big man with big hands. He wore an open-collared light blue shirt, a plain gold necklace, and a gold bracelet, and white slacks. We sat on high stools at a small, circular table on a level just above the bar, and frequently checked out a nearby movie-size screen to catch some college football action or scores.

He smoked a cigar — he said he smokes about three a day — and he drank Monterey Cabernet Sauvignon, a red wine from his native California. Gin used to be his favorite drink, but he has cut back on that consumption considerably, he said, as a concession to his age.

As a kid, I considered Kiner the greatest. I was delivering the *Pittsburgh Post-Gazette* during his latter days with the Pirates, and I used to devour the daily sports section, especially enjoying the special tabloid section about the Bucs before spring training opened each year.

I was writing for *The New York Post*, and had been on the baseball beat with the Mets and the Yankees, when Kiner was voted into the Baseball Hall of Fame in 1975. I made a point to go to Cooperstown, N.Y., for his induction ceremonies, asking for the assignment at *The Post*, because he had always been such a favorite of mine. We first met in New York in 1970, and my Pittsburgh heritage gave me an advantage in hitting it off with him right away. Heck, I was one of his fans. I was always in Kiner's Korner.

We both smiled as soon as we spotted each other in the lobby of the Vista, even though it had been 15 years since we were last together. He was coming off the elevator, following a post-golf shower. He looked fresh as can be. I didn't notice anyone in the lobby looking at him, or showing any signs of recognition. No one approached him for an autograph. That never would have happened back when he was the prime power-hitter for the Pirates.

Later on, I spotted John Franco, the $4 million relief pitcher for the Mets, signing some autographs for some kids at the entrance to the Vista, appearing bored and saying nothing to them. Cops signing traffic tickets do so with more enthusiasm. "It's all changed today," said Kiner, shrugging his round shoulders.

Toward the end of our conversation at the hotel bar, Kiner was approached by a gentleman who appeared to be in his 60s, and who spoke softly, but assuredly. "Ralph Kiner, right?" the man said for openers. "I just wanted to shake your hand. I used to watch you. There was nothing like seeing that ball go over the scoreboard. You were always a class act. I wish we had ballplayers like you today."

Then the man left. Kiner was quiet. Kiner's craggy face is still recognizable to ballfans around the country because many of them catch "Kiner's Korner" after Mets' telecasts on cable TV. But an appearance by Kiner in a Pittsburgh hotel lobby doesn't stir up the local citizens like it once did. So I asked Kiner how he felt about what the fan had just said to him.

"When people are like that," Ralph Kiner came back, "it's meaningful. It's nice to be remembered."

Kiner is a candid individual when he does his baseball broadcasts. He calls them as he sees them, for the most part. He is one of the few honest men in America when it comes to Bill Mazeroski's heroic home run to lead off the bottom of the ninth inning in the final game of that 1960 World Series.

So many men, and women, insist they were at Forbes Field when it happened. "The park held about 37,000 people at best," said Kiner, "and at least 500,000 were there that day, if you believed everybody who says they were there.

"I was here for the seventh game of the World Series, but I never saw Mazeroski's home run. I was on my way to the TV station to do the post-game report. I never saw it. Neither did Bob Prince see it. He was outside the Yankees' clubhouse, figuring they were going to win it. They told him to go to the Pirates' clubhouse. That's where the winners would be.

"After my show, I was part of the crowd that filled the city. It was the most unbelievable spontaneous scene or celebration I've ever seen. We were going to the LeMont Restaurant on Mt. Washington. We were going to have dinner with Bob and Betty Prince. It was usually about a 15 minute ride, but it took us an hour and a half to get there.

"Jim Blandi owned the LeMont; he still does. When I first met him, he ran a place called The Playhouse Restaurant. It was a private club at The Playhouse. It was the only place I could go in this town when I was playing ball where no one would bother me. After I left town, he opened the Park Schenley on Forbes Avenue, a block from Forbes Field, and I'd go there when I came to town. I would go to Klein's and the Cork & Bottle once in a while, too. Some days we went to the Nixon, where they had a supper club. Jim Blandi's place on Mt. Washington was the first of the real glamour spots in this city, as restaurants go."

I mentioned that I heard about how Prince talked Kiner into investing in a restaurant in Oakland, near the corner of Craig Street and Centre Avenue. "It was called The Cameo," recalled Kiner. It could have been called The Black Hole of Calcutta, the way money went down the drain for Kiner and Prince in that ill-fated project.

"I got traded to the Cubs soon after we bought the restaurant, so I was almost never there," recalled Kiner. "Prince was around all the time. He was buying drinks for everybody, which is one of the reasons we quickly went out of business. That's why we didn't make any money.

"Prince and I were very close. We got that way through osmosis, I think. He was the announcer, and he sorta latched on to me. We had a close relationship. He'd come out to Palm Springs and stay with me on occasion during the winter months. He was one of the ushers at my first wedding. He was sort of an agent for me. We shared an office in the Oliver Building."

Kiner wasn't that close to many of the Pirates who played on the 1960 World Series team. "I was never that involved with that bunch," he said. "Dick Groat was my roommate when he was a rookie in 1952. I had played a little with Bob Friend, and Vernon Law had been with

Kiner receives "high five" congratulations from his wife DiAnn at his night at Three Rivers Stadium as former teammates Pete Castiglione (left) and Frank Gustine look on.

Ralph Kiner for WWOR-TV

Kiner with Casey Stengel

"Gone . . . glimmering through the dreams that were."
—Byron

Ralph and DiAnn Kiner wave to crowd at Three Rivers Stadium.

us in spring training in my last year in Pittsburgh. And I played with Murtaugh; that's about it."

I mentioned to Kiner that Groat had told me he always appreciated Kiner's kindnesses when it came to dining on the road with the Pirates. "Kiner would let you pick up a check for breakfast or lunch," said Groat, "so you wouldn't feel like he was carrying you, but he always grabbed the big check at dinner time. I admired him for that."

When he heard that story, Kiner shrugged. "I always felt I should do that," he said. "I was making a lot more money than those guys. The whole infield that year was making about $24,000 total. They were all making the minimum of $6,000 a season. Wally Westlake and Murray Dickson were the only guys making any decent money. The whole payroll had to be less than a quarter million."

Kiner could not remember most of his teammates by name, off the top of his graying head, but he mentioned Murtaugh, an infielder who would manage the 1960 Pirates to a pennant and World Series championship, and Dick Cole. He mentioned two young men who came out of Pittsburgh's Hill District to stick with the Pirates, notably Bobby Del Greco and Tony Bartirome.

"As a ballplayer, Murtaugh was a hard-nosed second baseman," said Kiner, "who could run with a body that didn't figure to be able to run.

"He was one of the most subtle pranksters I ever met. He could spit tobacco juice better than anybody. He could hit your shoes from 30 feet away. He had a lot of fun on the train rides. He would have been the last guy I'd have thought would be a good manager. He was an Irishman's Irishman."

What was Kiner's impression of Roberto Clemente?

"I had him on Kiner's Korner once after a game when he went four-for-four against the Mets. And all he did was complain that he had been hurting for five days. He had a reputation for complaining about various hurts and ailments, and never being satisfied. Joe Durso of the *New York Times* asked me to read and review Clemente's book. I got the impression he felt he was never appreciated. He felt he was a much better ballplayer than anybody else who played the game.

"Bob Prince was close to him, and liked him. In his own mind, Clemente thought he was the greatest player in the game. I don't know about that, but I thought he was right up there with guys like Stan Musial."

Musial has always been a favorite in Pittsburgh because he came from nearby Donora. What did Kiner think of Musial?

"Stan Musial was a good friend of mine," said Kiner. "Stan Musial was Frankie Gustine with a better batting average. He was a terrific guy. Stan Musial was one of the greatest hitters who ever played the game."

Kiner's memory of Groat, in particular, was a positive one. "I remember him being extremely polite, and a well-mannered kid who was scared to death when he first came to the big leagues from college," said Kiner. Groat, who grew up in Swissvale, just east of Pittsburgh, was signed by Branch Rickey after he had starred in baseball and basketball at Duke.

"Groat was extremely competitive as a ballplayer, and extremely confident," said Kiner. "He was smart as hell, and he picked up quickly on what he needed to know. He asked a lot of questions.

"I always took a lot of extra batting practice, and he asked to participate. In my last season, in my last series in Cincinnati, we had an off-day, and I wanted to go out to the ballpark and take some extra batting practice. I wasn't hitting the ball well, and I wanted to lead the league in home runs. Dick came out and pitched to me. I hit a home run the next night and ended up tied for the league lead at 37 home runs with Hank Sauer of Chicago.

"I held out the next year because Branch Rickey wanted to cut my salary the maximum 25 per cent. He'd have cut me more if he could have."

That's when Rickey made the famous remark when Kiner complained about having his salary cut after leading or tying for the lead in home runs for seven straight seasons. "We finished last with you," Rickey retorted, "and we can finish last without you."

Kiner felt he deserved a raise because, individually, he had always done more than his share for the Pirates. At the close of the 1992 season, Kiner's seven-year streak of home run leadership was still unmatched in either league. Even Babe Ruth, whom Kiner regards as the greatest baseball player of all time, never did it. Kiner hit 23 home runs to lead the league as a rookie. Over the next six years, he hit 51, 40, 54, 47, 42 and 37 home runs. Kiner's 301 homeruns for the Pirates was second in team history only to Willie Stargell's 475 homeruns, who played for the Pirates a team record 21 seasons, three times longer than Kiner. Consider this, however: Kiner hit a homerun 7.1 times per 100 at-bats, second only to Babe Ruth in baseball history. His slugging percentage (extra-base hit totals per at bat) with the Pirates was .567, the best by a right-handed hitter, and Stargell's was .532, the best by a left-handed hitter.

In his 1990 book, *The Pittsburgh Pirates — An Illustrated History*, sportswriter Bob Smizik wrote that Kiner was the only player in Pirates' history who was a bonafide drawing card. "Attendance figures show that neither Honus Wagner nor Pie Traynor nor Roberto Clemente had a significant impact on attendance," wrote Smizik. "During Stargell's best years attendance declined. But there never has been a Pirate who so excited the fans, made them buy tickets, and then stay in the seats like Kiner."

Frank Gustine, a three-time All-Star performer and later a popular Oakland restaurateur, roomed with Kiner when Kiner first came to the Pirates. "It was amazing," said Gustine, shortly before he died in 1991. "If Ralph batted in the eighth, it seemed like the whole place would get up and leave afterward. But if there was a chance he could bat in the ninth, nobody left."

The 54 home runs Kiner hit in 1949 has not been surpassed since then in the National League, though Roger Maris did hit 61 for the Yankees in 1961.

The Pirates pulled in more than a million fans four straight years (1947-1950). The 1,517,021 they drew in 1948 held up as an attendance record until the 1960 season when the Pirates attracted a record 1,705,828. That stood up until 1988 when the Pirates drew 1,866,713 fans to Three Rivers Stadium.

"I was making $90,000 the year before (1952)," said Kiner. "There wasn't much in the way of endorsement money back then. I got $500 for being on a Wheaties box, and a case of Wheaties for every home run I hit.

"My wife Nancy (Chaffee, a former tennis star) and I did a Chesterfield ad, though neither of us smoked, and we got $1,000 for that. The only guy who made any money in those days was Bob Feller. He was the big guy in endorsements."

I asked Kiner for a critique on Billy Mazeroski. "We've met at some Old Timers' Day games," said Kiner. "I saw him play. He was the best doubleplay man I ever saw. Jerry Priddy was also pretty good at that, and Priddy came before Mazeroski."

Kiner said he has heard that Maz is a happy man, content with his lot in life, and doesn't require a great deal. "I think that's more important than having a lot of money," said Kiner. "I think Roger Maris was a lot like Maz. Maris never took advantage of having hit the 61 home runs to break Babe Ruth's record. He'd rather go fishing than to a sports banquet, or a business deal."

Why does Mazeroski's home run still have such a hold on people? When his home run is shown on the video screen of the scoreboard at Three Rivers Stadium it still draws strong and sustained cheering from the crowd.

"I've seen it a thousand times," came back Kiner, "and it has to be one of the greatest moments in sports. It sorta captures what baseball is all about. Plus, the Pirates hadn't been in a World Series for so long. It had been 33 years since the Yankees swept the Pirates in four straight with Babe Ruth and Lou Gehrig in their lineup. Revenge was a long time coming."

I asked Kiner what he thought of Mazeroski's situation in regard to the Hall of Fame. He had been eligible for 15 years, but never came close to getting enough votes to be inducted, and 1991 was his last year on the ballot.

"I never gave that any thought, to be truthful," said Kiner. "Nobody's ever asked me that question before. He certainly shouldn't get into the Hall of Fame on that home run he hit. He was the best fielding second baseman, but he was never an outstanding hitter."

What if Mazeroski had played for the Yankees?

"If Maz had hit that home run for the Yankees," said Kiner, "he'd be in the Hall of Fame."

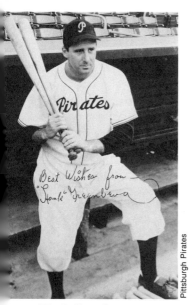

Hank Greenberg

Kiner with Greenberg

With Bucs' owner Bing Crosby

White Sox owner Bill Veeck in when he worked in Chicago

Hall of Famer Johnny Mize, died in 1993 at age 80

Flanked by Wally Westlake and Frank Gustine

Some of Kiner's critics believe he had an advantage into getting into the Hall of Fame himself because he was popular as a broadcaster with so many of the New York sports writers, and their number gave anybody associated with New York an edge in the voting.

"I think you should have to dominate the league in some category for a period of time in order to get into the Hall of Fame," said Kiner, defending what he did in a brief nine year career. "I don't think longevity should do it, either. To me, it's a mistake to think that just because a guy gets 3,000 hits he should be in the Hall of Fame."

I asked Kiner if Stengel ever spoke much about the 1960 World Series when he was managing the Mets. "Stengel said, 'I had the best players, and they beat us,'" recalled Kiner. "That was a weird World Series!"

It was one of the most incredible postseason encounters ever. The Yankees won Games No. 2, No. 3 and No. 6 by a combined score of 38-3. The Pirates used great pitching, defense and timely hitting to stretch the Series to a seventh game at Forbes Field (where the Pirates had lost two of three games). The Pirates took a 9-7 lead into the ninth — thanks to Hal Smith's three-run home run in the eighth — but the Yankees came up with two runs in the top of the ninth to tie the game.

"Hal Smith should get more credit," Kiner said. "That was the play of the World Series."

Kiner volunteered an anecdote involving Mazeroski. "I didn't know him that well, but I remember something he did once that impressed the heck out of me," said Kiner. "When they were filming the movie version of *The Odd Couple,* they wanted Roberto Clemente to hit into a triple play. They would pay him $1,000 to do it. He refused. So Maz said he would do it. On the first pitch, Maz hit it perfectly to the third baseman and he started a triple play. Usually, they'd have to film a sequence like that 10 or 12 times to get it right. But Maz did it in one take."

When Kiner mentioned a movie relating to baseball, it brought back a memory. "Do you remember when you were in that movie *Angels in the Outfield* at Forbes Field?" I said.

"I sure do," Kiner came back.

"Janet Leigh and Paul Douglas were both in that movie, weren't they?" I said.

"I ended up dating Janet Leigh for a few months as the result of making that movie in Pittsburgh," said Kiner.

"I still have some eight by tens of Janet and me at the batting cage," Kiner continued.

"I met her daughter, Jamie Lee Curtis, who's quite a movie actress herself, about six years ago. Jamie Lee Curtis married a guy from Philadelphia, and I spotted her. I told my wife, 'I'm going over and introduce myself to her.' My wife told me I ought to. So I went over and I said, 'My name is Ralph Kiner and I used to date your mother.' Jamie Lee Curtis jumped up, and she threw her arms around me, and she shrieked, 'Daddy, I've been searching for you all my life!' We bumped into each other later, and she said, 'Mother said to send her your child support payment.' Funny thing is she looks so much like my own daughter. My wife started to figure out when I dated Janet Leigh, and when Jamie Lee was born. She could have been my daughter because she looks like my daughter."

Kiner, of course, was shedding some light on his relationship with Janet Leigh in a light hearted way. That story had a familiar ring to it. I knew that Kiner had shared it with me before, more than once perhaps. It reminded me that he had also once had a date with Elizabeth Taylor when she was a young actress.

"Bing Crosby, who was a part-owner of the Pirates back when I was playing, fixed me up for a date with Elizabeth Taylor," said Kiner, picking up his cue as easily as he might spear a pop fly out of the sky in his heyday.

"A month ago, we were in San Francisco, and they had Eddie Fisher out to sing the National Anthem. He, of course, was once married to Elizabeth Taylor. He asked to come up in the broadcast booth, and we had a chance to say hello. I said, 'I dated Elizabeth Taylor before you ever met her.' And he said, 'You, too, huh. You also dated her before she married me."

Kiner has been married three times, and trails Taylor by a big margin in that respect. His first wife was tennis star Nancy Chaffee. They were married for 18 years, from 1951 through 1969. "She married sportscaster Jack Whitaker a year and a half ago," interjected Kiner. Then Kiner was married to Barbara Batchelder for ten years. She died of cancer after they were divorced. He had been married to DiAnn Sugart for nine years when we spoke.

He and Nancy had three children, a daughter named Katherine Chaffee Kiner. ("We call her K.C.," said Kiner. "Casey Stengel thought she was named after him. We never told him any different."); Scott, 37, is the general manager of two radio stations in Palm Springs, including KCMJ, a CBS affliliate; Ralph Michael, 39, was born in 1953. "He was born the year I got traded from the Pirates, and he was born in Chicago," said Kiner. "Nancy was eight months pregnant when I was traded to the Cubs."

I said, "You mentioned Casey Stengel. What was your relationship like with him? He was the original manager of the Mets, and he was still there in 1967 when they became the Amazin' Mets two years before they won the World Series. What was he like?"

"To me, Casey Stengel was a unique individual," came back Kiner. "I had known him for a long time. He was kinda a half-way scout for the Boston Braves when I was in high school. I grew up in Alhambra, just outside of Los Angeles, and he sorta tried to sign me.

"I ran into him as a ballplayer at World Series games. I found him to be like a father figure to me. He was always extremely nice to me. When I became the Mets' announcer, he was just great for Lindsey, Bob and I. He knew our job and was most gracious and helpful with us all the time.

"He was aware of everything that was going on. He was sharp, and very sensitive to a lot of things."

Kiner came back to his breakthrough in the broadcasting business, and how his short stint at the 1960 World Series led to some great opportunities.

"Gabe Paul, the general manager of the Cincinnati Reds, got to me and offered me the job in Cincinnati. He had seen my show in Pittsburgh. When the Pirates went to New York during the 1960 World Series I went to Cincy to see their agency people. Also off that show I was offered a job to do sports on the six o'clock news for a Pittsburgh TV station. I was also offered a job to work for the White Sox. It was really fortuitous. I turned down Cincinnati and Pittsburgh to work for the White Sox.

"I had signed for a second year when George Weiss, the general manager of the newly-formed New York Mets, called and asked me if I would like to do the Mets' games. I told him I would be interested if I could get out of my contract. The owners of the Chicago team were Bill Veeck and Hank Greenburg. The GM was Ed Short. Short let me out of my contract to go with the Mets.

"When Chicago contacted me initially I was doing the Bing Crosby Golf Tournament on TV. Crosby had called me to do that. I knew Bing well. I had played a lot of golf with Bing out at Palm Springs. I got to know him, to begin with, because of his ownership of the Pirates.

"I was interviewing Gay Brewer at the Crosby golf event, and somebody shoved Phil Harris in on me. I had played golf with him. I said, for openers, 'Phil, you know Gay Brewer, don't you?' Harris said, 'Yeah, he's a fag winemaker from Modesto.' I don't know what my reaction was. Off the air, I said, 'Good God, why did you say that?' And Harris said, 'You're only on for a short while and you've got to get their attention!'

"I was working that golf tournament on TV with Lindsey Nelson. He had already signed on to do the Mets games. And so had Bob Murphy. I asked Lindsey what I ought to do: stay in Chicago with my good friend Hank Greenburg, or go to New York. Lindsey said, 'I think it's the greatest opportunity in the world. We're not replacing anybody, we have no one else's act to follow, and we're in the biggest market in the country.'

"Lindsey was certainly right in what he told me. Lindsey Nelson, Bob Murphy and I stayed together for 17 years. That was longer than any three announcers anywhere stayed together.

"There was a period when the Mets were really pits. That's when M. Donald Grant was running the team, and they were losing 97 games a year. I was in Pittsburgh at one point when Tom Johnson, one of the Pittsburgh owners, asked me if I would like to come to the Pirates as an announcer. 'I'd like you to work for us,' Johnson said.

"Johnson also drank a lot, but he was not drinking when he said that to me. I would have worked for the Pirates if they wanted me. I think there was some objection to the offer, and nothing ever came of it. Bob Prince was pushing me for the job. But he was full of bullshit, too. He was always telling me we'd be a great team.

"The Dodgers were looking for a guy, too, at the same time. Peter O'Malley asked the Mets for permission to talk to me. I was one of two to be approached. But the job went to Ross Porter. I was looking to get out. Then the Mets were sold and the new owners eventually turned things around, and they have been great to me.

"New York is a tough market, and I've thought about how lucky I've been to have lasted so long. I think the reason I have lasted so long is that I started out with the Mets, and I am strongly associated with the team. Basically, people can believe what I say."

The day after I spoke with Kiner, I caught him and Tim McCarver doing a Mets game in Pittsburgh over WWOR-TV, which is available to TV watchers in Pittsburgh. They were critical of some moves made by Mets' manager Jeff Torborg, and reckless base-running by the Mets. Kiner also second-guessed some strategy employed by Pirates' manager Jim Leyland when he inserted a pinch-runner. "Nobody's perfect, even when you're winning," said Kiner. Even McCarver came in for some subtle criticism during my interview with Kiner. "Tim's good," Kiner conceded, "but sometimes he thinks that what he says is the only way."

When I asked Kiner about his broadcast style, he said, "I'm honest in my reporting. I don't think I make many enemies as a broadcaster, but I say what's on my mind. I still love the game, and it shows. I still enjoy doing the games, and I think that comes across to the viewers."

When the Pirates were splashing each other with champagne in the clubhouse, McCarver said, "I've played in a World Series, and that champagne burns your eyes."

Kiner came back, "I never played in a World Series, but I hate to see good champagne wasted like that."

When Kiner left Chicago in favor of New York, he was replaced as a White Sox broadcaster by Milo Hamilton. Yes, the same Milo Hamilton who replaced Bob Prince when Westinghouse officials got furious with Prince and bounced him from his post as the Pirates' principal broadcaster. It was a bad move that has been blamed on the Pirates, who merely went along with the wishes of the owners of KDKA.

Kiner said that Betty Prince was one of the few friends he retained in Pittsburgh from his playing days. "I see her a lot," I said. "She is such a nice person. She's so reserved, and such a contrast to Bob."

"She deserves every medal in the world for being married to Bob," said Kiner.

"I'd stay at their home from time to time. I don't know how she put up with him. But he was Pittsburgh.

"He was always getting me into one deal or another. They were always sure things. We were going to clean up. I put up everything I had on more than one occasion in one of his financial schemes.

217

Invariably, we lost our ass. He always had something going. He was in oil wells, you name it. They all went dry. He had one idea after another and, finally, I said, 'Bob, go get somebody else to bankroll this one.'

"Bob was always loose with money. Even if he was hurting financially, and he was more than a few times in his life, he always picked up the tab. No one else at the bar ever had to touch their wallet when Bob was around."

Kiner never called Pittsburgh home. "I never really lived here," he said. "I never stayed here after the season. It never appealed to me. I was playing golf in Palm Springs during the winter. My wife and I were from that area, and we never entertained any thoughts of spending time here during the off-season.

"Off the field, I couldn't go anywhere without attracting a crowd. It was like Joe DiMaggio in New York. The people here really knew their players and they wanted to talk to them, all the time. I couldn't walk these streets. There was a lot of stuff going on. I lived sort of a protected life here. I used to eat a lot in my room.

"Jackie Heller had a night club called the Carousel, and he'd put me up in the balcony away from the crowd. Lenny Litman had a place called the Copa. The first time I ever saw Sammy Davis Jr. was at the Copa when he worked with his father and his uncle. That was before he was famous. The Litmans looked after me pretty good, too. Prince was great at looking after me, too."

"Did they pick up the tab when you were there?"

"No, I paid my own way, and I expected to pay my own way.

"As a ballplayer, though, it was a great city for me. The people here treated me great.

"I always liked going to New York. I took Bob Prince with me and introduced him to Toots Shor at his restaurant and bar, and Bob went back there every time he was in New York. I went to New York in 1947, when the Yankees were in the World Series, and did a radio show with Prince. We were doing it from midtown Manhattan. One night we were stuck for a guest, and Mel Allen, who was at the height of his broadcasting career, came all the way from Yankee Stadium to do a show with us for $100."

While Kiner was sharing Bob Prince stories, I asked him what he thought of the decision to drop Prince from the Pirates' broadcast team before the 1976 season. Prince had been with the Pirates since 1948, and had been one of the most popular people in Pittsburgh, indeed, a local institution.

"I think it was the dumbest decision that they ever made," commented Kiner. "It wasn't the Pirates' decision. He rubbed some KDKA or Westinghouse executives the wrong way; Bob forgot that everybody has a boss. But the Pirates went along with the decision. It was stupid. He was Pittsburgh, and he was the man who put Pittsburgh into prominence into sports. He was a great front man. He was the best in the business. He was the greatest raconteur. He could tell wonderful stories all night. He was a legend in the business. He was one of those guys who come around once in a lifetime.

"We did a lot of crazy things together. I'll tell you one, though I probably shouldn't; Betty probably never knew about this one. We were driving from my home in California to spring training in San Bernardino. It's about a 50 mile drive. I had a back road route to get there, a road that had no traffic. It was a two-lane highway. Prince is following me in his car. We're driving about 90 miles an hour. All of a sudden, Prince is right behind me, and he's tapping his front bumper up against my back bumper. He keeps doing it, and I can see him laughing like hell in the rear view window.

"I can see a guy a mile down the road coming out just as Bob is passing me, and the guy is heading our way. Bob's eyes are on me alone. I see this car coming up closer and closer. And Bob is going 90 miles an hour in the same lane as the guy coming at us. I thought they were going to smash head-on. Prince went around him on the dirt to the left of the guy. If that guy had panicked and veered off to the right, Prince would have been dead. He had a heart of gold, but he was fearless. And sometimes foolish."

Kiner's tale brought another Prince story to mind. How about the time that Prince made a bet with some fellow travelers on a Pirates' road trip and dove out of the fourth floor of the Chase Hotel in St. Louis into the hotel pool. Prince bet he could clear the deck below, and dive into the pool, and he did. He could have broken his neck.

"I was at the Chase after that incident, and I went out by the pool to check it out, and have a look. He knew he could clear the cement and make it into the pool; he knew the angle because he had been on the swimming team at college."

"Do you think he had been drinking before he took his dare-devil dive?"

"I heard he had two drinks; that was nothing," Kiner came back. "There were some wires stretching across the area; it's a good thing he didn't hit them. They'd have lit him up pretty good."

I mentioned to Kiner that I had traveled to Cooperstown, N.Y. in 1975 with a neighbor of mine who was a big Mets' fan, attorney Bill Hodges, and what a great time we had meeting all the great baseball players of all time.

"I went in with Judy Johnson, a great player in the black leagues, and Billy Herman and Earl Averill," recalled Kiner.

We started talking about the merits of some of the players who have been inducted into the Baseball Hall of Fame, and some of the Pirates who have been snubbed, notably Mazeroski and ElRoy Face.

"I hear Face takes some real shots at me," said Kiner. "He tells people I wasn't a very good outfielder, and that I don't deserve to be in the Hall of Fame. I don't know why he picks on me; I'm not the reason he's not in there. It's like comparing apples and oranges. For one thing, I wasn't that bad an outfielder. One year I led the league in putouts by an outfielder."

The man who may have had the greatest influence on Kiner and his career was Hank Greenberg.

Greenberg, at 35, was ready to retire after leading the American League with 44 home runs and 127 RBIs in 1946. He agreed to play one more season at a salary of $80,000 for the Pirates, who purchased him from the Detroit Tigers. Imagine a player today thinking about retiring after putting up those kind of numbers. Imagine what a player today would make if he put up those kind of numbers.

To give Greenberg a break, and to take full advantage of his big bat, the Pirates built a bullpen in left field that stretched two hundred feet from the foul line toward centerfield. More significantly, the bullpen was 30 feet wide, and right in front of the left field scoreboard. The distant left field foul pole, once 365 feet away, was reduced to a more easily reachable 335 feet, which suited Greenberg and Kiner just fine. The bullpen became known as Greenberg Gardens.

Kiner cleaned up, hitting 51 home runs and driving in 127 runs that year. He more than doubled his home run total, and tied for the league HR lead with Johnny Mize of the New York Giants. Greenberg, playing in just 119 games, hit 25 home runs and had 74 RBIs. Kiner had been a big fan of Greenberg, and he was eager to get advice from him.

"The best thing that ever happened to me was when Greenberg came over in '47," Kiner has often said. "He just taught me some great work habits."

Greenberg played for the Pirates for just one season, but his presence left a lasting impression on Kiner. "I used to watch him every chance I had," recalled Kiner. "Hey, this is a guy who hit 58 home runs one year.

"When I was a kid, Babe Ruth was my favorite ballplayer. But then the Detroit Tigers of 1934 became my favorite team. Hank Greenberg and Charlie Gehringer were their two best ballplayers. Greenberg has been an influence on me throughout my whole life.

"It started in 1934, but I never met him until 1947 when he came to the Pirates. It changed my life. I'd just gotten out of the military service. We had a bunch of guys on the Pirates then who were more dedicated to having more fun off the field. Greenberg turned me around. He changed my stance. He got me going. He left a lasting impression on me. When I got married the first time, he was my best man. The second time he was my best man again. On the third time, he turned me down. 'I'm not going to jinx you,' he said. But he changed my life, no doubt about it. He hired me to work as a broadcaster with the White Sox when he and Bill Veeck owned the team. Hank died a couple of years ago, but I'll never forget him."

"I think I'm the luckiest guy in the world," Ralph Kiner told me during our meeting at the Vista. "My ambition as a little kid was to play major league baseball. When I decided that I was going to get out of baseball — now I know that was a mistake — it turned out to be a blessing.

"I have never applied for any job I ever got. They always came out of the blue. I enjoyed the job as general manager of the San Diego Padres for five years. I had no interest then of ever being in the broadcasting business.

"I was so lucky to get to go to New York for the Mets. Other than the two years I was in the military service, I have spent my entire adult life involved in a game I love.

"The 1969 season was a dream come true. After all those years that the Mets had been horrible, and now they won the World Series. The country was in turmoil that year. We were in Vietnam. New York's mayor, John Lindsey, was trying to ride the coattails of the Mets. There was deep love in the city for the Mets. It was sorta like life. The downtrodden Mets had come up and won it all. There was a great feeling.

"I remember in 1969, I had Kiner's Korner going strong in New York. Writers like Jack Lang and Dick Young were pissed because I had entree to the clubhouse 15 minutes before they did to get a ballplayer for a post-game interview."

I recalled a day in Atlanta when I was covering the Mets in a series against the Braves, during the 1972 season, and it began raining midway through the game. Dick Young spotted Kiner in the dugout during a rain delay, doing an interview for his radio broadcast.

Young commandeered all the New York sportswriters in the press box, and marched us in single file down through the stands, onto the field, and into the Mets' dugout. The crowd wondered what in the world was going on. Young had us all sit next to various Mets' players, and begin interviewing them. If Kiner could interview them during a rain delay, so could we. Young was militant about stuff like that; he insisted that the sports writers would get equal treatment, and he vociferously resented the invasion of his world by TV.

Young liked Kiner personally, but he wouldn't give an inch when it came to equal access in the clubhouse to the players. In those situations, Kiner was the enemy, like the rest of the TV guys.

What did Kiner recall of his first days at Forbes Field? "We opened the season in St. Louis, and then we came home," said Kiner. "I had never been to Pittsburgh in my life. My father was born and raised in Derry, Pa., but he moved to California before I was born. My first impression of Pittsburgh was a terrible one.

"We came in on a train from St. Louis. We arrived at 10 in the morning. I got off the train, and I just looked up. It looked like midnight. They were burning soft coal in those days in the local steel mills, and the smoke was so dark and thick. It was the most depressing thing I ever saw.

"We went to Webster Hall first, where we were staying, and later we worked out at the ballpark. I had come from California before they had smog, so I had never seen such dark skies in the middle of the afternoon. Then I looked out from home plate to the wall in left field and it measured 365 feet down the line. It was even deeper in center field. It was so far out they used to wheel the batting cage out there and park it there during the game. It was so far away nobody could hit it. I was ready to go back home. There was no way I wanted to stay in Pittsburgh. I couldn't believe you could live this way. I never saw the sun. My view was so negative.

"The next year Hank Greenberg came, and they put a bullpen in out in left field to give him a better target, and now it was 335 down the line. That was much better for both of us."

I asked Kiner if he continued to participate in Old Timers Games.

"No, I don't," he said. "I can't hit the ball anymore. That's no fun."

"Time is of the essence. The crowd and players are the same age always, but the man in the crowd is older every season. Come on, play ball!"
—From "Polo Grounds" by Rolfe Humphries

Greenberg (named for Hank Greenberg) Gardens was enclosed area in front of scoreboard in left field at Forbes Field. It shortened home run distance for Hank Greenberg and Ralph Kiner.

Where Were You?

"You just want to be there."
—Drew Balog

Dave Williams, Driver
John F. Slater Funeral Home
Baldwin-Whitehall

"I'm just an average guy, but I was present at two special moments in Pittsburgh sports history. I was at Forbes Field when Bill Mazeroski hit the home run, and I was at Three Rivers Stadium when Franco Harris had the 'Immaculate Reception.'

"I'm from Regent Square and I went to Taylor Allderdice High School with your brother Dan and I got into the funeral business as a driver soon after I graduated in 1955. I was driving for Reimer's Limousine Service on the side, and I picked up and dropped off Joe L. Brown, the Pirates' general manager, throughout the World Series. I remember people were crying for tickets, and Brown always had a fistful of tickets when I was with him. He gave me a ticket for the home games. I was sitting on the third base side in box seats right behind the Yankees dugout. The fellow who chased Maz home in the dark suit was sitting in front of me.

"Someone gave me a ticket to see the Steelers playoff game with the Oakland Raiders, and I was way up in the top of the stands behind the endzone, which didn't seem to be much of a seat. And then here came Franco running right toward me with the game-winning touchdown. For an average guy, I've been there for the two greatest things in Pittsburgh sports history."

Drew Balog
Ligonier, Pa.

"I was a sophomore at Duquesne High, and I was playing hooky. I was with two of my buddies and we went to it, and we didn't pay to get in. One of them was Johnny Clougherty, who became a big-time basketball official. We went in John's father's car. We eased in with 12 or 14 other people in the bleachers. We squeezed in the corner; we couldn't see much. When you're that young, you don't care if you can see or not. You just want to be there. I remember Yogi Berra running like the dickens out there. I didn't see much because people went crazy. The place was in pandemonium. But I didn't have any doubt it was going over."

Cleo Wilcox
Retired
Lehigh Acres, Florida

"It was the only office poll I ever won, when Maz hit that home run. I was working in the office of the B&O Rail Road in Downtown Pittsburgh. It was so exciting. I can remember exactly what I was doing when he hit it — I was counting money."

Neal Ryan
Bethel Park
Transportation Supervisor
Consolidation Coal Co.

"I still have the ticket stub from that seventh game. It cost $2.20 for a bleacher seat. I have been offered $100 for it, but I turned it down. I was 13 and a student at St. Anne's Grade School in Castle Shannon, and my parents called me in sick. The next day the nun asked me if I saw any of the game on TV when I was home sick. I said, 'Yeah, I saw it.' I just remember the people were so happy. I was at the game with my dad, whose name is Cornelius Ryan. You had to send in your money and you didn't know what game you would get tickets for. All my neighbors felt sorry for us because they didn't think there would be a seventh game. When Maz hit the home run over the left field wall, Yogi Berra just stood there and ran back in to the infield like it was just another inning. We went home on a streetcar and it took forever because the streets were so jammed with people. Everyone was so happy."

Carnegie Library of Pittsburgh

Streetcar on Fifth Avenue in front of Webster Hall Hotel, where Pirates held World Serie victory party, and St. Paul's Cathedral, the bishop's church in Pittsburgh

Frankie Gustine
He graced all playing fields

"He was a lovely man.
He always had a smile."
— Myron Cope

T his was a Saturday afternoon in February, 1991, and the
Piratefest was going full steam at the ExpoMart in Monroeville.
The annual mid-winter celebration of baseball had attracted thou-
sands of Pirates' fans, young and old.

I was having coffee and donuts with several Pirates from the past,
listening to wonderful stories from the likes of Vernon Law, Bob Friend,
ElRoy Face and Nellie King.

Suddenly it was 1960 again, I was 18 and a freshman at Pitt and
the Pirates were winning the World Series across the street from the
Pitt Student Union at Forbes Field.

Rick Cerrone, then vice-president for public relations of the Pirates,
was looking on as these former Pirates talked wistfully about the good
old days, and he said, "I can't believe how easy these guys are to work
with."

Cerrone, who is really into baseball nostalgia, and I strolled the
aisles together and checked out the many baseball-related activities,
and we came upon Frankie Gustine, another former Pirate. He was up
on a platform, signing autographs cheerfully, the only way he ever did
anything.

"We're paying these guys to appear here," said Cerrone, "but
Frank refused the money. He said we didn't have to pay him to do this.
I insisted, so he gave me the name of a charity to give the money to
in his name."

That Saturday was February 2, 1991. On April 2, exactly two
months later, I received a telephone call from Bill Gormley, the brother-
in-law of Frankie Gustine. He told me that Frankie had died the day
before in Davenport, Iowa.

Gustine, who made his home in Green Tree, was in Iowa as a guest
of one of his long-time business partners, John Connelly of the Gateway Clipper Fleet, who had begun a new enterprise that weekend, as
riverboat gambling debuted in Iowa. Frankie's sister lives in Davenport, and he had just finished calling to say he would be coming out to
her home for a visit when he collapsed and died of a heart attack.

His son, Frank Jr., has a framed photo on display that was taken
of his dad in Davenport, with a riverboat in the background, just hours
before he died. The color photo is in his offices at The Gustine Company, a highly-successful commercial real estate firm, in Birmingham Towers on the city's South Side. There are other photos of his father in a
Pirates baseball uniform adorning the wall by the windows.

Frank misses his father dearly.

One of the greatest honors I have ever had in my life was when Frank Gustine Jr. and his brother Bob asked me to serve as an honorary pallbearer for their father. "He used to talk about you like you were his son," said Bob, a Pittsburgh attorney.

Frankie Gustine was laid out at the Freyvogel Funeral Home in Oakland, on the border of Shadyside. In the midst of the three-day funeral, I traveled out to the ExpoMart in Monroeville one day to interview former Pirate Frank Thomas. On the way back to the funeral home, I heard the news that Pennsylvania Senator John Heinz had been killed in an airplane crash. Pittsburgh was losing two of its finest ambassadors in the same week. It hurt all of us.

Just prior to Gustine's death, the Pirates decided to honor his lifelong allegiance to their team. He was the recipient of the second annual "Pride of the Pirates" Award. Herb Douglas, a boyhood hero of mine from Hazelwood, who remains the only man ever to grow up in the city and win an Olympic medal (a bronze for the long jump in 1948), joined me at the Gustine table at the Pittsburgh Hilton Hotel.

The "Pride of the Pirates" Award was created in 1990 to recognize members of the Pirates family who have demonstrated the qualities of sportsmanship, dedication and outstanding character during a lifetime of service. Frank never knew that he was going to receive such an honor.

Accepting the award on Frank's behalf were his sons, Frank Jr., Robert and Mark, and his daughters, Joanne and Mimi. The award was presented by Carl Barger, then president of the Pirates.

"Frank Gustine embodied all of the qualities we in the Pirates organization strive for," Barger said in making the presentation. "He made outstanding contributions to the club as a player and embraced the Pittsburgh community by making it his home after his playing career. He was a successful businessman here and the contributions he made to the city and team he loved so much are too numerous to mention."

Frankie Gustine and I became friends during my freshman year of 1960 at Pitt. That is when I was privileged to meet him. He and Bill Gormley and Bill's brother, Owen, owned and worked the bar at Frankie Gustine's Restaurant, an Oakland landmark for over 30 years when the Pirates and Steelers were playing at Forbes Field. It is now called Hemingway's.

I remembered how he often offered to drive my mother from Pitt, where she worked in the mid-'60s, to Downtown Pittsburgh so she would have one less streetcar to ride in order to get home. He always inquired about her well being in later years. "Tell your mother I send my love," said Frank on so many occasions. "Tell her I was asking about her."

After Art Rooney died, Frankie Gustine gained the title of the finest person on the Pittsburgh sports scene. "We were all fortunate to know him," said Tom McDonough, an Oakland-born insurance salesman who tended bar on occasion for Gustine just for the hell of it. Gustine played nearly ten seasons for the Pirates, starting in 1939. He played every position but pitcher, anything just to be in the lineup. He played in three All-Star Games and had a lifetime batting average of .265.

"I believed in a higher power," he told me. "As a youngster, I prayed that if I could get one year in the big leagues I'd be satisfied. Later, I prayed for base hits."

He had a neighbor during his youth in Chicago whom he called "Mr. Roberts." He said Mr. Roberts introduced him, when he was only 15, to the likes of Honus Wagner and Pie Traynor, and later Paul and Lloyd Waner and Arky Vaughan. "It was Pie Traynor who got the Pirates to offer me a contract right out of high school for $85 a month," Gustine once related to a journalism class I was teaching at Point Park College. "But I didn't care about the money. I wanted to be a ballplayer; that's all that mattered."

He had been offered a four-year scholarship to the University of Chicago and his mother wanted him to go to school. "I was a very good basketball player and football player in high school, too," said Frank, "and I just wanted to be involved somehow in sports."

"If you prove to me that you'll finish high school and go to college," his mother told him, "I'll let you do it."

At Paducah, Kentucky, he was on a team that lost 19 in a row, and remembered how discouraging it was. "A lot of players were coming and going, and I made up my mind to hustle, to show them I belonged," said Gustine.

He stressed to the young would-be writers that they be as versatile as possible, and keep their options open.

"I went to Hutchinson, Kansas to play ball. I had been a third baseman all my life, and I had played some catcher. Well, the two best players on their team were the third baseman and the catcher. I said, 'Are there any positions open?' They said, 'Yeah, shortstop. What position you play?' I said, 'I'm a shortstop.' You never know where you're going to wind up. Back then, we'd have to sweep out the dugouts, and we'd get a $1 a day for meal money. We rode around in an old bus that didn't have seats. You had to sit on the bottom of the floor. We'd get malaria, and they'd give us quinine tablets. We'd go 360 and 400 miles on that bus for road games in Arkansas and Missouri. When it rained in Kansas, you'd have torrential rains. We had dust storms. Nothing was small in Kansas. But I loved it.

"Mr. Roberts told me, 'If you want to make it to the big leagues, you have to eat, drink and sleep baseball. You have to stay away from wine, women and song.' He told us not to drink or smoke. He said beer was the road to ruin.

"There was a great player named Luke Appling who played for the White Sox, and they were on a tour of Texas towns. I met him in Sweetwater, Texas. We played there on a real hot day; it was really hot out there. Appling advised me, 'Don't drink beer, drink whiskey. Beer goes to your legs. I carry a fifth of Scotch with me. Before I brush my teeth, I take a sip. Before I go to breakfast, I have another sip. Before I go to the ballpark I have another sip. When I come back to my room, I'd have three or four sips, and then I'd go to sleep.' I couldn't do that. I'd be drunk before I got to the ballpark.

"I did it my way, and it worked. I was called up to the Pirates in 1939 and I stayed with them until 1949, when I was sent back to my hometown to play for the Cubs. I played in the All-Star Game in 1946, 1947 and 1948, and, at 27, I had over 1,000 hits. And I played much of the time with a double hernia; I wore a truss. At 29, during the 1948 season, I was sidelined with nervous exhaustion. I couldn't run around the bases without getting exhausted. I couldn't even walk around the block without getting exhausted."

The Cubs sent him to the St. Louis Browns during the 1949 season and then he was optioned to the Pacific Coast League. That's when the Pirates signed him as a coach, and brought him back to Pittsburgh. He bought himself a bar in Oakland. He had two other locations before he found the site on Forbes Avenue, just a few doors up from Bouquet Street.

"Baseball set me up for life," said Gustine. "I loved every minute of it."

He was fiercely competitive on the field, and in basketball games at the nearby YMHA for many years after, but he was a wonderful and endearing gentleman away from the ballfield and ballcourt.

We teamed up one year, 1968, to broadcast Point Park College basketball games together on WEEP Radio. We also did a series of Pitt basketball games together on WEEP. He had coached basketball at Point Park, as well as at Waynesburg College. He also coached the baseball team at Point Park.

He got upset one day at practice when several players failed to show when the field was muddy from rainfall. "If I can come out on this mound every day," Gustine told the players assembled about him, "I'll be damned if I want to hear about anyone not being able to make it. If I'm here, I expect you to be here."

Nellie King of Mt. Lebanon, once a sidekick to Bob Prince on Pirates' baseball broadcasts on KDKA, said, "Branch Rickey told us all to be gentlemen. And he meant gentle men. That best describes Frankie Gustine. If you knew him, he was that kind of man."

Myron Cope of Upper St. Clair called Gustine "a lovely man. He always had a smile, and he was a wonderful story-teller. He was a ballplayer from a different time, and it was a better time. He never talked about money and contracts."

Frankie Gustine always made you feel better. When my wife Kathie and I attended the funeral of his wife, Mary Alice, he comforted us. And he made us smile.

Like Art Rooney, he always asked about your family, and told you to give everyone his love and regards. On Christmas Day, out of the blue, Frankie telephoned to offer season's greetings. He did things like that.

When I was a student at Pitt, I frequented his restaurant a lot. He may have been the best teacher I had at Pitt. He looked after you, counseled you, and made sure you behaved. He had four waitresses and a cook who worked for him over 25 years. That says a lot for him, too.

"I remember he used to sit down with you and Bob Smizik," said

228

Two of Pittsburgh's finest: Frank Gustine and Bob Prince at Forbes Field

Frank Gustine

Gustine's Restaurant placemat from 1959 season

Gustine in action

Posthumous "Pride of the Pirates" award to Frank Gustine was accepted by his family, left to right, Frank Jr., Joanne Gustine Bekampis, former Pirates president Carl Barger, Mimi Goff, Mark and Bob Gustine.

Gormley, "and talk sports for hours. I always had the impression that he had quite an influence on you guys."

He did, indeed. I courted Kathie Churchman in his restaurant, meeting her after she was done studying and I had put another sports section of *The Pitt News* to bed. She lived in an apartment on nearby Oakland Avenue while attending the Graduate School of Social Work at Pitt.

I loved the atmosphere in Gustine's. There was always a great group of old-timers at the end of the bar, bachelors from the neighborhood who loved to drink and sing and dance. And Frankie sang along with them. Frankie's favorite was "I Left My Heart in San Francisco."

There were always ballplayers and coaches and sports writers to be found in Frankie Gustine's as well, and Pitt used to hold its sports press conferences there each week. The basketball writers held weekly sessions with all the district coaches during the winter months. I would cut classes to be at those gatherings. I considered those press conferences as my journalism classes.

Gustine was the perfect guy to own a restaurant. He didn't just put his name on the window and walk away. He worked at it, and he greeted everyone, and said goodbye to everybody who came into his place. He made you feel like you had done him a tremendous favor. He seemed genuinely surprised when anyone asked him for his autograph.

The restaurant was one block north of Forbes Field, and it was filled with photographs and memorabilia of the Pirates, including the framed original contracts of players like Pie Traynor and Paul Waner, as well as his own. When you were in Gustine's, you felt like you were in the Pirates' clubhouse. Later, after the demolition of Forbes Field in 1972, there were actual lockers, and seats from Forbes Field to be found in the front of the restaurant.

Frank Gustine built his own Hall of Fame.

Frankie told fantastic stories about his early days in the minor leagues, and his travels through places like Hutchinson, Kansas and Paducah, Kentucky and Fort Smith, Arkansas.

Once, in Ponca City, Oklahoma, Frankie recalled that it was 120 degrees one day. "How do you fall asleep in this weather?" he asked a veteran player.

"You throw water on the bed sheets," the vet replied, "and hope you fall asleep before they dry."

Today's Pirates and young people everywhere could have learned a lot from Frankie Gustine.

He was so pleasant, so positive, so cheerful, so good-hearted, so humble, so down to earth. He grew up on the South Side of Chicago and wanted to play football for Notre Dame. But he became a Pittsburgher and was thrilled when one of his sons, Frank Jr., now of Mt. Lebanon, played football at Pitt, and against Notre Dame.

Frank Jr. is now successful with The Gustine Company in the commercial real estate world. His brothers, Bob, an attorney with the firm of Pietragallo, Bosick & Gordon, and Mark, associated with the department of athletics at the University of Pittsburgh, and sisters, Joanne Gustine Bekampis, a regional vice-president for Kaufmann's, and Mimi Goff, a homemaker now after a rewarding business career, have all been successful. And they are all chips off the old block.

I think it fitting and ironic that their father died in Iowa, out where they filmed "Field of Dreams," that wonderful 1988 movie about baseball and fathers and sons and life.

It is easy, and yet difficult, for me to picture Frankie Gustine coming through the cornfield to play some baseball with the game's greatest players, like Honus Wagner of Carnegie, his boyhood hero, and Pie Traynor and Ty Cobb. With a smile dancing on his face.

"Everybody loved Frankie Gustine."
— Ralph Kiner

I interviewed Ralph Kiner when he came to Pittsburgh with the New York Mets late in the 1992 season, and I asked him to reflect on Frank Gustine.

"Frank Gustine and I roomed together my first year with the Pirates," recalled Kiner. "He was one of the greatest guys who ever lived. If there was a saint in the sports world, it was him.

"Everybody loved Frankie Gustine. We had a writer in Pittsburgh then named Chilly Doyle, and he thought Gustine was the greatest guy who ever lived. One day I hit three home runs and we won by something like 15-nothing, and Gustine had an RBI single in that game. He featured Gustine's single in his story, and Gustine got the headline in the next day's newspaper.

"We had a good group of sportswriters back then. I recall Chet Smith and Al Abrams, Harry Keck and Jack Hernon and Les Biederman. Two guys who were kinda tough were Jack Henry and Vince Johnson, but they treated me and Gustine OK.

"It was different in those days. We traveled by train, and everyone hung together, the ballplayers and the sports writers. The cammaraderie is lost today. No one gets together anymore. Everyone goes their own way. Something special has been lost.

"It used to be a big thrill to go into different cities in those days. I don't know what I'd do today if I were a ballplayer, but I hit the best restaurants and nightclubs in every town in my day."

I was told that Frankie Gustine would start off every season with a bang, and be right up there with the league leaders at the All-Star break, but then tail off.

"He had a history of getting off to a great start, but he had two

231

hernias, and he never got them fixed, and he would weaken in the second half of the season," said Kiner.

"He was a great team guy. He was a handsome guy. People would say to him, 'Do you remember me?' and Frankie would always say, 'Sure I do.' Frank knew everybody. He was fantastic."

Hall of Famer Honus Wagner, left, joins Frank Gustine in welcoming Ralph Kiner to the Pirates in 1946.

Hall of Famer Pie Traynor talks to Rookie Frank Gustine in 1939.

View from the press box
Writers reflect on '60 Bucs

*"The magic of that moment
has a lot to do with the dream
of little kids everywhere."*
—Andrew Wilson
on Maz's home run

Pat Livingston,
Former Sports Editor, The Pittsburgh Press

"October 13, 1960, was a Thursday, I remember, because October 16 was a Sunday and it was my 40th birthday. It was the day I learned that my wife had Hodgkin's Disease, which would take her life in a few years. I stopped at our doctor's office at his home on my way to Forbes Field that day. I was covering a game between the Steelers and the Cardinals.

"I was in the composing room on the afternoon of October 13. I was writing the story on the seventh game of the World Series under Les Biederman's byline. Biederman was at Forbes Field, of course, and so were Roy McHugh and Bob Drum. We had a Western Union ticker-tape sending us a play-by-play of the game, and I was listening to the game on the radio. So I could double check my information.

"They wanted me to write the story so we could get it set in type as quickly as possible. Biederman would be interviewing the ballplayers after the game, and then he came to the office to do his over-night stories for the next day's newspaper.

"Two of our top editors, Vic Free and Wally Forster, were standing over my shoulders, saying, 'C'mon, c'mon.' They were on top of me to get the story finished. We wanted to have our last edition on the streets with the final score and the story that afternoon when the people from Forbes Field hit Downtown. We figured we could sell a lot of papers.

"The Pirates got off to a 4-0 lead after two innings, and we were really excited. But the game went back and forth. The Yankees came back and took a 7-4 lead after eight innings. The Pirates came back to take a 9-7 lead. Then the Yankees tied it in the top of the ninth.

"No sooner had Maz hit the home run than the presses started. I must have written ten different leads for that one. They had me writing because I happened to be there, and some of the guys couldn't write as fast as I could.

"I didn't give a damn about baseball at the time. I was at the first game at Forbes Field, and I didn't think I was missing out on anything.

"I see Maz on occasion at Groat's golf course. I know he was one tremendous ballplayer, a great ballplayer, and he was in a class by himself as an infielder. Just look at his fielding statistics.

233

"He was a quiet, unassuming guy. Unless you were close to Maz, you didn't know much about him, except his abilities as a ballplayer.

"I knew Groat better because he was a lot more outgoing. Groat would sit and talk to you. Maz would reply to your questions, but then he'd get the hell outta there before you could get a conversation going.

"I knew Dick Groat and his wife, Barbara. I used to see him at the Sandscratchers Club on Forbes Avenue near the ballpark. I think it was Eddie Cameron, a Pitt guy who became the athletic director at Duke, who got him to go down there.

"I interviewed Clemente many times. I had the most fantastic tape with Clemente, but I can't find it anymore. I was one of the few sports writers in the clubhouse (in 1972) after they lost the fifth and final game of a National League playoff series with the Cincinnati Reds on a wild pitch by Bob Moose.

"Moose was so disconsolate, and the room was so quiet. Nobody would have dared approach any of the players to ask any questions at that point. The players were all like zombies. Suddenly, Clemente erupted, and he started hollering at everyone. He's hollering, 'Hey, get your heads up! I don't want to see anybody in this place with their head down! Hey, Moose, get your head up! Those writers are going to be in here soon. I don't want them to see any long faces! Hey, we had a great year. Don't forget that! Everybody's going over to Bob Johnson's house for a party.'

"Most of the writers had run to the Cincinnati clubhouse, but I was writing a column, and I wasn't going to write about the Reds. There might have been a few other writers in the Pirates' clubhouse, but not the usual crush. Clemente kept hollering, 'I don't want to see any long faces!' He loosened the locker room up, I'll tell you. He must have hollered at Moose three or four times. 'Hey, Moose, get your head up! Don't look at the floor!'

"That was a good group of guys. You could feel comfortable in that clubhouse.

"I liked Clemente. I didn't know him when he was young. I knew him at the tailend of his career. But I do remember seeing him the first day he came to Pittsburgh. I couldn't take my eyes off him. He was such a charismatic figure. He looked like an athlete. He was there on a platform for a team picture. He was something of a hypochondriac, but there were few in baseball who were as good as him.

"Barry Bonds may be the closest in recent years. I met Bonds, I believe, when he was about 12 years old. I was in a golf foursome with his father, Bobby Bonds, at the Super Bowl when it was held in Pasadena, California. Deacon Jones was in the foursome in front of us. It started to rain, and I gave up, and went to the clubhouse. They got on me, at first, telling me I couldn't quit. But then they joined me in the clubhouse, and told me they should have come with me in the first place. Barry seemed like a nice kid. He was really thrilled to be in the company of all those athletes.

Al Abrams at 1976 opener

Pat Livingston with Art Rooney

Roy McHugh

Bob Smizik with Dick Groat

Myron Cope

Admiring new billboard at Fort Myers, Fla. training camp in spring of 1961 are (left to right) Frank Oceak, Joe L. Brown and Bob Friend.

"Bill Virdon and I were pretty good buddies, not good buddies, but I liked him a lot and I think he liked me. You never really know if they like you or not.

"I still don't think Maz's home run was the top moment in sports in Pittsburgh. I think Franco's 'Immaculate Reception' was the most magic moment. They hated the Raiders at that time. It's the one thing I did see. I saw it from the time it started till the time Franco caught the ball. I'm inclined to think it hit the Oakland player, Jack Tatum, because it really bounced back a long way. Something propelled it. It wouldn't have bounced that far if it hit Frenchy Fuqua's hands. So I think it was a legal catch and TD."

Andrew Wilson
Pittsburgh Free-Lance Writer
Allegheny Business News

"I was born the year after Mazeroski hit the home run, but my Dad talked about it so much and, of course, Mazeroski continued to play for the Pirates for a long time. When I was a kid playing baseball, I was always Mazeroski. This has probably occurred to you already, but I feel the magic of that moment has a lot to do with the dream of little kids everywhere. Every kid who has dreamed of being a pro athlete wants to hit the home run in the bottom of the ninth to win the World Series. Only one has actually done it, and he's a Pittsburgh Pirate forever. The only way Maz's home run could have been more dramatic is if the Pirates had been three runs down and the bases were loaded."

John Steigerwald
Sportscaster, KDKA-TV

"My dad, Bill Steigerwald, was there for Maz's home run and for Franco's 'Immaculate Reception.' If I know my dad, he was standing in the exit gate at Forbes Field when Maz hit the home run, and then he was out of there, and on his way home. He has always taken great pride in his quick get-aways from the ballpark. He knows when to start moving toward the door at just the right time. I was with him for 'The Immaculate Reception.' None of us really saw it. We were upset and looking down at our shoetops. We thought Bradshaw's pass was broken up by Jack Tatum. Then we heard the crowd roaring. I remember asking my dad which crowd was more vocal, and he said the one at Three Rivers Stadium. Of course, we were just coming away from that game, and the crowd was much larger than at Forbes Field. I also remember him pulling me hard after Franco scored the touchdown so we could get out of there in a hurry. I wanted to stick around for the celebration."

Earle Wittpen, Editor
Valley Mirror
Munhall, Pa.

"I lived in West Virginia at the time, and I was an ardent New York Yankees fan. I was working as a sports writer for the *Weirton Daily Times*, and our newspaper got a pair of tickets. I took a good friend, Pete Rodak, who owned a haberdashery in Weirton. His brother Mike had once played for the Steelers (1942). I'm watching the game and I'm not saying anything. I figured silence was the better part of valor. I haven't said a word the whole game. This guy next to me was from Pittsburgh and, finally, he turns to me and says sharply, 'Are you from New York?' I said, 'No, I'm from West Virginia.' He says, 'Are you a Yankees' fan?' I said, 'Yes, I am.' And he gave me a stern look, and says, 'I thought so.' When Maz hit that damn home run, I turned to my buddy and said, 'Let's go.' And we left town as fast as we could."

Myron Cope
WTAE Radio-TV
Pittsburgh, Pa.

"How could a man's day be ruined little more than two hours after Bill Mazeroski had slugged his unforgettable home run? Mine was.

"Eight months before, nearing 31, I had resigned from the sports department of the *Pittsburgh Post-Gazette* to attempt a new career. For several years, I had been selling articles to national magazines, so I made a decision to free-lance magazine articles full-time. Al Abrams, the long-time *P-G* sports columnist, told me, 'You'll starve, kid. You'll be back in six months.'

"As the Pirates neared the World Series, *Post-Gazette* Managing Editor Joe Shuman hired me to beef up the paper's coverage of the Series. Immediately after each game, I was to write a sidebar about any aspect of the game I chose, and secondly, I was to ghost-write a daily column for Bucs third baseman Don Hoak. I doubted Abrams was enthusiastic about Shuman having attached me to his staff.

"Game Seven, two innings remaining, Yankees leading, 5-4. No telling how the game would end. I decided to make notes of every remaining pitch, every swing, every gesture on the field, every movement that I could detect in that portion of the Pirates dugout within my view. Perhaps my notes would yield an interesting narrative of a tense finish.

"As soon as Maz struck his late-afternoon home run, I hustled to the Pirates clubhouse to interview Hoak for his column, then raced back up to the pressbox, determined to get the Hoak column and my own piece written in time to make the early 'bulldog' edition. Satisfied that I had, and pleased with myself, I drove to the *P-G* offices Downtown and walked into the sports department and grabbed the bulldog edition. 'Hey, where's my piece?' I asked Assistant Sports Editor Dan McGibbeny.

"He glanced sidewise at Abrams seated in a corner of the room and said, 'The boss killed it. He said you wrote the same stuff he wrote for his column.'

"I stormed into the city room to find Shuman. He repeated McGibbeny's explanation.

" 'Did you read my copy?' " I asked him.

" 'No. *Was* it the same stuff Al wrote?'

" 'The day I write the same piece Al writes,' I replied, 'I'll throw my typewriter out the window and never write another line.'

"I marched from the building to find the streets packed shoulder-to-shoulder by celebrating fans. The celebration, just beginning, was marvelous — no violence, just goodwill on all sides. In 1960 people — even kids — did not celebrate by smashing windows or cars.

"I walked the streets, head down, ignoring the greetings fans were calling out to one another. Once or twice, I responded with a snarl. There is no wrath exceeding that of a writer torpedoed by an editor.

"The next morning I drove to Daniels' Cleaners to pick up my laundry. Jack Daniels, the proprietor, said to me, 'Good story you wrote for the paper this morning.'

"Joe Shuman, it turned out, had retrieved my copy from the sports department trash can in time to get it into the later editions. As I drove home with my laundry, it was only then that I was able to savor Maz's home run."

Bill Guilfoile
Associate Director
National Baseball Hall of Fame and Museum, Inc.
Cooperstown, N.Y.

"It took me ten years to appreciate Bill Mazeroski's home run. When the ball disappeared over the Forbes Field wall at 3:36 p.m. on October 13, 1960, I was one of the most disappointed individuals in Forbes Field. All of us in the New York Yankees' front office delegation seated just beyond third base left the ballpark in a daze.

"Going into the Series, we felt we had the better team and we were *sure* we would put the Bucs away early. It was not until I joined the Pirates as the Public Relations Director in 1970 that I fully understood what Maz's home run meant to the Pirates and to the city of Pittsburgh. By the way, Bill was kind enough to loan his home run bat to the Hall of Fame some years ago, and it is one of our most prized artifacts and certainly one of the most popular conversation pieces anywhere in the museum.

"Maz and Roberto Clemente were still with the ballclub when I came aboard in 1970. Even in the twilight of his marvelous career, Mazeroski still showed the style and class that made him so very special around second base. I wasn't at all surprised to see him listed in *Total Baseball* as one of the 100 Greatest Players of All-Time and in the top ten among all second basemen who ever played the game.

"The day after I moved to Pittsburgh I was on my way to spring training. As I entered McKechnie Field for the first time, I was immediately confronted by a TV sports director and camera crew who asked for my assistance in arranging an interview with Clemente. I explained that this was my first day on the job, and that I hadn't even met Clemente yet, but that I would try to find him and see what I could do. Entering the clubhouse, I approached Roberto, introduced myself as the team's new PR director, and inquired as to his availability to be interviewed. Clemente launched into a ten minute tirade in a combination of English and Spanish in which he was most uncomplimentary toward the would-be interviewer. (Unknown to me, he had had a very rocky and negative relationship with this sports director over the years.) When he finally had vented his spleen, he took a deep breath, looked at me, and asked, 'Would it help you if I talked to him?' I replied, 'Roberto, as you know, this is my first day on the job and I'm trying to get off on the right foot with everybody. Undoubtedly, it would help me if you would do the interview.' 'For you, I will do it,' he said. He got dressed and kept his promise.

"If you check the record books, you'll find that, despite his tragic death during a still very productive career, Clemente is nevertheless the all-time Pirate leader in games played with 2,433 — one more than Honus Wagner. I still get a lot of satisfaction with the knowledge that I had a little something to do with this record.

"As the 1972 season came to a close, the Pirates already had clinched the Eastern Division title and Clemente achieved the milestone of his 3,000th hit on September 30. I had also been tracking his assault on Wagner's record for the most games played by a Pirate, and so I was aware that the two were tied with 2,432 games played going into the game of October 3. Having checked the lineup card in the dugout before the game that night and realizing that Clemente was not a starter, I approached Roberto and explained the significance of playing one more game. He shrugged and told me that Bill Virdon planned to rest him the final two games of the season in preparation for the upcoming Championship Series with Cincinnati. 'It's no big deal,' he said. 'I'll break the record on opening day next season.' To this day, I'll never know why I sought out Virdon and explained the scenario to him. Bill didn't hesitate. 'I'll see that he gets in the game,' he replied. Clemente went in to right field as a defensive replacement late in the game and thus became the Pirates' all-time leader in games played. It was to be his final regular season game for the Pirates."

Jim Kriek
Retired Sports Writer
Uniontown Herald-Standard

"Of the two greatest miracles in Pittsburgh sports history, I had to be content to hear the second. On the day Franco Harris made his 'Immaculate Reception,' I was laid up with the flu, and had to listen to the game on the radio.

"But I will never forget Bill Mazeroski's home run!

"I was then sports editor of the *Chatham (N.Y.) Courier*, and with the help of the late *Pittsburgh Press* baseball writer Les Biederman, and Joe Bradis, then with the Associated Press bureau in Pittsburgh, I secured credentials to cover the World Series.

"As Mazeroski came to bat in the ninth, I remember thinking, 'just get something going, get a hit, get on base some way.' I know sports writers are supposed to be neutral in the press box, but on that particular day I must admit to partisanship.

"When Maz connected, I followed the ball, mentally 'pushing' it toward the wall. When I saw it was gone, I remember thinking 'touch them all, don't miss a base!'

"As Maz crossed the plate, my next thought was of the long off-seasons of torment that I, as a Pirates follower, had endured from the Yankees fans where I was working, and then thinking to myself that it was now going to be a long off-season for them.

"It was, and they were glad to see me move to Connellsville shortly after The Miracle of Forbes Field."

Jim Lokhaiser
Sportscaster
WISR, Butler

"What I remember best about 1960 was that I started doing high school games over WISR in Butler, and I did a game in which Joe Namath quarterbacked Beaver Falls against Butler. The next year, 1961, I went to my first Pirates camp at Fort Myers, Florida. The Pirates were coming off winning the World Series and there weren't more than six reporters there the whole week. I remember Joe Brown saying, 'We're the world champions, and where are the newspaper and magazine people?' Bill Wilson was there from WJAC-TV in Johnstown, and Al Abrams and his entourage, the Litmans, Jack Hernon, were there, and Jimmy Klingensmith, the photographer, and Les Biederman and that was about it. If that were the Yankees and they had won the World Series, there would have been 55 or 60 media people there. The training camp facility at Fort Myers wasn't much to look at; it was an antiquated field. It was nothing like it would be at Bradenton when they moved there. Fort Myers was a little town then and there wasn't much to do, except sit out in front of the Bradford Hotel downtown and watch the people go by. The Litmans were nice to me and they took me everywhere they went, to restaurants and shows and such. Pie Traynor was there, and he didn't drive. So I started out driving him to and from the ballpark each day, and then to the dog track at night. That was the first time I ever saw segregation at work. They had a special section for blacks in the stands at the races. The blacks on the Pirates still ran into problems of that kind in Florida back then."

George Von Benko
WASP, Brownsville
KBL, Pittsburgh

"I remember my uncle Ted — his name was Ted Laskey — bet $600 on the Pirates. He owned a restaurant in Uniontown. My dad was a big Yankees fan, and he used to pick up the games on the radio from New York at night. When it came down to Game 7, my Uncle Ted wouldn't let my dad in his house. He was livid at my dad. He couldn't understand how my dad could be rooting for the Yankees when he had so much money riding on the game. My Uncle Ted always liked Mazeroski after that. I'm not sure he ever forgave my dad."

Joe Falls
Sports Columnist
Detroit News

"It was the greatest civic celebration I've ever seen. The joy I saw that day was unbelievable. People paraded through the streets celebrating. I left Forbes Field two hours after the game and I was in paper up to my knees. It was the most beautiful scene you'd ever want to see. I went to my hotel room to write. It was so hot. And it was so noisy outside my window. Fans were celebrating everywhere. There was no air-conditioning in my hotel room. I had a choice: open the window and be cool, but let all the noise in the room, or keep the window closed and sweat. I could get some fresh air or I could suffocate. But it was so noisy I couldn't hear myself think, so I closed the window."

Jack Lang
Retired Sportswriter
New York Daily News

"I can't remember what I got up and went to the refrigerator for . . . and now you want me to recall something that happened 33 years ago. I got that malady that comes at age 71 — CRS. I can't remember shit!

"But I do remember the '60 Series because I was ghosting a feature for *The Long Island Press* with Whitey Ford. I also was sleeping in a king-size bed with Charley Feeney, our baseball writer at the time, because *The Press* was trying to save money. That was the worst part of the Series.

"The Series was memorable for several things. Ford and the Yankees were sensational in the two games Whitey started. He didn't get to start until Game 3 and won, 10-0, with a four-hitter. Then he started again in Game 6 and won, 12-0, on a seven-hitter. Mazeroski was 1-for-6 against Ford in those two games.

"I remember the Yankees were not too pleased that Stengel started Art Ditmar in Games 1 and 5. Ditmar, a mediocre pitcher, did lead the Yankees with 15 wins that year. But he was never what you would call an ace who should be the starter in Game 1. The Yankees won the pennant by eight games over Baltimore and Ford, a wily old veteran,

241

should have been the starter for Games 1 and 5 and might have been able to come back for Game 7 if needed.

"The Yankees second-guessed their manager on the use of Ford and the front office probably did as well. They fired him a few days later.

"I also remember the whole town going beserk in Pittsburgh, I was staying at the Hilton and it took hours to get back Downtown after Game 7. I also remember Danny Whelan, the team trainer, and Bob Prince making so much about the Green Weenie hex.

"I think it was also a Series in which a manager showed up one of his players. Clete Boyer never forgot it. He still talks about it. Casey started Boyer at third base in Game 1 and then pinch-hit for him in the second inning before he ever got to bat. Bucs were leading 3-1 at the time. Berra and Skowron opened the second with singles and Casey sent up Dale Long as a pinch-hitter for Boyer, calling Boyer back from the on-deck circle, which was a long walk at Forbes Field, and embarrassing him in front of millions. Long flied out and Richardson lined to Skinner who doubled Berra off second. Yanks failed to score and Boyer was a basket case. A Stengel hunch went wrong. Boyer and McDougald alternated at third the rest of the Series.

"That's all I remember except for all the fans and the beer in the streets afterward. Was it Duquesne beer? I think they were sponsoring the Bucs in those days."

Bob Smizik
Sports Columnist
Pittsburgh Post-Gazette

"I was a sophomore at Pitt when the Pirates went into the 1960 World Series. Having grown up and been deeply attached to a team that was a big loser, this was quite an experience. Like the rest of the city, I was thrilled.

"The day of the first game I found myself wandering around Forbes Field during the lunch hour, just trying to share in the excitement. There was a television crew doing some filming which, back then, was quite unusual. I parked myself behind the guy doing the talking into a microphone and listened. To my astonishment, that Friday night I was part of a CBS show called 'Eyewitness to History.' I was on camera for a good 30 seconds, chewing like a cow on my gum behind the guy doing the talking.

"I remember sneaking a transistor radio into my 1 p.m. history lecture. I sat far enough in the back that the lecturer could not detect my radio. I passed information on to other students who were as interested as I was in what was going on about a quarter-mile away.

"I left school early the day of the seventh game. I don't think I had much confidence in the Pirates and I didn't want to hear the New Yorkers — and there were plenty of them at Pitt in those days — boasting. I had argued frequently and with much ardor with my New York friends during the course of the Series. I was home by myself —

my parents had tickets to the game — when Maz hit the home run. I remember going outside to our front porch looking for someone to celebrate with. But no one was out there.

"That night friends and I drove Downtown. We had to park at Duquesne University. It was a wonderful night. There was such joy. I don't imagine such a civic celebration could take place today. No sports victory will ever match that one in my mind."

Melvin Durslag
Sports Columnist, TV Guide
Los Angeles Herald-Examiner

"A person debarking in Pittsburgh for the World Series of 1960 was confronted at the airport by a garish sign reading, 'Beat 'em, Bucs.'

"You rode down the expressway towards town and cars passed bearing bumper stickers that said, 'Beat 'em, Bucs.' You saw it across the facades of factories, hotels and breweries, scarcely realizing that this was the lunatic index to the general dementia that gripped the city.

"When, in the seventh game of the Series, a fellow in a Pirates uniform struck a home run that beat the Yankees, the response that followed was worthy of discussion in a medical journal.

"People in the neighborhood of Forbes Field sprinted to the ball park and joined those inside in screaming, weeping and singing. The band played 'When Irish Eyes Are Smiling,' which was slightly unconventional, considering the guy who hit the home run was named Mazeroski and he was Polish.

"State troopers had to rescue the players from the mob and, for the next 12 hours, the scene in Pittsburgh was to suggest a revolution in a Latin American country.

"Early the next morning, I was awakened by snoring that seemed to be coming from my room at the Pittsburgh Hilton. I sat up, absolutely positive that nobody else was there the night before.

"A search disclosed an unauthorized body sprawled on the carpet outside the door, its hand clutching a glass containing a stale highball. Down the corridor, another man lay curled like a Guaymas shrimp on a couch too small for him. Outside, the streets were buried under tons of debris. Beer cans littered the gutters, and light poles, trolley wires and automobile tops were festooned with paper streamers.

"Plainly, Pittsburgh is a town not geared emotionally to success and should be excused from pennant contention for medical reasons. Pittsburgh was better adjusted to the type of teams inhabiting the place during the days of Fred Haney. Fred's club one time lost 12 straight. When the 13th game was rained out, the boys staged a victory celebration."

Roy McHugh
Executive Report

"During the 1960 World Series, I wrote sidebars (mostly clubhouse stuff) for *The Pittsburgh Press*, and I was a lot more interested in coming up with a decent story every day than I was in examining my emotions. There used to be a rule against cheering in the press box, and I never had any trouble obeying it. Objectivity, even feigned objectivity, helped me do a better job. I think it is unprofessional to write as a partisan. So, although at some level I was pleased when the Pirates won, I went about my business in the usual way. I remember that after the seventh game, while the Pirates were dousing one another with champagne and flinging wet towels from one end of the clubhouse to the other, a radio guy — Tom Bender, as I recall — asked me how come I was looking so preoccupied. The reason may have been that my Bill Mazeroski quotes were not the kind that would make riveting copy, and I knew it was going to be a problem for me.

"Mazeroski wasn't a player who gave sportswriters much to work with. Until late in his career, when he loosened up á little, he never had a whole lot to say, and hitting that home run hadn't exactly changed him into a chatterbox. In the middle of the celebration, Joe Brown handed him a bottle of champagne. He took one swig and handed it back, screwing up his face. One swig was more than enough. Eleven years later, when the Pirates won the 1971 Eastern Division championship, Mazeroski put away a quart of the stuff.

"The all-night street party touched off by Mazeroski's home run had already started when I left Forbes Field and drove to the office. I finished my piece and then joined the mob Downtown. It was one monstrous outdoor Animal House. Cars full of drunks, or of people just behaving like drunks, were bumper to bumper. And yet in comparison with what happened after the World Series victory in 1971 (rioting and burning, store windows shattered, the casualties dragged off to hospital emergency rooms, a hundred or so arrests) it was pretty tame. By 1971, the sixties generation had taken over. Smashing things was the way you expressed yourself."

Jerry Izenberg
Newark Star-Ledger

"Pittsburgh was a great, big, sweaty Cyrano of a town, holding off the Duke of Burgundy and his men with lightning parries and rapier thrusts while its shoulder blades were pressed tightly against the grimy outfield wall at Forbes Field.

"This city was a wall-to-wall ad for predestination. It stayed alive on memories of exceptions which prove the rule. It drew its strength from the vision of Bill Mazeroski circling the bases and Marshall Goldberg darting for the goal line out of a formation which lives only in old movies and Bill Dudley running over a linebacker in a world where everyone played a 6-2-2-1 defense.

"It bragged that it was a tough city and it always has been. It was loaded with action and with hustle and the only trouble was that after the hustlers handled the visiting slickers they went to work on each other and everyone wound up with someone else's back teeth in his pocket. This was a great source of satisfaction but the winners still had to pay the same dental tab as the losers.

"You can't explain Pittsburgh and the compulsion which drove it back to the ball parks when the track record told it over and over again that the best it could ever hope for was a tie. But those who persisted really enjoyed the success of the Steelers and the Pirates and the Penguins.

"Pittsburgh lived not off illusions so much as it lived off hope. Hope was its chauvinism. There were thousands of latter-day Jobs in Oakland and East Liberty and they wore their suffering with all the pride and joy of self-flagellants at a Mexican feast day. It was not a matter of vindication. It was simply a matter of showing up for war every time the roll was called."

Phil Musick
WTAE Radio
Author, Who Was Roberto?

"The 1960 season. The melding of a baseball team and a city that had awaited it thirty-three years and came to embrace it unashamedly. An affair of the heart between a team that could meet any demands and a town that wailed at its defeats and, literally, danced in the streets at its triumphs.

"The 1960 Pirates, the beloved Bucs, were a team for all time; all grit and hustle and daring. They snatched gut-wrenching victories from the brink of defeat. And they brought credibility to the basest of all baseball cliches — the one about 'the game never being over until the last man is out in the ninth.'

"Clemente hit .314 that summer, and led the club with 94 RBIs and 16 home runs, and thought he should have been the MVP in the National League. In the Series, he had nine hits and hit safely in all seven games. Clemente mixed with the fans and left his teammates behind after the seventh game. He didn't go to the post-game party. He never wore his 1960 ring. Clemente kept getting better and better from then on. He could never be ignored again."

Danny Murtaugh holds court with Pittsburgh sports writers, left to right, Chet Smith, Jack Hernon, Al Abrams and Les Biederman.

245

Where Were You?

*"That's when I became a serious fan,
and truly fell in love with baseball."*
—Gary Peck

Stanley Pittman
Monroeville, Pa.

"I remember one day that Roberto Clemente hit one out that just missed being a home run. The umpire said it was a foul ball. Danny Murtaugh and one of his coaches went out screaming into the face of the umpire. Murtaugh thought it should have been a home run. Roberto just stood at home plate, and leaned on his bat. He was so stoic. He didn't say anything. Then he hit a double. He didn't let it bother him. That impressed me."

Gary Peck
Attorney
Shadyside

"To me, Clemente was much more than just a baseball player. I have been a serious student of baseball for a long time, and I truly love the game. I talked my mother into letting me stay home from school to watch that seventh game of the 1960 World Series. It's my most vivid memory of baseball, and I was just ten at the time. That's when I became a serious fan, and truly fell in love with baseball. I'm a latecomer to Pittsburgh. I was in Washington, D.C., not in Pittsburgh, when he was playing. But, to me, Clemente was the greatest. For me, Clemente stands out. He wasn't just a magnificently talented baseball player. He was also an outstanding human being. Some of these ballplayers today seem so wrapped up in themselves. He was so different. To me, he really was a hero. He was genuinely interested in people. He cared. He suffered certain criticisms, much of which were intensified because he was a black Latin who was often misunderstood. Clemente was reviled when he was a star. He was accused of being a malingerer, of not going all out, of faking injuries and illnesses, criticisms which are more often aimed at black performers. There's been some revisionist history concerning Clemente in this city. He was not revered by everyone when he was playing. The memories are better now, and so is his image. It may be the same someday for Barry Bonds. People are critical of him now, but they will miss him as a ballplayer in this city. He is a great baseball player and people will miss seeing him in action at every game."

Larry Bush
Lake Shore Industries
Erie, Pa.

"I was working for a company called Sterling Seal out of Erie. The company officials asked all of us if they could use our names in submitting applications for World Series tickets. I was one of the lucky ones who got tickets. The company ended up having more tickets than it could use. So they had a raffle at work and you had to put up a buck to be eligible. I was one of the winners. The company provided us with a car, with food, and we got paid to work that day. You can't beat that. It was a great deal. That's how I got to see the seventh game of the World Series. We had seats — they were $7.70 apiece — right behind home plate. It wasn't until after we left the park that it probably registered what had happened. I still have the game program and the ticket stub."

Betty Dunn
Forest Hills, Pa.

"That's when I loved our athletes because that's when our athletes loved us."

Jim Titus
McKees Rocks, Pa.

"I grew up in Oakland, on Dawson, a road that led up to Forbes Field. Roberto Clemente was a great player, but he and Barry Bonds were clones. They didn't have a good relationship with the fans. Clemente used to push kids out of the way. I was one of those when I was 14. I'm amazed at how people have forgotten that. My favorite player was Dick Stuart, and I liked Gino Cimoli. You know who the kids really loved? Joe Christopher. He loved the kids. He tossed balls up in the stands to the kids, and had fun with them during the pre-game activity. I still have all the autographs of that year except — want to guess? — Clemente."

World Series ticket courtesy of Larry Bush

PITTSBURGH

PIRATS

NATIONAL LEAGUE CHAMPIONS

PITTSBURGH PIRATES

ROSTER

2—Oldis, Bob
4—Skinner, Bob
5—Smith, Hal
6—Burgess, Smoky
7—Stuart, Dick
9—Mazeroski, Bill
10—Trucks, Virgil
11—Schofield, Dick
12—Hoak, Don
14—Nelson, Rocky
16—Baker, Gene
18—Virdon, Bill
19—Friend, Bob
20—Cimoli, Gino
21—Clemente, Bob
22—Gibbon, Joe

23—Christopher, Joe
24—Groat, Dick
26—Face, Roy
29—Labine, Clem
30—Mizell, Wilmer
31—Haddix, Harvey
32—Law, Vern
35—Green, Fred

37—Cheney, Tom
39—Witt, George
40—Murtaugh, Danny
41—Burwell, Bill
42—Vernon, Mickey
43—Narron, Sam
44—Oceak, Frank
45—Levy, Lenny

NATIONAL LEAGUE UMPIRES

Lynton (Dusty) Boggess
William (Bill) Jackowski
Stanley (Stan) Landes

		1	2	3	4	5	6	7	8	9	10	11	AB	R	H	PO	A	E
Virdon cf 18		FLY o				GO			H				4	1	2			
Groat ss 24		FLYo GO							H				4	1	1			
Bob Skinner lf 4		W		GO			FLY o	SAC o					2	1	0			
Nelson 16 14		BB		W			GO	FLY o					3	1	1			
Clemente RF 21		FLY o	4-63 GO		GO		GO		H				4	1	1			
Burgess c 6 / Smith c		H	W		GO			H/	HR Smith				3	0	2			
Hoak 3b 12		W			4-C			FLY o	FLY o				3	1	0			
Mazeroski 28 9		A		FN o		GO		6-43 GO	K				4	2	2			
5in Law P 32		GO						H					2	0	0			
8in Face P 26									Friend				1	1	1			
		2	3	0	0	0	0	0	0	156 1			10	11				0

or Friend in 9th
in Haddix 3 in 9th (W)

Christopher — for Burgess in 7th
Cimoli — might for Face in 8th

PITTSBURGH

PIRATES

WORLD SERIES 1960

OFFICIAL SOUVENIR PROGRAM

50¢

Roberto Clemente
He has become a cult figure to his fans

"He had about him a touch of royalty."
—Baseball Commissioner Bowie Kuhn

Mostly they talk about some sensational throw they once saw him make. An opposing runner was foolish enough to test his arm and tried to score from second base on a single to right. They remember Roberto Clemente catching the ball off the base off the wall in the corner at Forbes Field and spinning and firing in one pirouette move, like an Olympic discus thrower, and hurling the baseball as if it were shot from a rocket launcher. It sailed on a jet stream to home plate, the Pirates catcher caught it and made the tag. Bam. Bam. Unreal. Clemente is recalled best for such great defensive plays. He had 19 assists from right field in one season, even though most baserunners respected his arm and accuracy so much they tended to be conservative and played it safe when the ball went out his way.

Others talk about him climbing that wall, or reaching up where the wall ended and the screen started and snaring the ball, or lunging into and along that wall, or catching one on the dead run in deepest right center field. They remember his reckless manner, his disregard for his own body's well-being, his daring, his flair and, yes, even his showboating. Some remember a home run, a base running maneuver, an extra base hit.

"I played mad all the time," Clemente once confessed. "It helped me. In all the years, when they talk about fielding, I am the best right fielder I have seen. But always it was, 'Roberto Clemente is ONE of the best.' "

Roy McHugh, a marvelous writer for *The Pittsburgh Press*, said, "I liked him better and better as the years went by. He got to the point where he could laugh at himself a little. He used to tell all the writers about his aches and pains, then get mad at them if they wrote about what he said. Myron Cope did a story about him once for *Sports Illustrated*, pointing up his hypochondriac tendencies, and Clemente didn't talk to him for about six years. And it was a great piece; it was hardly a hatchet-job.

"When Clemente was young, he was awfully difficult to deal with. Whenever you'd go to talk with him, he'd raise his voice and everyone in the room would look over, and he'd go into a five-minute denunciation of sports writers. I got tired of that, and stayed away from him. But he became more popular in Pittsburgh than Pie Traynor, which was hard to do, especially since Clemente never stayed here year-round. He became the biggest sports figure in this city. Maybe Mario Lemieux has replaced him as a revered sports figure."

The fans often chorused "Arriba! Arriba!" to encourage Clemente, and they were urged to do so by Bob Prince, leaning out of his press box perch above home plate at Forbes Field to lead the cheerleading.

The mind's eye can still see Clemente standing on second base, after he hit a double for the landmark 3,000th hit of his fabled career, waving his ballcap in that magic moment captured on film by *Pittsburgh Press* photographer Ed Morgan. It was his last hit in a regular season game for the Pirates.

Some talk about some special moment they enjoyed with him, his kindness, his personal attention, an autograph on a game program or picture that they treasure, seeing him visiting the kids at Children's Hospital. He was known to be generous in tipping clubhouse attendants, and gave money freely to friends and acquaintances who put the touch on him. Others speak of a snub, a time they waited for an autograph, and he brushed them off. They won't forget that experience either. It hurt. Clemente is recalled quite like no other Pirate of his era. Mazeroski is remembered affectionately. Clemente is remembered reverently. Clemente is a cult figure, especially to those who were young when he played and young when he died.

He died tragically in a plane crash while on a mission of mercy on New Year's Eve of 1972, taking medicine, food, and clothing to earthquake victims in Nicaragua. He was 38. In that respect he has a mystique about him, the way movie stars, rock musicians and other entertainers — Marilyn Monroe, Elvis Presley, Jimi Hendrix, Jim Morrison, Judy Garland, Jimmy Dean, Sal Mineo, John Belushi, John Lennon — who died too young, tragically or under questionable circumstances. There is something fascinating about such figures. Their deaths increase the appeal and strengthen the memories they might have otherwise left behind. The same is true of the Kennedys and Dr. Martin Luther King. Despite their sins, they enjoy a special sainthood. Harry Truman, talking about Abraham Lincoln, once said, "Heroes know when to die." Whenever there is a sports card show in Pittsburgh, collectors come from great distances, from New York, Maryland and D.C., seeking any kind of Clemente memorabilia they can come by. Seeing a photo of Clemente can light up their eyes. An English poet once wrote that "Nothing evokes sentimentality like an athlete dying young." It was that way with Clemente.

"I think the thing that I guess killed him," said General Manager Joe L. Brown the day after Clemente's death, "was his desire to do things for people. What he was trying to do for the people in Nicaragua was one of the few public things he did. He generally did things, kind things, few people knew about."

His real name was Roberto Clemente Walker, but like so many things about this man, someone got it mixed up at the outset, something got lost in the translation, and he never bothered to correct it. So he became Roberto Walker Clemente. In truth, it fit him better. There were other Walkers. There was only one Clemente.

"Misunderstood is the best way I can explain him," said Brown. "He was such a fine, warm, human being and yet I don't think he came across that way."

Brown understood Clemente. It was one of the rare employer-employee relationships in the cold bitter business that baseball has become.

Clemente was accused of being a malingerer and hypochondriac, sometimes in his own clubhouse. The business about hypochondria irritated Brown. "He played a good many times when most guys wouldn't play," said Brown. "Anybody who plays as hard as he does is bound to get hurt. I've seen him run into a wall head-first, split his chin, get eight stitches and be back in the lineup the next day."

You could look it up, as Casey Stengel used to say. Clemente went to bat at least 500 times 10 years in a row. He didn't know how to handle criticism. "He was extremely sensitive," said Brown.

"I have the same face all the time," Clemente once said. "You must understand that my mother, she is almost 80, and my father, he is 86, had to work so hard. When I grew up, one dollar meant a lot. My mother worked from sunup to sundown. It created something in my mind. It is why I never joke a lot."

He never forgot those humble beginnings. He loved kids. He thought that a kid playing ball was a kid who would not get into trouble, innocent and naive as that may sound. "I love the game," he would often say. Clemente had more confidence than anyone in the Pirates clubhouse. "From head to toe," he once announced, "Roberto Clemente is as good as the President of the United States. I believe that, and I think every one should believe that about himself."

Clemente can not be criticized for that observation. The President he was referring to was Richard M. Nixon.

Clemente was in right field when I first attended Pirates games as a member of the Knot-Hole Gang in my mid-teens. I never did a one-on-one interview with Clemente, and I regret that.

I wish I had gotten to know him better. I believe I could have gotten some good stories out of him. I take pride in my ability to get good stories out of sports stars regarded as difficult interviews, or controversial figures, such as Joe DiMaggio, Wilt Chamberlain, Joe Namath, Muhammad Ali, Thurman Munson, Franco Harris, Bill Bradley, Dave Parker, Billie Jean King . . . and I would have welcomed the challenge of Clemente interviews. But I did not come on the major league baseball beat until the year after his death.

To provide a composite picture of him here, I had to rely on interviews I did with those who worked with him, and from what I read about him in several books, magazine articles and newspaper stories. I have borrowed liberally from such sources, with proper attribution, to offer as many views of "The Great One" as possible. I would encourage readers to seek out such materials at Pittsburgh area libraries if you wish to learn more about the man.

One of his biographers, Phil Musick, felt he knew Clemente as well as any of his contemporaries, yet confessed that he wasn't sure he knew him at all. So Clemente remains a mystical figure in Pittsburgh sports lore. That is surely part of his fascination.

"You know all about him. But in real life he's even better."
— Brooks Robinson

He was always a heroic figure, a sleek, compact-muscled man who could do it all on a baseball field, whether it was Forbes Field, Three Rivers Stadium or some distant outpost in this country or his native Puerto Rico.

It took awhile for Pirates fans to truly appreciate him, and it took his untimely death in 1972 to properly focus attention on his marvelous feats, both on and off the playing field. Real fame came to Clemente late in life, and more so when he was gone.

He was something else, something special, an athletic marvel. Sometimes he was hard to understand, and to fathom, but this may have added to his mystique more than anything else. Clemente cried to be loved, to be lauded, to be cheered, to be crowned as one of the game's great players.

He came from Puerto Rico, but Clemente became a big part of Pittsburgh. "In a way I was born twice," Clemente said when honored in special ceremonies on July 25, 1970 at Three Rivers Stadium, his night at the ballpark. "I was born in 1934 and again in 1955, when I came to Pittsburgh. I am thankful I can say that I live two lives."

He didn't live either of them long enough, however.

He was with the Pirates so long, 18 seasons, yet he was gone too soon, leaving his wife, Vera, and their three children, as well as his many admirers, behind him. He left us with many cherished memories.

"You know all about him," said Baltimore's Brooks Robinson during the 1971 World Series. "But in real life he's even better."

For the record, Clemente was born August 18, 1934 in Carolina, Puerto Rico, and he died December 31, 1972 in an airplane crash in San Juan, Puerto Rico. He died with four others when an airplane carrying supplies to earthquake-stricken Nicaragua crashed.

Clemente was selected by the Pirates in the player draft when the Brooklyn Dodgers left him unprotected after the 1954 season, his first as a professional.

He appeared in only 87 games in the minors in Montreal, and batted .257. The Pirates paid the princely sum of $4,000 to get him from the Dodgers.

When he heard the news, he was in Puerto Rico. "I didn't even know where Pittsburgh was," he admitted later.

For the next 18 years, Clemente starred in the Pirates' outfield. He won four National League batting crowns and batted .317 for his career, with 240 home runs and 1,305 RBI. He also won 12 Rawlings' Gold Glove awards for his outstanding defensive abilities.

He hit safely in all seven games in both the 1960 and the 1971 World Series, winning the Series MVP Award in 1971 when he batted .414 with two home runs and two doubles against the Baltimore Orioles.

Clemente was a 12-time All-Star and the National League MVP in 1966. He ranks in the Pirates' Top Ten in 12 offensive categories.

His No. 21 was retired by the Pirates in 1973. He is featured, along with mementos of his career, in a wall display in the lobby of the Pirates offices at Three Rivers Stadium.

Clemente was characterized for a Latin-American variety of showboating. "Look at numero uno," he seemed to say.

His hard-headed reputation stemmed from a fabled episode that took place at second base in the late '50s. Cincinnati's Johnny Temple, taken out by Clemente on a double play two innings earlier, pivoted over the bag after a force play on Clemente and threw toward first from down under — the way Kent Tekulve would later release his pitches. The ball caught Clemente smartly right between the eyes. He didn't even blink.

He once ran over his manager, who was coaching third base, to complete an inside-the-park home run. It excited the fans, startled the manager and shocked the Cincinnati Reds.

Clemente explained afterward that he had sore feet that day, and wanted to get the game over with as quickly as possible. It was not the last time he would run over or by a third base coach waving his arms frantically with a stop sign.

It took him awhile to get his act together. His first five years with the team were marred by injuries and illnesses. He had a frayed spine that caused tortuous backaches. He also suffered flu attacks, a nervous stomach, malaria, spasms of diarrhea, infected tonsils, headaches, insomnia and bone chips in his throwing elbow. In his first five years with the Pirates, he missed 143 games for one reason or another. He did a hitch with the Marines at Parris Island and came away saying his back never felt better.

He even complained about Benny Benack's Iron City Six Band that played "The Bucs Are Going All The Way" over and over again at Forbes Field. Clemente called the band a jinx.

Clemente was called a good "bad ball" hitter. He was a free-swinger, but one of his most respected foes, Sandy Koufax of the Dodgers, said Clemente knew the strike zone well, but could hit pitches that were outside of it, and that he could hit with two strikes on him as well as anyone. He almost never drew a base on balls. In 1956, for instance, he went to bat 542 times and he walked exactly 13 times.

"All the good hitters are good two-strike hitters," claimed Koufax, "but no hitter is better with two strikes on him. I don't give Clemente a good pitch from my point of view, but he's liable to hit it anyway. To him, it's a good pitch. You just never know if you make a good one to that guy. He chases what I, or some other pitcher, might call a bad ball, but he hits them. It may not be a strike, but it's a strike in Clemente's zone, and also a base hit."

His teammates offer interesting insights into the man who was Roberto Clemente.

Roberto Clemente
acknowledges fans
after hitting
a double for
his 3000th hit.

Ed Morgan/The Pittsburgh Press

ElRoy Face: "I knew he was good when we won the World Series in '60, but I didn't know he was going to have the career he ended up having. He could do anything. He could hit, he could hit with power, he could run, he could field and he could throw with the best of them. He deserves to be in the Hall of Fame. But I don't think he should've gone in when he did. He should have waited the required five years like everyone else. His kids were too young to appreciate his accomplishment."

Bill Mazeroski: "When I first saw Clemente play in 1956, he wasn't the hitter he would become later, but anyone who saw him throw knew he was something special. During those first few years, he was always happy, full of vinegar, a guy who left laughter after him wherever he went."

Dick Groat: "He had the greatest God-given talent I ever saw. There was nothing in the game he couldn't do if he wanted to."

Bob Friend: "He had a good feeling for the fans, and felt we owed them another pennant. He'd get pretty windy on the subject, and you wondered how you could turn him off. A lot of players leave the game feeling the world owes them a living, but Clemente was an exception to the rule. He knew what baseball had done for him, and he often expressed his appreciation."

Bobby Bragan, one of his former managers, said of him: "The best way to describe Roberto Clemente is to say, if he were playing in New York they'd be comparing him to DiMaggio. I would say his greatness is limited only by the fact that he does not hit the long ball consistently, and by the fact that he is not playing in New York, or even Chicago or Los Angeles."

Former baseball commissioner Bowie Kuhn: "Somehow Roberto transcended super-stardom. His marvelous playing skills rank him among the truly elite. And what a wonderfully good man he was. Always concerned about others. He had about him a touch of royalty."

Clemente was neither the first black nor the first Latin American ballplayer on the Pirates. Curt Roberts, a capable second baseman, was the first black. Seven years after Branch Rickey signed Jackie Robinson to a contract with the Brooklyn Dodgers, he signed Roberts as the first black to a Pirates contract. Roberts was a slick-fielding, light-hitting performer. He had a brief career (1954-56) with the Pirates before giving way to Bill Mazeroski at second base. Carlos Bernier, a decent outfielder and hitter, was the first Latin American on the Pirates, playing for them in the summer of 1953. I saw a ballgame when I was 11 years old, one of the first games I ever saw at Forbes Field, in which Bernier hit a record-tying three triples against the Cincinnati Reds in May of that 1953 season. Roman Mejias, a Cuban outfielder, joined the Pirates in 1955, the same as Clemente, and they became close friends. But Clemente was the first star. And it was Rickey, significantly enough, who drafted Clemente away from the Dodgers' organization. The Dodgers were unsuccessful in their attempts to hide him.

Clemente's color and his Latin accent caused him difficulties, some real and some imagined, throughout his career, especially at the start when he was trying to find his way in Pittsburgh and with the Pirates.

Clemente comes in for mention in a play called *Fences*, written by August Wilson, who spent most of his youth living in a two-room apartment behind a grocery store on Bedford Avenue in Pittsburgh's Hill district, but lived for a few years as a teenager on Sylvan Avenue in Hazelwood. He lived across the street from Gladstone High School and just around the corner from a branch of the Carnegie Library, and there is a sign at the desk in the library acknowledging that it was Wilson's boyhood library. Many familiar characters and places from the Hazelwood area show up in his plays. Wilson won the Pulitzer Prize for drama in 1987 and 1990.

Fences is set in Pittsburgh in the late 1950s. Troy Maxson is a garbage collector, an embittered former baseball player in the Negro leagues, and a proud dominating father. When college athletic recruiters court his teenage son, Troy Maxson struggles against his son, Cory, his own wife, and his own frustrated ambitions.

Here's an excerpt from Act One, Scene One in the play:

CORY: The Pirates won today. That makes five in a row.

TROY: I ain't thinking about the Pirates. Got an all-white team. Got that boy . . . that Puerto Rican boy . . . Clemente. Don't even half-play him. That boy could be something if they give him a chance. Play him one day and sit him on the bench the next.

CORY: He gets a lot of chances to play.

TROY: I'm talking about playing regular. Playing every day so you can get your timing. That's what I'm talking about.

CORY: They got some white guys on the team that don't play every day. You can't play everybody at the same time.

TROY: If they got a white fellow sitting on the bench . . . you can bet your last dollar he can't play! The colored guy got to be twice as good before he gets on the team. That's why I don't want you to get all tied up in them sports. Man on the team and what it get him? They got colored on the team and don't use them. Same as not having them. All them teams the same.

CORY: The Braves got Hank Aaron and Wes Covington. Hank Aaron hit two home runs today. That makes forty-three.

TROY: Hank Aaron ain't nobody. That's what you supposed to do. That's how you supposed to play the game. Ain't nothing to it. It's just a matter of timing . . . getting the right follow-through. Hell, I can hit forty-three home runs right now!

CORY: Not off no major-league pitching, you couldn't.

TROY: We had better pitching in the Negro leagues. I hit seven home runs off of Satchel Paige. You can't get no better than that!

CORY: Sandy Koufax. He's leading the league in strike outs.

TROY: I ain't thinking of no Sandy Koufax.

CORY: You got Warren Spahn and Lew Burdette. I bet you couldn't hit no home runs off Warren Spahn.

Just as Bill Mazeroski and Sam Narron talked about hitting stones with sticks, and pretending they were ballplayers in their youth, Clemente often recalled hitting tin cans with a stick, and bouncing a rubber ball off the walls of his mother's kitchen.

Clemente started out with a slow-pitch softball league run by Robert Marin in Puerto Rico. Marin became one of his boyhood mentors, and Clemente publicly thanked Marin for his contribution to his development on several occasions.

When Clemente started to play baseball, he was an outstanding shortstop, but he couldn't hit, and often batted eighth. As a teenager, he was not an instant success with the bat, though he often made sensational plays in the field.

But his black eyes gleamed with a fondness for the game, and there was no denying his keen interest.

"I never saw a boy who loved baseball like he did," said Marin. "He spent every hour he could playing. He always carried that ball to squeeze, to make his hands stronger."

Clemente became an athlete to be noticed in high school. There was considerable speculation that he would, indeed, represent his country in the track and field competition in the 1952 Olympic Games at Helsinki as a javelin thrower. He could fling the javelin 170 feet. But nothing ever came of that; baseball was his overriding passion. Pittsburgh would later claim another nationally-recognized javelin thrower in Terry Bradshaw. Clemente and Bradshaw may have had the two greatest arms in Pittsburgh sports history.

Clemente first came to the attention of major league baseball scouts at a tryout camp, and it was Al Campanis of the Brooklyn Dodgers who first pursued him. The New York Giants got a look as well, but weren't impressed.

Both teams might still be in New York if either one of them had signed and kept Clemente. The Dodgers did sign him, but the Pirates stole him away from them with the first pick in the draft. Had Clemente stayed with the Dodgers, he would have been such a great draw for them with the large Latin American population in New York. It's unlikely the Giants would have gone to the West Coast alone. So Clemente coming to the Pirates may have changed the national baseball map for good.

Joe Brown came to Pittsburgh in 1956, following 16 years of administrative work at various minor league outposts, and his arrival came one year after that of Clemente. Talk about good timing. Brown became one of Clemente's biggest boosters, and remains so today.

"He was so emotional, so intense, so sensitive," said Brown. "He didn't understand a lot of things."

Most of his teammates didn't understand him, and few made the effort to befriend and embrace him in the beginning. He was never that close to any of his teammates.

Nobody knows any better than Brown the difficulties Clemente encountered as a newcomer in town. Clemente was homesick, for certain, and his best friend became a fellow named Phil Dorsey, who was introduced to him on his first day in town by Bob Friend, who had served in an Army reserve unit with Dorsey. Dorsey was a postal worker, but he became Clemente's closest friend in Pittsburgh, and remained so until Clemente's death. Dorsey was called "Pittsburgh Phil." Clemente's kids called him Uncle Phil. He accompanied Clemente everywhere, and they liked to go to movies together. As I was writing this book, I learned that Dorsey was doing time in a federal prison in Texas for his involvement in a major theft of stamps and services at a Pittsburgh post office in 1991.

Brown saw Clemente as "a driven athlete," and believes he not only had great natural ability, but pushed himself to be great. The Pirates were at the bottom when Clemente came to town, and stayed there awhile. Their lone representative in the 1954 and 1955 All-Star Game was Frank Thomas, who had grown up playing ball in the shadows of Forbes Field. Clemente started in right field in the seventh game of the 1955 season, going up against the Dodgers, ironically enough.

Forbes Field was a beautiful ballpark back then, a sylvan setting, with an ivy-covered wall — with no signs or billboards marring its facade — maple trees on the other side in Schenley Park, and towering overhead was the 42-story Cathedral of Learning, the skyscraper showcase building of the University of Pittsburgh. It was, indeed, a unique setting, befitting a great ballplayer like Clemente would eventually become.

Clemente came to the conclusion right away that Forbes Field was too formidable for him to try and hit home runs. It was a spacious ballpark, bigger than most in the major leagues, indeed, 457 feet to left center, 365 feet down the line to left to a 25-foot-scoreboard, 300 feet to the right field corner, where the foul line was guarded by a high fence.

It was a ballpark that brought out the best in Clemente as well as Bill Virdon, who played alongside him in center field. Both were defensive standouts.

"When I first saw Forbes Field, I said, 'Forget home runs.' I was strong, but nobody was that strong," recalled Clemente in an interview midway through his career. "I became a line-drive hitter."

Clemente was concerned about his physical welfare. He was involved in an auto crash before he reported to the Pirates, and it left him with back problems that persisted throughout his career. He was thought to be injury-prone, and was frequently rapped, in print and behind his back, for not being able to play more often than he did.

Clemente took care of himself, spending much time with the trainer, and frequenting the whirlpool bath, the way another gifted Pittsburgh performer, Franco Harris, would do years later with the Pittsburgh Steelers.

"I know Roberto was hurt deeply by the criticism he took the first few years here," said Nellie King, the former Pirates pitcher who became a broadcasting sidekick to Bob Prince and Jim Woods. "He was withdrawn partly because of the language. He had only been out of Puerto Rico one other time. Everything here was confusing him."

Roberto Clemente chats with Manager Danny Murtaugh during the 1971
World Series with Baltimore Orioles.

"Dying isn't important, it's the way we live that counts."
—Spencer Tracy

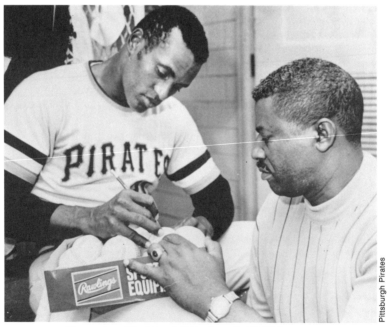

Clemente with friend "Pittsburgh Phil" Dorsey

*"Every time I hear
he has an ache,
I expect him
to go five for five."*
—Gil Hodges on
Roberto Clemente

Pittsburgh Pirates

With his youngest son, Enrique

Wide World

**Clemente climbs right field wall to snare shot by
Dodgers' Duke Snider during 1962 season.**

Street & Smith's Baseball

Among other problems, Clemente was an insomniac. He once told a friend, "If I could sleep, I would hit .400."

He loved to listen to music when he couldn't sleep, and Frank Sinatra and Nat King Cole were among his favorites. He had lots of record albums. He liked to go to the Crawford Grill in the Hill to listen to live jazz music.

Clemente felt the color of his skin, and the country where he came from, often made him an outcast in his own clubhouse, and in the city where he performed like few other outfielders or any athletes, for that matter.

"I don't believe in color; I believe in people," said Clemente. "I always respect everyone and thanks to God my mother and father taught me never to hate, never to dislike someone because of their color. I didn't even know about this stuff when I got here."

Curt Roberts and Roman Mejias counseled Clemente in that regard. It had only been eight years since Jackie Robinson broke the color line in major league baseball, and black baseball players still had difficulty being accepted.

"Most people who are good know it."
— Bill Virdon

Bill Virdon and Clemente were two of the finest outfielders in the league. Virdon's view of Clemente up close gave him a special appreciation for the young player from Puerto Rico.

"It was obvious he didn't doubt his ability to play the game," said Virdon. "He didn't brag, but he said things that indicated his confidence. Most people who are good know it. There are two kinds of confidence in baseball. I had one kind, he had the other. I didn't know if I could play in the big leagues. I struggled for five years in the minors. When you struggle, you have to be concerned. He hardly played in the minors. If I hadn't stayed here, I could've accepted that. He knew he was going to make it; he didn't even think about not making it."

In his outstanding in-depth 1974 biography of Clemente called *Who Was Roberto?*, Pittsburgh writer Phil Musick made the following observation:

"Like most players, Clemente did not read newspapers; but like most players, he had many friends who did, and they loyally kept him informed of what was being written. Through their devotion, they kept Clemente at odds with the media. He was daily and feverishly charging the news media with: implying he was a malingerer, accusing him of receiving preferential treatment, ridiculing his use of the English language and his style of play, ignoring him, unjustly denying him a Most Valuable Player award, and other crimes against humanity too numerous to mention.

"Every day of his professional life, Clemente sat in judgment on the news media. The verdict (guilty) and the sentence (his enmity) were unchanging. The press, he believed, portrayed him as a comic figure. He would tell reporters, 'My bad shoulder feels good, but my good shoulder feels bad.' The words were humorous, but the intent behind them was not, and to appear publicly cast as a buffoon rubbed Clemente's pride raw. Still, it is reasonable to conclude that he cherished his feud with the press; made it do his bidding; and drew forth from it inspiration."

He grew tired, for instance, of seeing himself referred to as "the Puerto Rican hot dog" in the daily newspapers.

Clemente once admitted, "If I would be happy, I would be a bad player. With me, when I get mad it puts energy into my body."

He also once said, "I feel better when I am sick." Yogi Berra attracted commercials for those kind of lines.

Another time, Clemente said, "I am tired, tired, tired. I am always tired. I never sleep."

Les Biederman, the baseball writer for *The Pittsburgh Press*, used to quote Clemente speaking phonetically, and Clemente felt he always came off as a comic figure. Al Abrams of the *Pittsburgh Post-Gazette*, who was more popular with the players, cleaned up Clemente's comments. Biederman made Clemente angry by frequently referring to the fact in print that "he didn't speak well."

But even Biederman recognized Clemente's ability, and offered him the usual qualified praise in an article he wrote early during Clemente's rookie season of 1955 for *The Sporting News*:

"There aren't many bright spots on the last-place Pirates but one of the brightest is Roberto Clemente. Although he has only a working knowledge of English and speaks with some difficulty, Clemente has no trouble at all playing the National Game. The Pittsburgh fans have fallen in love with his spectacular fielding and his deadly right arm."

And Clemente returned the affection. "I wouldn't play for nobody else," he was quoted as saying years later. "People are wonderful here."

George Kiseda came on the beat for the *Pittsburgh Sun-Telegraph* in 1958, about a year and a half before the demise of that newspaper, and wrote some of the best stuff, certainly among the most sensitive, that had ever been written about Clemente.

Roy McHugh of *The Press*, who was scolded by Clemente a couple of times without warrant, once suggested that Clemente ate reporters alive to fatten himself for winning batting titles in the National League.

In 1960, Clemente broke every personal record, hitting .314, scoring 89 runs, collecting 179 hits, 16 home runs and 94 RBIs. He was often compared to Willie Mays. "Willie is a very good ball player," said Clemente, "but why does everybody say I run like Willie, catch like Willie, throw like Willie and hit line drives like Willie? I am Roberto Clemente."

Jim Murray of the *Los Angeles Times* once wrote, "Willie Mays just might be better. On the other hand, he might not. Henry Aaron might have to move to the infield if Clemente were after the same spot in the outfield."

When Willie Mays was asked who was the best ballplayer he had ever seen, he responded. "I think I was the best ballplayer I've ever seen." Pushed to provide another name, Mays said, "The next one would be Roberto Clemente."

Musick sheds much light on Clemente's constant bickering with the media in his biography. When newcomer Dick Stockton came to town, and started shooting from the hip as an outspoken and unconventional voice in town, Clemente became unglued. Stockton, who would soon move on to Boston before beginning a long and prosperous career as a network broadcasting star, implied that Clemente was not a team player.

"You say maybe I no a team player," Clemente screamed at a group of newsmen prior to an exhibition game in Florida, according to Musick's account.

"I win four batting titles. I kill myself in the outfield. I try to catch everything that stays in the park. I play when I am hurt.

"What more do you writers want from me? Did any ballplayer come up to you and say that I am not a team player? Who say that? The writers, right? Well, I tell you one thing, the more I stay away from writers the better I am. You know why? Because they are trying to create a bad image for me. You know what they have against me? Because I am black and Puerto Rican. I am proud to be Puerto Rican."

Musick provided further detail:

"Did you ever see me loaf on the field?" continued Clemente. "I break my ass out there. Even Harry Walker say to me, 'Roberto, why you break your ass out there? Look at what the other fellows do, how they play. Take it easy.'"

Later, Clemente would say about Stockton's criticism. "Why that son-of-a-bitch say those things about me? Why he hurt my family? The year I come to this town I hurt my back, but I do my best. They call me a goldbrick, a mama's boy, a rotten fellow. I never do anything to that Stockton. He come in this clubhouse, I tell you, I kill him."

"I'd hit better than that for eight straight seasons, but I'm just Clemente."

Clemente would constantly complain to out-of-town newsmen about the treatment he got in Pittsburgh. In a story by Dan Hafner of *The Los Angeles Times*, after Clemente had led all major league hitters by a wide margin with a .357 batting average in 1967, that was reprinted in *Pittsburgh Weekly Sports*, Clemente said, "It took the .357 batting average to gain any credit for me. Other guys hit .309 and they are recognized as superstars. I'd hit better than that for eight straight seasons, but I'm just Clemente. It takes one great year to be recognized. I don't know what I have to do. Until the players started voting, I didn't win a fielding award."

Checking through Clemente's files at the Pirates offices, one is constantly coming across stories that carry headlines like the following: "Clemente Leads League In Aches And Batting." His ailments got as much space as his gaudy baseball statistics. Clemente would detail his difficulties to anybody with a pen and pad, then complain about the way he was portrayed in the stories that came out of these exchanges.

"I went to the hospital," Clemente once told Larry Merchant of *The Philadelphia News*, "and I try to go to sleep for the doctors. They find nothing. They sent me home and say, 'Go to sleep.'"

Clemente shrugged after he told Merchant about the docs' diagnosis. He said one of his tricks was to stay up all night watching television, and then play cards with his wife until dawn, and then pass out for four or five hours. Clemente said he could sleep well in some places, like Puerto Rico, Los Angeles and New York. "Chicago is fair," he said. "Everywhere else is terrible."

After he starred in the 1971 World Series, Clemente told a contingent of reporters, including Jerry Izenberg of the *Newark Star-Ledger*, that he had been a victim of benign neglect. "Hey, how come you guys don't know me?" said Clemente. "How come they call Pete Rose in Cincinnati Charlie Hustle? I hustle just like Pete Rose and they don't call me nothing."

Izenberg detailed all the baggage Clemente carried with him through the years . . . that people always found flaws in him, that he was a hypochondriac, that he couldn't pull the ball, that he failed to carry the whole franchise on his back.

"But now," wrote Izenberg, "after 17 major league seasons, 37-year-old Roberto Clemente is an overnight sensation."

Clemente wasn't the only one who vindicated himself in that Series. The Pirates were written off after they dropped the first two games to the Orioles. "There is not one among them who doesn't feel that this was their moment of vindication," wrote Izenberg after the Bucs battled back to beat the Baltimore team in seven games. "And there is not one among them who isn't right on that count. They ran a dandy crusade."

Roger Angell, writing for the *New Yorker*, did an essay that ended up in his book *The Summer Game* that captured Clemente's performance in the 1971 World Series. "Now and again — very rarely — we see a man who seems to have met all the demands, challenged all the implacable averages, spurned the mere luck. He has defied baseball, even altered it, and for a time at least the game is truly his."

In a book about Clemente, Kal Wagenheim wrote, "Unlike the Goliath-sized supermen of basketball and football, his physique was a really perfect match for the 'normal' ideal that one sees in time-weathered friezes and statues. He was strikingly handsome, with a superbly sculptured body: five feet, ten inches tall, one hundred and eighty pounds, broad-shouldered with powerful arms and legs, slender of waist, fleet of foot."

In my research I came across a revealing story about Clemente by Dick Young of the *New York Daily News*, who was then the most respected baseball writer in the country.

I selected Young's story to be reprinted in *Pittsburgh Weekly Sports*, a tabloid I edited and published on a shoestring in the '60s.

"Someone once said that if Roberto Clemente could sing, Harry Belafonte would have to learn to hit a baseball for a living, and it's true," Young's column began. "Clemente has more than a well-made face, and a hipless physique; he has eyes that sparkle, and a smile that captivates, and a Puerto Rican accent that sings. When he tells a story, he tells it with a zest that fills the room, and you listen and like him. Governor Wallace would like him."

Young provided a blow-by-blow account of a story Clemente told, in great detail, about an incident he experienced while playing winter baseball. The final series was played in Nicaragua. Clemente told of what a poor country it was, and how the people were impoverished. He said during the baseball series, the fans in the stands were throwing things at him. They really got to him, he said, when they tossed an iguana at him. Clemente said it was the ugliest thing he'd ever seen. Clemente kicked at the iguana. That was a mistake. "This thing suddenly jumps up in front of me!" recalled Clemente. "Now I run."

Young said Clemente ran while telling the story, to make his point.

He closed his column on Clemente — and mind you this was in August, 1964 — by quoting Clemente as saying of Nicaragua, "I never go back there again."

"He is vociferously resentful
of the fact that he is the
least known, least sung
superstar in baseball."
— Myron Cope

Cope wrote an article on Clemente for *Sports Illustrated* (May 7, 1966), the one McHugh referred to, which was reprinted in an outstanding collection of Cope's magazine pieces in a book called *Broken Cigars* (Prentice-Hall, Inc., 1968)

It was called "Aches, Pains, and Batting Titles." Cope certified Clemente as a real hypochondriac, and Clemente was so incensed by it that he didn't speak to Cope for several years after the article appeared. Again, something must have been lost in the translation because Cope's piece was largely highly complimentary of Clemente.

Cope could write with the best of them, and often wrote with tongue in cheek. He had wonderful lines capturing both sides of Clemente's character. He called Clemente "the Pittsburgh Pirates' marvelous right fielder and steadiest customer of the medical profession."

Cope visited Clemente at his home in Puerto Rico in the off-season, and wrote of him: "Relatively small at 5-feet-10 and 185 pounds when able to take nourishment, the chronic invalid has smooth black skin, glistening muscles, and perfect facial contours that suggest the sturdy mahogany sculpture peddled in the souvenir shops of his native Puerto

Rico. His countrymen regard him as the most superb all-around big-leaguer to emerge from their island, while many Pittsburghers concluded that the only thing that can prevent him from making them forget Paul Waner is a sudden attack of good health."

It was Clemente, of course, who provided Cope with a complete shopping list of all his ailments: headaches, heartaches, sore limbs, sore back, sleeping problems, you name it.

"My head still hurts," Clemente told Cope. "The pain splits my head. The doctors say it's tension. They say I worry too much. I've tried tranquilizers, but they don't work. My foot is killing me. I got this tendon in my left heel that rubs against the bone, and I cannot run on it at all. I'm weary, I tell you. All the time, it's go here, speak there, do dis, do dat. Always, always, always. When I go to spring training, that's when I take my rest."

Cope also chronicled what a community-minded, generous to a fault, charitable citizen he was, but Clemente's friends must have failed to relay that information to him when they told him what they didn't like about the article. Maybe the "dis" and "dat" offended them.

"For Roberto," wrote Cope, "life in the big leagues has been a series of outrages. He is by no means antigringo — in fact, his relationship with Pittsburgh fans is one of unwavering love stories of the national pastime — but, as a Latin, he feels persecuted. He is vociferously resentful of the fact that he is the least known, least sung superstar in baseball."

Clemente told Cope in no uncertain terms, "For me, I am the best ballplayer in the world."

At that time, that meant Clemente thought he was better than Willie Mays or Henry Aaron, among other all-time greats who were contemporaries.

Cope even defended Clemente against those who accused him of being a hot dog.

"In baseball, any player who obviously exaggerates simple moves is labeled a hot dog," wrote Cope in his *Sports Illustrated* article, "and, on two counts, Clemente seems to fall within this definition. First, he not only favors the basket catch made famous by Mays, but lends to it an added element of risk by allowing fly balls to drop below his waist before catching them. Secondly, while fielding routine singles he often underhands the ball to second base in a great, looping arc instead of pegging it on a line. Hotly defending himself, Clemente points out that both the low basket catch and the underhand throw are nothing more than natural habits carried over from his youth, for until he was seventeen he was a softball player, not a baseball player."

Cope cautioned the opposition to switch their strategy in competing with Clemente.

"For their own good," he advised, "they ought to warm the cockles of Clemente's heart with praise, commiserate with him when he has a hangnail, elect him to the All-Star team with a landslide vote, punch any sports writer who does not quote him as if he were Churchill on the floor of the Parliament, and campaign for him to receive his first Most Valuable Player award."

Cope concluded his article about Clemente by quoting him saying, "I like to work with kids. I'd like to work with kids all the time, if I live long enough."

Reading Clemente's comments now, knowing what happened to him six years later, gives one an eerie feeling.

"He could do it all and do it better more often than anybody else."
— Les Biederman

After he retired, Biederman rendered a glowing reflection on Clemente in a book called *The Pittsburgh Pirates—A Pictorial History.*

"I knew Roberto Clemente as a Pirate rookie in 1955, a 19-year-old Latin who spoke little, if any, English, but a young man with tremendous natural baseball ability. He was the best player I ever saw and I saw him in every game he played from 1955 through 1968, when I retired. He could do it all and do it better more often than anybody else.

"Clemente was his own man. He told you what he thought and why he thought that way. When you'd ask him to name the best player he ever saw, he'd tap his chest and say, 'me.' Then he'd explain:

"'I play the game as I think it was meant to be played. I don't think there's anybody who plays harder than I do and this is the way I play all of the time. All season, every season. I give everything I have to the game of baseball and I have a lot of pride. I just feel I'm the best.'

"In my opinion," Biederman concluded, "he was."

Clemente talked about himself to Milton Gross, a nationally-syndicated columnist at *The New York Post* and one of my mentors when I was on the staff there.

"I don't say I'm the best," said Clemente, "but I don't take second place from anybody in anything. If you think you're second, third or fourth, you're dead. It's a matter of pride and your mental state. If you don't have confidence, forget it. When I get on the field I think I'm number one and the more pressure the better I like it."

"The thing about Clemente is that he's the only guy to receive get-well cards after going five for five, throwing two runners out at the plate, and stealing second standing up."
—Jim Murray
Los Angeles Times

*"This was a ball park with character, a park
of dank inner passages and heavy iron beams,
of ivy-covered brick walls that bordered but
did not enclose. The new parks, machine-tooled
and symetrical, are bright topless cylinders,
as alike as Holiday Inns."*
— Roy McHugh on Forbes Field
In The Pittsburgh Press
November 11, 1971

On the day after the World Series ended in 1971, Clemente paid a visit to what remained of Forbes Field in Oakland. He wanted one last look before he returned home to Puerto Rico.

All work stopped when Clemente came on the scene, while Bud Trice, the foreman of the wrecking crew, gathered his men to pose for a picture with Clemente.

By the time Clemente departed an hour or so later, he had ordered a souvenir set of the faded blue chairs, uprooted from the stands. They were selling for $5 apiece.

Light towers were laying on the ground where Clemente and Maz and Hoak had once played. Bulldozers were at work, and a wrecking ball was slamming into the main stands. Scrap iron was everywhere. It was a sad sight. Clemente walked away and never looked back.

Reflections on Roberto Clemente
He showed the way for others

*"He said to be proud of who you are
and where you come from."*
—Al Oliver on Clemente

Two of the Pirates most productive hitters in recent decades, Al Oliver and Dave Parker, returned to Pittsburgh on a frigid February day in 1993 to sign their autographs at the U.S.A. Celebrity Sports Card Show at the A.J. Palumbo Center on the campus at Duquesne University.

Both were hard-hitting outfielders with speed who were often held up to comparison with Roberto Clemente, sometimes positively and sometimes negatively, and they know only too well the high standards for excellence that Clemente established when he played in Pittsburgh.

Both were personally fond of Clemente, and cherish the personal memories they have of time spent with him, and both recall counsel Clemente offered to them early in their professional careers.

One also gets the strong impression that they identified with Clemente in another way, complaining that Clemente was never fully appreciated when he was living and playing for the Pirates, as much as he was after he died in a tragic airplane accident in 1972. Like Clemente before them, Oliver and Parker both felt unappreciated in Pittsburgh.

They did not draw nearly as many baseball card collectors for their signing sessions as Henry Aaron and Pete Rose had at the same event the year before, so it probably only reinforced the negative feelings they had during their playing days.

Many of the people who asked Parker to put his signature on a baseball bat, a baseball, a glove, a photo, a program or simply a piece of paper often apologized to him about the indignities he sometimes suffered from fans who didn't care for him. "I let bygones be bygones," Parker assured them. "I've forgotten all that stuff. Time heals all wounds. That's in the past. I like Pittsburgh, and I had a great career with the Pirates. I have a lot of friends in Pittsburgh."

Oliver broke in with the Pirates as a fill-in for Clemente in right field in 1968 and stayed on through the 1977 season.

"Clemente and I had the same kind of personalities," said Oliver for openers when I interviewed him in the media room at the A.J. Palumbo Center on February 20, 1993.

"He was like a father figure. Like my father led me as a human being, Roberto ended up leading me as a major leaguer. I never had to be told what my job is, but he was my mentor; that's what he was to me.

"To see him hustle out ground balls, and the way he attacked the ball, the way he went after balls, the way he was reckless going for balls against the walls or fences . . . that's the same way I always played."

"Where were you when the Pirates won the 1960 World Series?" I asked Oliver.

"I was a ninth grader in Portsmouth, Ohio, which is about 90 miles south of Columbus. I collected baseball cards in the mid-'50s. That's when I got hooked on baseball. Of course, I was aware of Clemente. I didn't follow the Pirates as a team, but I knew about Clemente. Clemente and Dick Groat were the two Pirates I liked. Why? I don't know. With Clemente, I liked his own unique style and flair. With Groat, I think it was because he was such a great competitor, and he was smart."

I asked Oliver how he felt coming into a clubhouse where Clemente and Willie Stargell were the stars. Oliver was from Ohio, and I mentioned to him that Jack Lambert, who was also from Ohio, said he respected the veterans he found as a rookie when he joined the Steelers coming out of Kent State in 1974. Lambert would later complain that rookies didn't know their place, and came in cocky with little respect for their elders.

"I was like Jack in that respect," said Oliver. "I went to spring training for my first camp in 1966. When I walked into the clubhouse at Fort Myers, I walked into a room of men I admired and looked up to. But I was also confident that I belonged there, and I was comfortable. I knew my time had not come yet, so I knew my place. They put the young guys in a back room and gave us high numbers. I had 47, and you knew if you have 47 you're not going north with the team when spring training is over.

"I didn't do a lot of talking with Clemente, but there was a mutual relationship, and a mutual respect. Roberto saw something in me early, that I didn't think anyone saw, and that was one of his qualities. He said to be proud of who you are and where you come from.

"He saw early in my career that I was being platooned. He said, 'Al, don't worry about it. One day you'll get an opportunity to play on an everyday basis, and you'll be one of the best ballplayers in the game.'

"That couldn't have come from anybody except my father, who, unfortunately, died in 1968. I came from his funeral to the Pirates in September of that first season. He died of silichosis from what he breathed all those years working in a brickyard. He was a very religious man, and he was ready. He was Albert Oliver, and I'm Al Jr.

"The Pirates called me up from their farm team in Columbus, Ohio. It was ironic. I was not only coming from my father's funeral, but the Pirates were playing against the Cincinnati Reds, one of the teams I followed as a kid.

"In the second game of a doubleheader, I looked at the lineup card in the dugout and I was playing right field. I never played right field in my life. I could run and I guess they figured I could do it. 'Let's put him out there.' Number one, I was a nervous wreck. Not only had I never played the position, but right field was Roberto Clemente's place. That was real pressure.

"Right away, Vada Pinson hit a real shot to right center field. It was a bullet. I had no idea what I was doing. I ran like crazy and stuck my glove out and somehow got it. I think about that play sometimes.

271

I think about what might have happened to me if I had missed it. What would that have been like to break in on a negative note?

"Roberto Clemente was simply the greatest player or person I ever saw. I feel that by knowing him, and by playing with him, that I was a better person and a better player. I'm glad I had the honor of playing next to him.

"Not a lot of people knew where he was coming from. I did. Every day I wake up and put this ring on I think about him. He's responsible for it. In that 1971 World Series, he put on probably one of the best one-man shows anyone ever put on. He showed the world what he could do. We knew in Pittsburgh, but he let the world know what a unique talent he was, in every way.

"A lot of guys get on center stage and falter, but he put on an unbelievable performance."

Dave Parker was as pretty as ever. He wore a green leather outfit over a black jersey. He had gold jewelry around his neck, around his wrist, on his ear lobe, and on his fingers. He had a bracelet with his nickname "Cobra" spelled out with diamonds. Like Oliver, he wore a World Series ring, only his was from the 1979 Pirates.

Willie Stargell had been a greater influence in his career than Clemente, but he remembered Roberto in a revered manner, and paid him proper tribute.

"I was only nine years old when the Pirates won that 1960 World Series," pointed out Parker. "I was going to Garfield Elementary School. I grew up right across the street from Crosley Field in Cincinnati.

"Frank Robinson and Vada Pinson were my favorite players. I used to see them drive their cars to the ballpark. They both had white Thunderbirds with bright red interiors. I remember the porthole windows. They must have lived in the same apartment complex, because they usually arrived at the same time.

"When I first signed with the Pirates, I signed on as a catcher. I had a technique of throwing the ball, but it was a catcher's throw, and not an outfielder's throw. Robby first made me aware of the difference. 'You can get a lot more on that throw if you stretch your arm out.' He showed me how to throw the ball from the outfield."

Parker stood up and demonstrated what he was talking about. He reared back to throw the ball as an outfielder, whereas a catcher has to get rid of the ball quicker, and cocks his arm directly over his throwing shoulder, rather than reaching way back before unleashing a toss.

"Robby also showed me how to properly grip the ball before throwing it, and how you had to grab the ball out of your glove with that same grip each time. By gripping the ball a certain way with your fingers across the strings you could keep it from slicing. It had to be a routine.

"When you're getting this advice from a guy as great as Clemente it sinks in immediately. To me, the guy was God.

"When I started playing for the Pirates, he was a very loved guy by the other players. As great as Stargell was, Stargell just looked at him in awe. When Clemente walked into the room everything came to life. He respected everyone. He made you feel at ease.

"I was not an invited player when I came to my first Pirates camp. I was just there for a look-see, not as a serious candidate for the club. But he acknowledged me and he respected me.

"I learned more from Stargell than Clemente because I was around him a lot longer, and he was more my mentor.

"A lot of people praise Clemente now. What I saw as a young adult, though, was that he didn't get what he deserved. The true praise for Clemente came after his death. To me, he was every bit as good as Mantle and Mays, but they got more recognition on a national basis. Clemente was every bit as good as either of them, or anyone else. To me, he stuck out like a sore thumb. You knew he was a great baseball player."

Willie Stargell instructs Dave Parker.

Al Oliver

Al Oliver

Dave Parker

273

What A Neighbor
Clemente lived down the hall
at Pennley Park

"I'm ready to marry you for better or worse,
but this is ridiculous."
— Kathleen Churchman

My wife was concerned about her husband's mental health. "What's with you?" she inquired, as I sat on the family living room rug, clapping my hands.

"Clemente just hit a home run!" I replied. "The Pirates are ahead, one-to-nothing!"

My wife, who is called Kathie, glanced at the TV, then at her husband, and posed another question.

"How can you root for Roberto Clemente when he sued you for a million dollars?"

"Who cares?" I cried. "That's in the past. That's water under the bridge. That's money I never had in the first place. Hell, he made me look like a millionaire to all the guys in my hometown. I can't hold that against him for the rest of my life. You worry too much about petty things."

This was the seventh game of the World Series, the World Series of October, 1971. It was my day off. We were living in an apartment in East Rockaway, New York, alongside the tracks of the Long Island Rail Road. The apartment shook every time a train went past. I was helping the apartment shake this particular day. Pittsburgh was still my hometown. Roberto Clemente was still playing for the Pirates, my hometown team.

I wasn't going to let a little thing like a million dollar law suit spoil a life-long love affair. It wasn't going to turn me into a Baltimore Orioles booster. Nuts to that, I said.

So I sat on my magic green carpet, and rooted for the Pirates. This was no press box. Who had to behave? Who had to be quiet. Beat 'em, Bucs. No wonder the wife was worried.

Elrod Hendricks scored for the Baltimores, and now nervousness set in. I had not been that nervous, sitting on that carpet, since Jim O'Brien of the Baltimore Colts set up to kick the winning field goal in the 1971 Super Bowl.

I mean, most of my old neighbors in East Liberty were battling for the Bucs' glory. It was like rooting for a softball team from your favorite neighborhood bar. Clemente used to live in the Pennley Park Apartments at Penn and Negley, and so did Jose Pagan, who came through with some clutch fielding and the double that scored Willie Stargell with the winning run.

Roberto Clemente embraces wife Vera on airplane trip back to Pittsburgh after he was MVP in 1971 World Series won by Pirates over the Baltimore Orioles. He hit safely in all seven games in comeback triumph.

Vera Clemente is presented late husband's Gold Glove Award for 1972 by Bob Prince and Joe L. Brown at Three Rivers Stadium ceremonies at 1973 season opener.

I would always remember Pagan playing with his kids all the time on the grassy plot between the buildings of the Pennley Park complex. Al McBean and Maury Wills lived there. So did Juan Pizzaro. I remember playing basketball one afternoon in the playground, and looking up to Juan's window. There were no drapes and the blinds were drawn, and two women were massaging one of his shoulders. Ah, the tribulations of being a major league pitcher.

So no one was happier than I was when the Pirates won the World Series in 1971. I wanted to be in Pittsburgh that night. In retrospect, maybe it was better that I didn't go. I was on my way to Kansas City to see the Steelers play the Chiefs in the Monday Night game, and maybe I wouldn't have gotten there if I had stopped off in the old burg.

I was on my way to Kansas City to see the Steelers' Dave Smith spike the ball before he got into the end zone in one of the most famous foul-ups in football history.

Ah, the memories. . .

Just one month before moving into the Pennley Park Apartments with my new bride, one of my neighbors sued me for a million dollars. It was Clemente, of course. One of his pals on the Pirates, the same Stargell who scored the winning run against the Baltimores and sent me into sheer ecstasy, sued me for $750,000.

It was all over a story which I had written in my old newspaper, *Pittsburgh Weekly Sports*, about an alleged fight in the clubhouse between Clemente and Stargell. I only had two things wrong about the clubhouse fight. Neither Clemente nor Stargell was involved. Other than that, my story was right on the mark.

"What did I do wrong?" I wanted to know, when I learned that my neighbor had sued me for a cool million. "I haven't been playing my stereo that loud."

My future bride had the answer. "According to the paper here," she said, "he says you libeled him. Oh, what are we going to do?" My future bride broke down in tears. She was fearful in the first place over what figured to be an already tight budget.

"I'm ready to marry you for better or for worse," she sobbed, "but this is ridiculous. We'll be destitute the rest of our lives. You're going to have to go out and get a job."

Now I knew my bride-to-be was upset. "Brown-Eyes," I said. "I've told you a thousand times I do have a job."

"I mean one you make money on," she said.

"You always have to bring that up, don't you?" I shot back, we got into one of our first family feuds. "Don't worry, honey. I'll hustle a little harder this week. Let's see, a million dollars . . . that's only 250,000 new subscribers.

"But dear," she reminded me, preparing me for a lifetime of honest accounting, "your best week to date has been 75 new subscribers."

"True, honey, but I've never had an incentive like this before. First, Willie Stargell for $750,000. I no more than raise that, and now this has to come up."

It was midnight on a Friday, a few days after our initial conversation about Stargell and Clemente. "What's the matter, honey?" Kathie inquired. "Why, you're sweating!"

"Ah, I can't deal with this," I said, interrupting my efforts to move what little furniture we had into our newly-acquired apartment. "A guy just doesn't get sued for a million dollars every day. Listen, I'm going out and take a walk for awhile."

I left our apartment. It was on the fourth floor. I took an elevator up to the ninth floor. I wanted to see if anyone else was disturbed by the turn of events. I passed the door at F91 and there wasn't a sound inside.

I took the elevator down to the lobby, and went out and bought a *Post-Gazette*, my favorite morning newspaper in Pittsburgh. When I returned, I encountered the security guard and his German shepherd dog. "Is it true there are some ballplayers living in these apartments?" I inquired innocently.

"Sure are," he said. "See over there where the lights are out . . . Jose Pagan lives there. Over there, Juan Pizzaro. Andre Rodgers is down there, and up there on the top floor, the one with the lights on, is Clemente's place."

"You mean the great Roberto?" I shrieked.

"That's him," the guard said.

"Good," I thought to myself, knowing Clemente liked to get his sleep. "He can't get to sleep tonight. His conscience is bothering him."

I sat in the lobby and read the sports section of the bulldog edition. Clemente had one hit that day, but the Pirates lost.

I was leaving the building again, when I overheard the security guard talking on the intercom phone in the lobby. "Mr. Clemente, I'm sorry to disturb you," he said, "but you'll have to come down and move the car. I hope I didn't wake you up."

Sure enough, right at the top of the stairway outside was a dark green Lincoln Continental with a license plate on the front bumper which read: "RWC."

The car was parked on an area painted yellow with signs reading: "No Parking Here." That was two violations, blocking a walk and parking in a no-parking zone.

At 1:55 a.m., Clemente, his beautiful wife, Vera, and his friend Phil Dorsey came out of the apartment. They bumped into me getting on the elevator. They drove away into the night. I decided not to go home yet; I was still living with my parents in Hazelwood. The Clementes came back at 2:05.

I bumped into an old school chum in the parking lot, got invited to a party, and returned to our apartment with a gift of half a bottle of Old Crow. Then I drove home.

The next day I drove back to the apartment, picked up my bride-to-be and drove her to her parents' home in White Oak, out in McKeesport. She needed the reassurance that only a mother and a father could provide. I decided to spend the day at Forbes Field. Clemente and

Stargell both played well, and I was pleased. I didn't want them to show any ill effects from my story. The Pirates won a 16-inning game with the Giants. I wanted them to be in the Hall of Fame someday.

I checked with 32 youngsters who were hanging over the walls in right field, trying to get the autographs of their heroes before the game got under way. They all agreed that Clemente and Stargell were the greatest. I knew I could sleep that night, knowing that the images of Clemente and Stargell had not suffered because of my ill-begotten story.

I went to see the Steelers play the Chicago Bears the next day at Pitt Stadium, and I was happy to hear that Clemente had three hits, including the game-winning home run against the Giants.

The following day I found a violation ticket on my windshield in the parking lot at Pennley Park. I was parking in a restricted area — restricted for tenants of the apartment. I was paying $6 a month for that space.

The security guard who wrote out the ticket was the same one who called Mr. Clemente on the phone that night. They couldn't tell me there wasn't a star system in our country. There just wasn't any justice.

My friends were having fun at my expense, too. Someone sent me a renewal subscription for *Pittsburgh Weekly Sports* to be sent to Roberto Clemente.

Someone sent me a congratulatory wire on my wedding day, which read: "Eat, drink and be merry, for soon I shall have all your money. (Signed) Willie Stargell."

Four years had passed since that day and the Pirates had won another World Series, with me watching on TV from my family room in New York. Clemente and Stargell had the best of seasons, and Clemente won the Series MVP award, and deservedly so. No one was happier than I was. In time the law suits were dropped.

I returned to Pittsburgh to work in 1979, just in time to see the Pirates win the World Series again. In time, Stargell and I became friendly, and frequently met and talked to each other at various sports dinners and banquets. He forgave me for that foolish story. I became one of his biggest fans; he was easy to like.

Clemente died in that air crash when I was still living in New York. My mother was visiting me during the Christmas holidays. We celebrated her birthday Christmas Eve. She awoke me on New Year's Day to tell me about Clemente's death.

I never had a chance to get to know Clemente. Who knows? Maybe he and I could have put the problem behind us, gotten to know each other, and been friends. I'd like to think so.

"Whenever an old person dies,
it's like a library being burned down."
—Alex Haley
Author of "Roots"

Hal Smith
He could have been the hero

*"It was the most forgotten
home run in baseball history"*
— Dick Groat

Hal Smith said his dressing stall was near Roberto Clemente's in the clubhouse of the 1960 Pirates. "He was my buddy," said Smith. "I had been with other ballteams before I came to the Pirates. I had been with clubs in Kansas City and before that in Baltimore. But I had never been with a ballplayer like Clemente.

"After a month or two, he and I became good friends. I could talk to him. I could kid him. I could counsel him. He liked that. One day, we were changing clothes, getting into our uniforms at Forbes Field, and I moved close to him, and tugged at the lapel of his uniform shirt, and I said to him, 'Roberto, are you aware that if you play every day this year we're gonna win the pennant?'

"He said, 'Smitty, are you kidding?' And I said, 'I'm serious. You're that great. You're great!'

"He smiled at me, and he said, 'Smitty, I'll play every day.' And he did, or just about, anyhow.

"I had talked to Murtaugh about him before I said that. I said, 'What's the deal with Clemente?' I heard he had aches and pains and pulled himself from the lineup now and then. Murtaugh told me, 'He did that to me last year. This year I just put his name down on the lineup card, and I hide from him the rest of the time before the game starts. I don't talk to him the rest of the day. I don't give him a chance to tell me about his aches and pains.'

"Clemente was young. He was different from the rest of us. Maybe he wasn't always comfortable in the clubhouse or the dugout, in the beginning. But he needed a pat on the back, that's all.

"When he found out the team needed him, he really responded. He learned a lot that year, probably more than in any other year in his major league career. He learned a lot about himself, and about his teammates.

"I knew he was going to be great. I saw him make plays in '60 and I saw someone like Al Kaline try to make plays like that, and he couldn't. Clemente could throw the ball. There were few who could throw the ball like him. Rocky Colavito could and Kaline could, and Carl Furillo and Willie Mays could, but not many of them.

"He was such a great athlete. He could go stop and go. He could've played football. He was just a natural, instinctive ballplayer.

"If someone said, 'Hey, Roberto, let's go pitch horseshoes,' he'd probably win all the time. He had great speed, he was just such a natural athlete. I was in awe of his ability."

279

What prompted Smith's soliloquy on Roberto Clemente was that Smith, at first, had failed to mention Clemente when I asked Smith what made the '60 Bucs so special.

"I think there were six to eight guys on that team who were winners," Smith said. "You had Bill Mazeroski. Dick Groat. Bill Virdon. Don Hoak. Smoky Burgess. Bob Skinner. Vernon Law. Bob Friend. El-Roy Face."

"All white," I thought to myself. "What about Roberto Clemente? How could he not mention Clemente?"

"Hal, let me ask you something," I said. "You have mentioned nine guys on that team, and you didn't include Clemente. How's that?"

"He was my buddy," said Smith instantly, and with no apology, as if there had been no oversight. "He was in a league of his own."

Smith shared the catching duties with Burgess that year. The Pirates also platooned players at first base, with Dick Stuart sharing the position with Rocky Nelson. Once in a while, Gino Cimoli played in place of Bob Skinner in left field. It worked. Murtaugh made it work.

Smith nearly became the hero of that 1960 World Series.

The Yankees were leading by 7-4 going into the bottom of the eighth inning. Then an incredible series of events put the Pirates back in the game again. That's when Virdon hit what looked like an inning-ending double play ball to short, but the ball took a bad bounce and struck Tony Kubek of the Yankees in the Adam's apple, leaving him gagging on the ground.

It was a ball "spitefully steered by Dame Fortune," according to Arthur Daley, who would become a Pulitzer Prize-winning sports columnist for *The New York Times*.

Then Yankees' pitcher Jim Coates failed to cover first on a ground ball by Clemente to first baseman Moose Skowron that should have been an easy out. The Pirates put two runs on the scoreboard, for starters.

"The Yankees like to make a federal case out of the bad hop," Groat has said. "You never hear about Coates forgetting to cover first base. That's the kind of mistake the Pirates didn't make."

With two on base and two out, Smith, who had replaced Burgess when Smoky was lifted in the seventh inning for a pinch-runner, came to the plate. On a two-two pitch, he smacked one over the 406 mark in left-center field that gave the Pirates a 9-7 lead.

When I asked Pirates general manager Joe L. Brown what he remembered best about that 1960 season, he said, "The many late-inning winning rallies and Hal Smith's home run in the eighth inning of Game 7. We were dead before Smith hit the home run. It was the single most memorable play of my life, because it came when we needed it most, when we were behind."

Hoak had this to say after the game about Smith's home run: "Smitty comes off the bench and gives us the lead with a home run that Mantle himself might have hit."

It is often said that Smith was a forgotten hero in that 1960 World Series. Groat labeled it "the most forgotten home run in baseball

Hal Smith with wife Ann at Columbus (Ohio) Hall of Fame

Hal Smith heads home after hitting three-run shot over left field wall run in eighth inning of seventh game of 1960 World Series as Yankees manager Casey Stengel goes glumly to ound to make pitching change, calling in Ralph Terry from the bullpen.

history." His home run "passed into oblivion," according to one Pittsburgh newspaper account at the time. "It will be forgotten."

That has not really been the case, as I assured Smith when we spoke in late April, 1993. "Everybody I have interviewed for this book has mentioned your home run, and what you contributed to that club," I told him.

"That's good to hear," said Smith.

When I told him who I had talked to over the course of the previous year, mentioning the many players by name, Smith said, "You talked to a great bunch of guys. I could call Skinner or Maz or Face right now, and I'd be on the phone with them for an hour. That's how I feel about them. We became like brothers."

As I write this, I can see photographs of Smith hugging Mazeroski and Murtaugh in the clubhouse afterward. I can see Smith smiling broadly and shouting with glee as he goes by Frank Oceak, one of the Pirates coaches, at third base.

There is such joy in his face, such beacons of light in his dark brown eyes.

"It just felt like another home run," said Smith, sounding a lot like Mazeroski recalling his game-winning shot, "until I rounded second and started for third and saw the people. They were on top of the dugout. Then it dawned on me. I got quite excited."

Clemente, who preceeded Smith around the bases, traveled the final leg from third to home bounding like "a kangaroo," according to a magazine account of that game.

"I finally had a chance to be a hero," said Smith in 1960, "and then I didn't make it."

At the 1985 reunion of that team at Three Rivers Stadium, Smith told Bob Fulton of the *Indiana Gazette*, "Sure, I'd love to have been the hero in that World Series. My grandkids would love it."

"We have seen and shared in one of baseball's great moments." — Broadcaster Chuck Thompson

Put on the tape of the radio broadcast of that seventh game of the 1960 World Series, and here is what Chuck Thompson had to say about Smith's eighth-inning home run: "We have seen and shared in one of baseball's great moments. Hal Smith has just hit a home run to put the Pirates in front by a score of 9-to-7."

Thompson then turned the microphone over to Jack Quinlan. "I'm almost speechless," said Quinlan. "This is one of the most dramatic home runs of all time! Five runs are in and the Pirates again have the lead.

"A tremendous wallop by Smith . . . and the only reason that he was playing is that Burgess had been taken out earlier for a pinch-runner.

"He just drove a ball over the 406 foot sign in toward left-center. Berra went back and all Yogi could do was stand there and just be helpless and watch the ball sail out over the ballpark and into Schenley Park...

"A new pitcher, Ralph Terry, has come in, and Smith has delivered the cruelest blow off lean, lanky Jim Coates. Smith hit one out far into the afternoon.

"When Smith got to the dugout, it's a wonder he could stand up ... he was pummelled by his teammates."

But the Yankees, to their credit, came back with two runs of their own in the top of the ninth, to tie the score at 9-9, and set the stage for Mazeroski.

Instead of Smith hitting a home run for the ages, Mazeroski stole the spotlight with a home run of his own. Mazeroski's home run became a blast that was talked about the way baseball fans reflect on the 61st home run by Roger Maris, the "shot heard round the world" by Bobby Thomson in the '51 playoffs as the New York Giants beat the Brooklyn Dodgers, the three home runs struck by Babe Ruth — at age 40 and playing for the Boston Braves of the National League — including one over the right field roof at Forbes Field that was the last of his 714 home runs, struck a few weeks before Ruth retired for good from baseball.

Smith's home run was overshadowed by Mazeroski's blast, for sure, but it has not been forgotten.

"My dad made a statement after the 1960 World Series that I'll never forget," said Smith. "He said, 'I saw my son play in the major leagues, and I saw him help win a World Series. If I bowl a 300 game now, my life will be complete.'

"I didn't wear my World Championship ring for awhile. I'm not really big on jewelry. But about 20 years ago, I took it out, got it cleaned, and started wearing it. I'm very proud of it. It's a conversation piece. People come up to me and start asking questions. I mention Mazeroski's homer, and they suddenly remember the World Series that year. They don't always remember my home run in the seventh game that gave us a 9-7 lead. I have to tell them about that."

Smith sounded good, speaking from his home in Columbus, Texas, about 60 miles west of Houston. He was 62, happily retired, happily married, and sounding like a guy who had it made. He also sounded a lot like Mazeroski does when he reflects on his career and good fortune, and that is part of the charm of those '60 Pirates. They are pleasant, easy to talk to, grateful that the game gave them so much joy and pleasure, and perfectly satisfied with their lives after baseball. It wasn't always smooth, not in Smith's case, anyhow, but he's not complaining. He enjoyed his ten years in the bigs.

"I play golf and I fish," said Smith. "I like to go bass fishing, and I do a little salt water fishing, but I'm talking about in-shore fishing. I don't do any deep-sea fishing. In truth, though, I don't really do anything seriously. I just enjoy my life. I have a grandson — his name is Scott Perkins — and he's playing for the University of Southwestern Louisiana. I go down to watch him all the time. He's an excellent ball-player, he's an excellent student, and I am so proud of him.

"I'm spending time enjoying my family, which was sometimes difficult to do when you were playing ball. I have a daughter, Debbie, who's 42, a son Dan, who's 40, and a son Mike, who's 38. I enjoy them and their families. I'm 62. I play golf every day. I play at the Columbus Country Club. I'm a fair golfer. Dick Groat is a good golfer. Mazeroski is also a good golfer. Of course, they own their own courses.

"I have a house here in Columbus, and I have a condo in Houston that I lease to a lawyer. I have some acreage in between Houston and Columbus, and I tend to that all the time. I have been married to Ann for 15 years.

"I just became really retired this year. I had been working up until the first of this year. I was in steel sales for about 20 years, starting in 1964, my last year in baseball. I had a restaurant of my own after that. It was called K-Bobs, and it was in Houston. I had it for about seven years. I didn't do that well in the restaurant business, though I worked my whatchamacallit off. I have more respect for restaurant people. I had a place that seated 200, and it was rough."

"So now you respect Frankie Gustine more, huh? He had a place in Oakland for over 30 years," I said.

"I was always a fan of Frankie Gustine," said Smith. "But I didn't realize how much I respected him until I got in the restaurant business myself."

"Every time I see Bill, he thanks me."
— Hal Smith

I asked Smith if he had pictures from that 1960 World Series in the game room or a den at his home in Columbus. "I really have very little," he said. "I have my World Series ring and my World Series trophy, but my son Dan has a rec room in his home, and he has it all. He lives in Katy, between Columbus and Houston. He has all of my pictures. That's the way it should be, I guess. I had a lot of them on the walls in my restaurant, but after I gave that up he took all the pictures and put them up in his house. I'm proud that he likes to show them off to his friends.

"When I had them at the restaurant, people would check them out. The old baseball fans who knew the game would tell me they remembered my home run. They'd say, 'If it hadn't been for you, Mazeroski's home run wouldn't have won the game.' I would tell them, 'Every time I see Bill, he thanks me.'

"I have a story I want to tell you. In the '60 season, we were playing in St. Louis. We were in the top of the ninth and St. Louis had a runner on first and second, and a bunt play was coming. We had a meeting on the mound to discuss what we were going to do. We ended

Hal Smith gets hugs, at top, from Danny Murtaugh and Bill Mazeroski, and kisses from Bill Virdon and Bob Skinner after his heroics in seventh game of 1960 World Series. Bucs GM Joe L. Brown rates it as "my biggest thrill."

al Smith starts a Conga line after hitting 3-run homer that includes, left to right, Don Hoak 2), Roberto Clemente and Dick Groat.

up getting a double play. Hoak got the ball to Groat at second and Groat threw to Stuart at first for the double play. Murtaugh told us, 'I'll be out early every day from now on to make sure I don't miss anything.' "

Smith then mentioned a game that several of his teammates had pointed to as a tell-tale sign that something special was in store for the '60 Pirates. The tone for the season was set early. On April 17, the Pirates were losing, 5-0, to the Cincinnati Reds at Forbes Field, as the Pirates came to bat in the ninth. Smith hit a three-run, pinch-hit home run and Skinner hit a two-run homer and the Pirates produced another run to win, 6-5.

"It was exciting," said Smith. "I had a special feeling that night. I had been playing with second division teams before in Baltimore and Kansas City before I came to Pittsburgh. I had been a good catcher in Kansas City. I batted .311 or something like that, and I was the only catcher in the major leagues who hit over .300 that year. I held out for a $2,500 raise for Kansas City.

"I told the guys on the Pirates, 'We're going all the way,' after we won that Cincy game. All of a sudden it hit me upside the head. I was all pumped. On the way into the clubhouse after that game, I started asking the guys on our team, 'Hey, where do you buy your World Series tickets around here?' They laughed at me, but I told them, 'I'm serious. You'll see.' I heard Fred Hutchinson punched out all the overhead light bulbs on the way to the visitors' clubhouse, but I liked Fred, so I didn't feel good about hearing that. 'I know,' I kept telling my teammates. 'I've never been with a ballclub that had a chance to win, and this team is different.'

"They all hated to lose. It was the first team I was on where guys really cared about winning. On the rest of the teams I had been on, the guys just cared about their batting averages and their earned run averages and their home run counts. They just wanted to know about their stats. That's what happens on losing teams. They worry about things like that because that's the only way you're going to get a raise on a losing team. Winners think about winning.

"One of the highlights of my career in 1960 was what happened out in California. We happened to win a bunch of games over the Dodgers out there. They were playing in the LA Coliseum, which had a short left field fence because it was a football stadium."

"That's where Wally Moon hit all his home runs, right, that they called Moon Shots?" I interjected.

"That's right, but they still count," said Smith. "I had seven home runs as a visiting ballplayer. I hit five there in three days. Over that little left field fence. It was a record. It's a record that can never be broken because they never play there anymore."

I asked Smith if he followed the Houston Astros. "I do, but mostly on TV," he said. As a former catcher, I asked him if he got a particular kick out of what Nolan Ryan was able to accomplish as a 40-plus pitcher.

"He's incredible," said Smith. "I think he's a freak. Maybe that's a bad word to use, but he's just unreal. I don't think you can do what he's doing. He's inhuman."

I asked him if he thought Doug Drabek would be a big hit as a pitcher for the Astros. "Maybe," said Smith. "We'll see. Not necessarily."

I asked him what Murtaugh's role was in regard to the Pirates' success.

"He was a man's man," said Smith. "If he chewed you out, you earned it. He'd stand up in your face and speak his mind. Then it would be over. He didn't dwell on it. He was the finest coach at handling people I ever played for. He was probably the best."

"It's like an old dream."
— Hal Smith

Harold Wayne Smith came to the major leagues in 1955, a year before Harold Raymond Smith, who played for the Cardinals. So it was tough to distinguish himself when he wasn't even the only Hal Smith in baseball. He joined the Pirates the winter before the 1960 season.

Joe L. Brown got him during the interleague trading period. Brown gave the Athletics catcher Hank Foiles, who had represented the Pirates in the All-Star Game in 1957, and two farm hands — shortstop Ken Hamlin and pitcher Dick Hall — in exchange for cash and Smith. Smith was a catcher the A's were trying to convert into a third baseman. With the Pirates, Smith proved to be a capable receiver, and he hit close to .300 the entire season.

Smith hit 11 home runs during that 1960 season, and finished with a .295 batting average in part-time duty.

Then there was *the* home run. The one that helped win the deciding game of the 1960 World Series. It was his first World Series home run, and the only one he would ever hit.

"He was a great clutch hitter all season and he consummated it with his three-run homer in the eighth inning of the seventh game of the Series," said GM Joe Brown. "That baby was up in the trees."

"I was just trying to drive in the winning run," said Smith of what he hoped to accomplish when he came to bat that fateful afternoon.

"I can still visualize it," he said. "Yes, I can still picture it. It's like an old dream. It's not something I crave to do again, but it's something I'm glad I did."

Then Smith said some things that again brought Mazeroski to mind because he echoed sentiments that Mazeroski had stated when I visited him earlier.

"I'm a very contented person," said Smith. "I have a good wife; we absolutely love each other. I'm 62 and I accept it. I can do anything I want to do. I go out sometimes and I sign cards. It's fun for me. It's all life. It all ends.

"The one thing that's most important to tell the young players to-day is that you should enjoy it while you can. It ends soon! I enjoyed it all. That's the one thing they don't know until they're through.

"They think they're infallible. There's only one Nolan Ryan in history. Oh, Early Wynn and Hoyt Wilhelm and some of those pitchers with trick pitches lasted past 40, but not many do."

I asked him what it was like, even now, for his heroics to be surpassed by Mazeroski.

"He's one of the nicest people I've ever known in my life," said Smith. "I've told him, 'If it hadn't been you, I'd have been upset. But you were great.'

"We've had so many reunions in Pittsburgh. It's been great. They're like brothers and sisters. The Major League Baseball Alumni Association has fund-raising golf tournaments in most of the major league cities, and I have participated in a lot of those. So I've spent a lot of time together with my old teammates. Some of us go back farther than others. I played minor league ball, for instance, with Bill Virdon. We all exchange cards at Christmas.

"The thing I liked about that Pittsburgh ballclub is that we had so many super people on it. You take Wilmer Mizell, for instance. Have you ever heard him speak? I did, and I thought it was Will Rogers. Up close, he spellbinds people. I told him, 'Now I know why you won all those elections. I can see why people voted for you.'

"The accomplishment is one thing, but the people are what's really important in the long run. They were a great bunch of guys. Remember this: I played with other teams. The Pirates really came together. All of a sudden we got close. Most of us had been around a little bit, and we wanted to win. We had paid our dues. None of us were superstars, though one or two became superstars later on. We were good athletes, we were not second-rate athletes. Joe Brown did one heckuva job putting that team together. It was great. If you're lucky enough, it can happen to you."

Pittsburgh Pirates

Hal Smith is all smiles as he heads past third base coach Frank Oceak after giving Pirates 9-7 lead with a three-run homer in eighth inning of seventh game of 1960 World Series.

Yogi Berra
He remembers Whatzisname hitting the home run

"Nobody tries to lose."

There really is a Yogi Berra. There is a man in Montclair, New Jersey, who looks just like and talks just like the fellow you have seen in the TV commercials pitching potato chips. He looks funny and he talks funny, and he is the genuine article.

Some sports writers say Yogi Berra really didn't say all the funny things that are attributed to him — that Joe Garagiola, his boyhood buddy from Dago Hill in St. Louis, made up most of the stories and funny lines — but I regard most of them as spoilsports. Garagiola, who once played catcher for the Pirates when they were one of the worst teams in baseball, has embellished Berra's best lines, for sure, but Berra is capable of being funny and full of wisdom on his own.

There is always a grain of truth in the funny things Berra has said, or is supposed to have said.

On a well-known restaurant, Berra said, "Nobody goes there anymore. It's too crowded."

On receiving a check issued "Pay to Bearer" — "You know me all this time, and you can't spell my name."

On the merits of Little League baseball, he said, "I think it's wonderful. It keeps the kids out of the house."

I have been around Yogi Berra enough in my life to know what he is all about, and I have heard him say funny stuff. He still says funny stuff. It's just the way he thinks and talks. Some sell Yogi Berra short. He is a smart fellow, believe me, even though he didn't have much of a formal education, and he remains one of the most genuine people I have ever met in sports. Berra does his best to be helpful, and there isn't a wicked bone in his body.

"The writers described me as a funny person," said Berra, "but that isn't the case at all. No one was ever more serious about baseball than me, and no one in baseball ever worked harder to succeed."

You have to like Yogi Berra. "You're lucky when he is your best friend," said Garagiola.

That is at the root of his popularity. He is sincere. That is why companies like to have him promoting their products. Because people believe Yogi Berra. There is an honesty about him. That is why he was picked to peddle Yoo-Hoo chocolate drink and Jockey underwear, as well as so many other products through the years. He has a memorable face and delivery.

He has always been in demand and that is how he showed up with Johnny Berardino, the star of ABC-TV's "General Hospital" soap opera and a former player for the Pirates (1950 and 1952) and St. Louis Browns, as a brain surgeon in that soap opera.

I was covering the New York Mets at the spring training camp in St. Petersburg, Florida before the 1972 season when the team's manager, Gil Hodges, had a heart attack and died. That happened on April 2, Easter Sunday. I had just gotten to know Hodges, who had been a big, strong silent type, a truly private man, and this hurt. Berra, who had been one of his coaches and had previously managed the Yankees, was named to succeed Hodges.

I covered the Mets the first half of that season and the Yankees the second half for *The New York Post.* Berra was one of the best managers or coaches I ever dealt with. He knew you had a job to do and did his best to be helpful and accessible. He was always pleasant. He would get miffed once in a while, but he would get over it.

Whenever I passed him in a clubhouse, dugout, or office when I was covering his team, Yogi always offered a smile, a friendly remark, some kidding, and always a smile.

Berra knew something about motivation. I remember once when he was unhappy with Cleon Jones, one of the Mets' most talented players, and Berra blamed a multi-year contract for much of Jones' problems. "When I was with the Yankees," said Berra, "I knew that if I had a good season I would get a pay raise. The Yankees never disappointed me, and it kept me pushing harder every season. I don't know how it would have affected me if I didn't have to produce to be paid well the following season."

Berra always knew how to make a buck. And his wife of 45 years, Carmen, knew how to save a buck. They have always been a hugely successful combination.

Berra has been lucky, too, and everything he touches seems to turn to gold. He laughs all the way to the bank.

I remember being in the Mets' clubhouse one day at Al Lang Field in St. Petersburg when there was a large pot of clam chowder steaming in the center of the room. It was there for the players as part of the lunch offering. Red Foley, a sports writer for *The New York Daily News,* stirred the thin chowder, and said, "If there's a clam in here I'll bet it ends up in Yogi Berra's cup."

When I spoke to Berra in the winter of 1993, and reminded him of when I covered his club in New York, he said, "Geez, that was a long time ago." And when I asked him to reflect on the 1960 World Series, he said, "Now you're really asking me to go way back."

But Berra was equal to the test.

He was checking out the activity at his racquetball and health club in Fairfield, New Jersey, and talking to his son Dale, an infielder with the Pirates from 1977 to 1984, who looks after the place. Dale was on the team at the same time as Vance Law (1980-81), the son of Vernon Law, and they were both popular with the ushers, who remembered their dads from that 1960 World Series.

When I asked Yogi what came to mind when he thought about the final game of the 1960 World Series, he said, "I remember the bad hop that hit Kubek's throat . . . when Clemente hit the ground ball to Moose

New York Yankees

Yogi Berra in action as catcher and as outfielder, bottom left, watching Mazeroski's home run leave Forbes Field.

United Press International

at first base, and Coates didn't cover . . . and when that Smith fellow hit the home run . . . and when we tied the game in the ninth . . . and then Whatzisname hit the home run."

That, ladies and gentleman, is the real Yogi Berra.

Whatzisname!

Of course, Berra remembers Bill Mazeroski, and he knows it was Mazeroski who hit the game-winning home run — he said so a few seconds later — but when asked to recall what he remembered best about the seventh game of the 1960 World Series, he said Whatzisname.

That way there would be no mistaking that it came directly from Yogi Berra.

Keep something else in mind: Lawrence Peter Berra, better known as Yogi, played on more pennant winners (14) and more world champions (10) than any player in history. He played in a record 75 World Series games. He also managed the Yankees to a pennant in 1964. He went to the plate a record 259 times, delivered a record 71 hits and banged a record 10 doubles. He is second on the all-time Series records list with 41 runs scored and 39 runs-batted-in, and his 32 base-on-balls and 12 home runs rank third on the all-time list.

So it is not easy to remember what happened in one World Series when you have been a participant in so many of them.

But Berra remembered that 1960 World Series because it was so wacky and the Yankees outscored the Pirates in such a big way in the New York team's three wins, yet lost the Series.

The Yankees had set Series records for runs (55), hits (91), extra-base hits (27) and batting average (.338). They had drubbed the Pirates 16-3, 10-0 and 12-0. They did everything possible in the Series — except win it. "I can't believe it," Berra was reported to have moaned afterward.

Rocky Nelson made a tricky stop in the top of the ninth inning in the seventh game, backhanding a shot off Berra's bat that spun him around. Nelson stepped on first base in one of the more memorable sequences of the Series, and Mickey Mantle, who had been on first base, dove back into the bag to prevent a double play. It was a great move by Mantle. "Yeah, I hit that ball; it took a high hop," said Berra. Nelson had looked to second to double up Mantle, but Mantle had fooled him.

"Do you think Mantle knew exactly what he was doing when he dove back to the bag, or do you think it was just an instinctive move on his part?"

"Geez, I don't know," said Berra. "But he was a pretty smart fellow when it came to baseball."

What about the home run by Whatzisname? No one had a better view of it than Berra. He was playing left field that day because the Yankees went with Elston Howard and Johnny Blanchard behind home plate in that Series. Berra was the closest player to the wall when Mazeroski's home run sailed out of the ballyard.

"I didn't think the ball was going out," Berra told me. "I turned around and I was going to play it off the wall. I was going to play the carom (he pronounced it ca-rome) off the wall. It skimmed the ivies out there."

Berra might have been there, but his memory is playing tricks on him in that respect. The ball could not have hit the ivy on the wall as it cleared the wall with room to spare.

I had to smile, though, when Berra said he was going to play the "ca-rome" and when he said the ball "skimmed the ivies out there." They were authentic Yogi-isms.

Some people insist that Berra turned around and began walking toward the visitors' dugout before the ball was over the wall. "If a guy hits a home run, you start walking in," said Berra in our interview. "But I didn't think this one was going out. I turned back after it went over the wall."

He said he doesn't know Mazeroski that well, but that he has met him at a few golf outings, old timers games and baseball card shows. "I see him once in awhile," said Berra. "We laugh and kid about it. We thought we had a better team, sure, but in a short series anything can happen.

"A few years ago, Oakland had the better team, but Cincinnati beat them in four straight.

"With the Pirates, in the games we did beat them, we beat the hell outta them. I played for 17 years and I was in 14 of them as a player and we won ten. That tells you something. Somebody's got to win."

When I asked him about his racquet club, Berra said there were originally 14 racquetball courts. "But we tore down four of the courts to make room for some weight rooms; now it's more of a health club. I don't like lifting weights. They gave us hell if we lifted them when I was playing."

As for the Pirates of the '60s, Berra has no bad feelings toward any of them. He wouldn't know how to hold a grudge.

"We were all buddies," Berra said. "We used to play them in spring training all the time. Virdon was a Yankee to begin with. I knew him when he first broke in with us. I liked Smoky Burgess. They had Dick Stuart, and you had to like Dr. Strangeglove. And they had Friend and Face. They were good fellows. Face was tough. They call it a split-finger fastball today, but it's a fork ball, and nobody threw it better than Face. He was tough for everybody to hit.

"Joe Christopher was with that 1960 Pirates team, and we had him here with the Mets."

"I'm told that some of the Yankees are still angry about losing that series to the Pirates. That Ford never forgave Stengel for not starting him in the first game, and that Mantle cried in the clubhouse afterward, and said it was the worst defeat he ever suffered," I said.

"I don't worry about stuff like that," Berra said. "Whitey is liable to say anything, him and Mickey. Me, I'm fine. I play a lot of golf, and I'm going to play in an old timers game at Disney World for the United Negro College Fund.

"Maybe I'll see some of those Pirates at some old timers games this summer. Maz and Dick Groat are both good guys. Do they still have their golf courses? We used to have a lot of fun with them.

"What the heck you going to do? Somebody has to win. Nobody tries to lose."

Where Were You?

*"I missed one of the most exciting
moments in Pittsburgh's sports history."*
—Fred Graham

Travis Cutright
History teacher
Canon-McMillan High School
"I was a student at Cecil Township Junior High School, and someone had sneaked a transitor radio into the library. We'd whisper to each other what had happened in the game, and passed it on. When Maz hit the home run everybody went crazy in the room; the teacher couldn't understand what was going on. I got hooked with that '60 World Series. I don't think, since the end of World War II, there's been such a good feeling in this town. Now my daughter is infatuated with baseball. I've met ElRoy Face and his fingers are so huge for a guy his size. He's typical of the nice guys who were on that team. They're so nice."

Fred Graham
Retired, Civil Engineer
Allegheny County
Mt. Lebanon
"I was stationed in the U.S. Army at Aberdeen Proving Grounds. I was a graduate civil engineer from Carnegie Tech, and I was placed in an Army Ordnance Corps to help test, as I later discovered, weapons and ammunition used in the Vietnam War. After watching the first six games of the 1960 World Series on TV by thinking of many ways to get near a TV, I finally ran out of ideas and excuses, and I had to go to work at the test range during the 7th game. I borrowed a $120 radio from one of the civilian workers so I could at least listen to the game. The radio was quite expensive considering that I was drawing $99 a month in salary. I was in an observation tower, listening to the game on the radio, when I was surprised by a bomb going off without warning at the base of the tower. It shook the wooden tower and the radio dropped to the floor and broke. I had to return a broken radio to my civilian friend and was quite upset by the turn of events. As we entered the post, the military policeman said, 'Did you hear? The Pirates won the World Series. Mazeroski hit a game-winning home run.' I saw six games on TV and heard most of the seventh game, but missed one of the most exciting sporting events in Pittsburgh's history. However, I was in the stands for Franco's 'Immaculate Reception.' There is some justice after all."

Bernie Zuchelkowski
Merrittstown, Pa.

"I have treasured memories of the events in my life at the exact moment of the Billy Maz homer. The thought of it triggers so many warm and wonderful emotions and memories. I still have my 1960 Pirates yearbook, and my 1961 Pirates World Champion Yearbook, and look at them from time to time. My dad, whose name was Francis 'Zeke' Zuchelkowski, bought me a Bill Mazeroski model glove in the early '60s. It's still in decent shape today. Maz was my dad's all-time favorite ballplayer without a doubt. I remember my dad wearing a softball jersey with No. 9 on it when he kept score for my softball team in 1977. And he wanted everyone to know the significance of the No. 9. I remember Dad and I sitting on the glider on summer nights listening to the 'Gunner' and the 'Possum' on the radio. I inherited the family glider in 1979 when my folks moved from Filbert to Buffington (Dad's birthplace), another old mining patch. That old glider sits on my porch now and my son Zack and I skip the TV games once in awhile to listen to the Bucs on radio on our porch, just like Dad and I did 30-35 years ago. Dad and I had a close father-son relationship and our common love was Bucco baseball. I'm trying to raise Zack the way Dad raised my brother Ed and I. My dad died, at age 68, on October 7, 1992. I never see or listen to a Pirates' game that I don't think about my dad."

Forbes Field for opener of 1960 World Series

ElRoy Face
The Baron of the Bullpen

*"What I remember most about ElRoy
is that he was absolutely fearless."*
— Bob Prince

Baseball players from the past, including ElRoy Face, filled the lobby at the Green Tree Marriott. This was the morning of June 16, 1990 and these people were in town for a 30th anniversary reunion of the 1960 Pirates World Series champions and for an Oldtimers Game later that day at nearby Three Rivers Stadium.

I was lucky to come upon this scene. My wife Kathie and I had stayed overnight at the Marriott after attending a musical parody called "Forbidden Pittsburgh," a Don Brockett production that spoofed Mayor Sophie Masloff, and other local political, media and sports figures.

There were fans running around with bubble gum cards, asking the ballplayers to sign their cards. I did not have to look at any bubble gum card collection to recognize or identify those who were in the room that morning. The faces on those cards, as well as all the sports magazines I collected in my youth, and re-read until they were worn thin, were still stored in my mind.

I moved about the room and secured the autographs of several members of that 1960 Pirates team: ElRoy Face, Vernon Law, Smoky Burgess, Dick Schofield, Bob Oldis, Sam Narron, Mickey Vernon, George Witt, Rocky Nelson and Joe Gibbon. I also got the autographs of Maury Wills, Tito Francona, Eddie Mathews, Johnny Callison and Johnny Logan. Burgess died two years later. I wish I had talked to him at greater length. How was I to know it would be my last opportunity to do so?

I wanted their autographs for a book I was planning to write, so what if I behaved like I was 14 instead of 47?

What struck me most was the size of these ballplayers. Mathews and Callison were powerful home run hitters and I pictured them being much bigger than they appeared in the lobby. They were still big through the chest and shoulders, but not that tall. They had looked bigger on their baseball cards.

I am only 5-8 1/2 inches tall and have always thought of myself as being on the small side. Yet I was taller than Logan, Wills, Burgess and Face as well.

I was always a shrimp in grade school, the smallest kid in the class. I was at the front of the class for First Communion and for Confirmation at St. Stephen's, as they had us in a marching formation from the smallest to the tallest.

I was the littlest of the Little League players in my hometown of Hazelwood. I wore No. 1 when I played for the Moose Club, and then for the Hungarians Club. I wasn't much of a ballplayer. I think I was the first kid ever traded in the history of the Hazelwood Little League. My mother wasn't too thrilled about me wearing a uniform that read HUNGARIANS from shoulder to shoulder, but the Hungarians probably weren't too thrilled about it, either. As a nine-year-old, I remember I batted .167, with one hit in six at-bats, and that was a bunt where the ball rolled dead against the dropped hat, and the catcher couldn't get a good grip on it to throw me out. I did hit what appeared to be a single to right field that summer, but got thrown out at first base.

I always excused myself for my athletic shortcomings because of my size. And now I was standing next to Smoky Burgess, Johnny Logan and ElRoy Face, and I was as big as any of them. I had mixed emotions about that. I had spent most of my life as a sports writer walking through lobbies occupied by basketball players, football players and boxers, and most of them were much bigger than I am. Hockey players and baseball players, for the most part, are normal-sized people, which has always been part of their appeal to the populace.

That was certainly part of the appeal Face had for Pittsburghers. He was listed at 5-8, 155 pounds when he pitched for the Pirates — he was usually down to about 145 pounds by August — but he walked with the supreme confidence and arrogance of a giant whenever he was called into a game to put the fire out. He was one of the first premier relief pitchers, and he perked up his teammates and the crowd when he came striding in slowly from the bullpen. The sight of No. 26 coming to the mound put fear into the hearts of batters, no matter their size.

After batting against him in the 1960 World Series, Yogi Berra said, "I'm just glad I'm in the other league."

"Everybody said I was cocky," said Face. "I wasn't. I was confident."

"I like the way he struts to the mound," his manager, Danny Murtaugh, once said. "He's got a lot of moxie, and it picks up the club to watch him swagger out there."

Bob Prince said Face always strutted to the mound like he knew he was going to win. If he lost, he came in the next day with the same attitude. "What I remember most about ElRoy was that he was absolutely fearless," Prince said.

Face did not appear quite as fearless standing by himself near the front desk in the lobby of the Marriott. Like anybody in that situation, he was looking to make a connection with one of his former teammates, perhaps, eager to fit in.

I approached him and introduced myself and talked to him briefly. As I was talking to him, a man wearing glasses, came over and said hello to Face. He made some small talk, and then he caught Face off-guard with an off-the-wall remark.

"Maybe you can help me with something I'm trying to figure out," said the man. "I have a baseball at home that was signed by three Hall of Famers — you, Clemente and Mazeroski. . . "

"I'm not in the Hall of Fame," snapped Face, "and neither is Mazeroski. So you've got one . . . Clemente."

The man didn't miss a beat, nor did he seem to realize that he had just offended Face. Nor did Face hide his instant irritation very well. He was peeved.

"Would you have any idea," the man, continued, in a most serious manner, "what year you would have signed that ball?"

Think about that... How could anyone answer that question? How could anyone ask that question? Where do these guys come from? But people like this — and he didn't appear to be any dummy — come out of the woodwork whenever and wherever athletes or celebrities appear, and then people sometimes wonder why these ballplayers are not more friendly.

"I have absolutely no idea," said Face, making a pick-off move to get this man out of his life.

When the man moved on, Face just fumed for awhile. He was throwing off more heat than he did when he came in with the bases loaded, and fired a fastball or forkball.

"Did you hear that?" he asked me. "How the hell would I know when I signed it? How many baseballs do you think I've signed in my lifetime? If I had a dollar for every baseball I've signed in my lifetime I'd be a rich man now."

"In his book, Stan Musial said I was the best relief pitcher he ever faced."
— ElRoy Face

When Face attended that 1990 reunion of the 1960 team, he was still working as a carpenter at Mayview State Hospital in Bridgeville and he knew there were a lot of people out in the streets who had more mental problems than many of the patients where he worked.

He has since retired from that job as well, after 11 years there, and lives in retirement in an apartment complex in North Versailles, about 500 yards to the left after you cross the George Westinghouse Bridge, between East Pittsburgh and East McKeesport, if you are traveling east from Pittsburgh.

In the valley below that bridge, one can see the huge shell of what was once the largest Westinghouse plant in the world, where it all began. My father-in-law, Harvey Churchman, worked there for 42 years before retiring as an electrical tester, and his father had worked there for nearly 50 years. They never worked anywhere else; that's the way it once was among industrial workers in the Mon Valley. But the building and the workers in it became dinosaurs in the '70s and the plant has been abandoned. There is a sign at one end of the bridge pointing toward Turtle Creek, a community two miles away which produced a Heisman Trophy winner in Notre Dame's Leon Hart.

The people from places like East Pittsburgh and East McKeesport and Turtle Creek could identify with a tough little guy like Face. He, too, worked with his hands, whether he was firing a forkball, fixing a car or building a cabinet. He has huge hands, especially for a man his

Award winners ElRoy Face, Bob Bailey, Roberto Clemente and Bill Virdon in 1963

With broadcaster Red Barber

With Ed Sullivan on his TV show

Comparing biceps with Ted Kluszewski

With Vernon Law after '60 Series

Relief for ace reliever

size. He takes pride, for instance, that he and a friend, Frank Aquila, finished the basement in Bill Mazeroski's home. He was a little guy who undid giants, another David vs. Goliath story.

There are still two things that bug Face about his baseball career: that he missed out on the big money and that he missed out on the Hall of Fame. He was a candidate on the Hall of Fame ballot for 15 years, but never came close to making it for induction at Cooperstown. I voted for him, as well as Mazeroski, every one of those years, but he did not have the national backing he needed for such honors.

Only two relief pitchers have ever been voted into the Baseball Hall of Fame, namely Hoyt Wilhelm, who was a contemporary of Face, and Rollie Fingers, who came later. The induction of Fingers infuriated Face because he felt he belonged in there before Fingers did.

"I think I deserve to be in and a lot of my teammates do, too," offered Face in his defense. "In his book, Stan Musial said I was the best relief pitcher he ever faced."

There are times when Face comes off as being bitter about the way things turned out for him in baseball, but he remains a good-natured, personable individual. The Hall of Fame is just a sore subject with him.

"I just don't know what you have to do to get there," Face said of the Hall of Fame during our two-hour interview. "If Maz and I had played for the Yankees, we probably would have made it."

I traveled to the apartment in North Versailles where Face has lived the last 10 years on Friday, February 12. I was there at noon, as scheduled. When I got to the door, I noticed on the doorbell board outside the apartment that the name FACE appeared over the name FEENEY. That was Charley Feeney, or "the other" Chub Feeney, a former sportswriter for the *Pittsburgh Post-Gazette* who had covered the Pirates for over 20 years before retiring a few years earlier. Feeney also had an apartment in Bradenton, Florida, near the Pirates' training camp, where he stayed during the winter.

Feeney had come back to Pittsburgh a few days earlier, I knew, to attend the funeral of an old friend, Willard "Diz" Bellows, who had been the bartender and manager of the media lounge at Three Rivers Stadium and who had worked for the Pirates in one capacity or another dating back to 1924. Bellows was buried that Friday morning in Calvary Cemetery in my hometown of Hazelwood, following mass at St. Regis Church on Parkview Avenue in Oakland, near the boyhood homes of two Pittsburgh sports institutions, Danny Marino and Bruno Sanmartino, and near where Willie Stargell stayed during the baseball season early in his Pirates' career. Two of the all-time boxing greats, Harry Greb of Garfield, known as "The Pittsburgh Windmill," and Billy Conn, "The Pittsburgh Kid," are buried in Calvary Cemetery.

I had paid my respects to the Bellows family the night before at the John A. Freyvogel Sons Inc. funeral home in Oakland. Bellows was laid out in the same room where another barkeeper and former Pirate Frankie Gustine had been viewed a year earlier, and where Pete

Dimperio, a legendary high school football coach in the city, had been viewed the year before that.

Many of the same people were present to pay their respects as had been there for the funerals of Gustine and Dimperio, who had been life-long friends.

In the register, I noted many familiar names: Nellie King, Joe Gordon, Joe O'Toole, Jackie Powell, Ed Kiely, Sally O'Leary, Elmer Gray, and several former Forbes Field ushers, like Nick Pugliese, Nick Diulus, "Big Bob" DePasquale and his brother, Jeep, who had been a member of City Council as well as the head of the ushers union for many years.

Several members of the local sports media had come by, including Myron Cope, John Mehno, Pohla Smith, Evan Pattak, Bill DiFabio and John Duffy.

I bumped into Pat and Bob Friend when I walked into the funeral parlor. It was Friend who first told me about Bellows dying when I had talked to him a few days earlier.

Only six weeks earlier, on Sunday, December 27, I had interviewed Bellows for this book in the baseball press box at Three Rivers Stadium. He was working at the last regular season game of the Steelers.

I took some pictures of him. I took one of those photos with me to the funeral home, and gave it to his son, Willard, who had been a batboy for the Pirates in 1961 and 1962. It was the last photo ever taken of his father. I was so glad I had the opportunity to talk to Bellows about his baseball life before he died. I had just read a story about Alex Haley, the author of the Pulitzer Prize-winning *Roots*, in which Haley was quoted as saying, "Whenever an old person dies it is like having a library burned down."

Face was a good friend of Bellows, and every time Face would visit Three Rivers Stadium he would stop by to see his old friend and have a drink with him. But Face told me he had just found out from Feeney that Bellows had died.

Face told me that several former Pirates, including Richie Hebner and Bob Robertson, once resided in that same apartment complex. It is about ten miles from Forbes Field, and 15 miles from Three Rivers Stadium. It is a terrible drive during commuter rush hours, on the Parkway East, but a convenient drive during off-hours. Face had lived there for ten years in a two-bedroom apartment. He told me he has several plaques and photos and framed newspaper stories on display in his apartment, and I will have to take his word for it because I never got in to see it.

Face had come to the door less than a minute after I buzzed his apartment. "My wife has a cold and isn't feeling well," he said for openers. "Let's go somewhere for lunch."

He was wearing a black windbreaker jacket. It had a Pirates Alumni logo on the left breast. He wore a light blue shirt, his white T-shirt showed above it, and he wore light blue jeans and white sneakers. He was wearing glasses. He looked like he still weighed about 165 or 170 pounds.

We turned west coming out of his apartment parking lot, went over the Westinghouse Bridge, and drove a few miles to Forest Hills where he suggested we go to Drew's Family Restaurant. It was a rare winter day in Pittsburgh, with the sun shining and the temperature rising over 50 degrees.

Face made an early admission which certified how much time had passed since that 1960 World Series. "I'll be 65 next week," said Face, forcing a smile. "I'm into Medicare now."

Face had been my father's favorite Pirate, probably because they were about the same size. My father was 5-7, 135 pounds when he died at age 63 in 1969. When Face started smoking one cigarette after another following lunch, he really reminded me of my father, Dan O'Brien.

I asked Face about his chain-smoking habit. "I've been doing it for 50 years; I started from my mom and dad when I was 14." He was smoking Merit UltraLights. "I smoked Camels for years; then Phillip Morris, then Luckies," he said. The fingers he once used to grip a baseball were nicotine stained.

My dad always said that Camels were the only real cigarettes, but he realized they were too strong. He smoked Pall Malls, and I was frequently sent out to pick them up for him at a local store. Every time he went to a hospital he ended up with pneumonia, and one of the causes of his death was emphysema.

Face and my father bore a resemblance to one another. Only Face's salt and pepper hair was unkempt, like he had hurried to meet me at the door of his apartment, whereas my father had been so fussy about his hair. It always gleamed from Vaseline hair ointment, and was always impeccably combed straight back. He took great pride in his hair.

I asked Face how he felt when he heard a comment like the one offered by someone at the door of the restaurant — that "you were really something."

"I hope," said Face, "they enjoyed themselves. A lot of people say to me, 'I lost a lot of money on you.' I say, 'I'm glad I lost it for you.' "

I asked Face if he had been out to the Forbes Field site in recent years. "I've been up that road (Clemente Drive) that runs by what's left of the wall," he said. "It was about two months ago. I had to take my boy up to the Pitt dental school. He grew up with Forbes Field, so it seems odd to him."

"What's his name?" I asked.

"It was Gene until he was about 12 or 13," said Face. "But he came to me and asked me to change his name. He said, 'If my name is Gene Face, people are going to ask me if I'm your son,' he said. 'If my name is ElRoy, they won't ask me if I'm your son. They'll know.' "

I had to smile. It sounded like his son suffers inquiring people, or reporters, much like his dad.

"His middle initial is A, whereas mine is L," said Face. "His name is ElRoy Alan. He also lives in North Versailles. He has three girls and his wife is due with a boy; that's what they've been told by their doctor.

I also have two daughters to my first wife. There's Michelle, who will be 39 in July. She lives in East Liberty and she has two girls and a boy. My other daughter, Valerie, will be 30 in September. She lives in Penn Hills. She was married for a brief time. She has no children. She was in the Navy for four years.

"I think anybody who graduates from high school ought to be required to spend a year in the military service," interjected Face. "It gives them time to get themselves together, to see what they want to do, if they want to go to college or start a career. I have a grand niece who just went to the Air Force and she's stationed in San Antonio."

Face spent a year-and-a-half in the military service in 1946 and 1947 before beginning his pro baseball career in 1948. "I spent nine months in Guam," he recalled. "The war was over in December, and we got there in February for a clean-up effort. I was in ordnance; I was a mechanic in the motor pool."

Face was married to Jeanne Kuran, from Pittsburgh, for 25 years before they were divorced. They were married on July 15, 1953. He has been married for 14 years to Roberta, who is called Bo. "She has two children, a daughter, Debbie, 35, who lives outside Charlotte, North Carolina, and has a 12-year-old daughter, and a son, Bill, 32, who lives in North Huntingdon, and has a girl who is a year-and-a-half old."

I asked Face if he had been back home to Stephentown, N.Y. recently. "I was just there last Friday," he said. "My mother had a heart attack. She'll be 83 in July, and she seems okay now."

I later learned that some of Face's former teammates and friends had heard mistakenly that his mother had died. "I know, I got a sympathy card from Tito Francona," he said.

"I was there last July when they named a local ballpark after me. They had a parade in my honor and presented me with a plaque at ceremonies at the community park. The town is located at the intersection of Rt. 43 and Rt. 22, about 20 miles east of Albany.

"I never had any idea I'd play baseball professionally when I was 21 years old. I was the Pirates' No. 1 draft choice from Montreal two years before they came by Clemente in the same manner."

Face seemed a little subdued, perhaps because of his concern over the health of his mother and mother-in-law, and he probably had a case of cabin fever as well.

His former teammates say that Face always has a good time at their get-togethers, that he has a great sense of humor, an easy smile, and that he supports their activities and efforts more than most of the alumni.

Face insists he is not bitter about the snub from the Baseball Hall of Fame voters, just disappointed, that's all. He sees people gain admission such as relief pitcher Rollie Fingers, and feels his career was just as worthy of being similarly honored.

"I always said I wanted to get in while my parents were still alive," offered Face. "Now my dad is gone, and my mother is getting up there in years. It wasn't so much for me that I wanted it, but I thought it would mean a great deal to my parents and to my family. It means less to me now."

303

Face felt he also should have won the MVP Award for the 1960 World Series.

"I could have had a win in that seventh game if we had been able to hold the lead," offered Face. "It was between me and Bobby Richardson, and I'd probably have won it if I had gotten a win in that last game."

In the final game, Face pitched three relief innings and it was his pinch-hitter, Gino Cimoli, who started the Bucs' big eighth inning rally.

"I didn't think Richardson did anything in the four games we won. He only did something in the three games they won, and they blew us out. He had the hits and RBIs, but it was in games they would have won anyhow. The Yankees didn't win one game that was up for grabs in the seven game series.

"In the fourth or fifth game in New York, I came in and retired eight in a row, and I retired seven of eight in another game. I'm told (Bob) Prince kept saying forkball, forkball, but I was throwing few forkballs. It was mostly sliders right in on their fists. I was jamming them.

"In the first game of the Series, I struck out Mantle and Maris on a forkball. In that same game, (Moose) Skowron hit one to the wall, though, and Virdon went back and made a great catch. So I was lucky, too."

"He was accustomed to staring other men into submission. He was an athlete of the stare; he enjoyed the sport."
— From "The Lords of Discipline"
by Pat Conroy

Where did the walk to the mound come from? Was it something he did to intimidate the other side?

"Just a little ol' farmboy, I guess," said Face. "My father always had a team of horses. We all worked in the woods, cutting lumber. I never walked too fast. Who the hell's in a hurry to get into trouble? It's already there. You want to take your time getting to it.

"I guess I aggravated a lot of people the way I walked in. It wasn't cockiness, it was confidence. During that 18-1 season, I had a 22-game winning streak going over two years when I lost in L.A. About ten or twelve reporters came at me in the clubhouse afterward. One of them asked me, 'How do you feel about losing your streak?' I said, 'I'll have to start another one.' That was the end of the interview. They couldn't ask me anything after that.

"I hold two records that will never be broken. That's my 18-1 record in relief. I don't think anybody will touch it. And I made 802 appearances as a pitcher for one ballclub, tying the record held by Walter Johnson, and I don't think that will be broken. Guys don't stay with the same team long enough to do that anymore."

Face was thought to have the perfect demeanor to be a relief pitcher. He thrived on throwing the ball in tough spots. "A lot of people asked me how I could stand the pressure," said Face. "I don't think I had pressure. I had eight guys behind me. He (the batter) had no one to help him out."

Prince called him "The Baron of the Bullpen" and Jack Hernon of the *Post-Gazette* called him "Sam Spade."

Just to show that Face still has a sense of humor, he volunteered a story about himself. "I went 21 innings once without giving up a run. It's the bottom of the thirteenth inning, and I was facing Stan Musial in St. Louis. I threw a forkball to him down and away — it was a good pitch — and Musial went out and got it and put the ball on the roof in right field. Murtaugh walked by me in the clubhouse and said, 'Relief pitcher my ass!'

"Danny kept us all as happy and humble as possible. In '60, we just had a bunch of guys who never gave up. The team just pulled together. It was not a team of individuals. If a guy was benched, he'd root for the guy who took his place."

"Everybody liked ElRoy."
— Bob Skinner

On the eve of the 1960 season, Danny Murtaugh had a meeting with the pitchers.

"Listen, I don't want any of you having sex the night before you're pitching," he said to them.

"Hey, Danny, how about me?" asked Face. "I might be pitching every day. Am I shut out for the season?"

Like Mazeroski, Face remains one of the most respected and revered figures in baseball history, especially in Pittsburgh and western Pennsylvania where he makes his home. He is as well known nationally, and better known in some cases, than many of those who are enshrined at Cooperstown. He was most popular with his Pirates teammates.

"Everybody liked ElRoy," Bob Skinner said. "He was always friendly and personable, even with the pressure-type job he had."

When I asked Skinner which player on the '60 Pirates that he admired the most, he said it was Face. "He had the toughest job and handled it well. He never complained."

Face is a revered figure where it counts the most, in his own backyard. Face is proud to point out that he was voted to the Pirates All-Time Team for the first hundred years of the club's existence.

In an extensive interview with Pittsburgh writer Abby Mendelson, Face once said, "I thought it was the highlight of a ballplayer's career to be in the Hall of Fame, and I think it still is, but I don't think the meaning is there.

"In fact, when they put in Ralph Kiner I think they degraded the Hall of Fame. Because Ralph Kiner — all he did was hit home runs.

"To me, to be in the Hall of Fame you should be good at all phases of your position. Kiner couldn't run, couldn't throw, couldn't bat for average. All he could do was hit home runs. A Hall of Fame player should do everything well, but all he could do was hit home runs. He couldn't run and he couldn't play the outfield well. And I think he made it because of politics. Being an announcer (for the New York Mets) and traveling around the league, he could talk to the writers who he wanted to vote for him.

"There's another case — Ernie Banks. What could he do other than hit home runs? He didn't hit .300 lifetime. He couldn't play shortstop. He didn't have an arm. He couldn't run."

Conversely, however, Face felt that Reggie Jackson, who was the only player voted into the Baseball Hall of Fame for 1993, deserved the honor, despite a relatively low career batting average (.262). "He always came through in the clutch, and he was at his best in the biggest games," explained Face.

"If I had played for the Dodgers or Yankees or St. Louis," said Face, "I'd be in the Hall of Fame. I don't think there's any doubt in anybody's mind about that."

Kiner and Banks and Jackson, no doubt, all benefited from their popularity with the press. But his argument against a former Pirate, Kiner, is difficult to understand on several fronts. Kiner absolutely dominated the game in his day, leading the league in home runs seven straight seasons. It's difficult to follow Face's logic. It's like saying Face doesn't belong in the Hall of Fame because he didn't hit home runs. Kiner was a home run hitter and he came as close to Babe Ruth's record as anyone during his heyday, twice hitting more than 50 home runs.

And none of those guys got in at Face's expense. Maybe Kiner and Face both belong in the Hall of Fame.

Face is best known by Pirates fans for being an outstanding relief pitcher for a long period. His consistency was unparalleled in his time. In 1959 he posted an 18-1 record, a .947 winning percentage that is still the highest in baseball history, coupled with ten saves. Between 1958 and 1959, he won 22 straight games, all in relief.

From April 22, 1959 to September 11, 1959 Face won 17 games in relief without a loss.

In his trivia book, *The Answer is Baseball*, Luke Salisbury observed: "More attention should be paid to pitchers' winning streaks. Since 1945, only seven men have won 15 or more in a row. The man with the longest post-'45 streak also has the best season won-and-lost percentage of all time for 15 or more decisions. He is the Roger Maris of relief pitchers, ElRoy Face, godfather of the split-fingered fastball, then called a 'forkball,' won 17 straight games in 1959 and had an 18-1 record. Interestingly, Face had only ten saves."

In 1960, Face appeared in 68 games, had a 2.90 ERA, and all but won the World Series for the Pirates. He had three saves in the Series and almost got the win in the seventh game even though it was the one time in the Series he was not effective.

So he appeared in all four games won by the Pirates. He felt he deserved to win the World Series MVP Award, but he lost out to Richardson, the Yankees second baseman. Face has never hidden his disappointment over what he regarded as another slight in his career.

James G. Klingensmith/
Pittsburgh Post-Gazette

Three of his saves came with the tying or winning run on third when he entered the game.

"When I pitched, in order to get a save, you had to face the winning or tying run," said Face. "They either had to be at bat or on base, when you came in to pitch. Now, the rules are different. A pitcher can get a save when he comes in with a three- or four-run lead."

He led the National League in saves in 1958, 1961 and 1962 and in appearances in 1956 and 1960.

He was named to the All-Star Game in 1959, 1960 and 1961 and in 1963 *Sports Illustrated* put him on its cover and flatly called him "Baseball's Best Reliever."

Murtaugh once observed: "ElRoy had the uncanny knack of striking out the first batter he faced. Any reliever who can do that has to be something special."

On February 7, 1960, Face was honored as Dapper Dan Man of the Year at the Hilton Hotel for his performance in 1959. At the same dinner were Bobby Layne, Harvey Haddix, Ted Kluszewski, Hank Aaron and Ben Schwartzwalder, quite a lineup.

Haddix called him "one of the first of the great relief pitchers."

Between 1955 and 1957 Face started 14 games for the Pirates, but Murtaugh made him exclusively a relief pitcher.

Face pitched for the Pirates from 1953 to 1968. Then he was dealt to Detroit in a trade. Face found out from the ushers at Forbes Field that he had been traded. In his last game with the Pirates, manager Larry Shepard had him pitch in the first inning. He relieved Steve Blass who went to the outfield as Face pitched to one batter, and then Blass returned to pitch. That enabled Face to match Walter Johnson's record for 802 appearances for one club.

After a short stay in Detroit, Face was sent to Montreal, where he finished his career in 1969. Altogether, he appeared in 848 games, and had 104 wins.

Face had an occupational trade before he became a big league pitcher, and continued it during his career. Carpentry was familiar to everyone in the Face family.

"My whole family was full of carpenters — my grandfather, my father, my brothers — we all belonged to the carpenters union," said Face. He had remained in the carpenters' union the entire time he was in the major leagues.

"The hammering and sawing helped strengthen my arm during the winter months," he said.

Sometimes he tried something different, but not with satisfying results. He was a tire salesman in the off-season in 1956. His first entrepreneurial foray into the business world outside of carpentry was El-Roy Face's Bullpen, a restaurant-bar in Downtown Pittsburgh. It never caught on; he wasn't happy with it, and he soon abandoned the venture.

In 1978, Face passed a civil service test for his job at Mayview State Hospital.

"In my whole career, with all my jobs," offered Face, "I don't think I made a milion dollars total. Today, the average player is making it in one year."

During his heyday, Face supplemented his income with his music ability. He and catcher Hal Smith turned pro in the music business after the 1960 World Series. They both played guitar and sang, and their schedule included supper club dates at places like the Holiday House in Monroeville, an appearance, along with Casey Stengel, on the Perry Como Show on TV, and at sports shows and telethons, and they even made several records. They had road dates in Erie, McKeesport and Greensburg. It was all in good fun.

Two memories stand out for Face when he reflects on his long and storied career. He remembers a game in 1959 when a broken-bat single between short and third cost him a game and broke his 22-game consecutive win streak.

He remembers stuff like that. Eddie Mathews hit a home run off him once after Face had gone 18 1/3 innings in 14 games without giving up a run.

One of his most positive memories was the 1960 World Series.

He was proudest of his four appearances in the four games won by the Pirates in that Series.

Face stood to be the winning pitcher in the seventh game until Bob Friend gave up two runs in the top of the ninth when the Yankees tied the score. That, of course, set the stage for Mazeroski's place in baseball immortality.

That season Face's record was a more human 10-8, but he had 24 saves and a .290 ERA in 68 appearances. "That was my biggest year," he said.

Even more than his 18-1 season in 1959. He felt he was also more impressive in 1962 when he led the league with 28 saves in 63 appearances with a 1.88 ERA. "That's when I was named the Fireman of the Year," said Face.

"The most important thing about a reliever is that he's got to be the same every day. You can't go up and down with good and bad performances."

Before Face, relief pitchers were not respected much. "If you were a reliever, it was usually because you had failed as a starter," Face said.

"I think I was born 30 years too soon," said Face. "I'd probably me making three or four million dollars now. I'd sure like to be a free agent with my 18-1 record. I used to say if I were 30 years old and pitching today, the Pirates' owners would be working for me."

Actually, Face might have made even more than he thinks. Here's what the top four relief pitchers were making in the majors for the 1993 season: Tom Henke of the Texas Rangers ($4.25 million), John Franco of the New York Mets ($4 million), Rick Aquilera of the Minnesota Twins and Dennis Eckersley of the Oakland A's (both $3.9 million)

Face was a favorite among the sports writers, probably because they liked a little guy they could see eye-to-eye with during their interviews. Face frowned a lot, but he had an impish smile, and the light was usually on in his eyes. And he worked quickly, and sports writers liked that, too. He could warm up on eight or nine pitches.

ElRoy Leon Face was born February 20, 1928 at Stephentown, New York, about a two-hour drive from Cooperstown. He has gray-speckled brown hair, blue eyes. He is of English, French and German descent.

Face missed the big money, but he has learned to live with that. He tries hard to count his blessings. It helps him to remember where he came from.

"When I think back on it," said Face, "the town I grew up in had one gas station. Just one stop light in that town. Just a tiny town in upstate New York. To come from there and do what I did, I just feel I was lucky."

He was a natural, as an athlete, even though he got a late start as a baseball player. He had some instincts and skills for the game that he didn't recognize as a child.

"Even as a kid, I always had pretty good aim," he recalls. He describes seemingly endless summer days spent firing tennis balls at a circle crudely scrawled on the side of his grandfather's garage. He also threw stones and knocked out street lights.

Like many of his Pirates teammates, as a high school student, he starred in basketball, baseball and football.

"I never played Little League," said Face. "I never played baseball until high school."

As a kid, Face had a severe case of rickets, pneumonia five times, streptococcus and a weak heart. Even so, he once pulled his brother Leonard out of a pond when Leonard was going down for the second time. He was a brave lad.

When Myron Cope was writing for the *Pittsburgh Post-Gazette*, he reprinted parts of letters he received from ElRoy's brother Leonard and a separate one from his mother Bessie.

Leonard, a carpenter in Knoxville, Tennessee, shared this story with Cope:

"ElRoy was skinny and frail and had that blank look and quietness you always feel sorry for. He didn't make friends fast because he was hard to know. But when he made friends they always stuck by him. He has not or never had an ounce of conceit.

"When it came to Saturday, ElRoy didn't go to the baseball field like all the rest. He would stay at home and learn by himself how to play guitar by ear. He would stay home and play guitar and sing to himself.

"When ElRoy was in the seventh grade, we had a baseball game with Lebanon, N.Y., that day. Calvin Atwater was our manager. Well, ElRoy was ten minutes late getting there and Calvin wouldn't let him play. He put another boy in his place.

"It made ElRoy feel read bad, and as he started to walk away with tears in his eyes he said, 'Some day you'll be more than glad to have me on your team.' And he turned and walked a mile and a half home."

Several years later, ElRoy pitched Averill Park High School to the league championship by working four straight playoff games.

In a separate letter to Cope, Face's mother, Bessie wrote about an unfortunate aftermath to that achievement.

"Two days after the championship game, ElRoy was taken sick and the doctor said he had streptococcus. He was real bad with it for weeks. The drugs he had to take affected his heart, and the doctor told him he'd never play ball again. That almost done it for him.

"We talked to him and told him he would play ball and his brother Joe came home on furlough and he talked to him. And with all our encouragement and his determination, he did play again."

He was drafted by the Pirates from Montreal, then a minor league team, at the winter baseball meetings, December 1, 1952, the same way they would later get Roberto Clemente.

He was listed at 5-8, 155 pounds. "That's 155 pounds of dynamite," said Bobby Bragan, his first manager with the Bucs.

Sometimes, by late summer, Face would be down to 145 pounds, yet he remained one of the Pirates' strongest pitchers and one of their hardest throwers. He was a physical marvel. He once pitched in nine straight games.

He always had a good fastball and slider.

"Branch Rickey told him he had to get another pitch or he was through in the majors," said Bob Friend. "That's when he came up with the forkball. Today, they call it the split-finger fastball."

Face decided to throw the forkball after watching Joe Page, onetime Yankees relief ace, use the pitch during Page's comeback attempt with the Pirates when both were with the team's farm club in New Orleans.

"Page didn't show me how to throw it," said Face. "I learned that myself. I just thought if the forkball made Page so successful, I would give it a try."

To throw a forkball, a pitcher must hold the ball between the middle and forefingers. The only way that can be done effectively is by repeatedly jamming the ball in between the fingers until it becomes natural. Page and Face are among the few who ever mastered the pitch.

The motion is exactly the same as for a fastball, but the pitch is much slower and acts differently.

"It comes at you exactly like a fastball," said Dick Groat. "And when it got to the plate, it absolutely died. No way you could hit it.

"I can't describe to you the impact he had on a team when he entered a game," added Groat. "He lifted a ballclub right off the ground. You knew when he went in that somehow, some way, he would do whatever had to be done to win that ballgame.

"He did all the little things needed to win. He was an excellent fielder. He had the best pickoff move to second I'd ever seen. Only Roger

Craig had one nearly as good. He was the original stopper. The best way to describe him is to say he was the master of his trade.

"He was the greatest relief pitcher ever. He should be in the Hall of Fame. Over a four-year period, no matter what kind of jam we were in, you could look out to left field, and wonder what he'd do today to get us out of trouble. No matter how dark it looked, you knew something good was going to happen. He lifted the whole team when he came walking out from behind the scoreboard."

Face had also won his final five decisions in 1958. He compiled an astounding 22 consecutive victories in all. From May 30, 1958 to September 11, 1959, Face made 98 relief appearances without a loss

Hall of Famer Carl Hubbell of New York Giants holds the major league record with 24 consecutive victories over two seasons, but that was as a starter.

Face needed luck.

"If it's sinking right, I generally get em out," said Face of his forkball during that 18-1 season. "But if I'm getting it high — well, the other night Willie Mays hit one over the scoreboard for a three-run homer. To show you what kind of luck I'm having, we got five runs that inning and won it."

Once against the Cubs, Face made only three pitches and bang — three outs.

Once against Cincinnati, he came in with runners on first and second, none out. He picked the runner off second base. Then he picked the runner off first. He had two outs before he had even made a pitch to the plate. Then the batter hit the first and only pitch Face made for the third out. Thus he collected three quick outs on just one pitch.

Ed Bailey, Cincinnati catcher, said, "That little sucker would stand up to a mountain lion."

Face isn't sure what to do when fans fawn over him, or tell him what they remember him doing. "At times, I feel a little embarrassed," he said. "I know what I did; I don't have to be reminded."

Prior to retiring from his job at Mayview, Face bought a mobile home. He said he planned on traveling around the country and stopping to visit his old teammates. I asked him about that. "I put 10,000 miles on it each of the first two years, and 3,000 miles the third year," he said. "And last year I put only 500 miles on it. I'm going to get rid of it."

"Did you ever visit with any of your former teammates?"

"I stopped to see Ron Blackburn (1958-59) when we were visiting my step-daughter down in Charlotte. That's about it."

He said he has all the equipment, but he doesn't get out fishing much anymore. "I get a license every year," he said. He and Roberta have friends over from time to time to play cards, and he plays cards with friends when he goes golfing. He plays weekly in a golf league at Butler's, a local public course. He goes to just about all the golf outings he is invited to attend. "Ron Neccai ribs me about being the touring pro for the Pirates' Alumni."

He still visits Veterans Hospitals when called upon to do so. "I was just down there the other day with Steve Blass," he said. "We both signed autographs for the fellows."

As for his easy-does-it approach to life, Face defends himself:

"I earned the privilege. I worked hard, and I earned the privilege of taking it easy. If I had to do it over I'd be a baseball player. I have no regrets."

Face mentioned how the team cared for each other, and pointed to a sports card show hosted by J. Paul Sports Promotions, Inc. at Robert Morris College a few years earlier.

"It was a reunion of the 1960 Pirates," said Face. "The only ones who didn't show up who were scheduled to appear were Mizell, whose wife was dying of cancer, and Cimoli.

"The promoter wanted to know how we wanted to be paid, and we said to divide it evenly among everyone. He told us that was unusual, that when he did the Yankees, for instance, that Ford and Mantle wanted more than the others. We even gave Mizell a full share because of the circumstances that kept him away. The promoter told us it was one of the best groups he ever had for such a show.

"The players today are different. They seem to be out for themselves more. I don't know too many players today. I watch a game now and then on TV, but I'm not a fan.

"I think fans have a good feeling for us guys. I think they remember the '60 team better than the '71 or '79 team. I've had fans say to me, 'No team will ever beat the '60 Pirates.' That's the way I feel, too."

ElRoy Face (#26) comes in to relieve Vernon Law after meeting on mound involving, from left to right) Smoky Burgess (#6), Don Hoak, Danny Murtaugh (#40) and Dick Groat (#24).

John Blanchard
He was behind home plate when Maz hit the HR

"I should have called time . . .
I can still see it going."

The Yankees Yogi Berra had the best view of Bill Mazeroski's World Series-winning home run in 1960, standing to the right of the scoreboard at the wall in Forbes Field at 3:36 p.m. on October 13. Many Pirates fans can still envision Berra's behavior as Mazeroski's comet streaked over his head.

If Berra was the last to see the ball go over the wall, John Blanchard had the best view of the ball leaving Mazeroski's bat, and he knew instantly it was headed out of the ballpark.

Most accounts of the game have the fateful pitch being a fastball, but Blanchard says it was a slider. Blanchard wanted a fastball, but he couldn't convince Ralph Terry to throw one.

Blanchard has been second-guessing Casey Stengel, the manager; Terry, the pitcher; and himself, the catcher in that historic sequence, for more than 30 years.

Berra had given way as the catcher that year to Elston Howard, who was thought to keep baserunners more honest at that point in Berra's career. Howard got hurt just before the Series started, but was able to play in the first six games. He gave way to Blanchard in the second inning of the sixth game when he re-injured his wrist.

Blanchard went the distance behind home plate in the seventh game. It is a game he would sooner forget, like all of the Yankees, but he can't shake the memory. Especially when Pittsburghers persist in bringing up the subject.

"We didn't want Terry to throw a slider," began Blanchard. "I had played against Mazeroski in the minor leagues. I knew he could hit that high ball. If you throw Bill a fast ball between the letters and the belt, he'll take you downtown. I mean there's no tomorrow. We knew that, see. . .

"So Eddie Lopat, the pitching coach, in the ninth inning, said, 'Don't throw the slider. It's not working. It isn't sliding. OK?' I said, 'Fine.' I went down . . . I've got pictures . . . my mitt is about ten inches off the ground and I'm down on one knee. I'm as low as I can get to the ground.

"Anyway, I got in there, and the first sign I gave him was a fastball and Terry said no. I gave him a second sign, another fastball, and he said no. I thought, well, evidently he wants to throw the slider. So I put three down, three fingers, and he threw the slider. It was just about an inch above the letters, and Mazeroski took it, for a ball. Well, boy, I just closed my eyes back there and put my mitt up there and let the

314

ball stick. I said, 'I'm glad he didn't swing.' So I called time and went out to Terry and said, 'Hey, listen, throw the fastball. The slider is not breaking. Throw the fastball down low! Hit my mitt. Keep the ball down on this guy because, if you don't, we're going home early.' So he said, 'OK.' I turn around and went back behind the plate.

"And I put down the fastball sign and he didn't throw it. He shook his head. I put it down again. He shook his head again. Well, that's when I made my mistake. I should have called time and went out to the mound again. Maybe I should have gotten Eddie Lopat out there. But I didn't. I called a slider. Well, he threw it an extra inch, a little bit lower. About two inches lower. And Maz hit that thing...

"I can still see it going. As soon as it left the bat I knew that school was out and I headed for the dugout.

"After the game was over, Lopat came over to my locker. There was a five minute period when writers weren't allowed in and he said, 'Geez, I thought I told you not to call a slider.' And I said, 'I don't want to say anything. Ed, please, go over and talk to Ralph Terry about it.' So he went over and Ralph said, 'Yeah, I shook John off about three or four times. I just had more confidence in my slider.' Well, Lopat told him, 'You better leave that slider in Oklahoma, and don't bring it to spring training with you.'"

New York Yankees

Yankees catchers Yogi Berra, Elston Howard and John Blanchard

Vinegar Bend Mizell
He pitched for four Presidents

"The greatest year I had in baseball was that '60 season."

"To see, to remember, the power of words,
their power to move, to cause people to move."
—Maya Angelou
Poet, Winston-Salem

People still smile when they say his name. Vinegar Bend Mizell. Say it slowly, say it again, and let the words roll off your tongue like a change-up pitch. It is a baseball name that calls up visions of the past, of a purer, more colorful past. It is a baseball name for the ages. You don't put quotation marks before and after Vinegar Bend. It is as much his name as Wilmer David Mizell, his given name when he was born August 13, 1930 in Leakesville, Mississippi. He grew up on the outskirts of Vinegar Bend, Alabama, a rural community of 37 citizens about five miles across the state line from Leakesville, and drew his nickname from it. As a big league pitcher, he drew national attention to it. His remains one of the most recognizable baseball names.

"Sure, I remember Vinegar Bend . . . the baseball player," people are prone to say when they hear his name.

Even people who never saw him fire a fastball from the portside, as they said of left-handed flame-throwers back then, remember hearing that name someplace. There is something venerable about Vinegar Bend Mizell.

He was a big pitcher for his day, at 6-3½ — "when he stands up straight," said a scout — and 205 pounds. And he could throw hard. He was wild at the outset of his 14-year baseball career, but he learned how to control that speed, and he became an effective and winning pitcher. John Keane of the Cardinals swore Mizell could throw as hard as Lefty Grove or Wild Bill Hallahan or Dizzy Dean. Mizell posted a 90-88 lifetime major league record with 15 shutouts and a 3.85 earned run average. He won 13 games for the Pirates '60 champions. That would earn him at least two million a year if he were pitching these days. He was popular beyond his baseball statistics because he was a likable fellow, a southern gentleman whose homespun style was charming. He was as friendly as an old sheepdog, a decent sort who drew respect from his teammates and anybody who dealt with him. He has always been a "people person," a born politician.

He pitched for the Pirates for parts of two summers, coming to Pittsburgh from the St. Louis Cardinals in time to contribute to the championship season of 1960 — "the greatest year I had in baseball was that '60 season," he says now — and he stayed through the start of the 1962 season. He joined Casey Stengel's original New York Mets team that same 1962 season, but they soon gave up on him when they realized his arm was dead. He is better remembered for pitching for the Cardinals for six years, a stint that was interrupted by two years of military service.

"After the St. Louis Browns moved to Baltimore," he explained, "we were the only major league baseball team west of the Mississippi. So we represented a large region of the country, and our games were broadcast far and wide. That's why we were so well known."

It was an era when everybody had a nickname. The Cardinals included Stan "The Man" Musial, Enos "Country" Slaughter, Albert "Red" Schoendienst, Harry "The Hat" Walker, Harry "The Cat" Brecheen and Harvey "The Kitten" Haddix. It was a different age, a simpler age, when the grass was real, when the lines were drawn with lime dust, and the ballparks were built for baseball.

"I like the old ballparks," said Vinegar Bend, squinting his brown eyes as if he were staring into the noontime sun. "I loved Crosley Field, the Polo Grounds and the ballpark in Brooklyn, Ebbetts Field and, of course, Forbes Field in Pittsburgh. It was a beautiful ballpark with a beautiful backdrop. And Wrigley Field; I felt it was immoral to put lights in there."

Vinegar Bend was the only Pirate from the 1960 squad who didn't see Bill Mazeroski's Series-winning home run against the New York Yankees. Haddix, the pitcher, was due up after Maz and Dick Stuart was set to pinch-hit for him. Mizell had been warming up in the bullpen preparing to enter the game in the 10th inning. He was walking under the stands on his way to the dugout when he heard the crowd roar. "I knew somebody'd done somethin'," he said at the time. He saw Maz's home run on a TV monitor that was in the hallway on the way to the clubhouse. "I never got back out on the field," Mizell remembers now with a wink and a smile. "I was the only Pirate not to be part of the on-the-field celebration. I was set to pitch the tenth inning. Our bullpen was in right field, and the stands were so close to the field that you had to walk under the stands to get to the dugout so you wouldn't interfere with the game. There was a TV down there where they were monitoring the commercials or something like that. I got to the TV in time to see Maz hit the home run. I'll have to stay that was one time I was glad I didn't have to pitch."

When Vinegar Bend smiles, and he smiles often, his eyes are mere slits. So there are two smiles on his still handsome face. He is of French-Irish descent, and his black hair has turned gray with silver streaks, but it is meticulously coiffured.

"If anybody had told me when I left Vinegar Bend that I'd have had all the experiences I have had, I would have thought they were crazy," said Mizell.

At 62, Vinegar Bend still looks like a ballplayer. He walks like a ballplayer. He was wearing his 1960 championship ring on his right hand, and a relatively new wedding band on his left hand. During our four hour interview at his condominium apartment in Alexandria,

Virginia, he appeared relaxed in a white jersey with a red and blue Cracker Jack Old Timers Baseball Classic logo over the left breast. "I hear this is a collector's item because they don't have the game anymore," he said. Then, too, everything about baseball's past and present is considered a collectible today.

He wore cream-colored casual slacks, white sweat socks with red and blue stripes around his calves. "They look like baseball socks," I said. He smiled. "They feel like baseball socks; that's why I like 'em," he said. He wore white sneakers. He cupped his hands behind his head and leaned back comfortably on a cream-colored three-pillow couch as he reflected on his life in the big leagues — the National League, the U.S. Congress and federal offices in Washington, D. C. He has received many honors for his efforts.

Mizell's story is different from most of his teammates on that 1960 Pirates team. He served three terms as a U. S. Congressman, beginning in 1969, from the fifth district of North Carolina, and has parlayed that into several political appointments ever since. He was a Congressman during the tenure of President Nixon and has since served under three Presidents — Ford, Reagan and Bush. He is particularly proud of legislation he promoted to help the American farmers.

He won his Congressional seat, in the first place, on a law-and-order platform, plus his promise to try to do something for "the forgotten man of the Great Society," the guy who obeys the law, goes to church, pays his taxes and tries to keep enough cash on hand to take care of his family. His motto was "You have a friend in Vinegar Bend."

When he was first elected to Congress, Mizell said, "I know everybody's going to think I'm just a big-eared, funny baseball pitcher goin' to Congress. Well, I don't mind a little notoriety. But I've got a responsible job to do, and I'm going to be sincere and hard-working."

When Mizell called it quits as a ballplayer after the 1962 season, he moved to North Carolina, his wife Nancy's home, to a community called Midway, just outside Winston-Salem, and got a job with the Pepsi-Cola Bottling Company. In a round-about way, this led him to big league politics.

Mizell liked young people, and during the latter part of his career as a ballplayer he never skipped an invitation to appear before young people's groups. When he took the job in North Carolina, he accepted an average of 100 such speaking engagements a year.

This wasn't in his job description, but the bottling company encouraged such extracurricular activity. Before long, thousands and thousands of people had met or heard Mizell speak, and they liked what they saw and heard. Local political figures found him to be a natural, and they asked him to run for County Commissioner. Two years later, he was a candidate for Congress after the state had been re-districted. And he won.

"People thought I was gonna be Dean or Grove or somebody big like that," said Mizell. "I wasn't, but if I hadn't gotten into baseball, I'd still be behind a mule in Alabama. I got me a reputation.

"I've just been dead honest with folks. I tell 'em how I didn't wear shoes until I was 18, and then I wore 'em out because my feet were so tough."

Mizell was a man who could play roles. He sounded right as a Congressman, sincere as can be. He could change roles quickly. He was never the rube sports writers envisioned, but once he grasped his part in the fantasy, he filled it. The 1950's needed a new Dizzy Dean, and Wilmer was asked to fill the role. As a kid he knew only two baseball players: Babe Ruth and Dizzy Dean. "Those were the only names that floated around our place," he said in our interview.

"Ain't it great?" said Mizell after a year in the minors. "They give you two uniforms, all the steaks you can eat, and you live in a big hotel like an important person."

Or when he said, "These dadgummed parks are bigger than some of the farms I worked on. I'm afraid to cut loose with a pitch, 'cause I might kill somebody in these big crowds."

"It ain't braggin' if you done it."
— Dizzy Dean

I knew that when Bill Clinton became President it would mean that Mizell would be losing his political appointment in Washington, D.C. He had been appointed, after all, as a Republican by President Bush's administration as the deputy assistant secretary for intergovernmental relations at the Department of Veterans Affairs. "It's a long title, huh?" said Mizell, almost apologetically, when I asked him his job title.

I would be visiting Vinegar Bend on the Sunday before the Wednesday Presidential Inauguration ceremonies. I was pleased with the timing because it would represent a significant change in the life and affairs of the former Pirates pitcher, and it would provide fodder for conversation and reflection.

I first learned of this changing of the guard two months earlier when I was in Raleigh, North Carolina with my family to spend Thanksgiving with relatives. I had expressed an interest back then in checking out the possibility of interviewing Vinegar Bend at nearby Winston-Salem, should he have gone home for the holidays. But, as it developed, he really went home for the holidays, back to his boyhood home of Vinegar Bend, Alabama.

It seemed like quite a coincidence when I discovered a news article and an accompanying photograph of Mizell in the Thursday, November 26, 1992 issue of *The News & Observer* in Raleigh during my holiday reading. It was about how and he other North Carolinian appointed politicos were going to lose their jobs in D.C.

Mizell, as a former athlete, knew about wins and losses, and he was philosophical about starting over, according to the newspaper story by Elana Varon.

319

"When a new administration comes in, at any level that would be a policy position, they need to bring in their own team," said Mizell. "That is the way it should be."

After 12 years of Republican rule, some 3,000 political appointees would be relinquishing their posts beginning January 20 to make way for President Clinton's crew. Mizell, a Republican who represented North Carolina's 5th District in Congress from 1969 to 1974, was among those who would be losing out in the changeover.

"I didn't think he would lose right up to the end," Mizell said of Bush. "But I'm an old baseball pitcher, and you don't count the game over until the last out's made."

Sometimes you stumble onto something. Like Alice in Wonderland. Writers and observers like William Least Heat Moon (*Blue Highways*) and Charles Kuralt (*Life on the Road*) have taught us that we will find the unexpected in the way of people and places if we take to the road once in a while, and leave ourselves open to new discoveries.

I combined my visit to Vinegar Bend Mizell with returning my oldest daughter, Sarah, to school after the holiday break, along with another young man from our community, Todd Melegari. They were classmates at Upper St. Clair High School the year before, and now they were first-year students at the University of Virginia.

I drove from Pittsburgh to Charlottesville in seven-and-a-half hours, departing our home at 7 a.m. and arriving at the UVA campus at 2:30 p.m. I had a date in Alexandria, Virginia, in suburban D.C., with Mizell at 5:30 p.m., so I was able to take my time and make some stops along the way.

I left Charlottesville via Route 29 North, using the directions Mizell had given me over the telephone. The first big town I passed through, about 40 miles north of Charlottesville, was Culpeper. It reminded me of Parents Weekend at the University of Virginia, back in October, 1992, when my wife Kathie and I had stayed at a Holiday Inn in Culpeper because that was as close an accommodation we could get to Charlottesville on that busy weekend.

Soon after I passed Culpeper, I started seeing huge, neatly-printed placards on the media strip welcoming President-Elect Clinton and Mrs. Clinton. At first, I wondered what that was all about. And I wondered how Hillary would feel about seeing a sign that referred to her merely as Mrs. Clinton.

Then I heard a CBS Radio report that explained what I was seeing. William Jefferson Clinton — I had never heard him referred to by his full name at any time during his campaign — had made a symbolic trip from Monticello, Thomas Jefferson's home, to Washington D.C., following as best as he could the route taken by Jefferson 192 years earlier.

Jefferson's spirit, you must understand, is still very strong in Virginia. When I accompanied Sarah on her first tour of the campus the summer before, the tour guides did their best to convince us that

Jefferson was still strolling the grounds of the University he founded, and seeing the original building complex he had designed and built.

Earlier that day, William Jefferson Clinton and Hillary and their daughter, Chelsea, had attended services at the Culpeper Baptist Church. The sermon was delivered by Dr. Herbert O. Browning Jr., and his sermon was based on Daniel 6:1-17 in the New Testament, the passage about a man of faith thrown into a den of lions, and how he survived it.

Afterward, the Clinton bus tour proceeded on to Washington. Nearly two centuries after the nation's third president, Thomas Jefferson, had traveled to Washington, Clinton chose the same route. "It was a p.r. thing," as Mizell would say when I told him about what I had seen en route to our meeting.

Clinton's bus trip took him through some especially scenic landscape. Virginia is a beautiful state. The trip took Clinton & Co. past grist mills and rolling hills, across the Rivanna, the Rapidan, the Rappahannock and the Potomac, and past horse farms with names like Edgehill and Belcourt. I saw signs welcoming Clinton and his party to Ruckersville and to Madison County.

Then I saw some more road signs, most of them done in red, white and blue. One read: **GOOD LUCK BILL AND AL.** Followed by: **HILLARY & TIPPER, TOO.** Then I saw one that read: **PLEASE STOP IN GAINESVILLE**, quickly followed by **WE HAVE HOT CHOCOLATE FOR YOU.** This was about 30 miles south of Washington. I turned onto Interstate 66 East there, and started seeing permanent road signs about the Manassas Battlefield Park and Bull Run Park. They are reminders of the Civil War that once tore the country apart, the worst war with the worst casualties ever involving our people. I would bet that the history lesson was not lost on President-Elect Clinton.

I departed from the route of Thomas Jefferson and Bill Clinton as I got closer to Washington. Whereas Clinton walked from Virginia into the District of Columbia, I started looking for quick tricky turns I had to make to get to Mizell's apartment.

As I turned into his apartment complex it struck me that it was called Watergate at Landmark. I had to stop at a security gate, and there were four or five uniformed security guards inside the dark block booth. I was given a pass to display on my windshield. "I picked it out because of the security system," Mizell would tell me later.

I was to go to Building 3. There appeared to be at least four buildings of similar size and architecture in the complex. They were big apartment buildings, all 18 stories high, with several hundred units per building.

It was not the sort of place I expected to find Vinegar Bend Mizell. It seemed out of character.

Mizell could appreciate that perception. "We're comfortable here, though I never thought I would ever live in any place associated with Watergate," he said. "I'm told this building was built by the same developers. I was one of the many who lost an election because Watergate

321

was going on at the time. I had been voted in three times, but lost a bid for a fourth term because people were upset with the whole Washington political scene, just as they were this past year because of the downturn in the economy, and the different problems they had in Congress in recent years. I won the previous election by over 50,000 votes, and while Watergate was still going on I lost by 3,000 votes."

The biggest lesson he learned during his days in Congress: "You can strongly support your position, and you can disagree with others," he said. "But you don't have to be disagreeable.

"My philosophy, and I never got away from this, is that you're there to serve. Some of our bureaucrats have forgotten that. They want to rule; they want to dictate."

"Everybody likes him."
— Ruth Cox Mizell

Mizell's first wife, Nancy McAlpine, died of cancer in 1990, after they had been married for 38 years. They had met in 1950 when he was playing Class B ball in Winston-Salem, North Carolina, the second stop on his road to the big leagues. They married two years later.

Mizell met and married Ruth Cox of Corpus Christi, Texas, a year after he lost his first wife. They admit to being an odd couple. The only thing they seem to have in common are strong Christian beliefs. They are involved in national and world-wide church activities. Ruth is a refined woman who might be called a Washington socialite. She and her husband proved to be wonderful hosts. She set out coffee and a large plate of sugar cookies. It was my dinner, and I probably ate more than my share. Ruth and Vinegar Bend offered many positive comments about each other. "Everybody likes him," Ruth remarked more than once. "He's very popular. I'm still amazed at how many people recognize his name, and say they know him. I didn't know he'd been a ballplayer when I first met him."

Ruth was never into sports. As one of her friends said after she learned of Ruth's involvement with Vinegar Bend Mizell, "I know she didn't meet him at a game." Ruth has done her best to learn the sports vernacular, but still sounds awkward with the language. She constantly refers to what her husband once did as "ball" rather than "baseball," and she stumbled over some other sports terms as well.

"I remember once that I referred to the seventh inning stretch as halftime," she said, laughing at her own miscue.

At first, when she spoke to her friends and business associates of her new man friend, she simply could not refer to him as Vinegar Bend or Wilmer. "They're both awful names, I think, horrid," she said during my visit to their apartment. She made a face as if she had just swallowed some vinegar, or as if she had a case of the bends. "So I called him V.B. for awhile, but that didn't work, either. I'm getting used to it now."

322

Wilmer Mizell at ease in his apartment in Alexandria, Va. with wife Ruth Cox and, below, showing off *Pittsburgh Post-Gazette* issue the morning after 1960 World Series victory.

Jim O'Brien

She once invited Vinegar Bend to accompany her to an opera. He was interested because he misunderstood her, and thought she was talking about the Grand Ol' Opry. He figured it was a country and western concert. When she clarified what she had in mind, Vinegar Bend begged off.

She learned one thing in a hurry when she accompanied Vinegar Bend to ballplayer reunions and Old Timers Games. "I've never seen that many happy people before; they really enjoy sports," said Ruth.

"She was widowed eight years ago, and she came to Washington six years ago from Texas," Vinegar Bend began soon after I arrived at his apartment. "She ran the President's campaign down there when George Bush ran for the Senate. So she knew the President and Barbara.

"We met at a prayer breakfast sponsored by Here's Life Washington. I got a notice in the mail that Raymond Berry would be the speaker. I had met him briefly in Foxboro when Berry was the head coach of the New England Patriots. I wanted to go hear him. He has quite an inspirational story to tell. He was handicapped, with one leg shorter than the other, yet he was an All-Pro receiver for the Baltimore Colts and was Johnny Unitas' favorite receiver. Joe Gibbs, the Redskins' coach, said Raymond Berry was the man who led him to the Lord. I was impressed by that. The room was filled up and only one seat was still open.

"There was an attractive lady in the next seat. She told me, in no uncertain terms, that she was saving the seat for someone else. She was authoritative about it, though she denies that now when she hears me tell the story. I told her, 'I'll sit here until he shows up.' He never did show up. She won a prize for a free luncheon, and I invited myself to go along. That's how we met and how we had our first date."

"Soon after," interjected Ruth, "we were talking to some people, and they started making a fuss over him. That's how I found out what he'd done. 'Did you play ball?' I asked him."

"Last year," Vinegar Bend came back, "we went to Pearl Harbor for the 50th anniversary of the Japanese attack on Pearl Harbor. I was there as a representative of the Department of Veterans Affairs. We were there for a couple of days. And Ruth said, 'Why don't we see if we can give our families a Hawaiian Christmas?' I have two children and Ruth has two children and each of us has three grandchildren. So this Christmas (1992), we had all our families in Hawaii for the holidays. We just had a great time. When we came back, Ruth went off to China for a missionary effort.

"We are both very involved in the Christian Missionary Alliance Church. In fact, I am on the International Ministries' Board of Managers of the Christian Missionary Alliance Church. When I was playing for the Pirates, I went to a large church on the North Side. It was a Christian Missionary Alliance Church, and I enjoyed it quite a bit."

"I don't see all that. I see it like it was. That's the vision you have."
— Vinegar Bend Mizell
About his grandma's house
coming apart at the seams

While the Mizells spent Christmas in Hawaii, they spent Thanksgiving the past two years in Vinegar Bend, Alabama.

I asked him about his home town. "There was a railroad line that ran through there," he began. "There was a little river called the Escatawpa River, an Indian name for Dog River. We called it by both names. There was a bend in the river where the railroad ran over it. As the story goes, there was a barrel of sorghum molasses that went bad and turned sour. They emptied it into the water at the bend in the river, and they called it Vinegar Bend after that.

"At one time, Vinegar Bend had the second largest sawmill in the country. That was a great deal before my time. We didn't actually live in Vinegar Bend. We were out in the country, about four miles out. My address was Route 1, Vinegar Bend, Alabama.

"My Uncle Irvan Turner — he's the patriarch of the family — had us all over to his home this Thanksgiving. He's retired from the Game and Fish Commission in Mississippi.

"I grew up on a small farm. My dad died when I was a year-and-a-half old. My mother had a serious illness following the death of my dad. Grandma Turner, on my mother's side — she was a widow — took me in. Irvan was her youngest son. He was 14 and he was the bread-winner — he was working for 50 cents a day. The old log house where I lived, and which my granddaddy had built when he got married, had three fireplaces. Grandma Turner cooked in an old-fashioned wood stove. There were kerosene lamps. We didn't get electricity until I was 16. There was no indoor plumbing. We had an outhouse."

"That sounds like the same story that Bill Mazeroski told me," I said to Mizell.

He nodded knowingly. "Bill and I roomed together when we were on the road," said Vinegar Bend, "and he talked some about that when I came over to the Pirates. They put us together, and we had a lot in common. Maz was a great roommate. He was kinda quiet most of the time."

Getting back to his story about the family reunion in Vinegar Bend for Thanksgiving, Mizell said, "I think we had about 50 from the family there. They came out to Uncle Irvan's place. People brought all kinds of food and desserts. We had a great day for it. For dinner, we had venison that Uncle Irvan provided. We had turkey and pork, barbequed chicken and chicken and dumplings. Everyone brought their own specialty. My sister-in-law, for instance, always brings chicken and dumplings. My brother and his wife still live on what was my dad's old place. It's in great shape. My grandma's house is beginning to fall down.

325

We always go by it when we're there. Those old logs still look solid, but the porches are off, and it's falling apart.

"I don't see all that. I see it like it was. That's the vision you have."

Ruth was hoping she would fit in, and she felt comfortable with Vingegar Bend's family. "They're from there, they're from the country, but they're not country. They don't act country," she said.

As someone who represented North Carolina in Congress, I asked Vinegar Bend if Thomas Wolfe was right when he wrote a book called *You Can't Go Home Again.*

Vinegar Bend begs to differ with Thomas Wolfe. "Yes, you can," he said. "It's just different in some respects. We still have the post office. The old general store is closed. We still have the train station and the sign is still there on the side of the station — VINEGAR BEND — but the trains don't come by there anymore. The old passenger train doesn't stop there anymore. They use the siding to load farm produce and such.

"We used to have giant oaks along the streets, but Hurricane Frederick, I think in 1976, got a number of them. Out in the country, where we actually lived, the family is still close. That's what makes it special. A number of us grew up there together. That makes it home. And I still like to go back.

"Out in the country it's just miles of woods, and so forth. I still have a piece of property there I got when nobody wanted it. A stream runs through my property. It's spring-fed water and it's so clear. There's 320 acres on the plot.

"I bought it from the husband of the postmistress of Vinegar Bend. He cut all the timber off it. The value of land there is determined by the timber on it. I'm growing new timber on the land. The only problem in growing timber is that it's a long time between paydays."

Mizell smiled at his own observation. "It takes about 30 years before you have timber that can be cut," he said.

"But it's still my home and much of what I am is still there. We still have a little church out in the country. It's called the Pilgrim Rest Baptist Church. There's a cemetery there, where my parents and grandparents are buried. I visit that."

I asked Vinegar Bend about how he came to pitch for the Pirates. "When I was with the Cardinals, we were always close and in contention," he said. "We were second, third or fourth in an eight-team league. I really thought we could win the pennant in 1960. The Pirates traded for me one day before the trading deadline."

For the record, on May 28, 1960, the Pirates dispatched infielder Julian Javier and pitcher Ed Bauta to the Cardinals for Mizell and an outfielder named Dick Gray, who was assigned to the Pirates' farm team in Columbus, Ohio.

"It came as quite a surprise," remembered Mizell. "The Pirates hadn't won it in a long time. It was a big move for us. After I came out of the Army (following a two-year stint in 1956), I had bought a house in suburban St. Louis, in a Missouri community called Florissant.

Wilmer "Vinegar Bend" Mizell

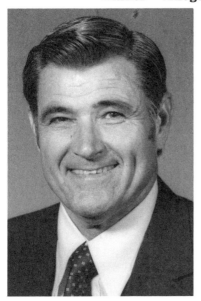

"I was disappointed, but I caught the first plane out of St. Louis for Pittsburgh the next morning. I was in before that night's game at Forbes Field. Three days later . . . it was in May . . . Danny (Murtaugh) started me."

Mizell brought with him a 1-3 record for 1960 and a career that was always bordering on the edge of greatness. He provided the Pirates with a fourth starter to go along with Vernon Law, Bob Friend and Harvey Haddix, and as a left-handed thrower needed to balance the staff.

"I had been a teammate of Haddix in St. Louis," said Mizell. "What a great individual. Harvey and I were there in 1956 when I first got out of the Army. He's a great fellow. He was just a great personality to be around, he was always upbeat, always laughing."

Mizell pitched three brilliant shutouts for the Pirates. His first, on July 29, was in Chicago when he gave up just two singles to win, 4-0. His next shutout was a 1-0 job over the Giants on August 5 in which he scattered four singles and a double. His final shutout was on September 18, in a must game for the Bucs, in which he limited the Reds to three singles in a 1-0 shutout at Cincinnati's cozy Crosley Field.

Vinegar's 14 wins, three shutouts, 211 innings and 113 strikeouts all represented his best records in those departments since 1956. At one stretch in 1960, Mizell pitched 30 scoreless innings, from the second inning July 22 in San Francisco through two shutouts and through four innings of a game on August 9.

"People still ask me what Maz was like," said Mizell. "He was just Bill Mazeroski, that's all.

"I've thought about that club a good bit. I know many of the players came up from the Pirates system, but we also had a lot who came to the Pirates from other teams. I played with several of them in St. Louis, like Ducky Schofield, Tom Cheney, Bill Virdon, Harvey Haddix and Rocky Nelson.

"To me, it was the greatest team effort of any team I've played with. The person who had a great deal to do with forging that team was Danny Murtaugh, and Joe Brown. I had a chance to play for a number of good managers, but I thought Danny Murtaugh was the greatest manager I ever played for. Not just because of the way he utilized players, but the way he managed men. That's why we won the World Series. If you lost today, tomorrow's a new day."

Vinegar Bend remembers the Yankees well. "That was a great team," he recalled during our interview. "They set the records in that Series, and blew us out three times, but we won the close games."

He thought the Pirates were pretty good, too, and volunteered some stories about game-saving catches during the regular season he won't soon forget that were made by Roberto Clemente in right field and by Billy Virdon in center field. "They were two of the greatest catches I ever saw out in the field," said Mizell.

"Clemente ran into the wall and cut his chin. Virdon made one on the dead run in left center. He ran into the wall, too, but just with his cleats. I think they were both in one-nothing jobs when I was pitching."

Almost on cue, Ruth returned to the room carrying a copy of the October 14, 1960 *Pittsburgh Post-Gazette*. She had bought it when she and her husband had visited Pittsburgh the previous year on behalf of the Department of Veterans Affairs. She bought it at the Shops at Station Square.

"I knew about everything that was going on that day," remarked Ruth, as she pointed out several front page stories, "except the World Series." Which dominated that day's newspaper in Pittsburgh.

Seeing that newspaper sparked several memories. When I was ten and eleven years old, I helped my brother Dan deliver the *Post-Gazette* each morning on an ambitious neighborhood route (just over 80 copies) before we went to school. Seeing the feature page which carried syndicated columns by Dorothy Kilgallen and Earl Wilson and a local column called Pittsburghesque by Charley Danver looked so familiar. I knew that the comics were on the flip-side of that section, like it was yesterday.

Back home in Pittsburgh, I also knew that the city's newspaper people were preparing the first daily paper after an eight month strike had idled the presses, and, to everyone's shocking surprise, put *The Pittsburgh Press* out of business. I had worked as a copy boy in the classified ad section on Friday nights at *The Press* when I was a junior and senior at Taylor Allderdice High School. I had worked as an intern on the city-side section after my sophomore year at the University of Pittsburgh, and I had written about the Pittsburgh Steelers for *The Press* from 1979 to 1983. I hated to see Pittsburgh lose one of its daily newspapers. The city was something less for its loss.

"We were in Pittsburgh with the Caring and Sharing Group, and we attended a party for the veterans aboard the Majestic," said Ruth, checking a logbook which she keeps on their social schedule. "They made Vinegar Bend co-captain of the boat, and I think he shook hands with all 700 of the guests who were aboard."

The couple also recalled a visit to St. Louis the previous summer, on June 11, Ruth noted, to celebrate the 100th baseball season for the Cardinals in that city.

"They had 65 of the former Cardinals come back for that event," said Mizell. "They had guys going back to Terry Moore and Johnny Mize. And there was Marty Marion and, of course, Stan Musial and Enos Slaughter. Harvey Haddix was there, and Dick Groat, Harry Walker, Red Schoendienst, Bob Gibson, Lou Brock. I pitched against my old teammate Wally Moon and when he swung at a pitch for the third time, the announcer said 'Strike two-and-a-half!' That got a big laugh."

Ruth also retrieved an August, 1956 copy of *Sport* magazine. Vinegar Bend was on the cover in a Cardinals uniform. It looked familiar. I was a big fan of *Sport* when I was a teenager, and collected copies and swapped them with friends.

The cover story was: VINEGAR BEND MIZELL — Will He Become Another Dizzy Dean?

There was a story about an aging Bob Feller in that issue of *Sport*.

Feller had been an idol of Mizell's. I also spotted a book about Bob Feller on the floor in Mizell's living room.

The article detailed how Vinegar Bend got his start in baseball, by attending a tryout camp in Biloxi with some of his buddies, sort of on a lark.

Thinking back on that story now, Vinegar Bend added, "It was just a fun thing for us to go to that tryout camp. Six of us loaded up in an automobile and took off; it was just a fun thing to do. I wasn't dreaming about a big league career."

He came by his nickname that first year at Albany, Georgia. "The sports editor of the newspaper in Albany was a fellow named Harley Bowers and he tagged me with the name Vinegar Bend."

The Mizells weren't sure about their future plans. Vinegar Bend would be leaving his job in Washington that coming Friday. "We hadn't had a chance to see all the things in Washington that a tourist would see," he said, "so we're going to take some time to do that."

He still has a home near Winston-Salem, and she still has two homes in Corpus Christi. "They're both waterfront properties," she said, proudly. "I love the water. He loves the mountains."

They want to do some reading, relaxing, and traveling. "I've been just about everywhere in this country," said Vinegar Bend, "but I was usually in and out. I'd like to travel across the country and see some of the great tourist attractions. I've never been to Yellowstone National Park, or Jackson Hole, or the Painted Desert, or the Grand Tetons. I'd like to see some of those places."

She is trying to convince him to come to Texas. His third stop on his minor league tour to St. Louis, after Albany and Winston-Salem, was in Houston where he played for the Houston Buffaloes in the Texas League, Double A ball. "They still love him in Texas," said Ruth. "So many people know him there. My grandchildren even know him; they have his cards."

They planned to attend some parties in D.C. before they left, though they would not be going to any of the Inaugural Balls that coming week.

"We went to an Elvis Presley party this past week," he said, "and Ruth talked me into wearing my Cardinals uniform. I can't get into my 1960 Pirates uniform. When I was in Congress, we used to have a baseball game every year. It was serious stuff. They play it to win; you'd think it was the seventh game of the World Series."

> *"You can disagree with others,*
> *but you don't have to be disagreeable."*
> —Vinegar Bend Mizell

Insiders
Behind the scene at Forbes Field

"We were the darlings of the world"
—Art McKennan

Nellie King
Former Pirates pitcher and broadcaster
Assnt. Athletic Director for Public Relations
Duquesne University

"I broke into the radio business during the 1960 season. I had my first job with WCNS in Latrobe. I would later work at WHJB in Greensburg before I became Bob Prince's partner on Pirates' game broadcasts.

"So I came down and interviewed all the Pirates and asked everybody who they thought would be the hero of the World Series. Guys were saying Mickey Mantle, Roger Maris, Roberto Clemente and Dick Groat. Harvey Haddix said he thought that Bill Mazeroski would be the hero. I asked him why. He said, 'I don't know. I just think he's going to be the hero, that's all.'

"After they won the World Series, some of the guys on the team were asking me to hide bottles of champagne for them. They were really sloshed. They were so caught up in the excitement of what they had accomplished. It was great.

"Another thing that comes to my mind is how big Bob Prince was back in the early '60s. KDKA had a 65 per cent share of the audience back then. People like Prince and Rege Cordic, their morning deejay, were so dominant in the market. Everybody knew them. With all the offerings on cable TV now, and the FM radio stations, KDKA is lucky to have a 20 per cent share today for Pirates broadcasts."

Jack Berger
Former Pirates Publicist

"I started working for the Pirates in 1947, working in the minor league system, and was in Brunswick, Georgia when Branch Rickey offered me the position during the 1954 season to be the team's publicity director when Jimmy Long died. I didn't think I had the background for the job. I wasn't a journalist. Rickey was perturbed with my hesitancy. 'I wouldn't have offered you the job if I didn't think you could handle it,' Rickey rumbled.

"My dad, who was also Jack Berger, was a sports cartoonist for *The Press*, and had played minor league ball. So I grew up with baseball. The 1960 World Series was special. For one thing, I had never been to a World Series before, and I had never been to Yankee Stadium. No one in our organization had ever been involved with a World Series, and it was my job to make all the press arrangements. So I had to call around the league and get some advice from people who knew what had to be done. Dave Grote of the National League office was particularly helpful. So was Bob Fischel from the Yankees. We had a stadium that seated just over 32,000 people. We had all kinds of special ticket requests from the commissioner's office and all the other teams for the best seats. Where would we put all our season ticket holders? We had no photo boxes.

"Our press box space was quite limited and inadequate for what we would need. So we had a major building program. We added box seats in front of the existing seats; we added several more rows. We put them in on a permanent basis. By the time we were done, we had increased our seating capacity for that time to 36,000. We hung some photo booths from under the second tier, and used them for TV as well. We put those in on a permanent basis, too. We also sold one or two of them as private boxes, which was, actually, the beginning of the private box era in Pittsburgh baseball.

"Our press box was so small. You had to duck under steel beams to get into it, and we put up padding so people wouldn't bang their heads against the beams. We could accomodate about 25 people in there, so that's where we had the Pittsburgh and New York writers and the Western Union people. The *Sun-Telegraph* went out of business that spring, or it would have been even tougher to take care of everyone. There was a press box on the top of the third deck which had been built by Bill Benswanger in 1938 in anticipation of a World Series, which never came to Pittsburgh because the Pirates faltered in the stretch run, and, of course, Gabby Harnett & Company (the Chicago Cubs) took care of that on the final day of the season. Hartnett hit a home run to win it all for the Cubs.

"Everyone had to have a Western Union wire operator next to them in those days. We put many of the writers out in the right field stands. We had writers from non-major league cities like Louisville and New Orleans out there. We made sure we took care of papers from places like Wheeling, Greensburg and Oil City. We took care of the area radio stations, too. We made sure we took care of the people who took care of us, both the media and our fans. All told, we had something like 750 news media. We had to provide box lunches for all of them. We had to put in a special p.a. system so they could hear the clubhouse interviews. There was no way everyone could get into those small clubhouses.

"With Clemente, for instance, we had many Spanish-speaking newspapers and radio stations covering the games. There was world-wide interest. We had a Japanese broadcast team there. We had to put up a tent for a dark room in the bowels of Forbes Field so that the photographers could develop and transmit photos right on the spot.

"We housed most of the writers at the Hilton, which was the press headquarters, but we had them at hotels all over the place. We had shuttle buses taking them to and from the ballpark. I also had to set up the entertainment for the games. I got Billy Eckstine through Lenny Litman to sing the National Anthem for the first game. I had to line up the bands, and you name it. I had no assistants, but I had a great

OLD
PRESS BOX

SUSPENDED NEW
PRESS BOX
AND RADIO BOOTHS

WIDTH OF
OLD BOXES

ADDITIONAL
SPACE FOR
NEW BOXES

Forbes Field had to be enlarged to meet seating needs for the 1960 World Series.

secretary, Emily Mulholland, and I had some help from the local media with press credentials, and so forth. Aside from our season ticket holders, we didn't sell tickets on a strip basis. We sold them on an individual game basis, which made for a lot more work, but we wanted to take care of as many people as possible. The Galbreaths wanted to make sure we were as fair as possible with our fans. We took great steps to make sure that tickets didn't get into the hands of scalpers or ticket agencies."

Nelson Briles
Director of Corporate Sales for Pirates
Chairman, Pirates Alumni Association

"No team is more revered in Pirates history than the 1960 team. The '79 team seemed to capture people's hearts more than the '71 team, but neither is close to that '60 bunch in popularity in Pittsburgh. None has surpassed the '60 team. It was kind of a special time, and that '60 team was a very close ballclub. They were so disappointed they didn't win in '59 after coming off a great year in '58. And they hadn't won anything important for so long. They were such underdogs to the mighty Yankees. It was big city versus small city. It really had all the elements of David slaying Goliath, and that's why I think it has lived so long."

Art McKennan
P. A. Announcer (1948-93)
Forbes Field, Three Rivers Stadium

"I grew up in Oakland, and I still live there. We lived on Ward Street and then Dawson Street, just a few blocks from Forbes Field. When I was a student at Schenley High School, I'd go to the ballpark during the summer at 11 o'clock in the morning, and sit outside and try to get someone to take me in. The ballgames started at 1:30 in those days. Billy Southworth, one of the ballplayers, took me in the first time. I ran errands for the guys in the clubhouse. I'd sit on the equipment trunks outside the clubhouse — they wouldn't let kids in — and they'd come out and get me when they wanted something. That's how I got started.

"Things were more primitive then. They let kids into the ballpark through the iron gate in left field for free after the sixth inning in those days. Now if you tried to get in the ballpark like I did as a kid there'd be nine guards descending on you. It's more of a business now.

"I've been with them since 1919, except for the 11 years I missed when I got polio. I was sitting in my wheel chair on the day (May 25, 1935) when Babe Ruth, playing for the Boston Braves in his last go-round, hit three successive home runs (numbers 712, 713 and 714). The last one went over the right field roof at Forbes Field. (Ruth, despite advancing age and an erosion of his skills, was the first person ever to accomplish that feat.) I also worked the scoreboard for several games for the old Homestead Grays, so I've sat in on some history.

"I was 23 when I was stricken with polio. I was playing golf in Schenley Park, playing the No. 9 hole, when my legs didn't feel so good,

Nellie Briles

Steve Blass

Nellie King

Nellie King interviews Roberto Clemente.

Concessionaire Myron O'Brisky with Pirates publicist Jack Berger.

and I wondered what was wrong. I've had to use a wheelchair ever since. I swam at the P.A.A. for 56 years as therapy.

"I started working the scoreboard in 1942. They had just put in an electronic scoreboard in 1940. A friend of mine gave up the job and asked me if I wanted to do it.

"I got the job as the p.a. announcer in 1948. Roy Hamey, the GM, said they liked my voice on the telephone. For many years, I ran the scoreboard, provided the music, and did the p.a. announcing. I was the full-time p.a. announcer from 1948 to 1986. Then I did Sundays after that, and some fill-ins and special announcements after that. I retired for good on Easter Sunday this year (1993) at the age of 86. I plan to go to the games about two or three times a week.

"When Joe O'Toole turned over the music to me, he gave me a charge account at the National Record Mart in Oakland. I built up quite a library of music. Les Biederman, the baseball writer for *The Pittsburgh Press*, told me we had the best music in the National League. I was proud of that.

"They wanted me to do something special for the World Series in 1960. So I arranged to have the Pitt band come to Forbes Field. I had them march through Oakland, and rather than have them come in through the center field gate, I had them march through the runway off Sennott Street, between the stands and the bleachers, and they just burst out on the field. They stood in formation in front of the scoreboard and Billy Eckstine came in from right field and he sang the National Anthem for the first game. I remember the musicians' union sent a telegram to the Pirates protesting that they didn't use a union band for the ballgame.

"Benny Benack's Band (The Iron City Six) wasn't allowed in to Forbes Field to play during the World Series because Clemente had complained and said they were a jinx. He said we lost every time they played. So Benny had his band on the back of a platform truck and they set up in front of the Board of Education warehouse building across from Forbes Field on Sennott Street. After the seventh game, the fans stayed there for hours and listened to his music as a celebration party. Pittsburgh was like a Halloween and Christmas party all in one that night.

"I remember little things, sentimental things. We hadn't had a World Series since 1927, and we were the darlings of fans all over the world. I have 'Beat 'Em Bucs' stickers in several foreign languages.

"I was working as an assistant director for the Parks & Recreation Department in those days, and our office was at the side of the Phipps Conservatory, at one end of the Panther Hollow Bridge.

"I remember going to my office early one morning and I was driving by the Mary Schenley Fountain, and I saw lines of people standing outside the center field gate to buy standing room only tickets. The line wrapped around the length of the outfield wall and out through Schenley Park toward Flagstaff Hill. I had never seen anything like that. It gave me a chill."

336

Fans line up outside wall at Forbes Field to buy standing room tickets for 1960 World Series.

Benny Benack's Iron City Six get fans revved up for World Series, playing atop a platform on Sennott Street.

Steve Blass
Former Pirates Pitcher and Analyst for KDKA-TV, KBL

"I was 18 and I had signed with the Pirates in June of 1960. I came home from working with a carpenter in my hometown of Falls Church, Connecticut. I was going to make about $1,000 for the summer on that job, which was important because I signed for $250 a month with the Pirates. I won $9 on a World Series poll at work because I had the bottom of the ninth inning. When Maz hit the home run, I thought what a clever guy I am to sign with this organization. I would be joining the World Series champions. Later on, when I came up to the Pirates, I would room on the road with Bob Friend and Bill Mazeroski. As private a person as Maz is, I remember he pulled a muscle, and he couldn't play, and he was in tears. Nobody was around, but I saw him cry because he couldn't play."

Joe O'Toole
Former assistant to GM Joe Brown

"I went to work at Forbes Field as an office boy in 1946, soon after I'd come out of the military service. I grew up in Oakland — we lived on Dithridge Street up from St. Paul's Cathedral — and I'd gone to Schenley High School. I worked my way up the front-office ranks, and was the assistant general manager to Joe Brown when we played in the 1960 World Series.

"I don't work for the Pirates anymore, but I still work at Three Rivers Stadium. I'm a consultant with ARA Services, Inc., and I'm involved with the food and beverage concession service. Part of my responsibilities the past few years was helping to get things ready in that respect at Camden Yards in Baltimore and now with the stadium to be built in Denver. I'm out there a lot now. I was the team's coordinator for the design and construction of Three Rivers Stadium, and made sure the Pirates had whatever we needed in place when we left Forbes Field.

"Getting the ring after the '60 World Series was my biggest thrill in baseball. I remember standing next to Billy Eckstine, the singer, just before he went out to sing the National Anthem for the opener of the Series with the Yankees. We were standing there, and we see this airplane flying low over the ballpark. A guy parachuted out of the plane, which sure wasn't in the pre-game program.

"Eckstine said — and the mike was open — 'What the hell's that?' I couldn't figure out what was going on. 'He's trying to land here!' I said. The guy drifted over the ballpark and landed on the roof of the Board of Education warehouse across the street. He landed on a ledge, and was hanging there.

"The police came and rescued him, and then took him to the No. 4 police station in Oakland. It turned out that he had come from the airport in West Mifflin. He made a bet that if we won the pennant he was going to parachute into Forbes Field. He had been a paratrooper in the service. The police called me to come over to the station.

Joe O'Toole

Art McKennan

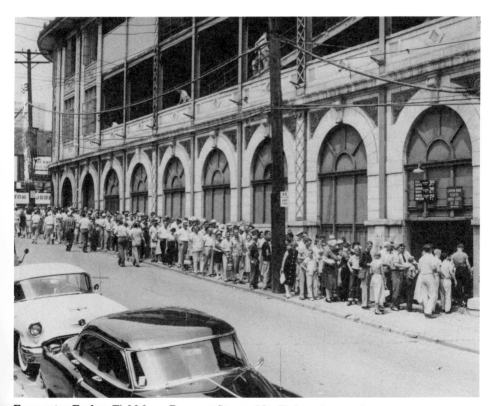

Fans enter Forbes Field from Bouquet Street side. Tickets for regular season games were $3 for box seats, $2.40 for reserved seats, $1.50 for general admission.

"They had been holding him. But everybody was in a good mood; it was a nice atmosphere in Pittsburgh because we were in a World Series for the first time since 1927. We let him go home.

"I don't have any souvenirs from Forbes Field, no chairs or anything like that, at our home in Westwood — that's between Sheraden and Crafton — which is in the city. I have a picture of that '60 team on the wall here.

"When Maz hit the home run, I was behind the third base dugout. I helped Dan Topping, the owner of the Yankees, get into their clubhouse. He wasn't too happy. Then I saw Bishop Wright, and he wanted to come into our clubhouse. He got hit with a wet towel, and I apologized, but he said it was OK. Mayor Barr came in, and he got doused by Dick Stuart with a beer. And they threw Mayor Barr in the showers. He wanted to be a part of the celebration, and they took him up on it."

O'Toole received the 1993 "Pride of the Pirates" award at the team's annual Opening Day luncheon at the Hilton. The award was created by the Pirates in 1990 to recognize people who have demonstrated the qualities of sportsmanship, dedication and outstanding character during a lifetime of service to the team. It had been previously awarded to Joe L. Brown, Frank Gustine and Art McKennan.

Bob Purkey
Former Pirates Pitcher
Owner, Insurance Agency,
Bethel Park, Pa.

"I was the best man for Maz when he married Milene. We hit it off because we're a lot alike. I liked the simple life, and I kept a low profile myself. Maz . . . I just like the guy. We respected each other. We just did battle out there, and that was about it. I really don't know why we became good friends. Maz and I had some experiences together . . . on and off the field. I grew up in the Duquesne Heights section of Mt. Washington, and it was a dream come true to pitch for the Pirates. I was with them from 1954 through 1957, and then I came back to them for the 1966 season. I was traded to the Cincinnati Reds for 1958. I couldn't feel bad about that. I was 11-14 in 1957 for the Pirates, and Bob Friend was our pitching leader with a 14-18 record, and we finished dead last. At the end of the year, Joe Brown was quoted in the paper as saying 'we have our starting pitching staff set with Friend, Kline and Law,' and I wondered where I figured in his plans. Two weeks later, I was traded to Cincinnati. In 1956, the Reds had set a league record for home runs (221) by one team. So I knew I was going to a team that would score runs behind me. They had guys like Gus Bell, Wally Post, Frank Robinson, Jim Greengrass, Johnny Temple and Ed Bailey. I faced Mazeroski that first season and it was early in the year. He'd been watching me warm up in the bullpen and he saw me working on a change-up. I was exaggerating the movement. And the ball's just supposed to float up there. Maz knew that I never had a change-up. Later, he said he knew I was going to throw him that change. I threw him a fastball and a slider for openers, like you would do. He's sitting there, waiting for the change. And I threw it on the next pitch. And he hit it off the scoreboard at Forbes Field for a double. He said he did it to teach me a lesson, to get me to stop throwing the change so I could last another five years in the major leagues. He told people he was doing a friend a favor. Obviously, I never threw it to him again. There were very few times I struck him out. He had probably one of the most dramatic changes for a batter I saw in baseball. When he first came up, all you had to do was throw him a breaking ball — a slider or a curveball — on the outside of the plate. He was such a pull hitter. But he made himself a better hitter. Pretty soon, you couldn't do that. He'd take you to right field or up the middle. He became more difficult to pitch to. He changed as a hitter more than any other hitter I faced in my career. (George Sisler, a Hall of Famer who was the Pirates' hitting instructor, got Maz to make the change, which Maz said hurt him as far as hitting with power.) Did I feel badly about not being with the Pirates in 1960? Well, we won it all in Cincinnati in 1961. Somebody just sent me a photograph the other day showing several of my Cincinnati teammates, saying they thought I would like to have it. I really appreciated it because it brought back a lot of good memories. Sometimes when I'm away on vacation, I will stop in at a card shop and go through the old cards. I'm not a collector, but I see the pictures and I see the names and it brings back the memories. I went into the insurance business the day after I retired in 1966, and I've been at it ever since out here in Bethel Park. My baseball reputation still serves me in good stead. I've had two good careers. If I could still do it, I'd still be playing baseball. I loved being a baseball player."

Pirates with Pittsburgh area roots included, left to right, Bob Purkey, Ronnie Kline, Tony Bartirome and Dick Groat.

Sam Narron
There Are Bats in His Attic

"Baseball is better than pickin' cotton."

"There was real beauty to the old idea of living and dying where you were born. You could hold a place in a kind of eternity."
— Annie Dillard
Pittsburgh-born author
"An American Childhood"

It was a warm and wonderful attic. Its dormered ceiling was finished from top to bottom in gleaming dark wood, in narrow, uniform slats, and it seemed like we were standing inside a giant-sized roll-top desk. It was in the home shared by Susie and Sam Narron on farmland just outside of Middlesex, North Carolina.

Sam Narron was the bullpen coach for the Pirates when they won the World Series in 1960.

Sam would mark his 80th birthday on August 25, 1993. "My mother lived to be almost 97," said Susie, hopefully. "If we can keep a good body and a sound mind, strong will, good spirit and attitude, we'd like to stick around a while longer."

Their comfortable nine-room Cape Cod home — once only the second brick home in a 25-mile stretch between Selma and Zebulon, according to Susie, when it was built in 1940 and 1941 — is a veritable baseball museum. Especially that attic. It was like entering a forgotten wing of the Baseball Hall of Fame in Cooperstown, New York. How many attics are there like that in America, where the precious past is stored with care?

The home where Sam was born, a gray-brown weather-beaten log farmhouse his father Troy Narron built in 1890, is located about 75 yards from the home now occupied by the Narrons. Sam can look out his back door and see his boyhood home. The skies were still gray and there was a light rain when I toured the grounds. "I have a lot of fun here," said Narron, standing in the door of his present home, with his bird-hunting dog Kate barking in the background, while I walked around, "but this is a good day to stay home. It's a good day to build a fire."

There is a mischievous twinkle in Sam's blue eyes. His bloodlines are Scotch Irish, and he's a good storyteller.

Susie insisted that I stay longer, as I was making a move to leave after a lengthy visit, and she urged me to go up the narrow staircase to the attic where their children's bedrooms and their son Richard's baseball achievements, in the form of plaques and trophies and autographed baseballs, remain in order. There were also rag dolls and toys that belonged to their daughter, Rebecca. Their children have children of their own now, and live elsewhere, but their spirit remains in those two bedrooms in the attic. So does much of the baseball history of Sam Narron. He is hailed as "Mr. Baseball" in that neck of the woods. There is even a green sign for Sam Narron Road near his homeland.

They are an absolutely wonderful couple, and you could stay with them a long time and feel right at home.

I knew beforehand that Narron had been a member of Danny Murtaugh's coaching staff in the late '50s and early '60s, but I never knew that Narron was a member of the 1942 St. Louis Cardinals — the "Gashouse Gang" — when they won the World Series. He wears World Series rings from both ballclubs. Those rings both have bandage tape wrapped around them now so they fit snugly. His fingers simply are not as big, or as swollen perhaps, as they were when he was catching fireball pitchers in his heyday and in the bullpen. Susie instructed him to hide the soiled tape when I took some photographs of his championship rings. Narron had also been a bullpen catcher for the Dodgers in the early 1950s, when they won several National League championships.

Narron made his major league baseball debut in 1935 before over 30,000 at Sportsman's Park in St. Louis. He came up as a pinch-hitter for his all-time baseball hero Dizzy Dean and faced Carl Hubbell of the New York Giants. Both Dean and Hubbell are in the Hall of Fame. What a memorable way to break into the big leagues.

"I hit a hard grounder back toward Hubbell who fielded the ball and threw me out at first," noted Narron.

So Narron was not only able to talk about, and provide insights, as anticipated, on a first-hand basis about the likes of ElRoy Face and Bob Friend and Vernon Law, but he sprinkled his conversation with personal reminiscences of some of the people he played with, or worked with, such as Frankie Frisch, Burleigh Grimes, Jackie Robinson, Stan Musial, Roy Campanella, Duke Snider, Marty Marion, Walker Cooper, Burt Shotten, Branch Rickey and Roberto Clemente.

The top of the staircase in that attic was rimmed by a waist-high U-shaped bat rack rather than a railing. There were at least 40 baseball bats in that rack. One of them belonged to Babe Ruth. Another to Joe "Ducky" Medwick. There were bats that were once wielded by Stan "The Man" Musial, Enos "Country" Slaughter and Sam Narron. There was one that had been signed by all the living members of the 1960 Pirates at one of their reunions at Three Rivers Stadium. A few of the bats were broken, and had been taped. I removed the one that had Ruth's signature on it, and squeezed it at the handle. It was light brown, and smooth and some of its label inscription had been worn down. I had just read in a book about how Ruth's bat was heavier than most others, 42 ounces, and it did feel heavy. Ruth's bats, or "war clubs" as they were called, were about a half pound more than most bats. I put it on my shoulder. I swung it. It felt great. I felt Ruth's presence in the room, the glory of his times. I had once been to Ruth's refurbished boyhood residence in Baltimore, while traveling with the New York Yankees as a sports writer in the early '70s, but this was even more poignant. I could pretend I was a big leaguer.

"When I was about ten years old, growing up in Middlesex," said Sam, "I used to take a tobacco stick — the kind that were used to hang out the tobacco leaves to dry — and use it to smack stones. I'd be walking down a dirt road, swinging that tobacco stick at stones, and pretending I was somebody big in baseball. I thought about the thousands of baseball fans packed into a big-league stadium somewhere far away, cheering as I knocked the balls way out of sight against some big-name pitcher. I dreamed of being somebody."

Narron's story reminded me of a similar one told to me earlier by Billy Mazeroski. As a youth, Maz said he used to swing a broom stick at stones as he was walking down a dirt road, and pretend he was Babe Ruth hitting a home run in the World Series. Clemente once recalled tossing tin cans into the air and swatting them with a stick as a youngster in Puerto Rico.

For the record, Babe Ruth's last home runs — three of them — came at Forbes Field in his final swing around the big leagues. He hit the first home run ever to clear the roof in right field in his last hurrah.

Sam had a story for every bat, including Babe Ruth's bat, and when he faltered or forgot a fact or a name or a nuance of his anecdote, Susie simply filled in the blank spaces with the right words and a kind smile, and kept his stories straight. It went that way for the four hours I was with them. Susie knows all of Sam's stories. They are a beautiful couple, sort of a song and dance team when it comes to recalling baseball folklore and the story of Sam Narron, and they complement each other perfectly. "When you have too many birthdays, you get mixed up," Sam apologized at one point. "We sit here and argue back and forth. We get upset sometimes." It made me smile about my own marital relationship. My wife always tells me she knows all of my stories; she has heard them all before. I told her, after spending an afternoon with the Narrons, that I can see where that could be helpful someday.

"Everybody's not so fortunate to dream about what they want to do, and be able to do it," said Susie Narron. "And that's what happened."

She was Susie Finney when they first met in Martinsville, Virginia. Sam broke into organized ball with Martinsville in the Bi-State League in 1934. He led the league with 125 hits in 78 games while playing third base. "She was such a pretty girl," Sam said of his early enthusiasm for Susie. For the record, she still is.

The following year, Narron was at Albany, Georgia, where he played third base and did some catching. He led the league in hitting with .349. He was called up to the St. Louis Cardinals at the end of the 1935 season and saw action in four games.

Sam and Susie were married on January 8, 1938.

During his early years, Narron caught for Sacramento, Asheville, Rochester and Houston, working his way up to the majors again with the Cardinals in 1942. He appeared as a pinch-hitter for the Cardinals in the 1943 World Series. Narron played at St. Paul, Mobile and Charleston in the Cardinals organization. He played a year after that at Smithfield-Selma in the Tobacco State League. Then he joined the Brooklyn Dodgers organization, playing one game in Montreal in 1949,

Sam Narron at the side door of his home . .   . . while his boyhood home is in the field out back.

Jim O'Brien

Narron holds up his World Series rings standing next to team pictures of 1960 Pirates, the 1949 Dodgers and the 1942 Cardinals. He and Susie show off special attic with its Hall of Fame bats.

and was a bullpen coach for the Dodgers in 1949 — when they won the National League pennant — and in 1950.

"I loved baseball all my life and played as I grew up with everyone that would play with me," said Narron. "Then I played at every school and semi-pro baseball team I could when I was old enough."

Branch Rickey, his boss in Brooklyn, brought Narron to the Pirates as a coach in 1951, Rickey's first season in Pittsburgh. Narron got to Pittsburgh in time to don a Phillies uniform for a small role in the 1951 movie, *Angels in the Outfield*, which featured Janet Leigh, Paul Douglas and the Pirates. During the winter, Narron would always return to his farm in Middlesex.

He always credited Rickey for helping him the most in his long baseball career. Except for one season of voluntary retirement in 1944, Narron was never without a job in baseball all his working life. He says the highlight of his baseball career was signing his first contract. He dropped out of school after ninth grade, so baseball provided a real opportunity for him. "Baseball is better than pickin' cotton," he often said.

It was the day after Thanksgiving, Friday, November 27, 1992. The Narron home was already decorated for Christmas with an artificial tree in the living room, and wreaths and other ornaments throughout the house. The grandchildren and their mothers do the decorating, said Susie, and one of the grandchildren, seven-year-old Ginny Richards, always calls the tree "Grandma's fake Christmas tree." Keeping company with the Narrons was a perfect start for the holiday season.

When I was ready to leave the first time, and had my coat on and was half-way out the door, Susie invited me to come into the kitchen where she served me a slice of pecan pie — "we call it pee-can pie, but you probably call it pee-con pie," said Susie. She also gave me a slice of sweet potato pie. "I'll bet you never had that before," she said. And she was right again. I ate at an antique lazy Susan dining table that had belonged to Sam's parents. There were napkins on the table that had the following message enscribed on them: "Friends Are The Flowers In The Garden Of Life."

There is an old black iron stove in the corner of the family room, an old-fashioned barber chair there as a decorative piece, a brass spittoon next to Sam's favorite chair. I asked if the barber's chair was a "Paidar" chair. I surprised myself when I asked that question. But somehow I had this flashback of the barber's chair I sat in as a youth, at Joe's Barber Shop, owned by my next-door neighbor, Joe Figoli. Sure enough, on the adjustable footrest, it read EMIL J. PAIDAR. My feet never reached that footrest when I was a kid. That's how I can remember the name.

The walls were filled with framed photographs of family members, and of former baseball teams with whom Sam Narron was associated in his long career in the big leagues. Just inside the front door, on the wall to the left, are team photos of the 1960 Pirates, the 1942 Cardinals and the 1949 Dodgers, all great baseball teams. There is more of the same throughout the room, throughout the house.

I was saying goodbye a second time when Susie suggested I might like to take a look in the attic.

"Sure. Everybody knows about Bill Mazeroski."
— Owner, Paper Heroes
Collectibles Store
Knightdale, N. C.

Sometimes it's scary for a writer. You never know the whole story, or all the stories. You never know what gem one more question might elicit. Or what's behind the next door. If you talk to one more person you might learn something that is critical, or special, or rounds off a good tale, or shades a story with a different slant or emphasis.

Sam Narron was on my list of members of the 1960 Pirates World Series team, but I had not planned on interviewing him for this book. I didn't think it would be necessary. I was dead wrong.

Here's how we got together:

I was driving from Pittsburgh to Raleigh the day before Thanksgiving for a family get-together. My wife Kathie and my youngest daughter, Rebecca, then 15, were with me. Our other daughter, Sarah, 19 at the time, a first-year student at the University of Virginia in Charlottesville, would join us in Raleigh.

My brother-in-law, Harvey Churchman, and his wife, Diane, and their children, Jason, 15, and Emily, 12, reside in Raleigh. His and my wife's mother and father, Harvey and Barbara Churchman, who live in McKeesport, just east of Pittsburgh, had come down a few days earlier. So we would all be together to celebrate Thanksgiving.

As we were driving through Winston-Salem en route, the thought struck me that one of the pitchers for the 1960 Pirates, the wonderfully-named Wilmer "Vinegar Bend" Mizell, had a home in Winston-Salem. I wondered if he was there for the holiday. He also had an apartment in Alexandria, Virginia, just outside Washington D.C. where he had been working in a political position during President Bush's administration. Earlier, Mizell had been a Congressman from North Carolina. Ironically enough, there was a story in the *Raleigh News & Observer* that same day about how Mizell was among the politicians from North Carolina who would be losing their jobs with the coming of Bill Clinton as President of the United States.

Sally O'Leary, who looks after the Pirates alumni in the team's public relations and publicity office at Three Rivers Stadium, had given me a list of names, addresses and telephone numbers for the 1960 World Series squad. It had a telephone number for Mizell in Alexandria, but not Winston-Salem. I found a number for him in a two-year-old Winston-Salem telephone book that my brother-in-law had in his home office.

But Mizell was not home. And he was not at his apartment in Alexandria, either. I learned, and I had to smile, when I got this message, that he had gone home to Vinegar Bend, Alabama for Thanksgiving. Good, I thought, that's his real home, and how he got his great nickname. That's where he ought to be for the holidays.

I wondered if there was someone else in North Carolina I might visit while I was there. So I checked out my Sally O'Leary list, and found Sam Narron's name with a rural address in Middlesex, North Carolina. Middlesex sounded as interesting as Vinegar Bend, and I was not disappointed.

I called Sam Narron on the telephone. We talked for only about two minutes. "It's a writer," Narron hollered to his wife while he was talking to me on the telephone, "and he wants to come down and talk to me." For Sam Narron, that was enough. We had a date, to meet at noon the next day at the post office in Middlesex. It was about 30 miles southeast of Raleigh.

As I was driving along Route 64 East, and passing through Knightdale, I decided to stop at a roadside card collectors shop called Paper Heroes.

A young woman behind the counter was eager to wait on me when I entered the store. There were several other men moving about the glass cases checking out the cards on display. "My wife is going to kill me," one man said to one of the sales clerks as he handed over some money. "If she asks you, tell her you've never seen me before."

"Can I help you?" said the one young woman.

"Yes, do you have any cards of Bill Mazeroski?" I asked.

"Who-ooo?" she said, stretching it to two syllables with a strong southern accent.

"Bill Mazeroski," I repeated.

"I never heard of him," she said, somewhat apologetically. "How do you spell his last name?"

The other woman clerk confessed ignorance as well.

But the woman who wanted to wait on me to begin with came back a few minutes later, and said she had found one. It was the last one, she said. It was a 1972 card and it cost me $1.75. It may have been the least expensive card in the store's inventory.

The storeowner came out from a back room and the woman asked him if he had ever heard of Bill Mazeroski.

"Sure," he said. "Everybody knows about Bill Mazeroski."

I found other cards from the cast of the 1960 World Series. Yogi Berra cards from 1962 and 1964 were selling for $40. A 1962 Dick Groat card cost $2. There were several Roberto Clemente cards (1959 — $50), (1960 — $90), (1962 — $75), (1972 — $23). A 1969 Mickey Mantle card was listed at $150. A 1961 Roger Maris card was available for $55, and a 1962 Maris card for $105. Then, too, among some not involved in that Series, a 1963 Joe Adcock was available for $60 and a 1954 Tommy Lasorda for $150.

"It's a town of hopes and dreams."
— James Earl Yates
Middlesex, N.C.

I arrived in Middlesex a half hour before my scheduled meeting with Sam Narron, so I nosed around the business district a little. There were only a few buildings, none higher than three or four stories, that comprised the downtown section.

I spotted five or six black men standing on a sidewalk, under the front roof of a hardware store, talking to each other, happy to be together and out of the rain. I got out of my car and approached them. I introduced myself and explained what I was doing in town, and picked out one of them — the one with a gleam in his eye and a look that invited conversation — to chat with about Middlesex.

His name was James Earl Yates. He was 43 years old and he worked at nearby Mortex, a clothing manufacturer, making shirts. He wore a brand new Duke sweatshirt under a well-worn black jacket, and gray stone-washed jeans. He wore a black baseball cap with a Malcolm X logo on the front. "That hat's new," I ventured.

"That's my daughter's hat," said James Earl Yates. "She's wearing my Chicago Bulls' cap, so I grabbed hers."

"Does she know who Malcolm X was, and what he stood for?" I asked. It was a question I had asked a few people since the movie about Malcolm X, and a re-issued copy of the *Autobiography of Malcolm X* written with Alex Haley, and all the fashions came out relating to it.

"She doesn't know anything about it," said James Earl Yates. "She's into fads. She has no idea who he was."

James Earl Yates didn't know Sam Narron, either, but he knew the Pittsburgh Pirates. "Didn't Roberto Clemente play for them?" he asked, not all that certain.

A young man nearby who was wearing a Georgetown sweatshirt under an Army jacket, and who had a gold earring in his left ear, shrugged his shoulders on the Clemente comment. The name didn't mean anything to him.

"He's one of the greatest ballplayers of all time," Yates told the young man. "But he's dead now."

"Tell me about Middlesex," I said. "What's this town all about?"

"It's a small town," Yates began. "It's a town of hopes and dreams."

As he said that, the hair stood up on the back of my neck. I picked a guy out by chance and he makes a thoughtful comment like that. Did I stumble upon James Earl Jones or James Earl Yates?

"What do you mean by that?" I went on.

"It's slow here," he said. "A lot of people want to do things, but they just don't get around to doing them."

That line would come to my mind later on when I was talking to Sam and Susie Narron. When Sam was growing up near Middlesex he dreamed of being a big league ballplayer someday. And he did it. His

349

hard working approach and dedication were among the reasons Susie admired him so much, and why she was attracted to him in the first place.

"Why not?" I asked James Earl Yates.

"This town is owned by a lot of big families," he said, "and it sorta squelches anyone else who wants to achieve anything. There aren't that many opportunities. There's only a few who hold the money."

James Earl Yates had played baseball in high school and during a short stint at Shaw University in Raleigh. I remembered a fellow from my hometown of Hazelwood who had attended Shaw University on a basketball scholarship for a year or so when I was in grade school. A lot of hot-shot athletes from my town went to college for a year or so, and then returned home with little to show for the experience except a sweatshirt or windbreaker.

"What's the industry in Middlesex?" I asked.

"Tobacco and cotton, that's it," he said. "There's plenty of that. If you stand here too long you'll see long trucks with lots of tobacco on them. And we make shirts just down the street."

I had seen some long trucks earlier carting Christmas trees through the main street of town. I crossed some railroad tracks to enter Middlesex. "The CCX, Seaboard and Norfolk Southern Railway Co. come through here," said Yates. "But no Amtrack."

"What do they talk about on this corner?" I asked.

"It's a corner spot for local news," said Yates. "Who got shot up or beat up and who won the money gambling. The whole nine yards."

"Is baseball big in this town?" I asked.

"There used to be a team involved here called the Middlesex Twins. It was just a county team. They had a knuckleball boy named Jughead who was tough to hit. It was composed of drunks — a bunch of boys who could throw the ball around all day. They could beat everybody around here back in the '60s and '70s.

"Then they'd go too far from home, like over in Raleigh. They had a team over there called the Raleigh All-Stars and they used to beat the death out of us. They had some guys who could play, but they also liked to drink a little liquor, drink a little wine and knock the ball outta the park.

"I used to go over to Durham a lot to see the Durham Bulls play. Now I go see the Mudcats play; their ballpark is just down the road. Our company has season tickets, and I'm lucky. Most of our workers are women and they're not interested in going to the games."

I asked him if he was a Duke basketball fan.

"No, I'm an N.C. State fan," he said. "But they've been having some problems. Just the other day, one of their kids (Tony Robinson), a real nice young man, shot and killed himself in a suicide. That's hard to figure out.

"When I was going to Shaw, we had a kid named James. And they found him dead in the dorm, just like that. He was a good young man. Good attitude. James was a fun-loving guy. They couldn't figure that one out, either."

350

I checked my watch and it was a few minutes before noon. I bid James Earl Yates and his buddies goodbye, thanked them for their time, and returned to my car. I drove down the street to the post office. It was still raining.

There was a man standing in front of the post office, just under a porch roof, and out of the rain, and he was wearing a baseball cap, pulled down tight to the top of his ears. It was red and it had the logo of the Carolina Mudcats, a Double A team that is affiliated with the Pittsburgh Pirates. He looked authentic.

It had to be Sam Narron and it was. He pointed to a nearby black Buick, a 1986 LeSabre Sedan, where a woman was sitting behind the wheel, waiting for him. It was his wife, Susie. I said I would like to take them to lunch somewhere they might normally go to for a meal in Middlesex. I was looking for more local color.

I followed the Narrons to the nearby Family Restaurant, right alongside the railroad tracks. On the sign outside the restaurant it boasted that it was "Family Owned and Operated." Under that line was another: "Jesus Is The Answer." The restaurant, I learned, was operated by a local minister. There were bottles by the cash register to toss change for a local orphanage and for a local ministry. Also by the cash register was an open Bible. Anybody who wanted to take the Bible to their table could do so. It was open to Gallatians. "We're in the Bible belt, you know," said Susie Narron. "We were here for a flounder dinner the other night. It's not bad."

I recalled once hearing Sparky Anderson, when he was the manager of "The Big Red Machine" in Cincinnati, say, "If you remember where you came from you won't go wrong."

Sam Narron can never forget where he came from. Narron has never left his boyhood stomping grounds.

"That's Sam Narron, the man who stays ready." — Branch Rickey

"A lot of people are still trying to learn about the '60 Pirates," said Susie Narron, soon after we sat down at a table in a rear room of the restaurant.

"You know Dick Groat spent the night with us before he signed with the Pirates. And his wife, Barbara, was a North Carolinian. She died about two years ago."

Sam took a cue from Susie's story and added, "Dick Groat . . . he worked baseball. He didn't play it. He was so smart. He was always ready."

Sam smiled over that observation, as it brought back one of his own favorite stories. "Mr. Rickey once asked me if I was ready to play. And I replied, 'Mr. Rickey, I stay ready.' And, after that, Mr. Rickey used to tell people, 'That's Sam Narron, the man who stays ready.'"

The Family Restaurant was a simple, no-nonsense place. The walls were exposed cinder block painted a rose color. The tables did not have

351

cloths on them. The floor was linoleum tile. The Narrons did not want anything to eat — they'd had a big breakfast, they told me — so they settled for coffee, and I had iced tea, unsweetened, thank you.

I checked out the menu, just for good measure, and spotted several items that identified it as a southern restaurant. They offered collard greens, black eyed peas, grits, catfish, pork barbeque, fried okra and peach cobbler.

None of it was more southern than Susie Narron. "I'm a Virginian, and proud of it," she said. "I'm from Franklin County, Virginia. I come from a big family; our roots are long up there. We still have our homeplace where our mother lived until she was almost 97. Her grandfather had owned the place, then her father, then her and my dad. Now their six living children own it."

She was also proud to say that she and Sam had been married for 55 years. Their home was 10 miles away, down Route 39, in Johnson County. "We live in North O'Neil Township, where our church and our own fire department are located," she said. "We've had a good life, so far."

She directed her next remark to her husband. "You're in pretty good shape for someone who's almost 80. Even if we don't think as fast anymore."

And Sam said, "I used to take smart pills, but I got immune to them."

I asked her what attracted her to him. "Going back, he was such a genuine person," said Susie Narron. "There was no pretension. He's just what he is. Just Sam, a natural person. He's not loud, just a good fellow. His desire to succeed at what he was doing, and his willingness to work so hard at what he was doing. It sounds a little boastful, but he had the right principles and, of course, his love for me. And his respect for people, old and young, and his kindness toward them. These are qualities that are worthwhile. We didn't have opportunities to get higher degrees at those stages of our life, in the late '20s and '30s, so we take what we have, and are grateful for our many blessings."

To which Sam added, "I've never been envious or jealous. When you pray, don't pray selfishly."

They have two children. Their daughter, Rebecca Narron Murphy, 52, lived in Buies Creek, where Campbell College is located. Their son, Richard, 47, lived in Goldsboro. He was a co-owner of a sporting goods store called Sportman's World Inc. in the Eastgate Shopping Center. A tornado had whipped through that area only the week before. It killed two people in Hillsborough, Joe Terrell, 53, and Josh Hall, just one day shy of his second birthday. Both were buried the day before Thanksgiving. People in those parts were still reeling from those deaths, as well as the scare and the devastation of the storm. "The wind was real bad here, too," said Sam. The Narrons felt fortunate for the near-miss. Sam has always felt fortunate.

"I grew up out in the country, on my parents' farm," recalled Sam. "I was a real greenhorn. Someone in the next community asked me if I wanted to go to school there."

Sam Narron and son "Rooster" talk baseball with Danny Murtaugh.

Branch Rickey was Narron's boss in
Brooklyn and Pittsburgh.

With Dodgers in 1949

With Cards in 1942

Sam had shown early promise as a ballplayer, and was recruited to play ball. "They had seen him play ball on the sandlots," said Susie. "His dad had died when he was 10, and it was just his mother who raised him. So he went to Zebulon to play ball and to go to high school. That's how he got away from home."

Because he was leaving his widowed mother, the 10-mile move was a big step in his life.

"I stayed in the teachers' dormitory and fired the furnace for my room and board," said Narron. "Getting home on the weekends was tough during those years. Sometimes, I was unable to catch a ride and walked the ten miles back to school.

"It was a big move because I left my widowed mother alone, as I was the youngest child. But she wanted me to take advantage of that opportunity and helped me in every way she could.

"When I was in high school," continued Sam, doing his best to explain his beginnings in baseball, "I saw an ad in *The Sporting News* about a baseball school in Hot Springs, Arkansas. Rogers Hornsby and Dizzy Dean were there. Burleigh Grimes was there for a week. So I went there."

The teachers and administrators at his school in Zebulon held a fund-raising basketball game to get the money to sponsor Narron so he could attend the Arkansas camp.

I asked Narron to reflect on his days with the Pirates, and some of their pitchers.

"Law and Friend both were so reliable," noted Narron. "They'd come down to the bullpen to throw between starting assignments. I had to protect them from overthrowing or getting upset when they didn't get the call.

"Now that little Face . . . When the game was in the late innings, you knew that little rascal was going to get the call. He had that terrific forkball. He took it up himself. And when he had that great year in 1959 (when he won 17 straight games in relief and finished with an almost incredible 18-1 record), you had to wonder how he did it, but he did. He had that great forkball and I don't think he weighed over 145 pounds. And everyone liked him."

Susie smiled while Sam was talking, and interjected, "One of the things you have to remember is the nice people you've met along the way in baseball. Pittsburgh is not a southern town, but the people there are really nice. It was a big city, but the people were not like big city people."

Sam started up again:

"I saw some great ones sittin' out there. I watched the great Roberto Clemente play right field. I saw Kiner hit, I watched Groat play shortstop. I was out in the pen in Milwaukee in 1959 when Harvey Haddix threw twelve perfect innings. That was a sight to see. I warmed him up before the game.

"Yes, he warmed up good and he was throwin' as hard as he'd ever thrown, but you never know. He went into that game and hit all the right spots at just the right time. We didn't mention the no-hitter, of

354

course; everybody's superstitious about that. We just sat and watched and when Adcock got the hit in the thirteenth inning, hitting the ball outta the park, that was a terrible ending to one beautiful baseball game.

"They switched the Pirates' bullpen from right field to left field while I was there. I could see Clemente up close from the right field bullpen. The best sight I ever saw from the bullpen was Yogi Berra, the Yankees' left fielder, turning and looking up at Maz's ball clearing the left field wall at Forbes Field in the 1960 World Series. I knew it was gone.

"That ball got me this ring on my right hand and that World Series trophy over there on the table. I had a sayin' when I was in the pen for moments like that one. I'd slap the players on the back and say, 'Boys, take me along with you. This here's better than pickin' cotton.' "

His son, Richard, nicknamed "Rooster," was a fair major league baseball prospect. In 1967 he was named to some All-American teams when he was playing at East Carolina University. He signed to play pro baseball with the New York Mets, and played in the Florida State League with Winter Haven, and later in the Carolina League and Texas League. Along the way he picked up a b.s. degree in business from East Carolina University.

"Richard was 15 when he was in the locker room at Forbes Field after we beat the Yankees in the 1960 World Series," noted Narron. "He carried out a case of champagne for them to have in the dugout after the game. He used to go out and shag flies in the outfield when he was kid. He was about six when he first went out in the field with the Pirates. He did well in college, but he was slowed down by his years in the military service. He kicked around the minor leagues for awhile before giving it up. He came up short of making the majors."

Three other members of Narron's family played pro baseball. A nephew, Jerry Narron, was named to be a coach with the Baltimore Orioles for the 1993 season, according to Sam, following a managerial stint in Rochester.

The ball park of the Carolina Mudcats is near Narron's home, about eight miles down the road on Highway NC 39. It is called Five County Stadium. There's a sign over the entrance that reads: "Our Field of Dreams." Narron put on his Pirates uniform for a summer exhibition back on May 17, 1992. The Pirates came to town to play the Mudcats. Narron remembered that Barry Bonds won a home run hitting contest before the exhibition game. Narron caught the ceremonial first pitch in pre-game festivities. Once again, Narron was proud to be a Pirate. "The Pirates players are something big in this area," said Sam. "We are real proud of the way Tim Wakefield, who was here two years ago, is pitching for the Pirates. We watched him pitch here for the Mudcats. It was good to see a guy from here make it big in the big leagues."

Sam Narron knew what that was all about.

Other Sports Voices

*"That home run is a bigger thing
to everyone else than
it is to Bill Mazeroski."*
—Kent Tekulve

Ray Mansfield, Insurance Broker
Cecil Twp., Pennsylvania
Pittsburgh Steelers (1964-76)
"When I think of 1960, I remember that our football team at the University of Washington won the Rose Bowl that season, beating Minnesota, the No. 1 ranked college team in the country. I was looking through one of my scrapbooks recently, trying to organize my stuff, and I saw on the back of one of the newspaper clippings a story about the Pirates winning the World Series. It was rather inconsequential to me when I was living in Washington. I was happy the Pirates won only because I was one of those Yankee haters, and there were a lot of them in those days because the Yankees were always winning. Now I can appreciate what it meant to the people here."

Kent Tekulve
Former Pirates Pitcher
Upper St. Clair
"I was 13 and in the 8th grade and living in Cincinnati. I wasn't paying any attention to it because the Reds weren't in it and I didn't care. Hopefully, I was worried about my homework. Now that I go out on the road representing the Pirates and helping to promote the team I am always amazed at how many people were in Forbes Field that day when Mazeroski hit the home run. If you believe them, there must have been over 300,000 there that day. Historically, it's never happened any other time — a home run to end the World Series — but what impresses me is the way Maz is content just to go hunting and fishing. It's almost as if that home run is a bigger thing to everyone else than it is to Maz. He's never been caught up with being Bill Mazeroski. He's just Bill."

John Banaszak
Former Pittsburgh Steeler
The Champions Advantage
McMurray, Pa.
"I was in grade school in Cleveland. I had one of the original transistor radios, which I won for selling newspapers. I had the wire in my ear, and was doing my best not to be detected in the back of the classroom. If you got caught by the nuns doing something like that in a Catholic grade school it was instant expulsion. Maz hit the home run and I started jumping up and down. They beat the Yankees! Everyone in Cleveland hated the Yankees. Plus, Maz was Polish. And I'm Polish. And that made it all the better. So I got caught."

'58 Chevy convertible catches fallout from '60 World Series victory demonstration in Downtown Pittsburgh.

Kent Tekulve

"Life every now and then becomes literature."
—Norman Maclean
"And The River Runs Through It"

Ray Mansfield presents check to Dan Rooney for the Art Rooney Scholarship Fund.

John Banaszak

The Cemetery Club
Reflections from Forbes Field ushers

*"Most of the oldtimers
are in Calvary Cemetery."*
—"Big Bob" DePasquale

It was a cold day in Oakland, a stone cold day. I was driving through the backstreets of this Pittsburgh community, searching for a parking spot. Oakland has always been a tough place to park a car. I was particularly keen on getting a space somewhere within a short walk of George Aiken's Restaurant because I did not fancy a long walk on such a cold day. I was not eager to leave the warmth of my wife's Jeep Wagoneer. The narrow streets were all familiar to me, but so were the unbroken lines of parked cars.

It had been one degree below zero when I awoke at 6:30 a.m. on February 18, 1993. The wind was whistling and howling outside our bedroom windows. It did not beckon one to take a walk in the park.

It was warming up, though, and was about 5 degrees around 8 a.m. as I drove into central Oakland, a block away from the University of Pittsburgh Medical Center.

It was Friday, and Pitt was marking Presidents Day a few days later than most institutions, and was closed for the day. This should have freed up some parking spaces, but that only seemed to be the case in the paid parking areas. It had snowed on Tuesday, and there were still sooty remnants of that snowfall along the curbs and where grass and shrubbery managed to survive. The streets and sidewalks were streaked and stained by rock salt residue. It wasn't pretty. The streets and sidewalks looked cold, too. Aiken's is located at 3600 Forbes Avenue, at the corner of Forbes and Meyran, about a half mile from the site of old Forbes Field.

I had a 9 a.m. appointment to meet an old friend I had not seen in years, Bob DePasquale, a.k.a. Big Bob and Tor, who had been an usher for many years at Forbes Field and at Three Rivers Stadium. His home was on Meyran Avenue. Big Bob was 73 at the time. He had promised to have a few other former ushers at Aiken's to talk with me.

His brother Jeep had been the head of the ushers union almost as long as Big Bob had been an usher, before becoming a colorful, controversial and outspoken member of City Council. Jeep headed the ushers union for 20 years at Forbes Field and for another 20 years at Three Rivers Stadium. Jeep and Big Bob were now in retirement.

I had thought about Big Bob when I was listening to a news report on the radio en route to Oakland that morning. There were structural problems with the pillars supporting one of the ramps on the Fort Pitt Bridge, and repairs would be necessary. I remembered that Big Bob had a succession of political plum jobs in which he was a building inspector, a bridge inspector and a mine inspector. I remember him telling us once how he was reluctant to actually enter a coal mine to check it out, so he'd stand at the entrance, stick his head inside and holler, "Is everything OK in there?" And then file his report on the safety of the mine.

"And do you think I'm going under one of those bridges to check the steel beams? Do I look crazy or what?"

His revelations weren't reassuring, but it gave you great insight into the political patronage system.

I had first met Big Bob during my student days at Pitt in the early '60s. Beano Cook made the introduction. Cook was caught up with all the characters in Oakland because they were all sports fanatics, and none was bigger in both respects than Big Bob, a garrulous, delightful fellow who was always good company at Canter's Restaurant. Unless you were trying to enjoy some matzo ball soup, and he was sitting across from you in a booth, spitting black-brown tobacco juice in one of those paper cups he always carried with him.

It was Bob who tipped us off to a fight in the Pirates' clubhouse that he said had involved Roberto Clemente and Willie Stargell. He swore by his sources.

I ran the report of a fight between the Pirates' two biggest stars under a **WORLD WAR II DECLARED** headline on the front page of *Pittsburgh Weekly Sports*, a tabloid that was co-published by Cook and yours truly, and it gained us a great deal of attention in the summer of 1967. "This is gonna make our paper!" declared Beano Cook. It was just another off-the-mark prediction in his career as a sports pundit and forecaster. What it gained us was a $1 million libel suit from Clemente and a $750,000 libel suit from Stargell. And I was trying to scrape up $25 to rent a tuxedo for my wedding. It's a good thing neither Cook nor I had any real money, or it might have been a real problem. It was reckless, irresponsible journalism that I blame on Beano Cook and myself for being too young to know better.

There had been a fight, all right, in the Pirates' clubhouse, but it had not been between Clemente and Stargell. Bob had the wrong dope on this story. But he remained a friend because it was impossible to get mad at him. And the suit was settled by Cook with an apology and a small payment for an attorney's fee. What hurt the most was that the attorney who brought the suit against us had been a loyal subscriber to *Pittsburgh Weekly Sports*. He, too, should have known better.

Bob knew something about the fight game, too. Just two days before our reunion at Aiken's, I had thought about Bob when I was watching the classic movie *Around the World in 80 Days* at a local theater. Many famous actors and actresses made cameo appearances in that Mike Todd production, and one of them was Victor McLaglen. It was McLaglen who prompted me to think about Bob and one of his classic stories.

Back around 1950, Bob saw an espionage movie at the Schenley Theater in Oakland in which Alan Ladd flattened Victor McLaglen with a single punch. "When he hit the floor, I hit the door," exclaimed Bob.

"I ain't been back since. That runt Alan Ladd was about five-foot four and he knocks out Victor McLaglen, a guy who once fought for the heavyweight championship of the world."

I knew Bob had been in ill health in recent years, and had some heart problems, but had bounced back after hospital stays. His wife had died years before, and so had his daughter in a tragic auto accident, and Bob was home alone on Meyran Avenue. He was not still going strong, but he was doing OK — he had good days and bad days, he said — and he managed to make it to Aiken's most mornings to compare aches and pains and sports stories and opinions with his life-long pals and former co-workers at the ballyards of Pittsburgh.

I arrived at Aiken's about 30 minutes ahead of schedule, and decided to have some breakfast, a fried egg on a bagel with a cup of decaffeinated coffee. You can get anything that can be fried at Aiken's. My mother used to eat lunch there frequently when she worked as a receptionist in a girls' dormitory at Pitt in 1965 and 1966. With all the deep vats of grease bubbling golden brown at Aiken's it was a warm and comfortable place to while away a few hours on an otherwise bone-chilling morning.

Two of Bob's buddies, Phil Coyne and Nick Pugliese, were sitting at a dining station — they don't have booths or full-size tables at Aiken's — sipping coffee and conversing, but I didn't know their identity at the time. Bob arrived on time, and promptly introduced both. Bob seemed smaller than I had remembered him. His cheeks seemed to be shallow, until he stuck in a large wad of Mail Pouch chewing tobacco. Then he looked more like his old self. He wore an electric blue sweater with a yellow-gold Pitt logo on the left breast, and had it buttoned down the front. The buttons at the bottom were under great duress. It was good to see him, and to talk to him, though his voice had gotten weaker and sounded older.

Two more ushers would show up within a half hour, namely Nicholas A. Diulus and Carl Giampolo, and they joined in the reminiscing session. Diulus would not divulge his age, but Giampolo said he was 77. "What was Red Grange's number?" Giampolo asked me. "That's how old I am." You didn't have to be Italian to be an usher at Forbes Field, but it helped. Most of them seemed to get usher's cards at birth. Coyne was among the few Irishmen who helped integrate the ranks. He looked after reserved seats on the third base side.

Coincidentally, the Pirates were opening spring practice that same day in Bradenton, Florida. When the players trotted onto the field at 9:30 a.m., the temperature hovered in the mid-30s. "We could have trained in Pittsburgh in this weather," pitcher Denny Neagle told a *Post-Gazette* reporter, blowing into his hands. Neagle did not know how cold it was in Pittsburgh that same morning, but he might have been warmed by the stories and observations offered by the five former ushers from Forbes Field.

"Big Bob" DePasquale struts
his stuff at Forbes Field

"Us guys in Oakland,
we never needed a ticket."
—Nick Pugliese

Phil Coyne was 74 and looked like a longshoreman. He had a dark blue tasselcap pulled down tight around his pink ears. Shocks of gray hair stuck out around his neck. His face was florid and well-lined, as if he had been walking against the wind. He smiled easily and the bright blue and white jacket he was wearing brought out the blue and white in his eyes. He was retired from Westinghouse Air Brake Co. in Wilmerding.

"They employ about 400 there now, all in one little division," he said, with a hint of sadness. "There were 3,000 there when I was working, with two foundries going full blast."

Phil is the older brother of Bill Coyne, the Congressman from the Oakland District, who still resides in his native Oakland. The Coyne family was living on Swinburne Street, and Phil was three when they moved to Halket Street. "I walked to Forbes Field for the '60 World Series," said Coyne.

Nick Pugliese, 73, had been talking shop with Coyne before Bob arrived on the scene. I overheard him telling Coyne something about a reduced payment on his retirement checks from Jones & Laughlin Steel Company, where he was a machine operator in the fabricating department for many years.

Pugliese came over with his family from Italy when he was seven, and had lived in Oakland ever since. He started ushering some games at Forbes Field back in the '40s. "I didn't have a union card for awhile, but I got to work some games," he said.

He did not draw an ushering assignment for the seventh game of the 1960 World Series. "I didn't work, but I was there," he said.

"Did you buy a ticket to get in?" I asked, teasing him.

"Us guys in Oakland, we never needed a ticket," said Pugliese, proudly.

"The Oakland guys never needed tickets for Pitt Stadium, the Pitt Field House, Forbes Field or Duquesne Gardens," interjected Bob.

Guys from Oakland, to be sure, have always thought they had a birthright to sports events in Pittsburgh, even since Three Rivers Stadium opened on the North Side in 1970.

"Does anybody from Oakland ever pay to see a sports event?" I asked Bob.

"In a word," Big Bob replied, "no. We got guys who say they're from the Internal Revenue Service and they're looking for tax dodgers. We got guys who get old chauffeurs' hats and wrap up a big empty box and say they are making a delivery. We got guys who know every entrance and every exit in every public building in Pittsburgh."

Everybody laughed at Bob's story.

"We get together like this every morning since we've retired," pointed out Pugliese. "We switched from Isaly's, when it closed."

Pugliese, whose silver white hair was parted impeccably and combed so carefully, appeared to be having some difficulty with my questions. "He's hard of hearing," each of his friends told me from time to time as we went along, each raising his voice as if I, too, were hard of hearing

"Do you guys ever walk over to where Forbes Field used to be?" I asked, raising my voice for everyone's sake. "Do you ever take a sentimental stroll?"

"Sometimes in the summer, when the weather is nicer," said Bob, "we go over to where Forbes Field used to be, where Pitt put up that Taj Mahal. They have a dining area on the second floor of the Forbes Quadrangle, and we have some coffee and sit around shooting the breeze there."

They can take an escalator down from the dining area, if the mood strikes them, and check out home plate from Forbes Field. There is a home plate under a plexiglass cover in the hallway, and the ushers say it is definitely positioned in the same place where home plate was at Forbes Field.

When I worked at Pitt as the assistant athletic director for public relations from 1983 to 1987, I once took a visiting media party that accompanied the Florida State football team on a tour of the Pitt campus. I took them to where Forbes Field was located, and showed them what remains of the wall, and pointed out home plate. Before I could say anything else, several of them started running down the hall and sliding — while wearing suits and sport coats and slacks — across home plate in that hallway. It was hilarious.

"When I can walk, I go over from time to time," said Bob, "when my legs can handle it. I've had a couple of heart attacks, and a couple of heart bypasses, so I don't always feel up to it."

"Do you get any other of your old friends to go up there with you?" I asked.

"Most of the oldtimers," began Bob, smiling and shaking his head, "are in Calvary Cemetery."

Diulus admitted to beginning his ushering career in 1938. "I lived on Boundary Street, down the hill behind Forbes Field, in what they called Sun Valley."

"Didn't they also call it Panther Hollow?" I asked.

"That's right," said Diulus.

"Or Little Italy?"

"You know your geography," declared Diulus.

Diulus told everyone he had been to see another former usher, Pete Argentine, in the hospital. Diulus was the district justice — they used to be called aldermen — and he had a hearing to preside over at the end of the hour, so his time at Aiken's was limited.

"We used to take a lot of people, especially visitors from New York, over to where Forbes Field used to be," said Diulus. "We used to be there all the time. The guys from New York couldn't believe it."

The conversation turned to how hard the surface used to be at Forbes Field, and how it was a factor in the outcome of the 1960 World

Series — when Tony Kubek got hit in the throat by an apparent double-play ball off the bat of Bill Virdon because the ball hit something and took a strange hop.

Bob told a story about how a former Pirates third baseman, Dick Cole, back in the mid-'50s, had explained away an error, blaming it on there being too many pebbles in the dirt around the bag. The ground-crew caught hell from management over that. The next day one of the members of the groundcrew dug up some pebbles outside the iron gate in right center field, and deposited a pile of them around third base. "He got fired for that," recalled Bob.

Eddie Dunn was the head of the ground crew that year, and George Kiseda, a maverick sports writer, voted for Dunn as the MVP of the Series.

They mentioned that another field in Oakland, Frazier Field, had really been a rockpile. "That's the one they renamed the Danny Marino Field because it was in his old neighborhood, overlooking the J&L," said Pugliese. "Some of the people up there resented that, and they keep knocking down the sign."

"Stengel lost his job over not properly using Ford in the Series."
—Bob DePasquale

During his days as an usher at Forbes Field, Bob was responsible for Box 66, the last one along the third base side. There was an alley way after that, which separated the reserved seats from the bleacher section in left field. Between Box 66 and the alley way, however, was a wide aisleway where Bob seated anywhere from 12 to 40 of his special friends. They sat on folding chairs and milk boxes and anything else they could find. It was called Box 67.

"I remember during the World Series that Joe L. Brown sent me a note," said Bob. "It said, 'Would you please give three of my friends seats in your private box?' I got a kick out of that. Of course, I took care of them, and they gave me a good tip. There were about 60 people sitting on milk cases in that runway during the Series."

Talk turned to the iron gate in right center, which rolled up and down as someone pulled a chain, and to the blue laws, and to garbage cans filled with dry ice, which fans brought in on Sundays to keep their beer and other drinks cold.

Diulus, the district justice, mentioned that once upon a time the blue laws forbade having a baseball game on Sunday. It was changed and games were allowed, but they had to be over before it got dark, and beer sales were not permitted on Sunday. So fans brought in beer and picnic baskets on their own. He recalled that fans were forbidden to bring in beer on Sunday a few years before the Pirates pulled up stakes at Forbes Field and shifted their operation to Three Rivers Stadium.

"They had some problems with fan behavior," said Diulus, "but I think they started to hate it because they weren't selling all that beer."

"Put something in the book about Myron O'Brisky's concessions," said Pugliese. "That's where Bob Prince got the idea for the green weenie. He said O'Brisky's hot dogs were often green. They kept all the supplies under the stands on the third base side. Prince kidded O'Brisky about keeping some of that stuff so long it turned green."

It was like these guys were playing pepper ball or something, the way they would bounce one story off the other, and they would field each other's tales, and either expand on them or completely change the subject.

"I remember how Stengel had two pitchers warming up in the bullpen in that seventh game," said Bob. "He's got Whitey Ford and Ralph Terry out there. There's no tomorrow and he brings in that friggin' asshole Terry. And Maz hits the home run off him. That was the last mistake Stengel made as manager of the Yankees. He lost his job over not using Ford properly in that Series. I didn't think he was much of a manager."

I mentioned that Ford has never forgiven Stengel for not starting him in the first game of the Series, which would have made him available for a third appearance as a starter in that seventh game. Then, too, if Ford had started that first game there might not have been a seventh game.

Along those same lines, I mentioned that Clete Boyer was still complaining about Stengel pulling him for a pinch-hitter in the second inning. Boyer said it was a long walk from the on-deck circle to the dugout.

"Yes, it was," said Bob. "Guys could get two bases on a wild pitch at Forbes Field. That's how far back the screen was behind home plate."

"That's where I worked," said Giampolo. "The players' wives all sat in my section, and so did Bob Rice, the team's traveling secretary."

"I remember," said Diulus, "that when Maz hit the home run Yogi Berra ran so far back and then just turned around and ran back in. He showed no emotion."

"So many people say they were there when Maz hit the home run," said Bob, "but people forget that the seventh game was not a sellout. They couldn't give away tickets to that final game. No one expected it to go that far, and there were lots of tickets available. They were about three or four thousand shy of a sellout that day. There were people outside trying to give tickets away.

"I also remember I saw Mickey Mantle hit two of the longest home runs I ever saw, and one of them was off Fred Green and one off Joe Gibbon. The one off Green went over the iron gate — he hit it right-handed, which was even more impressive — and no one had ever done that."

"He hit it left-handed, didn't he?" asked Diulus, but drew negative nods from all his former co-workers. "I think it hit my window down at the bottom of the Hollow. He was great when he wasn't all crippled."

"I remember Dick Stuart hit one over dead center, and it's still going," said Pugliese.

"He used to sign his autographs with '66' after his name," said Diulus. "He hit 66 one year at Lincoln, Nebraska before he came up to the Pirates. Talk about home runs, when Ralph Kiner first came up we called him 'Ozark Ike.' No one could hit home runs the way he could hit home runs. I remember him hitting one that went over the scoreboard and it was still climbing.

"Another thing about Forbes Field," said Bob. "You couldn't see first base from the third base boxes — and vice versa — the mound was that high.

"We liked it because it was nice and close to home," said Pugliese. "I could walk there in 15 minutes."

"The crowd was wild all the way for that Series," said Bob.

"It was a beautiful ballpark," said Diulus. "You could see the ball-players. When they came out of the ballpark you'd recognize them. You didn't have to see their uniform numbers."

"I hated Three Rivers Stadium all 11 years I worked there," said Bob, "until I retired after the 1981 season. I couldn't take that joint. I hated everything about it. I hated driving over there, the parking. It had no personality. The steps were so high over there. Traveling there was a pain in the ass."

Then they started telling stories about Gus Miller. I knew Gus Miller when I was a student at Pitt in the early '60s. He was a bald, bespectacled old man who had a store on the corner of Forbes Avenue and Oakland Avenue. His daughter's name was Myrtle Mae. I had seen photos showing Miller reviewing the ushers at Forbes Field before a ballgame back in the '30s.

In the early days, Miller managed the ushers and gave out the work assignments. "This was before the union," said Diulus, "and Miller would stand there and say, 'Yunz work, yunz work, yunz work . . . and you three ain't workin'.'

"If you bought something in his store when you checked in it helped get you an assignment to work," said Bob. "If he knew you chewed you better buy your chew at his store if you wanted to work. He was like that."

"If you caught a foul ball, you got to work the next day," said Giampolo. "He had a guy, Jay O'Neil, assigned to going around the park and reclaiming all the balls that were hit into the stands. He'd take your name if you turned in a ball, and you automatically got to work the next day.

"That Jay O'Neil lived on the Hill. Sam Waters, who was the vice president of the club, lived up there, and John Fogarty of the ground crew was a neighbor of his. So people were always looking out for their friends and neighbors. Guys brought their sons and daughters in to work at the park."

"I started to work there in 1933 and 1934," said Bob, "and I was there till it closed."

"The Norelco family tore down Forbes Field," said Giampolo. "Al and Norman, two brothers who lived in Oakland, who lived on Bates Street. They used to sell bags of peanuts at the park. I remember they auctioned off the seats."

366

Several of the players I had interviewed mentioned parking around a service station at the corner of Forbes and Bouquet, across the street from Frankie Gustine's Restaurant.

"That was owned by two brothers, Elsworth and Jimmy Stuckert," said Joyce. "Jimmy's son, has the place now, only it's been moved several blocks down Forbes Avenue toward Downtown now, at the corner of Forbes and McKee Place."

"I have a lot of great memories of Forbes Field," said Bob. "There were some great guys. Pie Taynor was one of my friends. I used to loaf with him, and we'd go to the track together a lot. He'd tell you some stories.

"Maz was a good guy. He liked my kid Petie. Petie worked in the visitors clubhouse from about the time he was ten years old."

"I remember the way the fans hit the field following Maz's home run," said Giampolo. "They were like sardines around home plate. Some guys I know were out there stealing the bases. They still have them in their homes. They must be worth a lot of money.

"The guy who's on Maz's heels as he hits home plate was an usher," said Coyne, who couldn't compete with the Italians for air time at our talkathon. "His name was Domenic Varratti. He lived on Bouquet Street, down in Little Italy. He comes in here a lot. He lives in Swisshelm Park now. But he's in Florida now on a two-week vacation."

I knew Bob liked to bet on sports events. "How did the betting go in the Oakland neighborhood for the '60 World Series?" I asked him.

"I got friggin' killed," said Bob. "I was bookin' it, and I took a beatin'. Everybody was bettin' on Whitey Ford and bettin' against Bob Friend."

"Why were they betting against Friend?"

"They just had his number; like it was over as soon as he went out there," said Bob.

"They were bettin' Harvey Haddix, too. They shoulda been bettin' against Stengel, too. That last game convinced me he didn't know what the hell he was doin'. He was an idiot."

"Has Oakland changed much since the days of Forbes Field?" I asked, knowing what was going to come next.

"You can't loaf around here at night anymore," said Big Bob. "It's a different time. Nobody respects anyone anymore. When I was a kid, everybody's parents had come from the old country. They were happy to be here, and they wanted to stay here. They were afraid if their kids misbehaved or got in any trouble that they'd be sent back. Now everybody thinks they own this country."

"The Janet Leigh bit was the best."
—Bob DePasquale

Big Bob DePasquale came by his nickname more honestly when I first knew him as a student at Pitt in the early '60s. He was six feet tall, weighed 285 pounds, with an 18-inch neck and 46-inch waistline. Forbes

Field was just a short walk from the Pitt Student Union, once the Schenley Hotel where visiting ballplayers had stayed, and I would go to the ballpark often after working on the sports pages of *The Pitt News*, the campus newspaper. Another student sports writer, Bob Smizik, would do the same. The Pirates would become Smizik's beat at *The Pittsburgh Press* in the '70s.

After Big Bob would get everybody seated in the boxes just beyond third base, he would sit down with his friends to watch the game. I sat next to him many a time. He was a tireless talker, always boisterous and garrulous, always interesting, and he could make you laugh.

He was great for filling in between pitched balls, changed pitchers and inning breaks. He would talk about the old days and he was delightful.

He always enjoyed telling the story about how Hollywood came to Oakland in the 1950s and made a movie called *Angels in the Outfield* in which God helps the Pittsburgh Pirates win a pennant.

"It was really a beautiful contest," Big Bob explained. He helped supply the semi-pro players who made up the visiting team. They were supposed to be the Reds but the first thing that happened was that someone stole the Cincinnati uniforms.

"Make it the Braves," the director said.

"I can't," the property man reported. "Somebody stole the Braves hats."

So the opposing team became the Phillies.

"Listen," said the late Paul Douglas, who played the manager in the movie. "I put my glove right down here on second base because I don't trust it out of my sight. It stays," he said, turning his head momentarily, "right here."

"What glove?" the director asked.

"Oh, no," Paul Douglas said.

Meanwhile a few of the boys from Oakland were busy cleaning out the Hollywood cast at gin rummy and across the field all hell was breaking loose because the paymaster was running out of money. "I don't know," he said, "we musta hired 9,000 extras. You could film Birth of a Nation with the number of guys I paid."

"What happened," Big Bob explained, "is that the guys from Oakland would get their pay, then run out this little gate by the left field bleachers, sprint 250 yards, and get in line again. It was beautiful, but the Janet Leigh bit was the best."

"I'm almost afraid to ask," I said.

"Well, what happened was that one of our boys was supposed to toss a ball to Janet Leigh. She has on this real tight sweater and he is throwing a little high.

"Each time he throws it, he throws it a little higher. And each time she tries to catch it, she has to reach. And each time she reaches, her sweater climbs higher and higher.

"But if it climbed high enough," someone said, "that would mean that. . ."

"Yeah," Big Bob said. "Yeah."

Hollywood has never asked for a rematch.

It's no wonder I missed Big Bob when I went into the military service and spent a year as an editor at the U. S. Army Home Town News Center in Kansas City, Missouri. While there, I went to a lot of football and baseball games. I picked up some extra spending money performing various statistical work or spotting chores in the press box at Municipal Stadium. I was never successful in finding Kansas City's answer to Big Bob. He was an original, a real Runyonesque character.

Bob was one of the big daddies of *Pittsburgh Weekly Sports*, and no newspaper ever had such a successful subscription agent. If he had been on commission, instead of doing it gratis, our circulation might have rivaled *The New York Times*.

The San Francisco Giants were in town one weekend for a two-game set. Big Bob emerged from the ballpark each day with 25 subscriptions. And Myron O'Brisky probably wondered why hot dog sales were off that weekend.

Our agent's tactics were about as subtle as Al Capone's "insurance" salesmen of the prohibition era.

"I was sitting in my seat, minding my own business," recalled Joe Scalise, a pal of Big Bob's who was also an usher, "and suddenly I was shy a deuce."

One night at a basketball game at the Pitt Field House, Big Bob comes over to where I was sitting, pushing this little guy. The man wore glasses and looked very meek and worried.

"Give him a deuce," says Big Bob.

The man gave me a deuce.

"Now give him your name and address," snapped Big Bob.

The poor man relinquished this information with all the relish of a POW in Viet Cong territory.

"What's it for?" the man rallied to inquire.

"Don't ask questions," snapped Big Bob. "You're a subscriber."

The man, looking bewildered, moved on. Big Bob winked, and returned to his seat.

Big Bob was, indeed, a sports writer's delight. He cared about the printed word. He picked up about six or seven newspapers a day at Yutsie's newsstand at Forbes and Atwood. Most of them were from New York.

Big Bob was by-line conscious, something few readers are. This does much for the ego of a writer. He not only could quote the best lines of a writer, but he'd say, "That story on Liston that Jimmy Breslin wrote in the *Herald-Tribune* was great. I liked that line where he said, 'he lay flat on his back with his hand in the world's pocket.' That guy's good. He said it got so contagious he stole a cigarette lighter from an AP writer nearby."

He was tough on baseball writers. "They ought to come down out of that press box once and see what the hell's going on," he said. "At least you see Al Abrams down here once in a while, talking with the guys in the stands. But most of them as soon as they hit the park, they're in the dining room for free refreshments. Then they're off to the press box. So they sit up there beside the rest of the idiots and they all think the same.

"They think all of us guys down here at third base don't know what's going on. Well, I'll bet there are a dozen guys down here who could take over for Harry Walker.

"Like Bill Veeck says about a club's general manager: he's got to sit with the fans. Find out what's on their mind. Move around the ball-park. The same goes for writers."

On Big Bob's advice, I sat in the bleacher section in right field from time to time in Kansas City. The Yankees were in town on this one evening, fresh from being chewed out over making a bad scene at the Newark Airport. Manager Johnny Keane had given them a stern talk about the Yankee image and public behavior, etc.

So some young fellows in Air Force uniforms started to heckle red-necked Roger Maris. And Maris turned on them like a tiger. Among other things, he shouted, "All you bums who sit in those dollar-fifty seats are idiots!"

It happened over 300 feet from the press box and I am sure no other writer in the place heard it. Even Maris wasn't that loud.

Big Bob always looked after me. I could not sit in the baseball press box at Forbes Field because our outlaw weekly newspaper did not qualify for membership in the Baseball Writers Association, and Les Bieder-man, the baseball beat writer for *The Press*, ruled the roost like a dicta-tor and he did not want any upstart college punks pressing in against him or his colleagues in the limited space.

So my large friend let me sit in box 54, which belonged to the ush-er's union, of which his brother Eugene was president.

This was much better since I could bring a date with me. And my seat was great — right behind the visiting team's dugout. And Big Bob really knew how to make a fellow feel like an authentic VIP instead of a free-loading sports writer.

As soon as I appeared at the top of the stairway with my date, Big Bob would cry out from below, as if he were hollering from the deck of a ship at sea in a storm, "Ho! Send Mr. O'Brien right down here!"

I would smile. My date would smile. Suddenly I was a big man at Forbes Field. "Good evening, Mr. O'Brien," Big Bob would cry with a delicious smile, all the time focusing his eyes on my date.

"And who is the lovely young lady?"

Upon being introduced, Big Bob would always curl his glad hand over my shoulder, and say, "You take care of my boy Jimmy-O now. He's a good man."

Then Big Bob would holler for yet another usher to escort us down to Box No. 54. He always hollered. Everyone in the place perked up to see what the fuss was about.

One night I was in Frankie Gustine's Restaurant with a new girl from Pitt. I was really trying to put on the dog. Her father was a doctor, she was in one of the best sororities, her family belonged to the country club, and I was doing my damndest to make a good impression.

Suddenly Big Bob and Beano Cook filled the front door. My heart sank. Sports talk had scared off girls in the past, and I didn't know what she would think of my Runyonesque pals. I was a heel, I suppose, for entertaining such thoughts.

Big Bob slid into the booth next to my date, and Beano pushed me over. Fortunately, we didn't talk about sports. At Beano's prodding (good ol' Beano), Big Bob relented to tell us a funny story about a groin operation he had just endured in a local hospital.

Things like that always happened to me in those days. One night at Dante's in Whitehall, a sports writer named Bob Drum opened my date's eyes with his theory that a certain four-letter word was not really bad. Big Bob's story was funny. Even the details of the operation, mind you. Finally, the party broke up. Walking down the street, I finally got up the nerve to ask the young woman, "Well, what do you think of my friend, Big Bob?"

She smiled a great smile, and said, "He's really a charming man. Different and funny."

That's why I enjoyed him so much at Forbes Field.

Jim O'Brien

Coffee club at George Aiken's includes former Forbes Field ushers, from left to right, Nick Pugliese, "Big Bob" DePasquale, Nicholas A. Diulus and Phil Coyne.

Where Were You?

*"I never thought I'd
get a chance to see it."*
—Lucille Fabbio

Ginny Mitchell
Commercial Artist/Homemaker
Oakdale, Pa.
"My Mom and I were big Pirates fans when I was growing up. I was a student in Samuel Hamilton Junior High in the North Hills during the 1960 season. We had a bus driver who was a big Yankees fan. So the kids on the bus made a bet with him for pizza on the World Series outcome. He said he would buy us all pizza if the Pirates won. We were riding the bus home from school on the day of the seventh game, and some of the rich kids on the bus brought along transistor radios. When Maz hit the home run there was a lot of shouting and screaming on the bus. The following week, the bus driver stopped at a pizza parlor on Babcock Boulevard and bought us all pizza. He had gotten special permission from the school, and our parents knew we'd be home a little later that day. It was reassuring to have someone like that keep their word. At first, we didn't believe he'd do it. We have a 10-year-old daughter, Kristin, who's a big sports fan now. She loves baseball. So we took her to Cooperstown last year, and she loved it. I've been there about five times, and I still enjoy going there. You feel good about being a Pirates fan when you're there."

Jack Bramer
Former WPNB banking executive
from Scott Twp., retired in Atlanta
"I was at the seventh game with my father-in-law, Vern Dowler. I got up to leave after the seventh inning. 'The Pirates are done,' I told my father-in-law. 'Let's go.' He pulled me back down into my chair. I'm glad I stayed."

Lucille Fabbio
Scott Twp., Pa.
"I was living on Mt. Washington and working in the produce yards in The Strip District. My boss, Al Wohleber, had been to the sixth game which the Pirates lost 12-0 and he was disgusted. He said he didn't want to go, and I asked for the tickets. I've been a big fan all my life, and used to go to lots of games at Forbes Field. I called my sister, Phyllis — we're twins — who was a waitress at Tambellini's. Bob Purkey, who used to pitch for the Pirates, was there and the place was jumping. So we got to see Maz hit the home run and the Pirates win the World Series. It was a highlight; I never thought I'd have a chance to see it happen. It was just an awesome thing. I'm 62 now, but I was young and foolish, 29, and it's something you never forget."

Jack Klepic
New Brighton, Pa.

"I was running a computer center in Downtown Pittsburgh, at Mechanized Accounting on the Boulevard of the Allies. My girls took all the scrap IBM computer punch cards and went up the fire escape to the roof, and threw all the cards off the roof. We had gone to the sixth game. My wife (Catherine) was teaching first grade at Brighton Elementary School and was at work and missed the seventh game."

Linda Filer
Recreation Department
Gettysburg, Pa.

"I was a senior in high school in Altoona, and I jumped off the bus and ran two blocks up a steep hill to our home, hoping to catch the end of the game on TV. I ran into our home just in time to see Maz hit the home run. I'll never forget it."

Nancy Bohl
San Bernardino, Calif.

"We were at the final game at Forbes Field, they were playing the Cubs that day. My three brothers, Bobby, Calvin and Timmy Kane were there. And I came away with three chairs and the PITTS sign from the scoreboard. Bob Prince made a plea on the air a few times asking for its return. I lived in Upper St. Clair at the time, and I took it with me when I moved to California. Now my brother Bobby has it in his gameroom. My mother, whose name is now Mary Fitzwilliams, was at Forbes Field for the 7th game of the World Series. I was too young to go; I remember crying because they left me with relatives."

Like bees in a honeycomb, fans rip out everything they can grab in scoreboard after final game played at Forbes Field. PITTS sign is missing.

Vernon Law
The Deacon

"Vernon Law is the nicest man I ever met."
—Joe L. Brown

Vernon Law still looks very much like Vernon Law. The once-blond hair has given way to gray, and curls up at the ends around his ears. There are a few lines in that once-porcelain face, but the chiseled jaw is as firm as ever. He still walks tall and carries himself with a certain dignity and grace that remains unrivaled among his former teammates on the Pittsburgh Pirates.

He still has the quick and reassuring smile, and eyes as cool blue as a glacier pool I once saw in Alaska.

He remains special.

"They talk about the nicest man I ever met in baseball," former Pirates general manager Joe L. Brown once said. "Well, Vernon Law is the nicest man I ever met. Period."

The values that Vernon Law preached and practiced when he was with the Pirates remain the pillars of his existence, as well as that of his family. The man who pitched for the Pirates for 18 seasons now has 18 grandchildren. He regards himself as a retired carpenter — just like ElRoy Face — and he has helped to build homes and barns. He is now working at improving his golf game.

He participates in many charity-related celebrity golf outings, and visits many elementary schools as part of the DARE program endorsed by the Major League Baseball Players Alumni Association, and puts on clinics throughout Utah in an effort to counsel youngsters and, hopefully, steer them in the right direction. "I enjoy helping them," he says.

Law was always looked upon, and written about, as a paragon of virtue, a role he was uneasy with because he did not want to come off to his teammates as some kind of saint.

He would not throw dusters, for instance, but insisted it was not because of his religious beliefs. He just felt it sometimes stirred up the opposing player, and he saw too many guys — Willie Mays and Don Hoak came to his mind — who got up from being knocked down by a high, hard inside pitch and promptly hit a sizzler in retaliation. "I don't think a duster does one bit of good," said Law.

Asked to point out the most significant or satisfying aspect of his life since he retired, Law responded, "Being able to spend time with my family and help them with their careers."

The Laws are Mormons, and there were not many Mormons in Pittsburgh when he was playing for the Pirates, and there still aren't, so there was always an air of mystery about him and his deep-rooted faith.

Vernon Law with Pie Traynor

With ElRoy Face in clubhouse after winning 1960 World Series.

Vernon Law won Cy Young Award as best pitcher in 1960.

He was nicknamed the Deacon because he was named a deacon in his church at age 12. He became an elder at age 19. As such, he was akin to an ordained minister. He was a tither in his church and an active member of the Fellowship of Christian Athletes.

He came from Meridian, Idaho, and he has been living in Provo, Utah for some time now. He was a physical education instructor and a coach on the baseball team at Brigham Young University there for nine years, when several of his sons were active in the school's athletic program. Mormons are in the majority out in Utah. So Law is not looked upon as being different, though he would set high standards for anyone associated with him.

"He was always a high-type guy."
—Gino Cimoli

Vernon Law and Gino Cimoli were waiting for a ride in the lobby of the Airport Holiday Inn in Coraopolis, just down Beers School Road from Robert Morris College in suburban Pittsburgh. How many times had they stood and waited in similar lobbies in their lives?

As retired players, they pack lightly, since they do not have anyone to carry their bags anymore.

Law and Cimoli had come back to Pittsburgh on April 17, 1993 to participate in a sports card and memorabilia show that was booked as "Pittsburgh IV Spring Classic," presented by J. Paul Sports Promotions, Inc. out of Sea Cliff, New York.

Law had come to similar weekend shows at the same site in the past, particularly the 30th year reunion of the 1960 Bucs back in 1990. Cimoli had skipped that one, as well as just about every other such sports card show in the country.

Cimoli, for personal reasons, some real, some imagined, has been reluctant to participate in such public events. As far as the baseball world was concerned, he had become a bit of a recluse, preferring to remain in Tiburon, a trendy waterside community near his boyhood home of San Francisco.

So Cimoli was in demand. Even by Law. When they were later signing posters of the team picture of the 1960 squad, Law allowed, "I have everybody's signature on the one I have framed in my home except Cimoli and Vinegar Bend Mizell."

If Law had come to Pittsburgh one day earlier, he could have had Mizell's as well. Mizell had been signing his autograph in the Saturday afternoon session. Mizell also missed that 1990 gathering because his first wife, Nancy, was dying of cancer and he was a late scratch.

Bob Friend had been to the show to sign his name to whatever was put in front of him on Friday night. "He is always so great to work with," said Elvira Stogner, one of the coordinators for the card show.

Baseball Hall of Famers Willie Stargell, Eddie Mathews and Johnny Mize had also appeared over the weekend, as well as National Hockey League star Kevin Stevens of the Pittsburgh Penguins.

Law looked the part of Vernon Law. He had turned 63 the month before, but he had aged gracefully. He looked as dignified as ever. He wore a gray glen plaid suit, a stiff-collared white dress shirt, a contemporary wide tie that was wine-colored, with traces of gray and green, a wine-colored silk handkerchief tucked smartly into the breast pocket of his suit. I had seen and spoken to Law two years earlier at the Piratefest in Monroeville, so he looked pretty much as I expected.

I had not seen Cimoli since he played for the Pirates, so there was, of course, more of a change in his appearance. Like Law, he had been a handsome devil during his ballplaying days. His hair was still dark brown, though it looked like he might have had a little help from Ronald Reagan's hairstylist to keep it that way, with the sideburns gray and bushy. Cimoli was also 63, about three months older than Law. At 6-2, Cimoli was an inch shorter than Law.

I told Cimoli that some of the ushers from his days at Forbes Field, like "Big Bob" DePasquale and Joe Scalise said to say hello. "DePasquale and Scalise, huh?" came back Cimoli. "Irish guys! That figures."

Cimoli was more casual than Law. He wore dark brown slacks and shoes, a beige cable-knit sweater over an olive shirt, and he had a huge, dark cigar clenched in the corner of his mouth most of the day. Law does not smoke or drink and it is fair to say Cimoli has always marched to the beat of a different drummer. Cimoli kids Law about his reputation as a clean-living individual.

"Ah, Vernon, are you still giving people that stuff? You were worse than anybody I ever saw in baseball."

Cimoli caught my eye, and added. "I like to get after him, just to keep him honest. But he has always been a high-type guy."

Later, when Law was talking about how Smoky Burgess was the perfect roommate for him — "He was a Southern Baptist and we had a lot in common" — Cimoli couldn't resist. "They were the rowdiest guys on our team," working that cigar and his comic lines as if he were George Burns.

Anybody who ever knew Law knew better. But Law laughed at Cimoli's wisecracks.

Law and Cimoli disagreed on another subject I introduced — Forbes Field. "I hated the place," said Cimoli. "It was too big." Law laughed. "That's what I liked about the place," he said. "It was a great place for a pitcher."

It was easy to see that Law was getting a kick out of being with Cimoli.

"One of the main reasons I like to come to these shows," allowed Law, "is the chance to see my old teammates, and friends from my baseball days. Just to see guys like Gino. It's been a long time since I last saw Gino. Most teams don't have a group of guys like we have from those '60 teams. We're a close-knit bunch. We like to keep in touch with each other."

Just a few hours earlier, in fact, Law had talked on the telephone to Dick Groat, Billy Mazeroski and ElRoy Face, who all live in the Pittsburgh area. "It's nice that we still care about each other," said Law.

"We enjoyed our friendships that way." Law told Cimoli that they all sent their regards.

I mentioned to Law that several of his former teammates had named him as the "teammate they most admired" from that 1960 team. They spoke of him setting high standards, and being a good role model who had a positive influence on everyone else, and for being the kind of pitcher who was reliable and who often stopped losing streaks.

Law never preached in the clubhouse, and he hated it if he was portrayed in any kind of superior manner to his teammates. "If you're going to be friends with people then you just want to be a friend," he said. "It's important to accept everybody for who they are, and what they are.

"Because of my religion, I didn't do a lot of things that the other guys did, but I was still a good friend. It was not hard for me to get along with guys who might have handled their own lives differently than I did. These guys were great to be with. I ate, slept and played ball with them. They become part of your family.

"If you're tying to influence others, the best way is to just be their friend. If there's something that they want to talk to you about, they'll ask you. If they wanted to know something about my faith and so forth, I'd tell them."

But he didn't force it on anyone else. I had heard, as a contrast, about another pitcher of that same era, a terrific relief pitcher named Lindy McDaniel of the St. Louis Cardinals, who had similar values to Law, but upset some of his teammates because he was trying to convert everyone on the team. Law did not care to comment on that when I mentioned McDaniel to him.

Vernon and his wife, VaNita, were about to become "empty nesters" out in Provo, Utah, to hear him report on his family activity. They have six children, five boys and a daughter, VaLynda, the youngest of the bunch.

"Our daughter is finishing up her schoolwork and getting a degree as a registered nurse, and her husband is going to medical school," said Law. "Our youngest son, Varlin, is gettting married May 29th, so we'll be losing him, too. He's the last one at home."

The Laws used to leave their home enmasse and go to spring training with the Pirates. They had a solid reputation.

"We're a very close family," said Law. "We do things together. We go down to Powell Lake in southern Utah, down near Arizona, and we have a house boat, and we do water skiing and fishing. Your family should be a big part of your life. We try to stick together as a family.

"One of the problems in today's world is that the family kinda comes second in a lot of people's lives. We're getting away from traditional family values in this country. The influence you have on your kids is so important. If they don't have close ties at home they'll find them in gangs and cults and drugs. We support each other. We have a great time together. It's time we cherish."

Law's message, no doubt, was one he delivered just the day before when he spoke at a clinic for 360 kids in Orem, Utah, near Provo. "I

Vernon and VaNita Law look after five sons at spring training camp at Fort Myers, Fla.

Pirates families, from left to right, include Gladys and Rickey Peterson; VaNita, Vance, Veryl and Veldon Law, Bernie King and Norma Hall and her child, strolling the beach at Fort Myers.

do a lot of work like that for the Baseball Alumni Association. We've got clinics every weekend for the next month and a half. It keeps me busy and I enjoy working with young people."

One fan, wearing a Pirates ballcap, caught Law up short when he asked him a question after getting an autograph from him in the gym at Robert Morris College: "I'm surprised that you're signing on Sunday . . . being that you're the Deacon."

"Yeah," said Law. "It was the only time they could fit me in."

"He was a leader in his own way. He was a leader in deeds . . . in performance."
—Bill Mazeroski

Provo is located 45 miles south of Salt Lake City. It is a college town of 87,000 in a valley of 275,000, at the western base of the Wasatch Mountains, part of the Rocky Mountain Range.

It is beautiful country, and a place where you can take a deep breath and let the fresh air fill up and clean out your lungs. I visited Salt Lake City on several occasions in the '70s while covering the New York Nets of the American Basketball Association who traveled there to play the Utah Stars. I have been to the Mormon Tabernacle, the showcase of the Church of the Latter Day Saints, heard the Mormom Tabernacle Choir perform there, been to the restored homes of Brigham Young and Joseph Smith, the early leaders of the church, and viewed the Great Salt Lake. I may have walked the same streets Roseanne Arnold did in her hellish youth. I have been to Ogden, Utah with a West Virginia University basketball team that played in an NCAA regional at Merlin Olsen's old school, Utah State. I remember playing tennis on an outdoor court there one afternoon, and being quite comfortable in the sunshine, while I could see snow-capped mountains all around me. The clean air is what I remember best. Having grown up among the steel mills of Pittsburgh, the air seemed distinctively different.

It is the kind of locale and environment one might expect to produce a clean-cut individual like Vernon Law.

On the wall of his study in Provo, Utah, the former Pirates' pitching ace displays pictures, plaques, awards and other memorabilia that tell the story of his years in the majors. There are pictures of Forbes Field where the fans were so close to the action, to the players themselves, where Law enjoyed some glorious days.

He still smiles when he studies these pictures from his Pirates' past.

He is a good man, and his clean-living habits were alien to many professional athletes of his time, yet no one was more respected on the club.

He was a strikingly handsome figure in a Pirates uniform. He was a 6-3, 200 pound right-handed pitcher with blond hair, blue eyes, of English-Swedish descent. He was a decent hitter, with 11 home runs to his credit, and nearly hit a home run down the left field line in that seventh game of the 1960 World Series. It went foul at the last second.

He was not a deacon, but an elder in the Church of the Latter Day Saints, by the time he came to the Pirates and as such was qualified to baptize, marry and perform other sacraments in the Mormom Church.

As a Mormon elder, he did not drink even tea or coffee, let alone whiskey or beer, because he regarded them as harmful stimulants. "If you don't take that first one, you don't have to worry about having a drinking problem," he said.

He has always been a man's man. He remains close to many of his former teammates, they still hear from him, and he is quick to catch a plane to return to Pittsburgh for reunions, Old Timers Games, and Pirates alumni golf outings and related activities.

"He was a leader in his own way," said Bill Mazeroski. "He was a leader in deeds . . . in performance."

The Deacon is still preaching. Asked if he had any advice for to-day's players, he told us, "Enjoy the game while you can as it's gone before you know it. And give something back to baseball, and to the community, instead of seeing how much you can take."

Asked what lesson he learned from his experience with the Pirates that has served him in good stead ever since, Law said, "Be nice to those coming up because you meet the same people going down."

He added another note: "If you know you've done all you can to win, and things go against you, there's no sense beating your head against the wall."

He said what he remembers best about the 1960 season was "how we won so many games in the late innings. I learned patience from that. And I learned to believe in other people. You have to show people you believe in them."

He has always been a strong family man, and no Pirates family was more photographed than his. They had a special appeal because of their size and sex. There were six of them and the five oldest were all boys. And their first names, like their parents, all began with the letter V. Vernon and his wife VaNita count these children: Veldon, 40; Veryl, 37; Vance, 36; Vaughan, 33, Varlin, 30 and VaLynda, 23. When spring training rolled around each February, the entire family would depart Idaho and head for the Florida sunshine. That was before VaLynda was born. There was not a spring training session that a pic-ture of the Law family did not appear in the Pittsburgh dailies.

"I have a lot of great memories of those trips," said Vance. "Mom and Dad were very careful to make us all feel a part of things. The fam-ily never took a backseat to baseball in our house."

Vance played two seasons as an infielder for the Pirates, in 1980 and 1981, and had modest success. He came into his own as a starting third baseman with the Chicago White Sox, Montreal Expos and Chicago Cubs later on. In 1988, at age 31, while playing for the Cubs, he was named to play in the All-Star Game. He, too, maintained the moral standards he learned from his family. He walked away from the last two months of the 1986 baseball season to be at the side of his then four-year-old daughter Natalie when she underwent surgery to remove a brain tumor.

"Winning a World Series is a great accomplishment. It's a team thing."
—Vernon Law

Vernon pitched for 18 seasons with the Pirates, in 1950 and 1951, then two years of military service — he was a sergeant in the U.S. Army — then from 1954 through 1967. Law later served the team as a pitching coach, and managed the Pirates Triple A farm team at Portland, Oregon in 1983 and 1984. He also coached in Japan for a couple of years.

His name still appears in just about all of the Pirates' Top Ten career pitching records. Law pitched in 483 major league games, all with the Pirates. He won 162 games, while losing 147 for a .524 winning percentage (the teams he played on had a .487 winning percentage) He completed 119 games and struck out 1,092 batters.

When Law retired as a player after the 1967 season, Les Biederman, the sports editor of *The Pittsburgh Press* wrote of him: "How do you say goodbye to a man who has meant so much to the Pirates and to baseball? Vernon Law — Pride of the Pirates. He lights up a room when he walks in. He leaves behind a legend worthy of any man who ever played sports. He has given more to the game than the game has given him."

His best season, of course, was 1960 when he won the Cy Young Award as the outstanding pitcher in the National League with a 20-9 record. But he was 18-9 the year before. He started in three of the seven games of the 1960 World Series. He was the winning pitcher in Games One and Four of the Series, and went to the sixth inning before giving way to ElRoy Face in Game 7. He was the most reliable starting pitcher that season, the stopper on the staff, the man who ended nearly every team losing streak. He had a 3.08 ERA and 18 complete games to his credit that campaign.

"My biggest thrill was playing in the World Series," he said, not surprising us with his answer to a stock question I posed to all the Pirates from that team. "I was very pleased about that year. The Cy Young Award wasn't that much compared to winning the World Series. I'm not degrading the award, but there were four or five others who deserved it. Winning a World Series is a great accomplishment. It's a team thing.

"Playing in the World Series is every baseball player's dream. I would have been satisfied to have pitched relief in a couple of ball games, but to start three and to win two was more than I ever bargained for."

He insisted he was not nervous when he went to the mound at Forbes Field with the double-decked stands filled to capacity. "But I admit that getting that first batter out was a big relief," he said. "It settled me down. Everyone was so awestruck by the Yankee lineup. But as a team we just considered them another opponent — like the ones we had been beating all year."

Ten days after the World Series had started it came down to Game 7 at Forbes Field, and Law went to the mound once more. The Pirates had a two-run lead in the fifth inning when the heart of the Yankees lineup came to bat. Law was looking at Mickey Mantle, Roger Maris and Yogi Berra, three of the most productive bats in baseball history.

"That inning was probably the most memorable part of the game for me," said Law. "I struck out all three of them. That's when I really felt we were going to win."

In the sixth inning, however, Law was lifted in favor of Face, the best relief pitcher in baseball then. But neither Face nor Bob Friend could hold off the Yankees. It was 9-9 going into the bottom of the ninth when Bill Mazeroski hit a home run to win it for the home team.

Law describes the moment. "I remember jumping up off the bench and running out toward home plate with my teammates as Maz rounded the bases. When he got to third, the stadium went crazy, and we all just disappeared into a sea of people."

In responding to my inquiries, Law looks back on that game and a 1955 game between the Pirates and Milwaukee Braves at Forbes Field (July 19, 1955) as the personal highlights of his career.

Law was called upon by Fred Haney to pitch with only two days rest when the scheduled starter became ill. Law took the mound at 7:30 p.m. and he was still throwing pitches well past midnight.

He worked the first 18 innings, leaving the game with the score tied, 2-2. He gave up nine hits, walked three and struck out 12. Going into the 1993 season, Law was the last major leaguer to pitch 18 innings in one game.

"It was an easy ballgame to pitch," recalled Law. "The air was heavy and everybody was striking out or popping up. Finally, Bob Friend came in and gave up a run, but we scored twice in the bottom of the nineteenth and won the game, 4-3." So Friend, of course, got credit for the victory. Sometimes there's no justice in baseball. Yet sometimes that's just the way things work out for you.

Law will never forget another game, either, an 11-10 victory over the San Francisco Giants on May 5, 1958. The Pirates were ahead 11-1 when the Giants came to bat in the bottom of the ninth inning at old Seals Stadium in San Francisco. The Giants came out of the inning with two home runs, three doubles, two singles, three walks, two Pirates errors and nine runs. The bases were filled when the game ended.

"My only regret is that I didn't attend college."
—Vernon Law

Vernon Sanders Law was one of ten children of Jess Law, a farmer and mechanic, and his wife, Melva, in Meridian, Idaho. He was born March 12, 1930.

"My father was a just, fair man with a strict sense of duty. When we did wrong he deemed it his duty to teach us a lesson. It came in the form of a leather strap," said Vernon.

"The only fight I had in my life was with a school mate and it didn't last long. I happened to knock him down and it was all over. When I got home my father was waiting for me.

"He said to me, 'You think you're a big shot because God made you stronger than that boy,' my father said. 'It didn't take a brave boy to do what you did. It takes a brave one not to do it.' He gave me my reward — a black and blue diploma. I haven't fought since."

Like most of the Pirates of the 1960 era, he was an all-around athlete as a schoolboy. Law lettered four years in baseball, football and basketball at Hillsdale High School in Meridian.

As a junior, he played on an American Legion baseball team that reached regional competition.

"Our banquet speaker at regionals was Babe Ruth." said Law. "From that point on, any doubts I had about which sport I should pursue were forgotten."

Shortly after he graduated from high school, his ballplaying heroics came to the attention of U.S. Senator Herman Welker of Idaho who contacted Bing Crosby, then a part owner of the Pirates, and told him about this terrific pitching prospect in his state. Crosby, in turn, contacted Roy Hamey in the Pirates front office. Law was invited to a tryout camp. He signed a contract for the major league minimum of $5,000 a season.

"I was 18 when I signed with the Pirates back in 1948," said Law. "And my only regret is that I didn't attend college. Education is a necessity in the business world today, and a college degree is something nobody can take away."

Walter Johnson was his baseball hero.

Law says his upbringing and basic values helped him handle the extreme pressures of the game, and, in fact, gave him an edge.

"I always felt I had two strikes against a hitter to start with," allowed Law, "knowing that many of them might have been out late at night and didn't care much about training. I just felt I was better prepared, emotionally and physically, for a game than they were."

When Law looks back, he recalls that early in his career that other ballplayers were not sure what to make of him. "A ballplayer with any type of religious leanings was looked upon as a sissy," he said.

"When I was with the Pirates, our announcer, Bob Prince, and I both loved reading westerns. He always used to bring me paperbacks after he'd read them and say, 'This one's okay for you, Vern — I screened it.'"

Bob Friend and Vernon Law look at fan mail.

Vernon Law and former roommate Smoky Burgess get together at 1990 reunion.

Vernon took pride in his religion and believed it was important to go out and talk to young people and try to steer them in the right direction. Law would visit churches and attend youth conferences throughout the Greater Pittsburgh area during his days with the Pirates.

"He was one of the finest men I ever met," said Pirates' owner John Galbreath. "He never gave anyone a bit of trouble."

"Our relationship was more than just manager and player."
—Danny Murtaugh

While winning the World Series was his greatest thrill, he could point with pride to another accomplishment that came years later.

"I had another big thrill after that," he said. "I had the arm trouble in 1963 and everybody thought I was through. But I came back, and proved everybody wrong. This was a great personal satisfaction."

Law struggled for several seasons after that sensational summer of 1960. Law hurt his ankle in horse play on a bus following a clubhouse celebration after the Pirates clinched the pennant in Milwaukee. Some guys didn't want to quit fooling around, and were acting crazy, and it cost Law dearly.

Law never identified the player who cost him three years and a lot of money. "There's no sense making a big thing of it," he said. "I like the man who did it. We've always been friends. I'm sure he didn't mean anything by it."

He was always a courageous athlete, and his ability to pitch so well in the World Series though he was in constant pain, and had to alter his delivery, and then to mount a comeback several years later only emphasizes his personal strength.

He pitched three times against the Yankees and beat them twice. But the records don't show how he could not push off the mound with his right ankle, how he put an unnatural strain on his right arm. The records do show that he did not have a good season for several years after that.

"Law was as fine a pitcher in 1960 as I ever saw," said Danny Murtaugh, the manager of the Pirates and a one-time teammate of Law. "If he hadn't hurt his arm after that season, I believe we could have won a couple more pennants."

Murtaugh was a veteran when Law first joined the Pirates as a rookie in 1950. "Our relationship was more than just player and manager," Murtaugh added. "I knew him and his family when I was a second baseman and he was a pitcher. We've eaten at each other's homes. I know all of his children and he knows mine. He even named his fourth son, Vaughan Daniel, after me. He has done a great deal for baseball and has been a wonderful influence on others."

Murtaugh often said he would be happy if his two sons would grow up to be like Law.

"Some of my best years were under Danny Murtaugh," Law once said. "Under him, we won the Series. Many times he took me out and I didn't agree. With a great reliever like Roy Face in the bullpen, though, you didn't hesitate."

Law pitched 11 times in 1961. He pitched 23 times in 1962. His ailment was diagnosed as a torn rotator muscle in his right shoulder. He pitched 18 times in 1963 and twice more in the low minors. He won 17 games for the Pirates over a three-year period. The Pirates doctors told him to go home and forget about baseball. He went home to Boise, signing the papers that said he had retired from baseball and went to work for a bank. That was in 1963. He was disillusioned because the Pirates quit on him.

Brown was asked why he set him down. "I wanted to keep him from getting hurt, physically and inside," said the Bucs' general manager. "I didn't want him getting booed. He wasn't helping us and he wasn't helping himself."

Law reached his salary peak after the 1960 season when he was paid about $40,000 for 1961. In 1962, he took the maximum 25 per cent cut and for 1963 was trimmed to $25,000.

"Those salary cuts hurt my pride," allowed Law at the time. "It conveyed the message to me that they had lost confidence in me. I've never argued about salary because money never meant that much."

Law came back in the spring of 1964, with no promises made by management. He pitched his way onto the roster. They stuck so many cortisone shots into Vernon Law, his right shoulder looked like the prize-winning needlepoint at the County Fair.

He came out to the ballpark an hour early every day and sat under a heat lamp. When it was his turn to pitch, they anointed his arm with "hot stuff." None of it calmed the pain that roared throughout his shoulder.

"I went out there thinking that today is the day it will stop hurting." said Law. "I had to finesse my way through a lot of games. Then, when I got behind, I had to dare them to hit the ball."

Smoky Burgess roomed with Law when he was trying to overcome his injuries. "I could see pain written all over his face every time he threw a ball," said Burgess. "Many a night he walked the floor in the hotel room after pitching because of the pain. Just being associated with a man like Law is a rewarding experience."

Most people do not come back from two injuries to the arm. "It takes an unusual man," said Brown. "But Vernon Law is an unusual man. Anyone but Vernon Law would have been released. But if anyone can come back it's him. This is the finest man I've ever known."

Law looked it from a different perspective: "I don't have a fatalistic attitude. I think things happen because you make them happen. If a person leads a good life, it's something you make yourself do."

Law bounced all the way back in 1965 with a remarkable 17-9 record and helped the Bucs finish third.

"I started out and lost my first five games, even though my ERA was just slightly over 1.00. I then won eight in a row, lost four and won nine in a row. I was really satisfied because some had written me off. It was a good year."

He did not wear his religion on the sleeve of his uniform, but he once disclosed, "Prayer is a daily experience with me and my family. We have found it a great source of strength. Humbleness comes from within. Many times after a winning game, I've looked in the mirror and said, 'You know you didn't do that alone.' Then I'd bow and say a quick prayer of thanks."

"Words To Live By"

He has collected thoughts and expressions that he uses in his talks:

"There is no 'I' in team."

"Keep your mouth closed — when you lose and when you win."

"A champion is not always a consistent winner. He may have been a one-time loser who would not quit."

"True sportsmanship is usually displayed following defeat."

"Counting time is not as important as making time count."

"It is better to be alone than in bad company."

"He that falls in love with himself will have no rivals."

"Impossible is a word to be found only in the dictionary of fools."

"There is no pillow as soft as a clear conscience."

"Never give advice unless asked."

"Wise men learn more from fools than fools from the wise."

"God does not want us to do extraordinary things. He wants us to do ordinary things extraordinarily well."

"I have never met a man who is not my superior at something."

"A good timber never grows with ease; it needs a strong wind and storms to give it strength."

"A discouraged man is not a strong man."

"Don't be satisfied with mediocrity."

"Deacon, c'mon, you can do it now."
—Don Hoak

Asked to name the player he admired the most on the team, Law said, "Don Hoak, our third baseman. He wouldn't let us get down on ourselves. If he didn't start a rally, he kept it going."

The funny thing about that is nobody on the ballclub swore as much as Hoak. "It didn't make a difference to me who did the cussing or how much," said Law. "It's difficult to judge a person without knowing the circumstances of his background. Don was the straw boss of the '60 Pirates. He always gave me 200 per cent every time I pitched. He'd march over from third base and tell me, 'Deacon, c'mon, you can do it now.'"

As far as his personal friends from that team, Law said, "It would have to be my roommate that I had for several years, Smoky Burgess. Harvey Haddix is a good friend and, of course, ElRoy Face. Gosh, I was with the team for so long that they're all good friends really when it comes right down to it. But I would say that probably the one I felt closest to at that time was my roommate Smoky."

As far as maintaining contact with other former teammates, he said, "Oh, yeah, we do every year, either at Christmastime, or we see each other at Old Timers' Games, things like that."

In an interview with Bob Hudson, the sports editor of the *Provo Daily Herald*, Law was asked if the stories about immorality among ballplayers were true.

"To a certain extent, I'd probably say that may be true. There are those who are committed to their families, to the game, that are just as strong as you would like to see among athletes. I always put athletes up on a pedestal myself when I was a youngster and I know that youngsters do today. I think the athlete ought to recognize that and accept it as a responsibility that they govern their lives and do the things that they're supposed to do, as athletes, to project the right kind of image for the American young people.

"I think it's important they do that because so many of them are endorsing products that they shouldn't be endorsing. All for the dollar. Money, I think, in a lot of cases is the root of that problem that they're having today, both in drugs and otherwise. They think they can buy and do and not have any scruples at all with what they do. But there are still good people playing the game. Now, you could scrutinize other businesses and find the same problems. But, because the athlete is in the limelight all the time, everything that he does is overblown to the point where everybody knows what he does."

Law was also asked in that same interview why drugs had become such a problem in sports.

"Money, I think, has a lot to do with it," he said. "There are certain pressures that athletes have. I don't understand anyone's thinking about drugs, that it's going to make them a better player. It's going to relieve the pressure. That will always be there. It's learning to be strong and deal with that kind of thing, without drugs, without alcohol and those kinds of things. I don't know. That's a tough question.

"It's something that each individual has to deal with. It seems like there are so many people out on the street who are trying to make the easy dollar and they keep throwing it at them and trying them. Sometimes you get mixed up in with the wrong group and they do it. And so, to be accepted, you do it. Maybe they don't have a good self-image. Maybe they don't have the right kind of background, moral or spiritual, to abstain from those kinds of things. I'm sure that's probably the root of the problem. I think where there are strong families you don't have that kind of problem — where the kids have been taught those things and understand them and know what they can do."

In recent years, Law has made public statements about being upset by how much money players were making, and how general managers were no longer involved with the players. "Joe Brown was very much a part of our team," he said Of course, he was upset when players were making $200,000 a season. Imagine how he must feel now.

Jim O'Brien

Vernon Law and Gino Cimoli are reunited at Robert Morris College in 1993.

Vernon Law looks after Brigham Young baseball players, Cam Killebrew, left, son of former major league power-hitter Harmon Killebrew, and his son, Vance Law.

Smoky Burgess
Oh, how he could hit

"You can wake Smoky up on Christmas morning and he'll get you hits."
—Birdie Tebbetts

S moky Burgess was behind the plate for the Pirates at Chicago's Wrigley Field.

Richie Ashburn was at bat for the Cubs.

Burgess was bugging Ashburn with his constant chatter. Finally, Ashburn could take no more, and he stepped out of the batter's box, and turned to the umpire red-faced and screamed:

"Now you tell him to shut up! You just tell him to shut up or I'll hit him over the head with this bat."

Smoky smiled. Once again, he had succeeded in getting the best of Ashburn. Richie was living up to his last name. Smoky had claimed another victim.

The 1960 Pirates had more than their share of non-stop talkers, with Rocky Nelson, Dick Stuart and Smoky Burgess leading the way. When they were on the bench together, players avoided them so they could pay attention to the game. They were always talking about hitting.

They would talk to anybody who would stand still for five minutes or more. Usually more. Stuart and Nelson spoke about themselves for the most part, while Burgess branched out into other subjects.

Burgess was best known for his ability with a baseball bat, more so than his defensive ability as a backstop, and for his penchant for sitting around hotel lobbies on the road and talking to traveling salesmen and old ladies he kept from sneaking an afternoon nap.

He especially liked to razz Richie Ashburn because he thought it distracted one of the game's best hitters, better known for his lengthy career with the Philadelphia Phillies.

Ashburn would get so aggravated with his jibes, Burgess contended, that he occasionally let pitches sail past him when he should have been swinging.

From time to time, Ashburn asked umpires if there were not some clauses in the rule book that could have put a cap on Smoky's freedom of speech.

Burgess did not talk to every batter. He knew better in some cases. You did not say anything to annoy Willie Mays, for instance. When Burgess played for the Cincinnati Reds, his manager, Birdie Tebbetts, a former catcher himself, forbid him to speak to Mays when he was at the plate. In fact, Tebbetts told everyone on the Reds not to talk to Mays from the moment he walked on the field.

When Mays was annoyed or enraged, he was more apt to smash the ball out of the park. Mays had a thin skin, but a thick bat.

Another player Burgess did not talk to was Stan Musial of the St. Louis Cardinals. "I used to talk to him and he'd answer me and then wear us out with his bat," Smoky said of the Donora Dandy. "So I quit talking to him."

Smoky was smart enough to know who to talk to and who not to talk to when he was behind the plate. He had a book on opposing batters as far as their strengths and weaknesses were concerned. He knew what pitches the pitcher and the catcher ought to employ.

"There's a lot of guys who don't like to be talked to," said Smoky. "Guys like Hank Aaron and Joe Adcock of Milwaukee. They say, 'Don't you talk to me. I'm trying to concentrate.' But I'd say to Aaron, 'Aw, now, Henry, you're hitting the ball just too hard and I'd like to get you out just one time today.'"

Burgess must have been talking to Aaron and Adcock pretty good on May 26, 1959 in Milwaukee when he was behind the plate for the Pirates when Harvey Haddix pitched 12 perfect innings only to lose in the 13th. Adcock hit the game-winner for the Braves, so maybe Adcock didn't care for any post-midnight conversations with the Bucs' catcher.

Burgess, for the record, also caught most of roommate Vernon Law's 20 victories when he won the Cy Young Award as the league's best pitcher during that memorable 1960 championship season.

He was a left-handed hitter whom Danny Murtaugh platooned with the right-handed hitting Hal Smith.

"I don't care how people remember me," said Burgess back in 1986, "just as long as they remember the good things."

With Burgess, that was not hard to do.

This was a unique man. He did not have the body for baseball, at 5-8, and around 200 pounds in the latter part of his storied 18-year career in the big leagues, but nobody could hit a ball any better than Burgess.

Once asked what his playing weight was, he responded, "Whatever it happens to be. I don't keep track."

Who wouldn't like a guy who was that honest?

He started in the league in 1949 and he lasted in the majors until he was 40, so he was especially popular with the geriatric set, much like pro football's George Blanda, because he was carrying the banner for a lot of pot-bellied 40-and-over folks. He looked like your favorite neighborhood slow-pitch softball player in some millworkers' league.

Myron Cope once captured his form this way: "He has a figure shaped like a head of cabbage, a slick of sparse black hair atop his head, and the small, fat hands that one sees folded across laps at luncheons of the Daughters of the American Revolution."

In another feature story on Burgess, Cope wrote: "There's teetotaling Smoky Burgess, who looks less like an athlete than like a traveling salesman for a farm-implement company. Burgess, a rotund little North Carolinian with a slick of sparse hair and small pudgy hands, sits by the hour in hotel lobbies chatting companionably with old ladies. At bat, he reaches over his head or down to his shins for pitches and clouts them into the right field seats."

In that latter respect, pitcher Lew Burdette of the Braves snarled at Burgess after he golfed one of Burdette's offerings into the right field stands, "If you didn't hit that pitch, it would have hit you on the ankle!"

Burgess was once described as looking like a walking laundry bag. But he surprised those who were fooled by his figure.

"You can wake Smoky up on Christmas morning and he'll get you hits," Tebbetts once said.

Joe Garagiola, borrowing from Tebbetts, no doubt, and embellishing the remark, once gave Burgess a similar compliment: "Smoky Burgess is the only man in the history of baseball who could be gotten out of bed at 3 a.m. in December, walk out into a driving snow and hit a line drive on the first pitch."

The only question about those observations, however, would be to ask who would be pitching at that hour, in that month, and in that weather.

But everybody seems to mention December and Burgess in the same breath when his name comes up for comment.

"You know how that came about?" Burgess asked a sports writer in 1973. "It was when we were going north in the spring of 1956. We stopped to play a game in Knoxville. It was about 32 degrees, and snow was layin' around on the grass.

"I was settin' on the bench wearin' three or four jackets and was all wrapped up in a blanket, too. It came down to the ninth inning. We were getting beat by a run. Camilo Pascual was pitching and that was when he was throwing real hard. Tebbetts called me to pinch-hit.

"So I took off everything and went up there. I usually went for the first pitch, not like other pinch-hitters. I had the gift of God that I never needed no warmups and I could swing hard on the first pitch. It was so cold this day that he knew I'd be swinging right away to get out of there.

"Well, I lined that first pitch over the right field fence to tie the game, ran around the bases and into the dugout and straight into the clubhouse. I wasn't taking no chances on Birdie wantin' me to play any more that day."

Rocky Nelson, when I interviewed him at his home in April, 1993, said one of the Pirates he enjoyed the most was Burgess. "He could hit you a line drive in December. That's all he wanted to do. We both did a lot of pinch-hitting."

The Pirates were blessed in their history by having several outstanding pinch-hitters, like Nelson, Manny Mota, Jerry Lynch, Vic Davalillo briefly and Bob Skinner, who was also a starter. Lynch held the Pirates record with 18 pinch-hit home runs. But Burgess had the best mark of all when he retired, with 144 pinch hits in 507 at bats for a .286 average. Mota later passed him, with 15 pinch-hits in 1979 to total 150. As a member of the Pirates, Burgess hit .302 overall and .364 as a pinch-hitter. His lifetime batting average was .295.

"He looks like a butcher in a supermarket," said Skinner, "but, oh, boy, how he could hit."

"He was the consummate clutch hitter," said Joe L. Brown, who was the general manager who obained Burgess, along with Don Hoak and Haddix from the Cincinnati Reds on January 31, 1959 in the best trade he ever made. "He hit so many line drives the opposite way, down the left-field line. He was worn down a little defensively from the wear and tear by the time we got him, but his bat was still strong."

Burgess came back to Pittsburgh in 1980 and again in 1990 for anniversary reunions of that 1960 world championship team.

"1960 was my greatest year in baseball," he said. "I may have had better years personally, but it was the only year I played in the World Series. It meant more to me than any of the other seasons.

"It's really incredible the way it happened. I still have the highlights film from that World Series. Every once in a while, I pull it out and look at it. My grandson still takes it to school."

I spotted Smoky in the lobby of the Green Tree Marriott the morning of the 1990 30th anniversary reunion and old timers game at Three Rivers Stadium, and was struck by his appearance.

He looked shorter than his listed 5-8, and the skin around his eyes was dark, and he did not look well. A year later, on September 15, 1991, he was dead from cancer.

"Without his ulcer, Burgess wouldn't be Burgess."
—Al Hirshberg

Burgess had never enjoyed good health. Even when he was playing for the Pirates, he was always nursing one physical problem or another. He could match Roberto Clemente for aches and pains and ailments.

He had ulcers throughout his career, and required an operation for same once he was finished playing. They took out two-thirds of his stomach. As a player, he often talked about something "stirrin' up my inside stomach."

Al Hirshberg interviewed Burgess before his final season in baseball. "He's a grandfather, fat, 40, gray at the temples, asthmatic, ulcerated and hypochondrial, but he's still the best pinch-hitter big-league baseball has ever known," wrote Hirshberg.

"Burgess has lived with his ulcer for so long that he speaks of it with the affection of a master for a pet poodle and coddles it in the same spirit. Without his ulcer, Burgess wouldn't be Burgess."

Burgess appeared to be a lot of things he was not. Despite his beer-barrel belly, for instance, he never drank beer or any kind of booze. Despite his nickname, he never smoked. He drew his nickname from the Smoky Mountains, near his boyhood home of Caroleen, North Carolina. And, despite all his ailments, real and imagined, he was never unable to swing a bat.

Smoky Burgess in 1960 . . .   . . .and at reunion in 1990.

*"There's no other sport except boxing that has such a
hard one-on-one confrontation as you get when a pitcher
and a hitter go up against one another."*
—Joe Torre

Smoky Burgess smashes a home run against Braves at Forbes Field. Umpire Augie
Donatelli and catcher Del Crandall have close-up view of his heroics.

"That Smoky Burgess," said Dick Groat when the two were together in Pittsburgh, "will hit left- or right-handed pitchers. He'll hit late in a game or early. He'll hit with men on base or with the bases empty. He just doesn't care."

The Pirates peddled Burgess to the White Sox in September of 1964. When he reported to the team in Detroit, where the White Sox were finishing a series, manager Al Lopez said, "I got you for your bat, not your glove. All I want you to do is hit."

That night, Lopez sent Burgess up in the ninth inning with two out, a man on and the White Sox a run behind. Burgess hit Dave Wickersham's first pitch into the upper deck of the right-field stands. It was foul by three feet. However, two pitches later, he hit a screaming line drive into the lower deck for a home run that won the ballgame.

"You got the idea," Lopez said as Smoky trotted into the dugout and was mobbed by his new teammates.

Burgess also listened closely to his manager on the last day of the 1956 season as a pinch-hitter late in the game, with the Reds needing one more home run to tie the single-season major-league record for team homers, 221, then held by the Giants.

"Home run or nothing," said Tebbetts, his manager.

Burgess hit the first pitch out of the park.

In the years between 1959 and 1962, he was the Pirates' regular catcher and rarely pinch-hit. During that period his batting average was never under .294 and once soared to .328.

With the Reds, he had been a regular for only one season, in 1954, but Ed Bailey came up that year and took the No. 1 catcher's job away from Burgess the following season. In that 1954 season, however, Burgess caught 108 games and hit a splendid .368. He didn't win the batting title that season because he was 55 at-bats shy of the required 400 to qualify for the league leadership.

He liked hitting in Forbes Field. "There's plenty of room in the park for balls to drop safely. I always hit well in Forbes Field, no matter who I was playing for."

"Smoky didn't like to catch," said Haddix when I talked to him in April, 1993. "It became more and more a tough job for him to get up and down, because of his build. He said he gained weight even when he wasn't eating. I told him, 'Smoky, you're the only one I know who gains weight just breathing air.' I don't think he felt good much. I don't think his health was up to par. I pitched more to him than I did to Hal Smith. My, how Smoky could hit that ball."

Once asked what the secret of his success was as a pinch-hitter, Smoky said, "The secret of any pinch-hitter's success is to swing at the first pitch if it's over the plate. How many times do you see a guy watch the first once come right down the middle? That puts him behind the pitcher, who then can monkey around. You don't want the pitcher monkeying around — you want to do that. You've got to make him come in with your pitch, not his. And most of the time, your pitch is his first one. You may not see another one like it."

But every pitcher in the league must have known that.

"I suppose so," Burgess said.

Then, weren't they likely not to give him much to hit on that first pitch.

"No, the pitcher isn't any more anxious for me to get ahead of him than I am for him to get ahead of me," said Burgess. "He'll try to get the first pitch over. If he doesn't, I'll let it go by for a ball and still have three swings left. He can't afford to let me do that."

"He was a great roommate."
—Vernon Law

Forrest Harrill Burgess was born on February 6, 1927 in Caroleen, N.C., a community of 8,000 citizens nestled in the western Carolina hills. His father worked in a textile mill during the '30s, earning twelve dollars and 50 cents for a six-day week.

When Smoky turned 12, he went to work in the fields, hoeing and picking cotton and harvesting corn by hand.

"Yes, we were poor," he said. "I quit school in tenth grade and went to work in the mill for a year. Then I went back and finished school, but worked 3 to 11 at the same time. I got twenty-two dollars and five cents for a week's work."

When he was playing for the Pirates, Burgess lived in Forest City, a few miles from Caroleen, where he owned a gas station on Route 74. Later, he owned an automobile agency, and he went to work as a scout and hitting instructor for the Atlanta Braves in 1976 and held that position for ten years.

He married Margaret Head on July 21, 1945, and they had two children, Larr Harold and Donice Carol.

He broke into pro ball with Lockport of the Pony League in 1944. He spent part of the 1945 and 1946 in military service, and then resumed his pro baseball career with Los Angeles.

After winning batting championships with Fayetteville in the Tri-State League in 1947 (.387) and Nashville in the Southern Association in 1948 (.386), Smoky was brought to the majors by the Chicago Cubs in 1949, but spent half the season with their Los Angeles farm club, and all of 1950 with the Cubs' Springfield farm.

In 1951, he was back in the majors for good with the Cubs. That winter he was traded from Chicago to Cincinnati, and Cincy in turn traded him to Philadelphia before the 1952 season began. Smoky was with the Phils until mid-1955 when they swapped him back to the Reds.

Before he came to the Pirates, Smoky played in the 1954 and 1955 All-Star Games. With the Bucs, he played in the All-Star Game in 1959, 1960, 1961 and 1964.

Burgess was quite serious about his religion. He took an active role in the Fellowship of Christian Athletes.

"He was a great roommate," said Vernon Law, when he visited Pittsburgh for a sports card show in April, 1993. "He was a practicing Southern Baptist, and we had a lot in common."

In an interview with Myron Cope before the 1960 World Series, Burgess talked about where he lived. "There's no nightclubbin' to be done in Forest City, but I'm not the nightclubbin' type anyhow.

"Last year, we had a little excitement. A new sheriff came in and tried to clean up the moonshiners. Caught twenty-seven in one night. Otherwise, there hasn't been much excitement 'cept the drag races the kids hold on the highway. They paint startin' and finishin' lines right on the highway and block off traffic till they're done. Folks are tryin' to put a stop to that."

He was an active member of the Holly Springs Baptist Church and never drank, smoked or chewed.

"I enjoy going to a good revival meeting," he said. "When the spirit of the Lord is there and you can feel His presence, then you have a good meeting.

"When I'm through with baseball, I just want to run my gas station in Forest City, be with my family, and do whatever I can for the church. That's my kind of life."

ElRoy Face, Bill Mazeroski and Smoky Burgess share joys in 1960.

Dick Stuart
Still Dr. Strangeglove

*"One time a pitcher lifted his hand
to his cap and I swung away."*

Dick Stuart was different, right from the first day with the Pittsburgh Pirates. He would later acquire a wonderful nickname which suited him perfectly and it remains appropriate even today. He was called "Dr. Strangeglove" after a Stanley Kubrick movie of 1964 called *Dr. Strangelove Or: How I Learned To Stop Worrying And Love The Bomb*, which starred Peter Sellers, George C. Scott and Sterling Hayden, and was nominated for an Academy Award as the best picture of the year.

Stuart merited the nickname for two reasons. He turned every ball that came his way at first base into an adventure, and he got up every day of the season hoping to hit a home run. No one loved baseball's version of The Bomb any more than Dick Stuart.

"All I remember about the 1960 World Series is that I was supposed to be the next hitter after Mazeroski," said Stuart when he showed up in Pittsburgh for an Old Timers Game at Three Rivers Stadium on August 2, 1980 for the 20th anniversary reunion of that championship team. "I was going to pinch-hit for Harvey Haddix. I was in the on-deck circle, and, after Mazeroski hit the homer, I almost got trampled to death."

Stuart had been dreaming of hitting a home run of his own to win that World Series. Maz messed up his plans. "Maz cost me some money," said Stuart, unabashedly.

Then, too, the Yankees scored the tying run in the top of the ninth on a ground-out that Rocky Nelson nearly turned into an inning-ending double play at first base. "If I had been at first, we'd have been out of the inning, and we wouldn't have had to bat in the ninth," Stuart told Nelson after the game. It was his way of endearing himself to his teammates.

"You couldn't stay mad at Stu too long," Nelson said when I interviewed him at his home in Portsmouth, Ohio, in mid-April, 1993. Of course, people used to say the same thing about Rocky Nelson.

"It seems like 100 years ago," said Stuart. "I come here to the ballpark and it seems like a million years ago. It's really hard for me to remember what happened that year."

Some things never change. At the 20th reunion, Stuart challenged former Yankee Moose Skowron to a home run hitting contest during batting practice before the Old Timers Game. Stuart did hit one out, high up on the inner wall in left field, during the pre-game workout.

Anybody who knew him will never forget Stuart.

"He was the most unique individual I ever met in baseball," said former teammate Vinegar Bend Mizell, himself an original, during an interview for this book. "You just never knew what would happen next with Dick around. You just never knew what he'd say or do next. But I liked him."

Harvey Haddix was paired with Stuart for one road trip. "He took my newspaper into the bathroom with him before I'd had a chance to look at it, and when I went in after him the paper was all over the floor," said Haddix. "It was scattered everywhere. That was it. I told Bob Rice, our traveling secretary, that he should never room me with Stuart again. He was a good guy — he could poke fun at himself, and you had to like him — but you wouldn't want to room with him."

During the 1960 World Series clubhouse celebration, Stuart spilled a beer over the head of Pittsburgh Mayor Joe Barr, who was not particularly thrilled by it. "He shouldn't have come in here if he didn't want to get wet," said Stuart with a shrug when told that the Mayor was unhappy with his shenanigans.

"I always had a lot of respect for Stuart's ability, and I mean that," said Bob Friend, one of the finest Pirates pitchers in that era. "He had pretty good hands, but he wasn't always serious. If you wanted a supporter in a fight you'd want Stuart on your side.

"He could hit, and he could hit under pressure. He broke up a few games for us. He was a man's man. He had a great sense of humor, and he kept you loose. Hell, there are more stories about Stuart that still make the rounds than anyone on that team."

Dick Groat, another former teammate, may have summed up Stuart best when he said, "He was one of a kind. They called him Dr. Strangeglove and he came by the name honestly. He brings up a strange situation. He was tremendously disliked by the Red Sox and Philly players when he later went with them. If you went back and questioned all the 1960 Pirates they all liked him. He was a good humor guy. He was good for the '60 club."

Stuart was a self-deprecating individual. He didn't spare himself when he was harpooning people. "One night in Pittsburgh, 30,000 fans gave me a standing ovation when I caught a hot dog wrapper on the fly," Stuart told the *New York Times* in 1960.

Frustrated by his own ineptitude in the field, Stuart once grabbed a ball he had fumbled and buried it alongside first base. Stuart's 117 home runs over five Pirates seasons fell short of expectations. The combination of too few home runs and too many strikeouts and errors shortened his stay in Pittsburgh. Plus, he had self-destructive tendencies away from the ballpark.

Joe Brown dealt away three-fourths of the infield after the 1962 season, after the Pirates had finished sixth and then fourth in successive seasons following their super 1960 accomplishment. He sent Stuart to the Boston Red Sox, Groat to the St. Louis Cardinals, and Don Hoak to the Philadelphia Phillies. Only Mazeroski remained. The Pirates fell to eighth place in 1963, completing the collapse.

Stuart was a handsome young man, and he would have made a great sports hero. He looked and talked the part. He combed his dark brown hair with much care, and slicked it back on all sides. When out

Stuart signs with Joe L. Brown.

Stuart swings at 1990 reunion.

"I tell you, I could make two hundred thousand dollars a year with Stuart's power and my brains."
—Roberto Clemente

Stuart signs autographs at the rail.

of uniform, he often dressed like "Fonz" from TV's *Happy Days* series, with wide collars turned up on his neck, and he liked driving around in big colorful convertibles. "Stuart was the biggest greaser in that pre-Beatles time when young men were sideburned, slicked-back sons of Elvis," wrote Luke Salisbury in his book, *The Answer is Baseball*. According to Salisbury, Stuart wore a uniform a full size too small because "if I look bitchin', it adds 20 points to my average." Stuart was an extra for TV and movies early in his career, and also worked as a salesman in the off-season back home in California.

He had blue eyes and he flashed them mischievously. He was 6-3 and weighed 212 when he played for the Pirates. He was of Scotch-Irish ancestry, and his hobbies included golf, water skiing and parties. His boyhood hero was Ted Williams. Richard Lee Stuart was born on November 7, 1932 in San Francisco, and still lives in that area today. He would not consent to an interview for this book, but, after three letters from us imploring him to cooperate, he did oblige us with his autograph for use in this book.

Former Pirates general manager Joe L. Brown called me on the telephone from his California residence as I was writing this chapter on Stuart. When I told Brown what I was doing when he called, he said, "Only one chapter?" Maybe Brown unwittingly tipped me off as to why Stuart was not more enthused about this book project. Stuart was a special project for Brown. Their relationship was a stormy one. Stuart often frustrated Brown, too. For Brown, there were several chapters to the Dick Stuart story, mostly with unsatisfying finishes.

"You were always fighting the organization and fighting yourself," Brown once said to Stuart.

I figured Stuart was still battling some demons, real or imagined, when he was being difficult with me when we had no previous dealings or interaction. I never had an opportunity to offend or upset him.

"He's always been a little strange," Brown reassured me when I mentioned my difficulties with Stuart during a telephone interview, just so I didn't take it personally.

Stuart wrote me that I was getting a real bargain. "I charge $17.50 per autograph — for Kids and Adults. No complaints yet. Plus extra for personal things about my life. So dig into your pockets real deep."

It is too bad that he did not want to talk about his life of late because Stuart was popular in Pittsburgh in his playing days, and he was a big contributor to the team's championship season, and his fans would be interested in knowing how he is doing these days. Danny Murtaugh called him "the big guy".

Stuart still has a lot of fans here.

"Stu was a personal friend of mine, and he was always a lot of great fun," says Miles Span, a former high fashion clothier who provided many of the Pirates with special wardrobes, and booked many of the Bucs for paid speaking and singing engagements at the peak of the team's success. Span, who has long been involved in politics in Monroeville, remains a big fan of Stuart. "He never meant anyone any harm. He was just full of himself," said Span, "and thought he was destined for greatness."

Span accompanied Stuart to a lot of social events and parties around Pittsburgh. Stuart was a legendary figure for his alleged sexual prowess. Apparently Murtaugh wasn't the only one who called him "the big guy."

Stuart was single when he first signed with the Pirates, and he listed himself in the form he filled out as a "bachleor." Even if he couldn't spell it properly, Stuart enjoyed his single status.

Stuart enjoys another distinction in baseball history. He was the first player to hit 30 home runs in each league.

Stuart showed up for the 30th anniversary reunion of the 1960 Pirates and participated in an Old Timers Game at Three Rivers Stadium. He got into a hassle with the Pirates front office over his airline tickets, according to club officials, and ran up some bills around town that the Pirates thought were excessive. In short, he was still difficult for them to deal with, just as he was as a young player with gargantuan potential.

"The Pittsburgh Pirates haven't changed in 25 years," Stuart said about the flap. "They're still cheap."

He still signs autographs "Dick Stuart (66)" to remind the ignorant or incredulous of his one-season record total of home runs at Lincoln, Nebraska in the minors. Stuart was said to have enough self-confidence to carry the entire club.

Stuart was one of the most colorful Pirates in the team's history, and he had a love-hate relationship with the fans in Pittsburgh. They loved it when he hit home runs — he had some swing — but they booed him when he struck out, which he did often, and when he flubbed plays at first base, which he did nearly as often.

Joe O'Toole, who was the assistant to Brown in the Bucs' front-office, remembers getting a telephone call from Tom Johnson, a Pittsburgh attorney who was one of the team's owners. Johnson had gotten a telephone call from a fan who was upset because Stuart had socked him in the nose and broken his glasses.

"The guy had been sitting behind our dugout, and the guy sticks his head in at one end of the dugout and is yelling into it," O'Toole tells the story. "Stuart thinks it's the guy who had been yelling at him throughout the game. Stuart hits him and knocks him down. After Johnson called me about the incident, I called the guy. I asked him if I could meet with him. He said, 'Actually, I was yelling at Murtaugh for something he did.' The guy showed me his broken glasses. We agreed to pay him for his glasses — I gave him a check for $48 — and had him sign a release. He was a law student at Duquesne University, and he didn't like the wording of the release, but he was a fan and he didn't want to be a problem. I gave him some tickets, and I brought him into the clubhouse and introduced him to Stuart. Stuart signed a baseball for him."

Sometimes Stuart responded to criticism with a smart-ass line, rather than taking a poke at someone. "Worst fielder I ever saw," was the superlative pinned on him by Bobby Bragan, who managed the Bucs in 1958 when he sent Stuart down to the minors. But Stuart later boasted to the press, "It took him an hour and a half to explain why he was sending me down." With that, a reporter cut in dryly, "Then he must have developed a terrible stutter. Because it only took him five words to explain it to us."

A later Bragan gem on Stuart went like this: "If he'd concentrate he could get good enough to be just bad."

Stuart regarded the fielding and throwing aspects of the game as unpleasant housekeeping chores anyhow.

Stuart was a favorite subject for Jim Murray, a delightful sports columnist for *The Los Angeles Times*, whether Stuart was botching balls for the Pirates, Red Sox or Phillies. Murray liked to write with tongue-in-cheek and he positively drooled at the sight or sound of Stuart. With him, Murray always had a field day.

"It has been conservatively estimated around the league that in order for the Boston Red Sox to come out even on Dick Stuart, he'd have to hit 84 home runs, bat .320 and drive in 236 runs. Unfortunately, he's only half that good," wrote Murray.

"For every ball Dick Stuart loses over the fence, he loses one at first base. He led the American League in runs-batted-in, but bottomed it in fielding last year (1963). His 29-error total was almost three times as many as his nearest competitor. He got exactly no votes in the most valuable player category.

"Asking a great artist to stoop for ground balls is like making Heifetz sweep the stage. In Richard's view, the ground crew should handle grounders. Managers, who have watched him do it, agree.

"At the bat, he has the nice level swing of a guy getting out of a sand trap. Manager after manager has shuddered in horror on first beholding it. Pitchers have pondered taking up a collection to keep him in the league. He gets fewer bases-on-balls than the bat boy. One part of the reason is, he swings at everything that doesn't hit the first baseman first. The other part is that pitchers reason that swing can't possibly hit something that's moving.

"His durability in the big leagues is a monument to his ego. Richard has more faith in himself than a gambler with his own deck. He plays his role as if it were written for him by Ring Lardner.

"He is the last of the .800 fielders. He fielded .889 in New Orleans in 1955. To give you an idea, the lowest fielding average in major league history is .954 and that was set back in 1884 when the gloves were small enough to slap a guy to start a duel."

Stuart hit 66 home runs in the 1956 season for the Lincoln Chiefs, the Pirates Class A entry in the Western League. At age 24, the San Francisco-born Stuart set minor league records with 383 total bases, 158 RBIs and 172 strikeouts. The following September, the Pirates brought Stuart to Pittsburgh for a week-long special instruction session with their hitting coach, George Sisler.

Sisler, a Hall of Famer, said at the time, "I feel that Stuart has tremendous potential and we will do everything we can to help him realize the fullest extent of his ability. I believe the important thing is to reduce his number of strikeouts without reducing his tremendous power. If this special work helps him, there is no doubt he will be an outstanding prospect."

Sisler had Stuart hitting home runs off a batting tee at Forbes Field, trying to get him to get his swing up, and across his middle. Stuart's normal swing was designed to hit a baseball off a golf tee.

Sisler was sent to the Dominican Republic League after the 1957 season to work some more with Stuart. In a letter to General Manager Joe L. Brown, Stuart wrote, "I want to thank you for sending George Sisler down here. He sure helped me a lot. He sure knows his stuff about hitting."

Stuart had hit home runs and struck out and made monstrous errors wherever he worked. He led his league in home runs every year of his first three full years of organized baseball. He broke in with Modesto in the California League in 1951, and then set the Pioneer League on fire the following year with Billings, leading the league in home runs with 31, runs scored with 115, hits with 161, total bases with 292 and RBIs with 121. Stuart spent 1953 and 1954 in the military service, but returned to baseball in 1955, again with Billings and again led the league in home runs with 32.

When Stuart came up to the Pirates for the 1958 season, the team's incumbent first basemen were Ted "Big Klu" Kluszewski, better known for being a big home run hitter in his heyday for the Cincinnati Reds, and Frank Thomas, second at that time in the Pirates record books only to Ralph Kiner for clobbering home runs. Willie Stargell has since surpassed both of them in career numbers.

Jack Berger, the Pirates p.r. man at the time, sent out a rather frank feature story about Stuart for possible use in newspapers at the outset of the 1958 season. It was more controversial than most sports columns to be found in Pittsburgh dailies back in those days:

"The California-born-and-bred clouter has had a stormy and tempestuous career thus far, even though he now is just beginning to play major league baseball," wrote Berger.

"Big Stu — as he is called by everyone — is perhaps the most colorful youngster to come into the National League since the famed Gas House Gang of the old St. Louis Cardinals. He first hit the headlines two years ago when he hit 66 homers for Lincoln (Neb.) in the Class A Western League. And he hasn't been out of the headlines since! For whatever Richard Lee Stuart — 25 years old, 6-2, 200 pounds of hulking muscle — does or says, he makes news!

"Dick is one of those rare individuals who is confident of his ability — and he's not too shy to talk about it. And he'll talk about his hitting accomplishments also — at the slightest drop of a bat . . . to this day, Stu'll talk about the 610-foot homer he hit at Pueblo (Colorado) two years ago. Or about the tremendous 550-foot-plus homer he hit at San Diego last year.

"Ralph Kiner, former Pirates home run king, predicted as far back as April, 1957, that 'Stuart could well be the next great home run king in the major leagues.' Big Stu, of course, had his troubles — like all long-ball hitters. Dick had a tendency to strike out much too often, but when he did connect the ball traveled out of the park in a hurry.

"He was sent out because of his lack of interest in the defensive phase of the game."

Larry Shepard, the manager of the Pirates' Salt Lake City team, once said of Stuart, "If he popped up, he'd go to sleep out there (at first base) wondering why he didn't hit the ball out of the park."

"His favorite subject is baseball and Dick Stuart."
—Al Abrams, Sports Editor
Pittsburgh Post-Gazette

Stuart was well aware of his shortcomings at bat and in the field, and made some admissions regarding same in a guest column he once did for the *Post-Gazette* in the space normally reserved for sports editor Al Abrams.

"When I first joined the Pirates, I was called talkative, brash, too cocky," Stuart confessed in his column.

He said he was trying to cut down on his strikeouts. "My objective is to cut down the same way as Babe Ruth, Ted Williams, Ralph Kiner and other sluggers did. No one likes to strike out too much," he continued.

"I was accused when I first came up of not having the right attitude. They thought all I was interested in was hitting home runs and in personal records."

On the subject of the 66 home runs he hit at Lincoln in 1956, Stuart said in his column:

"All the publicity went to my head, I'll admit. But there are times, too, when I feel sorry I didn't hit 73 to break the all-time baseball record. Hitting home runs is my business."

On June 5, 1959, Stuart hit a ball over the center field wall at Forbes Field, 457 feet away, and long-time observers said they had never seen anyone hit the ball over that part of the wall before. "One of his problems," said Bob Friend, "is he thought you had to hit 500-foot home runs all the time. One time, I remember Bob Skinner hit a home run on the road that traveled down the right field line, and just got into the seats, about 300 feet away. Stu asked Skinner if he thought that should really count as a home run. He said to Skinner, 'Are you going to take credit for that?' "

Al Abrams enjoyed Stuart. If you were a sports writer, you had to like Stuart. He was a sports writer's dream. He was flip, full of fun, and said outrageous things. He was way ahead of his time in that regard.

Abrams wrote the following evaluation of Stuart in one of his columns:

"Tall, handsome and articulate, the 24-year-old Stuart oozes personality and color from every pore. He would, indeed, be the delight of all typewriter jockeys if he makes the grade in the big leagues.

"At bat, he looks like a right-handed Ted Williams. He's 6-foot-3 inches, 212 pounds well distributed on his lean-looking chassis. He swings for distance every time up, home run or strikeout being his lot!

"Off the field, he'll sit down and talk to anybody who'll talk to him. His favorite subject is baseball and Dick Stuart, of course. 'If I don't believe in myself, who will?' he asks. As for the 172 strikeouts in 140 games at Lincoln, Stuart told Abrams, "it's nothing to get worked up about. If a fellow goes for the home run, he's gotta strike out a lot."

Stuart also made a confession to Abrams. "I'm not much of a glove man," he said. "I've played the outfield and first base and I have a lot to learn in both places."

Bobby Bragan said, "He reminds me of Bob Skinner, a good stick man, but no glove to speak of."

Abrams asked Stuart during the Pirates spring training session at Fort Myers what happened to him in the stretch run at Lincoln when it appeared he had a chance to hit more home runs in a single season than anybody in history. Stuart hit 61 home runs in the first 105 games, then only five in the last 45.

"That was the darndest thing," said Stuart. "Pressure and an injury to the third finger of my right hand did it. It was mostly pressure, I guess.

"I was sailing along hitting home runs by the bushel and minding my own business when I started getting all this publicity. Newspapers, television and radio started giving me the Mr. Big treatment. Branch Rickey Jr. came down to see me.

"Then it happened. I couldn't hit the side of a barn door anymore. To add to my troubles, a pitch hit me on the third finger and I couldn't grip the bat right.

"That made me all the more anxious to hit 'em out of the park. I was so anxious that some of the fellows used to kid me that I started swinging before a pitcher cut loose with the ball.

"I thought they were exaggerating but they weren't. One time a pitcher just lifted his hand to his cap and I swung away."

One day in the clubhouse, he turned his back to Abrams and asked, "Who's that number 5 remind you of?"

"I don't know," answered Abrams.

"Joe DiMaggio," Stuart snapped. "He was No. 5. I'm going to make you forget all about DiMaggio before I'm done."

What followed was a two-hour chat between Stuart and Abrams, with Stuart commanding most of the air time. Stuart was shipped back to the minors soon after.

Myron Cope maintained that Stuart took as much abuse from fans at Forbes Field as any Pirate since third baseman Bob Elliott back in the '40s.

Stuart insisted to Cope that it was more of a complimentary than a negative thing. "If they didn't boo me," said Stuart, "I'd be very disappointed. The day they stop booing me it'll mean they don't know I'm around. That'll be the time to worry.

"Heck, I've been booed everywhere I played, all through the minors. As soon as I'd join a new club I'd get a lot of publicity and then everybody would come out to the park to boo me if I didn't live up to the write-ups.

"I'll say this about being booed in Pittsburgh: I'd rather be booed here than in Salt Lake City or Lincoln, Nebraska. The money's better."

Stuart's style infuriated the fans, according to Cope. "He wouldn't show any signs that the booing was bothering him. He'd walk that walk of his, thrust out that strong jaw, and chomp on his bubble gum like a starved man."

Cope concluded of Stuart:

"What it boils down to is the fact that you have to know Big Stu, and once you meet him you have to grit your teeth for many weeks while listening to him say the wrong thing at the right time. Then, one day, you find suddenly that you are laughing and that you like the guy. You begin to root for him and you wish he'd get hot for a whole season and hit sixty home runs.

"You know, at any rate, that you are watching a ballplayer who has color, who resembles nobody but himself, a ballplayer you will remember long after he is retired and gone."

Nobody was more miffed than Cope when the Pirates sent Stuart packing to the Boston Red Sox. Cope wrote in a column for *Pittsburgh Weekly Sports* in late September of 1963, "It's more fun finishing in the second division with a Stu around to blame it on than without one. The worst part about watching the Pirates lose this year was there was not one player bonehead enough to get mad at and not one who was ridiculous enough to laugh at.

"Watching Big Stu loitering without a care near first base took me back to my youth when happy old geezers stood around on street-corners behind iceball wagons. 'Ice-a-balls!' they cried out from time to time, then returned to enjoying the midday sun," continued Cope.

"Babe Ruth wasn't such a hot fielder."
— Dick Stuart

Larry Shepard managed Stuart at both Salt Lake City and at Lincoln. He loved Stuart, even if Stuart often drove him nuts. "You had to like the guy," said Shepard. "Oh, I'll admit you couldn't talk to the guy. You'd try to tell him he was a lousy fielder, but he'd come right back and say, 'Babe Ruth wasn't such a hot fielder.'

"I had scouts come in time and again and tell me, 'I think I know this guy. Let me talk to him.' If I heard this once, I heard it a thousand times. But they all went away muttering.

"When Stu first came to my club, a scout in the Pirates organization told me, 'Get rid of the guy.' I think the only reason he said it was because Stu probably had a chance to talk to him and drove him nuts."

Dick Stuart and Don Hoak get some hitting tips from Hall of Famer George Sisler at spring training.

Stuart speaks to young fan during victory parade, and, at right, holds Dick Jr.

Stuart liked to sleep ten hours a night, and took a late afternoon health-nap. He would get to the clubhouse early before a game, and smoke a big cigar before taking the field. He did not drink whiskey or coffee, and he did not smoke cigarettes, but he enjoyed that pre-game cigar.

Once on the field, he would find a spot by the batting cage where he could needle everyone on the opposing team. He would accuse them of nightclubbing, loafing and whatever struck his fancy. They would needle him back, but it only served to make him worse.

When it was his turn to take some swings, he would step into the batter's box, and announce to one and all: "Bases loaded, two out, last of the ninth, Dick Stuart at bat!"

Imagine what Stuart would have been like to live with if it had been him instead of Mazeroski who hit that home run. Stuart was on deck, set to bat for Harvey Haddix, when Maz connected. Stuart would still be in the clubhouse talking about that home run.

Bob Clements, who was in charge of the Pirates' minor league farms when Stuart was with the team, once said, "Nobody can change Stu. Time may change him, but that would be a loss rather than a gain."

One time, when Stuart was sharing a room on the road with George "Red" Witt, he asked Witt what his salary was. "That comes under the heading of none of Stuart's business," said Witt.

"Well, whatever it is," said Stuart. "I should be making more."

He did not read Dale Carnegie's book, *How To Win Friends And Influence People.*

During the 1960 season, Stuart was often paired with Gino Cimoli as a roommate on the road. Cimoli did not hit a home run all year long. "How can a big guy like you not hit a home run?" Stuart was fond of asking Cimoli.

It was Stuart's way of gaining friends.

Les Biederman, the baseball writer at *The Pittsburgh Press*, wrote of Stuart: "If ever a player lived for the next time at bat, it was Big Stu. He did create excitement with his home run bat, and sometimes with his fielding. They don't call him 'Dr. Strangeglove' for nothing. But how he could hit a baseball."

"Don't ask me why, but I like the guy."
—Johnny Pesky
Red Sox Manager

Melvin Durslag, an outstanding columnist for the *Los Angeles Herald-Examiner*, once came upon Stuart at spring training in Palm Springs telling his new boss, Boston Red Sox manager Johnny Pesky, about his plans for the upcoming season.

Stuart, true to form, was assuring Pesky that he would be leading the American League in home runs, RBIs, total bases, batting average.

"And what about strikeouts?" asked Pesky.

"Ted Williams struck out a lot, too," said Stuart, using his boy-hood hero to defend himself as he often did. "What did he do to cut down?"

"When he got two strikes," said Pesky, a former teammate of Williams, who knew what he was talking about, "he choked up a little on the bat."

"Williams had it easier," said Stuart, as if he hadn't heard what Pesky said. "He never had to face the tough pitchers that I do."

"There were more 20-game winners in his time than there are today," the persistent Pesky pointed out.

"Maybe so," said Stuart, nonplussed, "but they had fewer pitches."

Pesky turned to Durslag, and whispered, "Don't ask me why, but I like the guy. There isn't a mean bone in his body."

Stuart could also defend himself against those who found flaws with his fielding around first base. Stuart prided himself in having fielded .973 or better in each of his years in the big leagues to that point. But, as one Red Sox official pointed out, "The averages only show the ones he muffed. They don't tell about the ones that go past him entirely."

Dick Radatz, one of the Boston pitchers, suggested Stuart should have a vanity license plate with one of those low numbers. "It should be E-3," said Radatz.

When a teammate accidentally stepped on his glove, Stuart picked up the mashed mitt and said with a smile, "there goes the pennant." So Stuart was capable of poking fun at himself.

Stuart was obsessed with statistics and with personal trophies. He could tell good stories about himself, too, and he peppered them with statistics, so many statistics, and he sounded so authoritative with them that it was difficult to doubt the truth of his tales.

"It's the last day of the season and I need six RBIs to tie for the title," Stuart was saying about one of his seasons with the Red Sox.

"It's a longshot. We get men on first and second base and there's a passed ball and they move up. We're playing Washington and Gil Hodges has me walked intentionally.

"They've got 99 losses and he doesn't want to lose 100. He's over there laughing at me. The next time up I hit a double and drive in two runs. We're ahead in the game, 13-6, and I've got one more time at bat and all I need is a homer with the bases loaded to tie for the RBI title.

"Well, we get a rally going and the bases are loaded. Ronnie Kline, a good friend of mine and a former teammate with the Pirates, is out there pitching for Washington. He throws a knuckleball low and outside and it bounces clear back to the stands. Here comes Felix Mantilla, scoring from third. His run makes it 15-to-8, and here he comes. I hollered at him, 'No, no,' but he's got his head down and he doesn't realize what he's doing.

"I figure there goes my chance for the RBI title. I just stood there and took three pitches down the pipe. Then I threw my bat against the bleachers and walked out to the infield.

"The thing is, I was going to go down and tell (third base coach) Billy Herman that if there's a passed ball don't let Mantilla score. But

Kline hasn't thrown a wild pitch since he's been in the big leagues. I didn't go down, and it might have cost me my chance."

That tells you a lot about Stuart. Talk about temerity. Can you just picture him shouting to too many base coaches, or managers, and telling them not to let a teammate score because he believes he's going to hit a grand slam homer in his final at bat for the season?

Then again, this is the same guy who grabbed Bill Mazeroski when he came into the clubhouse after hitting the home run that won the World Series for the Yankees and chastised him, even if only in a joking manner, for his heroics. After all, Stuart was on deck, ready to hit a home run to bring fame and fortune to you know who.

Maybe Stuart had taken his cues from the signs he saw at Forbes Field during the Series that read:

DON'T BOO STU — HE'LL COME THRU

The signs were not as inspirational when he went to Boston. Stuart did not see eye to eye with his manager in Boston.

"I've never said anything to any manager if I'm benched when I'm not hitting," he said. "Last year, I was leading the league in RBIs and Johnny Pesky benched me for four days without a reason. That's the maddest I ever got.

"A couple of times, Pesky had me bunting to move guys over. I had 40 homers. He had me bunt against Cleveland in Fenway Park when we were ahead, 11-7. The first two guys got on, and he gave me the bunt sign. I got mad, swung and popped up. He fined me $50. Danny Murtaugh would say that if he had his number four hitter bunting, he was in trouble. I'd look over at him, and he'd point to the fence."

Murtaugh won a pennant in Pittsburgh with Stuart playing first base, and he learned some things in the process. "There are words that look alike with different meanings," Murtaugh said, with his dry humor. "And there are different words with the same meaning. Well, I found out there's a difference between vision and sight.

"When Stuart went up there with a bat in his hands, he was a vision. When he went out there with a glove, he was a. . ."

Stuart had his own opinions about how he would be best handled, and he was never one to pass up an opportunity to offer an opinion.

"I don't think any manager should resent a regular player who wants to play," Stuart said. "The only arguments I've ever had were over that. As long as I start every game I'll be happy. If he thinks someone else can do a little better in the field in the late innings, that's okay."

When Stuart was playing for the Phillies, and Gene Mauch wasn't managing the club to suit Stuart, he started talking about the prospects of playing in Japan. In short, Stuart was not playing every day; he was being platooned. That was simply the way Mauch managed a team

"Why I'll be a national hero over there," Stuart told Bill Conlan of the *Philadelphia Daily News*, more recently with the *Philadelphia Inquirer*. "Maybe bigger than the emperor."

Then when Conlan and his colleagues on the Phillies beat wrote about what Stuart said, he was upset. "I didn't think you would write it," said Stuart.

He said he had been offered $110,000 for two years to go play in Japan. "That's $55,000 a year," said Stuart, never thinking that sports writers were too smart. "That's a lot of Geisha baths, baby. I wonder if they'll give me solid gold chopsticks."

Stuart said he didn't like the way Mauch would pull him off the field for defensive purposes late in a game. He would have preferred staying in the dugout when the Phillies took the field, which is understandable.

"It humiliates me when he takes me out of there while I'm on the field," he said.

"It's like telling me I'm no good in front of 30,000 people. If he's got to take me out, let him do it between innings."

Once when Mauch removed him from the field in that way, Stuart slammed his glove down on the floor of the dugout. Some felt that Stuart was aiming at the bench, but missed. No wonder they called him Dr. Strangeglove.

Pirate sluggers, left to right, are Dick Stuart, Dale Long and Frank Thomas.

Where Were You?

"It took a Polack to do it!"
—Anonymous Resident
Polish Hill

Patricia Easton
Children's Book Author
McMurray, Pa.
"I wasn't into baseball then. I was into horses. All I remember is the way Clemente ran. He ran with the grace of a horse. I was at Mt. Lebanon Foster School. We stopped what we were doing. My teacher was Margaret McBride; she was a legend, she was the first teacher who made me believe I could do anything. She was the vice-principal and a Pirates fan. She let us all listen to the game on the radio. There was no way she was going to miss the World Series."

Olin DiPolo
Former Assistant to Vice-President
Promotions and Marketing, Pirates
Bethel Park, Pa.
"Vinnie Smith, the National League umpire, was married to a relative of mine, and I got two tickets for the seventh game from Vinnie Smith. There was a guy in front of me who started crying after Maz hit the home run. If I saw the guy today I'd still know him. He was a Pittsburgher. He looked Italian. He was so happy, he hugged me. When I was working with the Pirates, we twice had reunions of that '60 team, and I was in my glory."

Nate Firestone
Political Science Instructor
Pitt and Point Park College
Squirrel Hill
"I was a staff sergeant and I was drilling an ROTC class on the lawn of the Cathedral of Learning, down toward the Stephen Foster Memorial Hall, when we heard the roar of the crowd at Forbes Field. I hollered out 'Dismissed!' We all ran over to Forbes Field to find out what happened. We wanted to know what was going on. Maz had just hit the home run."

J.E. "Jack" McCallister, Jr.
Area Manager, Sparkle Corporation
"I was about 13 years old, and I was playing hooky with two buddies of mine — Tom Tamburro and Frankie Carone — from Mother of Good Counsel Grade School, and we were at the bottom of the bleachers in left field. It was unbelievable. Number nine came to the plate in the

bottom of the ninth. I almost got killed, trampled, when he hit that home run. Three big guys ran over us. We never got to the field. But it was so exciting."

Jackie Poloka
Housewife
Coraopolis, Pa.

"I was ten years old, and my name was Jackie Paszkowski then, and I lived on Polish Hill, on the side of the hill between the Strip District and the Hill District. I was a student at Immaculate Heart of Mary Grade School, and we were coming home from school on the day of the seventh game of the World Series. There was no one else but students in the streets; everyone was in their homes watching the game on TV. We were walking on Downing Street, near the Immaculate Heart of Mary Church. Some of the kids had transistor radios. They started screaming when Mazeroski hit the home run. Then all the doors flew open on the street, and people poured out, celebrating. I'll never forget this one man, standing on his front porch, hollering as loud as he could, 'It took a Polack to do it! It took a Polack to do it!' We roped off the streets on Polish Hill that night, and people came out with peirogi and kielbasi and all kinds of food and drink, and we just had a great party. Everyone was so proud to be Polish. I've had World Series tickets here three times in the last three years because I wanted my son to know what it was like, but the Pirates lost in the playoffs all three years and didn't get to the World Series. I was pregnant with him in 1979 when the Pirates last won the World Series."

Office workers dance in Downtown streets after '60 victory.

Bob Skinner

At home in San Diego or Pittsburgh

"I love the Pittsburgh fans.
Even to this date the fans
recognize me and treat me great."

On a clear evening Bob Skinner can see Forbes Field from his boyhood home on Diamond Street in LaJolla, just outside San Diego. Skinner has stared into the sun for so many summers at baseball fields across America, and he has spent all his winters in sunny San Diego, so his hazel eyes are mere slits in his friendly well-lined face. Skinner has always seemed half asleep — talk about California laid-back — but his eyes brighten and his voice is full of enthusiasm as he speaks about his days with the Pirates, particularly that wonderful summer of 1960.

He can see Forbes Field even clearer if he closes his eyes. Memories. Skinner has over 40 years of them in the big leagues, but none quite as warm as the ones from his first title team. He enjoyed reminiscing.

He could not have been more affable and I was, frankly, caught off guard by the pace of his conversation, much more enthusiastic and boisterous than I had expected. Bob Skinner is not slowing down. If anything, he is speeding up. Maybe it was reminiscing about the summer of 1960 that made his blood pump faster.

"The Pirates hadn't won anything in so long," said Skinner. "It was really exciting. That city just went wild. It was one big party."

He retired as a player in 1966, but never left the game. He is a cheerful fellow. He would be good company on a baseball bench. That helps account for his endurance in baseball.

"Winning the 1960 World Series was the highlight of my baseball career," said Skinner, who was looking forward to his 42nd season in professional baseball. He was scouting major league players on the west coast for the Houston Astros.

The summer of 1993 would be the first time he would not be wearing some kind of uniform. He had been the manager of the Astros' A team, the Tucson Toros in his last on-the-field position. He began his career in 1951 with Waco, the Pirates Class B team in the Big State League. He spent the 1952 and 1953 seasons in the U.S. Marine Corps. He joined the Pirates the following season, and wore No. 4. His number is clearly visible in the welcoming committee of Pirates who awaited Bill Mazeroski as he headed for home plate after his game-winning home run in the 1960 World Series.

Skinner played for the Pirates from 1954 through 1963, going back to the minors for more seasoning in 1955, and he also played one season in Cincinnati and two in St. Louis during a 12-year stay in the big leagues. He came up to the Pirates for good in 1956; he became the club's regular left fielder when manager Bobby Bragan switched Frank Thomas from left to third base. Danny Murtaugh kept Skinner there when he became the manager. Skinner was named to the 1958 and 1960 All-Star teams. He was later a coach with the Pirates in the '70s and '80s under Murtaugh and Chuck Tanner, and was always a popular figure in Pittsburgh. Skinner was named the Pirates hitting coach in 1979 under Tanner and followed Tanner to Atlanta when Tanner was fired by the Pirates in 1988.

Skinner always had a slow, easy-does-it speech pattern. He was never in a hurry. He was easy going and instantly likable. Skinner smiled at the image he must have projected. "I don't imagine I'm the most energetic fellow around here," he once said. "It's not that I'm lazy. I just don't waste any steps."

He became a very good hitter. He challenged the likes of Stan Musial and Willie Mays for the batting title in 1958, and finished with a .321 average. On three occasions he hit over .300 with the Pirates.

Skinner had one of his best seasons in 1960, even though his batting average was just .273. His 145 games, 571 at bats, 15 home runs and 86 RBIs were all highs for him at that point in his career. He started off the season by hitting safely in the first nine games, and he had several similar streaks during the rest of the summer.

He had good speed, but he was not a particularly efficient outfielder. But that was traditional in left field at Forbes Field, as he followed in the not-so-sure footsteps of Thomas and Ralph Kiner. Skinner played with reckless abandon, and had more physical problems than even Roberto Clemente could claim, and Clemente was considered something of a hypochondriac.

Bullpen pitchers described Skinner's gait as "like a turkey," "like a giraffe," "like an ostrich." Not a pretty picture.

Skinner was enjoying a tremendous season with New Orleans in 1955 when he broke his left wrist in a sliding accident. With the Pirates in 1959, he crashed into the wall at Milwaukee County Stadium, and suffered a shoulder injury that nagged him for several seasons afterward. In 1961, when he tailed off considerably from his outstanding 1960 output, he suffered from allergies, he had colds, an attack of flu, pulled muscles, painful bone bruises on his ankles and a recurrence of stiffness in his shoulders.

Skinner had several nicknames that were popularized by broadcaster Bob Prince. They included Bob, Skin, Skins and Dog. He was tall and skinny — just like Prince — and his name, Skinner, fit him well. He was 6-4 1/2, 185 pounds.

His name remains in the Pirates record book. He was one of seven Pirates who have hit three pinch-hit home runs in a season (1956), and that list includes Willie Stargell, Jose Pagan, Gene Freese, Dick Stuart, Al Rubeling and Ham Hyatt.

"I was in Pittsburgh as a coach when the Pirates won the World Series in '79, and I was on a championship team in St. Louis in '64," said Skinner. "So I have three World Series rings. But my first experience with the World Series was in '60, and that first one sticks way out in my mind. I think most Pirates fans my age feel the same way."

"I have a lot of fond memories of that ballpark."
—Bob Skinner

There were many memories of those days that stick out in Skinner's mind. The lanky left fielder with the so-smooth pendulum swing speaks about it like it was yesterday. Suddenly, he could see the scoreboard that loomed large behind him — "you never knew when a ball would go through one of the holes in the scoreboard" — the ivy-covered wall, the iron gate in center field, the bleachers in left field, the fans out there, the feuds and fights that broke out in the stands, especially in the second games of doubleheaders, the smoke from the dry ice they brought in big coolers to keep their beer chilled, and how they might toss some of the dry ice his way whenever he flubbed one in the late innings, or when they simply grew restless.

"Shucks," he once said, excusing blame from the bleacherites who booed him, "if I had to sit up there and watch me, I'd boo me, too."

Thinking back on those days now, he said, "I have a lot of fond memories of that ballpark and of Pittsburgh. I can see Sennott Street and Bouquet Street, and I can remember when my wife told me she couldn't find a parking space. Hey, we drew 1.7 million to Forbes Field in 1960, and parking was at a real premium. I remember her parking down behind the ballpark in a neighborhood they called Little Italy. The ballplayers used to park their cars at that gas station (Stuckert's) at the corner of Forbes and Bouquet.

"I remember Schenley Park, and how my wife used to take our boys to Weinstein's Restaurant in Oakland, and how they'd feed them in grand style. They would take good care of us. I remember Frankie Gustine's Restaurant. I used to go in there. He was such a neat guy.

"I remember the bleachers on Sundays. We played a lot of double-headers on Sundays, and it was sort of a family day, a picnic for a lot of people. They'd be lined up outside the ballpark when I got there at 10 a.m. They'd have picnic baskets, and the guys would bring big coolers loaded with beer. They had their Rolling Rock, Duquesne, Fort Pitt and Iron City. That was when they had 'blue laws' and they didn't sell alcoholic beverages at the ballpark on Sunday. And you couldn't turn on the lights, either, on Sunday evenings and I remember playing when it was hard to see in the late innings of second games, especially if we went into extra innings."

One of my boyhood memories of my oldest brother, Richard, 15 years my senior, related to such activity. He had gotten married when he came out of the Navy, and lived in Bridgeport, Ohio — our mother's hometown. During the '50s, I can remember my brother stopping at our house for a visit when he came up from Bridgeport with all his buddies to see a Pirates' game at Forbes Field, just three miles from our home in Hazelwood. This was when I was in grade school. My brother and his buddies always bought an extra ticket, and stacked a few cases of beer in that empty seat. They also traveled to Cleveland to see the Indians and the American League teams. And they always brought their beer.

"And whatever they brought to the park they were going to drink," said Skinner, speaking about such guys in general. "They'd have dry ice, and if the game got out of hand, or something went wrong, they'd throw dry ice at you. You could see it smoking on the grass.

"It could get funny out there in left field. By the second game of the doubleheaders the beer was taking effect. You'd see guys arguing and fighting. It was no big deal. People would stand back and give them a little room and let them go at it for awhile. Some guys would throw a few punches, and that would be the end of it. They'd break it up themselves before the cops had to step in and do it. I'd watch 'em in between pitches. It always seemed to be the same people fighting, too. I kind of got to know them.

"I remember how in the seventh inning they'd open the iron gate out there in left field. And the college kids and school kids could come in for free for the late innings. In that '60 season, they saw some of the best baseball action. We were always coming back in the late innings that year to win games."

The Pirates managed on 29 occasions that summer, after trailing after six innings, to come on to win.

I asked Skinner if he had gone out to Forbes Field, or what remained of it, after the Pirates pulled up stakes there and shifted to Three Rivers Stadium. When he joined Chuck Tanner's staff as a batting coach in 1979, Skinner and his wife Joan went out to check out the wall from Forbes Field.

"There's just the wall now," said Skinner. "It was kind of an eerie feeling."

More has changed than the landscape for Pittsburgh baseball. It's a different day, a different era.

"I read a trivia item in the newspaper the other day that said our outfield — myself in left field, Bill Virdon in center field and Roberto Clemente in right field — was intact for the longest span, seven years — than any other in the history of baseball. I don't think that will ever happen again."

Pirates fans who cheered the outfield combination of Barry Bonds, Andy Van Slyke and Bobby Bonilla can certainly appreciate Skinner's prediction. Who knows what might have happened if the Pirates had been able to afford to keep them all here for a few more summers?

"In Pittsburgh every sports event was a big deal."

Robert Ralph Skinner was born October 3, 1931 in LaJolla, California, a posh suburb of San Diego, which has always been his winter home since he broke into big-time baseball.

San Diego and LaJolla were among my favorite places to visit when I was working as a sports writer for daily newspapers in Miami, New York and Pittsburgh over a 15-year period. They rank right up there with Montreal, Vancouver, Boston and New Orleans among my favorites.

In my family room, I have an arrangement of baskets on the wall which I picked up in a shop in LaJolla. I first traveled to San Diego with the New York Mets and remember staying at an old hotel in downtown San Diego called the El Cortez Hotel. I was covering the Mets for *The New York Post* in the early '70s.

I remember sitting at poolside while Dick Young of *The New York Daily News*, heralded by some as the best baseball writer in history, was also wearing swimming trunks, but was typing away at a nearby table.

He was scolding the other sports writers in the traveling party who had chosen to stay at a distant hotel complex that was more modern. "My paper didn't send me out here to be on a vacation," said Young, never one to miss an opportunity to offer an opinion.

Sure enough, the Mets made a trade that day, and Young and I were the first to get the news and relay it to our newspapers in New York. Young was a reporter first and foremost, even though he also wrote a column for the *Daily News*. The same was true of Milton Gross, the lead columnist for *The Post*.

It was just one of the many valuable lessons I learned from Young, and some of the other veteran sports writers and columnists when I first came to New York.

I remember seeing Mets roommates Tom Seaver and Bud Harrelson out on the streets of San Diego, heading for one of the city's best restaurants for lunch. Most players ate at fast-food joints, but not those two. I remember seeing an infielder named Wayne Garrett sitting in the lobby, just to pass the time away in the afternoon. That used to be a popular way for players to while away the day, but they don't do it much anymore. I remember visiting the San Diego Zoo, the best zoo I have ever visited.

I remember seeing the Padres' Nate Colbert clobbering the ball at Jack Murphy Stadium. Murphy was a revered sports writer for the *San Diego Union*. Not many sports writers have stadiums named after them.

On other occasions, I came back to San Diego to cover contests in both the NFL and the NBA, as well as with the Mets. My wife Kathleen came on one trip that cost me less than $200 for her airplane ticket when we spent five days in San Diego, three in Los Angeles and three in San Francisco on a memorable west coast swing.

I remember seeing Jack Lambert roller skating around a swimming pool on the eve of a Steelers' game in San Diego. My brother Dan was with me on that trip, and we had a great time together. I remember that we were out late one night, but that he got up before me on Sunday morning to attend mass. He walked a great distance to a church to do so. But that was Dan.

Sid Gillman, the inventive football coach who gave Chuck Noll his start as an assistant in the AFL, lives in LaJolla, and Skinner said he still sees him around town. "He's still going strong and he's still playing golf," said Skinner. "He's still very active, and he's in his 80s. He's a well-respected figure around here."

Bleacher crowd (at doubleheader with Cubs in 1961) is recalled fondly by Bob Skinner.

Bob and Joan Skinner go golfing with, left to right, Robert Mark, Craig, Andrew Ralph and Joel.

Joel Skinner with Pirates

The sun always seems to shine in San Diego. When I was speaking to Skinner, the weather forecast in Pittsburgh called for five inches of snow overnight. Skinner snickered when he heard that. Then he had to rub it in.

"It's a little overcast here today, but it was beautiful, and about 70 degrees," said Skinner, shortly after returning from playing golf at the Stardust in Mission Valley — that is also where those modern hotels were located — that day, which was President's Day.

"My oldest son, Mark (38), drove down from Sacramento for an extended weekend, and we got to play golf together," said Skinner. "I really enjoy that."

Skinner married Joan Phillips on February 4, 1954, and they have four sons. Craig, 36, lives in the suburbs, Drew, 34, lives in San Diego, and their youngest son, Joel, 32, is in Cleveland. He is playing for the Indians. Joel was originally drafted by the Pirates in 1980, and came to the Bucs' camp when his dad was a coach. Joel was the only one of Skinner's sons to pursue a baseball career. "He's the one who really wanted it," said Skinner.

"I live in the home I grew up in. I've lived in other places in San Diego, but I bought this place from my parents 20 years ago. It's a two-story cottage, the kind you'd find in the midwest. It's a local landmark; it was built in 1902. My parents bought it in 1935.

"We had a home in Pittsburgh when I was there, out near Blawnox, and I'd rent it to a Pitt student during the winter. We always came back here. We had two of our children in Pittsburgh, but my family would leave in September when school started. The latest I ever personally stayed was November, and it got so cold. I couldn't stand it.

"We loved Pittsburgh, though. We have a lot of friends there. I've lived all my life in San Diego, but I can go back to Pittsburgh tomorrow and person after person would come up to me and say hello and start talking about the Pirates to me. I can go downtown in San Diego and no one will know me. I really enjoyed people in Pittsburgh. They were great fans, and they knew their sports.

"Back in 1960, when you had fewer major league teams, when you had teams in Pittsburgh and in Detroit and in New York and St. Louis and Cincinnati you had real down-to-earth fans.

"In my early years in Pittsburgh every sports event was a big deal, whether it was baseball, boxing or football. But the Pirates and the Steelers were so down for a long time. When they saw our team start to put it together around 1957 they really got turned on to us, especially against the Yankees in that 1960 World Series. We were a very Cinderella team; we were heavy underdogs (6½ to 5). I think the fans just cling to that.

"The team had been down so long, whereas they had once been a dominating team in the 20s in the days of Paul and Lloyd Waner. The Pirates finished eighth five times and seventh the other three times in an eight-year stretch in the '50s. But the Pirates started coming back and finished second in 1958, and then fourth in 1959, cappping it off in 1960. We came from behind in so many games. The fans left Forbes

Field night after night talking to themselves about the great things that happened. We were making great comebacks; every night somebody else was doing something. We had a team that fans really grew to be part of. Damn, they can't get it out of their minds."

Skinner was injury-prone in his playing days. In the World Series against the Yankees, he jammed his thumb in the first game and sat out the next five, returning to action only in the last game.

"I was really disappointed, especially because I got hurt on a dumb baserunning mistake," said Skinner in our interview. "I was on second base and a ball was hit to short and I took off for third. You're not supposed to go unless the ball is hit behind you between first and second base. I shouldn't have run; it was a real bone-head play. I was just so excited. The ball was hit to Kubek and he threw to third to get me. I dove into third, a head-first slide, and my thumb just caught under the bag, and was bent back to my wrist.

"It really hurt. I told Murtaugh I had to play in the last game, though, if we were gonna win. I told him that. 'I'll help this team win,' I said. And I did. I had a sacrifice and I did some things that helped us. I only played seven innings in the field because my thumb hurt so bad."

Skinner walked in his first at-bat in the first inning and scored on a home run blast by Rocky Nelson. In the vital eighth inning of that seventh game, Skinner laid down a perfect sacrifice bunt to advance Virdon and Dick Groat.

"It was just fun for everybody."

"What do you remember about the way the fans reacted to the victory," I asked Skinner. "A sports writer named Joe Falls in Detroit told me it was the greatest spontaneous celebration he ever saw in sports."

"It was just the grand finale," said Skinner. "They let it all hang out. The city just stopped — over a baseball game. I don't know how you could can that kind of attitude, but everyone just wanted to be friendly. There was just joy. Everything was positive. It was just fun for everybody."

"How is life treating you now?" I asked him.

"I have eight grandchildren now and Joan and I have a lot of fun with them," said Skinner. "I'm 61 now, but I still feel young and I'm still in baseball. I enjoy playing golf in the winter. The only thing that's amazing to me is how the time flies. I've been in baseball for 42 years.

"You qualify for the maximum pension after ten years, so I have three times enough pension time. I started collecting it here a couple of years ago. I never made a lot of money in baseball. As a player, I made $33,000 late in my career. I never had a lot of extra money to put away. Now that I'm drawing on my pension, I'm getting a little money into the bank. We're able to save some at last.

"My son Joel is in his eighth year in baseball, and he's made more money already in baseball than I ever came close to making. That's fine for him."

Skinner managed San Diego to the Pacific Coast League title in 1967 when he was named minor league manager of the year. Skinner also managed the Philadelphia Phillies during the 1968 and 1969 seasons and he was an interim manager for one day with the San Diego Padres in 1977. He also coached for the Padres (1970-73 and 1977), the California Angels (1978) and for Danny Murtaugh with the Pirates from 1974 through 1976. He was on Chuck Tanner's staff from 1979 through 1988 in Pittsburgh, and with him after that in Atlanta. Skinner had managed for two years with the Tuscon minor league team.

"I've lived through a lot of changes. As a manager, I was young. That's when things started changing. The players' approach was different. As the years progressed, I've had to make a lot of adjustments. Managing a team today is different. You have the control, but it's not the same.

"When I was playing, the manager was the manager. I just looked for my name in the lineup. Now, if you're a manager, you have to do a lot of counseling, and you have to meet and talk with the players individually.

"Back then, the competition was such that you just played as hard as you could. If you didn't, they'd get rid of you. It's not that way anymore."

In 1967, when he was 36, Skinner was named the Minor League Manager of the Year by *The Sporting News* for the job he did with the San Diego Padres of the Pacific Coast League, which was the Phillies top farm team. The next year he replaced Gene Mauch as manager of the Phillies and resigned after several public conflicts with Dick Allen.

He then took coaching positions with the Pirates, Padres and California Angels.

"It was the biggest hit ever. It rocked the world."
—Bob Skinner on Maz's HR

Was there anyone Skinner was particularly close to on the Pirates of the '60s?"

"Harvey Haddix was my roommate," said Skinner. "I spent a lot of time with him. I was hoping to see him last year when the Cardinals had their 100th anniversary reunion, but I couldn't go. I was managing, working in Tucson.

"Haddix was really a fun guy. We were reunited on Tanner's staff when I came back to the team in 1979. I learned so much from him about pitching. He loved to read and he was into guns. He'd been raised on a farm and he was into hunting and fishing. To characterize him, I'd just say he was so down to earth. He was a real professional. When I was rooming with him, I remember he never spoke to opposing players in the field. They were the enemy. He'd talk to them in the hotel or in a restaurant, but not on the field. But he was a great guy; he was the kind of guy you liked to be around.

"I had a nice relationship with all of them: Hoak, Groat, Burgess and Smith. Hey, Hal Smith's home run in the eighth inning was a big home run. Clemente was our best ability player. He was good then, but he got better. He could hit, hit with power, field, throw, run; he had it all. He definitely had the most talent."

"Mazeroski said you were one of the players who came to him after the seventh game and told him you were glad he was the one to do it, that you were happy he was the hero?" I said to Skinner. "Do you remember that?"

"I certainly was happy for him," said Skinner. "To me, Maz was one of the better players we had on the team. He did all the things to help us win. He was great defensively and even though he didn't hit for a high average, he was a good clutch hitter. He always got key hits.

"It's too bad, but strangely enough in baseball everything is offensive. Even to the point of the Hall of Fame. Maz played baseball the smart way. I'm just so happy it was he that hit that home run. It was the biggest hit ever — it rocked the world."

"Maz told me he wished that someone else had hit it who could have explained it better," I said.

"There's not a heck of lot to be explained," said Skinner. "He hit it and it went over the wall in left field. I remember Yogi Berra going back to the wall.

"I think it was Maz's approach that made him a popular hero. He was just a blue collar Pittsburgh ballplayer. He just did a good job day in and day out. He has an easy-does-it approach to life. He was a steady, steady guy."

"It wouldn't be much fun being married to somebody who didn't like his job."
—Joan Skinner

Skinner says he has drawn the most satisfaction from staying in baseball as a coach and manager, and giving something back to the game through teaching. "My advice to the ballplayers today would be to have some fun and enjoy the game and give something back to the fans and to the game," he said.

"My mother and father were both school teachers, and I guess somewhere it rubbed off on me."

Before the children arrived, Bob and Joan had an apartment in East Liberty. Joan recalls, "I just hopped a trolley and went to every game." Later, they lived in an apartment in Baldwin Borough.

She was there once when he hit one over the right field stands in 1958. It was only the fifth time it had ever been done. "Bob and I were kidding about it before the game," said Joan. "I told him he couldn't hit it that far." After the game, Bob told the reporters he had done it for his wife.

"I like being a ballplayer's wife," Joan said back then, "because Bob is happy playing ball. But I'd be just as happy if he did something else. It wouldn't be much fun being married to somebody who didn't like his job."

The couple first met when Bob was an usher and Joan was a bridesmaid when her college roommate and his next-door neighbor got married. Joan was a student at San Diego State. Bob attended San Diego Junior College.

Skinner was a late bloomer in sports. He batted .200 in his junior year in high school. His coach said, "Of all the players I coached, I figured Bob Skinner was the least likely to succeed in baseball."

In the mid-40s, Skinner used to sneak into Lane Field to see the San Diego Padres of the Pacific Coast League.

He started his professional career in Waco, making $4,500 a year. He was once called a "butcher" in the outfield, but he became more reliable as he developed.

Skinner had some special moments throughout his career.

In his rookie season of 1954, he set a record for first basemen with eight assists in a game.

He went two-for-three for the Cardinals as a pinch-hitter in the 1964 World Series. He led the National League with 15 pinch-hits in 1965.

"We had the kind of club you want to manage."

Here's a synopsis of Skinner gleaned from a questionnaire he filled out when he was still playing for the Pirates:

His boyhood idol was Ted Williams, which makes sense. Williams was from the west coast and was a lean, mean hitting machine. His nickname was "The Splendid Splinter." It's a nickname Skinner could have worn as well.

In addition to winning the 1960 World Series, Skinner says the highlight of his major league career was signing his first big league contract. His most memorable moment was the seventh game of the World Series, specifically Mazeroski hitting the game-winning home run.

He listed Sandy Koufax of the Dodgers as the toughest pitcher he ever faced.

His favorite singer was Frank Sinatra. His favorite song was "Stardust." His favorite movie was "Gone With The Wind." His favorite food is Mexican and he loves Monday Night Football.

How can you not like a guy like that?

426

Back in 1974, Skinner made some insightful reflections on his days as a player at Forbes Field in an interview with Tom Rooney, who was writing for the *Times-Express Daily* in Penn Hills and Monroeville.

"We were something special. We all developed at the same time, at the same instance. We were so close, off and on the field, in restaurants, movie theatres, coffee houses on the road. It has left a lasting impression.

"I was out at the old Forbes Field site not long ago. It was my one and only trip back there since I quit playing baseball.

"I walked in front of what little remains of the outfield wall. Trailers pull in and out of the construction site. All that's left of Forbes Field, though, is a big hole. I stood in front of the left field wall like I had so many nights as a player. It was noisy and hot and a million thoughts went through my head.

"Hey, remember the nuns in the right field stands on Saturday afternoons? We always had a lot of nuns. They let them in free. I don't think we ever lost a Saturday afternoon game when they were there.

"We're all spread out now, all those guys who played on that '60 team. You only hear from them at Christmas time. We had a bond on that team. Nothing like winning keeps the memories warm.

"Baseball parks had charm then. They all had their own characteristics. The fans were closer to the field. We played on grass. Forbes Field had the rock hard infield. The Polo Grounds were so short down the left and right lines. Ebbetts Field on Bedford Avenue. 'Hit one out on Bedford!' they used to scream in the stands. Crosley had the inclined outfield toward the fence and 'goat's run.' The game is a little different now.

"We had the kind of club you want to manage. We did everything well. Run. Field. Hit. Hustle. The game's really not changed that much, though. Just the people. New names, new teams, new uniforms, new faces. They're out there making memories now. They'll have time to think about it someday."

Pittsburgh Pirates

Scoreboard in left field provided backdrop for Bob Skinner.

Mickey Mantle
"You can't go back."

"Nothing ever hurt as bad as that one."

Mickey Mantle took the defeat to the Pirates in the 1960 World Series very hard. Whitey Ford talked about the personal impact of seeing his good friend openly weeping in the clubhouse afterward.

Mantle and Ford conduct a highly-popular "Fantasy Baseball Camp" in Florida these days for adults seeking a special get-away vacation, a spiritual renewal, a chance to mix with big-time ballplayers, to get batting and fielding tips from them, and to listen to them reminisce about the good old days. Former Yankee teammates such as Moose Skowron and Hank Bauer come down to provide instruction.

Any Pirates fan tempted to pay the $2,000 or so fee for such frivolity is advised not to bring up the subject of the 1960 World Series. It could spoil a good time.

In his book, *The Mick*, written with Herb Gluck (Doubleday, 1985), Mantle detailed his disappointment over what started out looking like a great year:

"The 1960 season was particularly enjoyable because the team meshed in late summer, everyone pulling together, nobody slacking off," said Mantle in a tape-recorded reflection. "We had a superb bullpen, bolstered even further by Luis Arroyo, who came over from Cincinnati and saved a few games for us. Then Bill Stafford was brought up from Richmond. A gritty kid. He went 3-1 in the final weeks and had a low ERA.

"Our frontline pitchers were Ford, Ditmar, and Turley. Jim Coates did a good job during the early sledding, at a time when Ford and Terry were having their problems. With Whitey it was tendinitis. One game he'd throw a shutout, the next would be a struggle. In September he was never better, winning his last three starts.

"Ralph Terry's problem corrected itself once he stopped experimenting with an assortment of new pitches. I know Casey used to get hopping mad whenever Terry threw the slow curve as a sort of test against the hitters. At any rate, Casey demoted him to the bullpen and kept him there until he agreed to forget the experimenting and rely on his mainstay, a blazing fastball. The following spring Johnny Sain became pitching coach and under his direction Terry went from 10-8 to 16-3. So a fresh approach really made the difference.

"Without a doubt those teams from 1960 to 1964 were the strongest I had played on. In 1960 we had a great infield: Skowron might not have been the greatest defensive first baseman who ever lived, no argument there. But he did the job better than most. In fact, he led the league in putouts and I know he played first base thinking he was the best. So maybe he was, after all.

428

Yankees lineup included, left to right, Moose Skowron, Whitey Ford and Elston Howard.

rvey Haddix opposes Art Ditmar in 1960 rld Series match-up.

Mickey Mantle powers ball.

New York Yankees

MANTLE 7th INNING

MANTLE 5th INNING

UPI Telephoto

Diagram showing home runs hit by Mickey Mantle in second game of 1960 World Series at Forbes Field.

"People don't remember our pitching staff being really overpowering. But they led the league in saves, team ERA, and shutouts and Bobby Shantz won the Gold Glove.

"To complete the picture, we had Berra, Howard, McDougald, Maris, Lopez, Cerv, and I'm not about to skip over our center fielder, either. Altogether the offense generated 193 home runs to set a new American League season record. Maris led the league in RBIs and slugging average and I had the most home runs and the most total bases.

"When the season ended we were in front by the proverbial mile, which came off a fifteen-game winning streak. From mid-September right to the wire everybody was keyed up and ready for the Series against Pittsburgh, absolutely sure that we couldn't lose.

"Then a real mysterious thing happened. Casey didn't start Whitey in the opener. Here's the number one pitcher for World Series wins and our manager goes with Art Ditmar. Fate, circumstance, whatever — the decision either blows up in your face or makes you into a genius. I have always said this and I never second-guessed Casey in my life, but I believe the whole Series revolved around that decision. My hunch is that he was saving Whitey for the Stadium. Of course, you can't go back. Casey never explained why he started Ditmar. I don't think anybody knows. If he *did* make a mistake, you could wait a million years and still not get him to admit it.

"So we opened at Forbes Field and Ditmar got beat. Going into the sixth game, the Pirates were one up after Harvey Haddix and El-Roy Face held us to five hits and two runs. Meanwhile Ditmar took his second loss. Game six had us in Pittsburgh, where Whitey threw his second shutout and we bombed them, 12-0.

"The next day was the day of the Mazeroski home run. Nothing ever hurt as bad as that one. I remember Bobby Shantz pitching brilliantly in relief of Bill Stafford, who had relieved Bob Turley. We were ahead when Gino Cimoli came to bat in the bottom of the eighth inning. He singled. Then Bill Virdon hit a sure double play ball to Kubek, only it took a sudden hop and struck him in the Adam's apple. He was knocked dizzy. The ball trickled away. Cimoli went safely into second and Virdon made it to first. Meanwhile Kubek's on the ground, choking. What a scene. Gus Mauch was out there with his first-aid kit, Casey yelling. 'Give him room! Give him room!', and the rest of us walking around stupefied until Kubek got to his feet, appearing as though he had just disgorged a rock from his throat.

"Joe DeMaestri replaced him. The next batter was Dick Groat. He singled past Boyer for a run. We still held the lead, 7-5. Then Casey brings Jim Coates in from the bullpen. He pitches to Bob Skinner, who bunts the runners along. Rocky Nelson flies medium-deep to Maris. Virdon stays glued to third, knowing better than to challenge Roger's arm. Two out and Coates slows it down a bit, pitching carefully to Roberto Clemente, who hits a chopper to Skowron. I'm already on my way in from center field, thinking the inning's finally over as Skowron moves to his right, fields the ball, and turns.

"Hey! What the hell is Coates doing? I see him stop dead in his tracks between the pitcher's mound and first base! He didn't make the play. He *presumed* Moose would cover the bag. But Moose is standing helplessly by as Virdon scores. Right then and there — no question in the world — Casey should have pulled Coates out of the game. The situation demanded it. He was fidgeting like a man with ants in his pants. You don't let the man pitch.

"He worked a 2-2 count to Hal Smith, cranked up, eyeballed Groat at first, and threw a lovely fastball. Smith's bat whipped around and the ball jumped over the 406-foot brick wall in left field. They had three runs and a 9-7 lead.

"Then Casey brings in Ralph Terry, who holds off the inevitable by getting Don Hoak on a fly ball to end the inning.

"Bobby Richardson opens the ninth with a single. Then Dale Long pinch-hits a single, which sends Bobby on to third, and McDougald comes off the bench to run for Long. Next Roger fouls out. My turn and I single to right center, scoring Richardson.

"Yogi is our next hitter. He grounds hard to first. Fortunately, I'm leaning in and dive safely under Nelson's tag as McDougald scores the tying run.

"Bottom of the ninth. Bill Mazeroski is at the plate, taking the first pitch, a high slider . . . And the vivid memory of Johnny Blanchard going out to tell Terry to keep the ball down and me glancing at Yogi and Roger, the three of us breathing heavy sighs when Blanchard hunches down, gives Terry the sign . . . And the most tearing moment of all, seeing Mazeroski's hard line drive heading for the left field wall. Yogi moves toward it, me backing him up, but it keeps going, going, going. . .

"There's a sick sensation in the pit of my stomach. There's that unforgettable look on Yogi's face when he turns around, grim acceptance, expressed by a slow shrug of his shoulders. We walk off the field, a mob of fans already streaming past, and as Mazeroski crossed the plate his hysterical teammates grab at his uniform.

"In the locker room, all of us are wandering around in a trance, muttering, 'What happened?' I'm slumped on a stool, feeling so low I can hardly peel off my uniform.

"In all my World Series experience, that was the one time when I really thought the better team had lost."

Mickey Mantle dives back to first base in time to prevent a double play in ninth inning as Rocky Nelson tries to tag him.

Don Hoak
The Tiger at Third Base

*"Hoak epitomized blood and guts.
From the seventh inning on, there
wasn't a better player in baseball."*
—Joe L. Brown

Don Hoak's eyes were green and intense, and he liked to narrow them in a fierce scowl. He had a boxer's mashed nose, as it reportedly had been broken nine times. Hoak hailed from Roulette, Pennsylvania, a coal mining town, and his heritage was German.

His hair was reddish, and he wore it in a crew-cut when he played for the Pirates. Hoak had the look and demeanor of the least-favorite drill sergeant you could imagine, but he helped push the Pirates to a pennant and the 1960 World Series championship. He did not play catcher, but he wore a mask, to hear his teammates talk about him, and it was sometimes difficult to determine when he was playing baseball or when he was playing a theatrical role.

He was nicknamed "Tiger" by Pirates' broadcaster Bob Prince, and Hoak prided himself on being a former middleweight boxer, being part Comanche, and being an ex-Marine who had seen duty in the Pacific. It all added up to a tough-guy profile. He managed to drop those facts into most of his interviews with out-of-town writers. It made for a formidable package. One of his former teammates in Brooklyn, Gil Hodges, a strong silent type who was just the opposite of Hoak, once said, "Hoak is 0-for-15 when it comes to fights in baseball."

In truth, Hodges was much more feared than Hoak.

The one fight Hoak had in baseball that was officially recorded was a one-punch affair and Charlie Neal threw that one from the floor. Hoak went down, rolled over and the peacemakers didn't let him and Neal together again. After that, people started to wonder just how mean and tough Hoak really was.

Hoak came up the hard way, and it was a tough road to get to the majors, which might explain his pugnacious posture. He broke into the Dodgers farm system in 1947, following a trial in pro boxing and a hitch in the Marines. He bounced around the minors for seven years — Valdosta, Nashua, Greenville, Fort Worth, Montreal, St. Paul and Montreal again — before making the parent club in 1954. The Dodgers traded him to the Chicago Cubs in 1956 and the Cubs traded him to the Cincinnati Reds in 1957. He came to the Pirates in 1959.

Somebody once caught Hoak peeking to see if everybody was watching him brood into his locker. This tactic was branded "Hoak-um."

Even if he may not have been as tough as he wanted everybody to believe, he was quite a competitor and a real plus for the Pirates.

The best indicator of his contribution at third base and in the dugout was revealed by the voting for the National League's MVP in 1960.

Dick Groat, who played alongside Hoak at shortstop, was the top vote-getter, of course, but Hoak finished second in the voting by the Baseball Writers of America. After Hoak, in order, came Willie Mays, Ernie Banks, Lindy McDaniel, Ken Boyer, Vernon Law and Roberto Clemente.

Clemente coming in eighth in the voting still makes one wonder what the baseball writers were thinking about when they filled out their ballots, but they obviously had a high regard for Hoak, and he was no angel when it came to conversing with reporters so he was hardly a political pick.

He was described by Jack Quinlan on the network radio broadcast of the 1960 World Series as "the scrappy ex-Marine and former professional fighter." He would have approved.

He was regarded as a real red-ass by opposing players. He liked his reputation for being hard-nosed. Pitchers could not back him off the plate no matter how many times they leveled him with pitches at his head. Some thought he was overly aggressive. Some thought he was the team's MVP.

Hoak batted .282 and had 79 RBIs in 1960. He batted a career-high .298 with 61 RBIs in 1961.

His value to the Pirates was appreciated by the majority of his teammates.

Groat, for one, said of Hoak in my interview with him: "He was nail-tough. He never gave up and he was always thinking. Don never let you forget he'd been in the Marines. He was just a complete player, so competitive. He was a real winner."

Les Biederman, the baseball writer for *The Pittsburgh Press*, once wrote, "Don Hoak was one of the stars who made the 1960 Pirates click. He came to the Pirates in a trade from Cincinnati and was a terror. He was a good fielding third baseman, owned a strong arm and was tough in the clutch. Many times early in the 1960 season, he'd say, 'Carry me now, fellows, and I'll make up for it later on,' and he did."

Hoak came to the Pirates in what may have been the best trade ever pulled off by Bucs general manager Joe L. Brown.

On January 31, 1959, Brown sat down with Cincinnati general manager Gabe Paul in a New York hotel room and hammered out a seven-player exchange. Brown swapped slugger Frank Thomas — a homegrown Pittsburgh favorite — utility infielder Jim Pendleton, pinch hitter Johnny Powers and a one-eyed pitcher named Whammy Douglas for third baseman Hoak, catcher Smoky Burgess and pitcher Harvey Haddix.

All three of the players the Pirates picked up were over 30 years of age, which made the trade suspect at first. Burgess was a good hitter, but questionable defensively. Hoak was a fiery player and good third baseman but an ordinary hitter much of his major league career. Haddix had won in double figures, but his win total kept going down each year.

"The 1960 season could not have happened without those three," wrote Biederman.

Brown liked to talk about that trade in later years. As for Hoak, Brown said, "Hoak was a good hitter and a fine defensive third baseman. He finished second in 1960 to Groat as Most Valuable Player, but it was a coin flip. Hoak epitomized blood and guts. From the seventh inning on, there wasn't a better player in baseball, which is why I have always valued him so highly."

Hoak hit .294 in 1959, his best mark to that point. Burgess hit .297 and Haddix, of course, made baseball history that year by pitching 12 perfect innings one night in May in Milwaukee. It was Hoak who booted a ball to lead off the 13th that broke the spell, ala Jose Lind in the 1992 playoff finale with the Atlanta Braves. "Poor Hoakie. . .," Haddix says now in recalling that night in 1959.

"He waited in the clubhouse a long time after the game that night, and rode back in a cab with me to our hotel. He never apologized, but I didn't expect him to, either. He said, 'I made the error tonight, and I've made other errors. But I'll make a lot of good plays for you, too.' And I said, 'You're right, buddy.' And that was the end of it."

Hoak was a catalyst for the Pirates for a few seasons. He was good for the Pirates, and the Pirates brought out the best in Hoak.

"I'd say Don Hoak was the difference," said Vernon Law, looking back on that 1960 season. "He was the backbone. He had that fighting spirit that rubbed off on everyone. He just wouldn't let us lose."

Brown, during an interview for this book, was talking about the infamous incident in the seventh game of the 1960 World Series, when an apparent double play ball off the bat of Bill Virdon took a bad hop and hit Yankees shortstop Tony Kubek in the Adam's apple, and left him gasping for air on the hard infield surface, and permitted the Bucs to stay alive.

"Hoak always said till the day he died that 'if that sonuvabitch had charged the ball like he was supposed to, it never would have taken that bounce into his throat,' " recalled Brown. "Don thought you should charge everything. That's the way he lived."

Brown brought up another story about Hoak.

"Hoak was at a party in 1960 when he split his toe on a swimming pool ladder," said Brown. "A doctor who was there inserted eight stitches, but Hoak never told Murtaugh. He just continued to play day in and day out — he never even limped. Guys in the clubhouse said you could see the blood in his shoes after a game. But Don never missed a one.

"You won't find that competitive spirit in today's ballplayers, and Hoak wasn't making anywhere near a million dollars."

Hoak was at that party along with several other Pirates, notably Bob Friend, Bill Virdon and Gino Cimoli.

Hoak took the stitches without anesthesia. He played a doubleheader the next day against the Cardinals. "I was not going to let it knock me out of the lineup at a time like that," said Hoak in reflecting on the incident during the World Series.

Don Hoak

Popping champagne at '60 World Series celebration.

Don Hoak

Pirates third baseman and his wife, singer Jill Corey.

Asked who his most intriguing teammate was, ElRoy Face, said it was Hoak, who had been his roommate.

"I played alongside a lot of guys with natural talent." offered Face. "Don Hoak had only about 75 percent ability, but he gave 120 percent on the field and made himself a good ballplayer."

"He kept everybody stirred up, and on their toes."
—Harvey Haddix

Haddix knew Hoak as well as any of the Pirates because he had previously played with him in Cincinnati. "He wanted to put on a tough act, but he wasn't near as tough as his act," said Haddix, when I visited his home in Springfield, Ohio in mid-April, 1993. "He had soft spots.

"My wife and I used to baby-sit for his kids when he was in Cincinnati. He was married to Phyllis back then, a girl from his hometown in Pennsylvania, and we watched their kids when we were at spring training in Tampa, Florida. In 1960, he was getting divorced from her and dating Jill Corey, the singer. We met them in Pittsburgh at one of the Old Timers Games."

"What did Hoak bring to the Pirates?" I asked Haddix.

"Fire," said Haddix, without hesitation. "He kept everybody stirred up, and on their toes. He did a pretty good job hitting, too. His main contribution was fire. People talk about leaders, and we had several on that team. Hoak. Groat. Clemente. Clemente wasn't a star yet, but he was becoming a star and everyone could see that. Virdon could be a leader. Same was true of Vernon Law. We had a bunch of good hard-nosed guys."

Hoak liked to have a good time, too. Away from the ballpark, nobody had more fun.

"Back during the '60 season, Hal Smith, Harvey Haddix and I used to sit around the clubhouse after games playing guitars and singing," Hoak once recalled. "We ended up singing at a rally before the Series.

"When the Series was over, Hal and I got a request — through Bob Prince — to do a weekend show at the Holiday House in Monroeville. We were invited to go on the Perry Como Show."

"He gave so much of himself. . . he brought other people along with him."
—Gene Mauch

On November 28, 1962, Joe Brown traded Hoak to the Phillies for Pancho Herrera and Ted Savage. During that same off-season, Brown dealt away shortstop Dick Groat and first baseman Dick Stuart in a house-cleaning series of trades. Hoak played the 1963 season with the Phillies,

436

and just six games in 1964 before he was released. Hoak was hot about his dismissal from the Phillies, even though he had been struggling.

Though Hoak rejected an offer to take another job in the organization from the Phillies, and criticized the club, Gene Mauch, the Phillies manager, remained a big booster of Hoak.

"As a player," Mauch told Philadelphia writers, "he had fierce pride. He was so tireless in his performance. He gave so much of himself . . . he brought people along with him.

"I've seen him work up a 'mad' like nobody else. The only player I know of personally who does it any more is Jim Bunning. Bunning starts getting mad at 3:30 in the afternoon for a night game.

"Everybody realizes Hoak is a fine baseball mind. One day he intends to be a manager. The only thing people will be watching is whether or not he exhibits the self control I know he has."

When Hoak was released by Mauch, he fired a final salvo at the sports writers who cover the Phillies as "caustic, cryptic, cynical and unfair." He gave everything he had, he said, "every day, every game, every step." He was 36 when his career came to an end.

He lost the job at third base to a rookie named Richie Allen. Ask Allen what he remembers about Hoak, and he would say, "He was always staring at me. Always glaring at me."

Hoak returned to Pittsburgh and spent the 1965 and 1966 seasons working with Bob Prince and Jim Woods in the broadcast booth for Pirates games.

Hoak ended up changing his mind about his negative feelings for the Phillies, and accepted a job as coach of the Phillies for the summer of 1967.

Hoak became the manager of the Phillies farm club at Salem, Virginia the following year. His Salem club won a championship and Hoak was named Manager of the Year in the Carolina League. He had an eye on returning to Pittsburgh. The Pirates chief scout, Bob Whalen, said to him, "The only thing better than you is your wife."

His wife was singer Jill Corey, whom he married on December 27, 1961.

"Yeah," said Hoak, "but she can't manage."

Hoak went to Columbus in 1969 to manage the Pirates' farm team — the Columbus Jets. He was hoping to get the Pirates job the following year when Larry Shepard was let go. Brown brought back Danny Murtaugh instead and Hoak, ironically, died of a heart attack the same day after chasing some kids who had stolen his car.

"It was too late.
His heart had stopped."
—Dr. Mort Aronson

Hoak died under the most unusual circumstances. He died on October 9, 1969, the same day he learned that the Pirates were bringing back

Danny Murtaugh to manage the team for the following summer. Hoak had hoped that he would get the job.

Hoak died within hours after he and the town learned he was not the Pirates' choice. He said he had resigned from the Pirates' organization in an apparent dispute with Joe Brown over the manager's job with the Pirates. But Brown says today that this is not true. Hoak was struck down by a heart attack as he chased a car thief through the streets of Shadyside the same day the Pirates were announcing Murtaugh was back during a party aboard the Gateway Clipper.

Miles Span of Monroeville, who hung around with *Post-Gazette* sports editor Al Abrams and his cronies, as well as several of the Pirates, says he spoke to Hoak that morning at a breakfast meeting in the Carlton House Hotel.

Dr. Morton Aronson, one of the most loyal sports fans in Pittsburgh, was the first person to find Hoak after he died. Aronson has season tickets for the Pirates — front row center, directly behind home plate — and the Penguins and Steelers. He is a psychiatrist.

"In '69, I was living in the Amberson Towers on Bayard Road," Aronson said. "Our garage entrance was at the end of Bayard, across from the Winchester-Thurston girls school. One day I was coming home, and was going into the garage. I heard commotion outside, and I saw some people crowding around a car in the street. I went over to the car, and there was a man slumped over the wheel. I recognized him right away. It was Don Hoak. I tried C.P.R. Coincidentally enough, there was another fellow trying to help as well, and he was the son of Frank Scott, who had been a manager for one of Jock Sutherland's football teams at Pitt, and went to New York when Sutherland was coaching the Brooklyn Dodgers in pro football, and then became a public relations assistant for the Yankees. He ended up being one of the very first agents in sports. He started booking Mickey Mantle and people like that for appearances, and stuff like that. But his son and I couldn't do Don Hoak any good. It was too late. His heart had stopped.

"They took him to Shadyside Hospital where he was pronounced dead. His wife, Jill Corey, had a sister who lived around the corner from my apartment. I went to see his sister-in-law and tell her what I had witnessed, and offered my sympathy. She was appreciative. That's when I learned that somebody had stolen his car earlier in the day, and that he borrowed his sister-in-law's car because he somehow learned who had his car. He only got around the corner — a short block from her apartment — when he had a heart attack.

"It bothered me. I cared about these guys. I got in on the ground floor when they opened Three Rivers Stadium, and I still have seats in the first row directly behind home plate. The row is called AA. It's like being in the batter's box. You can talk to them when they're coming to bat.

"My father took me to the 1927 World Series, that's how far back I go with the Pirates," Dr. Aronson said in March of 1993, when asked to recount his discovery of a dead Don Hoak. "I've had season tickets for the Pirates ever since the 1960 season. Well, what happened in '60 prompted me to buy season tickets starting in 1961.

Don Hoak accepts champagne toast from Mayor Joe Barr.

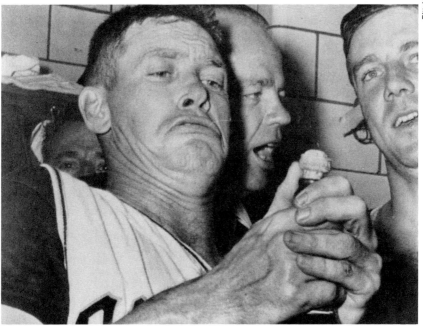

Hoak pops champagne as sportscaster Ray Scott and Bob Friend look on.

"I belonged to a special ticket club before then, and shared box seats on the third base side. When they had the '60 World Series, the Pirates wanted those seats for VIPs. So they put us up in seats on the roof, behind third base. I remember sitting in this box with my wife and the headmaster of Shady Side Academy; I don't remember his name. But I was there when Maz hit the home run and I'll never forget that."

"To me, baseball is war."
—Don Hoak

Hoak once told Myron Cope a whopper of a story for *Sport* in 1964 about the occasion in 1951 when Hoak claimed that Fidel Castro, while still a student, attempted to pitch against him. Castro threw hard and wild, and Hoak fouled off two pitches and perceived that a hit might cause a riot. So he had an umpire remove Castro and his supporters from the field before there was a confrontation. Even Hoak knew there were some times when it was best not to fight.

"Castro had two strikes on me and he was stomping pompously around the mound as though he had just conquered Washington, D.C."

At that point, however, a new factor entered the picture. The Hoak temper.

"I've got a wee trace of Comanche blood . . . I imagine I have a temper that can match any Latin's from Havana to Lima," he told Cope. "To me, baseball is war. In 1956, I played ball in the Dominican Republic, where I pleased the fans by hitting .394 and sliding into bases like a maniac. I am known there . . . as Crazy Horse. When I played for Pittsburgh, a broadcaster there named me The Tiger. Mind you, I don't care to fight Castro and three hundred Cubans under any circumstances, but if I have a bat in my hands, I know I won't be the only guy to get hurt."

In another story, Cope called Hoak "a former middleweight boxer who stalks in livid rage to the mound and censures his own pitchers in language that would raise the hair on a seal."

Hoak was what they call a "gamer" in sports parlance. That sobriquette is best explained by Tom Boswell, who wrote, "Baseball has a name for a player who, in the eyes of his peers, is well attuned to the demands of his discipline; he is called a 'gamer.' The gamer may scream and curse when his mates show the first hint of laziness, but he makes jokes and laughs naturally in the seventh game of the Series."

Where Were You?

"People were blowing whistles,
and everybody was so happy."
—Jim Walther

Tom Calamarino
Penn Hills
"It was either 1961 or 1962, and I was 11 or 12 at the time, and I was with my friend Gary Chick. His father and sister took us to a Pirates game. We sat on the third base side. His dad knew we were big Roberto Clemente fans. He tipped an usher a few extra bucks and we got seats up in right field by the foul pole in the upper deck. Clemente had 1,997 hits going into the game, and he needed three to reach the 2,000 hits mark. As we were driving in, I kept telling everyone that we were going to catch his 2,000th hit. 'He's going to hit a home run,' we were hollering in the back seat of the car, 'and we're going to catch it.' Clemente singled in the first, and then he got a double later on. He came up again, in about the fifth inning, I think, and he hit a home run. The ball bounced behind us, and this big guy dove for the ball, but Gary got it. The usher came up and talked to his dad, and took the ball. He said he would be back when the game was over and take us to the clubhouse. When we went in, I saw Maz on the training table. Clemente was getting dressed. He looked like black granite. Gary had his picture taken with Clemente. They gave him a ball signed by the players. And I was in the clubhouse. It was my first experience to be close to major league players like that."

Jim Walther
Scott Township
"I'm 39 now, so I was six years old in 1960. I was in the first grade at St. Paul's Cathedral Grade School. I lived on Oakland Avenue, so I walked by Forbes Field on the way to and from school every day. We got out of school around 3:15 that day, and we were close to Forbes Field when Maz hit that home run. The ballpark erupted. Horns started sounding. There was complete bedlam. We ran home because we knew something big had happened. Baseball was important in our house. My mother used to keep score of the night games for me, and give me this sheet at breakfast so I'd know what happened. My father took me into the middle of Oakland that night, up around Gus Miller's Newsstand, and Frankie Gustine's Restaurant. My dad, whose name is also Jim, wanted me to see what it was like when a Pittsburgh team wins a championship. People were blowing whistles and everybody was so happy. My dad said you didn't know when it might ever happen again. As it turned out, it was 11 years before we'd win a World Series again. It was great growing up in Oakland at that time. We used to stop at

441

Webster Hall on the way home from school, and there'd be ballplayers from the opposing teams in the hotel lobby. We'd check our bubble gum cards and recognize some of them and go ask them for their autographs. We had so many autographs. I've been lucky to grow up in Pittsburgh. I worked at the Allegheny Club at Three Rivers Stadium when I was a college student, and I've seen a lot. We'd had it great here. The Pirates won the World Series twice. Pitt — my alma mater — won the national football championship. The Steelers won four Super Bowls. It's been great."

Carol Helsey
At Monroeville Mall

"I was a student at St. Paul's Cathedral in Oakland, and they let us out early. We went over to Forbes Field for the late innings, and they let us in to see the game. My father, Dave Steele, who is now 82 and living in Swissvale, was the assistant manager back then at the Pittsburgh Athletic Association. He worked at the P.A.A. for 47 years. Bob Prince came walking in to the P.A.A. after the game, and he said to my dad, 'Hey, how'd we win that game anyhow?' My dad said, 'Maz hit the homer!' And Prince replied, 'Oh, no, I just treated him in the locker room like he was the team batboy!' I walked home from Forbes Field to Squirrel Hill because there was no way to get a street car. The street cars couldn't get out of town."

Scene outside Forbes Field, at corner of Bouquet and Sennott, in front of Tom & Jerry and Home Plate Cafe, during 1960 World Series.

Joey Diven
A tough guy with a big heart

*"The trick is growing up
without growing old."*
—Casey Stengel

*"If the world were perfect
it wouldn't be."*
—Yogi Berra

Joey Diven is a Damon Runyon character out of Oakland rather than Broadway. In his heyday, Diven was more likely to be found at Forbes Field rather than Times Square.

Billy Conn called him "Big Joey," which sounds a lot like Big Julie, one of the unforgettable characters along with Nathan Detroit in *Guys and Dolls*, the Broadway musical based on the characters chronicled in Runyon's popular newspaper column.

Diven did make it to New York in his youth where he met Frank Leahy, the legendary football coach at Notre Dame, and became a fan of the Fighting Irish forever, and he spent time with Toots Shor, the off-Broadway barkeeper. But he was more at home in Oakland.

He loved Forbes Field. "That was like my own house," he said when I spoke to him in mid-April of 1993. "You knew where everything was."

He palled around with several of the Pirates, and helped John "Hoolie" Hallahan, the team's equipment manager in the clubhouse at Forbes Field. Diven, indeed, was the doorman or bouncer at the clubhouse door after the seventh game of the 1960 World Series, making sure no one got in who didn't belong. Diven decided who belonged. So people like Mayor Joe Barr and Bishop John Wright were admitted. Hallahan, who hailed from "The Run" in nearby Greenfield and started his association with the Pirates as the visiting club batboy in 1941, knew he could trust Diven to do the job.

No one was going to mess with Diven. Diven was the doorman at the Irish Club for years, and they still tell stories about some of his skirmishes at the second-story joint, and how he pitched intruders and drunks head-first down the wooden stairs that were steeper than the Duquesne Incline.

Diven was voted in as constable in Oakland that same year. It was the first time he ever won an election. "It was the first time anyone had beaten 'the machine' to win there," Diven recalled proudly.

Art Rooney called him "Big Shot." The Steelers owner was always a political pundit, and he liked to poke fun at Diven and his difficulties in trying to get elected to public office, or to hold a job in Pittsburgh.

443

Rooney was close to Conn, and Conn and Diven were often a parlay as visitors to Rooney's office at the Steelers headquarters. Conn was called "America's Guest," and Diven didn't miss many social occasions, sans invitations or tickets, either.

"I always see you bringing your horses in," said Rooney in race track parlance, "but I never see you walk away with a winner. I never see you going to the window to collect."

Al Abrams called Diven a Dapper Dan with great frequency in the notes section at the bottom of his *Post-Gazette* sports column. Diven was among the regulars in the dot-dash world of local sports characters.

"Joey Diven was something special," recalls former Pirates pitcher Bob Purkey. "He was the only guy who had no money, no job, no income, and yet he showed up at every big event in the country. Every place you'd go, Joey Diven would be there. He was a beaut."

Some people, especially those who suffered his insults or punches, called him other less-flattering names.

Diven was always where the action was in Pittsburgh, but that was when he was hale and hearty and full of himself, one of the most feared street fighters in the city. Indeed, he was once profiled in a national magazine piece by Pittsburgh writer Roy McHugh as "the world's greatest streetfighter."

McHugh recalls today that Diven was a great interview. "He had a great memory for stories, and he could tell them well," said McHugh, who lives in an apartment on Mt. Washington with a good view of The Golden Triangle and Three Rivers Stadium. "I thought he was an entertaining fellow, friendly and a good story-teller. When Frank DeFord did a piece on Conn for *Sports Illustrated,* Diven was his main source. Now that he has those physical problems, he tries to make you think he doesn't worry or take life too seriously. He has a black humor. He tells people he's lost one leg, and he's working on the other. His lines are funnier when he says them than they may come off on paper."

Diven does not get around much anymore. He finally came up against a foe he couldn't handle — diabetes — and he lost his right leg to it in an operation in 1991, as well as much of the 280 pounds he once carried with great swagger on his wide 6-3 frame. In his day, Diven's back rivaled some billboards around Pittsburgh. When he was sick, Diven dropped down to as low as 170 pounds, but was back up to 218 when I talked to him.

"I can't hobble around on that cement over at the stadium; it's too hard," said Diven. "I watch the Pirates when they're on TV. I'm still rooting for them."

He palled around with Billy Conn when Conn was the light heavyweight boxing champion of the world, and they remained close friends.

Conn, once one of the most celebrated and popular pugilists anywhere, wasn't himself, either.

"He's 75, going on 76 real soon, and he's got Alzheimer's Disease real bad," said Diven, who is 63. "He's been in Veterans Hospital out in the East End for the past six months. I went to see him a month ago."

Joyous clubhouse lineup includes, left to right, John Hallahan, Bill Virdon, Joey Diven, Danny Whelan, Dr. Joseph Finegold, Don Hoak, Bill Mazeroski, Joe Brown and Dick Groat.

Two of Pittsburgh's all-time sports legends, Art Rooney and Billy Conn, check out photo showing Conn getting the best of Joe Louis in the first of their celebrated boxing bouts.

That was in March, 1993, just before St. Patrick's Day, a holiday that Conn and Diven always enjoyed to the hilt. Not this time. Diven went to visit Conn in the company of Billy Neumont, the second-best boxer ever to grow up in Garfield — a few furlongs behind the best, Harry Greb. (*Conn would die May 29, a month after I discussed his situation with Diven*). "With my leg gone, I need help to get around, and Billy Neumont called and said he'd pick me up if I wanted to go out and see Conn," recalled Diven.

Billy Neumont is a story in himself. He went out to visit Conn on several occasions, usually in the company of another ex-boxer, Ray Connelly. Neumont is a storied character, a legend in Garfield where he operates a carpet store on Penn Avenue.

Like the Pirates, Neumont made his mark in 1960, too. He did it on St. Patrick's Day, following a Downtown parade. They still tell the story about how he took a joyride in a fire engine — it was from Penn Hills and was parked outside a bar in Garfield following a parade — and drove it around his neighborhood until he failed to make a turn and crashed the truck into the front of his parish church, St. Lawrence O'Toole.

"I was loaded, and I didn't know what I was doing," recalled Neumont. "The priests weren't too happy with me. For years after that, my buddies would call my house in the middle of the night, and tell my wife, Betty, 'Get the captain up, there's a fire out on Frankstown Avenue!' I never heard the end of that."

Neumont was 31 back in 1960. He said that whenever he accompanied Conn, and his brother Jacky Conn, and Diven to New York, that Billy would build up all his friends. "He'd be talking to Toots Shor, and he'd tell stories about us," said Neumont. "He made us bigger than we were. He made it possible for us to feel comfortable in their company.

"Let's face it. Billy Conn and Joey Diven were larger than life in their day. Billy was a world champion, and Joey had a street-smartness about him, a charisma that attracted people. Big-shots would come to town, and the first guy they'd call to join them would be Joey Diven."

Neumont, who makes his home in Gibsonia these days, was asked what it was like to see Conn and Diven reunited at the Veterans Hospital. "It was a moving scene," said Neumont. "Billy is just a shell of himself, and he doesn't recognize anybody. But as soon as he walked in this side room where we were sitting, he said, 'Hi, Joey.' I couldn't believe he recognized him."

Earlier, I had asked Diven about seeing Conn at the hospital.

"Did he recognize you?" I asked Diven.

"He did," said Diven. "He said, 'Hi, Joey,' and then he went blank. He knew me, but he didn't know Billy Neumont at all. He's in bad shape. He weighs about 98 pounds. It's terrible."

"Does it hurt you," I said, "to see him like that?"

"It did. They can say what they want, but Billy was a helluva guy," said Diven. "He didn't want too many people around him. He didn't like people asking him for autographs, or bothering him. He didn't like people patting him on the back, and pestering him for favors, or getting in his face. He never showed up on two occasions when they were giving him awards at the Dapper Dan sports banquet. He knew he was special, but he was a good guy. He liked having me around, to keep the crowd off him."

I asked Joey how he handled his own situation, losing a leg. He is unable to drive an automobile, and he relies on other people to get from here to there. "I'm OK," said Joey. "Quitters never win, and winners never quit."

I mentioned to Diven that he had also served as a bodyguard or traveling companion with other celebrities or heavyweights who visited Pittsburgh.

"Oh, yeah, I looked after Bing Crosby, Pat O'Brien, Edward Bennett Williams, Joe Louis, guys like that, when they came here," said Diven.

Two days before I interviewed Diven, he had spent time with another old friend, Eddie Mathews, a Hall of Fame third baseman and home run hitter for the Braves — in Boston, Milwaukee and Atlanta — who was a favorite in their days at Forbes Field. They had gotten together at the Airport Holiday Inn.

Diven used to socialize with Mathews, as well as Henry Aaron, whenever the Braves came to Pittsburgh. Mathews was in town this time to sign autographs at a card and sports memorabilia show at Robert Morris College in Coraopolis, near Pittsburgh International Airport. When Aaron appeared at a similar sports card show at Duquesne University's A.J. Palumbo Center a year earlier, I saw Diven sitting behind Aaron as he was signing autographs. "He called me and asked me to sit with him," said Diven. "Henry and I are pretty tight."

Mathews was in a weekend lineup that included four former members of that 1960 Pirates world championship team, namely Bob Friend, Vernon Law, Vinegar Bend Mizell and Gino Cimoli, as well as Hall of Famers Willie Stargell and Johnny Mize, plus the Penguins' Kevin Stevens. (Mize died less than two months later.)

"When I walked across the floor, moving on my wooden leg," said Diven, "Mathews said, 'You do pretty good on that.' I said, 'Yeah, if you had the wood I have in my leg you'd have hit 600 home runs.' And he said, 'If I had stayed away from you, I would have been able to play another five years in the league.' We had a good time; it was great to see him again."

"I saw Mathews three years ago," I said, "when he participated in the 30th anniversary reunion of the 1960 Pirates. He played in their Old Timers Game. I always thought he was much bigger, and I was surprised at his size. He was smaller than I thought he would be."

"He used to be bigger than he is now," said Diven. "He's had some health problems. He was big through the shoulders. He could hit that ball a ton."

"If he has health problems," I asked, "why is he still smoking cigarettes?"

447

"Hoak was always on the muscle, but he couldn't fight his way out of a paper bag."
— Joe O'Toole

Harvey Haddix, who was one of Diven's favorites, told me a story when I visited him a week earlier at his home in Springfield, Ohio. Haddix spoke about an incident involving Diven and Don Hoak, which points up that Hoak — as tough as he thought he was — knew when to call for help. There was a restaurant a block from Forbes Field on the corner of Forbes and Bouquet, catty-corner from where the Original Hot Dog is today, called The Clock. Hoak got manhandled there one night, while playing cards upstairs with the usual occupants of the place. "Hoak got drunk and caused some trouble, and they gave him a hard time," said Haddix.

Hoak came back the next day with Diven.

"He used to hang around with Hoak and Cimoli, and I'd see him down at the Carlton House," Haddix said of Diven.

The way Haddix heard it, "Diven walked around the restaurant, under the anxious eyes of the Greek gentleman who owned the place. The man kept asking Joey, 'What do you want?' And Joey just ignored him and proceeded to tear a chandelier down from the ceiling, knock over potted plants, and turn the bar over on its side. He left the place in shambles. Then he and Hoak walked out." All that was missing were swinging doors to complete the scene.

"I broke the joint up pretty good," said Diven, when I asked him about that incident. "They'd given Don some shit in there one night. That 'Tiger' business went to Don's head. Bob Prince blew him up as a tough guy, and Hoak began to believe that he really was tough."

Diven had once turned a telephone booth on its side with someone inside it just a block away at the Oakland Cafe. He had also once beaten up a half dozen Pitt football players on the eve of a game in Oakland. One of the football players had made the mistake of roughing up one of Diven's Oakland buddies a few days earlier.

Diven got tired of defending his title as the toughest guy in Pittsburgh. "Those stories about me fighting five and six guys at a time are exaggerated," he said back in 1965 in an earlier interview. "I've never started a fight in my life . . . but I don't take any crap, either."

At the time, Diven was a handsome 35-year-old giant of an Irishman. He stood 6-3, weighed 280 and had a 19-inch neck. "I always stuck up for the underdog," he said for an interview I had with him for *Pittsburgh Weekly Sports*. "I've fought for the little guy all my life."

No one ever described Don Hoak as an underdog, and the only time Billy Conn was considered such was when he fought Joe Louis twice for the world's heavyweight title. Yet Diven put up his dukes on their behalf a few times.

They still remember the night Diven tore up the Gaslight, a dining club in Shadyside. He was there with Conn, and a patron got belligerent with Conn, as customers are prone to do whenever a boxer or a football player like Jack Lambert would belly up to the bar. Like Lambert, Conn didn't suffer smartasses too well. It didn't take much to set him off. These challengers had all seen too many western movies. Diven decked the bouncer at the club that night, and belted a TV announcer who said something he didn't like, and left the announcer with a nine-stitch gash.

A few years later, Conn escaped Mexico after refereeing a fight that ended in a riot, and told his hometown friends, "I sure wish I had Big Joey with me down there. We'd have banged a few heads together."

Conn was always trying to convince Diven to become a professional boxer, but to no avail. Diven preferred working without ropes and rules to restrain his style. "I'm not a good fighter, and I never had the desire," said Diven, begging off. "If someone bothers me, I'll bother them. That's my philosophy."

One time Diven bought a Shetland pony for $50 and led it down the mainstreet of Oakland and into a cocktail spot called the Cardinal Lounge. The pony promptly ruined the rug and ate all the plants, and the Joey Diven legend had a new chapter.

The same week, however, Diven took some Korean visitors home for dinner because "President Kennedy said we should do that sort of thing. It sends them home with a higher regard for us. I don't think there's enough harmony in The Great Society."

Diven always dressed his best, and had political connections. He also had political aspirations, but never was able to parlay them into the kind of respectable office he wanted to hold when he got older and more mature, and less frisky as far as street fights were concerned.

He did become a constable and later a county detective. He left the latter job to become a salesman for the Duquesne Brewery. Later on, he sold Schmidt's beer.

He ran unsuccessfully for the position of prothonotary in County government.

"I just did that to jag off Pete Joyce," recalled Diven. "He'd gotten rid of so many of us in county offices in the Monday Morning Massacre. I was working in the prothonotary's office when I got fired. I wanted to get back at him and spoil things for him. I didn't really work hard at getting out the vote; I didn't put a full-court press on."

When he was a detective, Diven single-handedly broke up the nasty business of winos buying beer for Oakland teenagers. His methods: "Constant harassment and a bust in the mouth!" He also put a crimp in the pill racket using the same methods.

He was often seen close by celebrity visitors to Pittsburgh. They felt safer with Diven on their side, and he scared off some would-be intruders. He was the perfect bodyguard. He was a big Notre Dame fan — it was part of his faith and upbringing in Oakland to root for The Fighting Irish; besides he liked their nickname — and he was often seen on the sideline looking after the well-being of the Irish coach.

He has been a fan ever since he met Frank Leahy at Yankee Stadium when Joey was just 18 years old. Leahy liked him, and the Notre Dame coach allowed Joey to sit on the Notre Dame bench for years after that. "He was warm to me," recalled Joey. "That's all that counts as far as I'm concerned." Not too many people ever described Leahy as being warm.

Diven liked to bounce back and forth between the Oakland Cafe and Pete Coyne's Shamrock Room whenever Notre Dame was playing a game that was on national TV. "There won't be too many guys there in uniform," said Diven, describing the scene on game day at those Oakland institutions, "but they'll all be playing. There will be more cheering and more confetti, and the girls will be there in their St. Patrick's Day finery. It should be some show."

I recall that Conn and Diven were at the bar in Coyne's when I went there one night with a group of friends when I was saying goodbye to them before moving to Miami in 1969. My friends were excited to see a former boxing champion, but I begged them to keep their distance. I didn't want any trouble. I didn't want my parting shot from Pittsburgh to be the fist of Conn or Diven. We smiled at them and they smiled back.

You would find Joey on the Steelers bench, in the Pirates locker room, in the classiest restaurants, at political and sports banquets. "Everybody liked Joey," said Joe O'Toole, the former assistant to Pirates general manager Joe L. Brown. "He was not only friendly with the Pirates, but with guys like Henry Aaron and Eddie Mathews of the Braves. He hung out with them when they were in town."

O'Toole, also an Oakland native, remembered the incident at the Gaslight, but drew a blank on the mayhem at The Clock, but he could appreciate how it could happen. "Hoak was always on the muscle," said O'Toole, "and he couldn't fight his way out of a paper bag. The guy who owned The Clock had a room upstairs which he kept open for card games after-hours. Hoak used to go there, I know that. They'd go to the Young Men's Thinking Club, the Greek Club, the Irish Club, the Sandscratchers, and a few other late-night spots. There were guys from Oakland who liked to take shots at them, make a name for themselves. It wasn't a bad idea to have Diven with you."

Most people think Diven lived in Oakland most of his early life. In fact, his family was living on Dawson Street, about eight blocks from Forbes Field, when he was born. But they moved soon after to Sheraden. The Divens didn't return to Oakland until Joey was 16. He attended Washington Vocational High School in Lawrenceville, alongside the 40th Street Bridge. "Another battleground in my life," recalled Diven.

While Diven lost a leg to diabetes, he did not lose his sense of humor.

Before he went into the operating table, he told the doctor, "Hey, Doc, save my leg and we'll give it to my father-in-law. He can have Leg of Diven for dinner tonight. He can chew something besides my ass for a change."

Haddix recalled that Diven did not look so good the last time he saw him, that he appeared to be in ill health, and had lost a lot of weight. I had the same impression.

Diven doesn't get around too well anymore. "Come on over and see me," he said, when I called him on the telephone. "I'm on my ass here; I'm not going anywhere."

Diven shows up for funerals from time to time, usually involving guys from Forbes Field or Forbes Avenue, more often than he would like. But he is at home on Woodburn Avenue in Brookline. He lives in a white-gray house across from a white public school, and a house once occupied by Madalyn O'Hair. "She was the world's biggest atheist," howled Diven. "Imagine me living where Madalyn O'Hair once lived."

At one of the more recent funerals he attended, he had a reunion with the likes of Jim Lally, who grew up in Oakland with him and is now an official with the Stadium Authority at Three Rivers, "Ditty" Rittmeyer, Tom "Maniac" McDonough and "Switch" Joyce, among others. The funeral mass was at St. Rosalia's in Greenfield.

The deceased was Jimmy Newell, who had worked for many years as a policeman for Gus Krop in Schenley Park. He was the cousin of John Newell, who owned the Oakland Cafe. "Jimmy had just one eye," said McDonough, "but it was always between him and Joey as to who was the toughest guy in Oakland."

Damon Runyon would have recognized the scene.

"That Ditty was the all-time scaler of the wall at Forbes Field," said Diven. "No one went up the side and over the roof of Forbes Field more often than he did. He had all the records. He went up that wall like an ant."

Runyon would have appreciated seeing Joey joining his 23-year-old son, Michael — "isn't he the spitting image of me?" — at his political campaign headquarters in a storefront on Brookline Boulevard. Michael was campaigning for his district's seat on City Council. He is one of three sons of Joey and the former Barbara Long, who has been married to Joey for 26 years.

"She's a wonderful woman," said McDonough. "She deserves to be canonized."

Diven was doing his best to stir up support for his son. McDonough said he had made his contribution to the fund, though Michael Diven was a decided under-dog in a five man race. The election was less than a month away. Young Diven would finish third in the voting.

"Diven for City Council!" Joey would say whenever he answered a telephone call.

Diven took time out, however, to discuss his beloved Bucs of that 1960 season.

"I could go wherever I wanted at Forbes Field," he said. "You could see the different guys: the ones who knew their baseball, and the ones who didn't know a damn thing about baseball. You knew where the good guys were; you knew where the jagoffs were. You could take your pick where you wanted to sit."

When I asked Diven to name his favorite Pirates from that team, he said, "Billy Virdon and Harvey Haddix. I liked the way Billy moved, the way he handled himself in the field. Off the field, he never looked for nothing. He wasn't a floater. He didn't say, 'I'm a ballplayer and you owe me a drink.' And The Kitten was a good guy.

"I remember The Kitten coming to me after the seventh game of that 1960 World Series, and saying, 'Joey, please, before they steal everything, will you wrap up all my stuff and hide it?' So I rolled up his uniform, spikes, glove and ballcap, and put them all away. Guys were taking everything that wasn't nailed down, and some were taking stuff that was nailed down. It was some scene.

"Hey, I've had an interesting life," declared Diven, as I was leaving. "I met people from Toots Shor to Eddie Arcaro. I wouldn't want to do it over any other way."

Two of Pittsburgh's toughest Irishmen, Billy Conn and Joey Diven, sit together at ringside.

Harvey Haddix
He was perfect for 12 innings

"You can't go home again."
—Thomas Wolfe

"Who the hell said that?
That's a bunch of crap."
—Harvey Haddix

I departed Pittsburgh at 7:30 a.m. on April 12, 1993, the day after Easter, and headed for the home of Harvey Haddix in Springfield, Ohio. He said it would take me four hours. His directions were short and simple. Take 79 South, he said, and get on 70 West going toward Wheeling, and stay on 70 all the way to Springfield. His home was about four blocks from 70.

Springfield is 222 miles from Pittsburgh.

Haddix, a little left-handed pitcher, had been one of the heroes of the Pirates championship season in 1960, with wins in the fifth and seventh games of the World Series. He was even better known for pitching 12 perfect innings in a 13-inning setback at Milwaukee the year before.

It remains one of the most talked-about ballgames in sports history.

While in Ohio, I was also going to visit and interview Rocky Nelson, who lives at the southernmost tip of the state in Portsmouth. Nelson shared first base duties with Dick Stuart in the early '60s, and hit a home run in that 1960 World Series and made some sparkling defensive plays.

After I left the Haddix home, I was to go east on 70, take the 270 bypass at Columbus, and get on Rt. 23 south and that would take me right into Portsmouth. Nelson lives about five or six blocks from the highway. He said it would take me about three hours to get to his place from Springfield. His directions were also short and simple.

I thought both of them had to be leaving something out. But the trip went smoothly, like clockwork, and it was an enjoyable way to spend a day, going back in time with two oldtimers who loved to talk about baseball. It was an overcast, gray Monday for the most part, but the sun came out in the afternoon, traffic was light and it was a good driving day.

There were reminders of the past along the way. Shortly after I got onto 70 west, for instance, off to the right I saw the Jessop Steel Company, where Pirates shortstop Dick Groat worked in sales and community relations during his playing days.

Then I saw a sign for Taylortown, just a mile off the road, where the Mel Blount Youth Home is located. There were reports on the radio that Blount, a Hall of Fame defensive back for the Steelers in the '70s,

453

was in trouble with legal officials once more, accused of roughing up some of the troubled boys in excessive disciplinary measures at his Washington County ranch. He was accused of ignoring a court order not to be involved with any disciplinary action. I felt badly for Blount. I had visited the home two years earlier, and thought Blount had the best of intentions, but might have been in over his head.

Wheeling is an hour from my home in the South Hills of Pittsburgh. I saw a new billboard hailing it as the home of Wheeling-Pittsburgh Steel Corporation. Wheeling was as far from home as I ever traveled until I went to school at the University of Pittsburgh in 1960.

Seeing the road signs sparked several personal connections. Wheeling is just across the Ohio River from Bridgeport, Ohio, the hometown of my mother. My oldest brother, Richard, still resides there, as do four nieces and a nephew of mine. Bill Mazeroski was born at Wheeling Hospital, and grew up in nearby Ohio, not far from Bridgeport.

Soon after I crossed the Wheeling Bridge, I saw a billboard off to the left hailing the Ohio Valley as the home area for former basketball star John Havlicek; one of baseball's all-time best brother pitching combinations, Joe and Phil Niekro, football's Bill Jobko, and each of them was pictured on the billboard.

Ohio is so flat compared to Pennsylvania. "Everyone from Pittsburgh says that," said Haddix. It is a drastic difference. The highway is straight, the farm fields are flat. It reminded me of driving across Kansas when I went to Witchita back in 1965 to interview Jim Ryan, the great long-distance runner. There is more sky in Kansas and Ohio than there is in Pennsylvania. One can imagine how easy it was to find ballfields on which to play baseball. "We used to cut them out of the farm field," said Haddix, who lived on a farm most of his life.

As I entered Ohio, I slipped a tape of the seventh game of the 1960 World Series into the casette player in my automobile, to refresh my memory about the details of how Haddix fared in that final game as a relief pitcher in the eighth inning, and to set the mood for my impending interview. There was more memorable action in that eighth inning of the Pirates-Yankees clash than some teams generate in a summer.

I need not have worried. Like most pitchers, Haddix has committed the details to memory. And Haddix is an enthusiastic subject. He is a good talker, and he has a snappy accent. If he needed any help as far as details were concerned, he could go to the huge gameroom in the basement of his pin-neat, spacious ranch home, and check the baseball he retained from that particular game.

Columbus is the capital of Ohio. It is the home of The Ohio State University. I saw the bright red and scarlet gray OSU sweatshirts wherever I traveled in Ohio that day. John W. Galbreath, the millionaire realtor who owned the Pirates when they won the World Series in 1960, 1971 and 1979, once lived there and raised thoroughbred racing horses on his Darby Dan Farm. He and Pittsburgh attorney Tom P. Johnson, Hollywood entertainer Bing Crosby and Frank McKinney of Indianapolis bought the Pirates in 1946. Galbreath soon bought out McKinney and assumed his position as president of the Pirates.

Pirates pitching aces: Vernon Law, Bob Friend and Harvey Haddix

Clubhouse celebration includes ElRoy Face, Bill Mazeroski and Harvey Haddix.

Columbus has outgrown Pittsburgh in population. The Pirates once had their top minor league team there, but since 1979 Columbus has been the home of the New York Yankees farm team. Cooper Stadium, named for a former general manager named Harold Cooper, can be seen from Interstate 70 off to the left on the way to downtown Columbus. It was called Jets Stadium and the team was the Columbus Jets when it was the Pirates top farm team back in 1960.

The Cardinal is the state bird, and Haddix broke into professional baseball with the Columbus Red Birds, then a farm team of the St. Louis Cardinals. He has one of their ballcaps on display in his gameroom.

"I can remember stuff back then even better than I can remember stuff from yesterday."
—Harvey Haddix

One of the most remarkable displays I found in his gameroom, which is full of photos, plaques, pennants, and all sorts of memorabilia and baseball paraphenalia — like the ballcaps from all the teams he has ever been associated with — was a glass-enclosed wall unit that contains a baseball from each of his 136 major league pitching victories. Most of the balls were ones he actually used in those games, but each has the score and other details handwritten in black ink on its rawhide surface. A trainer for the St. Louis Cardinals did the early ones, and Harvey's wife, Marcia, did most of the rest.

The one from his 12 "perfect innings" on May 26, 1959 stands out among the rest. A fan sent Harvey a ball that was done up like one of those hand-painted Ukranian Easter eggs, with a complete box score about the same size as would appear in a newspaper, all done by hand, from that famous game. And the ball was laquered to protect it, so it is shinier than the rest.

Harvey also has a set of 12 silver goblets, with a tray, that was given to him by the National League to honor his achievement. Each goblet contains the names of the three batters he faced in one of the 12 innings, and what they did.

The glove he wore that night is bronzed and displayed in the same case as the three Rawlings' Gold Glove Awards he won in 1959, 1960 and 1961. "I'm real proud of those," he said.

Haddix had a personally autographed and handsomely-framed photo of former President Richard M. Nixon, which he received only two months earlier. "To Harvey Haddix, with best wishes from one of his fans," wrote Nixon.

"Someone told me I was one of President Nixon's favorite ballplayers, so I signed a photo of mine, and sent it to him," said Haddix. "And he sent me this soon after."

There was also a "thank you" plaque that was presented to him by Willie Stargell when Stargell retired. It was signed to "one of the special people."

Haddix had just emptied several boxes worth of photos onto a table in one corner of the room, and allowed me to sift through them. He had personally autographed photos from all his teammates on the St. Louis Cardinals, his first major league team, including several signed by Stan Musial, Enos Slaughter, Harry "The Cat" Brecheen, Red Schoendienst, among others. "Hey, I was a fan myself, and I looked up to these guys when I came up," explained Haddix. "So I wanted their autographs."

He also had 8 x 10s of all his teammates from the 1960 Pirates, the best-looking collection of such photos I had seen in my research. Harvey had a story for each photo I flipped over. I surprised myself by identifying some of the Cardinals on photos that were not autographed, such as Del Rice, Gerry Staley, Ray Jablonski and Dick Sisler, remembering their images somehow from the trading cards I collected as a youngster. It always amazes me how the mind works. I don't remember where I put my car keys, but I can remember those faces. I had not seen those likenesses in nearly 40 years. I was ten when Haddix broke into the big leagues with the Cardinals in 1952.

"I can remember stuff back then even better than I can remember stuff from yesterday," said Haddix, when I told him I could not believe I could remember Gerry Staley.

I made my way about the huge Haddix gameroom, which is like a wing of the Hall of Fame at Cooperstown, New York. The only disturbing aspect of the visit was that Haddix knelt down and steadied himself by holding onto the billiards table for a prolonged period. He was short on breath. He said walking up the steps would take a lot out of him.

Haddix has emphysema. He often has a hard time breathing. He sprayed his throat several times with a hand-held breathalizer gadget.

"I loved cigarettes. They finally got to me. The doc said I was a dead man, but I came back."

As we sat in the living room upstairs for most of the interview, Haddix pointed out a nearby breathing machine, and said he sometimes slept with the aid of an oxygen-producing tank unit in his bedroom. "Some days you can breathe, some days you can't," he said with a shrug of his shoulders.

I had some bouts with bronchial asthma for a few years about ten years ago, and I know how spooky it can be when you are having difficulty breathing.

"I never knew I was going to end up like this," said the 67-year-old Haddix. "But I had fun getting here."

He blames his breathing problems, as do his doctors, on cigarettes.

"As far as cigarettes are concerned, I was a three packs a day man," said Haddix. "That was my friend. My wife and kids didn't travel with me. I could handle the drinking part of baseball, but not the cigarettes.

"I advertised for Camels when I was a young kid with the Cardinals. I got started smoking when I went to Winston-Salem. They gave us a box of locally-made products, and it included a box of cigarettes. That's how I got started.

"I loved cigarettes, but they finally got to me. They were my downfall. The doc said I was a dead man, but I came back. That happened in January of 1990. I woke up one morning and I couldn't breathe. He told me, 'You came back from the dead.'"

"The boys of Springfield"

He lives just a few miles from Westville, where he grew up, and which has a sign at its border hailing it as the "Hometown of Harvey Haddix," and from South Vienna, where he had a farm up until a few years ago.

"I was born about 20 miles from here in Medway," he said. "My mother went from Westville to Medway to have me because she had an aunt who was a midwife who lived there."

No matter where he played or coached during his 41 years in professional baseball, 26 in the major leagues — 13 as a player and 13 as a coach — Haddix always came home in the off-season.

"There were three of us on that Pirates team who live in Springfield," said Haddix, offering a trivia item. "Bill Virdon is in Springfield, Missouri, and Dick Schofield is in Springfield, Illinois. And all of us played for the Cardinals prior to being with the Pirates."

So many of the Pirates from that 1960 team returned to their hometowns and remain there. It goes against the title of Thomas Wolfe's book, *You Can't Go Home Again.*

"Who said that?" asked Haddix, when I mentioned Wolfe. "That's a bunch of crap.

"I always wanted to go home. I was always a farmboy. In 1959, we built our house out on our farm. My wife had most of it built while I was away. We had everything we needed there. We had a lake that was full of carp, and I loved to go fishing. We had woods nearby where I could go hunting. I've always been a hunter and a fisherman. It's something I love.

"Our three children live here in the Springfield area, and we are all in touch all the time."

In fact, while I was interviewing Haddix, one of his daughters telephoned him, and his wife also called. Marcia Haddix had been working for a few hours as a volunteer at nearby Community Hospital, and she wanted to tell him she was going to the local shopping mall. "There goes my money," said Haddix when he got off the phone. The daughters are Teri Lyn, 36, and Ann Elaine, 32, and the son is Harvey III, 29. There are no grandchildren.

"When I broke into baseball, most of the players came from farms or small towns," continued Haddix. "You don't see so much of that today.

I thought it was important to know where they came from. I loved certain players' names, like Arky Vaughan and Debs Garms, in Pirates history. Aren't they great names? You have to come from some place interesting to have names like that."

Harvey Haddix is a pretty fair handle in itself. Haddix had a farmer's look about him as we spoke. He was wearing blue jeans, a light blue shirt, and dark blue and red suspenders. The outfit brought out the blue in his eyes. He still has the familiar jug-ears and wide grin, and a few more lines on his forehead like any self-respecting farmer. He had on black baseball shoes, and black stockings. He was wearing wire-rimmed glasses and was red-faced. He looked fine, and talked animatedly, pausing only on occasion to catch his breath. He leaned forward from the front end of a couch, with his legs set wide apart, as if he were riding a horse, and waved his hands as he told stories.

"If you're brought up with nothing, like most of the guys I knew, being a baseball player and traveling around the country was a big deal," continued Haddix. "Most of the guys on the 1960 Pirates were making between $18,000 and $25,000 (or nearly three times the wages of the average Pittsburgher back then), and we thought we were doing pretty good. One of my best memories is how easy it was to be accepted by the other Pirate players."

"They want me to win . . . sending me something like that down here."
—Zip Payne
Winston-Salem, 1947

According to official records, Haddix broke into professional baseball with Winston-Salem in the Carolina League, a Class C loop, back in 1947, but that is not accurate, to hear Haddix.

"Actually, I started out in Columbus in Triple A that year, but I didn't get in a game. I was there several weeks and hadn't gotten to pitch. So I went to the team's president, Al Bannister, and said, 'Send me some place where I can play ball.' A few days later, he tells me, 'You're going to Pocatello, Idaho.' I said, 'No, I'm not, that's too far. You've got places closer than that where you can send me.' That shows you how cocky I was when I was 22. So he sent me to Winston-Salem, North Carolina. I had never heard of Winston-Salem, either, but I knew it was closer than Pocatello.

"My train ticket said my destination was Lynchburg, Virginia, and I thought Bannister had made a mistake. The Cardinals had a farm team in Lynchburg, too, a Class B team. They had the Winston-Salem Cardinals as well as the Lynchburg Cardinals. When I got off the train in Lynchburg, I grabbed a local newspaper, and saw a small item on the sports page that those two teams were playing an exhibition that night in Lynchburg.

"I was sitting on the visitors' clubhouse steps when a schoolbus pulled into the parking lot, bringing the Winston-Salem Cardinals. Only one guy on the team knew me, somebody I had been to spring training with at Columbus. He introduced me to the manager. The manager's name was Cecil 'Zip' Payne. He talked to me for awhile. I was about 5-6 or 5-7 then, and about 145 pounds. One of the guys on the team told me that Payne made a remark after I walked away that night, saying 'They want me to win . . . sending me something like that down here.'

"I was making about $350 a month because I started out in Triple A. Most of the guys in Winston-Salem were making about $75 to $100 a month. That year I roomed with our third baseman. We lived in a home and shared a bathroom with some old maids. Me and the third baseman slept in the same bed, and we paid about $7 a week in rent. When the season was over, he didn't have enough money to get home. I lent him some money, and he promised to send me the money. I'm still waiting for it.

"When I got to the Pirates, I roomed for the most part with Bob Skinner. We knew each other so well we could be at opposite ends of a room and we knew what the other one was thinking. They don't have roommates today. Some of them have their own suites. I think they're missing something. When I got up to Columbus again, they had guys on the team who had been to the majors and come back. They taught you a lot, too, and that doesn't happen much anymore.

"Bob and I used to order newspapers and coffee to be sent up to our room at the hotel, and then a while later we'd go down and have breakfast together. Today, most of the guys eat in their rooms, probably to avoid signing autographs in the hotel restaurant or coffee shop. In our day, maybe someone like Willie Mays had to do that, but that was about it.

"We traveled by train when I first got into baseball. We'd go from Milwaukee to Philadelphia, and we'd go through Chicago, and it would take us about 23 hours. You got to know the guys on the team, and the sports writers real well in those days. Some players would avoid certain sports writers for one reason or another. I'd tell the writer, 'If you need a story, come to me.'

"I bought the local paper wherever we went. I wanted to read that sports page. I wasn't into stats, or anything like that, but I wanted to see what was going on. I still do that.

"I think we had more fun in the days when I was playing," Haddix said. "Then, baseball was all we had. We didn't have the big salaries they have now. The guys can be more independent now than they used to be — they can go their own ways. But we had to share things together."

"To play in the big leagues, you got to be a man, but you got to have a lot of little boy in you, too."
—Roy Campanella
Hall of Fame Catcher

Harvey Haddix is proud to have made his mark in his hometown.

Haddix, Chuck Tanner and Tony Bartirome view game from dugout during Haddix's days as an assistant coach with Pirates.

Haddix and his former roommate Bob Skinner still share the sports pages as they did during their playing days.

"The hair stood up on the back of my neck."

Haddix recalled fairly well what he went through in the eighth inning of that famous final game against the Yankees at Forbes Field. "That's the only time in my life I was really nervous," he said.

"Bob Friend and I were both warming up in the bullpen. He got the call to go in for the eighth inning. Oh, was he throwing some good stuff in the bullpen. 'Go get 'em, young man,' I said to him as he left the bullpen. 'Just throw the same stuff.'

"But he gave up singles to the first two batters (Bobby Richardson and pinch-hitter Dale Long), and Murtaugh called me in to pitch."

Haddix got the call and the first batter he was going to face, with runners on first and third, was Roger Maris. And Maris had hit a home run off Haddix in the third inning of the fifth game. He was also going to face, in order, Mickey Mantle, Yogi Berra and Moose Skowron, the heart of the Yankees' formidable lineup. All had hit home runs in the Series. In fact, Berra had hit a three-run homer in the sixth inning to put the Yankees ahead, 5-4, after the Pirates had led 4-1.

"The hair stood up on the back of my neck," Haddix said. "I was nervous. I reached down on the way in from the bullpen and picked up a pebble in the grass behind second base. I kicked at the dirt in front of the mound. Check out the film from that game and you will see how long I kicked around at that mound. I was stalling. I had to get rid of that nervousness.

"Maris is in there, squeezing the sawdust out of the bat, and he can't wait to get at me. I'm talking to myself: 'This is something you've waited all your life to do, and now you're going to blow it because of nerves.' I finally whipped it. I don't think I threw a strike that inning. They were so anxious to hit.

"The first pitch was a wasted pitch to all of them. Down and away. They didn't give me a chance to work on them. They all went for the second pitch. I was going to bust him a fastball inside on the second pitch, and make him hit my slider going away on the next pitch. My second pitch to Maris was eight inches off the plate, and I jammed him, but Maris still hit the ball. He popped it up to Hal Smith, our catcher.

"Then it's Mantle. He's batting right-handed off me. He likes the ball up and away. I'm going to back him farther off the plate. I knew you had to pitch him inside. On my second pitch, he went down on one knee like this (Harvey slid out of his chair and down on one knee on the living room floor to make his point) and he blooped one over Maz's head. The ball was a foot off the plate and he reached out and hit it. That was just bait; that's all it was.

"Then Berra . . . it's the same thing with him. I wanted to go inside, waste a pitch. I wanted to set him up. But he hits my first pitch (Actually, Haddix had a 2-0 count on Berra, and Stengel sent in Gil McDougald as a pinch-runner for Long at third after the first ball to Berra.). He hits the ball hard to Rocky Nelson. Berra hit a one-hopper hard to Nelson. Rocky was looking to go to home plate (Rocky later said he was looking to go to second, but Groat was not covering the bag).

462

He tagged first base, and looked around for Mantle. Mantle slid back into first base behind him, and McDougald scored from third."

"Do you think Mantle recognized the situation and made the smart play?"

"The play was behind him. So how did he see it? I'd say he did it unconsciously. I know he surprised Rocky.

"Skowron . . . I threw the first pitch down and away for a ball. He hit the second pitch, a ground ball to Groat. And Groat flipped the ball to Maz at second for the force out. I went right to his weakness — inside. If you got the ball where you wanted it on them — like our scouting report said — you could get them out."

"It's 66 and a half feet from the pitcher's rubber to home plate," I said to Haddix. "How close could you put the ball where you wanted it?"

"When I had my control, I could put the ball within three inches of where I wanted to throw it."

"What happened to you immediately after the game?"

"We drank a lot of champagne in the clubhouse. We got pretty well loaded before we ever left the park. My wife was pregnant, and she was big, even though our child wasn't born until January. I wanted to get her home before our team party at Webster Hall. My parents were there, and they took her home. I went out in the runway between the stands and the bleachers to see them off. When I was standing there, some young girl jumped on my back, and was trying to rip a piece out of my sports jacket. I had to shrug her off and the police kicked her out of the park. I waited at the park a few hours before we went to Webster Hall."

"The Almost-Perfect Game"

Harvey Haddix has always been one of the most popular pitchers in Pirates history. When the team celebrated its 100th anniversary in 1987, Haddix was named the Pirates' all-time best left-handed thrower, while Vernon Law was voted the best right-handed pitcher, and ElRoy Face the best relief pitcher. "That's quite an honor," said Haddix, as he showed me a print of a painting that showed him with several of his teammates, plus the likes of Honus Wagner, Pie Traynor and Lloyd Waner that hung in a prominent spot in his gameroom.

Haddix was best known for his two wins in the 1960 World Series — one as a starter in the fifth game and the other in relief in the seventh game — and for his "perfect" game in 1959. On May 26 of that year in Milwaukee, Haddix pitched the longest "perfect" game in baseball history, 12 innings, only to lose in the 13th on an error, an intentional walk and a home run that was later ruled a double.

Afterwards, Haddix could not understand the fuss. "All I know is we lost in 13 innings," said Haddix. "What's so historic about that? Didn't anyone else ever lose a 13-inning shutout?"

Haddix won 136 games in 15 years (136-113), and those two World Series games, yet everyone remembers best the unique game he lost.

"I don't mind answering questions about it," Haddix said. "When I look back at it now, I realize how impossible it is to do. The only bad thing about it is that we lost the game."

Haddix was not feeling well the night he pitched the 12-inning perfect game. He was sucking on throat lozenges and cigarettes between innings, which would seem to be counterproductive. "Groat would come into the hallway behind the dugout, and light my cigarette and then take off," said Haddix. "No one would talk to me. They didn't want to jinx me.

"Speaking of Groat . . . did you know that Groat didn't play in that game that night. Neither did Clemente. I still wonder why they weren't playing. It might not have gone 13 innings if their bats were in the lineup."

Dick Schofield was at shortstop that night, and Roman Mejias was in right field.

Long-time Pirates fans still recall fondly staying up much later that night than they had planned, and following the pitch-by-pitch call over KDKA Radio. It was great theatre. Some people still regard it as the greatest pitching performance in baseball history.

"I really remember a lot about the ninth inning," recalled Haddix. "It was the only inning I tried for the no-hitter. I wanted to strike everybody out. I got two of the three on strikeouts and then went back to pitching my normal game."

"I was watching history. I was watching the greatest game ever pitched."
—ElRoy Face

Les Biederman, the long-time baseball writer for *The Pittsburgh Press*, wrote when he retired that his biggest thrill in baseball was not Bill Mazeroski's home run to win the 1960 World Series — that was too sudden, he said — but rather a toss-up between Haddix's 12 perfect innings, and Dale Long's home runs in eight consecutive games in May, 1956.

On his big night in Milwaukee, Haddix retired the first 36 batters he faced. He did not pitch from the stretch for 12 innings. Haddix fell behind in the count to only two of the 36 Braves he faced. And the Braves had one of the most feared lineups in the league.

Pirates infielders were flawless on the first 12 chances, but Don Hoak fumbled No. 13, a bouncer by Felix Mantilla that opened the 13th inning. It was an ordinary grounder, but Hoak threw the wet ball into the dirt to Rocky Nelson at first base, and Mantilla became the Braves' first base runner. Eddie Mathews sacrificed, and Haddix purposely walked Henry Aaron to set up the double play. Haddix threw a slider to the next hitter, Joe Adcock. Twice Adcock had gone down swinging at a slider, and had ground out twice. But not this time. This one was too high, too ripe, Haddix knew it as soon as he released the ball. Adcock

464

hit it over the fence — by a foot — in right-center field, just over the outstretched gloves of Joe Christopher, who had come in for Mejias, and Bill Virdon.

It should have been a home run. But as Mantilla scored, Aaron rounded second and cut across the diamond to the Braves' dugout on the first base side. Adcock, seeing the umpire's home run signal, simply kept on running and passed Aaron between second and third. Thus he was automatically out for passing a runner and was credited with only a double. The final score was 1-0 rather than 3-0.

It took another day, and a ruling from National League President Warren Giles, to determine the final score. "We didn't know for a day whether the score was 3-0, or 2-0 or 1-0," recalled Haddix.

For 12 innings, Haddix and Braves' right-hander Lew Burdette dueled to a draw. Burdette labored, giving up 12 hits but no runs over the same stretch.

There have been just 14 perfect games in baseball history going into the 1993 season, including Don Larsen's in the 1956 World Series. Haddix is the only one who did it past nine innings, and he is also the only one who lost. That is what made it even more memorable.

There was also an irony to Adcock being the Braves' hero. He figured in another setback in the career of Haddix. In 1954, Adcock lined a shot off Haddix's knee when Harvey was pitching for the Cardinals. The line drive not only damaged a nerve in his leg, it hurt Haddix in his bid for a 20-win season and altered his pitching style for the rest of his career.

"I was never the same after that," said Haddix, when I showed him a photo of him and Adcock smiling at one another. "I just wasn't right. I didn't have the same spring off the mound."

He said he didn't know until after the game that he had a perfect game going for him. "I knew I had a no-hitter, but I thought they might have gotten a walk somewhere," he said. "I didn't keep up on stats or anything, so I didn't know that nobody else had ever pitched a game like that."

Haddix had the flu going into that game and didn't feel very strong. There was some talk about scratching Haddix as a starter that night. Good thing someone thought better of that.

"Every batter, it was zip, zip — two strikes," Haddix went on. "I've had better stuff than I had that night — I only threw two pitches: the fastball and the slider. But I never had control like that."

His wife, Marcia, got a telephone call from her mother-in-law at about ten o'clock that night, telling her that her husband had a no-hitter going into the ninth inning. Marcia was in Springfield, and she couldn't get good reception on the Pirates' radio broadcast, as Springfield is over 200 miles from Pittsburgh. So she ran outside and sat in the family car, where the reception was better, and listened to the rest of the game.

"He'll still say that wasn't the highlight of his career," said Marcia. "He lost that game. He's more proud of the two games he won in the World Series."

Haddix got a lot of attention from national media after his pitching performance in Milwaukee.

Bob Prince and Jim Woods were working the game for KDKA Radio. "It was electrifying," said Prince. "Especially in the eighth and ninth. You could tell Haddix was going for it.

"I mentioned the perfect game at the end of the fifth inning," continued Prince. "People say you shouldn't talk about a no-hitter, but with all those zeroes on the board, I had to. The fans in the ballpark knew what was happening. The funny thing about it, in the sixth inning they were all pulling for Haddix.

"As the game went on, a number of stations called to see if they could pick up our broadcast. I said, 'sure.' Why not? This was history. By the time the 11th inning started, our game was being broadcast over a good part of the country."

The game was not on KDKA-TV. The original schedule called for the game to be televised back in Pittsburgh, but KDKA-TV switched its coverage to the following night because of a nationally-televised speech by then Vice-President Richard M. Nixon. (And, of course, Haddix became one of Nixon's favorite ballplayers.)

In a pre-game meeting to discuss how Haddix was to pitch against the Braves' awesome lineup — seven players who batted that night hit .300 — Hoak perked up and said, "Harvey, if you pitch those hitters like that, you'll throw a no-hitter." After that remark, they didn't even finish going over the rest of the hitters. "Whenever Hoakie said that, the meeting broke up," Haddix said.

Braves pitcher Bob Buhl claimed to have stolen signals off Pirates catcher Smoky Burgess. From his position in the center field bullpen, Buhl "told" Milwaukee hitters via pre-arranged gestures whether Haddix was throwing a fastball or a breaking ball.

Even so, Haddix handled the Braves with apparent ease. "There was nothing close to being a hit," said Haddix. "They hit some balls hard, but they were right at guys. There were no running, diving catches or anything like that."

Nobody talked to Haddix during the game about the way things were progressing. "I went to bat in the seventh inning, and their catcher, Del Crandall, said, 'You got a pretty good game going here.' Otherwise, nobody talked to me the whole game. I was a lonesome guy."

It was a strange night for a great ballgame. "It never did rain, but it was lightning and thundering, and the wind was blowing like crazy," recalled Haddix. "The field was damp from earlier rains."

Because Haddix and the Bucs were losers, the atmosphere was somber in the clubhouse afterward.

"It was quiet, real quiet," said Skinner. "The rest of us kind of had our heads down. We lost and we didn't score any runs for a guy who pitched his heart out. The only people talking were the sports writers who had gathered around Harvey."

Skinner admired how Haddix handled the disappointment. "I felt bad for him," said Skinner, who hit a ball he thought was out of the ballpark in the seventh but the wind blew it back in and Aaron caught

Harvey Haddix and Smoky Burgess check out story in *Sun-Telegraph* about Harvey's great pitching performance in Milwaukee.

addix shakes hands with Joe Adcock, the oiler.

Haddix says you had to like Dick Stuart.

it. "I have to give Harvey credit. He took it like a man. He was upset we lost as a team. That's the kind of guy he is. He's a real pro."

After the game, Haddix shared a cab with Hoak back to the hotel. "I was the last one out of the clubhouse," Haddix recalled. "And Hoak was waiting for me. He and I were sitting in the cab, and he said, 'I've booted 'em before, and I'll boot 'em again. But I'll also make some good plays for you, Harv.' That was it; no apologies, and I didn't want any.

"I went back to my room, and my roommate on that trip was R. G. Smith. After I got tired of answering the phone, it was about 2 o'clock in the morning. I said, 'Roomie, let's get out of here. If we get fined, I've got it.'

"So we walked the streets for a while, then we stopped for breakfast at about 6 a.m. And while we were having breakfast, I heard the people talking about the game.

"You know there were about 16,000 people at the park that night, but I swear about 100,000 people have told me they were at the game or saw it on television — and it wasn't televised.

"You've got to understand that I didn't get the full feeling of what was going on in the no-hitter until the players and everybody else gathered around me in the clubhouse after the game. That thrill was short-changed because we lost the game.

"But do you remember what happened in the game I pitched right after that at Forbes Field? Don Blasingame, first man up for the Cards, hit a single off me."

Harvey was too modest to add that he went on to shut out the St. Louis club, 3-0, on eight scattered hits. He was given a standing ovation by 28,644 adoring fans when he first took the mound.

Prior to the 1960 season, somebody suggested to Haddix that he had been a "hard-luck" pitcher. He was getting rubbed down by trainer Danny Whelan when the subject came up.

"I hate to associate tough luck with baseball," said Haddix. "A guy is no tough luck pitcher — he's just making mistakes out there."

Like Mazeroski and the home run, Haddix and his "perfect game" remain permanently sealed in the minds of baseball fans. Fans remember staying up late to listen to every pitch.

"Every day that I've put on a uniform since that night, I've been asked about the perfect game," said Haddix. "Every single day."

That was the same season that ElRoy Face posted an incredible 18-1 record as a relief pitcher.

"I didn't get off the bench all night," Face recalled. "I was watching history. I was watching the greatest game ever pitched."

"A part of me belongs in Pittsburgh."

He came to the Pirates in what is considered Joe L. Brown's best trade in his tenure as general manager. He was traded by the Cincinnati Reds along with Smoky Burgess and Don Hoak on December 31, 1959 for Frank Thomas, Whammy Douglas, Jim Pendleton and Johnny Powers.

Haddix was called "Kitten" because of his physical resemblance to Harry "The Cat" Brecheen, a veteran Cardinals pitcher when Haddix was a rookie with St. Louis in 1952.

The little lefty was also quite the fielder, and he was also considered a good hitting pitcher. He thought Forbes Field was "the best ball park in the league."

He loved the fans there. "I feel like a part of me belongs in Pittsburgh," he said.

Haddix was born September 18, 1925 at Medway, Ohio. He was 5-8, 160 pounds, of German ancestry, with brown hair and blue eyes. He was the son of Harvey Gebhart Haddix and Nellie May Haddix. He comes from solid stock.

He signed with the Cardinals orginally in 1947. He was a corporal in the Army September 1950 to September 1952 at Fort Dix, New Jersey. He married Marcia Williamson on December 10, 1955. During his playing career with the Pirates, they lived on the family farm in South Vienna, Ohio.

The 408-acre farm is located eight miles south of Springfield. Harvey used to retreat there each fall and winter, and worked the land. He was what he called a mixed farmer. He raised hogs, cattle and wheat. He came by his farming, naturally, as he was brought up on a farm in Urbana, and his dad owned a 436-acre farm adjacent to Harvey's when he was pitching for the Pirates. Harvey had to sell the farm when he had failing health.

As a rookie in his first full season with the Cardinals in 1953, Haddix posted a won-loss record of 20-9. He pitched 19 complete games, including six shutouts, high for the league.

He won 18 games his second season, then 12, and the Cardinals sent him to the Philadelphia Phillies during the 1956 season. He pitched for the Phillies the next season, then spent the 1958 season with the Reds. He pitched in the 1955 All-Star Game when he was with the Cardinals.

"Coaching is more fun than playing."

Haddix was let go as a pitching coach for the Cleveland Indians after the 1978 season, and joined Chuck Tanner's staff in time for the 1979 season, and a chance to be a part of another World Series-winning Pirates' organization.

Haddix had been the Indians' pitching coach since 1974 and earlier held the same post with three other clubs — the New York Mets (1966-67), the Cincinnati Reds (1969) and the Boston Red Sox (1971). He also handled minor league pitchers in the Pirates' operation in 1968 and 1970.

"A lot of guys coach because they need years for their pension plan," said Haddix. "Some guys just need a job. But me, I do it because

I enjoy it. Coaching is more fun than playing. When you play, you only worry about yourself. But when you coach, you worry about a whole bunch of fellas.

"To see someone else do a little something that you taught them, well, that's a really satisfying feeling."

I mentioned that you had to have a special metabolism to be a baseball manager or coach, because you did a lot of sitting. "The wheels are always spinning," said Haddix. "It might appear that you're relaxed, but you're not feeling so good if your guys aren't playing too good.

"But I loved it. I enjoyed it every place I was. I told myself, 'I'm going to play this game as long as I can play it.' The same went for coaching. As long as someone would have me, I would stay. I was with the Pirates for five years as a player, and six years as a coach. I was in baseball for 41 years, 26 in the big leagues. I had two brothers play professional baseball, but they didn't like it. And my son never wanted any of it."

I showed Haddix some photographs of himself as a young pitcher, and as a young father, with his wife and their daughters. "How young we were," said Haddix. "Isn't that a sight?"

When I showed him one that had him hugging Dick Stuart and smiling, he said, "See, I didn't dislike him. I just didn't want to room with him."

He said Stan Musial was the best ballplayer he was ever associated with. "He could really sting the ball; I saw him hit five home runs in one day," said Haddix.

A few other quickies from Haddix:

"I remember once that I was in the Carlton House when Kruschev, the Russian leader, came through the lobby. I was as close to him as I am to you. Imagine that today. How'd they know I didn't have a gun?"

What's the most satisfying thing that has happened to him since he retired?

"Being home with the family and not living out of a suitcase."

What player did he admire most from the '60 team?

"Vernon Law. He was steady all year long and was a good influence on all of us."

His advice for today's players?

"Learn more about how the game is played so you can make fewer mistakes."

What did he learn from his experience with the Pirates that has served him in good stead ever since?

"How easy it is to be a part of an organization that is very positive."

As I was leaving, Haddix walked me out to the car that was in the driveway. He pointed out his grounds, which are one and a third acres. There was a swimming pool in the backyard, and a golf course just across the street from him. "But I've never been a golfer," he said, almost apologetically.

470

As we spoke, I noticed for the first time that he had a hearing aid in his right ear. "Oh yeah," he said. "I've had that about ten years. It's hell to get old."

I got into my car and slipped the tape into the casette player. It came up, by coincidence, to the point where Haddix begins to pitch in the top of the ninth inning. He leaned against the car, and listened like it was a favorite song. Like the oldies I had been listening to on the radio as I rode along the Ohio highways. He was young again.

Then it came to the bottom of the ninth inning. . .

"Soon as Maz hit it," Haddix offered, "I said, 'That's gone.' I watched it come off his bat, and I knew what a home run ball looked like. I could see the angle and how well it was hit. There was no doubt about it."

From Haddix Family Album

Once upon a time Harvey and Marcia Haddix had two little girls, Anne Ellen and Terri Lyn.

471

Where Were You?

*"I saw one of the greatest plays
I ever saw in baseball."*
—Bill Steigerwald

Amy Jackson
Franklin Park
"We lived near the home of Harvey Haddix, on JoAlyee Drive in Allison Park, when he was pitching for the Pirates. He lived in a little yellow brick bungalow on the corner. After the Pirates won the 1960 World Series, I remember my dad driving our car by Haddix' home and honking his horn, over and over again. My dad just kept going round and round, honking his horn. I was seven, and I was with him. I never saw Haddix, but I was so excited. I remember watching the final game on TV with my dad."

Gerry Bosiljevac
Assistant Manager
Moraine State Park near Butler
Portersville, Pa.
"I have articles, posters, books, and everything I could get hold of about the Pirates through the years. Some of it has disappeared. I really admired Roberto Clemente. He turned me onto baseball. People didn't understand him. He couldn't express himself well enough. I was 12 in 1960 and that really sparked my interest in baseball. I admired Clemente for his intensity and the example he set for everyone on the team. I remember one morning my mother came to my room and woke me up. She told me Clemente had been killed in an airplane crash. I just went back to my room and cried. I cried for a good while. I thought about it for a long time afterward. It's still very upsetting to me."

Bill Steigerwald
Retired, Part-Time Manager, Mt. Lebanon Golf Course
"I used to go 30 to 40 baseball games a year back in those days. I saw all of the home games in the '60 World Series. In that seventh game, I saw one of the greatest plays I ever saw in baseball. In the ninth inning, Mantle was on first base when Yogi Berra hit a shot to Rocky Nelson, who made a tough pick-up and stepped on first base. Mantle dove back into first base. If he did that on purpose, rather than on instinct, he had to be the most knowledgeable baseball player ever. I never saw anything like it, then or since. A run scored on that play, and it kept the Yankees alive to get another run. Mantle did something else in that Series I never saw before. He hit a home run over the gate in right center — batting right-handed! — and that had never been done before. A few days after the Series, I read where Rogers Hornsby said he did it once. Well, I can remember sitting in right field one day when

472

I was in high school, and I saw Hornsby hit one — a line shot — that struck right above the iron gate on the fly and bounced back in. I can still see Lloyd and Paul Waner pinching in on it and closing it off. They held it to a double. I think that's the one Hornsby was talking about. I just think he embellished it; the way guys here tell you they hit one 300 yards when they hit it 200 yards. I remember Maz's home run, of course. I was still working Downtown at Gateway Center as a broker. We were Downtown before his home run landed, so we never got involved in any of that agony. A friend of mine, 'Red' Cipa dug up home plate after the home run and took it with him. He was then a bartender at the Little Red Door Bar Downtown. I saw three of Dale Long's home runs in his eight game streak, and he hit a few of those really high into the right field seats, and one of them, I swore, went through the lower deck and out the open end at the back. They were some shots, too. I saw Kiner hit a few. The year he hit 54 home runs . . . if he had been hitting at Ebbetts Field he'd have had 300 homeruns that year. And I'm not exaggerating."

Richard Fitzgerald
State College, Pa.

"Maz was my favorite ballplayer. I was 11 in 1970 when I became really interested in baseball. I wore No. 9 for our Burger King Little League team. The kids called me Maz. I had a brother named Charles, and they called him Chaz. So we were always known as Maz and Chaz."

State troopers come running to restore order as Bill Mazeroski is mobbed at home plate after hitting home run to win World Series in 1960.

Rocky Nelson
"Don't Knock the Rock"

"I consider myself an ex-Pirate.
They're the only team that gave me a chance."

The Scioto River runs from Columbus in central Ohio all the way to Portsmouth at the southern tip of the state, just above Ironton, where it empties into the Ohio River. The Ohio River begins in Pittsburgh, formed by the jointure of the Allegheny and Monongahela rivers by Point State Park and Three Rivers Stadium. The Ohio River is the border between Ohio and Kentucky, then flows along the southern borders of Indiana and Illinois and into the mighty Mississippi River.

These rivers run through our lives and they link us all somehow. There is something spiritual or mystical about rivers. The Ohio River still connects Rocky Nelson with Pittsburgh and its ballparks, and its best memories. Rocky and the rivers just keep rolling along.

Portsmouth seems like the perfect place to find Rocky Nelson with his wife, Alberta. Like Pittsburgh, there used to be smoky steel mills there, in an adjoining area called New Boston, and a huge shoe factory, but the industrial base has eroded in recent decades. There are still some chemical companies, like Aristech Chemical Corporation in nearby Haverhill, where Rocky worked before he retired in 1991. After his ball-playing days, Nelson also worked in the insurance business, wholesale distributing business, and owned Rocky Nelson's Steakhouse for several years. This is their hometown and they appeared quite comfortable there, in a cozy, squeaky-clean gray Cape Cod home, just a few blocks off Route 23. There were an assortment of flowers — roses, lilacs, daisies, mums — in the front yard, a shaded patio porch on the side of the house, and it has been their home since 1954. Both of the Nelsons grew up just a few miles away. "We have so many friends here," said Alberta. "We went to a lot of places to play ball, but we always came back here."

They live in the kind of eclectic for-real home where there are photos of children and knick-knacks displayed everywhere, things that are meaningful to the Nelsons. There are a few photographs of Rocky, rather unobtrusive, hanging in the hallway outside the powder room. The Nelsons said they had just taken down all the photos and mementos of Rocky's career that had been on display in the family room.

Alberta's maiden name is Burns, the same as my mother, and I suggested we might be related somehow, since my mother also comes from Ohio.

One of the Pirates all-time top hitters, Al Oliver, also grew up and continues to live in Portsmouth, and coaches the baseball team at the NAIA level there at Shawnee State University. It is the hometown of Chuck Noll's wife, Marianne, and some members of her family are buried in nearby Lucasville. It is more South than Midwest. ("We used to say I was from O-hi-o, and Marianne was from Ahh-hi-ya," Chuck cracked when I checked this tidbit out with him.)

I visited the Nelsons the day after Easter, 1993, after I had been to the home of Harvey Haddix, one of his teammates on the 1960 World Series champion Pittsburgh Pirates, earlier in the day at Springfield, just west of Columbus.

It took me a little over three hours, as I was told, to get from the home of Haddix to the home of Nelson, before I saw Alberta in the doorway of her home, making sure I would find them, since they took the address off the front of the house several years ago. It reminded me of how Bill and Milene Mazeroski had waited for me on the front porch of their home in Greensburg.

The Nelsons are the same kind of people as the Mazeroskis: homespun, humble, unpretentious, in comfortable but modest surroundings, obviously still much in love, happy with themselves, and content with their lives. "I think these are the best years, I really do," Alberta would say later on as I sat in their living room. "We've had a hundred times more good times than we've had bad times. It scares me sometimes."

The Nelsons are considered good neighbors, pillars of their church and respected members of the community.

She and Rocky had been married for 46 years, or since they exchanged vows on August 25, 1947 at home plate at Lynchburg, Virginia, where Rocky was playing in the Piedmont League. "I was a child bride," Alberta said. "I've always loved baseball. We traveled by train in the early years, and we got to see the world. He played in Canada, with Montreal and Toronto. Rocky played winter ball in Cuba six years, and I always went with him. We've had a wonderful life.

"We used to pull out of the driveway out there, and I'd be crying because we were leaving lots of friends behind. But wherever we went, we made new friends. I'd find me some golfing buddies, and we'd go out and play regularly — when we were with the Pirates, my golfing buddies were usually Pat Friend, Eleanor Kluszewski and Virginia Burwell — and I'd pass the time by quilting, and stuff like that."

Rocky Nelson still looked like Rocky Nelson. He was 68 at the time of our visit. He looked comfortable in a plaid flannel shirt, with blue jeans, and white socks and white sneakers. His hair was thin, but it had always been spare. He still squinted those blue eyes when bright sunlight streamed through the window. He was still chewing tobacco, though there wasn't the giant bulge in his cheek that used to be his trademark. He and Mazeroski used to compare cheeks for photographers just for fun. "Me and Smoky and him," added Rocky.

"It's Red Horse chewing tobacco," related Rocky. "I chew a pack every two or three days now. I used to chew one-and-a-half packs a day when I was playing ball. They used to give me Favorite when Maz and I were promoting it, but it was too strong for me. I used to give it all to Maz."

Alberta admonished him for continuing to chew at all. "That's one habit of his I never liked," she said. "I've always worried about it from a health standpoint."

She had good reason to be concerned about his health. Three years earlier, Rocky required surgery for ulcers. "They gave me 13 pints of blood," he said. "But I'm in good health now, and I'm out golfing all the time."

Alberta brought me some iced tea, and some strawberry shortcake which they had for dessert following dinner. I reached their home at 5:40 p.m., ten minutes later than promised. I had left the Haddix home at 2:20 p.m. I had stopped for some chili dogs and french fries at a Dairy Queen, hence the longer drive time.

The trip down Route 23 was uneventful most of the way. The terrain was still flat, one farmfield after another farmfield. I went through Circleville, then Chillicothe. That's where Elbie Nickel, a great end with the Pittsburgh Steelers (1947-1957), has lived for a long time. Then it was Waverly, then Wakefield. The land went from flat to rolling hills, and then I started seeing a series of big hills on the horizon on both sides of me.

Soon I was flanked by the Scioto River on my right and a rail road track on my left, heading down Route 23 to Portsmouth. It was hard to get lost. I felt like I was in one of those car tracks at an amusement park.

The whole day, I kept hearing radio news reports about a riot at a prison in Lucasville, Ohio. Six prisoners had been killed, and eight guards had been taken hostage. One of those guards would be killed and dumped in the prison yard two days later. I had no idea where Lucasville was located, and I had no map of Ohio to help me. Somehow I sensed that wherever Lucasville was I would somehow manage to end up there. Like a heat-seeking missile. To be honest, when I started my odyssey to Ohio, I had no idea that Portsmouth was so far south, just across the Ohio River from Kentucky. Sure enough, about ten miles north of Portsmouth, I passed through Lucasville. I saw road signs for the Southern Ohio Correctional Facility, where the riot was taking place, less than a mile to my left on the other side of the rail road tracks. It is Ohio's only maximum-security prison, with over 1,800 inmates, including death-row inmates who were secured in cells away from the affected area. (The siege lasted a national record-tying 11 days and, in the end, the death toll was nine inmates and one guard. It was a front page story in the nation's newspapers for nearly two weeks.)

It brought two thoughts to mind. Back in 1962, when I was working as a summertime intern in the news department of *The Pittsburgh Press*, my first major assignment was to cover a riot at the Western Penetentiary along the Ohio River in Pittsburgh. I was there for a week, observing activity in the prison yard from the roof of a nearby warehouse, during a protest for improved conditions. It was a front page headline story, a plum assignment, especially for a 20-year-old cub reporter.

Rocky Nelson is greeted by
Roberto Clemente after first-
inning home run in seventh
game of the 1960 World Series.

I also thought about a trip I had made just a year earlier, in 1992, almost to the day, with my daughter Sarah. She was on her college search, and we were going to see North Carolina, Virginia Tech and Virginia in our last sweep. We drove through West Virginia on the way there, and on the way back. Before we left Pittsburgh, the big story was about a breakout at the Moundsville (West Va.) Penetentiary. Three prisoners had escaped and were still on the loose. My mother warned me not to pick up any hitch-hikers, or to stop by any strangers along the highway, when I was driving through West Virginia. On the way home, after Sarah selected Virginia as The University of her choice, we stopped one night at a service station in Beckley, West Virginia. I went into the building to buy some snacks. I made sure to lock the car as she was sleeping in the backseat. When I came out of the store, I noticed that the back window of our car was wide open. That's great, I thought, I made sure the doors were locked and the window is wide open. Real security measures.

I learned the next day that one of the escaped prisoners had been apprehended in Beckley — on the same night we had stopped there!

"To me, the constant wonder has been
how strange reality has been."
—Norman Maclean, Author
"A River Runs Through It"

Glenn Richard "Rocky" Nelson knows something about going down some strange roads at night. He went down more roads, and to more countries, than most major league ballplayers in plying his trade. Nelson searched long and hard for places to play baseball, but it was never easy for him. Alberta went wherever Rocky went, and she says it was fun.

He had played for teams in Johnson City, Columbus, St. Joseph, Rochester, Lynchburg, St. Louis, Chicago, Montreal, Brooklyn, Cleveland and Toronto before he came to Pittsburgh.

Alberta can relate stories about when they lived in apartments in Bay Ridge and Flatbush when Rocky was playing in Brooklyn, and at the Schenley Hotel, Squirrel Hill and Green Tree when he was with the Pirates, and all the points in between.

Even though he began his professional baseball career in 1942, at Johnson City, Tennessee, that 1960 season with the Pirates was only Rocky's fourth full season in the majors. And it was his best year.

His hometown of Portsmouth gave him a hero's welcome after he helped the Pirates win the 1960 World Series.

Nelson shared duties with Dick Stuart at first base that year. Nelson started the first and seventh games of the World Series against the Yankees. In the first game, he collected two singles and it was his two-run homer in the first inning of the seventh game that gave the Bucs an early lead in that crazy clincher.

478

"Stuart was some ballplayer," recalled Rocky. "He could hit the ball. His problem was he always wanted to hit the ball 600 feet, like he did once in the minors. It was the worst thing that ever happened to him. In 1959, he was the best-looking hitter you ever saw. He had an infected eyelid, and all he was trying to do was make contact with the ball. He was hitting over .320, and then his eye got well and he started swinging for the fences again. And he went down to .280.

"He was a good-looking guy, and he was strong, for sure. Bob Prince had a standing bet with anybody in the country that they couldn't put Stuart's arm down in an arm-wrestling competition. Prince said he'd pay anyone $10,000 if they could do it.

"When we got together for a reunion in 1990, we all exchanged addresses and all, except for Stu. He wouldn't give anyone his address. He said he was afraid his ex-wife would find him."

Rocky got into 93 games and had a .300 batting average and 35 RBIs on 60 hits during the 1960 season. "Don't knock the Rock," recalled Robert Gustine, a Pittsburgh attorney and the son of former Pirate Frank Gustine. "That's what we used to say. And I remember the way he used to hold his front foot high, with his left foot back in the bucket."

And Rocky Nelson remembers Frank Gustine. "He was the greatest spring hitter I ever saw," said Nelson.

Rocky was a real favorite at Forbes Field, and there were always a few guffaws when he would get set at the plate. His batting stance resembled something out of the 1890s — but opposing pitchers did not see much humor in it.

His unorthodox stance, his lead foot pointing toward the pitcher, was like something out of "Casey At The Bat."

Nelson was the last of the gay '90s hitters. He placed his right foot parallel to the plate, left foot at a 90 degree angle to the right, bent his left knee, dipped his left shoulder slightly, tilted his chin back, and dared the pitcher to keep him from pulling the best fast ball ever thrown.

"I always just tried to get a pitch I could hit," said Nelson. "I never went for home runs. They just happened."

Nelson had more major league trials than most players, having played briefly with the Pirates, Cardinals, White Sox, Dodgers and Indians — and with some of the greatest players in the history of the game — before he really got a decent shot, after he was drafted by the Pirates at the winter meetings in December of 1958.

Joe L. Brown, the Bucs' general manager at the time, says it was one of the most fortuitous moves he ever made.

Rocky hit .291 with the 1959 Pirates and was the club's most dependable pinch-hitter. He proved he could hit and field with the best of them. And in the big leagues.

Prior to being with the Pirates, Nelson was a star in the International League with both Montreal and Toronto. He was the league's most valuable player in 1953, 1955 and 1958, and led the AAA loop several times in home runs and RBIs. He said his biggest thrill since leaving baseball was being named to the Canadian Baseball Hall of Fame. He was the first non-Canadian to be so honored.

When Gino Cimoli came back to Pittsburgh in mid-April of 1993 to participate in a sports card show, I mentioned to him that I had just visited with Nelson out in Ohio. "Ol' Rocky," said Cimoli, almost in song. "I was with him for two years in Montreal, and for two years in Pittsburgh. We were roommates at one time. He drove me nuts. He's the guy who introduced me to cigars. He used to buy these big $5 cigars. I can blame him for my bad habits. He could play; he could hit. He loved the horses, he loved to play cards, he loved the crossword puzzles. He could play anything. He liked the action. We were a good pair."

Rocky was a real joy to interview, as I had been told in advance. He remains outspoken, and Alberta cautioned him a few times to be careful about what he said. "Please don't quote him on that," Alberta advised me a few times.

"Rocky talked a lot and he talked loud," Haddix had told me when I mentioned that I had heard Rocky was a good talker. "I think it hurt him in his career at times. But you won't find nicer people than Rocky and Alberta Nelson. They are both beautiful people."

Haddix had a reputation for providing outstanding scouting reports, and he still had the knack for it.

When I mentioned to Nelson that I had visited Harvey Haddix earlier in the day, Nelson said, "Harvey was one of the better seven inning pitchers I ever saw. His arm would start coming down in the late innings. He kinda got tired, and he'd drop his shoulder, and he'd get the ball high. But I loved to watch him pitch. He was so smooth. I played with him in Columbus in 1950."

"At the drop of a subject,
he will talk incessantly."
—Jim Brosnan

Glenn Richard "Rocky" Nelson was a compulsive talker during his travels through baseball.

He was the subject of a full-length profile by Roy Terrell in the August 18, 1958 issue of *Sports Illustrated.* The article was entitled "The Man With A Million And One Alibis."

Rocky was portrayed as "one of the world's greatest living experts on food, travel and Cuban cigars, on bass fishing and card playing, on wing shooting and spitting, on handicapping horses and dogs and solving crossword puzzles, on religion and golf and pool and the modern novel — any subject that came up."

He was a colorful character, naturally, and the fans took to him wherever he worked. Jackie Robinson, Duke Snider, Roy Campanella and Don Newcombe all played in Montreal before Nelson, and none was as popular as he was. The same thing was true in Toronto. Then again, few of them remained there as long as he did. The Toronto Maple Leafs were owned by Jack Kent Cooke, a wealthy Toronto publisher, who would later own the Los Angeles Lakers and Kings, and more recently the Washington Redskins.

"Nelson was the greatest conversationalist in the history of the International League," wrote Jim Brosnan, the Cincinnati Reds pitcher who authored books *(The Long Season)* and articles on baseball. "At the drop of a subject, he will talk incessantly."

Nelson was known as the Babe Ruth of the minors. He had several chances at the major leagues before he went to camp with the Pittsburgh Pirates in the spring of 1959.

Dixie Walker, his manager in Toronto, said, "I think that most of his trouble was that most managers he played for in the big leagues never really had time enough to understand him. Last year I didn't understand him myself. You never have to wonder where Rocky is. You can always hear him. He does talk a lot. In fact, he spouts off."

In 1958, Nelson hit 48 home runs for Toronto. You would have thought every team in the majors would be after a guy with those numbers.

Yet there was laughter in the room when Brown tabbed him as the Pirates draft choice at the major league winter meetings that December.

When Brown named Nelson as the Pirates' draft pick, Chub Feeney, then the front-office boss of the San Francisco Giants and a man who remains a close chum, threw a verbal jab at Brown. "Don't you mean Ricky Nelson?"

Rocky had been in Pittsburgh earlier in his roller coaster career, back in 1951, but that was when Branch Rickey was the general manager, and responsible for the personnel. He played for the Pirates briefly that first time around, and he was traded to the White Sox for shortstop Stan Rojek. Even today, Rocky can relate what he did and what his competition, Billy Howerton, did, and when he was benched, and why he should not have been benched, and how he complained, and how he ended up getting traded. Rocky can relate stories and statistics about how he got the short end of the stick wherever he went.

"I never got a chance to play my way out of a lineup," he said during our visit. "I'd hit .395, and in ten days I'd be on the bench. When I got a chance to play, like I did in Pittsburgh, I paid my way."

In Brown's mind, Nelson was the best left-handed batter in the minors — it was that simple — and the Bucs needed to bolster their attack from that side of the plate.

"He was an outstanding platoon player, but his career was winding down by the time we got him," said Brown.

It was in Pittsburgh in 1959 that Nelson battled Stuart and Ted Kluszewski for the first base position.

"I've never been given a chance," Nelson said at the time when asked to explain his up-and-down experience in the majors.

He was platooned by Danny Murtaugh depending on whether the Pirates were facing a righty or lefty pitcher. Then, too, he replaced Stuart in late innings, if the Pirates were ahead, as a defensive measure.

481

In 1959, Nelson apppeared in 98 games, batted only 175 times and accounted for 32 RBIs and a .291 batting average.

"A lot of guys take home runs, or something like that, to be their biggest thrill," Rocky related in an interview back then. "I don't. You're going to get so many, and they can add up themselves. The big thrill to me here, more than anything, is just playing."

In 1960, he played in 93 games, had 200 at bats, 34 runs, 60 hits, 11 doubles, one triple, seven home runs, 35 RBIs, and a .300 batting average. Even so, Nelson was never satisfied. "The whole thing," he said, "is that if you're any good, you want to excel."

But the Nelsons still count their blessings as far as the Buccos are concerned.

"The Pirates were the only team that ever gave Rocky a real chance," advanced Alberta.

"That's why I think of myself as an ex-Pirate," said Rocky. "After I played for the Pirates, I went back to Toronto and finished up in Denver in 1962. But Pittsburgh remains a special experience for everyone in our family. When we went back for the 30th anniversary reunion of our team in 1990, our son Rick got to see me playing ball in a uniform for the first time. I was told that tears came to his eyes. It was great getting to see everyone again. We were really close."

"That '60 club was something special," added Alberta.

"They had wonderful people there, wonderful fans," said Rocky. "They were great."

"They were very generous to us," said Alberta."

"They had the best fans in the world," related Rocky. "They drew nearly a million the first year (1951) I played there, and we finished seventh. The year before, they drew a million and change and they finished eighth. In 1960, we set an attendance record for Pittsburgh with 1.7 million that held up for 30 years."

"The fans were always so nice; they weren't pushy," said Alberta.

The Nelsons still had a special spot in their hearts for Pittsburgh because they were renting an apartment in Green Tree when they adopted their son, Rick, on December 9, 1959. "That's a special memory for us," related Rocky. They also adopted a daughter, Laura. Rick, 33, lived in Hilton Head, South Carolina, and Laura, 31, was living in Duncansville, Pennsylvania, near Altoona. "She's beautiful, too," said Alberta.

They were looking forward to the birth of a grandson in June. Rick and his wife said they were going to name the child Glenn Richard Nelson II. "I didn't care for my own name," Rocky interjected, "but it's what they want to do."

"This is great," said Alberta. "Now, we'll have three grandchildren." Rick's wife, Christina, who is from the Pittsburgh area, has two children, Saralyn, 13, and Michael, 11, by a previous marriage. "It will be good to see the Nelson name carried on. Rocky had a brother Al, but he never had any children."

Rocky Nelson and Bill Mazeroski compare chewing tobacco jaws.

World Series celebration: Rocky Nelson, Hal Smith and ElRoy Face

Rocky and Alberta show off son Rick.

Alberta, at right, with daughter Laura and son Rick, who was working in the yard.

"We probably won more games in the late innings than anyone ever did."
—Rocky Nelson

Nelson smiled throughout his reflections on the 1960 season, and the World Series.

"It all started with Murtaugh, the shanty Irishman. He was probably the greatest guy you could ever play for," Nelson said. "He was the main reason we won."

"How so?" I asked Nelson.

"Because of the kind of person he was," Nelson said. "Everyone wanted to play for him. We had a lot of players from different clubs who all happened to jell in one year. We probably won more games in the late innings than anyone ever did. We'd be behind by three and four runs, and we'd come back to win. We did that in '59, too. Lookit how Face won 17 consecutive games and went 18-1 as a relief pitcher in 1959. In 15 of those, he came in and it was somebody else's game on our pitching staff to win. They'd tie it up or go ahead, and we'd come back and he'd be the winner.

"I remember hearing Face tell Bob Prince in our clubhouse that year, 'All I do is come in and let them have two or three runs and then we end up winning.' Law came in and said, 'Yeah, and eight of those were mine.' "

I asked Nelson to name the players he spent the most time with, and liked the best. "Vinegar Bend or Mazeroski, Smoky and Sam Narron. Bob Friend. We'd get together and chew and have a grand time."

I asked Rocky to provide the details of the much-discussed defensive play in which he was involved in the top of the ninth inning of that seventh game with the Yankees.

The Yankees had two baserunners with one out when Yogi Berra came to bat. Gil McDougald was sent in as a pinch-runner for Dale Long, a former Pirate who singled as a pinch-hitter, and was on third base. McDougald was inserted, sort of as an afterthought, when Harvey Haddix had a 1-0 count on Berra. Mickey Mantle was on first base.

Haddix served up another ball. With the count 2-0, Berra hit a line drive shot just inside the first base line, and Nelson speared the ball as it leaped over the bag. "I got to my knees and backhanded it," Nelson said. "I came up to throw to second to start a double play. But Groat had come in behind the pitcher's mound in preparation to take a throw from right field; he was on the grass instead of at second. He'd figured the ball had gone by me. So there's no one covering second. I cranked my arm twice, I was told, and then turned and stepped on the bag for a force out on Berra. But Mantle dove back into the bag and beat my tag at him.

"Yogi said I robbed him of a double. Mantle said he saw me catch the ball, and thought I caught it on the fly. Mantle might have been the goat if Skowron had followed with a single. Because if Mantle had gone to second he would have gotten there safely, and he would have

484

scored on a single. Mantle wasn't more than an arm's length off the bag. Stuart said I should've gotten Mantle at first base. He told me if he'd have been at first base, the ballgame would've been over, and Maz wouldn't even have had to bat. We'd have won, 9-8. That's the way Stuart was. He could give it and he could take it.

"But Murtaugh said I was the only one who could have caught the ball. I took one step off the bag with Yogi up; I couldn't take two steps off. The ball went over the bag and was in foul territory when I grabbed it. It was just one of the sequences in that game that stand out. It was probably the greatest game ever played in the seventh game of the World Series. It went back and forth. You couldn't ask for better drama."

Speaking of Stuart's second-guessing, I reminded Rocky that Don Hoak said that Tony Kubek should have charged the ball that Bill Virdon hit, and that he made a mental error on that play. "Everybody who watched the play thought Kubek let the ball play him," Nelson said.

Rocky showed me a photo of the 1949 St. Louis Cardinals. He was a rookie on that team and saw action in 82 games, and batted .221 in 244 at-bats. In the photo, he is standing alongside Red Schoendienst and Stan Musial, and directly behind both Joe Garagiola and Enos Slaughter.

"We lost by a half-game to the Dodgers for the pennant that year," recalled Rocky. "We were up by 2½ games on Brooklyn with six games to go in the schedule that season. Slaughter slid into second base, and hit Murtaugh with his spikes, and cut him pretty good. That Murtaugh; he'd challenge anybody. He came over to our bench, and hollered at everyone. He hollered, 'Boys, we would've laid over backwards to let you win it. We wanted you to beat out Brooklyn. But not now.' The Pirates beat us three in a row, and the Cubs beat us in the first two games of a three-game series. We won the final game. But Brooklyn beat Philadelphia in ten innings to win the pennant on the final day of the season. If Philadelphia had won we'd have won the pennant."

"Why did they want the Dodgers to get beaten?" I asked Nelson.

"All the other teams hated the Dodgers because they had black players; that was the thinking back then. You can't excuse it, but that's the way it was."

Alberta cautioned Rocky about talking that way. "The truth is not supposed to hurt anybody," Nelson said.

"Well, don't you say anything bad, Rocky," came back Alberta. "Talk about all the fun we had."

"I played in the Dodgers organization in the early '50s and the black-white thing was never a problem for me," Rocky related. "I was with the Dodgers when they lost to the Yankees in seven games in the 1952 World Series. So I was in two World Series, and I could've been in a few more. I started out with Cleveland in 1954, when Bob Feller was their ace, but I didn't stick, and the Indians won it all that year.

"In 1960, Jack Hernon of the *Post-Gazette* asked me who I thought was the MVP on our team. I told him Clemente. Hernon said Groat got it because Biederman boosted him with the writers around the league. Hernon said he agreed with me. There were very few players who could carry Clemente's glove. Maz and Virdon were great center fielders. But Clemente did everything so easy. He threw the ball better and more consistently than anybody else in the league.

"We had a play, which we worked on in Florida, where Roberto would throw the ball on the line from right field, and I'd either spear it at first and put the tag on the runner, or I'd let it go to home plate. His throw was good either way. I tagged out a few guys with that maneuver, if they rounded first base too much."

Nelson switched from one subject to another, as he spoke about that special summer in his storied life.

"My first teams never had the friendships that we had on the Pirates team in the early '60s," he said. "We had guys from all over the league on our team, and we all came together, and we beat everybody."

Nelson said something I had never heard before, or read about anywhere, that provided an interesting insight into Mazeroski's Series-ending home run.

Nelson said that as he was coming off the field at the end of the top of the ninth inning, Maz ran alongside him and asked him about Ralph Terry. Maz hollered out, "What's he going to throw?"

"I told him, 'A slider. Terry always throws sliders until he gets ahead of you.'

"We knew as soon as he hit it that it was going out. After Maz hit that ball, he jumped up as he was running to first base, and he shouted, 'Rocky told me! Rocky told me!'

"Maz was always a high ball hitter. You didn't want to get the ball up on him. And Terry threw high fastballs and high sliders. There's only one place for it to go, and that's out of the ballpark.

"When I came into baseball 80 per cent of the guys were low-ball hitters, and when I left 80 per cent were high-ball hitters. They learned how to hit high better. It's already up there, and it's easier to hit it out.

"I was so happy for Maz. He and Milene were our family's buddies. Maz and I used to play pool together on the road. We was real good at it; same with ping pong."

Rocky also related a story about how he beat Mazeroski playing horse shoes at Seven Springs Resort during a break in the schedule in 1959. "I hadn't played in years, but I bet him I'd throw more ringers, and I did," recalled Rocky.

He said he and Alberta were also close to Bob and Pat Friend. "We're godparents to Mary Ellen, their daughter," said Rocky.

It was time to go, and the Nelsons volunteered to lead me back out to Highway 23. Nelson slipped on a windbreaker, and went to the door. He pulled on a an old-fashioned soft baseball cap when he came out in his front yard. He winked at me. That is how I will always remember The Rock.

486

Tom McDonough
Tickets unnecessary in his sports world

"The world's gone mad.
Only those who laugh will survive."

Tom McDonough stands at the rail of his balcony in an apartment atop Mt. Washington and studies the landscape below. He can see the glow from the lights above Three Rivers Stadium on a night when the Pirates are playing, and he can hear the roar of the crowd. For McDonough, it is music to his ears, like an Irish lullaby.

He can see Point State Park, all the beautiful buildings that comprise the city's Downtown skyline, the Gateway Clipper fleet in the waters of the Allegheny, Monongahela and the Ohio. Different colored lights reflect off those waters.

It's an impressive view.

In the distance, he can see the Cathedral of Learning, out in his old boyhood neighborhood of Oakland, where he first fell in love with games and whatever sports they were playing at Pitt Stadium, Forbes Field, Schenley Park, Skibo Hall and Duquesne Gardens. He can see Duquesne University up on the Bluff.

It is a scene that both excites and saddens him. McDonough doesn't smile as much as he did when I first met him. He was 68, and had whipped some health problems, yet he was more aware of his mortality than he would like. He knew he wasn't a kid anymore.

No one is more of a Pittsburgh booster than Tom McDonough, known to his intimates as Maniac McDonough.

He got the nickname of Maniac in 1937 when he was 12. He scaled a 200-foot bleacher wall at Forbes Field to see a Pirates game and when the police spotted him, they shouted at him, "Come down, you little maniac."

At least that's one story that makes the rounds about how Maniac came by his nickname. It's a myth, however. I'll tell you the true origin of that nickname as we go on.

It is true that McDonough started sneaking into sports events without benefit of a ticket quite early in his life. He enjoyed getting into a game for free, and thus began a storied career of gate-crashing.

He can go to see the Pirates play anytime he desires these days. He still knows most of the guys who tend the turnstiles. Many of them got their start in the business at Forbes Field, and they smile and look the other way when McDonough approaches their gate.

Ted Simmons, who was the general manager of the Pirates at the time, was living in the same building. "Teddy can't believe the view," McDonough says with a familiar smirk. "He thinks he died and went to heaven."

Joe Gordon, the communications director of the Pittsburgh Steelers, lives in the same building and has been a long-time friend of McDonough. "I don't ask friends for tickets," said McDonough with more than a hint of pride.

He prefers to get in on his own. He has softened as he has aged. He has tickets for Pitt basketball games, I know, and he has tickets every year for the Big East basketball tournament in New York. He goes there with life-long pals like Bill Baierl and Tom Maloney and they have a ball. In his youth, McDonough loved to crash the gate at Madison Square Garden. "It was a piece of cake," he said. He felt the same way about the Palestra in Philadelphia.

"I pick my spots now," said McDonough.

"I can't understand the psyche of some sports fans in this town," he ventured. "There were 45,000 on opening day when it was a night game, and it was on the chilly side. I didn't go. I watched it on TV. I went two days later. They had an afternoon game against the same team in the sunshine. It was warm. It was great. There were 15,000 there."

McDonough has always moved to the beat of a different drummer.

"You've got to make your stories plausible."
—Jesse Stuart

During the Depression days, some things were hard to come by. Like meat. And sugar and butter. Like baseballs, even baseballs that were scuffed and lop-sided. The kids who played on Dunseith Street in Oakland usually had a few baseballs because they lived near Forbes Field. And they had baseballs the same way that kids in Oakland in later years always had ice skates and hockey sticks when Duquesne Gardens was still in business.

There was a crochety old man who sat in a chair behind a gray door in a gray house on Dunseith Street. And every time some kid fouled a ball off and it rolled onto the lawn outside that gray door, the old man would burst through the door and go down his porch steps quickly, seize the ball, and take it back into his house.

None of the kids could figure out why the man was so mean, and what he wanted with a baseball, especially one with the cover half off. But they were afraid of him, even the bigger ones. Except one day when a little boy named McDonough got fed up. Thomas Joseph McDonough was a small, broad-shouldered lad. His face was wide and so was his heart.

And when the ball trickled through the small bushes onto the lawn one afternoon, Tommy McDonough went through it. The old man threw back the door, and came down the porch steps. The boys in the street froze as Tommy scooped up the ball. The old man's outstretched hands just missed grabbing hold of Tommy's jersey. The old man cursed and yelled in a hoarse voice, "You . . . you little maniac!"

Tommy McDonough was celebrated as a hero on Dunseith Street that evening. Then one of the older kids started calling Tommy a "little maniac." Soon the chant was picked up and Tommy McDonough was no more. He was Maniac. Maniac McDonough.

"I did little in the years after that to erase that name," said McDonough.

I first met McDonough during my student days at Pitt in the early '60s. More often than not, I bumped into McDonough at Frankie Gustine's Restaurant on the Pitt campus. The restaurant was just below the then-new dormitories at Pitt, and a block away from Forbes Field. The Pirates and Steelers were still playing there.

McDonough was a successful insurance salesman. His specialty was selling insurance to young doctors and dentists, especially former Pitt athletes he had befriended during their student days on the campus. He would fill in on occasion as a bartender when Frank needed some help at his bar. McDonough had worked as a bartender there in earlier years.

McDonough was the father of seven children, an ex-war hero, a stand-up comic, a magician of sorts, and the greatest gate-crasher since Ghengis Khan.

When people asked him what his middle name was, he would say matter-of-factly that it was Maniac.

He told wonderful stories. He himself was a wonderful story. I was cautioned about writing such stories when I was a student at Pitt. At a writers' conference on the campus, I heard Jesse Stuart speak. He is a cherished writer of tall tales of Appalachia, and most of his short stories were drawn from real life incidents during his childhood in Kentucky.

"If I wrote the whole truth," cried Stuart, with a beefy grin, "no one would believe it. One thing you've got to remember: you've got to make your stories *plausible.*"

This is impossible when you're dealing with the story of Maniac McDonough. If you tampered with the story of Maniac McDonough it would be fiction. His life and foolishness are an epoch of incredulity. Like Scaramouche, "he was born with a gift of laughter and a sense that the world was mad."

Or, as he put it back then, "If you're not happy, you're terminal. The world's gone mad. Only those who laugh will survive."

The story of Maniac McDonough is the strange anomaly of the Irish "adventurous boy" who grows up to such an immature middle age that Jim Farrell wrote about in his *Studs Lonigan* trilogy.

"He looked like one of the waiters at the Last Supper."

Maniac McDonough is a healthy slice-of-life. He is Americana. He is incredible. Here is his story, a true one, and as Ripley put it, believe it or not.

Maniac McDonough is a sports nut. He used to go to every sports event — he usually had a reserved seat — even though he almost never bought a ticket.

He preferred his wits to tickets when it came to gaining admission to a ballpark or sports arena. In his 40s, he would have driven the Red Guard crazy going through the Berlin Wall every day just for kicks.

Maniac made his mark as a legendary figure among Oakland's sports crowd when, as a kid, he climbed the vent-shaped siding behind the right-field stands in Forbes Field to see a baseball game. A ranger who had climbed the Cliffs of Dover might have thought twice about climbing that 200 foot barrier, and all that Maniac remembers is that "there was a lot of cold wind blowing through those slats."

When the All-Star Baseball Game was held in Pittsburgh in 1958, Maniac stopped in at Frankie Gustine's Restaurant on the morning of the game. Gustine asked Maniac if he had tickets for the game. "Of course not," Maniac replied.

"Well, it's a sellout, you know," said Frank.

"That's why I came early," said Maniac. Then he left, and crashed the gate. Once inside, however, he got hungry. So he left the ballpark and returned to Gustine's for breakfast. Maniac returned to the scene of the crime, and crashed the gate again.

In 1963, he stood outside County Stadium in Milwaukee, plotting his entry. He noticed that the usher at the gate was an elderly man. "He looked like he had been one of the waiters at the Last Supper," said McDonough. "I knew he'd never chase me." So McDonough backed up a few steps, took a running start, and hurdled the turnstiles.

Another time, his long-time friend, Dick Groat, then a shortstop with the Pirates, invited him to a football game at the Stadium. Groat was turned away at Gate 1, and told that he would have to go around to the other side of the Stadium with the ticket he presented. Maniac knew the ticket-taker, so he asked Groat to give him the tickets. They entered the same turnstiles and on the other side McDonough presented Groat with the tickets. They were still intact.

Groat was dumbfounded. "I can't even get in this place with tickets and you can get in without them. What goes?" McDonough put a calming hand on Groat's shoulder, and told him, "Don't worry, Richard. If you ever have any trouble getting in Forbes Field, you let me know about it, okay."

In March of 1964, when I was completing my senior year at Pitt, I spoke to McDonough about his sports calendar. He said he was going to the NIT basketball tournament in New York. "I have no thoughts of tickets," he said. "Remember, it's at Madison Square Garden, and the bigger they are, the easier they are to get in."

McDonough went to New York to see Pitt play in the NIT, stayed over to march in the St. Patrick's Day Parade, and then went to see Duquesne play before returning home.

Although McDonough seldom spent a buck for a sports event, it wasn't because he was a bum, or that he didn't have the money. He had a highly successful run as a salesman for the National Life Insurance Company of Vermont. In fact, he was often a member of the Million Dollar Round-table, the higher echelon guys in the business who sell over a million dollars worth of life insurance a year. More often than not, he sold more than three million dollars worth of insurance a year. "All grind-'em out accounts, too," said McDonough. "I don't have accounts like Mellon Bank and U.S. Steel."

He has been one of the few insurance salesmen who doesn't have his friends ducking him. He never mentioned insurance to me for years when I first met him. Yet I ended up buying my first insurance policy from him. "I'm a friend," McDonough said back then. "I let a lot of people die without insurance. That'll teach them."

Before becoming an insurance man, McDonough had worked as a bartender in most of Oakland's cafes, and also had worked for General Motors, where he handled delinquent accounts. His approach was unique. He sent one fellow a letter, reminding him that he was 12 months in arrears of payment. The fellow sent a return note, thanking McDonough for the anniversary note. McDonough's next letter began: "Now look, we have already carried you three months longer than your mother." Another to a minister began, "GMAC giveth, but GMAC also taketh away." Needless to say, this didn't sit well with his superior, and when McDonough was criticized about his communication techniques, he just walked away and quit.

He worked longer hours as an insurance agent, but he liked the life better. "I don't sleep much," he said, "but I'm lucky because I faint a lot. A single guy would do better. It's a federal case for me to get out of the house."

The neighbors also complained because he didn't have time to work around the house much, either.

"They say I should plant grass," McDonough said at the time. "I think I'll just put an asphalt surface on the ground and paint it green."

His wife, Dorothy, said she understood. She said he had a nice disposition and that he was good with the children.

Where Were You?

"We went running wild,
all over the flight deck."
—Kenny Huffman

Denny Smith
Mt. Lebanon, Pa.

"I learned to play the piano back then. I was in high school and they were always playing Benny Benack's 'Beat 'Em Bucs' on the radio all the time. It was a simple song, and you could learn it by ear. I lived on Florida Avenue at the time, and every time the Pirates won I'd open the windows of our house and I'd play it real loud. I was 14 at the time. I also had a drum set. When Mazeroski hit that home run off Ralph Terry I grabbed a gong and went out and started banging it. I really tore up my finger."

Howard Kernats
Hair Stylist
Robinson Township, Pa.

"I'm 51 now, so I was 19 and living on the North Side and I was a student at Lattimer High School. I had a 1953 Ford convertible. About ten guys piled into my car and we went to town. We drove right into the middle of the celebration. We rode down Fifth Avenue. We got home at 11:30 or 12 that night, and my car was filled with paper and confetti. The guys in the back were sitting high on paper. I've been to the Super Bowls with the Steelers, but I was never in a celebration as wild as that one when the Pirates won the '60 World Series."

Kayss Sofaly
Irwin

"My late husband, Jerry, had played Legion Ball with Bill Mazeroski. I was very pregnant during the 1960 World Series. I was due in about two weeks when I laid down on the couch to watch the seventh game. I had been told to take it easy. When he hit the home run, I started screaming and ran through the house. I went crazy. My husband thought I was having the baby. I wore myself out and had to lie back down again. I ended up having a boy, after having two girls earlier. But I didn't name him Bill. I was looking up names and I saw John — 'a gift from God' — and I named him for John F. Kennedy, who was running for President, and for my doctor, whose name was John, and who delivered my baby."

492

Kenny Huffman
Brookline

"I was in the Navy in the Mediterranean, on the flight deck of the aircraft carrier *U.S.S. Independence,* just off the coast of Italy. I got a break and ran down to where I could hear a radio, and heard Hal Smith's home run. We went crazy. It was about 9 o'clock at night, and it was pitch black. There were about 4,000 guys on the ship, and a gang of them were from Pittsburgh or nearby. When we got the announcement that Mazeroski hit the home run and the Pirates won it, we went running wild all over the flight deck, shouting and hollering and celebrating as best we could. It's a wonder a few guys didn't fall over the side. The Steelers stunk in those days, and we didn't have a lot to get excited about. I was always into boxing, and it was the best thing we'd had to root about in Pittsburgh since Billy Conn. It was just great, running around the deck like we did. Smith never got the notoriety he deserved for hitting his home run. He brought us back from the dead. When he hit it, I just lost it. Mickey Mantle said that day was the biggest disappointment he had in baseball. In 1973, I was at a Pirates game at Three Rivers Stadium, and I had a chance to shake Mazeroski's hand. I said to him, 'I just want to thank you for giving me the greatest thrill of my life.' He was so nice and humble about it. You gotta love Bill Mazeroski."

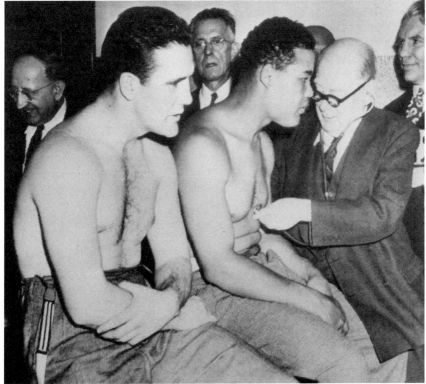

Billy Conn and Joe Louis receive pre-fight check-up before 1946 title fight in New York.

Joe Christopher
"Hurryin' Joe" is a work of art
"I made things happen."

Joe Christopher made a significant contribution to the Pirates world championship season of 1960 as a rookie reserve outfielder, hitter, base-runner and buoyant spirit. He had speed, and was often inserted as a pinch-runner, prompting broadcaster Bob Prince to call him "Hurryin' Joe."

Christopher seems to have slowed down considerably these days. He does not have a real job — one where he makes money — but he keeps himself busy by researching and doing what he calls pre-Columbian art.

He lives in Baltimore with his second wife, Karen Matthews Christopher, and their charming and precocious four-year-old daughter, Kameahle Loretta Christopher. They live in an apartment complex in the Mt. Washington section of the city. The daughter was just delightful in a brief conversation we had. She sounded so grown-up and polite. Karen, his wife of six years, works as a program analyst for the hospital section at the University of Maryland at Baltimore County. Joe draws on his baseball pension, and said he hoped to soon bring his art to the marketplace.

"I'm not ready to do that just yet," said Christopher in one of a series of telephone conversations we had in February of 1993. "I have a studio in our apartment."

Christopher's art renderings, which he calls pre-Columbian art, are not easily appreciated, but then the same could be said for Piccaso and Dali. They are different. But criticism is nothing new to Christopher. He can deal with it. He sees himself as an artist rather than a former baseball player. That is behind him, to hear him tell it.

Christopher's conversation is equally difficult to comprehend. He seems determined to demonstrate how different he has become since he hung up his spikes, how intellectual he is, and his observations are often long-winded, circuitous and not easy to follow. Friends and former co-workers who spoke with Christopher at the 30th anniversary reunion of the 1960 Pirates in 1990 came away shaking their heads. One of my favorite writers, Jimmy Breslin, would deal with such double-talk by snapping, "What the hell is this man trying to say?"

They did not know what to make of Joe Christopher. That is fine, if Christopher is to be taken at his word. He seems sincere enough. But he lost me a couple of times, like he had eluded me on a run-down between second and third base.

Christopher first discovered the real Christopher, he claims, thanks to Branch Rickey, who was the front-office boss of the Pirates when Christopher came up to stay from Salt Lake City for the 1960 season.

494

He had been up for a short stint in 1959 when Roberto Clemente was sidelined with a sore throwing arm. To hear Christopher tell his story, Rickey was as responsible for his breakthrough as he once was for Jackie Robinson's in Brooklyn. And it may prove to be as important.

"Branch Rickey had a guy talk to us one day at training camp about our futures, and discovering what we really wanted to do with our lives," recalled Christopher. "Everybody else was sleeping; the kids didn't want to hear it. But he was talking to *me*."

In time, a long time, at that, it brought Christopher to pre-Columbian art. "I have found out a whole lot about it," said Christopher. "And, from Rickey, I found out a whole lot about why certain people are successful. Rickey told me he chose Jackie Robinson (to break the color barrier in baseball) because of his birthdate. He believed that some people are pre-destined for success by their birthdate."

That was one of those points where Christopher lost me for awhile, and I quit taking notes on what he was saying, until he got to something I understood better.

Christopher confessed that he is reluctant to grant interviews because he does not like the way they come off in print, probably because he feels misunderstood. That is understandable. "I don't sound like a professional baseball player, do I?" he asked at one point in our discourse.

What confuses most people about Christopher is that he was such an outgoing, friendly fellow in his days at Forbes Field, and one of the most popular players with the fans, especially the young fans. Christopher spent a lot of time in pre-game workouts having a good time with the young fans in the stands. He'd play off the crowd before the games. Several fans told me about such positive experiences.

He did offer some interesting insights into his former teammate and friend Roberto Clemente. There were only four blacks on that 1960 ballclub, notably Clemente, Christopher, Earl Francis and Gene Baker.

Scars remain from slights they suffered as minorities in those days. For Christopher, they continue. "I'm the one person no one ever calls from that club," he said, "like I'm obsolete."

Mentally, Chistopher is not unique among the '60 Bucs. Several of them feel unappreciated in one area or another. Physically, Christopher sounds like he is in better physical shape than any of the other '60 Bucs.

"I'm 58 years old, and I can still run the 60 in 6.1," he was proud to say. "That's my point of reference. I still have my ability. Do I ever gain weight? You should always be in condition. I've never been out of condition. I can still offer batting instruction, and I could do it on a major league level. I'm into art now — that's what I do — but baseball has been my No. 1 passion. But in baseball we're dealing with a very narrow point of reference."

To demonstrate his independence, Christopher shot off on a different tangent. "If I were playing today, I'd never have an agent," he said. "All you need is a good bank. You pay the bank a commission to handle your money. Why would you let somebody with the backgrounds many of these people have handle your money? It's no wonder a lot of these guys lose their butts."

He was also eager to point up some of the unique contributions he made to the Bucs in that summer of 1960. Joe Christopher was a catalyst for positive action, there is no doubt about it.

"I made things happen," he said. "When I got on base, I made things happen. That's why Bob Prince called me 'Hurryin' Joe.' I was the one running when Virdon hit the ball that hit Kubek in the throat.

"I scored and I'm the only one who ever scored three runs in a World Series without one official at-bat. I got on twice as a pinch-runner and I got hit by a pitch by Bob Turley when I did come to the plate. And I scored all three times."

Christopher's memory must be playing tricks on him. He had come in as a pinch-runner for Smoky Burgess in the seventh inning of that seventh game. He did not score. Hal Smith replaced him in the lineup for the eighth inning, and ended up hitting a three-run home run. According to *The Sporting News* record book, Christopher scored two runs, not three, in that Series. But that's still pretty good.

"I'm one of only two players who participated in two perfect games. The first game I played in the major leagues was on May 25, 1959, when Harvey Haddix pitched his 12-inning perfect game in Milwaukee. And I was with the Mets when Jim Bunning pitched a perfect game against the Mets for the Phillies on June 21, 1964. See what I mean? I made things happen."

Christopher was one of the few players from the Virgin Islands in the big leagues.

"My greatest thrill was when Howie Haak signed me," he said back then. "My regular position is shortstop, but eventually they may change me because I have great speed and a tremendous arm."

Asked who helped him the most in his professional career on a form sent to him by the Pirates' publicity office, Christopher wrote at the time: "I helped myself." He listed his baseball hero as Phil Rizzuto.

"The first home run I hit came off Billy O'Dell," recalled Christopher in our stream-of-conscious conversation. "In a game in Cincinnati, I had five hits when Skinner wasn't able to play. I hit .300 one season with the Mets."

That was in 1964, his third season with the Mets. He was claimed from the Pirates by the Mets in the 1962 expansion draft. Some sports writers were calling him "Joltin' Joe" in their stories, while others had retired that nickname in deference to Joe DiMaggio. Christopher played the last 127 straight games of the '64 season for Casey Stengel, which was significant because Stengel liked to platoon. Christopher was the Mets' most consistent hitter, leading the team that summer in at-bats (543) hits (163), doubles (26), triples (8), total bases (253), slugging percentage (.486), runs batted in (76) and walks (48). Given his first real chance to hang in there against all kinds of pitching, Christopher had four 4-hit games. He set a club record with 12 total bases on a double, two triples and a home run against his former Pirate mates on August 18.

"Charlie Smith hit 20 home runs to lead the Mets that year, and I was next with 16. I led in every other offensive category," recalled Christopher. "I was a regular from June on. And I was making $10,000."

"The biggest joy I had in baseball was when I played in Pittsburgh for the Pirates."
— Joe Christopher

Joseph O'Neal Christopher was born December 13, 1935 at Fredriksted, St. Croix, Virgin Islands. In his playing days, he was 5-9, 175 and batted and threw right-handed. He lived in Puerto Rico in the off-season.

"I was the only player in the history of the Puerto Rican League to play on eight different championship teams," said Christopher, who always played winter ball.

He was a star in Puerto Rico, but a reserve or platoon player most of his career in the big leagues. Christopher felt he always adjusted well to his limited role, even though he believed in his heart he was better than some of the regulars.

"If they want you to be a fill-in, you have to be ready psychologically," he said. "The biggest joy I had in baseball was when I played in Pittsburgh for the Pirates. I was very close to the Rickey family. I was close to Joe L. Brown, Branch Rickey Jr., and Bob Rice, the team's traveling secretary. Joe Brown brought me up from Double A ball.

"They didn't realize how sensitive I was inside. The criticism hurt. I was from the Virgin Islands, and I spoke differently than the other guys. Alvin McBean also came from the Virgin Islands, but he was from St. Thomas and I was from St. Croix.

"I roomed with Clemente during the '60 season. I got to see the way this man really was."

Then Christopher lost me again when he started rattling off the birthdates of great baseball players like Clemente (8/19/34), Reggie Jackson (5/18/46) and Lou Brock (6/18/39), and how that affected their lives, but I didn't comprehend what he was driving at, or see any particular pattern in those dates. "You have to realize that there are things in nature," said Christopher. "Clemente was born a great player. The man was born with innate ability, therefore he was the best ballplayer every day. If he had the power of Aaron, he'd have been in a category all by himself."

There's no doubt about that, either. On a more personal level, Christopher was encouraged to discuss Clemente.

"When we played in Forbes Field," said Christopher, "Clemente's locker was next to mine. Sam Narron was next to him. They both helped me a lot. Clemente made me aware of so many things. There was a consistency in what he said. He would tell me, for instance, 'when the ball hits in the corner you have to play it to come out at a 45 degree angle. When the ball hits the screen, it comes right down.'

"There was so much to Clemente, but words don't do him justice. You have to use words, and it's hard to categorize what you're dealing with. You're dealing with euphemisms and they don't work with Clemente to capture his greatness. You can take words and change their meaning."

Clemente was considered a proud man, and Christopher came up with a story to pinpoint that attribute.

"Clemente said we could have gone to the victory party they had at the Webster Hall Hotel that evening after the seventh game," said Christopher. "But he said he should have been the MVP that year. Clemente carried the Pirates for the first two months of the season, but he never got the publicity and that's why he rebelled. The p.r. went to Dick Groat (who won the National League MVP that season) and Dick Stuart. Les Biederman (*The Pittsburgh Press*) was a good friend of mine, and Jack Hernon (*Pittsburgh Post-Gazette*) was a good friend of mine. 1960 was my happiest year. But they did favor other ballplayers over Clemente. He'd hit a home run or drive in several runs, and somebody else would get the headline.

"But he was so great. Can you imagine how much money a Clemente would get today? How much would you pay a guy like Roberto Clemente today? How much would you pay Willie Mays?

"You know how good Roberto Clemente played right field for the Pirates. He was the best right fielder I ever saw. Henry Aaron was the best home run hitter for consistency. When Willie Mays got hot, he was unreal. They called Pete Rose the greatest player of the century because he had over 4,000 hits. But he couldn't compare with Clemente.

"Clemente and I both decided not to go to the Series celebration party. Till this day I've never worn my World Series ring.

"They were supposed to do a movie about Clemente, but what happened to it? What's the reason they didn't do it? When they talk about Clemente, everybody goes to Manny Sanguillen to get the inside story. Because Manny is from a Latin country, Panama, but I knew Clemente better than he did.

"When Clemente went to Children's Hospital, I'd go with him all the time. He did a lot of charitable things in his spare time. I was the fourth or fifth outfielder, it depends on where you put (Gino) Cimoli, but I was as close as anyone on the team to Clemente.

"If you're on a baseball team, you get close to a few guys. The best friends I had on the bench were Smoky Burgess and Rocky Nelson. All we talked about was hitting. That's how I became so selective. Clemente helped me with that, too.

"Clemente was the best player pound for pound. He could throw, he could hit, he could hit with power, he could run. He was simply the greatest. I'm glad I knew him."

Supporting Cast
It was a team victory

"The 1960 season was a once-in-a-lifetime thing."

Dick Schofield

"I really believe if we would have played the Yankees in a 99-game World Series in 1960, we still would have won. We'd have probably beat them 50 games to 49. That's just the way I felt about that team. We just had the feeling late in the game that we were going to beat you. Somehow, some way, we were going to beat you."

Schofield, 58 in the summer of 1993, lives in Springfield, Illinois, and works for Jostens, a leading manufacturer of recognition products for education, business and athletics, such as championship and school rings, plaques and awards. Dick is responsible for sales efforts in central Illinois.

"The 1960 season was a once-in-a-lifetime thing," he said. "So many great games and so many wonderful players. Guys really got along well and we had fun. Groat, Hoak or Roberto could have been MVP! Friend and Law pitched great. We probably would not have won without Mizell. I enjoyed Pittsburgh and Forbes Field. I sure didn't want to leave. The '60 season was a team victory!"

On a personal level, Dick and Donna Schofield celebrated their 37th wedding anniversary in June of 1993. They have three children: Kim, 35, has three children (Jayson, 13, Hillary, 5, Hanah, 2); Tami, 32, has one child, Haley, 2, and both daughters live in Springfield. Their son, Dick, 30, who has one child, Gracie, 2, lives in California, and plays for the California Angels.

The Pirates infielder got his nickname "Ducky" from his dad, who never made it to the major leagues but was a long-time minor league baseball performer. Dick was signed by the Cardinals as a "bonus baby" right out of high school, and rode the bench for two years before he was traded to the Pirates in 1958. Joe Brown traded infielders Gene Freese and Johnny O'Brien to get him.

No one was under more pressure in the 1960 pennant drive than Dick Schofield. He had been in only 44 games until the night of September 6, when regular shortstop Dick Groat suffered a broken wrist when hit by a pitched ball by Lew Burdette of the Braves.

Schofield replaced Groat and came up with three hits, and made a sterling backhand stop to start a double play in the field to get rookie pitcher Joe Gibbon out of a jam. In the 19 games he subbed for Groat, the league's leading hitter and MVP that season, Schofield batted .368, and played well in the field. He came up with a single and a walk in four plate appearances as a pinch-hitter during the World Series.

"I had good friendships with many of the players and front-office people and the fans with the Pirates," recalled Schofield. "The fans of Pittsburgh were always nice to me."

His biggest thrills came when he got to see action in the 1960 World Series, and when his son, Dick, signed with the Angels right out of high school.

Schofield said the player he most admired on the '60 team was his good friend Bill Virdon. "He was a very professional player," said Schofield.

His advice to young players: "Remember where you came from and take care of the game of baseball. It's been good to all of us."

George Witt

This was a blue-eyed, freckle-faced, red-haired pitcher with great promise when he first came to the Pirates. He was a 6-3, 200 pound, hard-throwing right-handed hurler of Dutch-Irish ancestry. He turned the head of Charlie Dressen, the manager of the Washington Senators, one day at Fort Myers, training base of the Bucs back in 1957. Dressen said the kid looked just like Walter "Big Train" Johnson.

Witt, who grew up in Long Beach, California, and was a graduate of Long Beach State Teachers College, posted an outstanding record (18-7, with 2.24 ERA) at Hollywood that year, and came up to the Pirates the following summer to stay. He had a 9-2 record, with a 1.61 ERA, and was a strong candidate for Rookie of the Year honors. He appeared on his way to a great big league career.

He had it all — a fast ball, a tantalizing curve and pinpoint control. In his debut that season, he beat the Dodgers, who had originally signed him, 2-1, on six hits. He won seven in a row that 1958 season, the longest by a Pirates' pitcher since Rip Sewell in 1948. Twice Witt struck out ten batters in a game. He ran off 23⅓ consecutive scoreless innings.

Unfortunately, Witt, now lists that 1958 rookie season as the personal highlight of his career with the Pirates. "I gave up only ten extra base hits in 106 innings, and I had three shutouts, two against the Braves. In one of those, I struck out three Braves in a row, including Henry Aaron, in a two-hit shutout."

He came up with a sore elbow in spring training in 1959, and his record dipped to 0-7 in 15 starts. He was 1-2 in six starts in 1960, yet has fond memories of that championship season.

"My relationship with very special human beings" is his most cherished memory of his association with those '60 Bucs.

Witt was warming up in the bullpen, along with Wilmer Mizell, ready to replace Harvey Haddix if there was a tenth inning. Mizell got the nod, but never had to throw a pitch because Bill Mazeroski ended the game with a home run in the bottom of the ninth inning.

Witt, who would turn 60 on November 9, 1993, says the most significant event in his life since he left the Pirates was "meeting and marrying my soulmate and best friend, Ellen." George earned a master's

Pittsburgh Pirates

)onna and Dick Schofield with three little "duckies"
– Kim, Tami and Dick Jr.

Dick Schofield

Dick Schofield Jr.

George "Red" Witt

Pittsburgh Pirates

Dick Stuart douses Fred Green and George Witt with beer
in jubilant clubhouse after winning 1960 World Series.

degree in physical fitness instruction at the University of California at Irvine, and is a health teacher at Tustin (Calif.) High School.

He suggests that players spend the off-season doing physical training, but also schooling themselves or developing the skills they need for a new career to look forward to following their days in baseball.

The player Witt most admired on that 1960 team was Vernon Law: "He was a non-elitist, high-principled and non-judgmental. He saw all of us as valued individuals."

When asked what he had learned from his experience with the Pirates, he said somewhat philosophically, "That what you do relating to performance or job are only a small part of the unlimited possibilities of who you are."

Joe Gibbon

Mickey Mantle hit a home run off Gibbon in the 1960 World Series. Gibbon took some solace in the fact that Mantle did not hit it quite as far as the one he hit off Fred Green at Forbes Field.

"The one off me was also quite a poke," said Gibbon. "It went over the monument in center field. I took some kidding about that one for a long time. No, it didn't bother me. I don't care how many they hit off you in October; it's easy to forget when you're on the way to the bank."

Gibbon was a giant in his day, at 6-4, 210, and had been a standout basketball player as well as a baseball star at the University of Mississippi. He was known as "Jumpin' Joe" because of his jump shot and leaping ability. He lettered four years in basketball — he had been all-state as a schoolboy basketball player — and he lettered three years in baseball. He was a right-handed batter and a left-handed pitcher. He led his baseball team to a third place finish in the College World Series. He earned a b.a. in physical education. He had brown hair, blue eyes.

Stan Musial was his boyhood hero. He served six months in the military service in a reserve program upon graduation from college.

He was signed by Pirates in 1957 as a first baseman. Larry Shepard used him as a pitcher at Lincoln in Class A, and he remained a pitcher after that. He started nine games for the Pirates as a rookie in 1960 and posted a 4-2 record. He was hit hard, however, in the World Series, giving up four hits and three runs in three innings in the two appearances he made. He was 13-10 the following season when he had 29 starts. He dropped off to 3-4 in 1962.

He married Donna Jean Price of Hazelwood on September 28, 1962.

Gibbon's won-lost record was 5-12 in 1963, 10-7 in 1964 and 4-9 in 1965. At the end of that season, Joe Brown traded Gibbon to the Giants for Matty Alou — a great trade for the Pirates. Gibbon had a history of arm trouble and injuries, and proved to be a disappointment.

He came back at age 35 and helped Larry Shepard's team in 1964. The Pirates had traded Ron Kline to the Giants to get him and Gibbon became a Pirate for the second time.

Clem Labine

He was one of the Boys of Summer of the great Brooklyn Dodgers teams of the 1950s, and stayed with the team when it left New York for Los Angeles. At 67, he left Woonsocket, Rhode Island, where he wintered during his days with the Dodgers and retired to Vero Beach, Florida, where the Dodgers still conduct spring training. He was born in Lincoln, Rhode Island. He was always a natty dresser, as he was a graduate of the Rhode Island School of Design and designed, manufactured and sold his own line of men's clothing.

He was signed by Joe Brown on August 16, 1960 and helped the Pirates in the pennant race, but was a disaster in the World Series.

Prior to joining the Pirates, the one-time Dodgers relief ace was cut loose by Los Angeles on June 15, and signed by the Detroit Tigers. But he had no success in the American League. Hank Foiles, a former Pirates catcher who was then with Detroit, tipped off Brown that Labine was going to be released again, and Foiles said he was positive Labine could help the Pirates in the pennant drive.

Labine saw action the night after Brown obtained him, striking out six Phillies in three innings of relief. Accustomed to pennant pressure, the 10-year Dodgers veteran proved to be a cool competitor in the clutch. He was used mainly as a short relief man, spelling ElRoy Face. Labine appeared in 15 games for the Pirates, worked 30 innings, won three games, did not lose any, saved four games and had a 1.49 ERA. In the first three weeks he was with the Pirates, Labine won two games, saved four and allowed the opposition only three runs in 15 innings.

Labine had been in four World Series before the Bucs signed him. His most memorable game came, strangely enough, as a starter. In 1956, the Dodgers were stunned in the fifth game by Yankee Don Larsen's "perfect" game, a nine-inning, 2-0 no-hitter, the only one in World Series competition. The next day, Labine, who had started only three games all season, got the call and came through with a 10-inning 1-0 victory at Ebbets Field.

In the World Series with the Pirates, however, Labine pitched four innings, and gave up 13 hits and 11 runs, six of those earned, for a 13.50 ERA.

Fred Green

They still talk about the home run Mickey Mantle hit off Fred Green at Forbes Field in the 1960 World Series. Mantle drilled it over the wall in right-center, batting right-handed, the purists always add when telling the tale, and they swear that ball is still flying.

That is not what Fred Green gets the most satisfaction from when he recalls that October. "Winning the 1960 World Series," he says, when asked to name the personal highlight of his career with the Pirates.

"We were out-hit and out-scored in the World Series, yet we hung in there as a team and beat the Yankees four games to three."

He was a big pitcher, at 6-4, 190 pounds, a lefty reliever who did a fine job for the Pirates in their pennant drive that year. He was of Scotch-Irish descent, and he came from Titusville, New Jersey, where he had been a three-sport athlete (baseball, basketball and soccer) in high school. He turned 60 on September 13, 1993.

He spent two years in the Army (1956-58).

"Being able to play pro baseball is my greatest experience," he once said.

As far as the most significant event since he retired as a ballplayer, that is easy. "Watching my son Gary play in the big leagues," he said.

Gary is in the Red Sox farm system. Fred and his wife Mona have another son, Gregg.

The Greens still call Titusville home. Fred works in a hardware warehouse in the shipping and receiving department.

His advice for young players today is "Try to make yourself a complete player through hard work."

He did not single out any Pirates from the 1960 team, preferring to say, "I admired the whole team, as all of them were outstanding people."

As for what he learned from the experience that has served him in good stead ever since, he says, "How to get along with people and cope with ups and downs in everyday life."

Mickey Vernon

With the death of Lenny Levy in 1993, Vernon and Sam Narron were the only living coaches remaining from Danny Murtaugh's staff from the 1960 season. Bill Burwell and Frank Oceak had died earlier.

Vernon was living in Wallingford, Pennsylvania during the summer of 1993. He had retired from baseball after the 1988 season. His last job was as a minor league hitting instructor for the New York Yankees, and he had scouted the National League the previous two years for them.

He was proud to report that he has "been happily married to the same gal for 51 years," and that his daughter was a news reporter for a radio station in Boston.

He listed "being on the '60 team" as the personal highlight of his association with the Pirates. He was on the active roster during most of the regular season, but became a full-time coach for the Series.

What he remembers best from that year was "being associated with Danny Murtaugh on the same team for the first time since our American Legion team days back in Chester, Pa."

Asked if he had any advice for today's players, he said, "I don't give advice to players unless they ask for it, and very few ask."

He would not single out a player as the one he most admired from the 1960 squad, saying, "I admired all of them because they all rose to the occasion throughout the season."

Vernon was one of the best hitters in the game, with a super-smooth stroke.

Bob Oldis Today

Green   Bob Oldis

Joe Gibbon, Joe Christopher and Clem Labine get together at 1990 30th year reunion of '60 Bucs.

James G. Klingensmith/Pittsburgh Post-Gazette

n Labine, Vinegar Bend Mizell, Harvey dix go over pitcher's scouting report.

Joe Gibbon married Donna Jean Price of Hazelwood while he was pitching for Pirates.

Bob Oldis

At age 63, Oldis was still active in baseball during the summer of 1993, as a scout for the Montreal Expos. He continued to live in Iowa City, Iowa, which was his home when he played for the Pirates.

"I love signing kids and watching them grow," he said. "If they make it to the big leagues, well, I'm some kind of proud."

He was the third-string catcher for the 1960 Pirates, but Joe Brown always said he was the most important third-string catcher on any club. Smoky Burgess and Hal Smith split most of the time behind home plate that season, but Oldis managed to make some key contributions.

Oldis appeared in 22 games as a late-inning replacement for Burgess or Smith and batted just 20 times.

"I can't tell you how important he was to that team," said Brown, the Pirates general manager. "He was a funny guy, but through his wit he got a lot of truths across. Every team needs a Bob Oldis."

Oldis says the highlight of his Pirates' playing career was playing in two World Series games, the fourth and fifth, catching ElRoy Face and winning both games in Yankee Stadium. "It was the last inning of both games," points out Oldis.

Oldis was 32 when he joined the Pirates and had not played in the majors for five years, and then for only six games with the Washington Senators.

"I can't complain. Just being on that team was the biggest thrill of my career. I feel fortunate to have been in the right place at the right time that year. I tried to have fun and keep everyone loose. That role was natural for me. I just showed up at the park and cheered like heck. I've got to tell you I was a heckuva cheerleader.

"I wish my Dad could have seen me play in the majors. I always felt indebted to my wife, Rosemary, who made a lot of sacrifices so I could play big league baseball. She took care of our two boys, who both had muscular dystrophy, and our daughter, Susan (36), who has since given us two wonderful healthy grandchildren."

Asked to name his top personal memory from that 1960 season, Oldis recalled how the players gave him a record of the University of Iowa fight song — "I have always been a great Hawkeye fan" — and they all signed it. During the fall when he was in major league baseball, Oldis served as official time-keeper for Iowa football games. Oldis also officiated high school football and basketball games.

Oldis takes pride in having been elected to the Iowa High School Baseball Association Hall of Fame, and also being elected to the Basketball Officials Hall of Fame in Iowa.

The players on the Pirates '60 team that he admired the most were Don Hoak ("his desire to win when playing hurt") and Vernon Law ("he always could stop a losing streak").

Face tells a good story about Oldis. "We were in New York early in the season and Bob accidentally swallowed his chewing tobacco," said ElRoy. "I can still see him standing there choking and getting sick. Well, we won that day so we decided to make him swallow it again. He did it, too. He'd do anything if he thought it would help us win."

Oldis was a clown in the clubhouse, but often had a heavy heart at home. His good humor during his seven-year pro career masked the difficulties he had with his family.

During the spring of 1961, the year after the Pirates won the World Series, his oldest son, Bobby Jr., then 8, was diagnosed as having muscular dystrophy. He died at age 29 in October, 1982. Oldis discussed his difficult days with Pittsburgh sports writer Ron Cook in 1985.

"We watched the seventh game of the World Series between St. Louis and Milwaukee together," Oldis related to Cook. "He went to bed that night and never woke up.

"I'm so proud of that kid. He walked until he was 14, then had to use a wheelchair, but he never slowed down. He managed a Little League team from that wheelchair. They named a five-field baseball complex in Iowa City, Iowa, after him."

Bob's second son, John, also died from muscular dystrophy in March 1980 when he was 18.

"The same thing happened to him," Oldis told Cook. "He went to sleep on us and when we went to get him in the morning to get him ready for school, by golly, he had left us . . . He was good in school whereas the older one loved sports more."

Asked what he learned from his experience with the Pirates that has served him in good stead since then, Oldis told us, "To never give up. We came from behind in so many games and won them."

In an interview with Pittsburgh sports writer Bob Smizik prior to the team's 30th year anniversary reunion in 1990, Oldis showed that he had not lost his good sense of humor.

"Our World Series check was $8,400. After taxes it was $6,747. I'm certain of that. When I got my check I took it to the bank. They made a photo copy of it for me. I framed it and it's hanging on my wall. We bought the land we're living on with that check.

"But when people come into my game room, I tell them I never cashed my World Series check."

Gino Cimoli

Nobody was more popular than Gino Cimoli with the ushers at Forbes Field during the 1960 season. He was a handsome, fun-loving, blue-eyed, dark-haired Italian. He was custom-made for Oakland.

Myron Cope described him as "a strapping man with a thick pompadour, a flashing smile, and an easy way. He looks, in short, like a Latin lover, and Hollywood producers have asked him to take screen tests."

He was a favorite at Forbes Field, located alongside the "Little Italy" section of Oakland.

"Datsa my boy Geeno!" the fans at Forbes Field are reported to have shouted that summer, according to a story in one of the local dailies before the World Series. He played all three outfield positions, and is remembered for making some great catches to steal extra-base hits out of the ivy-covered walls at Chicago's Wrigley Field and the wind-swept reaches of San Francisco's Candlestick Park.

"He played all the fields," Dick Groat said, "and did a super job. He came through in the clutch in the seventh game, too."

In the seventh game of the 1960 World Series, it was Cimoli, pinch-hitting for ElRoy Face, who started the rally in the eighth inning with a single to right field. Minutes later, it was a startled Cimoli who stood safely on second base after Bill Virdon's grounder took that crazy bounce that hit Yankees' shortstop Tony Kubek in the throat on what appeared to be a sure double play ball.

It was Cimoli, always the outspoken good-humor guy in the club-house, who summed up the Series afterward by saying of the Yankees, "They set all the records, but we won the championship!"

At a later date, Cimoli made this comment:

"Let's face it, they didn't figure the 1960 Pirates were going to do anything, much less win a World Series. Some said we couldn't beat the cooks at the Carlton House Hotel. What did everyone have us picked to finish? Fifth? Sixth?

"I bumped into Chuck Tanner at an All-Star Game, and he was wearing his (1979) world championship ring and I had mine on. I told him, 'The 1960 model looks better. You guys were expected to win. We weren't.'"

Cimoli was signed originally into the Brooklyn organization, where he was also quite popular because of his heritage and high-spirited manner, by Branch Rickey Jr., then the Dodgers assistant general manager and later the Pirates' vice-president in charge of minor league clubs.

"Brooklyn was the greatest," recalls Cimoli. "You could be in a candy store or a delicatessen or a haberdashery or a five-and-ten or a meat market, and guys would corner you for autographs. One time there must have been 5,000 kids corner me on the street and tear the clothes right off the top of me."

Cimoli went back to Brooklyn in 1992 to appear at the first card collectors show he had ever agreed to attend. "I caught real hell there from a lot of the guys," recalled Cimoli on April 17, 1993 when he joined Vernon Law to sign autographs at a card and sports memorabilia show at Robert Morris College. "They wanted to know where I'd been.

"One guy said he'd been coming to such shows for ten years, and that I was the only guy whose signature he was missing from the 1957 Dodgers. I was keeping him from having a complete set."

I heard one man who had come from Johnstown to attend the card show at Robert Morris College saying he had 20 of the 25 signatures from the 1960 team, lacking two of those who had died, Roberto Clemente and Don Hoak, among others. "I don't want to buy Clemente's autograph from one of these dealers; it's not the same," he said. "Plus it can get real expensive for something like that."

Cimoli made his day. Cimoli, who works for UPS, might be convinced to do more such shows. Cimoli smiled at his popularity.

Gino Cimoli was a constant cut-up in the locker room, and nobody had more fun after Bill Mazeroski hit the home run to win the World Series in 1960.

Cimoli at card show at Robert Morris College in 1993.

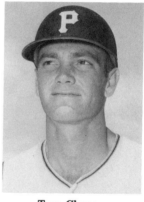

Tom Cheney

Joe Christopher

"I went through this in Brooklyn, too," said Cimoli. "One guy had me sign my autograph 30 times. He brought me home plate and seats from Ebbetts Field to sign. I was the last man to touch home plate, the last one to score a run at Ebbetts Field," said Cimoli.

Gino made good with the Dodgers in 1956 and appeared in his first World Series that season. He was traded to St. Louis for Wally Moon in the winter of 1958. The Pirates obtained him the following year, trading pitcher Ronnie Kline to the Cardinals for him and pitcher Tom Cheney on December 21.

He batted .267 for the Pirates in 1960, with 82 hits, 14 doubles and four triples. He had no home runs, and was constantly kidded about his lack of power by Dick Stuart. Cimoli was 6-2, 190. "How can a guy as big as you not hit a home run?" Stuart constantly asked him in front of the rest of the team.

"If you were a right-handed hitter, you had to hate Forbes Field," Cimoli said. "It was so big."

He came from the North Beach section of San Francisco. It was an Italian community of shrimp and crab fishermen in his youth. He came from a background similar to that of the Yankees' Joe DiMaggio. Gino's father, Papa Abramo Cimoli, a maintenance man, came over from Italy, where he had been a grape farmer. He made homemade wine, which he said was "the finest Dago red in San Fancisco."

When he came to Pittsburgh, Cimoli claimed he would be a starter or they should trade him. But Murtaugh platooned him, which was the game plan from the start. Cimoli liked the infield, if not the distant walls, of Forbes Field. "It's hard, like a paved highway," he said. "I got many a hit through it when I was with the Cardinals. Maz almost went crazy in one series because of my hits skidding past him."

Gene Baker

He had been a fine infielder for the Chicago Cubs for three and a half seasons before being traded to the Pirates during the 1957 season. He came with Dee Fondy in exchange for Dale Long and Lee Walls on May 1, 1957.

He got hurt after playing in 29 games of the 1958 season and was never the same after that. He was hurt on July 13 in St. Louis. He was playing third base and came in fast on a swinging bunt off the bat of Curt Flood. Somehow he caught his spikes in the infield grass, twisted his leg and tore the ligaments and tendons in his left knee. He was flown back to Pittsburgh and operated on and spent the remainder of the 1958 season and the entire 1959 season on the disabled list.

He rejoined the Pirates in 1960 to contribute to the championship season.

He was an Iowan, just like Oldis, from Davenport, and he continues to live there today. He is 58, retired, and loves to play golf.

He lettered in basketball and track at Davenport High School, and was an all-state guard in basketball during the 1943 season. He was

510

inducted into the Navy that same year, and spent 2½ years in the military service, where he played ball with the Ottumwa Naval Air Station.

He signed his first professional contract with the Kansas City Monarchs in 1948. His greatest thrill in baseball, he says, was playing in his first major league game at Cincinnati.

Gene Baker was recognized by Joe L. Brown at Pirates game at Three Rivers Stadium.

Tom Cheney

"You felt like you were on top of the world, that's the way I felt," said Tom Cheney in recalling what it was like to pitch for the Pirates in the 1960 World Series. "I was fortunate to be in the right place at the right time. It was the highlight of my career." Cheney was credited with eight years in the major leagues, including two years of military service. Like most of the Pirates of the '60 team, he was in the Army, was a three-sport star in high school. He was of English descent. Like Haddix, Schofield and Virdon, he had previously played for the St. Louis Cardinals. He was with the Pirates for only one full season, and was traded in May of 1961 to the Washington Senators. A right-handed thrower, the 6-foot Cheney pitched in relief in three games of the World Series, giving up four hits in four innings, posting a 4.50 ERA and striking out six batters with a blazing fast ball. He celebrated his 26th birthday the day after the Pirates won the World Series. His record in '60 was 2-2 in 11 starts. He works for Cordele Propane Gas Co. and lives in Albany, Georgia, about 25 miles from his family's farm in Morgan. The 59-year-old Cheney and his wife Jackie (they were divorced for 18½ years and remarried in 1988) have two daughters, Terri, and Lacie, and two grandchildren. His hobbies include golf and bass fishing.

What Readers Say About
Books About Pittsburgh Steelers

"I have recently finished reading your books, Doing It Right *and* Whatever It Takes, *about the Steelers of the '70s. I have always considered myself a loyal fan, but after reading your books, I almost feel as though I've known these players all my life. You've given them a depth and humanity all too rare in sports histories.*

"You have helped me understand something of their backgrounds and core beliefs, which in turn creates a greater understanding of what drives these men in their pursuit of excellence. It also helps explain how such a seemingly disparate group can come together for a common purpose.

"I have always sensed that there is something special about the Pittsburgh Steelers, and now I know I was correct. Thank you for a splendid history of the greatest football team of all time."

—Sean P. Duffy
Wheeling, West Va.

"I have learned so much about my teammates that I never knew before. I never knew what they were thinking."

—Bruce Van Dyke
Steelers (1967-73)

"Thank you for writing two such superb books on the Pittsburgh Steelers glory years. Your insights and appreciation for those teams — the players, the coaches and the management/ownership — is truly remarkable. I appreciate your effort and the quality of your writing."

—Andy Russell
Steelers (1963, 1966-76)

Gene Baker

Joseph Gibbon

Joe L. Brown

Dan Murtaugh

Joe Christopher

Gino Cimoli

Rocky Nelson

"Smoky" Burgess

George C. Witt